From **Carl B. Stilson, Jr., M.D.**:

As a junior in high school, my son Matt was struggling at the plate in varsity baseball, batting around .230. He was fearful of failing and had a negative mental outlook. Then he took a BRAIN TYPE-SPECIFIC lesson including batting practice with Jon Niednagel. Jon's instruction and confidence building helped him progress from being a ninth place hitter to becoming the premier leadoff hitter in the league. Matt made ALL-LEAGUE with an on-base percentage of over .500 and hit well over .450 since his "lesson" from Jon.

Jon has an uncanny and God given talent to understand and relate to people in real and very helpful ways, and I would consider it foolish for anyone *NOT* to consider what an understanding of Brain Types can do for their lives. Jon is an intelligent and caring person whose advice should be highly regarded in sports, spiritual matters, interpersonal relationships, business and life in general. .

From **Charles E. Ribak, Ph.D.**, *Department of Anatomy and Neurobiology, California College of Medicine, University of California:*

As a neuroanatomist who researches and teaches brain function to medical students, I've found Jon Niednagel's Brain Typing approach to be insightful and on the cutting edge of linking behavioral findings to regional activity in forebrain centers. Jon's book is truly the first to describe the use of Brain Types in sports. He provides an excellent instruction to the neurological basis of the various Types and attempts to show that data from positron emission tomography (PET) can be correlated to support his hypothesis.

In addition to the neuroscientific aspects of this book that have great interest for me, *Your Key to Sports Success* offers straightforward advice on how to help children select a sport and choose a specific playing position within that sport. As a coach in the local Little League and youth basketball programs in Southern California, I was very impressed with the predictive value that this approach showed.

Jon's information also enables you to understand why each athlete performs as he or she does, and how to get the most out of their abilities. I have become a believer in Jon's system and endorse his approach.

From **Richard J. Haier, Ph.D.**, *Professor of Psychiatry, Brain Imaging Researcher, University of California:*

Psychologists have known for some time that personality characteristics are strong predictors of vocational choice. *Your Key to Sports Success* takes this knowledge base and charts a new dimension in showing how personality is related to sports skills. This book is clear, clever, and a must read for aspiring athletes of all ages. Parents will read it twice before signing children up for lessons.

*From **Bill Westphal**, basketball coach of 25 years at the high school, college and NBA levels, and 16 years director of summer athletic camps:*

There's something for everyone in this book ...kids, parents, and coaches. I am amazed at how accurate and relevant Brain Typing is to life and sports. Everyone I have shared it with has been fascinated with the insight that it gives into how we function both on and off of the athletic field. It's incredible stuff!!!

God has created us as truly unique individuals. This book has helped me to understand people's uniqueness in a way that I never thought possible. I think that it will become a classic once people discover its tremendous potential. Be on the cutting edge . . . READ IT BEFORE YOUR COMPETITION!

*From point guard **Mike Coffin** of Biola University, 4th in assists nationally (NAIA), in 1992:*

I first heard Jon Niednagel speak at a team meeting at our assistant coach's house. It was just prior to the beginning of my senior season in college. The comments he made about people and their Brain Types piqued my interest about my own. He not only spoke of well known athletes, but told many of the players on our team about themselves, without ever having met us before.

After the meeting, Jon spoke with me privately. He told me that I was the only player on our team with a certain Brain Type, one with great potential in the NBA. I was excited to know the professional company I was in when Jon categorized my Brain Type. Although I was not the point guard at the time (I played the small forward position at 6' 5"), he informed me that with my particular Type, I should have been. After a few bad games with someone else at point, I was moved to that position. I feel that somehow Jon influenced the coach's decision.

Our team concluded league play with 34 wins and 4 losses, making it to the quarterfinals of the NAIA National Tournament! I contributed to my team as well as ending up the season as the nation's fourth leading assists producer.

I feel that this kind of study conducted by Jon can help coaches better understand and help place their players in proper positions. It also helps motivate players in ways that their performance then reflects on their coaches.

*From Assistant Basketball Coach **Scott Mossman** of Biola University:*

I want to follow up on Mike Coffin's testimonial. Jon Niednagel suggested after a team meeting that Mike could be an excellent point guard, that his Brain Type would be good for our team and its success. For various reasons, we had not used him at that position. Jon suggested that we allow Mike to play some point in practice, preparing him for the time that we might feel a greater need to use him. Well, that time did come.

Mike started our third game at point guard and held it firmly throughout the season. His invaluable contribution enabled us to win 26 games in a row! Mike was the glue to our team. He ran the show; he was a complete player. We couldn't have asked for a better point guard.

The techniques Jon describes in his book would be very beneficial to coaches at all levels. These

What People are Saying About Jon P. Niednagel, Brain Types®, and *YOUR KEY TO SPORTS SUCCESS*

Robert (Bob) Arnot, M.D., *bestselling author and Chief Medical Correspondent for NBC's Dateline and Today shows, says:*

When you conduct interviews for a living, you hope to be surprised by new and exciting information, but you're rarely prepared to be totally blown away. That's what happened to me when I interviewed Jonathan P. Niednagel and read his new book. Jon's scientific and 21st century approach to evaluating, developing, and motivating people is simply stunning. I've found it the most important and helpful information in the last 20 years of human understanding and development. Brain Typing is relevant for not only sports but every segment of society. Those who fail to use this new insight will be at a distinct disadvantage now and in the future.

From **Syd Thrift**, *former General Manager, Baltimore Orioles, former GM (New York Yankees and Pittsburgh Pirates), and honored as one of baseball's top 5 teachers in 1994:*

Holding leadership positions in major league baseball for many years, I have been inundated with new ideas on assessing baseball talent. Standing in a unique position is the scientific, invaluable, and new perspective Jon Niednagel brings to sports. The Brain Types method that Jon has pioneered has clear and dynamic relevance to professional sports organizations on many levels, from management to the individual player. Jon's expertise has made his work immediately applicable in predicting and developing athletic talent. To evaluate players as to their specific designs and then see them perform accordingly has added a new, revolutionary dimension to my field. Brain Typing has improved the quality of my evaluations and to see things I've never seen before.

From **Randy Myers**, *former All-Star relief pitcher:*

From my personal experience with Jon Niednagel, it would be a great competitive advantage for teams that are fortunate enough to have access to his Brain Typing system. His ability to precisely evaluate allows coaches to maximize potential of athletes, current and future.

From **Sammy Sosa**, *Chicago Cubs, 1998 National League MVP, All-Star outfielder and one of baseball's all-time home run leaders:*

I was struggling, really struggling. Jon helped me a lot. I like to talk to him because he's a good guy, and he can put you on track.

From **Sean Casey**, *All-Star Cincinnati Reds Infielder:*

When I talked to Jon Niednagel, I felt like he had been living in my head for 27 years. The Brain Typing Jon does is amazing. He really made me look at myself and others in a whole different light.

*From **Danny Ainge**, NBA Executive and former NBA Head Coach, NBA All-Star (14-year career), professional baseball player, and high school All-American football player:*

Jon gives me an advantage that no one else has. His methods and principles for selecting and developing players are the best.

*From **Pat Williams**, Senior Executive VP (former GM), Orlando Magic:*

We had the good fortune to have the number one pick in the 1993 Draft but the tough job of deciding what player to select. Jon Niednagel helped us with his unique concept to provide complete insights into the players we liked and really gave us thorough coverage. Jon has also written a fascinating book, *Your Key to Sports Success (formerly Your Best Sport),* that is a proven winner.

*From **John Gabriel**, Orlando Magic General Manager:*

To stay competitive in the NBA it's important that you make the right decisions about players. Utilizing Brain Typing and Jon Niednagel has helped the Orlando Magic in making some great decisions.

*From **Kevin McHale**, Minnesota Timberwolves V.P. of Operations, former NBA All-Star, 13-year career:*

I really enjoy talking to Jon. The next best thing is reading his book, *Your Key to Sports Success.* I find Brain Typing not only fascinating, but very accurate. I wish I had this information when I was playing. I use it now to help me evaluate and develop talent.

*From **Randy Pfund**, Miami Heat General Manager, former Head Coach of the Los Angeles Lakers:*

As a GM, coach or scout, you have to cover every angle. Jon's material provides insights that go far beyond conventional means, easily making the difference between winning and losing. This is a 21st century phenomenon that I especially recommend for coaches, scouts, sports organizations, and individual athletes. I've seen it work.

*From **Jim Harrick**, Head Basketball Coach of the 1995 National Champion UCLA Bruins:*

Jon Niednagel helped our UCLA basketball team tremendously in the 1995 season, where we went on to win the NCAA Championship. I've always stayed away from outside consultants, including psychologists and the advisors with little gimmicks. But from the moment I met Jon at the beginning of the 1994-95 season, I knew he was different from all the rest. His innovative, scientifically-based Brain Types explained in detail why everyone on the team acted the way they did, on and off the floor—even the coaching staff. Jon helped me to understand my players better this year than I ever have in all my life. He also told me how best to develop each player and which ones I could count on most—mentally and physically. I've never known Jon to be wrong about a person yet.

*From **Kerry Kittles**, NBA shooting guard, New Jersey Nets:*

"Jon Niednagel's Brain Typing helps you understand yourself better ... on and off the court."

From **Lorenzo Romar**, *Head Basketball Coach, University of Washington:*

I think your number one priority as a coach is understanding and managing people, working with people. Coaches wear a lot of different hats; you're a psychologist, you're a counselor, you're a father, you're a big brother. One of the things that Brain Typing does is that it allows you to understand people quickly—mentally and physically. Among other benefits, Brain Typing is really important in motivating players and developing team chemistry.

From **Brad Kullman**, *Director of Major League Operations, Cincinnati Reds:*

As a professional sports talent evaluator, I have had the blessing to be exposed to Jon Niednagel's Brain Tying and I have found it to be one of the most fascinating and invaluable concepts I have ever encountered . . . Brain Typing puts to rest the debate of nurture vs. nature, demonstrating that, while the environment in which you are raised has a significant impact on your personality and the way you live your life, each of us has an inborn genetic design that guides our basic behavior and beliefs. Learning and understanding this incredible technology should not only make us better evaluators, but also better parents and better members of society. Better understanding leads to more empathy and compassion, ultimately leading to better relationships and a better world for all of us. I strongly urge anyone who has the opportunity to learn more about Brain Typing."

From **Terry Donahue**, *San Francisco 49ers GM and all-time winningest football coach in NCAA Pac-10 history*:

Jon Niednagel's Brain Typing is a wealth of information for any coach, enabling him to do a much better job than he currently can. The recruitment and development of players based on the various Brain Types can be an extremely useful tool for amateur or professional teams. I found the information to be absolutely fascinating, almost scary, because it is so correct.

From **John Cappelletti**, *Heisman Trophy and Maxwell Award winner (both awarded to America's best college football player), NFL running back for 10 years*:

After reading the material given to me by Jon (which was the foundation for *Your Key To Sports Success*), I was amazed at how vast and important a field of science this is. I think Jon's research and conclusions in the field are fascinating. I couldn't wait to talk more about how Jon applied his findings in a practical manner. I wanted to know what Type I am and more importantly, why and how it affects me personally and professionally. Jon gave me that information and more.

I know my children are all different from one another, that's obvious. Why and how they are different, and how I can better understand them as young people and as athletes is important to me. I don't want to typecast them to a certain role in life, but would like to help them by understanding their strengths and weaknesses. Also, understanding what methods I can use with each individual child (I have four boys) to elicit a positive response will enable each child to reach their fullest potential. From a parent's viewpoint, there sometimes seems to be a very fine line between understanding a child, their wants and needs, and why they react a certain way to some things and not to others. Then there are other times that leave you thinking they were dropped on your doorstop by aliens. There is no doubt in my mind that if I apply this information, I will become a much more consistent and understanding person and father. I'm glad Jon thought enough of me to allow me to review his book. I know it is making a difference in my life, and feel it can for anyone who takes the time to read and understand the material.

From professional golfer **Larry Nelson**, *winner of 10 PGA tournaments, including the prestigious U.S. Open and 2 PGA Championships, and leading money winner in 2000 on the Senior PGA Tour*:

Personally, Jon's advice has enabled me to react in a more positive and constructive way to each member of my family. Professionally, understanding my Brain Type and how I react to the different elements of tournament golf has helped to improve my golf game and prolong my career.

Jon is the foremost authority in the world today on Brain Types as they relate to sports. After years of research and case studies, Jon has the knowledge of how different Types operate their body skills as well as respond to pressure, change, suggestions, assignments and discipline. Jon has helped thousands of people understand themselves and others better.

Although Jon recognizes each individual has his or her own God given, unique variations, he has logically explained the similarities of each Brain Type in a way that makes sense. Applying his knowledge will improve your game and your understanding of everyone around you.

From **Vic Braden**, *renowned tennis instructor, sports researcher, and psychologist*:

Research suggests that questionnaires derived from Jungian typology are less than 75 percent accurate in evaluating the 8 mental preferences. But in the 3 years I've done work with Jon Niednagel, where he's often only had brief conversations in over 100 cases, he's been right on the money determining Brain Type and body movements. Now that is amazing because sometimes a conversation is only 10 or 20 seconds long, but Jon's been extremely accurate and as a skeptical psychologist and a sports scientist, I've become convinced. This new science not only brings greater success and enables coaches to access each student's genius at a much faster rate, but it's truly enlightening and liberating.

From **Dr. Tom Amberry**, *World Free Throw Record Holder, 2,750 consecutive "Free Throws" without a miss!*:

The Brain Type information that Jon Niednagel has compiled is amazing. It would be helpful to any athlete or individual. To any coach in any sport or any teacher, this would be a wealth of knowledge.

From **Ted Newland**, *University of California at Irvine, Winningest Coach in NCAA Water Polo History*:

I obviously want to be the best coach I can possibly be, and at my age of 67 years, I don't want to stop growing; I want to continue growing and get better. Brain Typing has allowed me to be a much better coach and to better understand my players and myself. I'm super turned on to Brain Typing right now.

From **Ed Sorgi**, *father of Erica Sorgi, 3-Time National Jr. Diving Champion and youngest diver (age 14) in modern history to win the Women's Senior U.S. National Outdoor Championships, in 1996*:

I personally believe that regardless of what level you play at, whether you're a novice, intermediate or advanced athlete, the one common denominator is that everybody is trying to improve. So whether it's for the general population, the weekend athlete, or the professional athlete, there are benefits from Brain Typing. I believe Jon Niednagel's Brain Typing is going to be very pervasive going into the 21st century.

techniques can be used to determine everything from coaching compatibility to recruiting.

I know from personal experience that what Jon writes is very pertinent to today's coach and athlete. If you are a coach or an athlete who desires to obtain the winning edge, then this book and Brain Typing is for you.

From **Jeff Weltman** *of the NBA's Denver Nuggets (Assistant General Manager):*

I met Jon Niednagel at a very informal meeting arranged by our Director of Scouting. The three of us met in a hotel room and had only about a half hour to talk. Working in the scouting department for an NBA club, you come to be jaded by all the quick fix answers and promises that are thrown at you; the fattest file in my cabinet is one entitled: "Unsolicited Manuscripts." There's a whole litany of salesmanship in these letters, and each time I meet one of these guys I must make a conscious effort to approach the meeting with an open mind that's after I'm sure I can't avoid it altogether.

However, in no time at all Jon had my ear. In only a few minutes I was beginning to sense the validity of his research. The way he grabbed my attention so quickly was simple: after shaking my hand and exchanging small talk, he proceeded to give me a thumbnail sketch of something I think I know pretty well myself. He ran down many of my character traits, the way I approach people and work, and how I responded to certain situations. He was right on the money.

In the short time that followed, Jon sent me materials dealing with NBA players about the kinds of tendencies and reactions to expect from them under different situations, and once again, I found myself agreeing with the conclusions. They were thorough profiles that the casual fan would not be able to piece together. He listed the players by Brain Types, something I was unfamiliar with at the time. The more I looked at the lists, the more I began to feel the Brain Typing fall into place.

That was over ten years ago now. More than ten drafts have passed, and Jon's track record has remained strong in an area where they say "It's an art, not a science." I have bounced several ideas off Jon, and asked him questions both about myself and college prospects. I have come to know him on a more personal level, and I've seen how much time he dedicates to his research; really it is his life's work. I'm hopeful that many others will soon receive the benefits that have come my way through Jon and his Brain Typing. Of course, I hope they're not my competitors.

From **Dan Dyk**, *former CEO of The Sporting Way Trading Card Co. (specializing in Upper Deck), broker and collector (one of America's largest):*

Jon's material has really helped us "pick out" the hot Rookie cards—especially the ones that may not be as well known. Our card buying is targeted to certain "Brain Types" that excel in each sport.

Jon's insight has also helped us in building a business team, by combining the right Types, helping us gain an understanding of each other.

YOUR KEY

TO

SPORTS SUCCESS

JONATHAN P. NIEDNAGEL

LAGUNA PRESS

LP

Laguna Niguel, California 92677

YOUR KEY TO SPORTS SUCCESS
Copyright © 1992, 1997 by Jonathan P. Niednagel

Published by Laguna Press
Laguna Niguel, California 92677

All rights reserved. No part of this publication may be reproduced, stored in a retrieval system, or transmitted in any form or by any means, electronic, mechanical, photocopying, recording, or otherwise, without the prior written permission of the publisher, Laguna Press, except where permitted by law.

Library of Congress Cataloging in Publication Data
_____

Niednagel, Jonathan P. (Jonathan Philip), 1948-
Your Key to Sports Success / by Jonathan P. Niednagel
p.   cm.
Includes bibliographical references

ISBN: 0 916309 01 0 (pbk.)
1. Sports—Psychological and biological aspects. 2. Myers Briggs Type Indicator
I. Title
GV706.4.N54 1992
796'.01—dc20   92 60519
                                                          CIP

Printed in the United States of America

First Edition 1992, Reprinted 1993, Second Edition 1996,
Third Edition 1997, Fourth Edition 1998, Fifth Edition 1999,
Sixth Edition 2001, Seventh Edition 2002, Eighth Edition 2003,
Ninth Edition 2003, Tenth Ed. 2004

Scripture quotations taken from the HOLY BIBLE, NEW INTERNATIONAL VERSION. Copyright © 1973, 1978, 1984 by International Bible Society.

Cover design by Jordan P. Niednagel
Selected graphics by Jeremy J. & Jordan P. Niednagel

Refer to the back of the book for further information on Brain Types and how to order additional products.

Acknowledgments

Our Heavenly Creator Who made all this possible,

and
Vic Braden,
Dan Dyk,
Paul McDonald,
Ted Newland,
Jeremy and Jordan Niednagel,
Carl Stilson,
Kevin Warner: Your support, encouragement, and expertise have made all the difference. I'm in your debt. Thank you!

Toody: I'm forever grateful for believing in me from Day One!

Barbara: A loving appreciation for being my closest friend, for letting this quest of human understanding dominate our many years of marriage (1968), and for your tedious editing—bless you.

Publisher's Note:

The author has made Brain Type® assessments on thousands of people for more than 25 years. In this book, he mentions hundreds of well known people (both athlete and non) to better illustrate his insights. His evaluations are based on years of psychological, scientific, and empirical research. Though the author believes his appraisals are correct, he doesn't want them held as absolute—lest people profiled be unfairly judged by those who do not fully understand Brain Types. The author intends only for the positive application of this information and desires readers to grasp its essence—that each person possesses an inborn design, one of 16 individual Brain Types, which predisposes him or her to specific ***mental*** and ***physical*** traits.

Few of the numerous persons included in this book have been administered a written psychometric questionnaire by the author. He is skeptical of self-reporting instruments and explains his reasons herein. Nonetheless, whether appraised by questionnaire or empirically, Brain Types cannot yet be proved in the same way scientists validate laboratory experiments. Therefore, as the last validation hurdle to overcome, the author is presently testing the various Brain Types by DNA analysis. He believes genetic examination will identify each Type, removing any doubts of inaccuracy. In the meantime, though recent brain and genetic research complement the author's assertions, digitized video clips authenticate his biomechanical/motor skill claims, and numerous highly-respected persons attest to his exacting appraisals and results, it is not yet possible to fully validate scientifically the individual assessments.

Brain Typing has become the world's most accurate and sophisticated approach to understanding why people do what they do, on and off the field of play. Scientists are marveling at the new understanding this revolutionary technique brings—and its far-reaching implications. A good understanding of this 21st century system will enable you to appreciate and develop others like never before.

Contents

Testimonials
Acknowledgments

PART ONE: The Manual for Everyone Interested in Sports

    Where Are Your Interests?.. 16
    Introduction.. 18

    1. A Manual for Athletes, Parents, Coaches, Recruiters,
       Scouts, Sports Organizations Sports Media, and
         Trading Card Collectors.. 20
       Different Types Excel in Different Sports.. 27

PART TWO: The Mind, Brain, and Body

    2. Who Are You?.. 31
        Questionnaire.. 34
    3. Mental Preferences.. 38
      Summary of 16 Types.. 46
    4. Discovering Preferences in Children... 48
    5. You Were Meant to Fly!
       SJ Bees, SP Hummingbirds, NF Storks, NT Owls................................... 51
    6. "Personality" or "Psychological" Types vs. "Brain" Types..................... 58
      The Four Typological Functions... 59
      Introduction to 8 Brain-Related Functions... 62
    7. Neuroscience: How the Brain Works... 66
    8. Brain Types and Body Skills... 79

PART THREE: Sports and Brain Types

    9. Baseball... 89
    10. Basketball.. 126
    11. Bowling, Boxing, Cycling.. 154
    12. Football... 161
    13. Golf... 175
    14. Gymnastics, Hockey, Ice Skating.. 200
    15. Racing (auto), Snow Skiing, Soccer,
        Swimming and Diving... 211
    16. Tennis.. 220
    17. Track and Field, Volleyball, Water Polo,
        Wrestling.. 249

PART FOUR: Coaches and the Sports Media

    18. Coaches (and officials)... 259
    19. Sports Media... 275

PART FIVE: Portraits of the 16 Brain Types

  20. SPs
      ISTP.. 283
      ESTP... 290
      ISFP.. 295
      ESFP... 299

  21. SJs
      ISTJ... 303
      ESTJ.. 307
      ISFJ... 311
      ESFJ.. 313

  22. NFs
      INFP.. 316
      ENFP... 319
      INFJ... 323
      ENFJ.. 325

  23. NTs
      INTJ... 329
      ENTJ.. 332
      INTP.. 336
      ENTP... 339

PART SIX: Birds, Bees, and Temperament Groups

  24. The SJ "Bee".. 347
  25. The SP "Hummingbird".. 350
  26. The NF "Stork".. 353
  27. The NT "Owl"... 357

PART SEVEN: Helping the Mind

  28. The Performing Mind, Zoning, Relaxation, Visualization................................ 363
  29. Philosophical or Spiritual Foundation.. 370
  30. Goal Setting.. 377

PART EIGHT: Further Considerations in Type

  31. Other Psychological Methods and Accurate Typing.................................... 385
  32. Parents and Guardians... 390
      Using Brain Types to Improve Communication....................................... 394
  33. Putting It in Perspective.. 396

Notes.. 403

For Further Information.. 411

PART ONE

THE MANUAL FOR EVERYONE INTERESTED IN SPORTS

Where Are Your Interests?

Areas of interest in this book are many. Go over the following list and check the areas relevant to you.

_As an **athlete,** knowing:
- _the sport(s) and positions at which you are best.
- _why you are best at particular sports.
- _your own best, innate body skills.
- _yourself better, understanding your specific innate Brain Type and how it specifically works.
- _how to use your own uniqueness to:
  - _motivate yourself
  - _practice the best way
  - _handle pressure
  - _help others understand you better
- _how to gain an advantage over your athletic opponents by knowing their Brain Types.
- _which well known athletes have your corresponding Brain Type, and how they have learned to master their sport.

_As a **parent or guardian,** using your child's specific Brain Type to know:
- _which sport(s) your child is innately best at, and why.
- _how to understand your child better.
- _how to coach, motivate and encourage your child better in athletics, school, and life.
- _which professional or well known athletes have your child's specific Brain Type.
- _how to help your child understand himself better.

_As a **coach,** knowing:
- _which athletes to recruit or select.
- _at which position(s) a player would be best.
- _how to motivate each player according to his uniqueness.
- _in which body skills your players are innately best and least proficient.
- _how to gain an advantage over your athletic opponents by knowing their Brain Types.
- _in which academic subjects a player would have the greatest interest and excel.
- _which professional or well known athletes have your player's specific Brain Type.

Where Are Your Interests............................?

_As a **sports organization**, knowing:
    _which athletes would be best to draft.
    _at which position(s) a player would be best.
    _how to motivate each player and achieve his or her optimal playing level.
    _how to quickly get a player out of a slump.
    _which players are best to trade for.
    _how to gain an advantage over your athletic opponents by knowing their Brain Types.
    _how to select the best coaches.
    _how to better understand everyone in the organization, and how to motivate them.

_As a **trading card collector**, knowing:
    _which Brain Types are best at each sport.
    _which cards to buy and sell according to the athlete's Brain Type.
    _which athletes will excel before they actually do.

_As a **person**, knowing:
    _and understanding yourself better.
    _and understanding others better (at home, work, socially).
    _how to help others understand you better.
    _which professional athletes and well known celebrities possess your exact Brain Type.
    _the specific Brain Types of many well known athletes and celebrities.

Introduction

This book is for athletes, parents, coaches, sports teams (organizations and owners), the sports media, and trading-card collectors. It is equally addressed to every one of you interested in sports.

You, the reader, are about to embark on a journey into a new phase of sports science. Welcome aboard! You will find your perspective changing through a book which is quite unlike any other. The present and future potential of every athlete or would be athlete will be disclosed for your enjoyment and awareness. All you need for this journey is a little time and an inquiring mind.

Apart from one singular chapter, this book will be easy to read and understand. Unfortunately for those who do not like to spend a large amount of time reading, the information cannot be clearly understood in condensed form. Take heart, however, because the data's usefulness and relevancy will be invaluable to you who apply it. As in all interesting pursuits, we trust the time you spend herein will fly.

Years of scientific and empirical research have been consolidated to make this book possible. The data provided will not be just another person's theories on how to maximize athletic potential. Neuroscientific (brain related) facts, coupled with the most accurate and sophisticated psychometric approach in the world, will disclose details never before known about athletes. More than 15 years have been devoted to studying athletes from ages 3 to 83 with these scientific facts in mind.

This material will be immediately pertinent at every level, amateur or professional. Although this book does not highlight every sport, the principles are transferable. *Your Key to Sports Success* will soon become the sports manual for all who participate in or follow athletics.

Can Anyone be a Superior Athlete?

Would you like to be one of the best athletes in the world? Do you dream of being the next **Michael Jordan, Tiger Woods, Greg Maddux, Joe Montana, Carl Lewis, or Steffi Graf**? Or would you like to be proficient in a sport if only for recreation? If these goals speak to you, this book will give you the "how to" and discuss probabilities for success, based on your unique brain and body design.

There is tremendous hope for aspiring athletes. They need to discover their mental and physical predispositions, allowing them to pursue the sport(s) in which they are best able to perform. There are many young people out there who have the same potential as **Jack Nicklaus, Tiger Woods, Nancy Lopez, Emmitt Smith, Joe Montana, Dan Marino, Pete Sampras, Martina Hingas, Ken Griffey Jr., Larry Bird, John Stockton, Wayne Gretzky, Nadia Comaneci, Mary Lou Retton, Peggy Fleming, Michelle Kwan, Greg Louganis, and Janet Evans**, but who have little or no direction toward the sports in which they would most excel. This book can be their guide.

The vast majority of information presented has never before been offered to the general public. It is scientifically sound, providing a revolutionary approach to athletics.

All individuals are like snowflakes—uniquely different, yet sharing similar brain functions with other people of similar cerebral design. These same brain designs perform similarly in sports. Persons possessing comparable brain patterns are known to have a specific "psychological type," "personality type," or, more accurately, a "Brain Type."

Every person is cerebrally designed to excel in some sport or recreational event. Spending a lifetime in practicing the wrong sport or practicing the wrong way can be wasteful and discouraging. No athletes are precluded from pursuing any sports they desire, but they will perform much better at the sport(s) and position(s) within the sport for which they are mentally and physically designed.

Research reveals that a person will pursue physical

exercise if an activity is chosen to his or her liking. A person usually likes what he or she does best. A study of Harvard graduates by a Dartmouth Medical School researcher indicated that personality is a significant factor in determining whether an individual will stick with a sports or fitness program.[1]

This book will explain, in detail, the various Brain Types and how readers can discover their own. Each Brain Type excels in certain sports, has certain practice procedures that must be implemented, and needs certain kinds of coaches who will bring out his or her personal best. Therefore, athletes must know themselves, and those coaching them must know them if their athletic pinnacle is to be achieved. Being among the world's best results from athletes pursuing their naturally designed talents, plus giving years of devotion to their sport. Until now, knowing what a person is innately best at has been predominately guesswork. Success can now be more accurately and scientifically predicted.

Learning and Coaching According to Uniqueness

Have you ever been coached in a sport? If so, can you remember how you were instructed, particularly in technique? Were the other students or team members taught similarly to you?

Coaches have their individual philosophies which they impart to their students. Normally each coach treats his or her students alike, though the athletes differ from one another in fundamental ways, physically and mentally. This is equivalent to going to a clothing store which carries only one size. Individual athletes are unique and must be treated as such.

A variety of techniques are performed by top athletes in most professional sports. Different styles are used in pitching or batting a baseball, shooting a basketball, running a race or with a football, and swinging a golf club or tennis racket. This book will custom fit your inborn style to your sport. It will also tell you the fastest way to improve, based on who you are.

1

A Manual for Athletes, Parents, Coaches, Recruiters, Scouts, Sports Organizations, Sports Media, and Trading-Card Collectors

What if it were possible to know the following about athletes: their maximum potential, the sports and positions at which they would be best, and how they would handle pressure throughout their careers?

Parents would more than likely encourage their children to pursue a sport in which they would most naturally excel. A **coach** would be able to place athletes in their potentially best positions, working with them, not giving up so quickly with initial failure. **College recruiters or pro scouts** would be able to go far beyond the information they have traditionally relied upon to make a crucial selection. They would no longer have to play the guessing game.

Sports teams and organizations would be able to choose the specific kind of athlete who fit their master plan. Building a championship contender would be much easier. To them, this information would easily be worth millions of dollars.

Persons in the **sports media** would have greater insight into why athletes perform as they do. They would add refreshing new details to oft-times otherwise dull commentary. **Trading-card collectors** could predict with accuracy which untried athletes have the highest probabilities for success.

And what about the individual **athlete**? Think of the present excitement of being able to play a sport and position in which he or she could someday be among the absolute best.

Athletes

There are sixteen identifiable Brain Types. You possess one of them in a unique way. Discovering your personal cerebral genetic predisposition will enable you to perform to your highest potential, perform under pressure, find the best sport(s) and position(s) for you, practice correctly and efficiently, and implement mental exercises (left and right brain) that will enhance your athletic performance. You will discover which professional or well known athletes have your corresponding Brain Type, who provide you models for learning according to your specific physical and mental skills.

Parents

The most influential coach in a young person's life should be a parent. Who knows the child better and knows what makes him or her tick? It should be mom and dad. This book will supply information relevant to youngsters that you can find nowhere else. If you are a parent, this material will help you to understand your child (as well as yourself) better than ever before, to properly motivate your child, and to decide what sports and vocational careers he or she will do best in according to his or her unique personality and brain design.

Virtually every day, I become aware of situations in which parents could benefit significantly from this book. In April of 1991, I read of frustrated L.A. Dodger **Jeff Hamilton.** Hamilton was unhappy about being platooned at third base with two other baseball players. His hitting had been below Dodger expectations. What struck me most from this article was the interest Hamilton showed in his own son's future in sports:

If my boy wants to become a ballplayer, I am

going to do everything I can to make sure he is the best he can be. Maybe that way, he will never have to go through what I am going through now.[1]

Hamilton's son was less than two years old at the time. He already had a tiny glove, bat, and a pitching machine. Those items alone, his father knew, would *not* guarantee baseball success.

Hamilton's quote sums up the reason I wrote this book: to help my own and other children escape needless frustrations in athletics, as well as in life. Parents need to realize that understanding Brain Types is crucial. Providing our children all the high tech training and coaching is secondary to understanding their cerebral makeup and inherent body skills. If Hamilton's parents had understood his Brain Type when he was a youngster and how it related to sports, they would have known he would someday have difficulty hitting consistently at the major league level. He could have begun a specific batting regimen for his inborn design that would have been of unparalleled help as an adult. This is not to say that Hamilton still couldn't have improved his batting in 1991, only that he would have been much be better had he begun working on Brain Type characteristics at a younger age. Whether or not you have professional sports aspirations for your child, Brain Type information can greatly enhance your child's athletic pursuits.

Coaches

Have you ever coached athletes who later developed *beyond* your expectations? Perhaps you didn't play them much, or even if you did, you failed to see many of the hidden skills they later went on to demonstrate. Maybe you felt at the time the athlete was not ready to be given greater responsibility, when, in fact, he or she was, and only needed someone to see it. This book will enable you to discover abilities within those you now coach.

Have you ever coached athletes who later in their careers performed *below* your expectations? Perhaps you felt they were a sure bet to succeed as they reached the higher levels of competition. Longtime major league manager **Gene Mauch** said in 1992:

> In all the years I managed, one of my toughest disappointments is that **Dick Schofield** didn't blossom into a truly great ballplayer.

Mauch continued:

> Why he didn't come along as an offensive player has always been a sad mystery to me. As a kid, everyone thought the thing that would be his forte would be offense.[2]

Schofield's hitting instructor with the 1992 California Angels was seven-time American league batting champ and Hall of Famer Rod Carew. He said of Dick:

> Sometimes he goes through stages where he tries to pull everything, which is something I can't understand.[3]

Dick Schofield was one of the best defensive shortstops in professional baseball from the mid 1980s to mid-90s. Yet, as coach Mauch identified, his bat was a major disappointment. Had Coach Mauch known Brain Types, Schofield would not have been a "mystery."

If anyone should understand why hitters do what they do, it is Carew. Not only is he intelligent, he is among the top few batters of all time. This will explain why players with Schofield's Brain Type normally hit as they do, but also how to help them overcome their inborn tendencies which can be counterproductive. Even the best coaches will now be better able to understand and improve their players' deficiencies.

In 1994, I finally met Dick Schofield and sheepishly told him of how I had illustrated him and his Type in my first edition to this book. I also told him his hitting could improve, even after ten years in the major leagues. He agreed to give it a try, and we only had time for one hitting session before he was to leave for Spring Training. Within 15 minutes on the ballfield, Dick could quickly understand his disadvantageous Brain Type tendencies (primarily physical) and the need to overcome them. For the next thirty minutes I showed him two simple techniques. His improvement was dramatic. Not only could he now hit well to all areas of the field, but he was doing it more effortlessly and with power. Dick went on to have his best Spring Training ever, batting over .400. Though he was a backup player at the start of the regular season, Dick worked his way into the starting lineup and had his best year ever at the plate. He learned that he could hit much better with only minor adjustments based on his Brain Type; yet he also learned that it takes mental and physical discipline to practice these skills daily.

This book will tell of Brain Types who will not perform as well as expected as they climb the ladder of advanced athletics and what they can do to minimize poor performances. The problems of "tough disappointment, a sad mystery, and I can't understand" no longer need to plague coaches.

Coaches who have the opportunity to choose their players will gain a double advantage with this material. Generally, only a limited number of Types excel at each sport. Coaches can now select those athletes whose potential may be latent.

They can learn: why athletes perform as they do; how to get the most out of players, including where they will perform best (position, batting lineup, and so forth); how to help players handle pressure according to their unique brain designs; and the best way to motivate each athlete.

What did **Mike Ditka** and **Bobby Knight** have in common besides a tendency to be on the tempestuous side? These two coaches had similar cerebral designs.

How did **Pat Riley, Bill Walsh, and Lute Olson** appear similar (other than being "Dapper Dans")? They, too, are men of similar Brain Types, having many things in common.

This book has a chapter devoted to coaches, emphasizing their respective Types and coaching characteristics. This will enable you to see how they use their minds to implement coaching techniques and strategy. Many of your questions as to why they behave and coach as they do will be answered. You can also discover which coaches have your exact Brain Type.

One of baseball's smartest and all time best managers has been **Earl Weaver**. His autobiography, *It's What You Learn After You Know It All That Counts*, implies most coaches believe they have all the answers. Coaches who become familiar with the material in this book will find they can have even more. Just as doctors regularly continue their education to stay abreast of the latest scientific knowledge, so should coaches.

Sports Organizations

Catcher **Mike Piazza** was the National League top vote-getter in the 1996 All Star game, having been selected to the team for the fourth straight year. Yet Piazza was picked in the 62nd round of the 1988 Free-Agent draft! Had he not been chosen as a special favor from his godfather, big-league manager Tommy Lasorda, Piazza would have been overlooked. His Brain Type is one of the top few in baseball. Had baseball organizations understood this, Piazza would have been selected much sooner. This book will explain why the greatest athletes perform as they do, and how to pick out, in advance, the **Piazzas, Jordans, Montanas, and Nicklauses**.

In 1979, *Pro Football Weekly* said of draft pick, **Joe Montana**:

> Alarming lack of consistency and poor technique are most disturbing. [4]

Had they understood Joe's Brain Type, they wouldn't have been so disturbed.

Prior to the June, 1990, annual baseball draft, major league scouting directors said such things as:

- "These drafts are a crapshoot."
- "It's so difficult to project high school age players four and five years down the road."
- "Baseball is the most difficult of all games to predict future performance."[5]

Why do the directors make these kind of statements? First, they want to cover their mistakes when they make bad picks, and second, they often view drafts as "crapshoots."

In the late 1980s, when every NBA team was giving special notice to LSU's Chris Jackson, few were considering his teammate, seven-foot **Shaquille O'Neal**. The fact that O'Neal was a freshman explains part of this oversight, but the chief reason was he had not demonstrated his latent abilities in college.

Awareness of Brain Types allowed me to have high expectations of O'Neal the first time I saw him play. His television performance was unspectacular, but I couldn't have cared less. Actually, another seven-foot teammate with a similar stature played much better than Shaquille that day. (From my perspective, he did not possess O'Neal's top-notch Type for basketball at the center position.) Yet a well-known TV commentator said he believed Oneal's teammate would fare better in the NBA.

Soon thereafter, I told three NBA teams to draft O'Neal any way possible, even though he was a freshman. It was uncharacteristic of me to tout a frosh in those days, but I could see O'Neal would be a franchise. My jubilant recommendation fell on deaf ears, and O'Neal stayed in college. Then the 1990-91 season rolled around, and Shaq could no longer hide his talent. By mid season, he was regarded as the Number 1 pro prospect. He dominated games as a man among boys. Everyone now wanted Shaquille O'Neal. In 1992, he was the first player chosen in the NBA draft. In 1996, his talent was valued even higher—to the point where he was awarded a $120 million contract!

Though some believed O'Neal had a bright upside, what did I know about him that experienced basketball scouts and coaches did not? I knew about Brain Types and their incredible relevance to sports. I believe nothing can compare with their usefulness in determining future athletic potential. It may seem like it's no big deal to pick a stout seven-footer, such as O'Neal, to excel in the NBA. Size, however, is generally the last aspect I consider, whereas Brain Type is always preeminent.

Watching the 1991 and 1992 NBA playoffs, I was amazed at how many players excelled that few ever predicted would be there. Over the years, I have known of a number of players who were the best of Brain Types for basketball, regardless of size. I told key NBA personnel that, given the chance, these players would excel in the NBA. **Tim Hardaway** is one in particular. This small yet outstanding point guard caught virtually everyone by surprise.

In 1989, an NBA team gave me a videotape of their top 30 college prospects, which provided a minute or two of highlights on each player. After viewing the tape, I was to inform the team of each player's respective Brain Type, with corresponding strengths and weaknesses. (I am generally able to do this from watching film footage.) Tim Hardaway, from Texas at El Paso, was one of these players. His moves and ball handling abilities were good, but what most impressed me was his Brain Type. I told the team about his potential stardom as well as the other players' potential. This particular team passed on Hardaway, but the Golden State Warriors wisely drafted him. The coaching sage, **Don Nelson**, gave him the opportunity to play. Hardaway became an NBA All-Star.

In 1993, I was asked to help the Orlando Magic pick the Number-1 player in the draft. For the second year in a row, they had won the top lottery spot. My advice to them ran contrary to popular opinion; it was not an easy sell. I was high on another Hardaway; this time his name was **Anfernee Hardaway**. Of all the top players in the draft, I believed he would be the best complement (as a 2, not a point guard) to the Magic's Shaquille O'Neal. Though it was a very difficult choice for the Magic to make, they risked their fan's wrath and selected Anfernee. It didn't take long, however, for him to show his NBA talents. In only his second season, Hardaway made first team All-NBA. None of the other '93 draft picks performed so well.

Brain Types enabled me to make a bold recommendation and to help the Magic better understand Hardaway—how to best motivate and play him for his optimal potential. Brain Typing is not exclusive to my efforts. You, too, can use this information to bring out the best in others.

Prior to the 1996 NBA draft, I watched two players in a private workout. Both were graduating, one from college but the other only from high school. They were opposite in virtually every area imaginable—including Brain Types. The college player never stopped hustling; the kid cruised a bit, and I vividly recall the comments of some NBA staff watching who were turned off by his perceived passiveness (and game). Later I heard a senior NBA scout comment that the kid was a great high school player who would probably become a good college performer but a doubtful NBA contributor. This comment troubled me. When asked what I thought of the young man's future, my response was that even though this was the first time I had ever seen him, I believed that due to his 6'6" frame, athleticism, developing skills and Brain Type—which was undeniably one of the NBA's best—he should become an an NBA All-Star (barring injury and provided he kept his nose clean). Most of those who heard me speak that day had never heard of Brain Types and naturally thought my comments were not to be taken seriously. Who was this controversial kid? **Kobe Bryant**.

In 1997, by looking at a video clip for a few minutes with an NBA coach, I realized the high-schooler soon entering the NBA draft had **Michael Jordan**'s Brain Type, as well as similar size and athleticism! Though he lacked some of MJ's other assets, I was exceptionally high on him (much more than other NBA "experts"), and told my NBA bosses. **Tracy McGrady** was one of my top two rated players (Tim Duncan was the other—who was picked first in '97 and McGrady 9th), and it didn't surprise me that within a few years, T-Mac became one of the few dominant NBA superstars, leading the league in scoring in 2003 at 32 p.p.g!

In 1998, my work was profiled on an ABC TV Saturday night news special, broadcast nationally. I was put on the spot and asked to forecast how highly-touted quarterbacks **Peyton Manning** and **Ryan Leaf** would fare in their upcoming NFL rookie seasons. I boldly stated that only one of the two had the top Brain Type for QB, but was not at liberty to tell the viewing audience which. Behind the scenes, I told the NFL team which hired me, and was looking to draft one of the two, much more in detail as to the sharp contrast between the QBs (based on Brain Type). Years have since passed, and needless to say, my once-maligned prediction proved uncannily true.

The first time I ever met with an NFL coach regarding QBs was with legendary **Tom Landry** of the Dallas Cowboys in August of 1986, thanks to a referral by a mutual friend. With less than an hour to meet at the Cowboys' training camp, I attempted to apprise him of my sports and Type research. He was reserved, cautious, and polite as he heard another "great" idea. Who could blame him or any other sports expert for being skeptical?

Following our meeting, I sent Coach Landry three letters throughout the remainder of 1986, each adding information regarding typology and specific football players. In January of 1987, he wrote:[6]

I continued to send him information throughout 1987. Rather than trying to tell him about numerous players and positions related to Type, I focused on the critical position of quarterback. The Cowboys at the time had a QB in the twilight years of his career; I felt it imperative for the Cowboys either to trade for or to draft the top Brain Type for QB.

UCLA's **Troy Aikman** was a college junior at the time who had not yet gained fame for his QB abilities. Watching him play here in Southern California, I was able to discern that he was the Brain Type I was looking

Tom Landry

January 13, 1987

Mr. Jon Niednagel
Type Dynamics
Country Club Drive
P.O. Box 6171
Laguna Niguel, California 92677

Dear Jon:

I read your summations of quarterbacks with interest. Your evaluations of each of the quarterbacks seems to be fairly accurate. It is always difficult to really point out those qualities that make the difference in that important position.

I am sure that as you continue to send me information, that I will better understand your Jungian Type Theory. I am not sure that I am ready to pursue it at this time; however, in the future something might come up that will be worthwhile for us to discuss.

I do appreciate your efforts in this field and the progress that you have made.

Sincerely yours,

Tom Landry

TL:bg

The gracious Mr. Landry was at least to "first base." Unlike many sports aficionados who believe they have all the answers, he was open to new information. I knew it was only a matter of time before he would see validity in my work.

for. I notified Coach Landry of his Type and potential. It wasn't long, however, before Aikman began to show his wares to the whole nation.

Prior to the NFL draft in 1989, Mr. Landry wrote again:[7]

Tom Landry

February 6, 1989

Jon Niednagel
Type Dynamics
P.O. Box 6171
Laguna Niguel, California 92677

Dear Jon:

Just a note to let you know how much I appreciate your letters from time to time and your discussions concerning the quarterbacks in the NFL. Most all of the people involved are very positive concerning Troy Aikman. I have not had the opportunity to see him work other than one time before the Cotton Bowl game. He is surely an impressive looking player because of his size and his movement.

It was encouraging for you to write and say that he is an ESTP type quarterback. We are leaving this weekend to go to Indianapolis and check out all of the college players who will be eligible for the Draft in April. Troy Aikman will be there and I will have a good chance to see him work.

Thanks again for writing and for your interest.

Sincerely yours,

Tom Landry

TL:bg

Following the Indianapolis workouts, Coach Landry phoned me and said Aikman was now high on the Cowboys' priority list. My predictions were being validated. I was happy for Mr. Landry, too, because I felt his critics at this late stage in his career had not taken into account the limitations of his personnel.

Only a month later, Coach Landry was no longer head coach of the Cowboys. Nevertheless, my three years of contact with him were not wasted. He learned about Types and I was further exposed to professional organizations. Mr. Landry was a class act.

The Cowboys went on to take Troy Aikman as their Number-1 pick in the 1989 draft. It took two years, but by overcoming injuries and a marginal team, Troy finally became recognized in the 1991-92 season as one of the best quarterbacks in the NFL. His subsequent Super Bowl rings have since proven his greatness.

Every year I go through similar routines with coaches and pro organizations when it comes draft time. Scores of players are involved, each with a specific Brain Type and athletic potential. With the advent of this information, teams can better understand their players, present and future, and draft and trade more wisely.

Each year players go high in the professional drafts that never should, according to Brain Types. They look good statistically, but they're not wired to be as productive as team expectations. Large amounts of money are needlessly wasted as teams look for the competitive edge. Many coaches are needlessly fired as a result of these ill-advised draft selections and the players' subsequent poor performances.

Sports Media

Persons in the sports media, generally gifted at seeing the "big picture," can see how our subject matter holds promise for them. The benefits are many.

As we just witnessed, most teams initially overlooked **Shaquille O'Neal**, as did the sports media, by and large. Some very prominent sportscasters said things about the big man during his freshman year they would probably like to correct.

Prior to the 1991 NCAA Basketball Tournament, sophomore guard, **Bobby Hurley** of Duke, was much maligned. After he led his Blue Devils to the '91 National title, his praises were heard everywhere. If the media had known our subject, they would have sung his praises even after Duke's NCAA tournament loss to UNLV in 1990. Bobby Hurley's exceptional Brain Type for basketball was the same in '90 as it was in '91 and '92. So was Shaquille's. This book will explain this Brain Type and its maturation process.

When watching TV or reading an article, we will often be told players seem to have exceptional body skills or traits. Yet the media persons can't quite put their finger on why or how the athletes excel the way they do.

Why do broadcasters **Dick Vitale, John Madden, Vin Scully and Dick Enberg** announce as they do? Is it what Vitale eats for breakfast that gives him his creative energy? This material will give you strong clues to how his brain operates, as well as those of other well known sports media persons.

Trading-Card Collectors

I can remember as a kid in the 1950s trying to scrounge up enough money to buy a bubblegum pack containing baseball cards. My brother Roland and I would walk to wherever they were sold, which wasn't always close. Roland was a fanatic about cards. He knew every player, their averages and especially their uniforms. His motto was always "It's not how you play that counts, but how you look." To him, the cards had life. They were people, and he liked to pretend he was every superstar. Because he was older, I was always left to emulate the lesser talents.

To me, the cards were for practical use. On rainy days, I would use them to play baseball indoors. I made a field on the basement floor with fences 8" high (2" x 8" boards). I'd prop up a card at each position in the field (each player in his real spot), and we'd hit marbles on the ground with a ruler. If a card was knocked over, the batter was out, and so on. We had some great games during which we learned some skills of coaching and disputing bad calls ala Billy Martin. We survived the conflicts and retain memories of fun times.

Roland and I collected cards for years, each for different reasons. We had scads of **Mantles, Aarons, Williams**, and all the big names in that era. Some of the cards ended up pretty thrashed (especially mine); after all, they had suffered some wicked line drives. We outgrew that stage, and the cards were relegated to shoe boxes in the attic. After years of college and marriage, Roland and I returned home looking for our cards. You guessed it, Mom had thrown them out believing they were worthless.

Collecting baseball and other athletic cards (and sports memorabilia) isn't done naively anymore. There is still sentiment attached by some to their heroes, but for many the attachment is financial. When **Honus Wagners** sell for half a million bucks and **Mickey Mantle** rookies for $50,000, we are no longer looking at collecting cards for recreation only. From 1982 to 1992, baseball cards in general increased in value about 1,000 percent. By comparison, the Dow Jones industrial average increased approximately 250 percent.

In 1980, only one company, the Topps Chewing Gum Co. of Brooklyn, N.Y., was making collector cards, with one set each in baseball, basketball, football, and hockey. In 1991, five companies printed some 7.5 billion cards, with multiple sets in almost every sport.

The information supplied in this book can assist card collectors as they assemble their collections. Depending on your proficiency with this material, you can predict with surprising accuracy who is going to make it big in any of the major professional sports. I've been doing it for years.

Summary

Athletes at any level have to practice, have to play, have to mature, have to work hard if they expect to reach their potential. And those who guide them—parents, coaches, managers, as well as athletes themselves—would be wise to know what makes them tick. They would also do well to take advantage of the knowledge that can help any athlete, at any level, know what sports and what positions offer the best potential for success.

To gain this insight, they have to discover what Brain Types they are. More about the process is soon to be explained on our journey.

Different Types Excel in Different Sports

Have you ever wondered what enabled **Magic Johnson** to play NBA basketball as he did? What allowed him to see the floor like a helicopter pilot, and pass the ball as if he were Merlin the Magician?

How has **Dan Marino** thrown a football like Grandma threads a needle? Does he have any inborn abilities beyond yours (or mine), or could you have accomplished the same with commensurate coaching, practice and play?

Was Olympic diving great, **Greg Louganis**, that big of a deal, or could you have achieved the same, given equal training and commitment?

Each of these three great athletes has a separate, unique cerebral floor-plan and circuitry pattern that differs from the others. Each has a Brain Type that is designed to excel at his respective sport and position. If these three could swap brains with one another, they would not perform anywhere near their previous performances. Practice, coaching, stature, discipline, and so on, all played critical roles in their greatness. Yet, without their specific brain design, they would not have achieved their level of greatness.

Did you know the NBA's **Michael Jordan, Hakeem Olajuwon, John Stockton, Larry Bird, and Shaquille O'Neal** are a few of one specific Brain Type?

The NFL's **Joe Montana, Joe Namath, John Elway, and Brett Favre** all have similar cerebral and physical patterns within another specific Brain Type.

Baseball's **Barry Bonds, Nomar Garciaparra, Ken Griffey Jr., and Tony Gwynn** also possess inborn make ups similar to each other.

These athletes, however, who possess the exact Brain Types of others, often have very different personas or personalities from one another. Upbringing, friends, experiences, and cultural environment will significantly shape one's unique personality or temperament. So will other genetic differences. Brain designs are not the same as personalities and are not changeable. More on this later.

In the pages ahead, we will view well known athletes, discussing how their cerebral make ups empower them to perform at such high levels. You can also learn what sport it is in which you have the greatest potential.

Of a possible 16 distinct Brain Types, each excels at one (or more) sport more than another. The inborn mental, physical, and spatial characteristics of each innate design determine this phenomenon. Once you get a handle on the unique attributes for each Brain Type, you'll readily understand why some hardwirings are better than others at certain sports.

Certain Types excel at different positions as well. Although many of the 16 Types are found in professional football, one Type above all generally excels at quarterback. Not only can this Type be the most proficient at passing, it can consistently handle pressure better than any other QB Type on the gridiron. Handling pressure is a critical point in any sport.

Certain Brain Types can physically shoot, pass, dribble, throw, or kick the ball as well as any other. Unfortunately, some of these Types are not designed to see peripherally as well, or evaluate matters as logically as others, thereby making them less effective in game or pressure situations.

Some Types are less proficient at physical dexterity and adroitness, but can be very good athletes, relying on their mental acumen. They'll need to work overtime developing their motor skills, but ultimately they will depend primarily on their capable mental skills.

The best athletes in each sport combine superior physical and mental dexterity. We will see which Types they are after we build a foundation for your new typology neuroscience understanding.

PART TWO

THE MIND, BRAIN, AND BODY

2
Who Are You?

Understanding Self and Others: A Key to Success in Athletics and Life

Have you ever left a social gathering knowing you had really made an impression, only to find that your spouse had a list of things you shouldn't have said? Have you ever gotten ready for a party, spent a lot of time on your appearance, rushed to get there on time, only to stand in the door looking for a familiar face, someone safe with whom you could feel at home?

Do you try to get things done but the distractions around every corner entice you away from completion? Does that bother someone close to you?

Do you plan for impending doom because it usually comes?

Do others say, "Relax, lighten up"? Are you too busy to notice the complexities of life? Do people around you seem to come up with suffocating rules and regulations?

Does the world seem too abstract, with the theoretical courses you're forced to take boggling your mind? Do you wish you could be more practical, face reality, and deal with it?

Are you having trouble with those around you, wishing they would accept your constructive suggestions? Or are you on the receiving end of those suggestions and having a hard time accepting criticism? Do you feel you are not loved or appreciated for who you are, only for what you accomplish for the team, organization, or family?

We have many responsibilities and roles to play. We want to meet the needs of others as well as our own. Some of the biggest obstacles in each of our lives come from the clashing of personalities. In whatever role we play, during any part of the day, we use our God given designs and personalities. With them, we interact with other people who seem vastly different from us.

Psychologists and others who study people have discovered wonderful differences. People are not alike. We all have gifts and abilities that are unique. We differ in our attitudes, our beliefs, our wants, our skills, and our needs.

Can We Change Others?

No matter how hard we may try to mold or reshape an individual, we will not be able to effect another's basic design. It would be like trying to change an elephant into a giraffe. Typological and genetic research now concur that certain aspects of personality are paramount and unchangeable. It is believed we are created with basic characteristics formed from the time of conception which remain with us throughout life.

Traits or mannerisms of others frequently irritate us. These characteristics are usually different from our own. It would be easier to live with those who are like us. Many of us want to correct the differences we see in others, but most attempts to do so would be doomed to fail.

Instead of trying to change others, we would be better off trying to understand them. What are their interests and needs? What are their preferences and goals? It will take time and effort on our part. Trying to make others something they can never be will not work. Understanding others from their points of view will revitalize our relationships.

The "Real" Person is Hidden

Michelangelo, the Renaissance sculptor, painter, architect, and poet, is said to have looked upon a freestanding mass of gleaming Carrara marble one day and exclaimed, "There's an angel in that stone and I am going to liberate him!" In the same way, we might think of those around us as beautiful designs to liberate and help them become all they can be.

You will find it highly advantageous to discover the designs of those with whom you associate. Not only will you gain a new sense of appreciation for others, but you will be better equipped to meet their needs. People often camouflage their real needs by expressing their perceived needs; most onlookers lack the insight to discern the difference.

Before we can evaluate others, we must first study ourselves. A preference quiz (questionnaire) is provided here for you to complete and an answer sheet to record your answers. There are no *right* or *wrong* answers. You can neither *pass* nor *fail* this questionnaire because it is designed to help you see who you really are. "*Help*" is the key word here, not guarantee. Keep in mind that regardless the accuracy of any particular mental or psychological analysis, self evaluating questionnaires (such as the MBTI™, Keirsey Temperament Sorter, or this one) cannot be considered foolproof—or close to it. Even when test takers answer as honestly as possible, there are numerous reasons why they often score contrary to their true Type. (Some of these reasons are covered in the "Accurate Typing" section of this book.)

Taking a questionnaire is only one step in the process to determine your true Brain Type. (The Brain Type Institute offers other and more reliable helps, such as CD-ROMs, video tapes, and personal evaluations.) Consider your questionnaire results with objectivity and caution. You've only begun the process of Brain Type self discovery.

In the following questions you must make one of two choices: *a* or *b*. You will find that a third choice, *c*, is provided as well. It wants to know if the person who knows you best (spouse, relative, friend, and so forth) would disagree with your answer. If you feel he or she would disagree, then check *c*, too. Therefore, on certain questions you may have two answers checked, either *a* and *c*, or *b* and *c*.

The questions are not meant to be difficult. They are straightforward and require simple honesty. Set aside some time for yourself without interruptions. Perhaps, in some cases, you will feel like choosing both *a* and *b*. Even if you agree with both answers, check the one with which you agree more.

To yield an accurate description of yourself, it is imperative that you answer the questionnaire honestly. Answer as you really are, not as the person you would like to be.

As much as possible, try to make choices *outside* the context of your job. In other words, questionnaire results can be altered if you interpret too many questions with your job in mind. The fact that we all have certain job responsibilities and strong interests should not be used to cloud the results. Therefore, try to think of situations in which you are most free to be yourself.

Again, there are no right or wrong answers. Just be honest with yourself as you read and make choices. Once you have completed the survey, you will be on your way to making some exciting discoveries.

QUESTIONNAIRE

Questionnaire

Answer on each of the following 20 groupings of phrases and word pairs, which choices most accurately describe you. Record your answers in the columns following the questionnaire.

1. a. higher energy level, sociable
   b. lower energy level, reserved, soft spoken
   c. close associate probably disagrees

2. a. interpret matters literally, rely on common sense
   b. look for meaning and possibilities, rely on foresight
   c. close associate probably disagrees

3. a. logical, thinking, questioning
   b. empathetic, feeling, accommodating
   c. close associate probably disagrees

4. a. organized, orderly
   b. flexible, adaptable
   c. close associate probably disagrees

5. a. outgoing, make things happen
   b. shy, do fewer things
   c. close associate probably disagrees

6. a. practical, realistic, experiential
   b. imaginative, innovative, theoretical
   c. close associate probably disagrees

7. a. candid, straight forward, frank
   b. tactful, kind, encouraging
   c. close associate probably disagrees

8. a. plan, schedule
   b. unplanned, spontaneous
   c. close associate probably disagrees

9. a. seek many tasks, public activities, interaction with others
   b. seek more private, solitary activities with quiet to concentrate
   c. close associate probably disagrees

10. a. standard, usual, conventional
    b. different, novel, unique
    c. close associate probably disagrees

11. a. firm, tend to criticize, hold the line
    b. gentle, tend to appreciate, conciliate
    c. close associate probably disagrees

12. a. regulated, structured
    b. easygoing, "live" and "let live"
    c. close associate probably disagrees

13. a. external, communicative, express yourself
    b. internal, reticent, hold things in
    c. close associate probably disagrees

14. a. consider immediate issues, focus on the here-and-now
    b. look to future, global perspective, "big picture"
    c. close associate probably disagrees

15. a. tough-minded, just
    b. tenderhearted, merciful
    c. close associate probably disagrees

16. a. preparation, work-minded
    b. go with the flow, play-minded
    c. close associate probably disagrees

17. a. active, initiate
    b. reflective, deliberate
    c. close associate probably disagrees

18. a. facts, things, seeing "what is"
    b. ideas, dreams, seeing "what could be," philosophical
    c. close associate probably disagrees

19. a. matter of fact, issue-oriented, principled
    b. sensitive, people-oriented, compassionate
    c. close associate probably disagrees

20. a. control, govern
    b. latitude, freedom
    c. close associate probably disagrees

2....Who Are You?

> You have the capacity to fly, but we don't know what kind of flying creature you are. In a way, you're an "Unidentified Flying Object." That's why you need to take the:
>
> ### "U.F.O." TYPE DETECTOR

	I			II			III			IV		
	a	b	c	a	b	c	a	b	c	a	b	c
1				2			3			4		
5				6			7			8		
9				10			11			12		
13				14			15			16		
17				18			19			20		

    E I   S N   T F   J P

How to Score Your Questionnaire

To find your Type profile, add the number of *a*, *b*, and *c* responses in each column. (There are four columns and five numbers in each column.) In column 1, simply total the number of checks of *a*, *b*, and *c* in the boxes below. This shows your E (Extraversion) versus I (Introversion) score.

Add the results of columns 2, 3, and 4 as you did in column 1. This shows your S (Sensation) versus N (iNtuition) score), T (Thinking) versus F (Feeling) score, and J (Judging) versus P (Perceiving) score.

Next, circle the one letter of each pair that is the highest number. Your Type is now expressed as a four-letter combination.

What About the "c" Responses?

The number of *c* responses you find will tell you two things. First, it will serve as a tiebreaker if your *a* and *b* responses are equal. Second, it will tell you to use caution in evaluating your own preferences. For example, if you checked three J responses, two P responses, and three *c* responses, you will have to take some additional time considering your true preferences. You will have to pay special attention to the responses the *c*'s were opposing. For example, if all your J choices also have *c*'s marked, you evidently think someone who knows you well would consider you a P. Your score would actually differ if your friend's *c* responses were tallied. As you can see, the *c* responses serve as a warning that your self perception may not agree with the way others see you.

So What's Your Type?

Now that you've taken the questionnaire, you are probably anxious to know the meaning of the results. You have a combination of four letters that describes your typological design, one that is different from 15 other Types. For a brief description of your Type, turn to the summary chart of the 16 Types found on pages 46 and 47. There you may read about your own Type and see how it compares to a few others. Keep in mind this is only a brief description, not a summary of your whole personality. Once you've read it, continue reading on page 37.

You may not agree with everything (or anything!) that is written about you, but if you have answered the questionnaire according to your true Type, the majority of traits and habits will be accurate. If you really have a struggle with the description of your personality, it is likely that one or more of your preferences are wrong. If this is the case, don't be concerned. Accuracy cannot be guaranteed by a questionnaire. It is only the first step in discovering your inherent characteristics. Accurately evaluating yourself will be discussed later. For now, we want to begin the process of discovering your inborn Brain Type.

The following chart lists the specific Types and their opposites. You may want to read the chapter describing your opposite as well as your own Type. Seeing the differences in perspectives and understanding them will be essential in maximizing the information in this book.

Type	your opposite is............................	**Type**
ESTP	....	INFJ
ESFP	....	INTJ
ESTJ	....	INFP
ESFJ	....	INTP
ENTP	....	ISFJ
ENTJ	....	ISFP
ENFP	....	ISTJ
ENFJ	....	ISTP

Once you have read about your possible Brain Type and its opposite, continue reading with the next chapter.

3
Mental Preferences

This book is devoted to helping you know and understand yourself and others more fully. By discovering your God given design, you will understand why your mind works as it does—why you view matters and make decisions as you do. You will also better understand your emotional makeup. Presented with the physical and athletic perspective, you will know what you are capable of doing and to what degree. Socially, you will better understand why you tend to regard others as you do, and, spiritually, you may see why you view God as you do.

The study of human behavior has attracted many theorists over the course of time. The field of psychology is more than simply the study of the psyche or mind; it is preeminently the investigation of human behavior. Those who study the behavior of others have tried for ages to explain both the rational and irrational acts of humankind. Or, as someone put it, "Psychology is the study of what makes people tick—and what ticks them off."

Most of us tend to have many questions about the area of personality. What do I mean by *personality*? It is the *sum total of the various traits, attitudes and characteristics of an individual that can be identified and described.* There are definite patterns of behavior among people. These patterns set people apart from others who demonstrate a different set or pattern of behavior. Thus, what appears to be random behavior in people is in fact quite orderly and dependable. Dr. Walter Lowen, scientist and engineer, stated:

> I marvel at the order in nature. Whenever some new secret of nature is revealed, what is uncovered is a new, beautiful, simple ordering scheme, be it a periodic table, the structure of crystals, the atom, or DNA.

I believe intelligence, too, has its explanation in some basic order.[1]

Researchers have discovered these patterns translate into "personality types" or "psychological types." In the next chapter we will see that "Brain Types" is the most accurate way to categorize people and understand why they behave as they do. For now, we will continue to use personality Type terminology. (People are infinitely complex. No model can explain all there is to know about a person.)

We will leave the world of sports temporarily in order for you to grasp the essence of personality Types. Keep in mind that the understanding of this material will lead you to improved athletic performance.

A word of caution: Do you sense that ascribing specific personality Types to people is like putting them in boxes, providing them little or no room for growth or flexibility? Do you suspect the practice could become demeaning or restricting? It is true that categorizing can be counterproductive; therefore two questions must be asked: (1) Is the categorization true and accurate and (2) is it used in a constructive way?

Have you ever considered how you might categorize people? After all, most everyone does. Many use cultural distinctions such as social, financial, and educational status, or religion. Some use physical classifications like race, sex, and stature, or mental labels like "smart," "dumb," and "average." If you can't think of any of your labels, ask the persons who know you best; they may be able to help you remember.

This book is solely intended for constructive use. I hope we all are able to view others in a rational, appreciative fashion, without making disparaging conclusions.

Jung-Myers Typology

We owe much of what we know about individual differences to the Swiss psychiatrist and psychologist, **Dr. Carl Gustav Jung**, who is regarded as the founder of the modern theory of psychological type, or typology. Jung said:

> It was one of the greatest experiences of my life to discover how enormously different people's psyches are.[2]

Jung believed that specific patterns, types, or combinations of preferences in humans could be described and categorized. *Please note that we will be discussing Jung's typology as opposed to his psychology—of which I am not an advocate.*

In all, there are four pairs of preferences which he, and later, **Isabel Myers**, explained and developed. A preference is the conscious or unconscious choice an individual makes in a certain designated realm. The eight preferences (also called "processes") are Extraversion (E), Introversion (I), Sensation (S), iNtuition (N), Thinking (T), Feeling (F), Judging (J) and Perceiving (P). (The symbol for iNtuition is "N," since the letter "I" is used as the symbol for Introversion.)

Each preference is paired with its opposite. Thus an individual is either Extraverted or Introverted, Sensing or iNtuitive, Thinking or Feeling, and Judging or Perceiving. Every individual's personality is a combination of four preferences, expressed as a series of four letters. An ISFP, for example, is an individual who is an Introvert, Sensate, Feeler, and is Perceptive. In all, there are 16 different combinations of the preferences making up the different personality Types, each with a unique description.

The Type analysis does not involve questions of good and bad. There are no superior Types and no inferior Types. Rather, the study points out major differences in people's perspectives and throws substantial light on why they behave as they do and perform as they do in athletics.

Everyone has all eight preferences to some degree. However, in each pairing, one preference is more prominent than its opposite. For example, an ISFP would prefer to use the process of Sensation more often than iNtuition. No person is evenly balanced, that is, equal in both parts of a preference pair. In fact, students of typology strongly support the contention that in any sort of pressure situation, one will quickly choose one's stronger or dominant preference. "Thinkers," therefore, particularly under pressure, will react with impersonal, logical reasoning and may not have an awareness of their Feelings or the feelings of others when making a decision. Similarly, "Feelers," when under pressure, will resort to a more subjective means of evaluation, placing a greater emphasis upon the Feelings involved (theirs or others') to the possible exclusion of logical deduction. Outside of pressure situations, we tend to maintain a better balance of our preferences, especially as we mature.

The best way to understand the eight preferences is to define and describe each one. The following pages discuss the eight preferences in pairs. You may find it helpful to reread the following portion from time to time. These definitions and descriptions are foundational to your own personal success in using typology.

Extraversion (E) and Introversion (I)

The terms "Extravert" and "Introvert" may be two of the most misunderstood words in our vocabulary. When we hear these terms, we think of stereotypes, usually negative ones. Introverts have come to be considered wallflowers, loners, bookish, bores and self absorbed hermits. Extraverts are described as loud, overbearing, social, talkative, and domineering. Let's erase our prejudices and replace them with the terms' original meanings. "Extraversion" and "Introversion" are terms coined by Carl Jung to identify how people are energized. (Jung preferred the spelling extr**a**version." Typology literature follows his lead, differing from the dictionary's extr**o**version.) The question is, where do people get their energy—the outer world of people, action, and things (E), or the inner world of ideas, contemplation, and reflection (I)?

Extraverts prefer to focus on the outer world and are energized by their contact with it. Their batteries are charged by talking and interacting with people, with activities, with living out their plans and dreams. It is believed by many type theorists that approximately 70 percent of the population in America is Extraverted. Extraverts look for stimuli outside themselves and have a wider scope of activities and interests. They usually say what they think or feel. They live life outwardly to gain inner understanding and generally need to be with others, but as active people they still need some time alone so they don't become rundown. Confident Extraverts can enjoy time in the inner world, but their talents are best used for relating to others.

Extraverts are consistently more energetic than Introverts. They generally have a quicker response time when asked questions. They tend to have better eye contact during conversation. Many clues, verbal and physical, distinguish the Extravert from the Introvert.

Introverts, in contrast, are compelled to recharge their batteries from within. Many Introverts are inclined to keep their real selves hidden until they fully trust a confidant or until they know others will take the time to hear them out. Introverts thrive in contemplating, thinking before they act. Introverts build their energy when they have time and space to be alone. It is estimated only 25-30 percent of Americans are Introverted.

Introverts are not as distracted by activities around them having better concentrating abilities. Introverts conserve energy and delve deeply into interests and relationships. They have fewer acquaintances, since they become drained by too much interaction. Through practice, or by being in an Extraverted family, an Introvert may develop an adequate facility for Extraversion. Introverted Feelers may seem more Extraverted because of the use of relational and people skills. Extraversion, however, is something they will continually seek in order to relate to other people.

In a family setting or when with close friends, Introverts may be loud, outgoing, vivacious and apparently Extraverted. Their preference for Introversion will be seen more clearly, however, when they're in unfamiliar situations. Extraverts can appear Introverted when they lack self confidence or concern for others.

There are different degrees of Extraversion and Introversion. People who display extreme Extraversion will be absorbed in action, crowds, business, rushing from place to place, and speaking extemporaneously. They would rather "do" than "wait." Introverts with extreme tendencies will be reclusive, painfully shy, and retiring. Most of us are somewhere in between. We can use our Extraversion or our Introversion at any time, but we will feel more comfortable using one more than the other. It is always best to work toward being a balanced person.

KEY CHARACTERISTICS

Extraversion:	**Introversion:**
outer world	inner world
active	reflective
energy-expending	energy-conserving
expressive	reserved
aggressive	defensive
expanding	conserving
many acquaintances	a few close friends
conversational	passive conversationalist with strangers
intrigued by surroundings	more concerned with self
inspired by public activities	inspired by private, solitary activities
responsive before reasoning	responsive after reasoning
public	private
congregate	meditate
reasons out loud	needs time to express

Sensing (S) and iNtuition (N)

Sensing (S) and iNtuition (N) show how you perceive the world around you. They indicate which senses you prefer to use first—the five senses or the sixth sense, iNtuition.

Are you more interested in reality, what actually is observable and measurable? Or are you fascinated by the possibilities in a situation, following hunches, imagining what could be instead of what is? Do you prefer fiction or nonfiction? Do you walk through the forest examining the detailed variety of flora and fauna or do you float above the trees, seeing "the big picture"?

The "N" is used for iNtuition since the "I" stood for Introversion. iNtuition should not be confused with our common notions of the word. Instead, iNtuition is the reliance upon one's own insights into the world of possibilities, concepts, significance, to take in information. The **iNtuitive** enjoy symbols, daydreaming, and mental gymnastics that focus on the future. For the iNtuitive, the here and now take second place to the past and future. Facts are useful only to develop patterns that lead to further discoveries or that support thoughts and ideas already held.

The driving force inside the iNtuitive is to invent and create. Therefore, the iNtuitive is the dealer in ideas—the inventor, the novel writer, the research scientist, the journalist, the movie director. It's believed iNtuitives approximate 30-40 percent of the American public. Being in a minority, they sometimes feel out of step until college, which is more iNtuition oriented. Higher education leaves more Sensates behind, and the balance of the two evens out on campus. You will find the iNtuitive reading more fiction and fantasy.

The **Sensate** lives in the real world of the present. Sensates are pragmatic and enjoy the impressions from their environment taken in through the five senses. They're observant and factual. They're most interested in the immediate usefulness of knowledge and they tend to shun the theoretical. One of their questions is, "Will it work?" Sensates go through life trusting the tangible, the visible. They pay attention to detail and follow directions step by step. Direct conversation is their style and they generally say what they mean.

The difference between Sensates and iNtuitives is wide and various, and they need great tolerance of one another. Sensates see iNtuitives as flighty, impractical, out of touch with reality. iNtuitives see Sensates as short-sighted, nit-picking and unimaginative. Using one function or the other exclusively can lead one astray. We need the input of both functions, facts with possibilities and dreams within reach of reality.

KEY CHARACTERISTICS

Sensing:	iNtuition:
informed by the five senses	informed by the "sixth sense"
inspired by the real, the practical	inspired by the imaginative, the ingenious
found in the present	found in the future
"Will it work?"	"Is it possible?"
perspiration driven	inspiration driven
motivated by usefulness	motivated by inventiveness
evidence seeking	potential seeking
the way it is	the way it could be
yesterday and today	tomorrow and beyond
directions	hunches
literal	figurative
tangible	intangible
observant	imaginative
down to earth	visionary

Thinking (T) and Feeling (F)

Decisions must inevitably be made, and people find themselves most comfortable making them based on either the "Feeling" preference or the "Thinking" preference. One person may choose an impersonal, objective approach that seems to be clear and logical. Another person may be prone to "feel a situation out" and then decide based on personal, subjective values. This person usually considers how the decision will affect the people involved. The first person would be declared a Thinker and the second a Feeler.

Here we have a major point of contention between opposite Types. Thinkers have feelings and Feelers do think, but they do not speak the same language. In a situation affecting both a Thinker and a Feeler, they often clash.

For example, a Thinking parent may want a child to study for an exam since the child is behind in that subject. Thus the parent is Thinking logically. The Feeling parent may want the child to spend the night with a best friend who is leaving town the next day for many months. In terms of relationships, that parent is also being logical. A conflict is unavoidable.

Both Thinking and Feeling are rational processes, and both are necessary. In dealing with inanimate matters, numbers, and principles, we need logical Thinking. In dealing with people, Feeling is the most effective function.

Thinkers are more apt to make decisions based on logical, impersonal reasoning. They can be objective and rational, considering rules and policy, and they can remove themselves personally from the decision. To the Feeler, the Thinker may seem distant and hard-hearted.

Thinkers seek objective truth, using the terms "true" and "false", "right" and "wrong". They use emotions and values only to validate logical conclusions. Thinkers must be careful their deductions are based on true statistics. In some cases, too, tact is preferable to bare truth. To avoid hurting a friend, a wise Thinker will learn at an early age to be tactful when telling the truth.

Most men in our society refer to themselves as Thinkers, probably because they see this description as more masculine. Statistically there appear to be no more Thinking men than Feeling men; the discrepancy is not as once believed; the ratio approximates 50-50. Typology questionnaire results are often incorrect in this area due to cultural bias.

Feeling oriented persons makes judgments or decisions subjectively, placing extra emphasis on personal values. They consider how a decision will affect people. They are more apt to be totally and personally involved in decision-making. They use persuasion rather than argument to convince another person to see things their way. Softer, friendly expressions and ready smiles give us clues to their Feeling preference.

To Thinkers, Feelers appear wishy-washy, unable to come to or stand by a firm decision that's tough on people. Feelers show their thoughts in body language and are often seen as too emotional, too soft, and too illogical. It is harder for them to express their logic.

Feelers may need to see the logical side of issues and get input from Thinkers. If the values of Feelers are solid, however, and true, they will be just as "on target" as logical Thinkers.

Feelers are sympathetic to the emotional pain of others and show special sensitivity to those in need. They are more interested in people than in things, preferring tactfulness over directness in most situations. Feelers flourish under appreciation and "good vibrations." Recalling past encounters and reminiscing are Feeling traits.

Women tend to see themselves as Feelers even when they are not. Thinking females often find it beneficial to soften their image whenever possible. For all women, motherhood and cultural female behavior bring an extra measure of personableness. Society often rewards a "warm-natured" woman with its approval.

Remember, all people use both Thinking and Feeling, but one is innately stronger in each person. This preference is especially used when experiencing pressure.

Few people are at the extreme ends of the spectrum of Feeling and Thinking. An example might be seen in a morning walk taken by two neighbors. The first person is there to talk, to relate, to build the friendship, and secondarily to exercise. The second person mentions that she may have to start walking alone because when she tried it, she seemed to walk much faster. She was out for increased metabolism and exercise, secondarily for the relationship and conversation.

We may see the difference in the example of the couple deciding how to spend the weekend. The wife wants to have friends over, and the husband wants to paint the house. The Feeler is drawn toward relationships, the Thinker toward projects. Thinkers, however, often have a strong affinity toward their own family members. Feelers tend to broaden their scope of loved ones.

KEY CHARACTERISTICS

Thinking:	Feeling:
objective	subjective
impersonal	interpersonal
just	merciful
lawful	circumstantial
critical	appreciative
rational	non rational (not necessarily irrational)
principled	value driven
systematic	relational
cool	caring
commanding	persuasive
concerned with issues	concerned with effects on people
logical reasons	personal reasons
unconcerned with emotional aspects	concerned with emotional aspects
firm managers	sympathetic managers
direct	tactful

Judging (J) and Perceiving (P)

The "Judgment" and "Perception" preferences show how people choose to live their lives. When a J or a P is at the end of the four-letter Brain Type, it refers to the outer world of a person, the side he or she chooses to reveal to others.

The P and the J tell whether one prefers keeping options open and flexible or organized and closed. Judging does not necessarily mean judgmental but rather conclusive and decisive. The person is uncomfortable until decisions are made. Perceiving does not mean perceptive as we normally think of it but rather becoming aware, absorbing information without experiencing pressure to arrive at closure. Both are rational ways of living, though one is more planned and the other more and the other more spontaneous.

In determining whether you are a P or J, don't put too much emphasis on how you behave at work. Work arenas demand we act a certain way. Think about your total person, how you choose to live during the time that you call the shots. Then add the complication that what you show the world is often the opposite of what you are at home, in your Introverted world. Moreover, Extraverts appear to be extreme one way or the other, unless they are exceptionally balanced through experience or determination.

For example, a man at a meeting or social event may be decisive, scheduled, and controlling. When at home or on vacation this same person may have a messy desk or closet and may not want to make as many decisions. Therefore he is a J in the Extraverted world, P in the inner world. The J would go at the end of his Brain Type (ENT**J**, for example) because that is what he shows the world.

Another person may be spontaneous and open ended in a group setting but opinionated about the important things in her inner world, maybe even hiding these traits from her friends, especially if she is Introverted. She would be a P (for example, ISTP) in her designated Brain Type.

So what exactly is a judging person, a judge, a J? How would one be recognized?

Judgers prefer to take action and come to a decision or conclusion as soon as possible. They are driven to closure in their outer world. Judging persons are organized and decisive, and they value advanced planning. They are geared toward making decisions about what they should do as well as what others should do. They prefer to plan, maintain order, and control events and people around them.

The danger for these people is that they tend to become too rigid in their effort to keep the world on its axis. They need to seek balance, loosening up so they can experience greater freedom. This may lead to more creativity, less stress, or both.

J's do better with deadlines and living by the rules. They want to get their work done before they play, believing play must be earned. Watching a J athlete on a basketball court, you may notice a stilted motion, more rigidity, and less fluid movement. Their golf swings and their baseball pitching will appear more mechanical. They may be accurate, but they're normally less graceful than a P person. The J's may tend to break more bones and have more accidents due to their inflexibility. The P's will have accidents due to greater risk taking. If you want to do something on the spur of the moment, call the spontaneous P person.

Perceivers are those who need additional time dealing with the outer world before making decisions. They feel the need to gather more information and make observations, keeping their schedules and viewpoints fairly open-ended. In this way, they are in a position to experience the new and exciting. This is true for both the Introvert and the Extravert. Perceptive individuals are more flexible and adaptable. They shun the attempts of others to put them in a box. They avoid confinement and desire greater freedom with little or no restraints.

The Perceiving (P) person is flexible, spontaneous, fun-loving, and adaptable. When opportunity knocks, the P is ready!

The Judging (J) person is organized, decisive, and values advanced planning. The J's ethic: "Work now, play later."

If taken to the extreme, P persons may stray off course and lose control of their outer lives. P's need a degree of Judgment (J) so they can know what their boundaries are.

Last, P's tend to receive new information in a non-judgmental, open-minded way, whereas J's are inclined to make new information conform to preconceived knowledge, hesitating if it doesn't. It is estimated that approximately half the American population is innately Perceptive, and the other half is Judging.

KEY CHARACTERISTICS

Judging:	**Perceiving:**
organized	flexible
decisive	exploratory
"let's finalize"	"let's wait"
closed	open
work-oriented	play-oriented
planned	adaptable
control-loving	freedom-loving
deliberate	spontaneous
driven to decide	driven to understand
enjoys finishing	enjoys beginning
rigid	wishy-washy
avoids surprises	welcomes surprises
step-by-step	hurry it up
enjoys results	enjoys the process
"get to the point"	"explore the tangents"

How long will you lie there, you sluggard?
When will you get up from your sleep?
A little sleep, a little slumber,
a little folding of the hands to rest—
and poverty will come on you like a bandit
and scarcity like an armed man.   Proverbs 6:9-11

Better one handful with tranquility than two handfuls with toil and chasing after the wind.   Ecclesiastes 4:6

Summary of the Eight Preferences

The research of Carl Jung and, later, Isabel Myers into psychological types reveals eight personality preferences paired as opposites within four categories. Each of the four categories is concerned with basic, fundamental questions.

Category 1: Introversion or Extraversion

The first category of preferences deals with the direction of attention and interests, whether inward or outward.

Introvert (I) Do I reflective on life? Do I prefer to ponder and delve more deeply into life's encounters (few deep relationships, greater introspection, and more energy invested in myself than others)? I like people, too, but I'm normally reserved or shy (especially with strangers). I prefer to "charge my batteries" by not having to relate to people (other than close friends and family). Conserving energy, saving it for when I'll really need it, is important to me.

Extravert (E) Am I chiefly interested in the outer world where I can deal with people and things (many acquaintances, relationships, and a variety of interests that are broad in scope)? Normally, I get "charged up" when I am around others, and I enjoy the company of others. I also tend to share with others what's on my mind. Continually expending energy is part of my inherent nature.

Category 2: Sensing or iNtuition

The second category of preferences deals with how one becomes aware of things in the world, whether through the five senses or through the sixth sense.

Sensate (S) Do I stay in touch with the world by using my five senses? Do I place a high value on facts and practicality? Am I more down-to-earth than visionary? When reading or listening to conversation, do I tend to interpret matters literally more than attach special meaning and significance?

iNtuitive (N) Do I rely on my innate ability to view things creatively, looking for possibilities and meanings? Am I an idea person who prefers to view the future and what it might become rather than be stuck in the "here and now?" Am I more imaginative than observant?

Category 3: Thinking or Feeling

The third category of preferences deals with whether one makes decisions objectively or subjectively.

Thinker (T) Do I make decisions based on logical reasoning, objectivity, justice, policy, and principles—judging what I think is right or wrong? Do I like to take systematic approaches to solving problems?

Feeler (F) Do I make decisions based more on subjective reasoning, highly valuing interpersonal relationships and how decisions will affect others? Is it very important to me that I have harmony with others?

Category 4: Judging or Perceiving

The third category of preferences deals with whether one is controlled or flexible in living the outer life.

Judger (J) Do I live my life in a planned, organized, controlled, and self-disciplined way (preferring to bring matters to a close and valuing a strong work ethic)?

Perceiver (P) Do I live my life in a spontaneous and adaptable manner (preferring freedom and exploration and choosing between play and work)?

Introverts

Sensate

ISFP
"Artisan"

appreciates beauty and texture; artistic, athletic and graceful; reticent, not verbally expressive; realistic; sensitive, modest, kind; sympathetic; impulsive, enjoys freedom; service-oriented; *gross motor skilled.*

ISFJ
"Assistant"

concerned with others' welfare; responsible, reserved, patient, practical, friendly, orderly, inquisitive regarding people, harm-avoiding; conscientious, thorough, loyal; service-oriented; *gross motor skilled.*

ISTP
"Athlete"

artful with machines, tools, and hands; seeks action and excitement; superb tactician—seizing the moment; athletic, competitive, witty but usually not wordy; street smart; ever-thinking; can be intense with deep convictions; adaptive; *fine motor skilled.*

ISTJ
"Investigator"

gatherer of data; compelled to identify reality and bring order; stable, conservative, dependable, reserved, logical, fastidious, systematic, painstaking, thorough, dutiful; *fine motor skilled.*

iNtuitive

INFP
"Idealist"

deep internal values; idealistic, romantic, appears calm; generally reticent; creative, avoids conflict, sensitive, aware of others' feelings; sacrificial, welcomes new ideas; flexible, interested in learning and writing; composer; *language skilled.*

INFJ
"Wordsmith"

potential gifted writer; imaginative, conscientious; has concern for the needs and development of others; empathetic; enjoys enriching inner life; methodical; quietly forceful; counselor; *language skilled.*

INTP
"Logician"

master of conceptual logic; problem-solver; scientific—desires understanding of universe; designs logical models; seeks precision; introspective; adaptable; tends to excel in theoretical, philosophical subjects; *logical abstraction skilled.*

INTJ
"Inventor"

applicator of ideas; builder of theoretical systems; self confident; independent, reserved, single minded, conceptual; seeks knowledge; not impressed with authority; determined, analytic, stubborn, skeptical, scientific; *logical abstraction skilled.*

Extraverts

Sensate   iNtuitive

ESFP
"Entertainer"

performs to entertain others; enjoys creating party-like atmosphere; spender—not a saver; expressive; down-to-earth; radiates warmth and optimism; impulsive, enjoys promoting and business; rhythmical and athletic; *gross motor skilled.*

ESFJ
"Facilitator"

hospitable, focuses on usefulness; energetic, realistic; develops and nurtures relationships; sensitive to praise and criticism; expresses feelings; conscientious; orderly; friendly promoter, commerce oriented, *gross motor skilled.*

ESTJ
"Supervisor"

excels at organizing and running activities and orderly procedures; matter-of-fact; consistent, efficient, energetic, pragmatic, critiquing; likes rules and laws; values traditions; commerce oriented; *fine motor skilled.*

ESTP
"Opportunist"

"smooth operator," deal-maker; tactical, enterprising; adaptable, persuasive, energetic; seeks fun and excitement; athletic; enjoys the moment; realistic, good natured, self-focused; body- and clothes-conscious; entrepreneur; negotiator; promoter; *fine motor skilled.*

ENFP
"Motivator"

highly energetic; enthusiastic, charming, imaginative, improvisational; sees possibilities; spontaneous; easily bored with repetition; enjoys solving people's problems; catalyst, marketer, *language skilled.*

ENFJ
"Educator"

teacher/pastor; socially sophisticated; expressive, ambitious, catalyst, cooperative, devoted, fluent, imaginative, emotional; opinionated; interested in ideas and possibilities; seeks order, *language skilled.*

ENTP
"Strategizer"

"precocious planner," imaginative, alert to possibilities; quick thinking; likes complexity; computer proficient; enjoys one-up-manship; enthusiastic, outspoken, artistic, comedic, manipulative, spontaneous, entrepreneurial; *logical abstraction skilled.*

ENTJ
"Chief Executive Officer"

born "CEO," driven, takes charge; harnesses people to a distant goal; strategic; expressive; potential good debater and public speaker; seeks vision and purpose; political; self-focused; structured; *logical abstraction skilled.*

4
Discovering Preferences in Children

The benefits of knowing and understanding your children's specific cerebral design are many. This information will help you and your children understand their innate strengths and weaknesses in social relationships, academics, athletics, vocations, marriage, and much more. Actually, there is not an area of life in which this information does not relate. Even the spiritual realm is affected.

This information can give parents direction, comfort, and assurance as they seek to raise their children properly. Fathers and mothers should be reasonable with their children and consider their unique Brain Types. Persons with different Types may have poor communication styles. Many disagreements between people are *not* a matter of right or wrong, but they are typological instead.

Let me provide an example. Pick out a book that has print on the front and back covers. Stand the book upright on a table and pretend 16 people are sitting around the book in a circle. Each person is looking at the book from his or her unique angle. Now change seats and describe what you see from another person's perspective. Each person sees the same book differently from his or her vantage point. No one is wrong in describing the book, but some people have a better angle to see what kind of book is on the table. They are the ones we should most rely upon for an accurate description. The others are not lying; they just do not see enough to give an accurate perspective even though their insights are still valuable.

This illustration is relevant to the various Brain Types in people, including children. Each Type is especially gifted to perceive and judge matters according to his or her unique cerebral design. I have learned that wise people, including parents, rely upon each of the other 15 Types for insight, because input from all Types is important. Different Types are skilled in different areas. No one Type has the best viewpoint in all situations.

If we know and understand our children's specific Brain Types, we can more effectively communicate with them. We can present information in the best and easiest way for them to understand. This should also provide us greater tolerance. I can remember trying to teach my child mathematical principles. Before I knew she was a Feeler and I was a Thinker, I was too impatient in how I tried to instruct her. After realizing our typological differences, my patience improved appreciably (according to her), as did my tutoring methods. Wise parents will do all they can to understand the unique cerebral makeups of their children.

How can they accomplish this? It can be more difficult to figure out children's Brain Types because they are usually not as conversant as adults. Nevertheless, there are steps for going about the process. For those who prefer questionnaires, there is the *Murphy-Meisgeir Type Indicator for Children* (*MMTIC*). It is designed to be used by teachers and is administered to children ages 7 to 12. Although the instrument is well researched and highly regarded, it should be used as an indicator, not as an accurate evaluator. It is helpful in trying to understand children better, but it is just one of many tools that provide good but incomplete insight without the aid of a Brain Type evaluation.

The best approach for accurately evaluating children (and adults) typologically is by careful observation of their conversations, behavior, attitudes and motor movements. Parents can learn to view these traits to various degrees, depending upon how much time they are willing to devote and how well they use this material. It is important to listen in depth to the thoughts, syntax, diction, voice inflection, and so forth, to get a good typological reading on children. This takes time. Let us begin with some questions that will provide you clues for better understanding your children.

The following questions are far from comprehensive and are not intended for thorough accuracy. Since personality preferences are found in people in combinations rather than singly, they can be difficult to distinguish on a questionnaire. Therefore, the following questions are merely a guide.

1. Does the child . . .
__ have a high energy level, looking for places to expend his or her energy?
__ welcome new situations?
__ become more sociable in large group gatherings?
__ tend to be a leader in groups?

These are only a few Extraverted characteristics. However, you need not answer affirmatively to all of these for your child to be Extraverted. The child's energy level is a significant determinant.

2. Does the child . . .
__ seek many opportunities to conserve energy?
__ cautiously approach new situations?
__ act more reserved in large group gatherings?
__ like to spend large amounts of time alone reading, watching TV, or playing computer/video games?

These are only a few Introverted characteristics. You need not answer affirmatively to all of these either for your child to be Introverted. The child's energy level is significant here as well.

3. Does the child...
__ like to participate in action games?
__ like nonfiction more than fiction?
__ prefer to hear new stories rather than old stories repeated?
__ seem to be more practical, a user of ordinary language?

These are only a few Sensate characteristics.

4. Does the child...
__ enjoy fiction more than nonfiction?
__ like to have the same stories and tales repeated often?
__ have a vivid imagination?
__ enjoy being different?
__ seem to be verbally precocious?
__ do things in creative, unusual ways?

These are a few iNtuitive characteristics.

5. Does the child...
__ ask "Why?" a lot?
__ act uneasy with affection?
__ seek logical explanations?
__ tend to sacrifice harmony with others to get his or her point across?

These are a few Thinking characteristics.

6. Does the child...
__ seem to get along easily with others?
__ act sad or hurt when criticized?
__ seek to please others?
__ smile a lot?
__ need and enjoy affection?
__ try to promote harmony whenever possible?

These are some Feeling traits. Feelers, however, are not always peacemakers.

7. Does the child...
__ seem to want to regulate and organize matters?
__ seem to be judgmental and opinionated?
__ seem to be mechanical or rigid in his or her motor movements?

These are a few Judging traits.

8. Does the child...
__ seem to be flexible?
__ seem to be open-minded?
__ seem to be fluid and smooth in his or her motor movements?

These are some Perceiving traits in children. Perceiving children like to "go with the flow" and are known to have infectious laughs.

Accuracy of Questions

Your answers to the preceding questions can provide good indications, though they are not fool-proof. Here are some reasons. Question groups one through eight deal with each of the eight typological preferences. If a child possessed only one preference rather than the combination of all eight, he or she would be easy to figure out. A person who had only Thinking with no Feeling preference, for example, would be rather easy to type. We must remember, however, that all persons have a combination of each trait in various degrees, affecting the impact of the other traits.

Question 6 asks, "Does the child seem to get along easily with others?" Even though the question seeks to determine whether the child is a Feeler, in many instances it will fail to do so. Some parents do not view their children realistically. Thinking parents will generally not be as sensitive to their children's relationships with others as Feeling parents. Also, Thinking Perceivers (or TPs) will generally be more tolerant and easy to get along with than Thinking Judgers (or TJs). The combination of Perceiving with Thinking can greatly lessen the T in a Thinker's personality. And if a Thinker (P or J) places value on people and treating others kindly, he or she can get along easily with others. You can see this question, like all typological questions, can be an indicator but is not fool proof.

Properly Using Typological Information

As we have discussed, there are many reasons for attempting to know a child's exact Brain Type. The prime reason, as far as this book is concerned, is improved athletics. Yet most parents will seek to apply this valuable material in any way they can to help their children. Therefore, discretion should be used when considering how much to tell children.

At this initial stage of the game, it would be unwise to tell your children what you believe to be their Brain Types. If you are incorrect in your assessment, you will be feeding your children data that will cause them to view themselves erroneously. The results could prove to be detrimental. If your appraisal is correct, you still need to take time to understand this material more thoroughly. Then you may wisely present the information in an understandable, relevant, and edifying fashion.

Some typologists suggest that parents should never "label" their children. When they label, they essentially think of their children as Introverted or Extraverted, Sensing or iNtuitive, and so forth. Even if their children are Extraverted, they may overlook their children's reflective or Introverted side and not give time and value to this less developed cerebral trait.

Wise parents will seek to learn their children's Brain Types and preferences and use this information constructively. As I shared about helping my daughter with mathematics, I would not have been successful had I not known or "labeled" her Type and mine. A day does not pass that my knowledge of my children's Types does not help me to be a more understanding father. My children are thankful that I am aware of who they are typologically, and what makes them tick.

I informed my teenage son at the age four of his inborn and purposeful Brain Type. Over this time period he's loved to hear me tell about adults of his same Type and how they have developed and used their gifts. He appreciates knowing who he is and why he likes to do certain things and not others. He also wants to know the lesser-developed areas of his Type so he can devote more time to becoming a complete person. I regularly point out other Types to him, so he can better understand and appreciate the kids around him. He loves knowing why his classmate, an INTP, corrects the teacher when she makes a mistake. He enjoys knowing why an ENTP friend acts so precociously and calls him with nothing in particular to talk about. He likes knowing why other kids perform in sports as they do. He persistently has typology questions for me. *Type information has made my son more sensitive and compassionate to others, even empowering him to encourage those who lack certain motor skills in sports.* The benefits to him personally have been numerous.

I will say it again: Brain Typing is a wonderful subject to explore. Unfortunately, valuable information of any kind can be used destructively, regardless of how valid it is. There will always be persons who will misuse and pervert that which is inherently good. This must not stop those who would use beneficial information for constructive use.

I believe that the principles of Brain Typing can be discussed with children, provided parents convey it in the proper way. *If you do not believe you can present typological material favorably, then do not share it with your children.* Just retain the knowledge so you yourself can put it to beneficial use. On the other hand, if you see positive opportunities to share this information with your children, by all means do so. All three of my children are glad their parents did.

5
You Were Meant to Fly!
GETTING TO KNOW THE FOUR TEMPERAMENTS

Researchers in Jung-Myers typology have discovered a number of temperaments—categories into which the 16 Types fit. Today, such temperaments have been clearly identified and have come to be accepted within the community of psychologists and other professionals who study Type. Four of these temperaments, described by David Keirsey and Marilyn Bates in their book, *Please Understand Me*, are the SJ, SP, NF, and the NT. After careful research, I have adopted the Keirsey Bates model as one that is particularly useful for life situations but *for sports analysis, I rely on the SF, ST, NF, and NT.*

Within each of the four temperaments there are four Types; sixteen Types in all. In this section, we will consider the four temperaments; we will study the sixteen Types in subsequent chapters.

Since most persons who become acquainted with typology want to know the frequency of each Type found in the American population, statistical percentages have been included. Do not consider them as exact, but as estimations that are only approximations. A number of sources have attempted to estimate the frequencies of the Myers-Briggs Type Indicator (*MBTI*) Types, including Isabel Myers and the Center for Applications of Psychological Type (CAPT). This book has taken these and other reputable sources into consideration to provide "ballpark" percentages.

To illustrate the differences found in the four temperaments, I have chosen four creatures from the world of animals, specifically flying creatures. Many striking similarities exist between the four temperaments and the creatures chosen to illustrate them. Naturally, there are many characteristics that will be dissimilar, too. The comparisons are given to help you see the overall picture of each temperament more clearly.

The Birds and the Bees

This chapter covers very briefly what is described more comprehensively in Part Six. There you may read in greater detail about each of the four temperaments. Many readers will want to consult Part Six to gain a more well rounded picture of the four temperaments. Similarities between the four temperaments and four flying creatures, the honeybee, hummingbird, stork, and owl, are described.

U.F.O. Detector

Another reason for using flying creatures to illustrate the temperaments is to draw attention to the fact that we all have the capacity to "fly" or soar above our present circumstances, athletically and in life. Each individual is special and unique, capable of accomplishing great and wonderful things. In a manner of speaking, you are capable of taking off and flying high. From my experience with all kinds of individuals, I have met no one who cannot "fly." With the right amount of will, desire, determination—whatever you may call it—all individuals can soar and become something spectacular.

Knowing that each one of us has this tremendous potential for becoming something more, I would like you to consider each and every person a "flying creature." What, then, kind of flying creature are we?

Until we discover our own unique Type, we are "Unidentified Flying Objects," or "U.F.O.s."

Your principal task in taking the questionnaire was to make your choices accurately and honestly so your Type might be correctly identified. Taking the "U.F.O." Type Detector helps you learn more about yourself and, in the long run, everyone else you may know.

Consider the illustrations below. Note that the creatures inside are about to become free of the confines of their shells. Once they are free, they can fly. What about you? Learning all you can about your temperament and your Type should be a freeing experience—one that launches you into flight.

Anyone who has ever flown knows that air travel is an exhilarating experience. The perspective of seeing activity on the ground with a bird's-eye view is marvelous. It gives you the "big picture," and puts a different light on the temporary nature of life. Indeed, being airborne may allow you to see things moving below (oncoming collisions, disaster, threats of danger) that an earth-dweller could not see. It's all a matter of perspective. You will come to more fully appreciate yourself and your giftedness. You'll learn how to help others find their strengths and capitalize on them, too. Let's begin by looking at the first of four temperaments, the SJ.

Introducing the SJ Temperament

The SJ (Sensing, Judging) temperament is one that is usually so responsible that it has been called the backbone of society. The practical, dutiful, and faithful SJ is one who also values tradition and abides by the rules and standards of the social unit. A tireless worker, the SJ is most like the honeybee, a flying creature with which it shares many attributes.

There are four SJ Types: **ESFJ, ESTJ, ISFJ,** and **ISTJ**. Being Sensates, SJs are drawn to the world through their five senses. They are at home in the arena where facts, numbers, and details are of concern. As for their knowledge of products and their usefulness, none is better in judging quality than the observant SJ. SJs are generally commerce oriented, pragmatic, and independent.

An SJ believes that hard work is necessary to earn rewards. Work must precede play, and the rule is generally not broken. SJs are guardians of time honored institutions. They value, support, and perpetuate the home, social club, church, company, and country. They like to be prepared and may be considered the most protective of all the temperaments. Their somewhat pessimistic bent prods them to prepare for the worst or expect impending doom and plan for its arrival. It is believed there are more SJ and SP Types than NFs and NTs in the U.S. population.

Introducing the SP Temperament

The SP (Sensing, Perceiving) temperament is made up of a variety of Types of individuals. This variety makes it seem that its members have little in common. For example, it is common for SPs to be fond of using tools to express their personalities. On one hand, a careful orthopedic surgeon might be an SP; on the other hand, a daring and reckless motocross racer might also be an SP. Both individuals are skillful and both have a deep need to work with tools as an extension of themselves in their chosen professions. Yet, to the average person, the orthopedic surgeon and the motocross speedster seem light years apart.

The tendency to use tools and employ the use of their extremities as a means of self expression is consistent with the SP temperament. Many athletes, artists, dancers, mechanics, dentists, construction workers, and racers are of the SP design. As you can see, all have some means of projecting their Type: athletic equipment, paintbrush, dance step, wrench, dentist drill, hammer or bulldozer, and car, boat, or plane. Athletics, with its bat, hockey stick, rackets, and balls, is a natural outlet of expression for the SP.

As with the other temperaments, there are four Types of SP: **ESTP, ESFP, ISTP,** and **ISFP**. There is perhaps no other temperament that combines the desire for freedom, independence, opportunity, and action than the SP. SPs want to set their own hours, and work with those they like. They love travel, and they want the freedom to enjoy life as it comes.

SPs show their boldness by taking risks; they live for the moment and tend to shun long range planning. They may become restless if they see no hope for immediate action. Whether performing tirelessly before others or saving their strength for the next opportunity, SPs love action for action's sake. It is believed there are more SP and SJ Types than NFs and NTs in the U.S. population.

Introducing the NF Temperament

The NF (Intuition, Feeling) temperament is one that joins the need to form interpersonal relationships with the desire to communicate, often through various forms of media. For this reason, NFs are found in teaching, acting, writing, pastoring, and the professional communications media (television, radio, journalism, and so on).

Closely akin to the NF temperament in the world of flying creatures is the legendary stork. The NF temperament group includes the **ENFP, ENFJ, INFP, and INFJ**. NFs believe the best about others and value relationships. They're devoted to friends, family, and their vocations. They tend to be romantic, and visionary, and they're often optimistic about future possibilities. NFs see potential good in nearly everything; hence, many NFs subscribe to the possibility thinking found in success and motivation books that urge their readers to adopt a positive attitude.

The Feeling function in the NF draws him or her to others. Concern for the welfare of others marks the NF, accounting for the number of NFs in nursing and missionary work. They live life as a quest for purpose, meaning, and for finding themselves. They require recognition for a task or duty well performed or their interest will wane. Having a flair for language, NF communicators excel in both the written and spoken word. They prefer frankness and personal warmth to pretentiousness. It is believed there are fewer NF and NT Types than SJs and SPs in the U.S. population.

Introducing the NT Temperament

If you have ever known anyone interested in science and technology or someone who has an insatiable interest in finding out how and why things work, you've probably met up with an NT. NTs are inquisitive, inventive, skeptical, logical, and ingenious. They're often the scientists and philosophers of society. In this book, the NT temperament is associated with the wise ol' owl.

The four Types who belong to the NT temperament are: the **ENTJ, ENTP, INTJ,** and **INTP**. The NTs' iNtuition draws them to consider the big picture. They have the desire to know, to understand, to predict, to delve into the future, and to ponder the abstract phenomena—interests which often escape other temperaments. Since NTs are also Thinkers (instead of Feelers), they have the tendency to be more concerned with the theory behind something than its effect on people. As NTs ponder and act, their chief desire is to prove themselves competent in whatever they do. In sports, this burning ambition to demonstrate competency can be harnessed to produce a tireless dynamo of activity. For this reason an NT will often stay up late at night, burning the midnight oil, to seek greater understanding through study and inquiry.

NTs are tempted to carry logic to the extreme, assuming others around them understand the logic involved in every situation. NTs demand much of themselves and others, particularly in areas where the NT is strong. They are adept at manipulating their environment, seeking solutions to a variety of problems. They exhibit a passion for knowledge very early in life. It is believed there are fewer NF and NT Types than SJs and SPs in the U.S. population.

Principal Characteristics of the Four Temperaments

The SJ "Bee"	The SP "Hummingbird"	The NF "Stork"	The NT "Owl"
Rulesdriven	Graceful	Devoted	Competent
Stable	Free	Optimistic	Inquisitive
Authoritative	Whimsical	Idealistic	Critical
Conservative	Adventurous	Harmonious	Knowledgeable
Saver (stores-up)	Active	Interpersonal	Inventive
Bound, obligated	Daring	Purposeful	Enigmatic
Responsible	Performing	Motivational	Skeptical
Practical	Impulsive	Nurturing	Logical
Giving, not taking	Optimistic	Romantic	Asks "why?"
Worker	Precise	Transparent	Remote
Traditional	Lives for today	Spiritual	Conceptual
Realistic	Adaptable	Influential	Visionary
Should, ought-driven	Restless	Contributing	Hard-working
Prepared	Skillful w/Tools	Visionary	Futuristic
Logistic	Tactical	Relational	Strategic
Thorough	Independent	Desiring Uniqueness	"Burns Midnight Oil"
Industrious	Appearance Conscious	Communicative	Controlling

Frequently Chosen Professions:
- Commerce
- Teaching
- Accounting
- Law enforcement
- Law
- Nursing

Frequently Chosen Professions:
- Athletics
- Marketing
- Construction
- Transportation
- Art

Frequently Chosen Professions:
- Counseling/human services
- Writing/Journalism
- Education
- Ministry/Clergy
- Music

Frequently Chosen Professions:
- Science
- Medicine
- Computers
- Law/Politics
- Business Management
- Acting

6
"Personality" or "Psychological" Types vs. "Brain" Types

When the eight mental preferences are paired into four categories, one preference from each category can be selected to provide 16 classifications of people. ISFJ and ENTP are just two of the 16 possibilities. In typology circles, these classifications are referred to as psychological or personality types. Before we look briefly at the sixteen Types, let us consider how we might most accurately describe them. This can have a major bearing on how you will view and discuss Types for the rest of your life.

Many Jung-Myers typology advocates have loosely used the terms "personality types" to describe the 16 different kinds of people. I am uncomfortable with this expression. Over the years I have tried to help others understand and identify the 16 personality psychological Types. Inevitably, many have gotten hung up when two persons I am discussing fall within the same Jung-Myers Type yet appear to have very differing personalities.

Jung coined "function types" and "psychological types," being quite precise in his labelings. He knew he had identified common behavioral characteristics in the myriad of people he had studied. His era did not possess 21st century neuroscientific evidence; therefore, he had to rely on evidence from psychology (the study of the mind). Thus, "psychological types" was a most appropriate label. Before long, however, people started using personality types to describe his classifications, rendering a vernacular more relevant to the layperson, removing it from the mysterious and abstract world of psychology.

"Personality" to the layperson conveys the sum total of the physical, mental, emotional, and social characteristics of an individual. The term "personality," however, originates from the Latin "persona." It corresponds to the Greek word for *face*. Actors in ancient Greece could perform more than one role on stage by donning different *personas* or masks. But Type behavior is not dictated by the faces we choose to wear. Instead it is the orderly, systematic function of the brain. I therefore coined and prefer the term *Brain Types* to both personality and psychological types.

I also use the term since there are many personalities within each Brain Type. We will discuss reasons for this in the following few pages. Certainly not all ENFPs or ISTJs or any other Types act just alike. There are vast distinctions within each Jung-Myers personality or psychological Type. For instance, let's consider the ISTP, who is Introverted. Not all ISTPs (or all Introverts for that matter) act shy or reticent. Even though Introversion is innate and cerebrally immutable (from a Brain Type perspective), it has many external looks among people. Generally speaking, an Introvert living in an environment of Extraverts will appear much more outgoing than an Introvert raised or living among Introverts.

We've seen that Jung coined *Introversion* from the Latin, meaning *turning inward*. Neuroscience tells us that an Introvert's brain is physiologically and neurologically structured to *reflect* more than *act* on matters. Therefore, regardless of whether ISTPs are more on the outgoing or reserved side, they are far more *reflective* than their closest cousins, the ESTPs.

Former baseball stars **Ted Williams** and **Pete Rose** possessed the ISTP Brain Type. Williams was widely known in his playing days for his laconic and withdrawn style; whereas Rose became known for his gregariousness. Their personas were very different from one another, yet they shared the same ISTP inborn design. You need to look carefully behind the personality to see the authentic Brain Type.

The Four Typological Functions

It is not vitally important to grasp the following explanation of Type functions and their respective strengths. It will, however, enhance your understanding of the material in this book.

Function theory is a position held in typological circles, suggesting that all 16 Types possess a *dominant* function that overshadows the other three. There are four functions found within the eight preferences. The four are Sensing (S), iNtuition (N), Thinking (T), and Feeling (F).

1. The most developed function of our four-letter Brain Type is called the **dominant**.
2. The second most developed is the **auxiliary** function.
3. The third function is labeled **tertiary**.
4. The fourth function is called the **least preferred** or **inferior** function.

What is the significance about knowing one's dominant and auxiliary functions? The dominant function serves as the captain of one's ship of destiny. It gives unity to one's life and proves to be the strongest function in the life of the individual. The auxiliary function serves as an aide to the dominant function, working along with it to support and balance the individual. It is not nearly as well developed, however. A chart which summarizes the dominant function of each of the 16 Types provides further clarity.

DOMINANT FUNCTION OF EACH TYPE

ISTJ	ISFJ	INFJ	INTJ
ISTP	ISFP	INFP	INTP
ESTP	ESFP	ENFP	ENTP
ESTJ	ESFJ	ENFJ	ENTJ

E - Extraversion
I - Introversion
S - Sensing
N - iNtuition
T - Thinking
F - Feeling
J - Judging
P - Perceiving

Each bold letter signifies the dominant function in each of the sixteen Types. The auxiliary function is the other middle letter—the one in lighter print. Thus the dominant function for ISTJs is Sensing. Their auxiliary function is Thinking.

One final note about the discussion of dominant and auxiliary: Extraverts display or use their dominant function (suppressing their auxiliary), thus showing the world what they're really like, but Introverts don't. Therefore Introverts' friends probably know them for their auxiliary function, not their dominant ones which they protect within their inner worlds.

For example, in ISTJs, the dominant function of Sensing is most often hidden. Instead, they show and deal with the external world in their Thinking function. ESTJs, on the other hand, show the outer world their dominant Function—Thinking. Their auxiliary function—Sensing—is used less often and appears hesitantly displayed because it is used primarily in the inner or Introverted world of ESTJs.

The fact that both ISTJs and ESTJs show the outer world their Thinking function makes them appear quite similar to one another. Do not be misled. Coming to quick decisions by the Thinking function is much more valued by ESTJs than ISTJs. Conversely, ISTJs prefer gathering Sensing data and making a final decision sometime in the future.

A Helpful Hint

To help her determine the dominant function of each Type, a creative 18-year-old friend, Amy Williams (ENTP), created this diagram. We hope it helps you visualize this important concept.

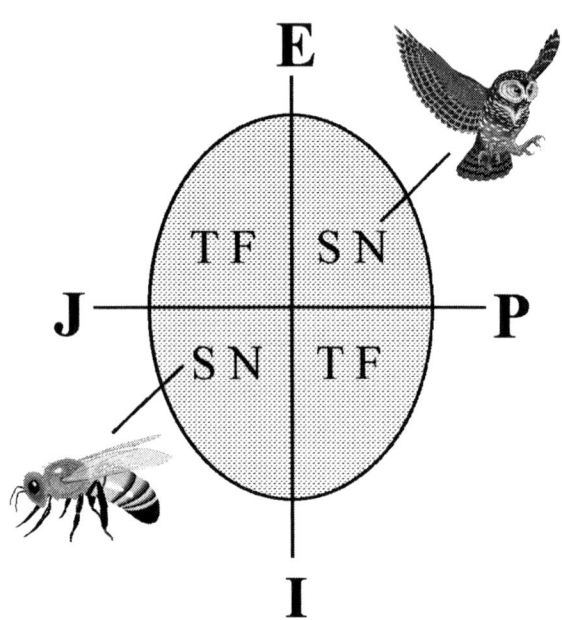

Example: If you are an **ISTJ**, your Type would fall in the area between the "I" and "J" (which is illustrated by the use of a honey bee). The dominant trait of the ISTJ is the Sensing (**S**) function—which is the only letter contained in your **ISTJ** letters in that quadrant. Conversely, if you are an **ENTP** (illustrated by the owl), of the two letters in the quadrant between "E" and "P", only the **N** applies, and thus reveals the dominant function as being iNtuition (**N**).

This model can also identify the secondary function of each Type. After you have established the dominant function and the quadrant in which it resides, just look to the only other quadrant (above or below) on that same side of the pie (either right or left) and find the other letter contained in the Type in question. This will be its auxiliary (or second strongest). For instance, the ENTP's auxiliary function is Thinking (**T**).

Tertiary and Least Preferred

Opposite the dominant function is the *least preferred* or inferior function. If the dominant function is a Perceiving one (Sensing or iNtuition), then the least-preferred function will be the other one. For example, Thinking is dominant in ESTJs and Feeling is least preferred. If the dominant is a Perceiving function (Sensing, iNtuition), the auxiliary will always be a Judging one (Thinking or Feeling).

The opposite of the auxiliary function is the third or *tertiary* function. Auxiliary and tertiary functions are of the same mode. If one's auxiliary is Sensing, the tertiary is iNtuition (the other Perceiving function); if the auxiliary is Feeling, the tertiary is Thinking (the other Judging function).

Caution

Now that you have been made aware of function strengths espoused by many typology enthusiasts, I want to sound a word of caution. There is research that suggests function strengths are of a slightly different order than just mentioned. This does *not* affect which functions each Type shows the outer world and conceals in the inner world. Rather, it speaks to the magnitude of mental energy attributed to each function. For the purposes of this book, I will use the Myers order of dominant and auxiliary functions. They are sufficient to illustrate my points. Regardless of which is correct, it is important to remember that each Brain Type contains typological functions in varying strengths. Knowing the proficiency order of your mental functions can help you see more clearly the areas you need to work on in order to strive for balance.

Developmental Stages of Functions

Some type theorists have observed the development of functions in stages. They generalize that the dominant function develops from birth to teens; the auxiliary matures during adolescence; the tertiary function develops somewhere near the ages 20 to 35; and the least-preferred function emerges last—after 35 or so. This is not to suggest that the functions are inoperative until these timetables occur, only that they find greater development in these time frames.

Assuming there are developmental stages of functions, an ENFP, for example, would gather information and make decisions differently at age 18 from the way he or she would at 38. This principle would add greater diversity even within each Type.

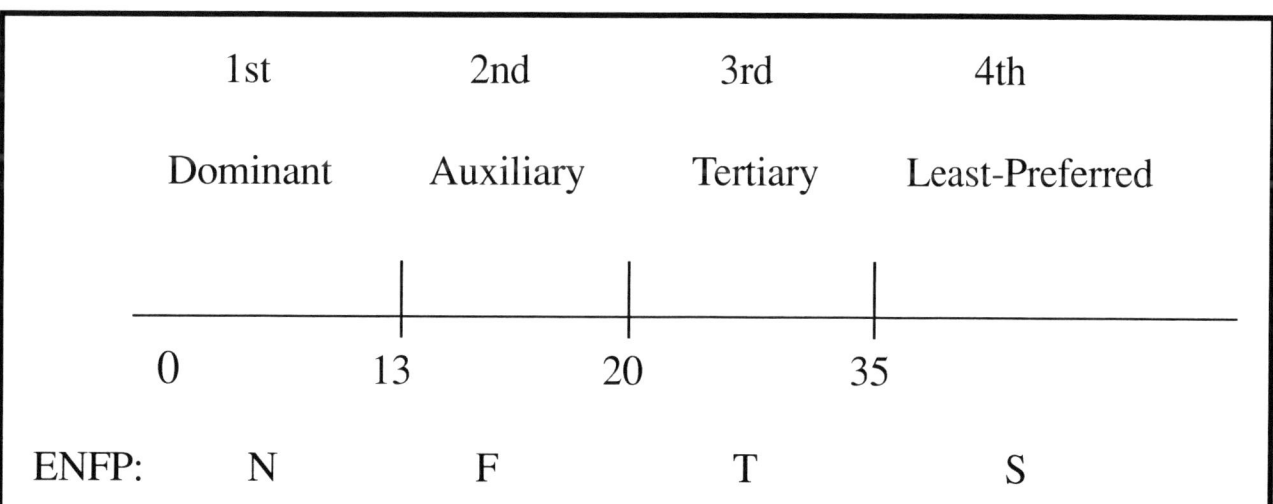

For an ENFP, iNtuition would be dominant, and develop first. Feelings would be secondary and mature during the adolescent years. Thinking is the ENFP's tertiary function, and Sensing the least-preferred function.

Introduction to and Explanation of Eight Brain-Related Functions

Nearly 30 years of Brain Type-related research has identified eight brain functions that correspond with the aforementioned eight "personality" preferences—both paired as opposites within four categories.

Popularized and expanded in recent years from the early 20th century are the typological findings of Swiss psychiatrist, Carl Jung. Unlike Jung's oft-errant psychological theories, his personality evaluations were insightful and based upon observing "normal" behavior in thousands of people over the course of his lifetime.

Independent studies and experiences have led me to concur that there are sixteen "types." However, this belief concerning the various types is quite different from the norm. I distinguish these differing designs as Brain Types—found in all people the world over—each with unique and inborn cerebral/cognitive, physical/motor and visual/spatial proficiencies. The short definitions below of each Brain Type are only simple summaries—generic descriptions for the majority within each category. Though personas can vary significantly within individuals of each Brain Type (due to *nurture*: parenting, upbringing, etc., and *nature:* genetic variances), I believe that differing inborn neural circuits in each Brain Type affect specific cognitive, physical, and spatial skills and that these similarities within each design are due to genetic hardwiring—*nature*.

I have built upon the empirical data collected by Jung and subsequent protagonists of his by applying neuroscientific, genetic, and biomechanical studies implemented by others, those with whom I work, and myself. My attempt has been to take Jung's "soft' typological findings into the 21st century "hard" sciences for verification. These efforts have me convinced that Jung, including his modern-day devotees, was (and are) on the right track—though I believe they are far removed from the accuracy and scientific understanding now available for evaluating human behavior (cognitive, physical, and spatial).

Not only do I believe that Jung's original "type" preferences and functions can be attributed to specific regions of the brain, but that they can be directly linked to specific motor (via the brain's motor cortex) and spatial skills. Whereas Jung's followers have devoted their attentions to outward personality characteristics, my studies and experience has led me to minimize outward persona and fixate on internal biological and physical characteristics that dictate cognitive, physical, and spatial behaviors. I am not interested in the typical "psychological" aspects of mankind but rather the quantifiable and verifiable biological behavioral dimensions—to be applied pragmatically to living life.

I am not a psychologist, nor do I practice psychology. It is for this reason that I desire to distinguish all aspects of Brain Typing (in the minds of my readers) from that of psychology. The following few pages contain descriptions *similar to* but *distinct from* the 16 personality types and corresponding mental preferences we've just discussed. This is to give you a "heads up" for where Brain Typing is going and what you can learn to expect. I am introducing new terminology and nomenclature for Brain Types, distinct from the 8 letters espoused by Jungian enthusiasts. I hope and plan to integrate this more thoroughly in future editions and publications. Though I find no fault in Jung's 8 terms, I believe there is a far more accurate and scientific way to describe man's inborn skills. Though I have privately used these more scientific descriptions for years, I feel it is time to begin sharing this information with the public—which is generally disinterested in these kinds of technical terms. Nonetheless, I believe it is necessary in order to assist you, the reader, in achieving a greater understanding of Brain Types and how the brain directs our various inborn "behaviors."

I believe Brain Typing is the most accurate methodology for evaluating and describing man's inborn "normal" behavior—cerebrally and physically. I strongly suspect each of the 16 Brain Types will soon have subclassifications—based upon other genetic variables. I have recently finished collaboration on another genetic study regarding a particular brain neurotransmitter. With similar results, outside studies have already demonstrated that various neurotransmitter polymorphisms affect personality and behavior. Consequently, since 1996 I have been pursuing this course—examining differences within like Brain Types (e.g. a sample group of ENTPs).

To be sure, my recent collaboration with geneticists has furthered my resolve to give greater credence to the genetic diversity within each Type. This has helped to give an account for the minor differences I find within each inborn design—though I still believe that all people clearly fall into only one of the 16 Brain Types. I encourage you to keep abreast of not only what I espouse, but to notice published genetic studies that are strongly demonstrating that man's "normal" behavior is more than 50% genetically-based.

Now let's have a look at this *similar* but *distinct* nomenclature that I trust will provide us a greater scientific understanding of and appreciation for our inherent designs.

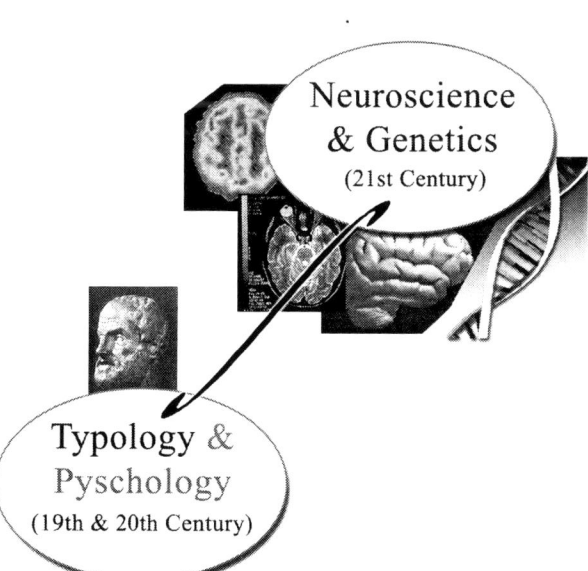

Definitions by Comparison:
Jung-Myers and Brain Typing

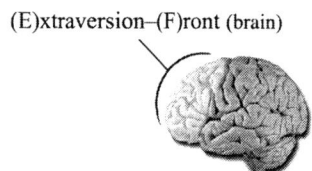

(E)xtraversion–(F)ront (brain)

(**Extraversion**) *equivalent to* **Front "F"**: anterior, forepart, energy-expending, external, expressive, broad, many

(**Introversion**) *equivalent to* **Back "B"**: posterior, rear, energy-conserving, internal, reflective, deep, few

(**Sensing**) *equivalent to* **Empirical "E"**: observe, experience, literal, concrete, actual, realistic, 5 senses, pragmatic, "what is"

(i**N**tuitive) *equivalent to* **Conceptual "C"**: imagine, envision, figurative, abstract, theoretical, idealistic, 6th sense, visionary, "what could be"

(**Feeling**) *equivalent to* **Animate "A"**: living, persons, emotion, compassion, encourage, feelings, deductive, subjective, relational

(**Thinking**) *equivalent to* **Inanimate "I"**: non-living, things, logic, justice, critique, issues, inductive, objective, systematic

(**Perceiving**) *equivalent to* **Right "R"** (brain): synthetic, holistic, universal, adaptable, multiple, graceful, artistic, spatial adeptness—peripherally, etc., pattern-skilled, sufficient solution, welcoming of interruptions, skilled at drawing and sculpting, spatial and visual logic, play-oriented

(**Judging**) *equivalent to* **Left "L"** (brain): analytic, divisible, local, ordered, sequential, mechanical, detailed, speech-skilled, exact solution, resistant to interruptions, skilled at reading and writing, numerical and verbal logic, work-oriented

Below are both the eight Jung-Myers mental processes and the eight Brain Type functions (and their respective acronyms) depicting cerebral locales based upon neuroscientific studies:

The 8 Left-Brain Dominant:
Jung/Myers — Brain Type

ENFJ—FCAL (Front, Conceptual, Animate, Left)
INFJ—BCAL (Back, Conceptual, Animate, Left)
ENTJ—FCIL (Front, Conceptual, Inanimate, Left)
INTJ—BCIL (Back, Conceptual, Inanimate, Left)
ESTJ—FEIL (Front, Empirical, Inanimate, Left)
ISTJ—BEIL (Back, Empirical, Inanimate, Left)
ESFJ—FEAL (Front, Empirical, Animate, Left)
ISFJ—BEAL (Back, Empirical, Animate, Left)

The 8 Right-Brain Dominant:
Jung/Myers — Brain Type

ENFP—FCAR (Front, Conceptual, Animate, Right)
INFP—BCAR (Back, Conceptual, Animate, Right)
ENTP—FCIR (Front, Conceptual, Inanimate, Right)
INTP—BCIR (Back, Conceptual, Inanimate, Right)
ESFP—FEAR (Front, Empirical, Animate, Right)
ISFP—BEAR (Back, Empirical, Animate, Right)
ESTP—FEIR (Front, Empirical, Inanimate, Right)
ISTP—BEIR (Back, Empirical, Inanimate, Right)

Jung-Myers

Typology	Brain Typing
Extraversion	**Front** (Anterior)
Introversion	**Back** (Posterior)
Sensing	**Empirical**
iNtuition	**Conceptual**
Thinking	**Inanimate**
Feeling	**Animate**
Judging	**Left** (brain-dominant)
Perceiving	**Right** (brain-dominant)

Where we are heading ⟶

6...."Personality" or "Psychological" Types vs. "Brain" Types

Jung-Myers and Brain Types® Comparison

(general area of cerebral strength)
Jung-Myers

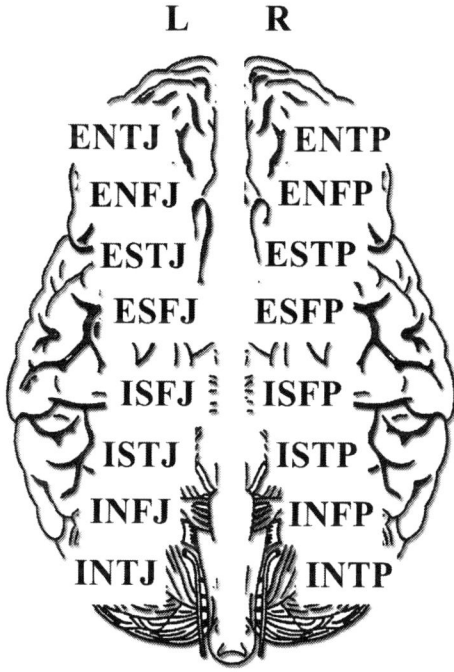

(general area of cerebral strength)
Brain Types

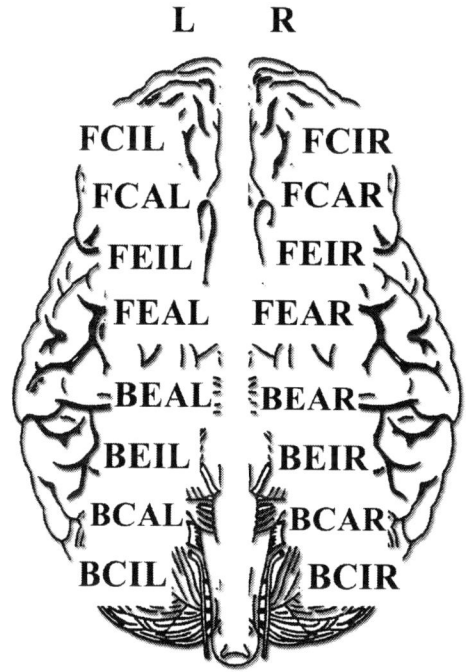

Jung-Myers	Brain Types
Extraversion	Front
Introversion	Back
Sensing	Empirical
iNtuition	Conceptual
Feeling	Animate
Thinking	Inanimate
Perceiving	Right
Judging	Left

7
NEUROSCIENCE
(how the brain works) and BRAIN TYPING

A thorough reading of this neuroscience section is not necessary for understanding the essence of this book. This section lends scientific support to Jung-Myers typology, but more pertinently, Brain Typing, and the claims made herein. If your reading time is limited, you should skim this material and proceed to a more relevant section. However, make sure you spend most of your time reading "Judging and Perceiving" in this section before proceeding. It is necessary to understand the dynamics of these brain preferences as they relate to the right and left hemispheres. You will later need to return to this segment, however, in order to build a solid base for your understanding of Types and the brain.

The levels and regions of cerebral activity are different in Introverts than Extraverts. The Perceiving functions (Sensing, iNtuition) and Judging functions (Thinking, Feeling) often involve different neurons and cerebral regions. *Each Brain Type has a primary residence and cerebral circuitry unique to itself.*

Knowledge of the brain has changed monumentally over the past few decades. Neuroscience, which studies the nerves and nervous system, has found new doors for researching the brain's untold mysteries. Through the use of sophisticated brain-mapping instruments and other high-tech monitoring devices, scientists are achieving remarkable insight into cerebral activity. The latest findings supply critical data for those involved in applying this information to everyday life.

Brain Research Advances

Brain imaging devices include such names as CATs, MRIs, PETs, SQUIDs, SPECTs, and EEGs. Many of the breakthroughs in brain awareness have come from the recent advances in *PET* technology. PET, which stands for positron emission tomography, was used by some 70 centers in the United States, as of 2001, for both research and diagnostic purposes. The technique was originally developed in the early 1970s, yet only since the late 1980s have new methods been used to accelerate our understanding of the brain.

PET technology utilizes a scanner that makes pictures of the brain's activity. These images are of molecules, blood or glucose, tagged with radioactive isotope. The isotope is intravenously administered to the patient where it is then taken up by blood to the active regions of the brain. The newer PET Scan differs from the CAT Scan in that it reveals brain function (doing its work), rather than showing basic structure or anatomy. The processes of seeing, hearing, thinking, and so on, all become visible on the scan in a full spectrum of color. Red, for instance, indicates high activity. Neuroscientists are now able to conduct experiments with fully conscious patients, indicating which areas of the brain are most active for each task assigned.

Persons having brain surgery in which the nerve connections (*corpus collosum*) have been cut (*commissurotomy*) between hemispheres are known as split-brain patients. (This surgery is to combat advanced, life threatening convulsions in epileptic patients.) These persons have taught us much pertaining to brain *lateralization* (the limiting of stimuli to one hemisphere). There is virtually no change in personality or normal behavior, yet cerebrally there has been significant change. Upon close examination, the patients appear to have two separate minds inside one body. In 1981, **Roger W. Sperry** of the California Institute of Technology shared the Nobel Prize in Medicine/Physiology for his research in this area.

Let's now consider neuroscience more closely, beginning our understanding of this subject by considering fundamental aspects of the most magnificent mechanism in the universe.

7....Neuroscience: How the Brain Works

The Brain

The adult brain is about the size of a grapefruit, weighing roughly three pounds. It consists of a myriad of cells; evidence suggests some 10 billion are nerve active. The number of possible interconnections between these cells in a single brain is on the order of 10^{14} (100 trillion). Chemical messengers send charged impulses throughout and from the brain. Not only is the brain involved in profound cognitive matters, it manipulates the body in amazing and complex ways. There is no better explanation for the existence of the human brain than that an infinite God created it.

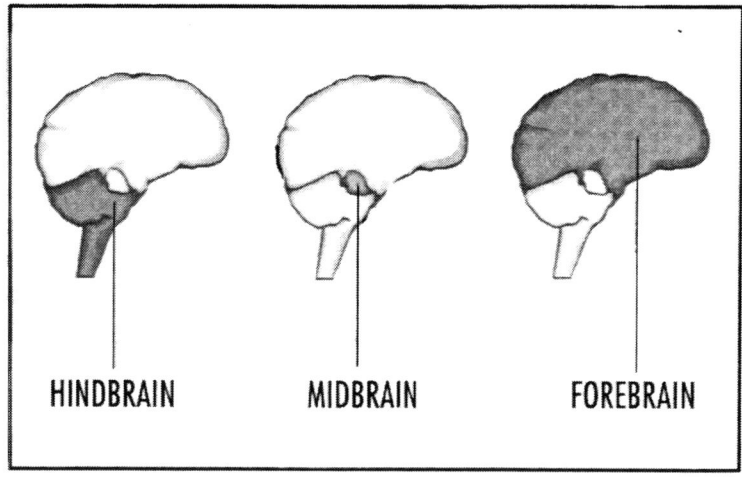
HINDBRAIN   MIDBRAIN   FOREBRAIN

The brain resides at the top end of the spinal cord. (The spinal cord receives all the information from the muscles and skin. It also is a sending station, particularly controlling motor commands for movement.) The three parts of the brain are the *hindbrain* (consisting of the cerebellum and parts of the brainstem), the *midbrain* (the top of the brainstem), and the *forebrain* (primarily the cerebral hemispheres).

The *brainstem*, the extension of the spinal cord, receives skin and muscle information from the neck and head while coordinating the movements in these areas. The brainstem also contains the centers for our senses (including balance), except for smell and vision. Smell and vision link directly with the cerebral cortex and limbic system. Thus, the reason for their strong influence on us.

The *cerebellum* and *basal ganglia* together coordinate the complex body movements, especially the limbs. The cerebellum is intimately involved in running, swinging, jumping, muscle tone, and posture, as well as hand and eye movements.

The *cerebrum*, the largest part of the human brain, is divided into two halves, or hemispheres. Often referred to as the *right brain* and the *left brain*, each controls its opposite half of the body. Sitting atop each hemisphere is a one-eighth-inch-thick layer of nerve cells named the cortex. The *cerebral cortex* contains billions of neurons, more than all the rest of the brain put together. Its structure consists of six layers of nerve cells running horizontally and columns of cells vertically. The vast superiority of the human brain over beasts' lies in the internal complexity of the cerebral cortex.

Connecting the two cerebral hemispheres are a bundle of some 300 million nerve cell fibers called the *corpus callosum*. It acts as a power transformer, regulating activity between the two hemispheres.

The Cortex Lobes

The cortex of each hemisphere has four divisions called lobes. The *occipital lobe*, residing at the back of the forebrain, is devoted to vision. Moving forward, we next come to the *parietal lobe*, largely devoted to the entire body and receiving sensory information. Residing below the parietal lobe is the *temporal lobe* (near the temples) which has several important functions, including memory, hearing, and perception. As we approach the anterior (front) of the forebrain we find the *frontal lobe*, the largest cortical lobe. Among other things, it is actively involved in purposeful behavior, decision making, planning, and adapting.

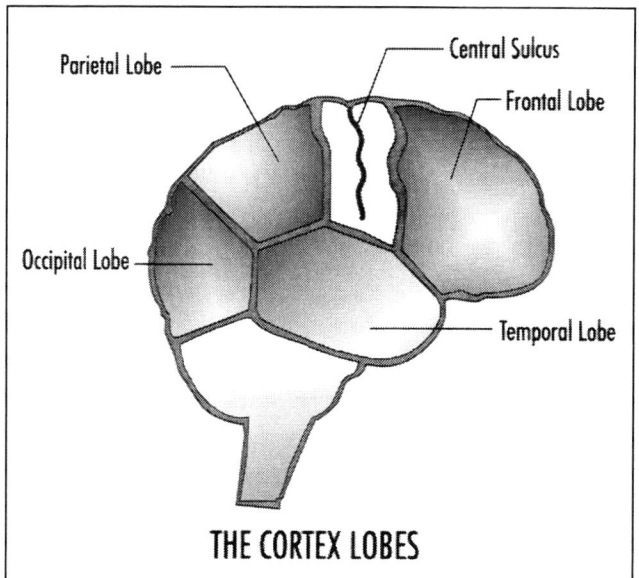
THE CORTEX LOBES

Brain Processing—including Introversion and Extraversion

Let's now consider how the forebrain processes information. Simply stated, the work of the **back** of the forebrain is to focus and *reflect* (Introversion) on the external world. The job of the **front** of the two cerebral hemispheres is to *act* (Extraversion) on these reflections or internal needs, having already considered external circumstances.

The **back** section of the forebrain (posterior to the central sulcus) gathers and handles input from the outside world. This external information is received via the senses (sight, smell, sound, hearing, and taste), and the rear of the brain prefers to translate this input into meaning.

In addition, "Fragments of knowledge are scattered around the brain, especially in the back of the cortex."[1] This locale clearly handles the preponderance of what could be described as Introverted processes.

Areas closer to the front of the brain assemble information from the rear; the location of these "convergence zones" varies among people.[2] The **front** of the forebrain (anterior to the central sulcus) receives input from the *limbic system,* which is often called the *mammalian brain.* This complex organization *regulates our internal needs* and other matters that pertain to our personal survival, such as: feeding, fighting, fleeing, and procreation.

Of the four cerebral lobes, three deal essentially with Introversion. The *occipital* lobe processes visual information, the *temporal* lobe deals with sounds, and the *parietal* lobe masters tactile sensations. Principally handling Extraversion is the lone *frontal* lobe which deals with voluntary movements—activated by the primary motor cortex.

The prefrontal cortex is the most significant area for creating one's outward "personality." Persons with specific kinds of frontal lobe damage speak with flattened inflection, lacking personality. Broca's area in the frontal lobe is responsible for the expression of speech. This helps explain why Extraverts are generally more verbose and speak with louder tone.

PET Scan data suggest the anterior portion of the *cingulum* (a bundle of association fibers), located near the medial part of the frontal cortex, as crucial to our very ability to act. Patients with lesions to the cingulate gyrus are essentially creatures without a will. Their brains can work perfectly well; they can converse with and understand others. Yet they have lost their volition.

The brain consists of distinct components serving distinct functions. Unequivocally, the take-charge part of the brain—the CEO, general, and Extravert—is the frontal region. Typology and neuroscience combined correlate *Introversion* with the *back* of the brain (**reflecting** on external, Extraverted matters), and *Extraversion* with the *front* of the brain (**acting** on internal, Introverted matters).

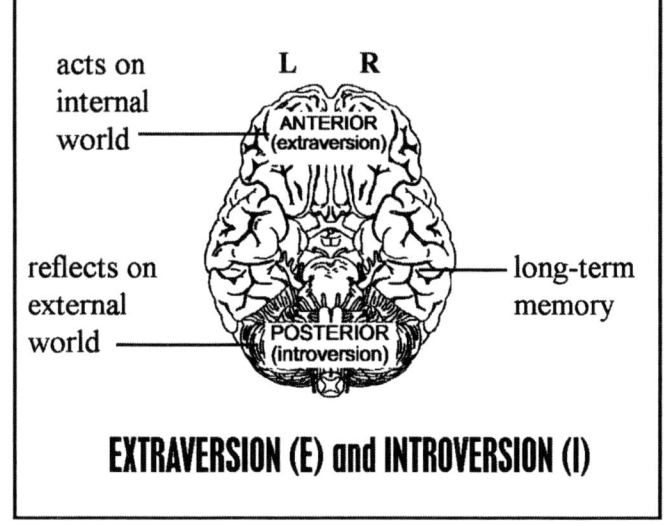

EXTRAVERSION (E) and INTROVERSION (I)

Sensing and iNtuition

Humans possess twin cerebral hemispheres, often referred to as the right and left brains. We will study this more fully under the heading "Judgment and Perception." For now we will only look superficially at these brain halves, which appear the same anatomically yet function in dissimilar ways.

Sensing and iNtuition are two distinct ways in which the brain perceives matters. Research suggests these two brain functions (S,N) take place in both left and right cerebral hemispheres, though in different locations within each.

"*Semantic processing,* the comprehension of word meanings" (involved in Sensing and iNtuition), "is severely disrupted in patients with damage to posterior regions of the left hemisphere."[3] This condition is often referred to as Wernicke's aphasia.

Research has shown the *posterior* (back) region of the left forebrain demonstrates comprehension of *abstract words with meaning* (for example: justice, compassion or hate). Damage to the *anterior* (front) region of the left brain, as in Broca's aphasia, retards the *articulation of speech* but not the understanding of it.

Thus, Sensing and iNtuition (Perceiving brain functions) in the left hemisphere appear to take place primarily in the posterior region. As we just learned, Introversion is a posterior forebrain process which would then render *left-brained Sensing and iNtuition as Introverted functions.*

We now traverse to the *right hemisphere* and discover where *intonation patterns and emotional tones are deciphered and produced.* Persons with right forebrain damage speak with flattened inflection, and have difficulty judging the emotional tone of speech produced by others.

Intonation is a dimension of the iNtuitive (N) brain function. (Right-brained NFs [or NFPs] are most in touch with the mental dynamic, intonation. Thus, *we witness iNtuition in the right hemisphere as well as in the left.*

Comprehending *metaphor, another aspect of typological iNtuition, is performed in the right brain.* Persons with right forebrain deficit (leaving only left brain intact) pick literal interpretations of metaphorical statements.

Persons with left-hemisphere dysfunction have severely impaired voluntary speech, reading, and writing abilities. In that same person, the unimpaired right hemisphere, however, shows a surprising amount of verbal comprehension, though lacking the abstract understanding of its left counterpart. Research strongly suggests **spatial/visual** right-brained Sensing and iNtuition, whereas *the left is* **verbally** *predisposed to Sensing and iNtuition.*

Research demonstrates damage to the right frontal lobe creates an impairment of pictorial stimuli sequences. The anterior right forebrain is especially adept at design and spatial fluency in contrast with the left's verbal fluency. Many aspects of *visual perception and visual imagery* are right hemisphere duties.

Music is also associated with the right brain, particularly as it relates to melody recognition, tonal memory and timbre.

We can conclude that Sensing and iNtuition are found in both hemispheres but possess varying abilities within the same S and N typological function. In other words, *Sensing and iNtuition in the right hemisphere are different than Sensing and iNtuition in the left.*

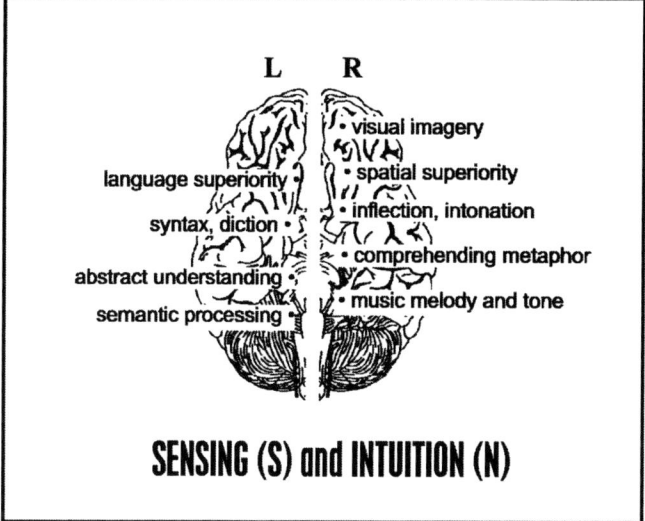

Thinking and Feeling

Typology describes Thinking as a "logical" process. Current talk among right and left-brained dabblers says logic is confined to the left hemisphere. Nearly every book at the neighborhood bookstore which tells you how to use your right brain more, simplifies the brain's complexity and disseminates much misinformation—such as logic is limited to the left brain. Modern science proves otherwise.

Neuroscientific research reveals logical processes take place in both hemispheres, yet only the left half is capable of dealing with logic at the verbal level. *Logical, analytic, verbal reasoning* takes place in the **left** anterior (front) hemisphere; whereas *logical, synthetic, spatial reasoning* is engaged in the posterior **right** forebrain. (Damage in right parietal areas results in spatial reasoning deficits.)

Albert Einstein

Albert Einstein was the most famous scientist of the twentieth century and considered by many the greatest genius of our time. If anyone ever had the ability to reason with logic, it was Einstein, an INTP right-brained person.

Einstein is a real life example of the verbally logical left brain and spatially logical right brain phenomenon. He spoke little before the age of three (Introverted Perceivers [IPs] are the last to naturally develop speech), but later in life, after his scientific discoveries, he said:

The words or the language, as they are written or spoken, do not seem to play any role in my mechanism of thought. The psychical entities which seem to serve as elements in thought are certain signs and more or less clear images which can be "voluntarily" reproduced and combined.

Einstein was best at utilizing his Thinking in the spatial realm. As an iNtuitive, he was always imagining and thinking what could be, not what is, as would a Sensate Thomas Blakeslee says in his book, *The Right Brain*:

> The real innovators in the precise and abstract science of mathematics rely heavily on visual thinking in their work.[5]

Typological Feeling is the other way in which certain Brain Types are predisposed to making decisions. *Feeling, like its cerebral counterpart, Thinking, is also a reasoning process.* As we have seen, it specializes in relational and interpersonal matters, preferring to focus on animate objects (such as people). The Feeling function appears to be centered in the same vicinity as Thinking, in both hemispheres.

In the 1980's, comprehensive electroencephalographic (EEG) recordings in patients indicated the *left-frontal region showed higher activity during negative emotions*. These same studies likewise demonstrated the *back regions of the right forebrain as especially adept for evaluating emotion and feeling.*[6] In 1997, brain mapping technology more clearly validated a long-held theory of mine: the posterior right brain is highly involved in sensing and storing emotions. Recent brain scan analysis has demonstrated a significant finding: *the right amygdala is the brain's emotional center.* Fascinatingly, the *left* amygdala (in men) is *not* involved with emotion, whereas adrenaline and the right amygdala interact to create emotional memory. Researchers have discovered that by clinically restricting right amygdala activity, Post Traumatic Stress Disorder symptoms can be alleviated. The two Introverted, Feeling, right-brained Types (ISFP and INFP) are particularly right amygdala adept. These Types are the most sensitive to emotional or feeling issues.

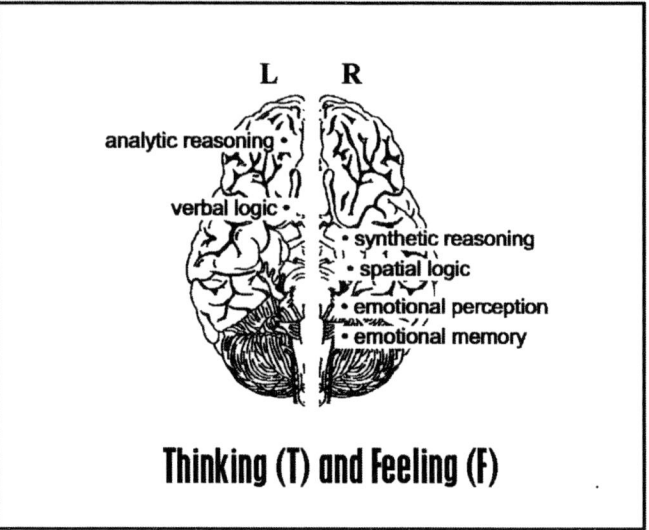

Thinking (T) and Feeling (F)

Judging and Perceiving

Since the discovery of two brain hemispheres many years ago, man has had many questions regarding this strange anatomical quirk. Why would humans need two similar yet distinct cerebral lobes? Neuroscientists have discovered that the **left** specializes in concentrating on *one issue* at a time whereas the **right** focuses on *many issues* at once. *Both hemispheres process Introversion, Extraversion, Sensing, iNtuition, Thinking and Feeling.* Each hemisphere handles these typological processes differently from the other.

Thus, in Jung-Myers parlance we could equate the *left brain with Judging (J)* and the *right brain with Perceiving (P)*. Typology describes Judging as deliberate, seeking closure, and other terms highly compatible with the left brain and Perceiving as adaptable, spontaneous, and other terms harmonious with the right brain.

To my knowledge, Dr. Walter Lowen, State University of New York at Binghamton professor emeritus, is the first researcher to suggest the Judging left brain, Perceiving right brain association. The postulations in his book, *Dichotomies of the Mind*, not only make logical sense, but the latest brain mapping data provide convincing supportive evidence. (Dr. Lowen has also suggested a link between Type and motor skill activity.)

J & P Differences in Athletes

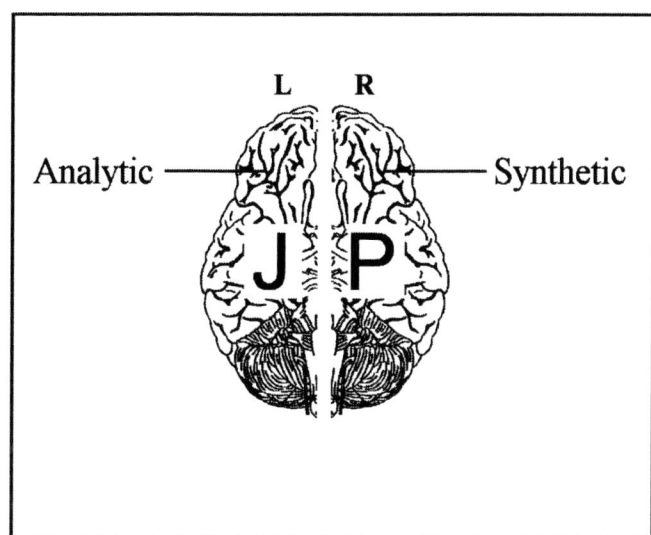

I have witnessed the unequivocal Judging (J) and Perceiving (P) distinctions in athletes for years. J athletes tend to be more mechanical in their movements. Desiring quick conclusions, they act faster than their P counterparts, who demonstrate more grace, smoothness and spontaneity, waiting as long as possible to make their moves. For example, the P basketball player who dribbles into the lane and jumps will normally wait longer to decide to shoot or pass the ball than the J hoopster. In a sport like basketball, it is usually better to hold off making a decision until the last possible moment. This is one reason why Ps are your best point guards in the NBA; rarely does a J point guard make the starting team.

J athletes are cerebrally designed to see *one part* of their field of play in an *exact* fashion, whereas Ps see the *entire field* of play in an *inexact* way. Given their other brain processes (E,I,S,N,T,F), not all Js and Ps perform alike. The differences in Brain Types are quite dramatic in athletes who operate from the same side of the brain.

Key Characteristics of the Two Brain Hemispheres

J (left brain)

speech-skilled
exact solution
sequential processing
analytic
resistant to interruptions
skilled at reading, writing
abstract categorizing
verbal, numerical logic
generally positive
work-oriented

P (right brain)

pattern-skilled
sufficient solution
parallel processing
synthetic
welcoming of interruptions
skilled at drawing, sculpting
understanding metaphor
spatial, visual logic
generally moody
play-oriented

RESEARCH DEMONSTRATES THE **RIGHT BRAIN:**

- qualifies as a mind in itself: solving problems, remembering matters, implementing actions with full personality.
- is generally nonverbal; "it thinks in patterns, or pictures, composed of `whole things,' and does not comprehend reductions, either numbers, letters or words."[7]
- dominates in nonverbal, spatial, and visual thinking. This helps explain why Introverted right-brained persons are generally the least communicative.
- is inferior to the left hemisphere in the processing of consonants. It does, however, handle vowels equally well with the left brain. (The bulk of the information content in speech is in the consonants.)
- has less of a vocabulary than the left and is inept at syntax (structure of word order in sentences).
- produces intonation patterns and emotional tone (major contributions to speech). ("Patients with right-hemisphere damage . . . speak with flattened intonation; they also have difficulty judging the emotional tone of the speech produced by others.")[8]
- is involved in aspects of metaphor and some qualities of humor. (Right brain damaged patients frequently pick inappropriate endings to cartoon strips and pick literal interpretations of metaphorical statements.)
- "plays the more significant role in stereoscopic vision" (three-dimensional depth perception).[9]
- "to be markedly superior" with split brain patients" studying the ability of each hemisphere to match two- and three-dimensional forms on the basis of common geometrical features, especially on the difficult matches."[10]
- has an advantage in visual, spatial matters largely due to its "superiority in being able to manipulate spatial relationships in the environment."[11]
- regulates the left hand, which performs consistently better than the right hand (controlled by left brain) "on matching unseen objects by touch with geometric shapes presented in free vision." (In addition, the left hand superiority increases as the shapes become less geometric and more free form.)[12]
- "superiority is not just in spatially related hand activities but also in visual mental manipulations."[13]
- when damaged, results in impaired performance of spatial tasks, such as the ability to draw.
- when damaged in front lobe, incurs impairment of pictorial stimuli sequences.
- specializes in both visual and imagery perception.
- views an entire image "in parallel."
- is better at recognizing faces.
- excels in music.
- is largely responsible for personality, imagination, and initiative.
- specializes in the perception of emotion in the posterior region.
- is more emotional, negative, and pessimistic than the left brain.
- looks at the whole situation in problem-solving.
- quiets down when the person is writing.

RESEARCH DEMONSTRATES THE LEFT BRAIN:

- controls speech in the vast majority of the population.

- is seen to have a verbal consciousness, essentially unaware of the right brain's nonverbal thoughts. This is proved by the surgical removal of the right brain in a conscious person without the patient noticing any difference! (The brain feels no pain, thus no anesthesia is required in brain surgery.)

- reduces matters to words, letters, or numbers.

- is superior in the processing of consonants, yet equal in the processing of vowels with the right brain.

- is specialized in language functions, due to its analytic skills, of which language is one manifestation. Experiments have shown that words briefly projected on a screen are correctly recognized nearly twice as often on the right side, in the right visual field (by the verbal-oriented left brain) than on the left. Recognizing faces or pictures is just the opposite, with nearly twice as many correctly identified in the left visual field (by the visual oriented right brain) as the right.[14]

- seeks the organization of separate material rather than the right brain's picture of the entire scene.

- is less expressive in intonation than the right, more monotone, dull and colorless.

- is unable to detect things such as the emotions of joy and anger communicated by voice intonation. Even discerning the difference between male and female voices is difficult.

- is essentially optimistic and cheerful, even amid difficult times.

- in the frontal region, is more active during negative emotions.

- when damaged in the frontal lobe, incurs impairment in recent memory for order of occurrence of verbal stimuli sequences.

- quiets down when arranging building blocks.

Brain Types and Cerebral Locations

Because the brain is infinitely complex, we cannot say for certain, at this juncture, where all the mental processes take place. We can say, however, where certain processes demonstrate high levels of activity. These were discussed earlier.

It appears that each of the 16 Brain Types has a particular region of the brain in which it most excels. This certainly does not limit any Type's access to other cerebral regions. Nevertheless, each Type feels most at home in a specific brain locale. This information is especially meaningful as it relates to body skills and how each Brain Type will perform athletically under pressure.

Let us view where all the Brain Types seem to have primary residence in the cerebral cortex. The significant areas of efficiency in the brain for each Type can be seen in the following map.

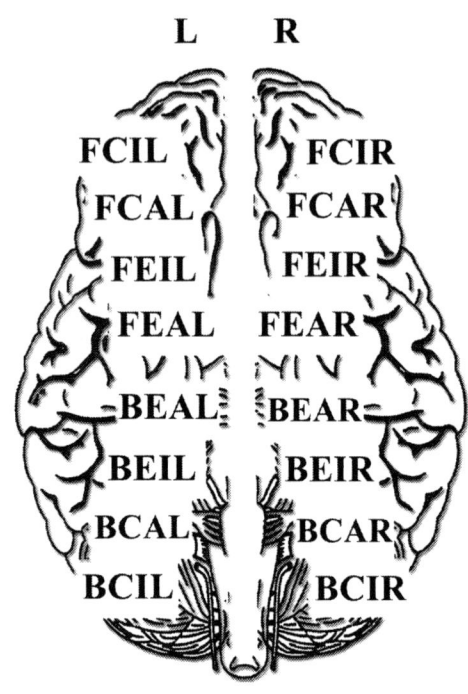

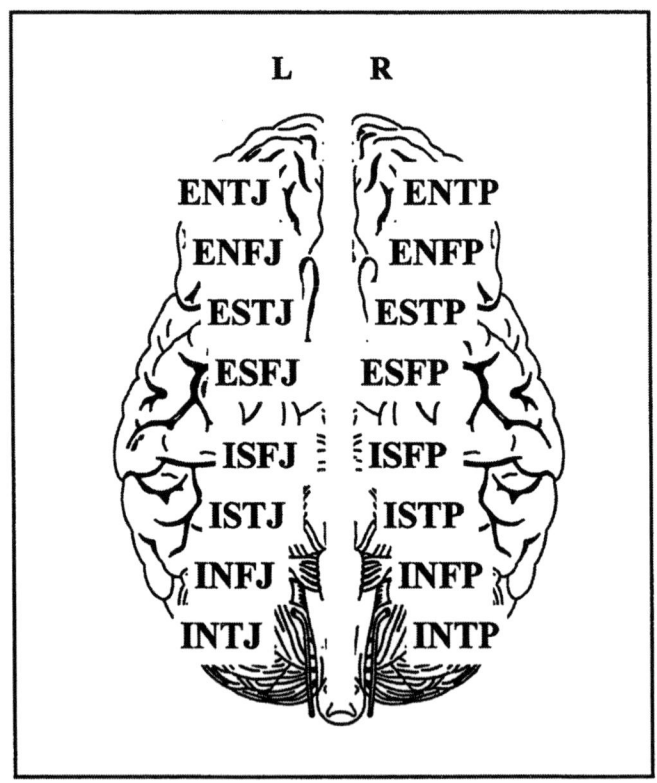

Therefore, the *front-right hemisphere would be most efficient for the EPs, the back-right for the IPs, the front left for the EJs, and the back-left hemisphere for the IJs.*

Noting the eight Brain Typing definitions for the Jung-Myers processes, it can be easier to understand their locales and significance in the brain. (Extraversion—**Front**, Introversion—**Back**, Sensing—**Empirical**, iNtuition—**Conceptual**, Thinking—**Inanimate**, Feeling—**Animate**, Judging—**Left** brain, Perceiving—**Right** brain.)

Typology and Body Skills

Research reveals that the cerebral cortex has four typologically significant areas, each regulating a distinct part of the human body. The individual 16 Brain Types are most proficient in one of these four areas. Thus, each of the 16 Types is most skilled in a specific part of the body. The various Types and their areas of body specialty can best be understood by the typological quadrants SF, ST, NF, and NT.

The typological grouping most active in the motor cortex level closest to the spinal cord and forebrain's center is the Sensing Feelers (**SF**). These persons have the greatest proficiency with the *gross motor skills*, such as basketball's **Magic Johnson and LeBron James**, baseball's **Barry Bonds and Tony Gywnn**, golf's **Annika Sorenstam**, tennis' **Serena Williams**, and track's **Carl Lewis, Michael Johnson, Florence Griffith Joyner and Jackie Joyner-Kersee, and Marion Jones**.

7....Neuroscience: How the Brain Works

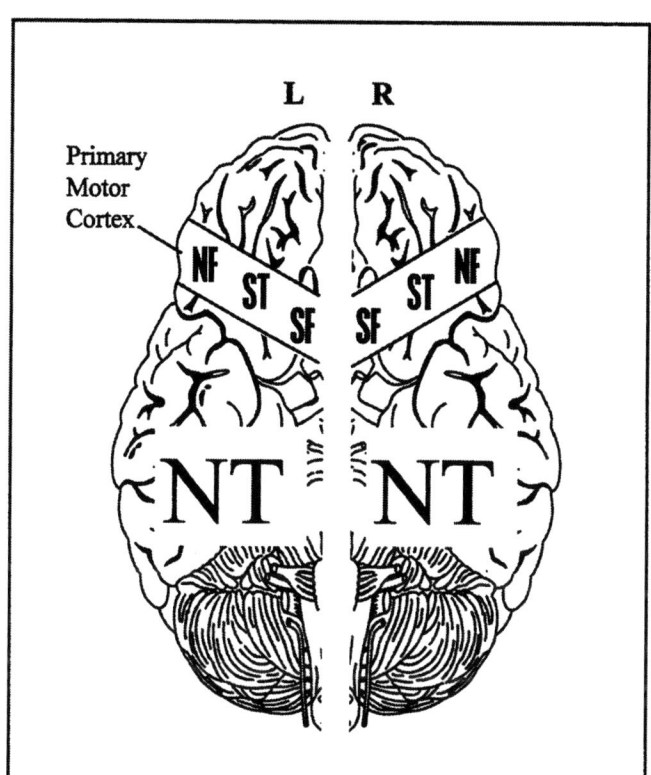

STs specialize in the second region of the motor cortex as we move away from the cerebral core, responsible for *fine motor skills*. **Michael Jordan, Larry Bird, Jack Nicklaus, Andre Agassi, Wayne Gretzky, and Wade Boggs** represent STs.

The third region from the brain's center is specialized in by the **NF**s. *Verbal and hearing skills* are mastered by this group as well as aspects of athleticism. Basketball's **Kevin Garnett**, football's **Jerry Rice**, baseball's **Sammy Sosa**, ice-skating's **Michelle Kwan**, boxing's **Evander Holyfield**, and golf's **Tiger Woods** are NFs.

Last, we come to the **NT**s, who appear to excel in the cerebral rather than motor cortex. NTs excel at *logical abstraction skills*, mastering inanimate reasoning. They, too, can be excellent athletes. Intellectual areas do not show up when the brain is probed as physical properties do, for they are mental. Muscular movements are not necessary to regulate the NTs mental skills. NT athletes include these former greats: **Bill Bradley, Jim Palmer, Tom Seaver, Johnny Bench, Jack Kemp, and Roger Staubach.**

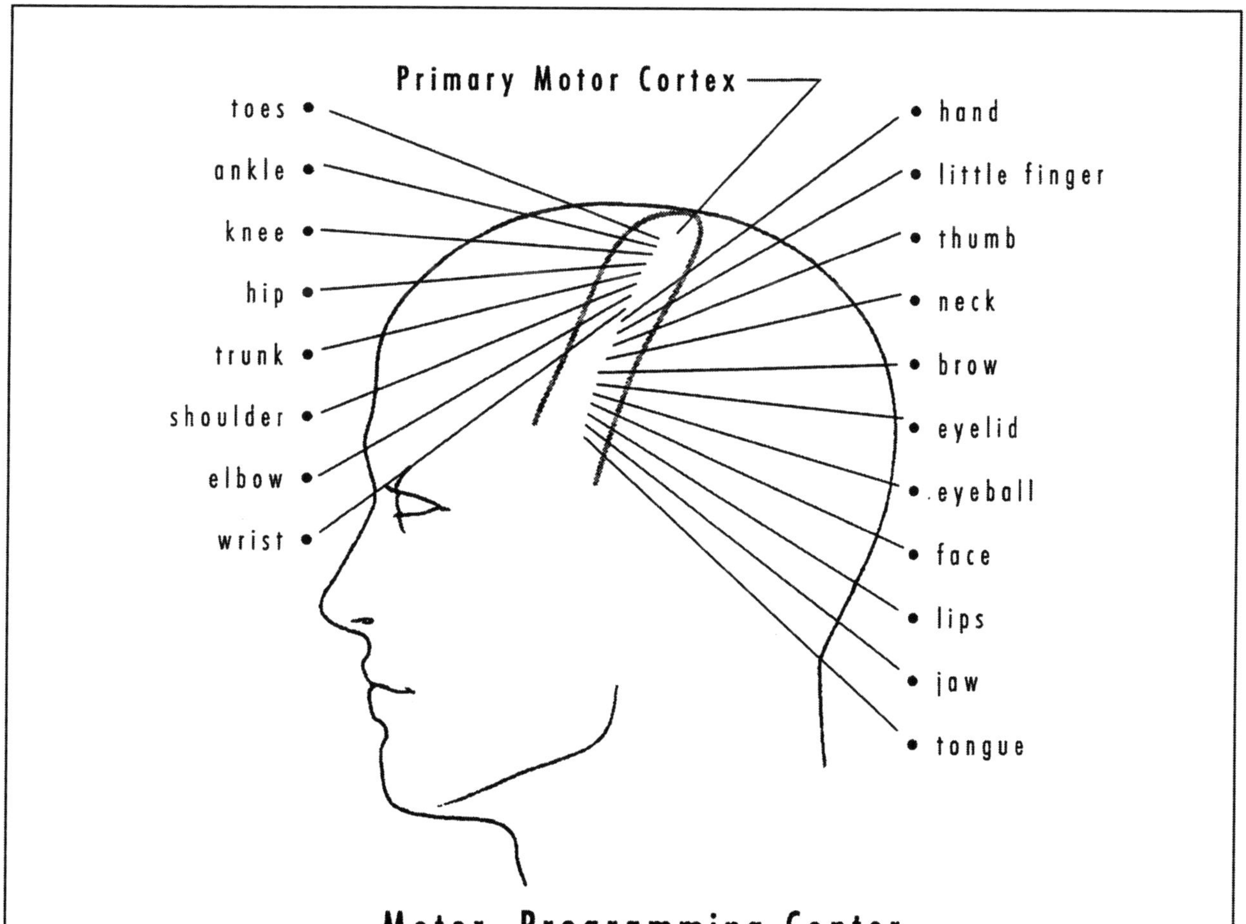

Anatomical and Physiological Aspects of the Brain

We now want to consider a drawing from the previous page that illustrates the left hemisphere of the brain. (The left hemisphere controls the right side of the body.) The picture displays the site and space devoted to commanding the muscles in various parts of the body.

Notice, as you view the picture, the *primary motor cortex* regulates three major areas of the body. Beginning with the area closest to the brain's center and spinal cord, the brain regulates the large muscles that control *gross motor* skills. They control such areas as the legs, trunk or torso, and upper arm. As we traverse outwardly from the spinal cord, we find the next area regulates the wrist, hand, fingers (*fine motor* skills), and then the eye. Continuing outward and downward, we see the face and mouth's region of control (*language and hearing* skills).

All normal people throughout the world are able to regulate the three areas of the brain with relative ease. However, they tend to be more proficient in one of these areas than the others. SFs (Sensing Feelers) specialize in gross motor skills; STs in fine motor; NFs in facial, oral, verbal and hearing skills; and NTs in logical abstraction skills.

Is it environment or training that determines the dominance of one of these areas? Or do genetics specifically design a person's brain to excel in a certain area? Although training can improve brain functions, I have come to see that *genetics* play the largest role is this puzzle.

This neuroscience section is not intended to provide every known piece of research to support these suppositions, but to provide ample amounts of data to deepen your understanding of the brain's inner workings as it relates to body skills and typology. Actually, the masses of empirical evidence I have collected by associating with athletes give me more than enough support to know which Brain Types possess the various body and mental skills. Brain and genetic research has provided the icing on the cake.

Visualization

The following picture shows some regions in which the human neocortex processes sensory information and governs movement. The primary visual cortex at the back of the brain is where the process of visual imaging begins. Hearing and touch centers also have their specific residences as shown. Taste and smell are processed from areas not visible from the outer brain.

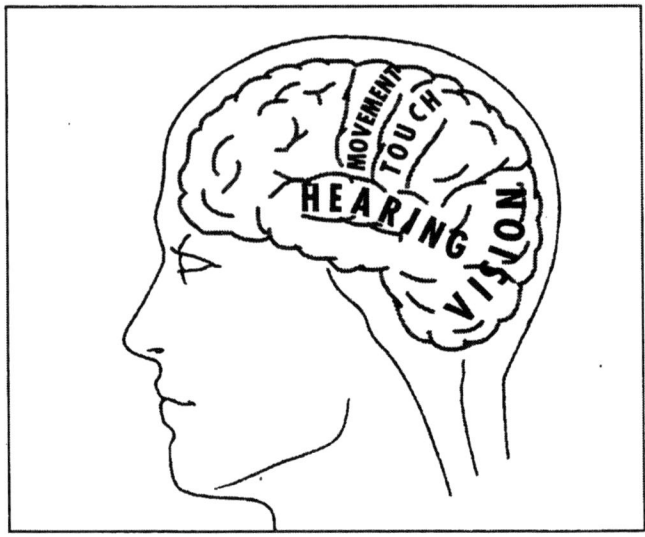

The *parietal cortex* integrates sensory inputs, handling spatial relations among parts of the body and between the body and objects of the outside world.

The *primary motor cortex* regulates body movements, whereas the pre motor cortex is now thought of as a general *motor-programming region* that controls a variety of coordinated movements.

If you were to only imagine moving your hand, with no actual movement, there would be no activity in the primary motor cortex. Yet, imagining or visualizing such movement would activate neural activity in the motor programming region around Broca's area (the speech center), at the base of the motor cortex.

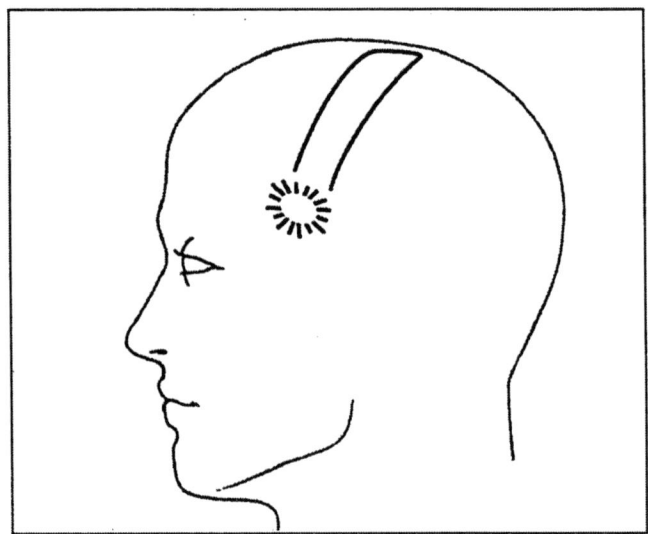

Thus, to imagine movements, we use areas of the brain controlling actual movement. This has been proven by experiments with PET scanning instruments. This finding lends support to those who use certain aspects of visualization in sports.

The Brain's Division of Labor

There is an inherent left-right division of labor in the neural "wiring" of all mammals. Each brain hemisphere is connected to the opposite side of the body. The left hemisphere controls vision, touch, and movement on the right side of the body and vice versa. The neural connections (*corpus collosum*) between hemispheres allow both to communicate with one another, enabling each to directly or indirectly participate in actions on either side of the body.

There are methods for estimating the activities of the two hemispheres in humans. When these experiments are implemented, one finds that reaction time is faster when the material is presented to the hemisphere where the process occurs than when it must first be detoured across to the opposite hemisphere.

The center of the body has neural connections to both left and right hemispheres. As we move away from the center of the body, we see the left-right separation becoming more pronounced. Arms are connected *primarily* to the opposite lobe, while fingers have connections *only* to the opposite lobe. (If you wish to move your left-hand fingers right now, your right hemisphere is doing the work.)

There is evidence "that the right hemisphere can control the right hand as well as the left in a simple pointing task."[15] *Contralateral*, or crossed descending nerve fibers to the spinal cord allow each hemisphere to control the hand opposite it. Nevertheless, "a much smaller number of same side, or *ipsilateral*, fibers allow each hemisphere to exert some control over the hand on the same-side of the body. Ipsilateral motor control, though, is generally quite coarse and limited to movements of the whole arm or hand. Fine finger movements require the use of the contralateral hemisphere and generally cannot be controlled by the ipsilateral hemisphere."[16]

The same is true for listening. Even though both ears have projections to both hemispheres, the transmission time is longer for one when stimuli are presented simultaneously to both ears.

Exciting Data

Perhaps this information concerning the two cerebral hemispheres is more than you need to know. Yet if you plan to explore further the application of this subject to sports, you'll find these data most relevant.

Persons already familiar with Jungian typology need to consider this material carefully, as well. It opens up another world of comprehension. The *Journal of Psychological Type* reported a study in 1990 examining "the relationship between MBTI personality type and member perception of nonverbal cues and feeling states exhibited in group settings."[17]

One finding confirmed:

> ... significantly more peripheral body movements were reported by Ps [Perceptive types]. Ps were more attentive to nonfacial cues in their assessment of nonverbal behaviors."[18]

It is the marriage, if you will, of typology and neuroscience that helps us make statements such as: Because Ps are right-brained dominant, they have peripheral vision capabilities superior to those of their J counterparts.

Type Functions Differ According to Hemisphere

Once again, S, N, T, and F are found in both hemispheres, yet each function varies according to hemisphere. Let's consider, practically, how this might look in real life.

For example, Type theory says INTJs (dominant iNtuitives [N], a Perceiving function) would actually prefer to spend the majority of time iNtuitively taking in information in an open-ended way. Amalgamating neuroscience, their iNtuition is stronger when Introverted in the left hemisphere than Extraverted in the right. Therefore, INTJs have a tendency to soak up new information in a methodical, analytic, and "J" kind of way. Actually, their left brains don't mind at all the open-ended desire to accumulate info, so long as they can do it one step at a time.

Let's look, however, at what happens when you have NTs who are dominant iNtuitives in the right hemisphere such as the ENTP Brain Type. Blending neuroscience, their iNtuition will be stronger when Extraverted in the synthetic right hemisphere than Introverted in the analytic left. Their N preference in the right brain is not as interested in gathering information as much as it is in expounding it to the outer world or living out often unorthodox ideas. In other words, ENTPs want to tell or show others what they believe in a creative way. Their right hemisphere says it's okay not only to Extravert in this fashion but to deal with more than one issue at a time. In fact, the more issues they can deal with, the more exciting life will be! The dynamics of the brain are "mind blowing," to say the least.

Typology/Neuroscience Paradox

If you happen to be a Jung-Myers typology buff, you might be perplexed over a seeming typology-neuroscience paradox. According to typology, Sensing and iNtuition are Perceiving functions, while Thinking and Feeling are Judging functions. Thus, if neurophysiological evidence suggests Judging as left-brained activity, T and F would have to be limited to the left hemisphere. Conversely, S and N would be limited to the right brain. Yet we have just witnessed a number of pages devoted to the contrary. You may ask, what gives?

As has already been stated, neuroscientific data would suggest that the four Jungian functions (S,N,T,F) are found in both cerebral hemispheres. Let's try to further understand this dilemma.

First, let me say up-front that I certainly do not comprehend all the complexities of neuroscience or even typology, for that matter. No one knows exactly how the brain works, but we do know many aspects of its functioning. I could leave some of these ambiguous areas alone but have chosen not to, for they are future areas to understand and verify. Therefore, why not raise the issues now?

Second, understanding this paradox and other difficult areas within this subject is not necessary to derive benefits from typology. Unfortunately, they could become a hindrance to some, but to open minded truth seekers they are valuable considerations.

Third, I want to make a distinction between *typological* Judging (J) and Perceiving (P) differences, and *neurological* left-brain and right-brain dissimilarities. By reviewing the contrasts between J and P in the typology section, and the contrasts between the left hemisphere and right hemisphere in this section, you will notice varying classifications. They do not fit hand in glove.

For example, typology states that the functions Thinking (T) and Feeling (F) are decision making processes. This is correct. Typology also states that T and F are associated with the structured, controlled preference of Judging (J). This is not always correct. Combining neuroscience with typology still keeps T and F as decision makers, yet (the neuro/type connection) would also suggest that *left-brain Thinking is structured and analytic but right brain Thinking more flexible and synthetic. Left-brain Sensing and iNtuition would also be structured and analytic, whereas right-brain S and N more flexible and synthetic.*

I have supplied this superficial explanation to acknowledge ambiguous areas and to offer possible steps to solving them. Again, let me reiterate, the essence of this material will remain unaffected by what is still to be known on this subject.

Remember, it is possible to have a typological Judging Function, such as T, in the Perceiving right hemisphere, or a Perceiving function, such as N in the left half. It appears Thinking and Feeling are primarily found in the front of the left brain and the back of the right brain. In contrast, Sensing and iNtuition are mainly found in the areas of the rear left forebrain and front right forebrain.

Conclusion

We have just considered many facts and educated speculations pertaining to the brain. The purpose has been to gain a greater understanding of neuroscience, particularly as it relates to typology and athletics. The more we learn regarding neuroscience and Jung-Myers typology, the more we see their inevitable matrimony. They complement one another, shedding infinitely more light on the mind and brain than when viewed separately.

8
Brain Types and Body Skills

Neuroscience and typology can be integrated successfully with athletics. In this chapter, we will combine Jung-Myers Type preferences along with neuroscientific data. Our goal is to observe athletes' mental and physical traits. There are a number of ways we could observe Type and brain preferences. I have chosen to illustrate with the temperament groups formulated by Isabel Myers. In simplifying the 16 Types, she chose four groupings of preferences—the **SF**, **ST**, **NF,** and **NT**. They provide clear insight into the dynamics of Brain Types, body skills, and sports. Later on in the book, we will also look at SJ and SP groupings to gain a broader understanding of temperament.

I want to recognize Walter Lowen's book, *Dichotomies of the Mind,* and Susan Scanlon's interpretive work of Lowen's book, published in *The Type Reporter,* for the scientific direction of this chapter. Lowen's work provided the final framework for my empirical and scientific research into sports.

SFs *(Gross Motor Skills)*

SFs are made up of those persons who possess Sensing (S) and Feeling (F) as their dominant and auxiliary functions (iNtuition and Thinking are less preferred). These Brain Types are the ESFP, ISFP, ESFJ, and ISFJ. The ESFP and ISFP are members of the SP temperament group (hummingbird), whereas the ESFJ and ISFJ are SJ temperaments (bee).

SFs are gifted in the use of their **gross motor skills**. The large muscle groups such as the arms, torso, and legs fall in this category. The two major aspects of body coordination are: (1) **control**, which comes from the *left brain* and tends to specialize in the separate parts in a movement; and (2) **rhythm**, a product of the *right brain* which processes multiple parts of movement into an artistic, graceful flow.

SFs (Gross Motor)

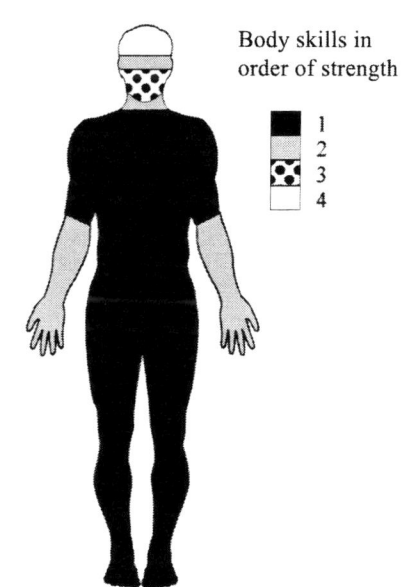

Body skills in order of strength

1
2
3
4

The average person has no difficulty exercising gross motor skills with both sides of the brain. All unimpaired adults can lift a grocery bag out of the car, walk next door to borrow milk, and sweep the kitchen floor. SFs are masters of *gross motor* skills. They like to have body involvement in whatever they do.

We must remember that athletic weaknesses come in two varieties. One is the individual who is inherently weak or deficient in particular body skills. Developing these skills takes many years of practice. The second kind of weakness is the result of an innate strength gone too far, generally occurring when the athlete is too tense or nervous. The gross motor skills of SFs can become too rigid, a liability when the SFs do not control their anxiety. A tightening of the muscles can cause the big muscles to lose suppleness and fluidity. This weakness can be corrected if the individual can learn to control his or her thoughts. Unfortunately, few athletes have this ability.

SFJs

The **left-brained SFJs** are controlled in their body movements. Since all left-brained persons deal with matters in successive order, the SFJ has a special ability to **control** body actions. Prior to SFJs moving their bodies, they tend to analyze how and when specific body movements should be implemented.

SFJs learn best from practical and simple teaching, emphasizing how the body movements are performed, step-by-step. This is an important fact to know when coaching SFJ athletes. Without this approach, SFJs will experience needless frustration and sub par performances.

In the mid-1990s, I attended an NBA team's training camp. The coach was an iNtuitive Brain Type, and one of his players was an SFJ (rare in the NBA). As I watched several full practices, the SFJ had tremendous difficulty understanding the coach's iNtuitive instructions. As a result, this player took some verbal abuse. The coach would have been better off using the time to offer clear, simple instructions.

SFPs

In **right-brained SFPs, rhythm** is dominant (in contrast to control for the left-brained SFJs). *SFPs are found much more frequently in professional sports than SFJs.* Their brain (and body) functions are not as conducive to professional performance. This is not to say that SFJs can't be good athletes or make it to the pro ranks, however.

Like SFJs, *SFPs learn by receiving practical and simple teaching. Unlike SFJs, SFPs enjoy receiving information in a wholistic manner.* A few months into the 1992 season baseball's **Mark McGwire** (ISFP) was hitting home runs at a record pace. He said about the teaching style of his new batting coach, Doug Rader:

> Right away, I liked his approach. He keeps things simple: See the ball, hit the ball. The first time he spoke to the guys in spring training, he asked us, 'What is the object of being a hitter?' There was silence; then finally someone said, 'To get a hit?' And Doug said, 'Correct.' [1]

SFPs approach movement as a whole, integrating parts instead of segregating them as SFJs do. Thus, SFPs are able to attain rhythm, grace, and flow. Their bodies reflect rhythmic coordination. They may not manifest this ability in every action but, with a little practice, it will soon develop.

One athlete who demonstrated superior gross motor skills was Extraverted SFP (ESFP) **Walter Payton**, former running back for the Chicago Bears. Not only did Walter set all-time NFL rushing records, but he also performed with an artistry the game had never seen. He could cut on a dime, lift his legs like a graceful high hurdler, and sail over the defense with the style of an Olympic broad jumper. No one but the ESFP could add such flair and beauty to the game with total body control. Payton also demonstrated his big muscle proficiency by carrying the football almost 4,000 times, nearly 1,000 more than anyone in NFL history.

SFPs are process-oriented (as opposed to result-oriented). They tend to use their bodies just for the pleasure of it. The actual movements that a sport provides can bring resounding gratification to these individuals.

Years ago I coached a twelve-year-old ISFP in basketball who loved to hold his follow through after a shot. He was actually demonstrating two important factors. First, the held follow through improves the chance of making a shot, and, second, enjoying this maneuver adds fun to the game, which is essential for this Type to continue with a sport.

I once asked a successful SFP golfer on the PGA Tour if a parent should steer his or her child into golf. He said:

> Unless the child wants to do it on his own and enjoys doing it, he shouldn't play.[2]

In other words, let the child make the choice. Other parent Types (such as STJs) have a tendency to make children participate regardless of their desire. How parents were raised will influence their values regardless of Type, but the Brain Type will have a strong bearing on the motivations of both parents and children.

Extraverted SFPs have included **basketball's Magic Johnson and Charles Barkley, baseball's Willie Mays, Frank Thomas, and Barry Bonds, and track's Carl Lewis, Jackie Joyner-Kersee,** and Marion Jones. *Introverted SFPs are* **the NBA's Scottie Pippen, Tim Duncan, and Kobe Bryant, baseball's Mark McGwire, and track's Michael Johnson.**

STs (Fine Motor)

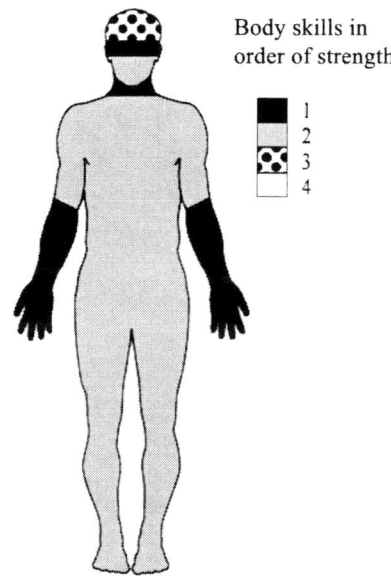

Body skills in order of strength

1
2
3
4

STs (*Fine Motor Skills*)

STs are those individuals who have Sensing and Thinking as their dominant and auxiliary functions (iNtuition and Feeling are less preferred). These Brain Types are the ESTP, ISTP, ESTJ, and ISTJ. The ESTP and ISTP are members of the SP temperament group (hummingbird), while the ESTJ and ISTJ are SJ temperaments (bee).

STs have a special inborn ability to master **fine motor skills**, especially as they relate to hand-eye coordination. Two significant aspects are associated with hand-eye coordination: Calculated **dexterity** is the special skill or adroitness in using the hands to manipulate objects in a controlled fashion. The ability to handle detailed movements comes principally from the *left brain*.

The other major aspect of hand-eye coordination involves spontaneous **positioning**, or placing the hand in the proper location at a given moment. The *right brain* primarily regulates this skill.

All normal persons exercise hand dexterity and positioning, but STs do exceptionally well with them. Each of us routinely uses fine motor skills in such activities as brushing teeth, putting on clothes, driving a car, or throwing a ball. The more we exercise these movements, the more skillful and artistic we become.

Because of their brain specialization, STs have the greatest potential for mastery of the fine motor skills. Anything they pick up will become an artistic tool. The construction worker with a hammer and nails, the dentist with instruments, the architect with a pencil, and the athlete with a baseball, glove and bat, or golf club, are just a few examples.

The ST will not always have the best fine motor skills compared to the other non-ST athletes. For example, an NF athlete who practices a lot more than the ST can develop a greater skill in fine motor movements. However, the ST athlete who practices as much as the non-ST will develop the greatest fine motor proficiency of all the Types. STs have the greatest potential for excellence with hand eye coordination and other fine motor skills.

Body skill strengths can become weaknesses, especially when the athlete is affected by anxiety. In the case of STs, the forearms, wrists, hands, and fingers can change from an asset to a liability. Mental stress stiffens up their fine motor movements, particularly on the dominant side. If ST athletes are right-handed, they must attempt to stay relaxed and loose with the dominant right hand, regardless of what sport they are playing. Likewise, left handed STs need to stay loose with the left side.

As an aside, STs often have a hawk- or eagle-eyed look. Their brain regulated, hand-eye proficiency can be seen on the face. When they concentrate, they'll often emulate the eyes of a preying bird, able to spot a scurrying rodent from a mile above.

STs can be defined even further, but for now let's see which STs specialize in dexterity and which specialize in positioning.

STJs

For the **left-brained STJs** (ESTJ, ISTJ), **dexterity** is dominant. They are able to manipulate their wrists, hands, and fingers with ease. They possess extra aptitude for hand-eye coordination in the dexterity realm. Since STJs rely heavily on the left hemisphere, they can be very patient in problem solving (especially ISTJs). Typically, STJ athletes will approach sports with a more calculated and defensive style. If an STJ athlete participates in a sport for a long period of time, however, he or she can become much better at reacting quickly and offensively. The STJ will never become as proficient as the STP (who practices equally as hard) in processing many things at once, reacting quickly, and attacking the opposition in an offensive mode. Nevertheless, STJs can develop these right-brained characteristics to the point of performing first-rate even at the professional level.

Not all sports and their respective positions of play require right-brained athletes. **Dick Schofield** played the 1988 baseball season with the highest fielding percentage of any American League shortstop. As an STJ who naturally played defense better than offense, he is proof that left-brained STJs can excel at the professional level.

Extraverted STJs include **baseball's Nolan Ryan, golf's Nick Faldo, tennis' Pam Shriver, and football's Ryan Leaf.** *Introverted STJ Brain Types include* **baseball's Orel Hershiser, the NBA's Jeff Hornacek, golf's Jack Nicklaus and Betsy King, and tennis' Chris Evert.** (Remember, Brain Types are not necessarily synonymous with the personas or personalities that people show others.)

STPs

For the **right-brained STPs (ESTP, ISTP), positioning** is superior. It provides them the special facility to place their hands in the right place at the right time which helps their split-second ability to process many things at once—a must for fast-moving sports. STPs have a superlative God-given gift of hand-eye coordination, utilizing their hands to manipulate and position sporting objects.

STPs are inherently more offensive minded than STJs, and they continually look for ways to score, whereas STJs instinctively look to prevent the opposition from scoring. STPs can play excellent defense and STJs can be prolific scorers, but these roles do not come naturally.

Michael Jordan, the legendary scoring machine of the NBA, is an STP. Jordan could always play defense but found it difficult to play both ends of the floor equally well. In his initial NBA years Michael figured his 35 points per game were his greatest contribution to the team. When he was criticized by the media, Michael determined to prove he could play defense expertly as well. Thus, in 1988, he won the NBA Best Defensive Player award (taking it from perennial STJ winner Michael Cooper of the L.A. Lakers).

Though offensive minded, if STPs give extra attention to defense, they can master it, too. Unfortunately, the human body and brain have limitations. It is virtually impossible to play offense and defense equally in a tiring sporting contest. One will ultimately give way to the other.

Extraverted STPs include **the NBA's Karl Malone, football's Joe Namath and Dan Marino, baseball's Mike Piazza and Rickey Henderson, tennis' Andre Agassi and Martina Hingas, and golf's Greg Norman and Fred Couples.** *Introverted STPs are* **the NBA's Larry Bird and Michael Jordan, football's Barry Sanders, baseball's Wade Boggs, hockey's Wayne Gretzky and Mario Lemieux, tennis' Steffi Graff and Monica Seles, and golf's Karrie Webb and Ben Hogan.**

NFs (*Oral, Verbal and Hearing Skills*)

NFs are persons who have iNtuition and Feeling as their dominant and auxiliary brain functions (Sensing and Thinking are less preferred). These Brain Types are the ENFP, INFP, ENFJ, and INFJ. All four Types are members of the NF temperament group (stork).

NFs are most gifted in speech, hearing, and verbal skills. Do not assume they are therefore weak in gross and fine motor skills. NFs are better with fine than gross motors, but they can develop excellent coordination between the two—although INFJs can struggle with synchronizing complete body movements.

NFs, more than any other temperament group, increase and decrease motor movements based on their moods. The Extraverted NFs (ENFJ and ENFP) are especially susceptible to hyperactivity when they are excited about a game or event. This can work to their advantage or disadvantage. In basketball, it can lead to foul trouble and errant shots. In figure skating, a world or Olympic championship can be attained by pulling off a daring, difficult triple axle.

Let us look more closely at NFs most natural body skills. Speech and its related functions are where they excel. There are two major aspects to speech. **Words** are created by an intricate series of undertakings in the head's sound chamber, and originate primarily in the *left side of the brain*. **Intonation** is a resonant component cultivated by the *right hemisphere*. Intonation is "the pattern or melody of pitch changes in connected speech, especially the pitch pattern of a sentence."[3]

NFs (Language and Hearing)

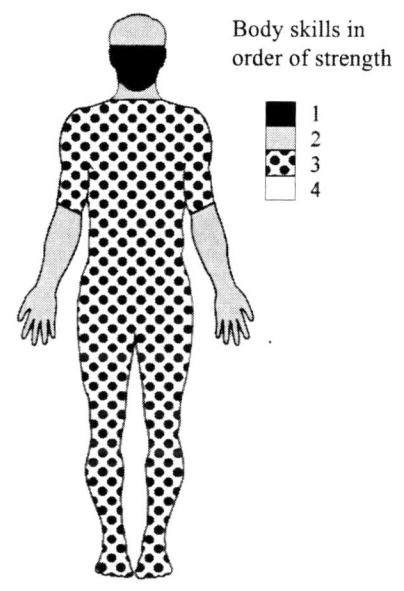

Body skills in order of strength
1
2
3
4

NFJs

NFJs (ENFJ and INFJ) process language principally in the **left brain** and are more interested in **words** themselves and their meanings than in the intonations of words. Diction or finding the precise word they want is most important to NFJs. Thus, they say or write the same thing in a number of ways.

NFJ athletes are often quoted by reporters and journalists. They are refreshing and unique, articulating matters cogently and creatively. Some past and present NFJ television commentators who are former athletes are **Frank Gifford, Pat Summerall, Bob Griese, and Pat Haden**. They demonstrated their prowess on the field of play and can be even better in the TV booth (with practice).

NFJs are more controlled and mechanical in sports than their right-brained NFP counterparts. Because NFJs rely more on the left brain, they process matters more cautiously and calculatingly. The faster the pace of the sport, with split second decisions to be made, the more difficulty NFJs have coping compared to NFPs. NFPs are cerebrally designed to facilitate rapid movement in athletics.

Extraverted NFJs include baseball's **Mark Grace and Jeff Kent, the NFL's Drew Bledsoe and Vinny Testaverde, golf's Nick Price and Julie Inkster, and tennis' Jim Courier**.

Introverted NFJs include **the NBA's Chis Dudley** and **Jim McIlvaine**.

NFPs

NFPs (ENFP and INFP) process information principally in their **right brain**, being most in tune with **intonation**. Intonation involves harmony, which for our purposes is the ability to evaluate things by Feelings, not Thinking. NFP athletes operate by their subjective feeling of what is best to do. They do not possess the logical reasoning abilities of Thinkers. Nevertheless, they can become exceptional athletes by utilizing their spontaneous iNtuitive and Feeling functions of the brain. To perform best in certain sports such as basketball and baseball they will need to rely a little more on their less preferred Thinking function. Yet they will perform best in sports such as figure skating, diving, and gymnastics when implementing their most natural iNtuitive and Feeling functions of the right hemisphere. Here they are more fluid and artistic than their NFJ counterparts.

NFPs can also speak very well, like NFJs. Take, for example, **Bob Uecker**, the affable sport's broadcaster who is a former big league player. The ol' "he missed the tag" man is colorful, creative and spontaneous in a world of predominately left-brained broadcasters.

Like all P's, NFPs are predisposed to using the right hemisphere and have tremendous aptitude at processing many things at once. The fact that NFPs reside naturally in this portion of the brain ensures a greater chance for success in many sporting endeavors.

NFs, especially NFPs, can attain remarkable jumping abilities. I do not have all the answers to why this is true; a few are obvious. First, NFs perform athletically according to mood. They generally take their enthusiasm for life into competition.

Second, NFs seem to excel at coordinating or harmonizing body movements, blending the gross and fine motor movements. They do not possess the natural dominance of motor skills as do the SFs and STs, yet they have an uncanny knack for synergizing these muscle movements.

Third, NFs (particularly NFPs) tend to walk on the toes or front of their feet. After a lifetime of this, and the Achilles tendon and calf muscles can generate extra leaping abilities.

Some Extraverted NFPs include **the NBA's David**

Robinson, the NFL's Jerry Rice, baseball's Sammy Sosa, figure skating's Kristi Yamaguchi, Michelle Kwan, and Scott Hamilton, and diving's Greg Louganis and Fu Mingxia.

Introverted NFPs are the **NBA's Grant Hill, Julius Erving (Dr. J), and Dirk Nowitzki, baseball's Derek Jeter, Mariano Rivera, and David Justice, golf's Tiger Woods, and track's Said Aouita.** All these INFPs have had creative feel for their sport, demonstrating harmony in motion when performing.

NTs (*Mental Skills*)

NTs possess iNtuition and Thinking as their dominant and auxiliary functions (Sensing and Feeling are less preferred). These Brain Types are the ENTJ, INTJ, ENTP, and INTP. They all are members of the NT temperament group (owl).

Whereas SFs are exceptionally gifted in gross motor skills, STs in fine motor skills, and NFs in language and hearing, the NTs dominate in logical abstraction skills. NTs can excel in speech and motor skills, yet find logical reasoning easiest to come by.

NTs are more gifted in and reliant on fine motor skills than gross motor. The use of the large muscle groups (gross motor) is the NT's least proficient body skill. To perform best athletically, NTs need to adequately develop their legs, lower body balance, torso, and upper arms.

The adage that it is "better to work smarter than harder" is implemented daily by NTs. They believe in "brain over brawn." **Planning/exploring** and **conclusion** are the two major dimensions to the NTs' mental prowess. **Planning** involves how a problem can be solved and necessitates iNtuitive awareness of the complete scenario, processed by the *right brain*. Attaining a **conclusion** requires sequential processing, which comes from the *left brain*.

NTs (Mental)

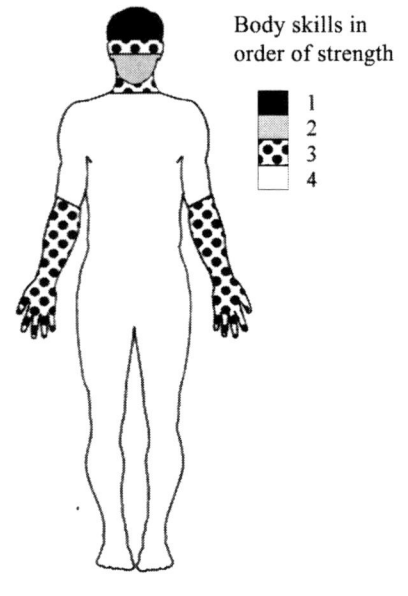

Body skills in order of strength

1
2
3
4

NTJs

NTJs (ENTJ and INTJ) work enthusiastically to reach a **conclusion** to matters. Whether they work backward to prove a conclusion or forward to discover it, finality is always in mind. Concepts are either put together or broken apart piece by piece by NTJs. They use their step-by-step logical abilities to get the upper hand on all problems, even in athletics.

NTJ athletes are more mechanical and controlled than their NTP counterparts. Having a greater facility with the left brain, the NTJ methodically deals with sporting events. Extraverted NTJs act faster than Introverted NTJs in their systematic left brain processing. To the casual observer, ENTJ athletes act almost right-brained due to their speed of maneuvering and excessive practicing, despite the singular processing of information.

Some well-known ENTJ athletes have included **basketball's Kevin McHale, Tom Chambers, and John Paxson, baseball's Ryne Sandberg, Greg Maddux, and Tom Seaver, football's Roger Staubach and Steve Young, golf's Tom Watson and Phil Mickelson, tennis' Gabriela Sabatini and Billy Jean King, and figure skating's Peggy Fleming and Dorthy Hamill.**

Tom Kite, the most consistent PGA star of the 1980s, represents the INTJs. Golf is certainly a sport that allows INTJs to excel in their methodical, abstract, analytic ways. *Other INTJs include* **baseball's David Cone and Randy Johnson, and basketball coaches' Phil Jackson and Don Nelson**.

NTPs

NTPs (ENTP and INTP) find fulfillment in the **plan**, or the process of designing an intellectual game plan. An INTP relative of mine personifies the NTP. As a medical researcher, he enjoys collecting and studying data and watching what it eventually reveals. If it does not come out as he exactly planned, it isn't the end of the world because he enjoyed the journey. In addition, a wrong conclusion affords the exciting opportunity to reexamine the old evidence and discover the new. The NTP prefers researching and exploring the data as much as anything.

NTPs also tend to visualize formulas and patterns. They apply creative, synthetic, logical abilities rapidly with less emphasis on sequence and structure. Their *right-brained dominance* can facilitate many things at once. Introverted NTPs are rarely found in professional sports, though they can be acclaimed athletes. They are the most logically abstract of all the 16 Types. Thus, they are the most naturally gifted academics in our educational systems. **Albert Einstein and William F. Buckley** are two INTPs who come to mind. With inordinate cerebral acumen, it is no wonder few INTPs pursue the concrete world of athletics.

One INTP who made the headlines in 1986-87 did so in a tragic fashion. Her name is **Kathy Ormsby**. She is a record-setting distance runner from North Carolina State who attempted an apparent suicide during the 10,000-meter run at the 1986 NCAA track and field championships in Indianapolis. Ormsby found herself in eighth place as the race progressed, with no chance to win the event in which she was favored. In utter frustration she ran out of the stadium, climbed a 7-foot chain link fence and leaped from a 30-foot bridge. She eluded death, but was paralyzed from the waist down.

What would make this person try to take her life who, in 12 years of elementary and high school, never received one grade lower than an A? How could this prodigy be overcome by such pressure? Ormsby graduated Number 1 in a class of 600 with an unprecedented grade average. Her former high school principal said:

> She was the classic overachiever, doing nothing but the best. Track just seemed to be a sidelight from her pre-med studies, we thought.[4]

Following her tragedy, Kathy told reporters she felt that by falling behind in this crucial race, she was failing God, her parents, and her coach, and that something was wrong with her. In retrospect, she was shocked by her own behavior. It was atypical of her cool, calm, level-headed demeanor. Her friends knew her as a perfectionist, which is common for INTPs, the sages of conceptual logic. Kathy was so used to her intellectual dominance she couldn't handle her athletic "failure" (which would have been a major success in most anyone else's book). A teammate who wished to remain anonymous said:

> [Ormsby] always put pressure on herself when she went to meets. She had to be the best and she had to do the best. If she didn't, she got upset with herself. But I never thought she'd try something like this.[5]

Another acquaintance said:

> We kept saying she needed to get loose, but she never, never did. She set tremendous goals for herself.[6]

Ormsby's rash behavior is not typical of INTPs. But due to their tremendous inner resolve to be the most competent at whatever they take seriously, INTPs can lose temporary perspective when they fall short. Having a *stronger* iNtuitive than Sensing perception, INTPs (like all iNtuitives) can distort reality under pressure. Kathy made her tragic, hasty decision on the spur of the moment. We all wish she had taken time to think of what she was doing. Let this be a lesson to all of us parents and coaches to make sure we keep matters in perspective for our athletes.

Ormsby proved that INTPs can excel at long distance running if they choose (as in other sports). They have the strong inner (Introverted) focus, the NT mental prowess, and the right-brained abilities to handle many things at once and smoothly. Like other iNtuitive Types, however, INTPs need to maintain a balance in the real world, the here and now.

ENTPs, who also possess a right-hemisphere dominance, can excel in athletics. Far more ENTPs than INTPs are professional athletes. (ENTPs are also found much more frequently in the U.S. populace.) They lack the intense inner focus of Introverted Types but can make up for it by avoiding "paralysis by analysis." Their energetic and more go with the flow approach works well in many sports.

Pro golfer **Fuzzy Zoeller** has routinely typified the ENTP on the golf course. He is a competitor, audacious and generally good natured. When tied by Greg Norman's 40-foot putt at the 1984 U.S. Open, Fuzzy stood on the 18th fairway waving his white towel, acknowledging Norman's fantastic comeback and conciliating a defeat or play-off to Norman standing on the 18th green. This "un-golflike" humorous gesture classically illustrated the ENTP. Often called the "masters of one-upmanship," they rarely leave themselves in a position of not having the final say-so or showing their wit.

All NTs will one up others with their mental giftedness, but none can do it with the quickness and flair of ENTPs. Their Extraverted, right-brained dominance has a capacity for dealing with iNtuitive cognitive matters faster than any. **Bill Russell**, the former Celtic star center and ENTP, accentuated his physical skills by his meteoric mental dexterity.

ENTPs make outstanding coaches. Their cerebral keenness is clearly manifested in this role. **Lou Holtz, Jim Valvano, Frank Layden, and Chuck Daly** are just a few of the well known ENTP coaches.

Other ENTP athletes have included **figure skating's Tara Lipinski, swimming's Melvin Stewart and Amy Van Dyken, tennis' Pete Sampras and Guillermo Vilas, golf's Dave Stockton, baseball's Babe Ruth and Kevin Brown, basketball's Bob Cousy, Glenn Robinson, and Vince Carter, and football's John Brodie, Dan Fouts, and Kurt Warner.**

A few INTP athletes include **tennis stars Arthur Ashe and Mary Joe Fernandez, and basketball's Dikembe Mutombo.**

For you created my inmost being;
you knit me together in my mother's womb.
I praise you because I am fearfully and wonderfully made;
your works are wonderful,
I know that full well.
(Psalm 139:13-14)

PART THREE

VARIOUS SPORTS AND BRAIN TYPES

Some Issues to Consider Before You Begin

In this section, I have limited my attentions to the most popular sports in America and the Brain Types that perform best in each of them. We will find some Types mentioned regularly, while others are rarely discussed. My research exposed which Types excelled most often in these sports. My hope was to find all sixteen well-represented, with each Type proficient in at least one sport. Unfortunately, this did not happen. Rather, I found a few Types dominating most sports, with the remainder showing proficiency to various degrees, depending upon the sport.

This is not to say all the evidence is in. Patterns continue to emerge in my research. At the same time, I have spent thousands of hours studying athletes as they relate to Brain Types. Associates of mine have exhorted me to reveal the many answers I do have, and write sequels to include the depth of material I cannot include in this book, as well as the new discoveries I make. This I do reluctantly.

There are lingering, nagging questions in my mind, such as, "How many patterns must I see?", "How many athletes must I type?", "How many sports must I cover?", and so forth. I suppose they'll never leave me in my desire to exhaust this fascinating subject. *I say all of this especially for the Types seldom mentioned in this section.* Do not give up your dreams of reaching professional status, if that is your desire. I am sure there are sports in which you can attain professional success. Be patient as your areas of proficiency are unearthed. At the same time, take the valuable information in this book and use it. Think of sports and positions in those sports which would match your Brain Type, those which would be compatible with your motor and mental skills.

A concerted effort is made throughout this book to show the distinction between Brain Types and personality. Even though persons possess the same Brain Type as other persons, their personas will be distinct due to environmental factors (upbringing, culture, friends, and so forth). All persons within each of the 16 inborn designs will share some common personality characteristics with others of their same Type. The differences will be manifold in many cases. Therefore, this book is chiefly interested in distinguishing Brain Types in sports, not in personalities.

With these thoughts in mind, let's consider some patterns that I have observed regarding various sports and the brain.

9
Baseball

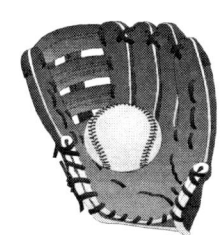

Baseball has become a lucrative sport for modern players. In 1997, the average major league salary was over $1 million. By the year 2000, Alex Rodriguez signed a contract worth $250 million! Ever since the days of Babe Ruth, Ty Cobb, and the "Gas House Gang," many folks have wondered just what makes some professional baseball players so exceptional. We must remind ourselves that they have put in countless hours of practice. The old timers, as well as modern players, have been made to comply with the simple axiom: hard work = success. Though practice procedures have changed dramatically over time, working hard on the fundamentals is still necessary. All baseball greats, past and present, have had to put in the necessary time.

Another significant factor for baseball greatness is, you guessed it, Brain Type. The old timers had the intrinsic cerebral factors working for them as well, giving them that edge over the other hard workers who weren't blessed with ideal baseball brains. Though a number of Brain Types have made it to the major league level over the years, we see that certain ones tend to dominate.

ISTP

The Brain Type you will encounter most often throughout this book is the ISTP. There is no innate design more gifted athletically, virtually no sport in which they cannot excel. Professional baseball is no exception.

ISTPs can be the best, or among the best, at every position on the field—a difficult claim that can only be made by a few Brain Types. Versatility accompanies their extraordinary baseball-giftedness. To pick a 1980s or 1990s ISTP All Star team would not take long. We might choose: first base—**Don Mattingly, Will Clark, Jim Thome** or **Jeff Bagwell**; second—**Pete Rose**; shortstop—**Cal Ripken Jr.**; third—**Wade Boggs, George Brett,** or **Chipper Jones**; outfield—**Darryl Strawberry, Lenny Dykstra,** or **Eric Davis**; pitching—**Roger Clemens, Tom Glavine, Bret Saberhagen** or **Trevor Hoffman;** catching—**Terry Steinbach.**

We could choose an ISTP team of the past that would include such stars as: **Ty Cobb, Lou Gehrig, Ted Williams,** and **Henry Aaron.**

ISTPs are highly logical players who approach the game as tacticians. Their introspecting, *everthinking* minds continuously attempt to figure out baseball matters to perfection. **Wade Boggs** was such a player. Upon retirement in 2000, Boggs was a five-time American League batting champion. He hit over .300 for 14 of his 15 big league years and was voted as a starter in 11 consecutive All-Star games.

Extraordinary Concentration

ISTPs are able to devote tremendous concentration to matters that have their interest. First baseman, **Will Clark**, demonstrated this in the 1989 National League play off series against the Chicago Cubs. Not many baseball aficionados will forget 62,000 fans on their feet, bases loaded with San Francisco Giants, and Cubs star reliever and wild man, **Mitch Williams**, exemplifying an executioner on the mound. Clark was batting for his life.

It was a classic confrontation of ISTPs. Both men had indomitable spirits. But someone had to lose the battle, and it ended up being Williams. **Will "The**

Thrill" Clark, said afterward:

> I heard nothing, I felt nothing. I didn't know what the fans were doing, I didn't know what the pitcher was doing. I couldn't have told you what Mitch's eyes looked like. I didn't even know if he was wearing a beard. What it was, was just me and the ball.[1]

That, sports fans, is concentration. No one can exercise it in baseball better than the ISTP.

Risk Takers, Intrepid

One aspect of ISTPs' Brain Type making for star athletes is their ability to deal with fear. When ISTPs concentrate on the subject at hand, any previous fear they may have had is lost. This is especially seen as they mature and gain more confidence in their sport.

Consider ISTP **Lenny Dykstra**. Growing up as a kid in Southern California, Lenny and friends would sneak into empty Anaheim Stadium (home of the Angels), where he would practice diving into the outfield fence. In high school, he would challenge the pitching machine, moving up on it until he was within 20 feet. Anyone who's ever watched Lenny play, knows he was a fearless fighter, willing to sacrifice his body to win.

Offensive-minded

"Offensive" is defined by **Ty Cobb, Ted Williams, Pete Rose, Henry Aaron, George Brett,** and **Wade Boggs**. These are just a few of the ISTPs ranking with the greatest hitters of all time. ISTPs have cat like reflexes, extraordinary hand eye coordination, and the aggressiveness of a pit-bull. No Brain Type has greater hitting potential than the ISTP. **Ty Cobb** is the all time batting champion in major league baseball, a career .367 hitter. **Pete Rose** holds the major league record with 4,256 career base hits. **George Brett** became the first player to win a batting title in each of three decades.

Wrist Generated Power

ISTPs are able to generate tremendous power, regardless of their stature. Bigger ISTPs just hit the ball harder and farther. The wise ones learn to use their power for line drives and base hits rather than going for the fences. This hitting philosophy produces a healthy batting average and extra base hits. Most home runs will come when ISTPs do not try to hit them. **Henry Aaron** was an astute ISTP hitter who went down in the record books with the most career home runs, 755, averaging 33 homers for 19 straight years! Henry was an All Star in each of the 23 seasons he played, a career .305 hitter who won two batting titles, and an adept outfielder, winning 4 Gold Gloves.

ISTPs' right brain activated, fine motor movements create their inordinate power. Hammerin' Hank demonstrated this as much as any baseball player in history with his graceful, wristy swing. ISTP **Roger Maris** was able to employ his powerful wrists to set the major league single season home run record, 61! ISFP, Mark McGwire broke Maris's record in 1998.

In 1994, ISTP basketball superstar **Michael Jordan** hung up his Air-Jordans to give hardball a try. A little more than a year later, Jordan bowed out of a game that most felt he could never play, particularly as a hitter. In one season, Jordan batted only .202 with two home runs as a 31-year-old outfielder at double-A Birmingham, Alabama.

Michael suffered from the ills of every ISTP right-handed hitter (who's also right hand dominant). He tried to swing too much with his right side. He triggered those high-powered ISTP wrists—especially the right hand—and was always vulnerable to off-speed pitches, especially breaking balls. Unfortunately, Michael appeared to try to pull the ball virtually every time at bat. Though he had "expert" instruction from some of baseball's top coaches, he never got the teaching that could have made his baseball a much better experience. Had Michael been taught how to properly hit to the opposite field according to his Brain Type, his batting average would have been much higher. Jordan's rusty baseball skills were good enough to work with and make him a success at baseball, too.

Spatial, Logical, Quick-Reacting

ISTP batters can have, bar none, the best eye at the plate of all the 16 Brain Types. A few other Types may have as high a batting average, but they do not have the innate abilities of the ISTP for swinging at the best pitches. ISTPs' Introversion enables them to wait longer on the ball before they react. Their dominant, visually oriented right brain allows them to see the ball in flight as an owl sights a field mouse. Then, waiting as long as possible before deciding to swing at the ball, their spatial Thinking function reasons whether or not it is going to be a strike. If so, the ISTPs' lightning-fast, fine motor reflexes kick in and attack the ball with their superior, ST hand-eye coordination, positioning the bat in the right place at the right time.

Remember ISTP **Wade Boggs** at the plate? His ST hawk eyes followed the ball all the way into the catcher's mitt when he decided not to swing. They were trancelike, deeply focused on the ball and nothing else.

James L. Breen has written a report titled, *What Makes a Good Hitter?*[2] He assumes that if a ball is in the air for .54 seconds from the pitcher to the catcher, more slowly responding Major Leaguers require .28 seconds to swing the bat. This leaves them only .26 seconds to make up their minds as the fast-moving ball approaches. Conversely, a quickly responding hitter needs only .19 seconds to swing the lumber and is given .35 seconds to contemplate hitting the ball. This split second time difference is nearly 17 percent. It may not seem like much of a difference to fans in the stands; but to the hitter in the batter's box, it is significant.

The knowledge of Brain Types can provide us greater insight into these reaction times. Although there are many factors to consider, a right-brained Perceiver will see the ball better and react more quickly. Ted Williams, Ernie Banks, Hank Aaron, Mickey Mantle, Willie Mays, and Stan Musial were the quickly reacting hitters in this study. All were Ps.

Not all ISTPs adequately utilize their cerebral abilities at the plate. Bigger-in-stature ISTPs tend to be impatient with their batting. They like to perform to the expectations of others by trying to hit home runs (lowering their batting averages and raising their strike-outs).

Base-stealing

Not all ISTPs are base stealing threats, but they're some of the fastest. Throughout baseball history, many ISTPs have demonstrated their prowess.

Years ago I coached my son's Little League team and drafted a nine-year-old ISTP. It was only his second year of organized ball, so he was far from his potential. I was able to select him in the last rounds on draft night because the other coaches overlooked him. They were not impressed with his tryouts. I wasn't either except that I determined his Type on tryout day. He was a diamond in the rough, from my perspective. (I'll rarely pass on an ISTP, even if he or she has little or no experience.) He started out the season slowly, but by the season's end he was my lead off hitter, starting second baseman, and best base runner. Not only did he possess deceptive speed, but he was as cunning as Wile E. Coyote. Opposing teams could not contain him. Given the opportunity, ISTPs have the potential to be among the best base stealers.

Defensive too

ISTPs can also be the best defensive players in baseball. They generally prefer playing offense, but as they develop they see the importance of honing their defensive skills as well. With concerted effort, they can become Gold Glovers.

One exceptional defensive shortstop was ISTP **Cal Ripken Jr**. Former great Brooks Robinson, winner of 16 Gold Gloves, could not believe Ripken didn't win a Gold Glove in 1990:

> It's incomprehensible to me that he could play every day and make three errors and not win the Gold Glove. And that's not to take anything away from Ozzie Guillen, because he's a very good shortstop. Cal is not as dazzling, not as spectacular, but nobody plays the position like he does. Nobody puts as much thought into playing the position. He's the best I've ever seen when it comes to playing the hitters, and I think that's the reason his defense is overlooked.[3]

The astute Robinson perceptively acknowledged Ripken's "thought" in playing shortstop. Like all ISTPs, Ripken excelled in his dominant Thinking world. His defensive skills were even more remarkable when you consider his 6-foot-4 frame. Ripken holds the Major League record for consecutive errorless games by a shortstop. In 1991, he won his first Gold Glove and second American League most valuable player award, batting .323—34 homers and 114 runs batted in. In 1995, Ripken demonstrated his ISTP perseverance and indomitable will by surpassing ISTP **Lou Gehrig's** extraordinary record in consecutive games played. Ripken's record streak finally ended in 1998, at 2,632. Cal retired in 2001 at age 41.

Upon his retirement in 1995, first baseman and six-time all-star **Don Mattingly** had won the Gold Glove award 9 times. Some ISTPs capturing Gold Gloves at the turn of the 21st century included **Pokey Reese** and **Steve Finley**. Though not the fleetest of foot, Finley utilized every ounce of his ISTP grit, complementing his Type's superior hand-eye coordination, to run down and snag balls in centerfield.

Clever on the Mound

Dave Stewart, Roger Clemens, Bret Saberhagen and **Tom Glavine** are some of the many outstanding ISTP hurlers in baseball history. **Roger Clemens** won his third Cy Young in 1991, his fourth in 1997, and his record-setting fifth in 1998, leading the American League all three times in strikeouts and ERA! In 1996, Clemens struck out 20 batters in one game for the second time in his career.

Tom Glavine had a superb 1991: was appointed the National League's starting pitcher in the All-Star game; helped the Atlanta Braves to their first World Series in history; won the National League's Cy Young Award; and tallied a 20-11 record, with a 2.55 earned run average. He was baseball's winningest pitcher from 1991 to 1996 with 106 victories. In 1997, Glavine became baseball's highest-paid pitcher, signing a four-year contract worth $34 million. He didn't disappoint his employer in 1998, when he won his second NL Cy Young award. Glavine continued his excellence into the 21st century (2000), where at age 34, he won 21 games.

In 1998, hard-throwing **Kerry Wood** (ISTP) won the NL Rookie of the Year award. He had a 13-3 record with 233 strikeouts and a 3.40 ERA. ISTPs pack aggression in their pitching. Preferring to overpower batters, they attempt from an early age to throw hard. Bigger and stronger ISTPs find this approach highly successful; smaller ISTPs learn to rely on pin point accuracy, off speed pitches, and moves that outsmart batters. ISTPs, with their dominant right hemisphere and superb hand-eye coordination, can be Houdinis with a baseball.

If ISTPs continue their pitching careers beyond the age of thirty-five, even the previously overpowering ones learn to rely on off-speed pitches.

Incidentally, ISTPs not only excel on the mound, they generally have the highest batting averages among pitchers.

Controlled

If you follow baseball, you know that not all hard-throwers are accurate or control pitchers. Bob Feller, Nolan Ryan, and Ryne Duren would not be winners at dart-throwing contests. None of these three had an ISTP Brain Type sitting under his cap. Those who possess ISTP brains have the potential for superb control, even when throwing hard. When pitching, however, they must be careful to not rely excessively on their dominant upper body fine motor movements.

OBSTACLES

ISTPs incur batting problems like any other Brain Type. They just will not have as many. ISTPs find difficulties when they try to swing too hard, pull the ball, or hit home runs. They can hit as many round trippers as any Type, but that should not be their goal. It will lead to their demise at the plate. ISTPs hitting from the right side have greater difficulty than lefties. Batting from the left side enables ISTPs to hit balls to the opposite field more easily. Their gross motor movements become more active.

ISTP **Cal Ripken Jr.** was the first shortstop to hit 20 or more home runs in nine consecutive seasons. He once said:

> I generally don't like to hit home runs in batting practice because I think they produce bad habits.[4]

For ISTPs in particular, the best way to hit the long ball is to try to bang out hard line drives in the gaps, trying to keep the ball in the park. When the fences are the goal, the batter success will suffer.

(The ESTP is arguably the purest of home run hitters. They are much more apt to knock it out when they try to, though that isn't generally smart for them, either.)

Superstitious

Superstitions are common for ISTPs and sometimes debilitating. When on a hitting streak, **Ty Cobb's** superstitions consisted of: taking the same route to the ball park, eating the same breakfast, hanging his shower towel on the same hook, and refusing to clean his uniform. **Wade Boggs** was known for eating chicken exclusively for dinner.

Too Intense

As you read about ISTPs in the various sports highlighted in this book, you will discover a number of them have been known for their excessive intensity. ISTP boxer **Mike Tyson** has been allowed to act barbaric in the ring because it is expected. In other sports, baseball being one, temper tantrums are not as welcomed.

ISTP **Ty Cobb** was one of baseballs most disliked players. Ty was known for spiking opponents, punching umpires and fans, and hell raising off the field.

A well-known ISTP pitcher has had a short fuse reputation. It's been written of him:

> The sign over his locker . . . reads "Possessed Rebel," and he is just that. Possessed and obsessed. Driven by inexplicable demons. Wound so tightly he seems ready to shatter. Unable to enjoy his talent and fame. Respected by teammates who admire his competitiveness and ability, but not widely liked because of his intensity and abrasiveness.[5]

A teammate of his says:

> I worry about [him] because he always seems ready to detonate.[6]

The Rocketman **Roger Clemens** is our fiery ISTP. Red Sox pitching coach Bill Fischer said in 1991:

> No one is harder on Roger than Roger himself. He accepts no excuses, no alibis. Second place isn't good enough. If you had to fight him, you'd have to kill him to win. He's that strong, that determined.[7]

Roger continued his volatile ways into the 21st century. In the 2000 World Series, the 38-year-old New York Yankee hurler was throwing against the Mets. Clemens jammed the power hitting Mike Piazza on an inside pitch. Piazza hit a broken-bat foul ball, causing the bat to split in three pieces. As Piazza was running to first base, Clemens picked up a fragmented section of the bat (virtually a lethal weapon) and slung it in front of the perennial All-star catcher. Not only did this astound the massive audience but Piazza as well. After the game, Yankee manager Joe Torre said Clemens' antic was a spontaneous and emotional act and nothing personal: "Why would he throw the bat at him? Nobody's adding any common sense to this?"[8] What Torre forgot to mention was that Clemens had beaned Piazza in the head (thought to be deliberate by many) with a pitch only three months prior, during the regular season.

Not surprisingly, ISTP Clemens couldn't understand why people were questioning his bizarre bat-throwing actions. "Is this all they have been talking about? What a joke."[9]

Piazza didn't see it as humorous, however, believing that he had been thrown at intentionally. "It was bizarre," Piazza said of the incident. "I asked him what his problem was, and he really had no response."[10]

Needless to say, Roger Clemens was involved in an event that wasn't all that surprising for an ISTP in the heat of battle. This Brain Type has not gained a reputation for winning at all costs for nothing.

And by the way, in his last two starts in the 2000 post-season, Roger Clemens threw 17 shutout innings, allowing three hits with 24 strikeouts. While many other Brain Types struggle with their composure in post-season competition, ISTPs are usually at their best.

Helping ISTPs

Perhaps it is now clear that the greatest assistance you can give ISTPs is mental and emotional. A calming influence in their lives will yield tremendous dividends. Teach sportsmanship to your ISTPs, not winning at all costs. (See ISTP Stefan Edberg in the Tennis chapter.)

As you teach the sound fundamentals, the best physical advice you can normally provide ISTPs is: "relax and see the ball." If they can relax and watch the ball all the way to their mitt or bat, their ISTP Type will take over from there. No Type can position a bat or glove in space and time better than an ISTP.

If ISTPs do not relax, they can perform poorly in the field and at the plate. They will become impatient and try to make things happen too quickly.

I would recommend teaching ISTPs to be switch-hitters. There is no Type that can adapt to switch-hitting better. If they decide at a later point in time to stick with one side, that's fine, but they will be thankful they learned both ways. Switch hitting ISTPs generally end up being more effective from the left side, especially right-handers.

ESTP

ESTPs are known in life for their brashness, confidence, brawn, chic style, and zest for living. ESTPs **Sylvester Stallone, Arnold Schwarzenegger, Madonna, Cher, Hulk Hogan, Joe Namath, Wilt Chamberlain, Sugar Ray Leonard**, and most likely the Biblical **Apostle Peter**, have all demonstrated their Types vividly during their lifetimes. **Reggie Jackson, Rickey Henderson,** and **Jose Canseco** are few of baseball's ESTPs in recent years.

ESTP great **Mickey Mantle** was known for his

off the field escapades. Former Yankee Whitey Ford described his years of rooming with Number 7:

> Anyone who roomed with Mantle lost five years off his career.[11]

In Mantle's 18-year career with the Yankees, he hit 536 home runs, had 1,509 RBIs and a .298 batting average. Mickey's chronic knee problems forced his early retirement at age 36. Nevertheless, his baseball reputation grew, making his trading card one of the most valuable of the post 1950s players. Mantle became a star at autograph shows, making more money in a weekend than he did in his first four years with the New York Yankees.

In 1996, at the age of 63, Mantle succumbed to cancer. Bobby Murcer eulogized his former teammate:

> He was the greatest player I ever saw. I don't think to this day that Mickey realized how much he touched the hearts of fans.[12]

Home run king Henry Aaron said of Mantle:

> He played 10 years on one leg . . . . He was a tremendous athlete.[13]

Power Galore

The Extraverted ESTPs, equipped with high powered fine motored skills, are the power athletes, regardless of the sport. Especially when they have the size, they are normally the hardest servers and ground strokers in tennis and the longest hitters in golf and baseball. ESTPs are consistently among the top home run hitters in baseball. In 1996, ESTP outfielder **Juan Gonzalez** won the American League's MVP Award. He tallied 47 home runs and a .314 batting average despite spending nearly two months on the disabled list. In 1998, Gonzalez won his second AL MVP, batting .318 with 45 homers and a whopping 157 RBIs. Young ESTP sensation **Alex Rodriguez** came in second in the '96 American League MVP voting—his first full season in the majors. His 36 homers and league-leading .356 batting average were exceptional for a shortstop. In the National League, third baseman **Ken Caminiti** won the 1996 MVP, batting .326 and hitting 40 home runs.

ESTPs do not mind chalking up strikeouts in their pursuit of punishing the ball. **Reggie Jackson**, ESTP, struck out once every 3.7 times at bat. Normally possessing great physiques, ESTPs feel obligated to the crowd (which they love to play for) to go for the fences.

In 1996 ESTP **Eddie Murray** launched his 500th home run, the first American leaguer to hit 500 since Reggie Jackson in 1984. National Leaguer and ESTP third baseman **Mike Schmidt** hit his final and 548th career home run in 1987.

Love Limelight

ESTPs love to be noticed. **Mike Schmidt** wanted to be on the cover of *Sports Illustrated* so much he conspired with teammate, Tug McGraw, at the 1980 World Series. At the final out, pitcher McGraw raised his arms, walked toward home plate, then turned toward third base and greeted a leaping Schmidt. This seemingly spontaneous celebration was in fact preplanned. Little did *SI* or the world know!

Said Reggie Jackson, when he saw ESTP **Deion Sanders** with all his jewelry:

> He had on his Mr. T starter set.[14]

Mr. Octobers

When ESTPs become bored, they seek another exciting adventure. Regardless of what presently enthralls them, it generally isn't long before this interest wanes, and they feel they must find another thrill. When baseball becomes boring for ESTPs, they easily lose concentration and motivation for playing.

The autumn wind and leaves, pennant fever, and baseball playoffs are generally the perfect antidote for slumping ESTPs. They like to rise to the occasion, to perform for the crowds; they crave showtime. Who can forget injured ESTP **Kirk Gibson's** dramatic pinch-hit home run in the 1988 World Series? It was his only at-bat in the series, but it sparked the underdog Dodgers to the title.

Reggie Jackson belongs in the "Mr. October Hall of Fame." ESTPs don't always come through at playoff time, however. When they don't, they may be trying too hard to impress the fans. If they contain their energies and use their heads, they will be the ones to watch at playoff time.

Base Stealers

ESTPs, like all SPs, are often blessed with running ability. Yet speed alone is not the key to ESTPs' ability to steal bases. Their spatial right-brained Thinking function enables them to outfox the pitcher and get a quick jump. ESTPs do not mind sliding into a base at full speed. The more thrilling and dramatic the play, the better they like it. This is the same Brain Type that dominates professional wrestling—the **Hulk Hogans, the Brutus "the Barber" Beefcakes**. They love to strut their stuff before the crowds.

Rickey Henderson is one flamboyant player who's personified base stealing prowess. Henderson is an ESTP who broke Lou Brock's all-time base stealing record of 938 bases on May 1, 1991.

Rickey Henderson realizes his hitting is not what got him to the big leagues. He has said:

> I wasn't really a hitter then [when he became a major league player]. My legs got me here.[15]

Henderson's running and batting skills won him the American League's most valuable player award in 1990. Unlike Henderson, ESTP **Jose Canseco** has been known for his hitting ability. Nonetheless, Canseco was an exceptional base stealer, and became baseball's first 40 40 man (forty home runs and 40 stolen bases).

Often Brash and Studly

Rickey Henderson, in ESTP fashion, took on a new look when breaking the all time base stealing record. He decided to wear sunglasses. When asked if he was trying to look cool, he responded:

> Cool? I'm cool without the glasses. I style pretty well, don't you think?[16]

Speaking to the packed stadium on his record-setting day, Rickey said:

> Lou Brock was a symbol of great base stealing, but today I am the greatest of all time.[17]

A number of ESTPs, like Henderson, would be well served to practice humility.

ESTPs have also been known for their antics following a home run. As the ball leaves their bat they may stand and watch, or trot the bases in some way that draws attention to themselves.

Spectacular but Sometimes Inconsistent with Glove

ESTPs need to stay continually attentive to their defensive efforts. Being offensive minded and sometimes easily distracted, their fielding can suffer. When concerted devotion is given to the glove, their right-brained fine motor superiority can enable them to achieve gold glove status. Hall-of-Famer **Mike Schmidt** won 11 Gold Gloves in 16 major league seasons! Schmidt was the third player in history to be voted the National League's Most Valuable Player for a third time.

First base is the position ESTPs generally feel most comfortable playing in the infield (followed by third base). ESTP **Eddie Murray** had the highest fielding percentage in a season for an infielder in American League history, fielding .999 as a first baseman for Baltimore in 1981. It generally takes more time, however, for ESTPs than ISTPs to perfect the proper handling of the glove.

ESTPs can make the impossible play, dazzling the crowd with their boldness and flair. But sometimes their unnecessary recklessness creates problems. The ill advised, unsuccessful diving catch for the outfield fly can leave the ball going to the wall, yielding unearned runs. Managers may turn prematurely gray waiting for their ESTPs to mature defensively.

Pitchers with Great Stuff and Control

ESTPs can develop into outstanding big league pitchers. They are known to throw fast and are masters of the breaking ball and change up. Some ESTP hurlers have included: **Dennis Eckersley, Doug Drabek, Dennis Martinez** (who pitched a perfect game in 1991), **Dave Stieb, Don Sutton,** and **Pedro Martinez**. Thanks to their Extraverted, right brain Sensing region, ESTPs generally get into the flow of the game quicker than any other Type.

Dennis Eckersley was a top ESTP hurler in the 20th century (among his accomplishments were the 1992 American League Cy Young Award and MVP). He repeatedly demonstrated the abilities of his Brain Type as a relief pitcher. The "Eck" went 150 innings in the 1989-1990 season without giving up a walk! This epitomizes ESTPs' outlook on life. They're always ready to get involved with "action," not having to get psyched up or do something to activate their energy level. ESTPs continually look for situations that provide excitement.

ESTPs, especially in relief pitching, tend to work fast on the mound. They have much energy to release and are quick to make decisions. Consider Eckersley, who worked so speedily on the mound a batter didn't have time to think.

In 1998 and at the age of 44, Dennis Eckersley was the oldest player in major league baseball. Amazingly, his arm held up for 24 seasons before he retired with an A.L. career record for most saves—323.

In 1991, ESTP **Dennis Martinez** set down 27 consecutive batters to become the second oldest big-league pitcher to throw a perfect game. In 1998 and at age 43, the first Nicaraguan to play in the majors completed his 22nd season. Dennis Eckersley and Dennis Martinez have proven the pitching excellence and durability of the ESTP.

In 2000, ESTP **Pedro Martinez** won his third Cy Young Award in four years. Standing only 5-foot-11 and 170 pounds, he was baseball's best pitcher, having a vast array of pitches.

Outstanding Catchers

Catching is one of the best positions to play for an ESTP aspiring to make it to the big leagues. They have all the inborn mental and physical tools to excel. Whereas ISTP catchers tend to have difficulty shutting off their dominant Thinking between their catching and batting duties, ESTPs generally make the transition from defense to offense more easily. ESTP catchers **Gary Carter and Lance Parrish** were two of the best in their prime. ESTP **Benito Santiago** was acclaimed as the best catcher in the business in 1991. He had won three Gold Glove and three Silver Slugger Awards. In 1993, ESTP **Mike Piazza** won the National League rookie of the year. He was the National League top vote-getter in the 1996 All Star game, having been selected to the team for the fourth straight year. His first four years in the majors, he averaged .330, 32 home runs and 100 RBIs. Beginning the 21st century, Mike Piazza continued his prowess as one of the premier hitters in the game. No ESTP hitting from the right side, especially in modern baseball, could match Piazza's ability to hit to all fields for batting average and power. At the plate, he established himself as a role model for all aspiring ESTPs.

OBSTACLES

Controlling Aggression

If ESTPs can learn to just see and meet the ball at the plate (which often tests their patience) they can have a high batting average and hit many homers. **Mickey Mantle** learned this principle.

A great piece of advice for ESTPs comes from one of their own, the loquacious **Tommy Lasorda**. Manager Lasorda told the press in mid-season 1991 about the progress of his Dodger second baseman, ESTP **Juan Samuel**. At the time, Samuel was second in the league in batting average at .333, and a leading candidate for the National League's comeback-player-of-the-year award. Lasorda spoke of his most consistent Dodger, who had tallied hits in 51 of his 61 games:

> On the opening day in Atlanta, I told Samuel that I wanted him to be our No. 2 hitter, but that he wouldn't succeed unless he changed his style. He had to be more patient. He had to cut down on his swing. He had to be more selective and hit the ball to the opposite field. Well, he's doing all those things for us.[18]

ESTPs are wise to learn to hit the ball to the opposite field, meaning left-handed hitters should hit to left field, and right-handers should learn to hit to right field. ESTPs have a strong tendency to pull the ball, controlling the bat too much with their dominant hand. The gross motor or big muscles of the body aren't involved enough, which results in sub par performance. Batters can often use the muscles properly by hitting in practice from the opposite side of the plate. Right-handers may like it so much they'll stay on the left side.

Tommy Lasorda continued to address Samuel's and, unwittingly, other ESTPs' problems at the plate. Though not large in stature, the ESTP Samuel hit 28 home runs in 1987 and had, like all ESTPs, a tendency to try to knock the cover off the ball. Lasorda said:

> Ted Williams [ISTP] once told me that he was the most surprised guy in the ballpark when he hit a homer. I told Samuel that I wanted him to be the most surprised guy in the world when he

hit one.[19] (Insert added.)

Striking Out

ESTPs, due to their free swinging approach to baseball, tend to strike out more than they should. Desiring to punish the ball and impress the crowd with flashy hits, they will often chase bad pitches. With experience and maturity this can be improved. Large ESTPs are apt to exhibit this weakness. Smaller ESTPs, like **Luis Polonia**, learned to concentrate on their batting average, knowing they can't put the ball out of the park too often.

HELPING ESTPs

Coaches and guardians would do well to teach ESTPs aspects of humility and regard for others. This need not lessen their competitive drive, only complement it. ESTPs have the potential to win awards and trophies on the field, as well as friends and admirers.

Final reminders for this Brain Type are to have them play under control, as Tommy Lasorda suggested, and have right handed ESTPs learn to hit the ball the other way—which doesn't come easy. Also, it's helpful to their careers to hit from the left side, even if this is limited to practice sessions only.

ISFP

ISFPs are among the top athletes in most sports, including baseball. Their prowess with the right brain controlled gross motor skills enables them to perform with the utmost grace and ease. To the eyes of the beholder, ISFPs are smooth operators when throwing, hitting, and running. They can play every position, demonstrated by their success in the major leagues.

Varied Personas

Though ISFPs have multiple looks, as do all Types, they generally have endearing natures. But because they are private persons, this trait is not always seen. Likable ISFPs have included catchers **Roy Campanella** and **Yogi Berra**. Sparky Lyle, former New York Yankee pitcher, said of Berra:

Yogi's supposed to have said a lot of funny things, but I don't know how anybody hears the funny things he says, because he doesn't talk.[20]

Yogi Berra-isms are plentiful, but this one is memorable:

Eighty percent of baseball is half mental.[21]

Defensive Specialists

ISFPs master defense with their speed, body coordination, spatial giftedness, and willingness to take risks. They are especially fun to watch in the outfield where they can show their stuff. **Gary Pettis** and **Devon White** have been prime examples. By mastering their gross motor skills, ISFPs can also be among the top defensive catchers. **Charles Johnson** (ISFP) won his third consecutive Gold Glove in 1997, and set a major league record for catchers with 171 consecutive games without an error, including none in 123 games during the 1996 regular season!

ISFPs like to play offense, too, though they are normally better at defense. Only a few will achieve high batting averages at the professional level. As you read the list of ISFP names at the end of this baseball section, past and present, you will see this illustrated.

Fleet-footed Stealers

Adept at exercising the gross motor skills, svelte ISFPs run the bases. ISFP **Maury Wills** won the National League's most valuable player award when he stole 104 bases in 1962. He broke Ty Cobb's 1915 record of 96 steals. Wills was the most exciting player on the base paths since Jackie Robinson.

Fastball Hitters

ISFPs are excellent fastball hitters. Their right brain dominance enables them to see the ball expertly, swinging with quick reactions. Their big muscle skills enable them to create tremendous bat speed and power, hitting the ball hard.

Shortstop **Ernie Banks** wore a Cub uniform for 19 years, winning two consecutive MVPs in 1958-59. Banks was a career .274 hitter with 512 home runs. In 1955 he hit 44 homers, the most ever for a shortstop. ISFP Mr. Cub won a Gold Glove in 1960 and was Chicago's most beloved ballplayer.

In the year 2000, ISFP outfielder **Moises Alou** finished second in the batting race with an average of .355, including 30 home runs.

Excellent Pitchers

ISFPs excel in the big leagues as pitchers. Their Brain Type enables them to use the big muscles for pitching velocity, rhythm, and control, with a predisposition for mastering breaking balls. Their curves, split fingers, and forkballs make many good hitters look bad. ISFPs **Mike Scott, Frank Viola, Bruce Hurst,** and **Chuck Finley** have demonstrated the strengths of the ISFP.

Frank Viola was a Cy Young winner in 1988, when he went 24-7 for the Minnesota Twins. **Mike Scott's** major league career spanned 13 seasons. In his first few seasons, he lost almost twice as many games as he won (14-27). On a trade that sent him to the Houston Astros, he turned his career around with the split fingered fastball. He tallied 86 wins and 49 losses from 1985 to 1989. In Scott's best year, 1986, he won the Cy Young award after leading the majors in strikeouts (306), innings ($275^{1}/_{3}$) and ERAs (2.22).

Durable Players

ISFPs are occasionally known for their intrepid ways in the batter's box. They may crowd the plate, seemingly oblivious to the possibility of getting beaned. Former ISFP big leaguer **Don Baylor** was hit by pitches 267 times in his playing career, a major league record. Only once did the muscular Baylor call time to ask the trainer to spray him with pain killer. Who was responsible? The flame thrower himself, Nolan Ryan. ISFP **Lonnie Smith** was hit nine times in 1991. It was reported he stood only eight inches from the plate.

Coaching youth baseball in the past has shown me this pattern with ISFPs. Fearing for their safety, I often told them to stand farther from the plate. One particular year a 9-year-old ISFP virtually stood on the plate the whole season—after numerous directives to do otherwise! I generally had to tell my young SJs to stand closer as they cautiously approached the plate.

Long ball Hitters

Mark McGwire's career has epitomized many larger ISFPs'. In his 1987 rookie season, Mark knocked the cover off the ball, batting .289 with 49 home runs and 118 RBIs. It wasn't long before pitchers quit throwing him fastballs, trying slower pitches instead. McGwire's statistics began to fall. Although his home run production stayed high (he was the first person to hit 30 homers in each of his first four major league seasons), his batting average nose-dived. His average slipped to .260 in 1988, .231 in 1989, .222 in 1990, and in 1991, Mark batted .201 with 22 homers.

As the opposing pitchers played smarter with McGwire, he demonstrated his ISFP tendencies at the plate. Oakland's batting coach in 1991, Rick Burleson said, at the end of the season, that Mark is the friendliest of the A's—as long as hitting isn't mentioned:

> He's elected to stay with what he has. He talks to me the least about hitting of all of them. . . . Mark wants to pull. He gives up the middle of the plate. . . . He looks to turn on everything. That's why he doesn't hit for average. . . . He had so much to improve. Obviously, he hasn't.[22]

In 1992, McGwire began to turn things around. He learned to accept the walk and take the opposite-field single. His new approach resulted in 42 homers and 104 RBIs. Then his sculptured body began to betray him. He sat out 242 of 420 games from 1993 through 1995. On the verge of retirement, Mark gave another try in 1996. Despite missing over 30 games, he became only the 13th player in major league history to hit 50 home runs in a season. Mark ended up with 52 homers, a .312 batting average, and was among the league leaders in walks. He also set a season record with a ratio of 7.8 at-bats per home run. Babe Ruth was the former record holder. In 1997, McGwire bashed 58 homers—joining Babe Ruth as the only players to hit 50 dingers in consecutive seasons.

*ISFP **Mark McGwire** turned the sports world upside down in 1998 when he eclipsed Babe Ruth's 60 home runs and Roger Maris's 61.* His strength and home run consistencies have not only come from a massive body size but an SFP Brain Type. Unlike the Brain Types of Maris (ISTP) and Ruth (ENTP), which rely more on fine motor movements, McGwire utilized his dominant SF gross motor skills. As a right-handed hitter, he has demonstrated this by the pulling of his front side and left arm while releasing the right or top hand shortly after impact. In contrast, the fine motor hitters are more apt to keep both hands on the bat throughout the swing, including the follow-through. Not surprisingly, ISFP and power hitter **Fred McGriff** demonstrated as much as any contemporary hitter, the pulling of the front side while minimizing the action of the top hand.

As Mark McGwire has clearly demonstrated, defense does not have to be the ISFP's prime strength.

OBSTACLES

ISFPs' greatest weakness as hitters originates from their dominant Introverted Feelings. Rather than logically responding to the approaching pitch (as do ISTPs), response comes from their subjective, gut level Feeling function. In effect, they do not watch the ball long enough; they pull the trigger too soon. ISFPs have greater ability to see the ball, in some respects, than the eight left-brained Types. Nevertheless, they do not fully utilize this potential when overusing their Feeling function. This problem is especially revealed on breaking balls or off speed pitches.

If ISFPs would watch the ball longer, trusting their innate abilities to swing the bat quickly when necessary, they would improve their hitting. Hitting to the opposite field as often as possible is recommended. ISFPs are capable of implementing these two important dimensions of hitting.

HELPING ISFPs

ISFPs are capable of being good switch hitters. Encourage them while they are young to try hitting from both sides of the plate. Switch hitting will minimize their fear as well as improve their batting average.

ISFP youngsters tend to swing at pitches outside the strike zone. Under pressure, their dominant Feelings often supersede their spatial awareness. Waiting for good pitches is beneficial practice for ISFPs.

ISFPs are capable of playing every position on the diamond, though few are found at third base in the majors. There has been a diversity in talent among big-league ISFPs. Work habits, physically and mentally, have been an influence. The ISFPs listed at the end of this chapter will reveal their varying successes.

ISFPs are often known for their self effacing and self doubting ways. Negative thoughts are debilitating to their athletic performances. ISFPs need encouragement. It is worth repeating; they are self-doubters, becoming discouraged when they fail. They may not show or express it.

ISFPs are grounded in the present, desiring to enjoy life to its fullest and to enjoy security in their treasured values. When their prized relationships or values are threatened, despondency is at the door. They need to see hope and receive the encouragement of others at this juncture.

ESFP

"If you were starting a baseball team, who's the first player you would take?"[23] In 1991, *Sports Illustrated* polled professional baseball general managers with this question. Twenty two teams responded and *SI* "got an astonishingly consistent response."[24] The top four vote getters were Reds shortstop, Barry Larkin (9), Mariners centerfielder, Ken Griffey Jr. (5), Pirate outfielder, Barry Bonds (2), and Twins centerfielder, Kirby Puckett (2).[25] **Larkin, Griffey, Bonds, and Puckett** are all ESFPs!

Needless to say, ESFPs are designed to excel at baseball.

Great Hitters

ESFPs can be among major-league baseball's top hitters. One in particular has shown this on a consistent basis: **Tony Gwynn**. By the time Gwynn was 30-years old, he had earned four batting titles, five Gold Gloves and five All Star selections. In his first full season in the big leagues, 1984, he hit .351 and led the National League. By 1998, Gwynn had 8 NL batting titles, and the highest lifetime batting average among active players.

How do ESFPs stack up against the great ISTPs? Though both are right-brained, their batting approaches contrast markedly. Whereas ISTPs break the swing down to a science, whereas ESFPs rely on instinct - quick and gut reactions. Don Mattingly and Wade Boggs have personified ISTPs in baseball. Tony Gwynn compared himself to Boggs, Mattingly, and other top performers in 1986:

> They can all hit. People put me in the same class. Personally I don't feel I belong there. They all know a lot about hitting. They're great mechanical hitters. I just go up there and hit the ball.

Added Gwynn:

> The last thing I think about at the plate is technique, where your elbows are, weight transfer.... I'm a scuffler. What I do might not look pretty, there's nothing scientific about it.[26]

At this stage of Gwynn's career, he wasn't looking for the *perfect* pitch; he was looking for *any* pitch. He'd see it within hitting distance and try to whack it. Gwynn became more scientific in the '90s than he was in the mid '80s. Nonetheless, he and other ESFPs will always be a far cry from the ISTPs. Why do you think ESFPs generally choose the less technical approach?

ESFPs' prime decision maker is their right-brained, Introverted auxiliary Feelings. They are principally spatial as opposed to verbal. Instead of using the ISTPs' deeply Introverted, logic, they innately choose their mildly Introverted Feeling function. This function is not going to approach matters scientifically. Instead, it will be triggered by a good or bad feeling based on past experiences. This explains why ESFPs have difficulty explaining why and how they do many things, including hitting a baseball.

ESFP **Kirby Puckett** was at or near the top of the American League in batting average many times before his retirement in 1996. **Barry Bonds**, ESFP, was the NL MVP in 1990, 1992, 1993, 2001, 2002, and 2003!

In the year 2000, shortstop **Nomar Garciaparra** won the AL batting title with a .372 average. The 2003 season witnessed budding star and ESFP **Albert Pujols** lead the NL in hitting, with a .359 average.

Total Body Control

ESFP catcher **Tony Pena** was poetry in motion behind the plate, having more body contortions than a yoga instructor. His body control and balance defied normal human abilities. The few who could imitate his improvised positions would need help extricating themselves. Pena also had catlike quickness coming out of one of his catching positions to gun down a runner stealing second. Tony Pena was one of the few players who drew fans to the ballpark just to watch a defensive performance. The sweet rhythm and expert control of his gross motor movements made it all possible.

Pena's ESFP abilities also made him the king of squat. In 1991, he caught more innings than any other AL catcher (1,156). In 1992, Tony caught all 19 innings in a 6½ hour game! Tony Pena continued his remarkable play into the twilight of his career.

Ivan Rodriguez has become the next ESFP catching sensation. A perennial All-Star, "Pudge" won his 10th consecutive gold glove in 2001; it was also his 7th consecutive .300 season.

Great Swings with Power

ESFPs utilize the big muscles of the body for their artistic swing. It's a liquid swing, entirely fluid, generating terrific bat speed. Their hands give way to the large muscles, providing a graceful whip to the swing. ESFP's **Barry Bonds, Ken Griffey Jr.,** and **Albert Belle** all won league home-run titles in the 1990s. Bonds hit 46 homers in 1993, 40 for Griffey in 1994, and Belle hit 50 dingers in 1995. In 2001, ESFP **Barry Bonds** spectacularly broke Mark McGwire's single season home-run record, bashing 73.

Though ESFPs possess great power, they do not focus on hitting home runs as ESTPs do. They prefer making solid contact. Said one young ESFP superstar, 6-foot-5 **Frank Thomas** in 1991:

> I know people look at my size and say he could hit a lot more home runs. But that's not my game. I'll hit 25 or 30 home runs but average and RBIs are more important to me.[27]

Thomas is not only talented, but wise. In 1997, he proved his strategy by winning the AL batting title (a .347 average), including 35 homers and 125 RBIs.

Quick Reactions

ESFPs have the quickest response time to Sensing, external stimuli of any Brain Type in athletics. When batting, they can hold off on pitches until the last possible instant and still be able to whip the bat into place for ball contact. Kent Hrbek spoke of Minnesota teammate **Kirby Puckett** in 1991:

> I just don't know what to say about Kirby except he's one of the best players in the game, if not the best player. He does everything well. It's a joy to go up to the plate after he hits and listen to the catcher talking to himself, about how he was able to hit a certain pitch or that guy can really hit. I've been watching this guy for several years and he just amazes me.[28]

Tough in the Clutch

With the game on the line, ESFPs are difficult to retire. They love to perform for the crowd, to capture center stage at the most critical time. Their concentration heightens; they become focused in an atypical ESFP manner. After ESFP **Dave Henderson** smacked 2 homers and a double in game 3 of the 1989 World Series, his Oakland A's manager, Tony La Russa, commented:

> It's in the book. The guy loves that situation,

where there's a game to win and he's at the plate. This year I think he's had more hits to send games into extra innings than anybody in baseball.[29]

Young or inexperienced ESFPs may perform just the opposite. They become too emotional and often fail in tight situations.

Potential for Speed

Baseball pundits were always baffled by **Tony Gwynn's** speed despite his large frame. At 6'3" and 225 pounds, All-Star and '97 NL MVP **Larry Walker** (ESFP) has possessed surprising speed. Again, the ESFP's conquest of the large muscles provides a solid, scientific basis for this physical skill. Speed is best generated by the large muscles of the body. (The world's fastest human beings in recent history have included ESFPs **Carl Lewis, Maurice Greene, Florence Griffith Joyner,** and **Marion Jones!**) Switch-hitting ESFP **Roberto Alomar** stole 53 bases in 1991.

Superb Gloves

When we chose up teams in the side lot as kids (back in the '50s), I always wanted to be Willie Mays. For those of us old enough to remember, ESFP **Willie Mays** was amazing with the glove. I now realize why I could never be another Mays. Mastering my gross motor and spatial skills to the same degree would be impossible. Mays made the most of his God-given physical abilities.

Willie Mays is not the only great ESFP glove to come down the pike. We've already seen where **Tony Gwynn** has been a perennial Gold Glover. In 2001, **Andruw Jones** won his 4th consecutive Gold Glove, whereas **Ivan Rodriguez** bagged his 10th consecutive, tying Johnny Bench for the most by a catcher. **Ken Griffey Jr.** ('97 AL MVP) quickly became recognized as the best defensive centerfielder in baseball. In 1999, he captured his 10th consecutive Gold Glove!

Consider ESFP **Barry Larkin**. Opposition team coach Larry Bowa, a former All-Star shortstop, said of shortstop Larkin in 1990:

> I'll tell you what, Larkin could win a Gold Glove. Ozzie Smith gets a lot of it on reputation now. Ozzie gets all the attention. But if you're looking at the whole picture, Larkin's a better player. There's nothing, really, that he can't do. He can even do Ozzie's favorite stunt, the running front flip.[30] (Insert added.)

Larkin adds: "I've been doing it since I was a kid."[31]

Control Pitchers

Although few ESFPs are on the mound in the majors, they have the potential to be there in larger numbers. I suppose they're not as drawn to pitching as they are to other positions. ESFPs' rhythmical mastery over the big muscles enables them to throw the ball with high velocity, good control, and action. ESFPs **Dizzy Dean and Satchel Paige** were magicians on the mound. **John Candelaria**, ESFP, is one of the top control pitchers of all time, walking a minimum of batters.

OBSTACLES

Although their demeanor is generally warm, charitable and accommodating, some ESFPs can be considered moody and enigmatic. ESFP **Kal Daniels** was one who has been described as such. He has said:

> People who don't know me, they think I'm tough, and that's fine. It's not true, but let them think that.[32]

His sister, Faye, commented:

> The person we read about in the newspapers and the person we know is so different, we laugh about it. The person we know isn't nearly so tough as people think ... although probably people will never believe it.[33]

I believe Faye. ESFPs' strongest decision-making function is Feeling, which acutely senses the emotional vibes of themselves and others. Reacting quickly to situations emotionally often causes them to be misunderstood.

Lenny Harris has been known for the way most ESFPs show preference. His coach in 1991, Tommy Lasorda, stated:

> Lenny is a breath of fresh air.[34]

In 1991, Minnesota's rookie Chuck Knoblauch spoke of ESFP teammate **Kirby Puckett**:

> He's impressed me a great deal. I can't find words to describe how much. You can be having

a bad day and he's always smiling and laughing, and he tries to get you going, even if he's having a bad day. Although, most of the time he's going good.[35]

Ken Griffey Jr. was considered the most talkative player with the 1990 Seattle Mariners. He told his teammates after he saw the movie, "Darkman:"

> It was so good I didn't say a word during the whole movie.[36]

His coach, Gene Clines, remarked:

> It must be the greatest movie ever made.[37]

ESFPs are generally talkative, energetic, warm and positive. Nonetheless, their personalities can very radically, like all Types. What remains consistent, however, is their cerebral schematic.

HELPING ESFPs

Naturally gifted for baseball, ESFPs do not need as much physical assistance as many other Types. They may, however, need encouragement to stay mentally alert and in control. It is important for them to learn patience when playing both offense and defense.

ESFPs need to trust their right-hemisphere dominant instincts at the plate. Reasoning should be kept to a minimum and emphasis placed on seeing the ball all the way to the bat.

When ESFPs lose interest in or don't feel good about their sport, for whatever reason, their attitudes go south in a hurry. Help them see the "big picture" and keep a good attitude. Things could easily turn around.

ISTJ

The inherent dexterity skills of ISTJs gives them a natural coordination for baseball. Hitting and fielding are not difficult for them to learn. Yet baseball, like other sports, involves more than physical skills; mental toughness is imperative for long-term success. ISTJs are generally not intense competitors when they're young and developing their dominant Sensing function. As they head into the high-school years and rely more upon their auxiliary Thinking function, they become tougher competitors and lose many fears they once had. If they continue playing sports in college, they will make excellent competitive athletes.

ISTJs play the game of baseball as they live their lives—in a meticulous and cautious manner. They prefer to maintain control, which generally dictates a more conservative approach to the game.

ISTJs are found in the big leagues playing infield positions (but rarely first base), and pitching and catching. (They can play a good defensive outfield, but their offensive production is usually too low for those positions.)

Excellent Defensive Infielders

Dick Schofield and Jeff Blauser are recent major league examples of ISTJ infielders. By age 21, **Dick Schofield** earned a starting position at shortstop with the California Angels. With only five years of play, Schofield's 1988 season gave him the highest fielding percentage of any American League shortstop—for the third time!

Analytic, Perfectionistic Pitchers

Orel Hershiser has been the epitome on an ISTJ pitcher. Hershiser began his pitching debut for the Los Angeles Dodgers in 1984 and was third in the Rookie of the Year voting. In 1985, his first full year as a starter, he tallied a 19-3 record. His career soared even higher in 1988 when he pitched an astounding 59 consecutive scoreless innings, breaking ENTJ Don Drysdale's record and winning the 1988 Gold Glove Award. He had 23 wins during the regular season, won the National League Cy Young Award, MVP in both the National League championship Series and the World Series, *Sports Illustrated* Sportsman of the Year, and the Associated Press Professional Athlete of the Year. Not bad for the mild-mannered ISTJ who turns enforcer in the heat of battle. Hershiser made pitching a science, analyzing every component he could find. It's reported that he was the first pitcher to carry notes about hitters on computer disk.

ISTJ **Mike Witt** pitched the 13th perfect game in big-league history in 1984, retiring 27 straight Texas Rangers.

OBSTACLES

Hitting Deficiency

ISTJs have excellent hand eye coordination as members of the Sensing, Thinking (ST) family. They can swing hard at the ball, though their power is generated by the lower arms and hands and not the body. This practice curtails their power and batting average. Unfortunately, as left-brained batters, they tend to make premature decisions, swinging too soon and failing to watch the ball travel farther before pulling the trigger. The result is often an overstride or an early release on the ball, yielding a pulled ball or a weakened swing (depending upon the pitch).

ISTJs would do well to emulate most ISTP hitters and be more adaptable to pitches. They should go with the ball where it is pitched: if it's outside, they should hit to the opposite field; inside, pull it; or down the middle, hit it back up the middle. This will take much practice, but it can and must be learned if the ISTJ is to reach his or her hitting potential. ISTJs tend to pull the ball too much, greatly hurting their batting performances.

ISTJ's also need to work on seeing the ball better and longer. Concentrating on the pitch will increase the awareness of the spatial right brain and slow down their left-hemisphere Thinking function. They should trust their innate abilities to get the bat on the ball by holding off that extra fraction of a second. By delaying, they can still hit the ball, albeit they may foul off some by waiting. This approach will result in going with the pitch and generating a higher batting average.

HELPING THE ISTJ

ISTJs' natural physical dexterity helps them adapt to baseball quickly. Though they don't possess the smooth SP motor skills, physical limitations should not be a problem. Their chief hindrances will come from the mind.

One of their biggest obstacles in continuing the game is fearing the ball. ISTJs and ISFJs sense pain more acutely than any other Types (though they may not express pain), and once being hit by the ball, they do not cherish the experience again. In addition, ISTJs' inherent conservatism and non aggression does not bode well for standing in the batters' box against a wild, hard-throwing pitcher. This concern is something they can overcome, but it may take some time.

The fear of being hit by the ball can inhibit ISTJs from maximizing their skills on defense. The apprehension of putting their nose lower to the earth on a grounder or failing to watch the ball all the way into the mitt are common for them. By concentrating on seeing the ball, they will lessen the left brain's control and activate the more subconscious, athletic right hemisphere.

Shortstop, pitcher, and *catcher* appear the prime positions ISTJs play at the major-league level. (Shortstop is where they will most likely be found.) ISTJs' offensive statistics usually preclude them from the outfield.

ESTJ

ESTJs are gifted athletes, masters of wrist and hand dexterity in particular. Their dominant, Extraverted Thinking function makes them extra tough competitors, not the Type to quit in a game.

When ESTJs participate in youth sports, they normally are one of the most successful Types. Their superb hand-eye coordination and physical dexterity give them a head start over many other Brain Types. Second, most children are not too competitive, and when ESTJs compete, they have the attitude of "take no prisoners." Sports are approached with vigor and tenacity. Coaches rarely have to tell young ESTJs to try harder. In youth baseball, ESTJs play well at all positions, including the difficult shortstop.

But things change for ESTJs as they get older and decide to make a career of baseball. As I have studied hundreds of major league players, I've found ESTJs primarily in one position. Their ability to master the various fielding positions appears to lessen dramatically by the time they reach professional ball. Can you imagine the primary position that the dominant, left-brained ESTJs play? If you guessed they usually stand 60' 6" from home plate, atop a pile of brickdust, you're a winner. The hard-throwing ESTJ is gifted in pitching and loves to intimidate batters.

Hard Throwers

There may be some, but I know of no ESTJs who are finesse pitchers. They do not come to the park to trick batters; they come to overpower them. At the major-league level, they learn they have to throw other pitches besides their fastball if they want to keep getting paychecks.

Who would you say was the ultimate sultan of smoke, the flame-thrower, the human cannon? You'd more than likely choose ESTJ **Nolan Ryan**. Ryan racked up statistics that may never be equaled again at the major league level. After 25 years of professional ball, Ryan, at age 44, recorded his seventh no-hitter! (His closest competitor, Sandy Koufax, threw four no hitters.) In May of 1991, Ryan stuck out 16 Toronto Blue Jays, almost pitching a perfect game, allowing two walks on full-count pitches. His last pitch that evening was his 122nd, a 93 m.p.h. fastball. In 1989, Ryan registered his 5000th strike-out, a record that should stand the test of time.

Evidence shows that ESTJs could be voted the hardest throwers in baseball. Their high energy level, ST fine motor skills, dexterity, and desire to dominate the opposition all contribute to their ability to wing it.

Few pitchers can dominate the opponent with the fastball; Nolan Ryan and a few other ESTJs have given it their best. Yet even Ryan learned that to be most effective, he had to be a pitcher, not a thrower. Developing control with off-speed pitches is essential to becoming a good pitcher, and that's true for the ESTJ, too.

If baseball fans are looking for the next Nolan Ryan, the most likely candidate is **Josh Beckett**, who won the World Series MVP in 2003. I scouted Beckett when he was in high school and realized then that the flame-throwing ESTJ had the same intimidating presence and potential upside as did Ryan.

Wildness

ESTJs have difficulty with control. In their zeal to win and overpower the opponent, they tend to throw too hard, sacrificing smooth tempo and accuracy. This especially happens when they face good hitters who can handle the fastball. ESTJs then miss the strike zone by throwing too hard or from fear that they may get tagged.

ESTJ pitcher **Bryan Harvey** was the American League's Rookie of the Year runner-up in 1988 with the California Angels. But 1989 put extra pressure on Harvey's Brain Type. By midseason he was averaging nearly a walk per inning. Harvey attributed his wildness to off-season surgery, not because it weakened his arm but because it strengthened it! His three-year minor league career had demonstrated good control, but his arm had hurt continually. Then Harvey had bone chips removed from his pitching elbow following the 1988 season. Harvey said:

> Now that I ain't hurtin', I can't find home plate.[38]

According to Harvey, his arm then felt so good and strong he could not help overthrowing (his ESTJ tendency). Harvey did discover an ESTJ solution to wildness, the forkball. (More on that soon.) Bryan Harvey went on to become one of the top relievers in baseball.

Nolan Ryan also set some records in his career that he would just like to forget. He led the league in walks eight times, a major league record. At the end of his career, Ryan had walked 2,795 batters, over 950 more than anyone else. Wildness played a key factor in Ryan's never winning a Cy Young Award. His fastball not only made him the most overpowering pitcher of his era, but also the wildest. He has had the lowest winning percentage of all 300 game winners.

Improve with Age

ESTJs should take hope. Their pitching control improves as they get older. By developing the less preferred functions of their Brain Type and gaining greater control over anxiety in competition, ESTJs can be among the best pitchers in baseball.

Nolan Ryan got better with age. At age 44, he had increased his pre-40 strikeout ratio from 9.4 per nine innings to 10.7, and lowered his walk ratio from five to 3.5. Those are significant numbers. Jim Kaat pitched 25 seasons in the majors, a record for pitchers. He commented on the 43-year-old Ryan in 1990:

> The thing is, he's pitched better overall the past two seasons than he did the previous 20.[39]

Pillars of Intimidation

Most good hitters overcome the fear of being hit at the plate. They realize they must concentrate on the ball, not on the pain they'll experience if they get hit by a pitch. ESTJ pitchers are normally best at sidetracking the necessary concentration of good hitters. Their often errant fastball helps them do it.

Dick Sharon, a former light-hitting outfielder for the Detroit Tigers, said of **Nolan Ryan**:

I call him the Exorcist, because he scares the devil out of me.[40]

Reggie Jackson, in his best days with the Oakland A's, said of Ryan:

He's the only guy in baseball I'm afraid of. If he hits you, you're dead.[41]

Jackson was quoted again as saying:

Ryan's the only guy who put fear in me. Not because he could get me out, but because he could kill me.... You just hoped to mix in a walk so you could have a good night and go 0 for 3.[42]

Ryan admitted he often, "had no idea where the ball's going."[43]

Jimmy Reese, longtime California Angel coach and friend of Ryan, said:

There were many times visiting players would see that Nolan was pitching and start walking around the clubhouse, saying, 'I don't feel good today. I've got a bad leg. I've got a sore throat.' I can readily understand that line of thinking.[44]

Not all ESTJs terrify batters as Nolan Ryan did, but, rest assured, those standing at the plate won't dig in as much with an ESTJ on the mound.

Throwing vs. Pitching

ESTJs can usually get by with being a hard thrower until they hit pro ball; then it is imperative they learn to pitch if they want a long, successful career. Even **Nolan Ryan** learned this lesson late in his career. Ryan perfected not only his fastball, but curve and changeup. Following his 7th no-hitter, at age 44, Ryan said:

I had the best command of all three pitches. This is the best. This is my most over-powering night.[45]

Reflecting the following day on his 7th no-hitter, Ryan said:

Last night was more a reflection on me as a complete pitcher than any other time, as far as no-hitters are concerned.[46]

Ryan acknowledged that his most overpowering and best pitching performance came not in his early 20's when he threw 100 m.p.h., but in his mid-40's with the aid of three pitches, all under control. His fastball averaged 93-m.p.h. this historic evening.

Forkball or Splitter

ESTJs get really anxious at game time, especially early in their careers. Their control goes awry. Their fastball goes everywhere but over the plate, and their curve balls usually hang high, out of the strike zone. If they can make it through the first few innings until they calm down and regain control, they'll be in good shape. Until then, there are the split-finger and forkball pitches.

If the ball is clearly out of the strike zone halfway to home plate, hitters will generally lay off the pitch. A successful pitcher must therefore make most pitches look good until the very end. The fork and its cousin, the splitter, start off ostensibly as fastballs, causing a lot of hitters to swing. But they don't stay straight for long; their trajectory descends rapidly approaching the plate—much to the batter's dismay. ESTJs' wrist and hand dexterity enable them to master the fork and splitter, providing them a salvation pitch that will keep many of them in the majors for a long time.

ESTJ **John Smoltz** won his first Cy Young award in 1996, having pitched brilliantly through most of the 1990s. His fastball and slider have always been nightmarish for right-handed hitters, but his new-found splitter in '96 created havoc for lefties.

Bryan Harvey found an answer to his ESTJ wildness in the forkball. Manager Jim Lefebvre said of Harvey in 1991:

Harvey has the stuff to be one of the premier stoppers in the league. He's built like a bulldog and goes about it like one. If his forkball is working, he's almost unhittable.[47]

Only four relievers have recorded 17 or more saves in each of their first three big-league seasons. Harvey is one. His strikeout ratio was superlative, one of the highest of all time. Harvey said of his forker:

The best thing about it is that even I don't know which way it's going to break. I just spread my fingers and throw it as hard as I can. The more my arm speed looks like a fastball, the better it is for me.[48]

Harvey also credited the forkball to saving his career:

> I don't think that I could have made it with just the fastball, and until I changed my delivery the forkball wasn't doing anything. Now I'm confident to throw it at any time, no matter what the count is.[49]

Harvey's fastball was generally in the 92 to 95 m.p.h. range. His forkball—85 to 88.

A final thought: We learned how ESTPs (ESTJ's right-brained counterpart) often have the best control in a relieving situation. If we can only get ESTJs to access their right hemisphere more often (there are ways), they will better control their non-forkball pitches. By the way, with much practice (and relaxation), ESTJs can master the slider. Their wrist action is nasty.

Durable Catchers

The other most likely position in which you might find an ESTJ in major league baseball is catcher. The ESTJ is like the old Timex watch commercials, "It takes a lickin' and keeps on tickin'." ESTJs are not afraid to get dirty and banged up, catch ricocheting balls in the dirt, and endure all the other unpleasantries associated with catching.

Once I coached a Little League team that had two ESTJ boys (ages 8 and 9). These two wanted to play catcher more than any of the other kids on the team, so I let them. What impressed me most about them their natural instincts. Wherever the ball was thrown, they dove for it. This was great until the pitcher threw the ball short. Then my ESTJs dove forward, sometimes catching the ball before the batter could swing! I repeatedly warned them to wait for the ball, never to dive forward, but their physical well being was the last thing on their minds. ESTJs are born to catch, having tenacity, dexterity, and good hand-eye coordination.

Defense and pitch orchestration distinguished **Bob Boone's** 19-year major league career spanning 2,225 games behind the plate. He collected 5 Gold Gloves. Boone, like other ESTJs, improved with age. *The L.A. Times* said of the 40-year old in 1988:

> Boone is a better catcher now than he was when he came up to the majors with Philadelphia in 1972.[50]

Veteran pitcher, John Candelaria, said of Boone:

> The best catcher I ever worked with.[51]

Teammate Kirk McCaskill said of Boone in 1987:

> He's the best catcher in the game.[52]

Mike Witt spoke of Boone when he played with the California Angels:

> He was a steady, settling influence on me. He did have a clue and, over a period of time, that became a reinforcement to my way of thinking. He gave me a lot of confidence.[53]

Having many strengths, Bob Boone will best be remembered for framing pitches or "stealing strikes," turning borderline pitches into called strikes.

Top Relievers

ESTJs are among the top relievers in baseball. 6-foot-4 **Duane Ward** was clocked having the fastest pitch in baseball in 1991, according to *Sports Illustrated*. In 1991, he held opponents to a .208 batting average and allowed only 80 hits in 107 innings, striking out 132. Ward summed up his ESTJ philosophy:

> I have the same mentality every time I'm out there, and that's to kick [butt].[54]

In 1993, Ward co-led the American League in saves with 45.

Team Players

ESTJs, like all SJs, have an innate desire to support and protect the institution or team; they are often willing to make personal sacrifices. On top of that, they manifest the kind of behavior which represents their team well.

HELPING ESTJs

Rarely will you find an ESTJ at a position other than pitcher or catcher in the majors. They generally do not hit high enough or play most positions adequately at this level. (At pitcher and catcher, these are not major concerns.) If ESTJs do get the opportunity to play field positions, they can hit for power. ESTJ **Tom Brunansky** hit 20 or more home runs in 6 consecutive seasons. The key for ESTJs to make the bigs, and stay there, is to develop the ability to hit the ball to all fields at will.

ESTJs will find it helpful to seek out someone who can help them to relax and maintain their composure on the ball diamond. ESTJ pitcher **John Smoltz** was 2-11 with the Atlanta Braves in the first half of the 1991 season. At wit's end, he sought the counsel of a sports psychologist who could help him relax. The result? Smoltz went 12-2 the remainder of the season, helping his team to the World Series. ESTJs will battle anxiety as long as they play sports. Learning to remain cool in competition is of prime importance.

ESTJs tend to start off the season and each game on shaky ground; their anxiety runs high. As pitchers, they need to establish a smooth tempo as quickly as possible, throwing *under* 100 percent velocity.

When batting, they need to concentrate on seeing the ball and delay pulling the trigger. Otherwise curves and other off speed pitches will be their downfall. ESTJs should learn to hit to the opposite field to neutralize their powerful ST wrists and pulling the ball. A few have mastered this and even batted over .300 in the majors.

INTJ

Not only are INTJs infrequently found in the general populace, they are rare in the major leagues. The positions they play in the majors are greatly limited. INTJs make it essentially as pitchers. Evidently, they are unable to master the motor skills and hand-eye coordination to make it offensively at the major league level. Nevertheless, their NT cerebral dexterity complements their lesser physical skills to the point that they can be excellent pitchers.

David Cone, Randy Johnson, Mike Mussina, Eric Show, Ed Whitson, Tim Burke, and **Mark Wohlers** are some past and present INTJ hurlers.

Pitcher **David Cone** led the majors in strikeouts in 1990, totaling 233. In 1991, he finished with 241 strikeouts, tying Roger Clemens for the major league lead. In 1994, Cone won the American League Cy Young Award.

Randy Johnson is a 6-foot-10 imposing figure on the mound. His near-100 m.p.h. fastball and sometimes lack of control keep opposing batters on their heels. Johnson pitched a no-hitter in 1990 and finished second in the American League in 1991, with 228 strikeouts. This intimidating INTJ went on to lead the majors in strikeouts over the next four seasons, 1992-1995.

Johnson won the American League Cy Young Award in 1995. In the year 2000, and at the advanced baseball age of 37, Randy Johnson won his third Cy Young Award—posting a 2.64 ERA while racking up an amazing 347 strikeouts. In 2001, Johnson earned his fourth Cy Young, with 372 K's! In 2002, at age 39, Johnson won his fifth Cy Young, his 4th in a row!

Abstract, Intellectual Ballplayers

INTJs are often known for their intellect and eccentricities. They are devout learners, always gleaning new knowledge. They choose theoretical subjects; they're not your typical baseball jocks. INTJs will study philosophers, scientists, historians, and theorists. **Randy Johnson** is a skilled photographer:

> The pictures I take are nothing in particular, a lot of abstract stuff, stuff that makes a statement. I've been in a lot of cities I never would have been without baseball, but I don't go out and try to take your basic skyline picture.[55]

Johnson's intellectual abstraction carries over into his hobbies.

When **Eric Show** was in his second season with the San Diego Padres, he gave rookie Tony Gwynn (ESFP) a dose of his INTJism. Gywnn recalled:

> I get an off day in Pittsburgh, so during the game I am kicking back on the bench when Show comes over and sits next to me. He looks at me and says, "There's 10 questions every American should know. Do you want me to ask you those questions?"
>
> I figure, I got nowhere to go, so fine, ask away. And he does. Who was the fourth president of the United States? What is the capital of Montana?

After a few questions, Tony pondered:

> We're in the middle of a game, and he's giving me a history test. I wasn't getting any of those questions right. I didn't know a single answer.
>
> After missing all 10 of them, Tony sat there confounded. Then, unexpectedly, he was called into the game:

I run into right field and Jason Thompson hits me a fly ball, I break the wrong way, I have to dive to catch it, and I land right on my wrist. I was so messed up over that quiz, I am out for four weeks.[56]

Eric Show and other INTJs often put people in situations where they must think, even when they don't want to. Tony Gwynn learned quickly what happens when an ESFP leaves his comfortable anterior right hemisphere and delves into his subordinate Thinking function and left brain. Gywnn lost his ESFP style of play, resulting in poor performance and, in this case, injury.

INTJs' uncommonalities may cause others to wonder what planet they're from. Just when you've got them figured out, INTJs may throw a curveball of sorts. They demonstrate contradicting styles. On one hand, they can be irascible ballplayers, yet other times pranksters, or else sensitive to those down on their luck. INTJs wear many masks. Be ready when they change from one to another.

Win with Their Smarts

INTJs have intricate reasons for everything they do, analyzing everything they're interested in to the nth degree. **David Cone** once explained a pitch he gave up for a home run to power hitter Kevin Mitchell:

I threw a four-seam fastball that you have to keep down. But when I overthrow that pitch, my elbow has a tendency to drop and the pitch flattens out. That pitch is designed to strike out a power hitter, but if it flattens out, it's particularly conducive to home runs.[57]

OBSTACLES

Because INTJs set such high standards for themselves and others, they can easily be disappointed with incompetencies and imperfect results. INTJs are prone to showing their disfavor in competition. Seattle catcher Scott Bradley recalled a time when **Randy Johnson** thought he saw a batter stealing his signs:

He thought the hitter was peeking back, and all of a sudden he got this glazed look in his eye. The next pitch he fired right behind the guy's head, all the way to the screen.[58]

Johnson said of himself:

When I first came up through the minor leagues, I was very animated, fierce, high-strung. When someone made an error or I made a bad pitch, I used to get down on myself or upset.

But I came to the conclusion that that's not going to help me. I don't let that bother me. I've come a long way in that category, and hopefully I can get better.[59]

HELPING INTJs

It is rare to find an INTJ in the majors at a non-pitching position. Pitching is where they perform best at the highest levels of baseball. INTJs should begin at an early age developing their motor skills. They will require more time for this than Sensate children.

Mental and emotional exercises should also be given high priority. Considering INTJs live life in their minds as much as any Type, it is crucial they learn to keep their tensions and thoughts in check.

ENTJ

As Extraverted, left-brained Thinkers, ENTJs begin their young baseball careers with great potential. If Mom, Dad, siblings, or friends have spent time with them playing ball, ENTJs can start out as one of the top players on the team. Not possessing the motor skills of the SFs and STs, ENTJs need to give extra work to mastering them. Additional time fielding and hitting balls will yield great dividends in the years ahead. ENTJs are found at all positions in professional baseball—often excelling at all phases of the game. Their tireless work habits usually overcome any motor skill deficiencies, enabling them to become complete ballplayers.

Intellectually Precocious

NTs' logical abstraction and reasoning skills are superior to the other Brain Type groups (SJ, SP, and NF). In 1984, Ed Lynch of the New York Mets spoke of teammate and ENTJ **Ron Darling**, a Yale graduate:

I don't understand the questions of things he can answer.[60]

At an early age, ENTJs demonstrate their ability to one-up others mentally on the ball diamond. They'll pull off the ol' hidden ball trick, the surprise pick-off move, or the drag bunt when least expected. I can vividly remember, years ago, coaching a Little League team when the opposing ENTJ shortstop used his mental acumen to trick my ISFP base runner (the ENTJ's opposite Type) who had just stolen second base. As most youngsters do when stealing, my ISFP had his head down as he slid into the base. The ENTJ who had caught the high throw over the bag yelled, "It's going to center field." Without batting a lash or looking to see if in fact the ball were "going to center field," my base runner took off like a mouse across an open field, only to be swooped down upon by a merciless owl. It was no contest; the ISFP (dominant Feeler) had not developed his street smarts yet and was easy prey for the wily ENTJ.

A similar circumstance took place in the 1991 major league baseball season. In the seventh and final game of the World Series, Atlanta's Terry Pendleton hit a ball toward the wall in left-center field. ISFP Baserunner, Lonnie Smith, was on his way from first to second when Minnesota's ENTP second baseman, Chuck Knoblauch, feigned a double play move with ISTP shortstop, Greg Gagne. Smith, who had taken his eye off the ball, fell for the wiles of the ENTP. (Both ENTPs and ENTJs rely heavily on their smarts for sports success.) Lonnie hesitated at second base, then continued to third base where he stopped. In this critical eighth inning, he would have scored had he not paused. The Braves eventually lost in the tenth inning, 1-0. Smith later admitted he had been fooled, and that he had made the mistake of watching Knoblauch rather than the ball. I felt sorry for Smith; he was too trusting. Knoblauch later commented:

> That's my first instinct in a play like that, to [decoy] them.[61]

Remember, regardless of the ages of ENTJs or ENTPs, they are quite capable of outfoxing you!

When ENTJs who persist in their sporting endeavors are ready to leave high school, they will have developed a motor skill proficiency to fully complement their innate mental skills. They soon have the potential for the professional ranks. Though they are in the minority in professional baseball, they are among the best players.

Steve Jacobson of *Newsday* wrote of ENTJ **Dave Magadan**, once again reminding us of the ENTJ's keen mind. Fellow teammate and Mets reliever, Jeff Innis, said of Magadan:

> "He'll point out things others don't see and point it out in a unique way."

The article continues:

> During spring training, the FBI gave its annual talk, warning against the dangers of drugs and gambling. Innis recalled Magadan's pointing out that on the bulletin board behind the agent was the grid of the Mets' annual Final Four pool.[62]

Defensive Aces

ENTJs have tremendous innate, defensive abilities. We have already seen that left-brained, Judging persons tend as a whole to be more defensive than offensive minded. Though ENTJs have exceptional defensive abilities, they generally prefer the accomplishment and glory of the offense.

By 1991, **Ryne Sandberg** had won 9 consecutive Gold Glove Awards for his spectacular fielding for the Chicago Cubs. On April 12, 1990, Sandberg made history by eclipsing Cincinnati's Joe Morgan's record (set in 1977-78) of 91 consecutive errorless games by a second baseman. Sandberg finally made an errant throw on May 19, 1990, ending an errorless streak of 123 games and 584 chances, the longest ever by an infielder, excluding the first basemen. Sandberg has also been gifted offensively, which was evident when he won the National League's most valuable player award in 1984. Cubs manager Don Zimmer said of Sandberg in 1990:

> He's just the best I've seen at that position in my 42 years, and I've been around guys like Jackie Robinson, Joe Morgan, Red Schoendienst and Bill Mazeroski.[63]

Steve Garvey, ENTJ, won the Gold Glove four consecutive times. Garvey was nicknamed the Senator, relating to his post-baseball political aspirations. He was aptly named, considering his ENTJ bent. In 2001, ENTJ **Greg Maddux** won his 12th consecutive NL Gold Glove. (It was the 14th straight year that Maddux had won at least 15 games!) The last pitcher to win a NL Gold Glove, way back in 1989, was ENTJ Ron Darling.

Hitters

ENTJs can hit for average and home runs, usually doing much better against pitchers who throw from the opposite side. They are excellent at hitting fastballs and guessing which pitches will be thrown. **Ryne Sandberg** hit 40 home runs in 1990 (the 3rd second baseman in history to hit 40 in a year) and 26 in 1991. In 1995, NL first baseman **Eric Karros** hit 32 and AL outfielder **Tim Salmon** hit 34 round trippers. Playing second base, ENTJ **Jay Bell** hit 38 homers in 1999.

ENTJ **Dale Murphy** was a 7-time all star and the National League's MVP in 1982 and 1983. Murphy hit 30 or more home runs and had at least 100 RBIs in five of six seasons from 1982-87. He also won 5 Gold Glove awards.

In 1996, ENTJ **Paul Molitor** hit at a .341 average in the AL; he also collected his 3000th hit. In 1997, Molitor batted over .300 for the 12th time in his career—his 20th year in the majors!

Bunters, Sacrifice Hitters

ENTJs, particularly those smaller in stature, often realize the importance of bunts and sacrifices in winning ball games. Utilizing their NT acuity, ENTJs learn when and where to take advantage of another team's defense.

Brett Butler was an ideal leadoff hitter. During his career, he got on base some 300 times a year and stole 40-50 bases. In 1990, he batted .309 with 192 hits and stole 51 bases. He was also one of baseball's foremost bunters. Butler realized he didn't possess the motor skills of the greatest hitters:

> I can't manipulate a bat like Wade Boggs or Tony Gwynn.[64]

Butler relied on his mind and moxie. The bunt was part of his repertoire.

ENTJ shortstop **Jay Bell** led the majors in sacrifices in 1990 and 1991 with 39 and 30 respectively.

High Expectations, Hard Work

Former Cub manager Don Zimmer said of **Ryne Sandberg**:

> I've never really seen Sandberg angry, but when he does make an error it's like the end of the world.[65]

As employers or leaders, ENTJs insist on competency from their subordinates as well as from themselves; as ballplayers, they insist on personal competency.

According to the Cubs coaching staff, no one worked harder at the game than **Sandberg** (a common characteristic of ENTJs). In 1990, Cub third base coach Chuck Cottier said of Ryne:

> He's the best I've ever seen, and there's a reason for it. He works at it.[66]

Cub General Manager Jim Frey spoke of Sandberg:

> Never in my seven years here have I heard or seen him make an excuse or look for an out. He plays sick, he plays hurt, he plays hard.[67]

In 1997, Ryne Sandberg finally hung up his glove and cleats for good.

Steve Garvey was the most durable player of his era, setting the National League record for playing in the most consecutive games, 1207.

After playing in his first 1991 intrasquad game at spring training, veteran player, **Brett Butler**, commented on his over the shoulder, diving catch:

> I can't do anything but play like that. I get in a game, any game, and I go all out. I play one way. I want the pitcher to know that if the ball is in the ballpark, I'm going into the wall after it, I'm going into the ground after it, I'm doing whatever it takes.[68]

Top Notch Catchers

ENTJs possess extraordinary skills for the catcher position. Their mental dexterity excels at calling for the proper pitches, often outwitting the opposition. Couple this with the defensive and offensive skills of the ENTJ and you come up with probably the best overall Brain Type for catching in major league baseball.

Carlton Fisk begins our list of ENTJ catchers. Fisk caught more games than any other player in baseball history. He hit the most home runs as a catcher, breaking Johnny Bench's career home run record in 1991, surpassing 327. Fisk was Rookie of the Year in 1972, the first to be chosen unanimously. He also won a Gold Glove that same year. He played 23 years in the majors, and was chosen to the All-Star game in eleven of those seasons. In 2000, he was inducted into the National Hall of Fame in Cooperstown. But "Pudge" will always be remembered in the hearts of Red Sox fans for especially one moment during his illustrious career.

Tim McCarver, a career .271 hitter, played major league baseball in four decades. In ENTJ fashion,

McCarver has taken his post-baseball playing day's intelligence into the broadcast booth, and at last count he's also penned three books—the most popular of these being "Baseball for Brain Surgeons and Other Fans."

Joe Torre won a Gold Glove behind the plate in 1965. An All-Star catcher in the 1960s, Torre moved to third base in the 1970s and won an MVP in 1971, batting .363 with 137 RBIs. He was a career .297 hitter with 252 home runs.

Mike Scioscia, ENTJ, was regarded as one of the best catchers in the early 1990s. He hit for a good average with power, called excellent games behind the plate, and was a top-notch defensive player, known for blocking the plate better than any catcher in baseball. (Just ask some runners who tried to run him over.) Scioscia holds the L.A. Dodgers club record for games played as a catcher, exceeding John Roseboro, Roy Campanella, and Steve Yeager. As you can see, ENTJs are one of the best catchers in baseball.

Superb Pitchers

ENTJ pitchers are among the top hurlers in the big leagues and arguably the most frequently successful. Some modern ENTJ pitchers include: **Greg Maddux, Barry Zito, Jimmy Key, Denny Neagle, Tim Belcher, John Wetteland,** and **Rob Nen.** Consider the likes of retirees **Don Drysdale, Tom Seaver,** and **Jim Palmer.** All three former greats epitomized the ENTJ pitcher: brilliant NT strategists, super competitors, and born leaders. They had excellent control, mastery of the breaking ball, and the ability to throw hard. Every big league team would be prudent to have at least one ENTJ on their pitching staff.

ENTJ pitchers seem to have an uncanny ability to work themselves out of trouble when they are on their game. Trouble activates ENTJs' brains to bring the game under control, thus applying greater concentration on their Extraverted tendencies. In this situation, the ENTJ will often throw pitches that fool the batter and end the inning. Veteran infielder Willie Randolph, who batted .327 in 1991, spoke of ENTJ hurler, **Mike Boddicker**:

> Boddicker is real crafty. You can't think with him.[69]

ENTJs are determined fighters on the mound. They must win. Coming out of the game before they've sealed the victory is torturous to them. When **Kirk McCaskill** was in his second year with the 1986 California Angels, he demonstrated his Type in tangible fashion. Pitching coach Marcel Lachemann was sent to the mound by manager Gene Mauch to remove McCaskill. The *L.A. Times* reported:

> "What are you doing here? I'm not leaving. Go away," McCaskill told Lachemann.
>
> McCaskill persisted. "Go back and tell Gene I'm all right," he said. "He'll understand."
>
> ... McCaskill continued his plea. He tried disgust. He tried reason. He tried a few words. Lachemann could not be persuaded, even if he wanted to be.
>
> "I'm going," Lachemann said, "and you're going with me."
>
> So off they went—a grateful Lachemann and McCaskill, who had thrown, Mauch would later say: "140 something, hard, grinding pitches."[70]

Tom Seaver won three Cy Young awards and five times won 20 or more games for the New York Mets. He was the first ever to win Rookie of the Year honors for a last place team. ENTJ Seaver posted a superb 25-7 record in 1969, and won 311 games over his outstanding career. He was elected to the Hall of Fame in 1992.

Jim Palmer was another three-time Cy Young winner. He won 15 games his first year in the majors and, at age 20, he became the youngest player to pitch a World Series shutout. Palmer won 20 games in eight seasons. In classic ENTJ fashion, he was known to ask umpires for a new ball seven times, knowing fully that umps only carry six.

ENTJs are best when they employ their fierce concentration. Junior Ortiz, ENTJ pitcher **Scott Erickson's** regular catcher in 1991, said:

> I've never seen a pitcher so much focused and prepared for every inning. You can't say anything to him on the mound. You can't joke with him. It's amazing how he does that.[71]

Not all successful ENTJs demonstrate Erickson's seriousness (he was 20-8 in 1991, tops in the A.L.). Nonetheless, they are all business when taking the field or mound.

ENTJs are among the best relief pitchers in baseball.

They've included: **John Wetteland, Robb Nen, Jay Howell, Rick Aguilera,** and **Roger McDowell.** Six-foot-five **Rick Aguilera** converted 32 of 39 regular season save opportunities in 1990, and 42 of 51 in 1991, tying a major league record for saves in a month, with 10 in June. In 1996, **John Wetteland** led the AL in saves with 43. **Rob Nen** had 41 saves in 2000 and 45 in 2001.

Over his career, **Dave Dravecky** pitched in an All-Star game, 2 National League championship series, and a World Series. Tragically, Dravecky had his left arm and shoulder amputated in 1991, following a prolonged bout with cancer. Despite his big-league setback, he has since relied upon his ENTJ determination and spiritual convictions to continue with his life, speaking of his faith and authoring a book, *Comeback*. Dravecky is a legitimate baseball hero and model to whom we can direct our children.

In 1992, ENTJ **Greg Maddux** had a 2.18 ERA and won 20 games for a below .500 Chicago Cubs' team, earning him the National League Cy Young Award. By 1995, Maddux had won a remarkable four successive Cy Young Awards. His 1994 and 1995 ERA's were 1.56 and 1.63! In 2004, Maddux won his 300th game.

As NTs, ENTJs have looser motor skills than the eight Sensing Types. This seeming deficiency enables ENTJ pitchers to get outstanding movement on the ball. ENTJs are also capable of being superb control pitchers.

OBSTACLES

ENTJs without the superior physical tools often need time to develop in the big leagues. Their intensity and drive to be the best can work against them. Always seeking perfection may lead to great discouragement when they develop slumps. They'll tend to press even harder. By relaxing and playing within themselves, ENTJs flourish. The Pittsburgh Pirates acquired **Jay Bell** in a 1987 trade, when he had a .223 career average and double figure errors at every level. In the 1990s, he became one of the best shortstops in baseball.

HELPING ENTJs

ENTJs, like all iNtuitives, should work hard on developing motor skills. Lots of running and learning body balance will improve the gross motor skills, while performing hand-eye coordination drills will enhance the fine motor movements and dealing with spatial visual aspects of the game.

When nervous at the plate, ENTJs, particularly the younger ones, tend to take the dominant hand off the bat prematurely when swinging. This results in missing the ball and strikeouts. Practicing with both hands on the bat through the complete swing will correct this trait.

When ENTJs get in a batting slump, they would be wise to follow the strategy of former all-star, ENTJ **Steve Garvey**. Dodgers' coach Tom Lasorda spoke of his former first baseman:

> If he stopped hitting, Garvey would snap out of it by laying down a couple bunts and going to the opposite field more often.[72]

Though this advice is good for all Types, ENTJs often have the self-discipline to pull it off.

ENTJs must be careful not to come across as arrogant and pedantic with teammates. Otherwise, they may develop strained relationships in a team sport that necessitates cooperation. Learning and practicing mental techniques will help enable ENTJs to handle game anxieties.

ENTP

Outstanding Pitchers

Using their NT sagacity and smooth, right hemisphere throwing motion, ENTPs can become outstanding pitchers. Though their dominant body skill isn't fine motor adeptness, ENTPs rely more on their fine motors than gross motors. They can grip a baseball lightly, enabling pitches to have good velocity and significant movement. Some modern ENTP pitchers include: **Curt Schilling, Andy Pettitte, Kevin Brown, David Wells, Mike Hampton, Tom Candiotti, Rod Beck, Jeff Montgomery, Norm Charlton, Jeff Brantley, Sid Fernandez, Hideo Nomo,** and **Jesse Orosco.**

Hideo Nomo encapsulates many ENTP nuances. When he first came to America in 1995, he was regarded in his homeland as a spoiled brat, a rebel who quit Japanese baseball when his team refused to give in to his multi-year contract demands. But after taking American baseball by storm in only his first season, Nomo became a national hero and romantic symbol for many Japanese—a youth who discarded a safe career to pursue a dream. Nomo had opened the door for other Japanese players to follow.

Hideo Nomo has perfected some ENTP pitching skills like few others. For one, his contorted windup could only be achieved by a few Brain Types—righted-brained iNtuitives (NPs). These Types have the greatest potential for body flexibility. Nomo brings both arms high over his head and keeps them there seemingly forever. With his back arched inward, he coils his body like a circus performer—with his back to the batter—then throws. Nomo's twisting delivery has contributed greatly to his success. No one else pitches that way.

Nomo threw his first National League no-hitter in 1996. It came in Denver on a rainy and cold evening. It was 46 degrees at game time, and the humidity was 97 percent. ENTPs have exceptionally high pain thresholds. They can perform superior athletic feats in the worst of weather conditions—focusing on the event with all their mental and physical energies. (In football, ENTP field-goal kickers are the best in nasty weather.)

In 1995, Nomo was voted National League rookie of the year. He was the first rookie since Fernando Valenzuela to lead the league in strikeouts. Nomo's forkball has been considered his best pitch.

Youngster **Andy Pettitte** went 21-8 in 1996, winning the coveted Cy Young Award in the American League. The 24-year-old left-hander posted an impressive 33-17 record after only two big-league seasons. ENTP closer **Jeff Reardon** was the only relief pitcher ever to save 20 games in 10 straight years. In 1992, Reardon broke the all-time mark for career saves held by Rollie Fingers. ENTP **Gaylord Perry** frustrated batters and umpires for 22 years with great pitching, disconcerting mannerisms, and illegal pitches. Umpires would nearly undress him at times, looking for prohibited substances. Ol' Gaylord outsmarted them all. Like a great magician (a popular endeavor for ENTPs), he never let them in on his bag of tricks. During his major league career he racked up 314 career wins, was a 5-time All-Star, and won the Cy Young Award twice.

Masters of the Knuckleball

Over my years of baseball research, it didn't take long to learn that ENTPs are the premier knuckleball pitchers. Possessing hands like those of the great artists, ENTPs can get exceptional movement on their pitches. Breaking balls or knucklers, the pitches of ENTPs can be the most difficult to hit. **Tom Candiotti** was the workhorse and ace of the Toronto pitching staff in 1991, with a 2.65 ERA. Tom spent 6 years in the minors before perfecting his knuckleball. There, in ENTP fashion, he developed his knuckler because he needed a new practical joke to fluster his friend, catcher Bill Schroeder. Knuckleball specialist **Phil Niekro** was elected to baseball's Hall of Fame in 1997. Niekro was the first knuckleball pitcher to win 300 games.

Comedians

ENTPs are not only the best comedians in show business, but generally in baseball. And now, he-e-e-ere's **Gaylord Perry, Bill (Spaceman) Lee, Jay Johnstone, and Steve Lyons.**

Known for his uninhibited clubhouse antics, **Jay Johnstone** was a career .267 hitter over his 20 seasons in the majors. At a ball game in 1990, **Steve Lyons** dropped his pants and the fans dropped their jaws. Lyons, known as "Psycho" to his Chicago White Sox teammates, slid into first base on a single and then proceeded to drop his drawers to remove the dirt. The fans roared. Lyons then pulled his pants back up and went on with the game. Some believe Bill was completely aware of his actions while others believe he inadvertently lost his train of thought. Either way would explain ENTPs' Extraverted iNtuitive behavior.

Sports Illustrated reported that prior to the Steve Lyons incident:

> ... the closest anyone had come to taking off his pants was when **Spaceman Bill Lee** reportedly shagged flies before a college game clad only in a jockstrap.[73]

Former pitcher, ENTP Bill Lee, was the clubhouse comedian in his major league playing days. As a part time philosopher, he left a pearl for us to contemplate:

> Baseball is the belly button of society. Straighten out baseball and you'll straighten out the rest of the world.[74]

Defensive Aces

ENTPs who make the majors in non pitching positions often do it with their defensive abilities. Their right-brained dominance enables them to see the ball well, while fluidly fielding it.

At 6-feet-4 and 250 pounds, **Kent Hrbek** was a power hitter and, surprisingly, a graceful, outstanding fielder. Hrbek's reputation broadened at the 1991 World Series. The ENTP first baseman one-upped Atlanta's Ron Gant by artfully lifting him off the base and tagging him out. Hrbek's move resembled a Hulk Hogan maneuver in front of his "Hulkamaniacs." The umpires were hoodwinked but not the viewing public. Some avid fans didn't take a liking to his antics. Hrbek did what was natural for an ENTP, and it worked—sort of. The incident helped Hrbek's team on the field but hurt his image off the field. Knowing his Brain Type at least adds another dimension to the event. Hrbek retired in 1994.

Steve Lyons was a utility fielder, displaying his defensive versatility. He played all nine positions in the majors, including pitcher. Lyons discussed common behavior for ENTPs:

> I'm a hyperactive person anyway, so it's hard for me to sit on the bench.[75]

This is particularly visible when coaching ENTP youngsters. When it is their time to ride the bench, they will test the coach's patience, particularly by their constant chatting and asking questions.

Power Potential

Body strength and size are key ingredients for power hitting; nonetheless certain Brain Types without these body attributes can hit with greater power. As a rule of thumb, the Extraverted right-brained Types (EPs) generate the greatest power in sports—baseball not excepting.

As one of the four EP Types, ENTPs have superior power potential. When I first attempted to assess the legendary **Babe Ruth**, I believed he was an ESTP. The Babe was before my time, and the only information I had on him was incomplete. His public persona fit that of an ESTP. In recent years, however, I've read biographies and watched video clips on the great Bambino. He was an ENTP. This Brain Type and the ESTP have many similarities.

Hitting for power is one physical commonality. (For example, ENTP Pete Sampras has been one of tennis' biggest servers.) ENTPs generate explosive power by their high energy, flexible body movements. They can develop a whipping motion like few others.

Ruth's motor skills were ENTP, not ESTP. His motor movements were much looser and pliable than the ESTP. Ruth's speaking style was also very ENTP. His diction, syntax, and facial expressions were very ENTP.

Babe Ruth tallied 714 round trippers over his career. Not only did Babe hit as many as 60 home runs in a single season, he hit 50 or more homers 4 times.

No ENTPs since Ruth have come close to making his impact on power baseball. In fact, there's been an absence of ENTP superstars. One ENTP, though, who's shown Ruthian potential in modern baseball is **Mo Vaughn**. In 1995, Vaughn hit 39 homers and in 1996, 44 round trippers. In the year 2000, ENTP **Jason Giambi** won the AL MVP, banging 43 homers; he also had a .333 batting average and career-best 137 RBI. In 2001, Giambi posted a .342 batting average.

ENTP sluggers are also highly susceptible to the strikeout. As dominant iNtuitives, they often imagine the ball in a certain swing zone rather than actually seeing it to their bats. Mo Vaughn was the American League MVP in 1995 while striking out 150 times, the most by an MVP in either league.

Great Variation

No Brain Type demonstrates more variation in personality than the ENTP. This helps explain why ENTPs are the top actors in Hollywood, dominating the movie industry. They also reveal significant differences in their baseball styles as well. Though all ENTPs are proficient in the same regions of the brain's cerebral and motor cortexes, the plasticity of the ENTP mind and body enables them to show multifaceted looks. Since ENTPs are often unsound in their body mechanics, proper coaching and training is crucial for optimal success.

HELPING ENTPs

ENTPs like to challenge conventional wisdom. As you instruct them in the game of baseball, allow them to play the game their way (within limits). They will quickly learn the intellectual side of the game, but need to spend extra time developing motor skills.

Though spatial right-brained persons, ENTPs often have difficulty watching the ball travel to the bat. They've already visualized a base hit. Practicing bunts will assist young ENTPs in concentrating on the ball and improving hand-eye coordination. ENTPs can become detrimentally nervous at the plate in big game situations. Practicing spatial and mental techniques can pay off when these situations occur.

A Batting Tip for Young ENTPs

Unless ENTPs are developed athletically at an early age, they will normally possess mechanically unsound and disjointed motor movements. For many unfamiliar with the multiple nuances and intricacies of Brain Typing, they may have difficulty understanding how ENTPs can develop into such excellent hitters with superior hand-eye coordination. Consider the likes of **Ichiro Suzuki, Todd Helton, Jim Edmonds, and Jason Giambi**—all with high batting averages entering the 21st century. Though many explanations can be offered, a prime one is that these four ENTPs all swing from the left side—a distinct advantage for them. Since ENTPs are much more fine than gross-motor dominant, they will often use their arms and wrists too much in the swing, especially creating problems when attempting to hit breaking balls or off-speed pitches. By batting from the left side, ENTPs use more of their gross motors, minimizing hand movements and generating more power. Though it's possible for ENTPs to be successful from the right side at the professional level, it will not be as easy as from the left.

INFP

The INFP can be an excellent athlete, including baseball player. Having a proclivity for academic matters, the INFP will generally not pursue and stick with athletics unless encouraged by others. (INFPs are not guaranteed academians without encouragement to apply themselves.) INFP children show remarkable coordination and fluidity in athletics.

Baseball is a sport at which the INFP can excel, both offensively and defensively. **Roberto Clemente, Rod Carew, Fred Lynn, David Justice, John Olerud, Raul Mondesi, Derek Jeter,** and **Mariano Rivera** are some of the INFPs who have left their mark on professional baseball. Hall-of-Famer **Roberto Clemente** had a remarkable 18-year career, tallying 3000 hits. A perennial All Star, he won 4 National League batting titles.

Sometimes Lighthearted, Sometimes Not

INFPs possess rich, meaningful Feelings. They treasure their values and convictions, taking them seriously. As long as INFPs are not threatened in these areas, they are easy going, friendly people. When their values come under attack, however, INFPs may react with tremendous passion and seriousness. *Sports Illustrated* said of **Roberto Clemente**:

> Clemente was thoughtful and very quiet. He'd answer questions, but he wasn't the type to initiate conversation. He always had a serious expression . . . .[76]

Roberto's persona was not like all INFP's. Nevertheless, he demonstrated a side of his Type that occurs when INFPs get deep into their Feelings. Roberto could not escape from his convictions. He remembered the poverty of his youth and country; he quested to make things better for others. How tragically fitting it was for Roberto to lose his life when trying to make a life for the less fortunate. He was killed in a plane crash on a mercy mission to earthquake stricken Nicaragua in 1972.

INFPs are often noted for their melancholic ways. Many observers fail to realize that INFPs are exceptionally sensitive persons who hone in on the intonations and vibes of those about them. As long as the vibes are good, INFPs are upbeat. When they're not, INFPs are greatly affected. They are champions of causes, with hearts for helping out the underdog. **Mother Teresa** of India's slums was an INFP.

Silky, Smooth Swings

No Brain Type has a more graceful swing than the INFP. In 1991 *Sports Illustrated* wrote of young INFP, **John Olerud**:

> Olerud's Lou-ish [Gehrig] left-handed stroke seems almost an extension of his character: easy, even and seamless.[77] (Insert added.)

All-Star Don Mattingly was so impressed with Olerud that he studied his swing to pull himself out of a batting slump in 1990. In 1993, Olerud won the American League batting title with a .363 average.

INFP **David Justice**, 1990 National League Rookie of the Year, adorned his new Mercedes with vanity plates reading "Sweet Swing." His team manager said:

> With that kind of swing, the only way he isn't going to hit the ball is bad luck.[78]

Fred Lynn demonstrated his INFP sweet swing in the majors 17 years. Along the way, he had a career average of .283, with 4 seasons over .300. In 1979, Lynn led the American League by hitting .333 and achieved career highs with 39 home runs and 122 RBIs. He hit more than 20 homers in nine different seasons. Lynn played in 9 All Star games, won 4 Gold Gloves, and was the American League's MVP as a rookie.

Hit to All Fields

INFPs have an extraordinary ability to hit the ball in the direction where it is thrown. Hall-of-Famer **Rod Carew** was a master at going with the pitch. Carew was a career .328 hitter and seven-time American League batting champion. He hit .300 or better for 15 consecutive seasons! In modern times, only Carew has won a batting title by more than 40 points, and he did it 3 times!

As iNtuitive right brain persons, INFPs are quite adaptable. Former catcher Gene Tenace said of Carew:

> Like all great hitters, he was quick to adjust. There was no one way to pitch him.[79]

Power hitting **Roberto Clemente** was gifted at spraying the ball to all fields. In 1995, **Lance Johnson** used his INFP skills to lead the American League in base hits in 1995. Toronto manager, Cito Gaston, spoke of his young INFP **John Olerud** in 1991:

> The first day he took batting practice, right out of college, every middle to outside pitch he took to left, every inside pitch he pulled, and everything he hit was a line drive. Guys who have played 10 years can't do that.[80]

From my experience of coaching young INFPs, I have noticed this innate ability from their first swings. It is amazing, considering how improbable it is to teach this to some Brain Types, regardless of their age.

All-Star **Derek Jeter** was one of the top few shortstops at the turn of the 21st century. He excelled in all phases of the game. For a right-handed batter, he superbly hit the ball to all fields, with a smooth inside-out swing. In 1998, he hit 324, in '99—.349, and in 2000, his average was a stellar .339.

Deceptive Power

The INFP's suppleness and body coordination trigger inordinate power in a swing, whether it be golf or baseball. Bobo Brayton, **John Olerud's** college coach at Washington State, said of his former 6' 5" star:

> He's got great coordination. My goodness! He just barely swings and the ball jumps.
>
> Little Oly looks kind of pale on the bench, but then he'll jump up when it's his turn and hit one out of the park like it was nothing.[81]

INFPs do not get their power by maximizing their gross motor movements as the SFs do, or the fine motor skills as the STs. INFPs have lesser domination over these particular skills yet *coordinate* these independent movements with perfection. John Olerud's college coaches suspected he had Herculean strength after watching him hit a ball deep over the centerfield fence as a freshman. Therefore, they figured he would be a master of pull-ups, like a monkey in the trees. Wrong. He couldn't make it to two.[82] Some Brain Types do not need dominating motor skills or big muscles to generate power. Just watch INFPs. (Golfer **Tiger Woods** is an INFP.)

Defensive Play

It bears repeating, right-brained INFPs have speedy reflexes, with flexibility and flow throughout their movements. They are especially adept in the infield, particularly at shortstop, and can play any outfield position superbly. Hall-of-Fame outfielder **Roberto Clemente** is third on the all-time Gold Glove winner list at 12. The last place you will find an INFP on a ball diamond is behind the plate.

INFPs generally are unafraid to put their nose down on a hard hit grounder. Much of playing well in the infield has to do with not fearing the ball, an advantage to the INFP.

INFPs are gifted shortstops; they are "poetry in motion." INFP **Tony Fernandez's** career average of only one error in 51 chances is the best ever in baseball history. Needless to say, he won multiple Gold Glove awards. In 1991, San Diego Padre general manager Joe McIlvaine said of Fernandez:

> He has great range, that's the thing I love about him. He can cover an acre.[83]

A couple of years ago, I was watching my son's Pony League team play another all star team with an INFP at shortstop. My discovery came when the boy made his first putout. I thought for sure the ground ball was through the infield, when this cheetah quick kid sucked it up like my Hoover on a dust bunny. He then waited until the runner was almost to the base before gunning him down with the fastest, most graceful release I had ever seen for a player of his age. The boy repeated his wizardry at shortstop the rest of the game, yet he had more in store. He batted third in the lineup, drilling the ball every time up, and capped off the game pitching the last few innings. He proceeded to strike out the hitters with his fastball and wicked curveball. This INFP was something, defensively and offensively.

Not all INFPs are this phenomenal. Yet if they start playing at an early age, they can be splendid ballplayers. That is simply the way God designed their brains and bodies to perform.

OBSTACLES

Passivity

INFPs are basically mellow persons. They look to appreciate life and people, seeking harmony in their surroundings. This is not always possible, but it is their preference. Mustering the ISTP's mentality of destroy the opponent at all costs is not the INFP's normal style. Manager Cito Gaston commented on **John Olerud's** slump in 1991:

> He'll show signs of coming out of it, but then the next day he just won't be aggressive. I can't figure it out. He'll get a 3-and-1 fastball down the middle and take it. I don't understand it, because tonight he may be aggressive and tomorrow he won't be.[84]

HELPING INFPs

Manager Cito Gaston and the rest of us who deal with INFPs need to realize an essential point. INFPs generally perform according to how they feel. Therefore, it is important that we do all we can to make them feel their best, physically, mentally, and emotionally.

INFPs are not always aggressive. It is helpful to provide them inspirational reasons for giving their best each time they play. Daily sharing the same song and dance will not cut it; INFPs respond best with creative variety. If you broaden your motivational techniques, you and your INFPs will be helped.

Even on their passive days, INFPs come involved defensively on the field. They can be quick as cats as they happily dive for balls and make artistic catches.

INFPs can adapt to switch hitting. They find switch-hitting minimizes fear at the plate and generally improves their batting average. Batting from the left side is especially important for INFPs to learn.

Like all Brain Types, INFPs must remember to not get into the habit of pulling the ball. Great hitters have always been able to hit to all fields. Hitting to the opposite field is usually the easiest way to pull yourself out of a batting slump. **John Olerud** hit .274 in 1996, almost 20 points below his career average. He commented after the season:

> Last year I tried to pull the ball too much.[85]

Last, INFPs can be good pitchers. Their loose and fluid motor skills can not only achieve good breaking balls but deceptive fast balls. INFP star reliever **Mariano Rivera** has been known for lulling batters with a slow, easy delivery, while his INFP motor skills cause his fastball to accelerate or explode at the plate. Rivera laid claim as the best closer in baseball with another terrific regular season in 2000. He limited hitters to a .176 batting average and allowed just two home runs in 69 innings. He succeeded in 45 of 49 regular-season save opportunities, including his final 22, and didn't allow a run over his final 28 appearances. He was even better in the postseason, collecting six saves in eight scoreless appearances. He earned World Series MVP honors while lowering his career postseason ERA to 0.38 in 47.1 innings.

ENFPs

ENFPs, for the most part, are personable and charming individuals. They carry this aura to the ballpark. Resident motivators and cheerleaders, ENFPs are usually fun to be around.

Acrobatic Athletes

As we repeatedly witness throughout this material, ENFPs are powerful, acrobatic athletes. They possess phenomenal muscle coordination throughout their entire bodies, thanks to their NF dominant right hemisphere. This enables them to run fast, jump high, and react quickly (depending upon physical stature). Their Extraversion infuses additional zeal, energy, and power.

The vivacious Venezuelan, **Ozzie Guillen**, has personified the ENFP. Once regarded by many as the best shortstop in baseball, he resembled a supercharged acrobat. Guillen is a rare ENFP big-league shortstop, earning his position with boundless effort and grace.

At age 31, switch hitting **Terry Pendleton** won the 1991 National League's MVP, his first. ENFP Terry hit .319—52 points above his career average and 89 points above his 1990 average, with a career-high 22 home runs and 86 RBIs.

ENFP Hall-of-Famer, **Joe Morgan**, a .271 lifetime hitter with 268 home runs, won consecutive MVP titles in 1975 and 1976, leading the Cincinnati Reds to the World Series victories each year.

Can Hit for Power

For reasons already mentioned, ENFPs can tag the ball. They are especially adept at coordinating large and small motor movements, producing tremendous swing force. ENFP **Ron Gant**, only 170 pounds, smacked 32 home runs in 1991. A major factor explaining Gant's home run production, besides his Type, is that he's been a dead-pull hitter. Gant hit from the right side. It was reported in '91 that 80 percent of his base hits were to left field!

Baseball produced its most amazing ENFP in 1998, when the personable and energetic **Sammy Sosa** surpassed both Babe Ruth's and Roger Maris's single-season home run records. Sammy was able to improve his batting and power by pulling the ball less and giving more emphasis to hitting to all parts of the field. This approach enhanced his gross motor movements while restricting his more dominant and naturally aggressive fine motor skills.

Fast Runners

In 1991, track's **Leroy Burrell** (ENFP) lowered the world record for 100 meters, eclipsing Carl Lewis' (ESFP) previous mark. In baseball, ENFPs can run the bases, generally possessing a good jump, quickness, and sound judgment.

ENFP **Vince Coleman** led the National League in steals in each of his first six seasons in the majors. His streak ended in 1991. Coleman stole a truck load of bases with an amazing 83 percent success rate, stealing third base 87 percent of the time (according to 1991 statistics). He set a rookie record of 110 stolen bases as his St. Louis Cardinals won the pennant in 1985.

In 1991, ENFP **Ron Gant** became only the third player in major league history to accomplish consecutive 30-30 years (30 steals and 30 home runs). In 1996, **Sammy Sosa** recorded his third 30-30 season in four years. In 1997, Sosa was rewarded for his consistent outstanding play, signing a 4-year contract extension at $42.5 million—becoming the third-highest paid player in baseball. Before moving to the National League in 1997, fleet-footed **Kenny Lofton**, ENFP, led the American League in stolen bases five consecutive years (1992-1996).

Visualizers, Dreamers

Visualizing is easily learned by ENFPs, who use it as a valuable mental tool for their athletic success. Vince Coleman said:

> When I'm running, I'm watching a big picture that's been frozen in time. Second base looks like a huge pool. As I get closer, the image becomes larger and larger. I tell myself: You're almost there.... As I dive in, I think, it's my bag, my territory, my world. I own it. Nobody can stop me.[86]

Terry Pendleton said, following his 1991 MVP award:

> I'm a dreamer, and this is a dream come true.[87]

Defensively Versatile

Initial efforts with the glove may be disappointing to ENFP youngsters. By persisting, they can eventually perform expertly with the mitt. **Ozzie Guillen** has been a prime example. Guillen grew up in a country, Venezuela, which reveres baseball (especially shortstops). He was noticed playing in the streets at age 11 by Ernesto Aparicio, uncle of former big-league star, Luis Aparicio. This baseball sage encouraged Ozzie to take formal instruction from him, which he did, before and after school. *Sports Illustrated* provided insight into ENFP Guillen, beginning with his love for baseball and high tolerance for pain:

> When Ozzie took a grounder in the lip early in his apprenticeship, Ernesto found he could barely persuade him to leave the game for his seven stitches.[88]

Guillen said:

> Ernesto was building another shortstop. Grounding balls to me every day before school, teaching me little tricks. He was the only one who believed I could be a shortstop at the professional level.[89]

Ozzie's greatness was formed by expert instruction, daily hard work, and strong encouragement. Former major league shortstop and fellow Venezuelan, Chico

Carrasquel, said of Guillen:

> He worked hard. When he started as a pro, and the games started at 7:30, he would be in the ballpark at 2:00, taking grounders.[90]

I repeat, ENFPs are found infrequently at shortstop in pro baseball. Yet Ozzie Guillen has demonstrated what is necessary for his Type to succeed at this position and level.

Switch-hitting **Tony Phillips** (ENFP) became the first player in history to start at least 10 games at 5 different positions (counting the outfield). **Terry Pendleton** was a frequent winner of the Gold Glove as the National League's best defensive third baseman.

Heading into the 21st century, another ENFP (and Venezuelan!) had become heralded as the best defensive shortstop in the game. ENFP **Omar Vizquel** won his eighth consecutive Gold Glove in 2000.

Pitching Potential

Though they may not be naturals on the mound as youngsters, ENFPs can become first-rate pitchers. Learning to control their energy and emotions is important in this process. They also need to give extra attention to attaining smooth and rhythmical motions. **Dwight Gooden**, ENFP, led the National League in strikeouts twice (1984 and 1985). In 1985, he posted a NL low 1.53 ERA.

Dwight Gooden dominated the National league in the mid-1980s with just two pitches: a fastball and overhand curveball. As major league baseball heads into the 21st century, a pitcher's arsenal needs greater variety than in former times. With more sophisticated batting and strength techniques, hitters have increased bat speed. It is more important than ever that pitchers keep batters off balance. ENFPs must work hard at developing this strategy, physically and mentally.

HELPING ENFPs

It appears that ENFPs have found major league success at all positions, not a claim most Brain Types could make. Though not commonly found at certain positions, ENFPs are versatile players. They are able to develop impressive defensive skills, yet ENFPs need lots of training with hand-eye, fine motor drills. They will not have the innate Sensate (S) proficiencies.

Exuding boundless energy, ENFPs need to contain themselves at the plate. Patience is a virtue when batting, like waiting for a good pitch, watching the ball to the bat. (If ENFPs are despondent, however, they may wait too long. NFs are greatly affected by their emotional status.) The *L.A. Times* reported on the resurgence of Atlanta Braves' **Terry Pendleton**, after his winning the National League's 1991 MVP:

> Pendleton, who never hit more than .286 in seven seasons with St. Louis, said the difference stemmed from "a feeling of being wanted again" and a determination to swing only at strikes.[91]

After playing in his first inter-league games in 1997, Ozzie Guillen was asked the difference in American and National League strike zones:

> I don't have a strike zone. I see the ball and swing.[92]

ENFPs tend to pull the ball too much, weakening their batting averages and hurting their chances to produce in pressure situations. Learning to hit to the opposite field will be of significant benefit. Switch-hitting will also be helpful to their long term success.

ENFPs must be careful to use their cerebral talents as well as athletic talents on the field. It is necessary for them to Introvert and analyze matters in key situations, particularly when running the bases or with fielding that requires heady play.

ENFJ

The verve and enthusiasm ENFJs bring to sports are their greatest assets. They express devotion for their sport by giving it their all, both emotionally and physically. Baseball is no exception; when they love it, they embrace it with a passion.

As youngsters, ENFJs appear a little stiff and mechanical. Their motor skills are undeveloped and their strong left-brain dominance is not conducive to grace and dexterity. Nevertheless, if ENFJs persist, they can develop accomplished motor skills as they grow older.

ENFJs are greatly interested in people, past and present. They have a special ability to live vicariously through others, to relate and place themselves in others' shoes. In baseball, this can translate into having idols of their revered players, learning their many statistics, even copying the way they play. An ENFJ who understands Brain Typing once told me that, in life and sports, form precedes function. How one looks or performs is most important, sometimes even at the cost of substance. This attitude can be detrimental to the ENFJ if it is not balanced when performing under pressure.

ENFJs are infrequently found in the majors, yet they have the potential, unlike many other Brain Types, to make it and stay there. They are not found nearly as often as ENTJs in the big leagues, and the positions they play are more limited. As professionals, pitcher, first, second, and third bases, and right field appear their most common positions.

Aggressive

Competitiveness with too much anxiety can create problems in baseball. The intricacies of the game, including finesse, are stymied. Too much emotion is hazardous, especially to the ENFJ swing. Consider ENFJ **Robin Ventura** who hit only 5 home runs his 1990 rookie season for the Chicago White Sox. The first three months of the '91 season brought 4 more for Ventura. He then attained a level of relaxation that enabled him to crank out 12 home runs in one month! Fireworks lasted the whole month of July for Robin Ventura. He finished the '91 season with 23 homers, batting .284.

ENFJ **Jeff Kent**'s career took considerably longer to blossom than Ventura's. In the year 2000, **Kent** finally hit over .300 after 9 years in the bigs, with an average of .334, including 33 home runs; his all-around excellence won him the NL MVP. He was the first second baseman to win the award since ENTJ Ryne Sandberg in 1984. In 2001, Kent established himself as the National League's premier second baseman by posting his fifth consecutive 20 home run and 100 RBI season, clubbing 22 home runs and driving in 106 runs. He also turned in Gold Glove-caliber defense, leading National League second basemen with a .987 fielding pct. (668 chances, 9 errors at his position).

Former third baseman **Doug DeCinces**, ENFJ, had his best year in 1982, batting .301 and hitting 30 home runs.

Mark Grace may qualify as the consummate ENFJ in modern baseball. In many ways he has defied his Type, as Jim Courier (ENFJ) did in tennis. Grace has performed with seemingly right-brain fluidity, in the field and at the plate. As a left brain ENFJ, how has he done it?

First, Mark's "grace" was not always been apparent. In 1985, he was drafted by the Cubs in the 24th round, far down the list for a big league star. He proved to be a late bloomer.

Second, when ENFJs devote many years and extended hours of practice to a sport, they can achieve NF "harmony" in their gross and fine motor skills.

Third, Mark is a natural lefty at throwing and hitting. Since the right hemisphere controls the majority of left-side body movements, a left-handed J is able to exercise more P movements than right handed Js.

Lastly, I discovered perhaps the prime reason for Grace's hitting success at Spring Training in 1993. Mark told me that hitting to the opposite field was a major emphasis of his.

Potential as Pitchers

From their Little League years on, ENFJs are hard throwers. Unfortunately, their accuracy is not as good as the strength of their arms. As youngsters, they can even be dangerous to the opposition. I remember as a boy growing up watching my ENFJ brother pitch. An unforgettable outing came when he pitched a no-hitter in Little League, striking out 16. His 15 walks and hitting 3 batters were his undoing, however, as he lost the game 8 to 6!

Following a roller-coaster career, my ENFJ brother gave up pitching upon graduation from high school. His last pitching performance ended it in a blaze of glory, pitching a one-hitter. He did it in a somewhat ENFJ fashion, hitting the first batter squarely in the head (who was thankful for batting helmets). Settling down, my brother went on to strike out 16 with only two walks. He even won the game! (He was undefeated his senior year.)

ENFJs, like ESTJs, have the special ability to put fear in every hitter. Their pitching can cause unspiritual batters to pray before they go to the plate. ENFJs are not always wild, but it will be their tendency, particularly when younger.

Years ago I was coaching a Little League team, standing on the bench, leaning over the screen to get a better view of my team who was up to bat. The opposing team's pitcher was an ENFJ. The boy was pitching wildly and the walks were adding up. He proceeded to throw a pitch where the ball flew out of his fingers so errantly that it flew just past my head and out onto the street. Mind you, I was at least 20 feet right of home plate! If he were an ISTP he may have been deliberately throwing at me, but the Feeling ENFJ was embarrassed and apologetic. Do not misunderstand me, ENFJs have the ultimate potential to be excellent major-league pitchers. They must, however, weather the storms of wildness in their youth and practice throwing the ball a little easier, for the sake of accuracy. Unfortunately, prone to wildness, many ENFJs give up their pitching careers before reaching their potential.

One ENFJ who stuck with pitching and brought credibility to ENFJ hurlers is **Mark Langston**. The hard-throwing lefty (whose fastball has been in the 95-m.p.h. range) fought the ENFJ lack of control and consistency throughout his career. Under pressure, he tended to get a little hasty, speeding up his motion while kicking his leg higher than ex-punter Ray Guy. This hurt Mark's ability to put the ball in the strike zone. In 1990, he had a dismal season, going 10-17 with 104 walks, fifth most in the league. He yielded a 109 earned runs, the second most in the league. Langston explained:

> I just started to get behind on the count. It's very hard to make your pitches when it's two and 0 or three and one on the hitter. The hitter has all the advantage.

He continued:

> The art of pitching is pitching from ahead. What happened was, I became more of a defensive pitcher. I didn't lose my fastball, I lost my confidence.[93]

Fortunately for Langston, he had a turnaround year in '91, compiling a record of 19-8 and an ERA of 3.00, while fanning 183 batters. With the proper mental approach, Mark Langston and other ENFJs can be highly successful pitchers.

ENFJs, like all NFs, are capable of attaining wonderful body coordination, harmonizing both gross and fine motor skills. Yet as NFJs (left-brained NFs), they will require more time than NFPs (right-brained dominant) to achieve this coordination. ENFJs will get better the longer they pitch, particularly physically. They must work just as hard on the mental side of the game.

ENFJ **Andy Benes** was the No. 1 pick in the 1988 draft. Though showing star potential his first two professional years, Andy didn't reveal his capabilities until halfway through the 1991 season. In mid July, he was a miserable 4-10; by mid September, he had run off 9 straight victories. Andy ended the season with 15 victories, striking out 167 and earning an ERA of 3.03. Andy's major league career continued into the 21st century, quite an accomplishment. Nonetheless, his tenure in the big leagues demonstrated his ENFJ tendencies.

Love to Play Defense

Playing defense is fun for ENFJs; they particularly show this in basketball. In baseball, it is not as apparent to the fan, though just as real. With hard work and grit, ENFJs can be Gold Glovers.

Playing infield is not as conducive for ENFJs in the major leagues as it is for some other Types. When ENFJs play the infield, they usually play at the corners, first and third. A distinct advantage for ENFJs with developed defensive skills is that they will do whatever it takes to be successful, including sticking their "chin out" and getting hit by balls.

In 1991, **Robin Ventura** won his first Gold Glove at third base; his fourth came in 1996. Pitcher **Mark Langston** won five consecutive Gold Glove awards between 1991 and '95.

HELPING ENFJs

Though capable of playing every position in lower leagues, ENFJs' best chances for professional success appear at the positions of pitcher, first and third bases, and right field.

Throwing accuracy is of prime importance for ENFJs, even if they have no aspirations for pitching. They are designed to have strong arms, but arm control is often a problem, particularly when ENFJs are younger, inexperienced, or under pressure. Whether they be on the mound, third base, or right field, throwing accuracy is essential for success. Throwing accuracy can be developed at home by hanging a tire in the back yard and trying to hit the bulls-eye. Older ENFJs generally improve their pitching accuracy by simplifying their delivery.

ENFJs can hit for power by utilizing their NF muscle coordination skills. Yet this is not where they need to devote attention. Their biggest nemesis at the plate is not waiting on the ball and watching it to their bat. They tend to pull the trigger too soon, often getting suckered on off speed pitches. ENFJs would be wise to try to learn how to hit to the opposite field as much as possible. This would ensure waiting longer on the pitch, watching the approaching ball as long as possible, and improving the batting average.

Right-handed ENFJs can learn to hit from the left side, though not as easily as some other Types. Nonetheless, this can be of benefit in the long run. Right-handed **Robin Ventura** became proficient from the left side of the plate.

One ENFJ who has excelled from his natural right side at the plate in recent years has been All-Star **Jeff Kent**.

ENFJs are susceptible to losing confidence in their abilities when things are not going well. They view their circumstances more subjectively than Thinkers, having a tendency to get down on themselves. They welcome encouragement and a positive outlook from their associates.

OTHER BRAIN TYPES (ISFJ, ESFJ, INFJ, INTP)

We have considered some major attributes of the most commonly found Brain Types found in professional baseball. The ISFJ, ESFJ, INFJ, and INTP appear to be the least represented. Any baseball players possessing any of these remaining four Types (or Types already mentioned but infrequently found in the majors) should not give up their aspirations, but realize working harder and smarter will be necessary to reach the highest levels of baseball. They should consider the true life stories of persons who overcame unfavorable odds to attain athletic stardom. Reading the accounts of the disciplines and rigors that enabled them to reach their goals would be helpful.

If persons who constitute any of these remaining Types are unwilling to undergo the hard work necessary to reach the upper limits of baseball, yet they desire to reach them, perhaps they should choose a sport more accommodating to their respective Types.

Conclusion

Each Brain Type excels at specific phases of the game, mentally and physically. The more time you devote to observing and understanding these differences in Types, the more exciting and beneficial this study will become for you.

It is wise to investigate the players of your specific Brain Type. This will enable you to see the various ways persons of the same Brain Type play baseball. Look for articles where they share their methods of success, mental and physical. If you have typed yourself correctly, you should relate to what they are saying. Remember the adage "different strokes for different folks." You will generally do best by emulating those most like yourself.

Though far from complete, here is a list of well known players and their probable Brain Types that will provide a perspective on the most successful Types in professional baseball.

ISTP
1st: Jeff Bagwell, Jim Thome;
    R: Lou Gehrig, Don Mattingly, Will Clark, Wally Joyner
2nd: Ray Durham, Pokey Reese;
    R: Pete Rose, Steve Sax, Rob Thompson, Mark Lemke, Jeff Treadway
ss: **R:** Alan Trammell, Robin Yount, Walt Weiss, Cal Ripken Jr., Shawon Dunston
3rd: Chipper Jones, Matt Williams, Dave Hansen;
    R: George Brett, **Wade Boggs**
C: **R:** Terry Steinbach
OF: Brady Anderson, Rusty Greer, Steve Finley, Jeromy Burnitz, Todd Hollandsworth;
    R: Ty Cobb, **Ted Williams**, **Henry Aaron**, Carl Yastrzemski, Roger Maris, Darryl Strawberry, Jim Eisenreich, Willie McGee, Mike Greenwell, Jay Buhner, Chili Davis, Eric Davis
P: **Roger Clemens**, **Tom Glavine**, Bret Saberhagen, Charles Nagy, Kerry Wood, Rick Helling,
    RP: Trevor Hoffman, Billy Wagner, Troy Percival;
    R: Dennis "Oil Can" Boyd, John Tudor, Dave Stewart, Steve Howe, Danny Jackson, Jim Abbott, Randy Myers, Steve Avery

9....Baseball

ESTP
1st: Phil Nevin
  R: Dick Allen, Jack Clark, Cory Snyder, Glen Davis, Eddie Murray
2nd: Craig Biggio;
  R: Bobby Grich, Juan Samuel, Mickey Morandini, Craig Grebeck
ss: **Alex Rodriguez**, Edgar Renteria,
  R: Mike Gallego, Mariano Duncan, Rafael Belliard, Jose Offerman,
3rd: R: **Mike Schmidt**, Pedro Guerrero, Steve Buechele, Gary Gaetti, Ken Caminiti
C: Mike Piazza, Benito Santiago;
  R: Gary Carter, Lance Parrish, Steve Yeager, Darren Daulton
OF: Juan Gonzalez, Gary Sheffield, Rickey Henderson;
  R: **Mickey Mantle**, Reggie Jackson, Dusty Baker, Andre Dawson, Jesse Barfield, Dave Winfield, Kirk Gibson, Brian Downing, George Bell, Luis Polonia, Deion Sanders, Jose Canseco
P: **Pedro Martinez**, Todd Stottlemyre, Darren Dreifort, Ricky Bones, Byung-Hyun Kim;
  R: Don Sutton, Dennis Martinez, Doug Drabek, Dennis Eckersley, Dave Stieb, Juan Berenguer, Julio Machado, Pete Smith, Juan Guzman

ISFP
1st: Fred McGriff, John Jaha;
  R: Jason Thompson, Sid Bream, Joe Carter, **Mark McGwire**
2nd Damion Easley; R: Harold Reynolds
ss: Jose Hernandez, Julio Lugo;
  R: **Ernie Banks**, Maury Wills, Alfredo Griffin, Rafael Ramirez, Manuel Lee
3rd: Fernando Tatis, Dean Palmer
C: Charles Johnson, Jorge Posada;
  R: Yogi Berra, Roy Campanella, Pat Borders
OF: Moises Alou, Jermaine Dye, Richard Hidalgo, Henry Rodriguez, Juan Encarnacion, Devon White, Shane Spencer ;
  R: Don Baylor, Lonnie Smith, John Shelby, Gary Pettis, Derrick May
P: Chuck Finley, Frank Castillo;
  R: J.R. Richard, Mike Scott, Mike Davis, Dave Smith, Bruce Hurst, Storm Davis, Alejandro Pena, Heathcliff Slocumb, Ken Hill

ESFP
1st: Frank Thomas, Carlos Delgado, Andres Galarraga
  R: Carlos Quintana
IF: Barry Larkin, Roberto Alomar, Jose Vidro, **Nomar Garciaparra**, Edgardo Alfonzo, Tony Batista, Junior Spivey, Miguel Tejada, Luis Castillo, Adrian Beltre, Luis Sojo;
  R: Mike Sharperson, Lenny Harris, Jose Oquendo, Junior Felix
OF: **Barry Bonds**, **Ken Griffey Jr.**, Larry Walker, **Albert Pujols**, Manny Ramirez, Andruw Jones, Garret Anderson, Magglio Ordonez, Dimitri Young, Vernon Wells, Jose Guillen, Geronimo Berroa, Al Martin, Felix Jose;
  R: **Willie Mays**, Willie Stargell, Dave Parker, Dave Henderson, Kal Daniels, Kirby Puckett, Willie Wilson, Bobby Bonilla, Brian McRae, Glenallen Hill, Albert Belle, **Tony Gywnn**
C: Ivan Rodriguez; R: Joe Garagiola, Tony Pena
P: Bartolo Colon, Livan Hernandez, Jose Rijo, C.C. Sabathia, Armando Benitez, Freddy Garcia, Jose Acevedo; Jennie Finch, Lisa Fernandez
  R: **Dizzy Dean**, Satchel Paige, Doc Ellis, John Candelaria, Ben Rivera, Alex Fernandez Wilson Alvarez

ISTJ
IF: Craig Counsell;
  R: Bill Russell, Dick Schofield, Jeff Blauser
P: **Orel Hershiser**; R: Mike Witt

ESTJ
IF: Ed Sprague
OF: Austin Kearns   R: Tom Brunansky
C: Damian Miller, John Flaherty; R: **Bob Boone**, Brian Harper, Ernie Whitt
P: John Smoltz, Jason Bere, Roberto Hernandez, Josh Beckett;
  R: **Nolan Ryan**, Jeff Russell, Bryan Harvey, Duane Ward, Kevin Gross, Jim Gott, Willie Frazier, Danny Cox, Mike Harkey, Doug Henry

ISFJ
1st: Derreck Lee

ESFJ
C: Chris Jones, **R:** Greg Olson

INFP
IF: John Olerud, Derek Jeter, Chris Gomez, Wilton Guerrero;
  R: **Rod Carew**, Tony Fernandez
OF: Dave Justice, Raul Mondesi, Harold Baines, Lance Johnson, Dave Martinez, Doug Glanville;
  R: **Roberto Clemente**, Fred Lynn, Earnest Riles
P: **Mariano Rivera**, Steve Trachsel;
  R: Jose Melendez, Kevin Foster

ENFP
IF: **Alfonso Soriano**, Omar Vizquel, Eric Young, Mark McLemore;
  R: Lou Whitaker, Terry Pendleton, Cecil Fielder, Tony Phillips, Ozzie Guillen, Joey Cora
OF: **Sammy Sosa**, Vladimir Guerrero, Darin Erstad, Bernie Williams, Kenny Lofton, Torii Hunter, Roberto Kelly, Reggie Sanders, Greg Vaughn, Alex Ochoa;
  R: **Jackie Robinson**, Hubie Brooks, Shane Mack, Billy Hatcher, Milt Thompson, Mel Hall, Ron Gant,
C: Sandy Alomar Jr.;
  R: Bob Uecker, Lenny Webster
P: Dontrelle Willis, Pedro Astacio, Chan Ho Park, Carlos Perez, Chuck McElroy,
  RP: Danny Graves, Shigetoshi Hasegawa
  R: **Dwight Gooden**, Alvin Morman

ENFJ
1st: **Mark Grace**
2nd: Jeff Kent
ss: Gary DiSarcina
3rd: Robin Ventura
  R: Doug DeCinces, Kevin Seitzer
P: Andy Benes, Jaret Wright, Dan Plesac, Bob Scanlan, Jeff Austin;
  R: Mark Langston, Shawn Boskie

INTJ
P: **Randy Johnson**, Mike Mussina, Andy Ashby, Shane Reynolds, Mark Wohlers, Gregg Olson;
  R: Eric Show, Tim Burke, Ed Whitson, **David Cone**

ENTJ
1st: Eric Karros, J.T. Snow, Jeff Conine, Travis Lee;
  R: Steve Garvey
2nd: **R:** **Ryne Sandberg**, Marty Barrett, Jody Reed
ss: Jay Bell, **R:** Tony Kubec
3rd: Travis Fryman, Todd Zeile, Russell Branyan;
  R: **Paul Molitor**, Dave Hollins, Dave Magadan
C: Javy Lopez;
  R: Joe Torre, Tim McCarver, Carlton Fisk, Mike Scioscia, Damon Berryhill, Mike Stanley, Mike MacFarlane
OF: Tim Salmon;
  R: Bobby Valentine, Dale Murphy, Kevin McReynolds, Brett Butler, Paul O'Neill, Chad Curtis
P: **Greg Maddux**, Barry Zito, Mark Prior, Denny Neagle, Jeff Fassero, Scott Erickson, Shawn Estes, Bobby Witt, Kevin Tapani;
  RP: Robb Nen, Matt Mantei
  R: **Don Drysdale**, Jim Palmer, **Tom Seaver**, Dave Dravecky, Steve Stone, Tom House, Ken Brett, Joe Magrane, Kirk McCaskill, Scott Sanderson, Jimmy Key, Jay Howell, Ron Darling, Mike Boddicker, Rick Aguilera, Roger McDowell, Tim Belcher, John Wetteland

ENTP
- 1st: **Jason Giambi**, Mo Vaughn, Rafael Palmeiro, Tino Martinez, Todd Helton, Sean Casey, Lee Stevens, Richie Sexson, Doug Mientkiewicz;
  R: Frank Howard, Kent Hrbek, Bob Hamelin
- 2nd: Chuck Knoblauch, Delino DeShields, Todd Walker; **R:** Jose Lind
- ss: **R:** Bill Ripkin, Pat Listach
- 3rd: Troy Glaus, Paul Konerko, Tyler Houston, Aaron Boone, Mike Lowell;
  R: Doug Rader, Sal Bando, Scott Leius, Scott Brosius
- C: Jason Kendall, Joe Girardi, Jason LaRue;
  R: Mike LaValiere, Charlie O'Brien, Jim Leyritz
- OF: **Ichiro Suzuki**, Jim Edmonds, Luis Gonzalez, Shawn Green, Marquis Grissom, Brian Giles, Hideki Matsui, Geoff Jenkins, Derek Bell, B.J. Surhoff, Ryan Klesko, Cliff Floyd, Johnny Damon, Mark Kotsay, Turner Ward, Marty Cordova;
  R: Jay Johnstone, John Lowenstein, Steve Lyons, Otis Nixon, Chuck Carr,
- P: **Curt Schilling,** Kevin Brown, David Wells, Andy Pettitte, Brad Radke, Hideo Nomo, Mike Hampton, Jason Schmidt, Russ Ortiz, Kevin Millwood, Orlando Hernandez (El Duque), Hideki Irabu, Eric Milton, Joey Hamilton, Carlos Perez, Matt Clement, Mike Remlinger, Ben Sheets, Dave Burba, Turk Wendell, Rick Ankiel;
- *RP:* Eric Gagne, Mike Williams, Scott Sullivan, Norm Charlton;
  R: Gaylord Perry, **Phil Niekro**, Charlie Hough, John (The Count) Montefusco, Bill "Spaceman" Lee, Jeff Reardon, Tom Candiotti, Chad Ogea, Chris Bozio, Carl Willis, Jeff Montgomery, Sid Fernandez, Jesse Orosco, Doug Jones, Jeff Brantley, Rod Beck, Terry Mulholland

10 Basketball

Growing up in Indiana amid Hoosier hysteria and playing basketball into college, I developed an affinity for the sport. Being able to practice alone, working on a myriad of shots, passes, and dribbles, all to the ultimate appreciation of large, enthusiastic audiences were enough to interest me in hoops. Of course, there are many more motivations for lacing up the Air Jordans.

Professional basketball experienced remarkable development in the 1980s. The NBA averaged 15,690 fans per game for the 1989-90 season, marking a 46 percent increase since the 1982-83 season. The advent of **Bird, Johnson,** and **Jordan** worked wonders in capturing the public focus. As a result, salaries skyrocketed and virtually every aspiring basketball player dreams of playing in the NBA.

What does it take to make it big time in basketball? Unlike tennis, golf, or even baseball, pro basketball requires height. Admittedly, there are the exceptions with 5-foot-3 **Muggsy Bogues** and 5-foot-7 **Spud Webb.** The average height in the NBA is 6-foot-7. What other sport requires such stature?

Who will be able to play high school and college ball? I have observed all 16 Types playing at every level. Each of the 16 Brain Types has the potential to earn a college scholarship in basketball. College basketball consists of many levels of competition, from NAIA to NCAA Division 1, with a wide range of athletic talent.

By the time athletes reach the NBA, however, the variety of Types found are far fewer, especially from a percentage basis. A few Brain Types dominate the NBA in numbers found, with another four or so making up the majority of the other players. Let's look at the top Types.

ISTP

Again we see the ISTP having the best overall potential to succeed to the heights of athletic professionalism. In the NBA, more top-notch players are ISTP than any other Brain Type.

Whereas some designs are found only in the positions requiring great height, ISTPs can excel equally well at every basketball position. Their right brain, fine motor skill proficiency allows for mastery of every dimension of the game. Modern ISTP players have included **Hakeem Olajuwon, Patrick Ewing, Alonzo Mourning, Shaquille O'Neal, Larry Bird, James Worthy, Michael Jordan, Tracy McGrady, John Stockton, Jason Kidd,** and **Allen Iverson.** You can see that ISTPs can play every position on the basketball floor with excellence.

Einsteins on the Court

Basketball ISTPs are often regarded as less than bright in their formative years. Their Introverted, ST right-brained dominance does not place a high priority on verbal expression and proper syntax. Therefore, many perceive the ISTP incorrectly. Few recognize the exceptional basketball intelligence of the ISTP hoopster.

True basketball skill involves "seeing the floor" (including players and basket), calculating the angles and trajectories, understanding the strategies, and so on. ISTPs are much more proficient at their own understanding and mastery of these aspects of basketball than communicating in words. NBA great **Larry Bird** once said of himself:

> I'm not the smartest guy in life, but on the basketball court I consider myself an A plus. Not that I'm dumb. . . . I just don't explain myself to people very often.[1]

Others saw Larry's basketball genius, too. *Sports Illustrated* polled NBA coaches and general managers in 1992, asking "Who is the league's smartest player?"[2] Bird won, followed by ISTPs **John Stockton** and **Chris Mullin**.

Remarkable aspects associated with the ISTP's brain are the ability to see multi dimensionally and peripherally and to make logical split second decisions. ISTPs, like all Sensing right-brained persons, are more inclined to trust their spatial abilities than their verbal left brain. After much practice, they are able to see virtually everyone on the floor, while making rapid, precise, and logical decisions. They can then make wise passes and shots, while remaining adaptable to almost any situation that presents itself.

NBA great Magic Johnson said of his long time ISTP adversary and friend, **Larry Bird**:

> They say he's not that quick, but he makes up for any quickness he lacks with his guts, intelligence and determination.

He continued:

> Of all the people I play against, the only one I truly fear—or worry about—is Larry Bird.[3]

Hard Workers

As we saw the ISTP's tireless work ethic demonstrated in baseball, we also find it in basketball, or in any sport or interest about which the ISTP is excited. NBA All-Star forward **Chris Mullin** was known as the ultimate gym rat when growing up in New York. Yet ISTP Mullin admits he met his match in the 1984 Olympic trials. His name was **Michael Jordan**, ISTP. Mullin spoke of those days:

> At the trials in Indiana, we were working out three times a day. After a while, guys would come to the evening workout and sit there until the coaches showed up. Not Michael. He'd be out there doing 360-degree jams. And I'd sit there thinking, I've got to guard this man for two hours and I can't move.[4]

One ISTP outdid another. Magic Johnson also acknowledges the work ethic of ISTPs when he says of **Larry Bird**:

> He's got to be the most dedicated athlete imaginable. A lot of guys I've played with and against are not really that dedicated. To them, it's just a job. With Larry, basketball is his life.[5]

Intense Competitors, Focused

ISTPs are the fiercest of competitors. To whatever sport they are devoted, they give their all in competition. They hate to lose or even to perform poorly. Some athletes are so competitive that they will even try to beat their own mother or grandmother. They are most likely ISTPs.

Everyone knew **Michael Jordan** for his scoring and dunks, but few realized his competitive spirit and intensity for the game. Former NBA competitor and guard, Doc Rivers, said of Jordan:

> He plays every game like it's his last.[6]

ISTPs respond consistently to pressure better than any Brain Type. They have their choking moments, too, but overall they handle pressure well. Coaches play a major role in how ISTPs perform. They must instill confidence in ISTPs, allowing them to handle the ball often, even making some mistakes. Otherwise ISTPs may perform poorly.

In 1990, Portland Trail Blazer coach Rick Adelman said of his ISTP point guard, **Terry Porter**:

> Terry just seems to play consistently, game by game. Then we get into a big situation or big game and he asserts himself. He has always risen to the occasion. He's been doing it for years.[7]

In the 1990 post season playoffs, Houston Rocket coach Don Chaney spoke of L.A. Laker **James Worthy**,

ISTP:

> We have not conquered James Worthy yet. To be honest with you, no, I didn't think he was that good. But in the playoffs, he just gets better. He's been the key factor.[8]

Worthy earned a reputation around the NBA at playoff time. He was dubbed "Big Game" James.

Hank Gathers, the late college star at Loyola Marymount, was an ISTP bound for success in the NBA. Following his sudden and tragic coronary failure, Gather's high school coach, Rich Yankowitz, said:

> Of all the players, I have never had a player whose life was so centered in basketball. His every dream was basketball, to be a top quality player. Every day in practice he would work as hard as possible and then beg to stay on the floor to work more. He was the hardest working player I ever coached. He was never satisfied with his performance.[9]

Prolific Scorers

ISTPs can be outstanding scorers and shooters. They have the God given Type expertly designed for shooting, ball-handling, and outsmarting their opponents. They also can develop extraordinary work habits. **Larry Bird** often arrived three hours before a game to practice.

In the 1991-92 season, **Michael Jordan** won his sixth consecutive NBA scoring championship and was named the league's most valuable player for the third time in five years. Jordan's highest seasonal average came in the 1986-87 season, tallying over 37 points per game. Upon his retirement in 1999, Jordan had won a record ten NBA scoring titles.

LSU's **Pistol Pete Maravich**, ISTP, not only set the NCAA scoring record in three seasons (1968-70) with 3,667 points and an average of 44.2 points per game, he did it before the advent of the three point shot. Consider the NCAA career records the Pistol established in three seasons: most points, highest scoring average, most games scoring at least 50 points (28), most field goals made, most field goals attempted, most free throws made, and most free throws attempted.

ISTP **Jerry West** made a profound impact on the NBA from 1960 to 1974. As a scorer, he averaged 27 points per game over his career. He made the All NBA Team 12 times, and the NBA All Defensive team five times. He even led the NBA in assists in 1972.

One of basketball's most memorable individual performances took place in the 1973 NCAA championship game. Junior center **Bill Walton** hit 21 of 22 field goals and scored 44 points, leading his UCLA Bruins over a tough Memphis State team. Before graduating, Walton collected 3 College Player of the Year awards. ISTP Bill later led the NBA in rebounding and won an NBA championship with the Portland Trail Blazers in 1976-77.

The 2002-2003 season saw the closest ISTP comparison to retiring Michael Jordan in **Tracy McGady**. T-Mac proved his dominance as he led the NBA in scoring at 32.1 points per game.

Three-point and Foul Shooters

ISTPs consistently shoot the three point shot as well as any Brain Type, particularly under big game pressure. A few other Types shoot the threes as well in normal situations, but ISTPs are arguably the best at crunch time.

ISTPs are also at the top among free-throw shooters. They have the cerebral and body potential to be the supreme foul shooters. Other Types can be excellent at the foul line as well, but ISTPs have the ultimate goods.

As of 2001, three of the top five free-throw shooters of all time, in career percentage, were ISTPs. **Mark Price** led the list. (Price retired in 1999, with a career percentage of 90.4!) **Scott Skiles** and **Larry Bird** complete the list; ENTJ Rick Barry and Calvin Murphy are the only non-ISTPs.

In 1991, ISTP **Ricky Pierce** connected on 75 free-throws in a row. **Pete Maravich**, ISTP, holds the NCAA record for most free throws made in a game, 30 in 31 attempts.

These statistics do not mean that all ISTPs are good free-throw shooters. In reality, some ISTPs have been dismal. (Consider Shaquille O'Neal.) With lots of practice, however, they can make great strides. The younger they begin practicing foul shots, the better they will become. ISTPs, along with their coaches and guardians, should never give up if they don't see early shooting success. With proper ST technique and practice, it's only a matter of time before they get the right results.

Ball-handlers

ISTPs can be remarkable ball handlers, employing their right-brained fluidity and ST fine motor skills. No Type is better. Consider the ball handling skills of some

ISTP guards in the NBA: **Jason Kidd, John Stockton, Tim Hardaway, Allen Iverson, Stephon Marbury,** and even a big guard by the name of **Michael Jordan**. ISTPs are the preeminent point guards.

As Sensing, spatial, right-brained P's, ISTPs are able to see every detail "on the floor." Their logical Thinking function, with split second timing, lends critical assistance in determining the best possible time to implement a move. ISTPs are able to make the fewest passing errors, particularly under pressure.

ISTP Byron Scott of the Lakers had the ill fated task of guarding **Michael Jordan** in the 1991 NBA finals. One would expect Scott to have been most impressed by Jordan's dunks or dazzling moves, or incredible passes or shots. Rather, Scott said of Jordan:

> The thing that impresses me most about him is his awareness. He knows where everybody is on the court . . . .[10]

John Stockton, ISTP, broke his own NBA single season assist record in 1991, while averaging 14.2 assists per game. In 1992, Stockton led the NBA in assists for the fifth straight season, with 13.7 per game. **Scott Skiles**, ISTP, holds the NBA record for most assists in a game, with 30 (set in 1990).

Defensive Aces

ISTPs can be superb defensive players. Their cerebral makeup enables them to have highly aggressive, must win attitudes, catlike reflexes, and lightning hands and be able to anticipate moves and passes by the opposition. Watching the L.A. Lakers play for years, I was amazed at how many passes were stolen by 6-foot-9 **James Worthy**, ISTP. Despite his size, he was a master ball snatcher on the court.

Not only does ISTP **John Stockton** hold the NBA career record for assists, but he's the all-time steals leader. These feats are even more amazing when one considers Stockton's physical makeup and his low recognition when entering the pros. He could not have accomplished so much without his ISTP Brain Type.

Even the prolific scoring machine, **Michael Jordan**, demonstrated the ISTP's ability to play defense. In 1988, Jordan was voted NBA Defensive Player of the Year. Nearly a decade later (1997), he became the second player in NBA history to be selected to the all-defensive first team eight times. Jordan has proved that ISTPs can be the best at both ends of the floor.

Coach Doug Collins compared Michael Jordan and two time Defensive Player of the Year, Dennis Rodman:

> I love Dennis Rodman, but Michael plays tougher defense than Dennis. If you polled the NBA guards and asked them to pick the man they would least like to have guarding them in the last 24 seconds of a game, I bet most of them would pick Michael.[11]

Regardless of whom the guards would pick, Michael Jordan has proven it possible for a basketball player to excel at both ends of the court. ISTPs have this potential like no other Brain Type. By the way, Dennis Rodman was concerned primarily with defense, averaging fewer than 10 points per game over his career. We have seen Mr. Jordan's ability to do it all.

Rebounders

When you consider outstanding rebounders in the NBA, ISTPs **Hakeem Olajuwon, Shaquille O'Neal**, and **Ben Wallace** naturally come to mind. Their innate aggression, tenacity, and athleticism enable superb rebounding.

ISTP Moses Malone led the NBA in rebounding six times, five times consecutively. His record is second only to Wilt Chamberlain's eleven seasons. Offensive rebounds have only been compiled by the NBA since 1973 74. Here, Moses Malone is the career leader. He holds the NBA's record for the most *offensive* rebounds in a game, 21, set in 1982. Malone was the NBA's MVP in 1979, 1982, and 1983.

At age thirty-six, Malone signed a two year contract with the Milwaukee Bucks. Coach Del Harris commented:

> Moses is an intense competitor with the heart of a lion and the spirit of a thoroughbred. He will give us a big lift in our rebounding and inside game.[12]

Unheralded ISTP **Larry Smith,** only 6-foot-8, was one of the NBA's best rebounders. He was known throughout the league as "Mr. Mean." Columnist Mike Downey wrote of Smith in 1991:

> Mister Mean means business. He has one mission in life. He tracks down rebounds. Mr. Mean goes after a basketball the way a Patriot missile goes after a Scud. He senses it. He sights it. He nails it. Nothing deters Mr. Mean. . . .[13]

All-Stars

With long hours of practice and learning, ISTPs can play the total game of basketball better than any other Type. Magic Johnson spoke again of **Larry Bird**:

> The reason I love to watch Larry play is that he can dominate a game without even taking a shot. He is truly a guy who can make other players better.[14]

Bird made the All-NBA First Team in each of his initial nine years in the league with the Boston Celtics (1979 through 1988). Heel surgery helped break this streak. The jacket cover of Bird's book, *Drive*, says:

> When it comes to hoops, folks agree that Larry Bird is the best there is. Magic may have the moves, Dominique the slam dunk, Michael Jordan the speed—but no one puts it together like Bird. Arguably the greatest all around player the game has ever known. Bird led the Boston Celtics from the basement to three world championships, collecting three NBA MVP awards along the way.[15]

Michael Jordan became basketball's next ISTP premier player. He finally got his just recognition for being the most complete player in the game by carrying his Chicago Bulls team to the NBA title in 1991. He was unanimously voted the MVP of the series against Magic Johnson and the Los Angeles Lakers. Michael did a curtain call in '92, carrying the Bulls to another world title while winning another series MVP. Retiring after the 1998 season, Jordan's career accomplishments included six MVP's in the NBA Finals as well as five regular season MVP's.

Further demonstrating ISTPs' basketball excellence, nine players of this Brain Type won the NBA Rookie of the Year award from 1985 to 1997!

Masters of Deception

ISTPs are masters at the cunning use of deception. Whether on offense or defense, they employ trickery. Before shooting the ball, ISTPs have a full repertoire of fakes: when passing, the no-lookers, when dribbling, through the legs or around the back. In ISTP **Kenny Anderson's** playing days as a Georgia Tech point guard, he said:

> I'm so deceiving, it might take four or five years for me and my teammates to be on the same wavelength.[16]

Brain Type Versus Persona

Once again, the personas or personalities within each particular Brain Type can be manifold. Contributing to this are environment and cultural influences. For example, two of the many ISTPs who have been known for their Extravertedness in the NBA are **Reggie "Hollywood" Miller** and **Gary Payton**. They have been influenced by their own unique experiences, which shape their gregariousness, evident only at certain times.

Reggie was exposed to plenty of Extraversion in childhood with little sister and basketball star, Cheryl, an outgoing ESFP. I also know that Gary felt it was necessary for survival in Oakland, California, to talk tough when being hassled. Environment impacts one's persona beginning early in life, whereas Brain Type is entirely genetic. ISTPs reveal their Type when performing athletically, as do all other Types, regardless of their varied personalities. They cannot hide their body movements.

In addition, Extraversion and Introverson—from a Brain Type perspective—pertain to the front and rear regions of the brain. Brain Type "Extraverts" are hard wired to use more of the energy-expending regions of the frontal lobes, whereas Brain Type "Introverts" rely more on posterior brain locales which master concentration and conserve energy in physical activities—until it's absolutely necessary to give full effort.

ISTPs may act Extraverted on the basketball court, too. When I spoke with players who have played against the likes of **Larry Bird** and **Michael Jordan**, they convey these two, as well as some other big-name ISTPs in the NBA, can seem far from Introverted on the hardwood. These ISTPs have been known to do some serious "jawing," articulating their basketball superiority toward their foes, "talkin' trash."

Sports Illustrated wrote a piece comparing Magic Johnson (ESFP) and **Michael Jordan** during the 1991 NBA Finals. Magic was portrayed as the "charismatic showman." It was said of Michael:

> For all the hearts he stops when he walks down the street, Jordan is quiet, even close to hermitlike at times. He has a wife and two young sons and

hangs around mostly with his "homeboys" from North Carolina . . . ."[17]

Trust me, Michael and Larry Bird are Introverts (from a Brain Type perspective)!

HELPING ISTPs

ISTPs will perform best when they can keep their aggression and intensity under control. They must remember these assets can become counterproductive if not kept in balance. ISTPs must make sure not to overuse their Thinking function (which most of us should use more often). Excessive logical introspection will cause ISTPs to lose their smoothness and adaptability on the court. Not only can this occur with superstar ISTPs but especially when any ISTP is in a new or pressure situation—causing him or her to overly think rather than operate on automatic pilot.

Remember, inexperienced ISTPs may not perform well. Despite their inherent potential, they must devote many hours of practice to developing their basketball skills.

ESTP

We will witness throughout this book the athleticism of ESTPs. They excel in basketball, too. ESTPs perform similarly to ISTPs, yet differ in significant ways. ESTPs tend to force matters and play a little more out of control. Sometimes it works for them, many times not. They will not give as careful consideration to a shot or pass as ISTPs. This can become most problematic for ESTPs in big games or pressure situations. Turnovers or ill advised shots must be guarded against.

Scorers

ESTPs like to make things happen, to conquer the opponent with flair. They like to play offense, their mind-set geared to putting the ball in the basket. Coaching youth basketball for years made me especially aware of ESTPs on the hardwood. They have that confident, stylish, look and are not shy about shooting the ball.

In a youth league game, I once witnessed a nine year old boy on the opposing team take at least five shots just beyond midcourt (on a shortened floor). Nevertheless, they were all at least 25-foot shots! Not all ESTPs are so bold and confident, but they all like to shoot.

When Darryl Dawkins played for the Detroit Pistons, he said:

> When it comes to shooting I use a tip taught to me by **World B. Free**—just keep shooting.[18]

ESTP "World" was an expert at getting off shots. There were no shots he didn't like. ESFP Dawkins was a willing disciple despite his awesome size.

ESTPs are dominant right-brained persons with excellent hand-eye coordination and fine motor skills. With practice, their shots becomes picturesque and threatening, with plenty of backspin. ESTPs love to jump, which make their shots difficult to block.

Larry Bird spoke of former teammate and ESTP, **Danny Ainge**:

> Some people pick the ball up and they automatically get great rotation. They are true "natural" athletes. Danny Ainge is one of those people.[19]

ESTPs are proficient at utilizing their anterior (front) right hemisphere. It does not take them long to warm up. Their Extraversion has them already in an active mode, their Sensing function is ever ready for the here and now, and their Perceiving right brain is ready to handle any motor task with artistry and grace. Day in and day out, ESTPs can shoot as well as any Type. (Big game pressure will generally affect their outside shot more than ISTPs, however.)

Karl Malone, the NBA's 6' 9", 250-pounder with a strapping physique, was second only to Michael Jordan in scoring for the years 1989-92. ESTP Malone averaged nearly 30 points and 11.5 rebounds per game in the five years of 1988-92. In 1999, after 14 NBA years, Malone became the oldest player to win the MVP (his second). He also set a league record for starting in his eleventh all-star game.

In years past, I viewed youngsters in the annual Pepsi/NBA Hotshot competition. Verdant basketball players must shoot from five different spots on the floor, ranging from 12 to 21 feet. They have one minute to achieve their scores. The youngsters feel pressure as they perform before their peers and parents. One can visibly see the result of tension on their shots in this unfamiliar competition. Their warm up shots contrasted with their shots in competition are often markedly different, especially for the left-brain, Judging Types. They become much more mechanical and rigid when shooting. In contrast, I have noticed that the ESTP is the most cool, calm and collected of all the Types in this event. They generally win the beginning rounds of competition, being harder pressed as they approach the pressure-packed national finals.

Streak Shooters?

By the time ESTPs reach the college or professional level, many regard them as streak shooters (if they're hot, they're hot; if they're not . . . .). The prime reason is that ESTPs like to shoot whether or not the ball is going in the basket. Every basketball player, regardless of Brain Type, will have bad shooting days. Most other Types will reduce the number of shots they make when they can't hit the basket, but ESTPs will normally keep right on shooting. Sometimes they will even shoot more, attempting to break out of a slump. If anything, ESTPs tend to battle overconfidence, not underconfidence.

The pressure of the game is another cause for the appearance of streak shooting. In big games, ESTPs have a tendency to get too hyped, speeding up the tempo to the point of adversely affecting shots and passes. When they do maintain their composure, ESTPs are consistently good shooters, even from long range.

ESTP **Danny Ainge** was one of the NBA's top long-distance shooters before his retirement in 1995.

At the end of the 2002-2003 season, ESTP **Steve Nash** was 7th on the all-time leader list in 3-point shooting percentage, canning 41.8% of his 1361 attempts.

Drive to the Basket

ESTPs have an alternative plan for scoring when their outside shots do not score. They are extremely gifted at taking the ball aggressively to the basket. The rim almost becomes magnet to ESTPs' bodies; they feel pulled to it. ESTPs are aggressive, normally strong, athletic, and love to jump. Add these to ESTPs' exceptional ability to put the necessary spin on the ball off the glass and you come up with supreme drivers to the hoop.

Some of the ESTPs that have shown superior driving abilities throughout their careers include **Elgin Baylor, Gail Goodrich, Walt Frazier, Paul Westphal,** and **Karl Malone.**

ESTPs usually see another benefit of driving to the basket—drawing fouls and going to the charity stripe. ESTPs master this style of play. In 1992, **Karl Malone**, "the Mailman," shot more free throws per minutes played than any other NBA player. ESTP **Sarunas Marciulionis** was second.

Rebounders

ESTPs are bangers; they're not about to back down from anyone. Especially when playing the big man positions, their hulking physiques are capable of moving opponents out from under the boards. Consider the likes of **Wilt Chamberlain, Maurice Lucas, Charles Oakley, Karl Malone,** and **Amare Stoudemire**—typical ESTPs. ESTPs are always at or near the top of the list of the NBA's leading rebounders.

Many people think **Wilt Chamberlain** rebounded superbly due to his stature alone. His size was advantageous, but what made Wilt exceptional was his ESTP Brain Type. Give another Type Wilt's body and, in most cases, you would get far fewer rebounds. (All Extraverted Perceivers [EPs] are designed to be excellent rebounders, ESTPs especially.) Chamberlain led the NBA in rebounding 11 seasons compared to ISTP Moses Malone's 6, ENTP Bill Russell's 4 and INFP Abdul-Jabbar's 1. Wilt averaged nearly 23 rebounds per game during his career! In one game, "the Big Dipper" hauled down 55 rebounds, an NBA record.

Speaking of Wilt, I am reminded of how ESTPs are often big-time dressers and performers (a la **Madonna and Deion Sanders**). Former NBA coach and player, Tom Meschery, said of former teammate, Chamberlain:

> Wilt once told me that if he could be granted one wish in life, he'd like to be invisible for a day, a week, maybe a month. The next time I saw Wilt he was wearing lizard-skin pants and a flowing, multicolored African shirt and we was leading two enormous Afghan hounds down the street on silver chains.[20]

Catalysts

ESTPs are able to come off the bench and create a lot of excitement in a hurry. Their energy, aggressiveness, daring-do, showmanship, and superb fine motor skills are galvinizers to the team.

HELPING ESTPs

As kids and adults, ESTPs are free spirits. They desire to make their own decisions, eschewing close supervision. They are best served by listening to others' *constructive* suggestions and guidelines. At the same time, they will perform best by not introspecting too much. They need to keep in their Extraverted high-energy mode and avoid deep analysis when playing.

ESTPs need to concentrate on playing a controlled game, putting a "governor" of sorts on their tempo.

ISFP

Scorers with Soft Touch

As with all Perceiving types, ISFPs love to shoot the ball. The Introverted, Feeling Perceivers (ISFPs and INFPs) have the softest shooting touches in basketball. INFPs display this many times even with an unorthodox shot, whereas ISFPs have the velvety touch with the more traditional shot. Because ISFPs are adept with their gross motor skills, they can easily achieve an excellent vertical jump and extraordinary body control on a shot. Their shots are fluid, with hand movements secondary big muscle use, which enables them to shoot the ball with the best form possible. **Dale Ellis, Clyde Drexler, Eddie Johnson,** and **Joe Dumars** have been living proof of this.

ISFP **Bob McAdoo** led the NBA in scoring three consecutive years (1974-76). He averaged over 30 points per game in each of those seasons. **Scottie Pippen, Anfernee Hardaway, Kobe Bryant** and **Tim Duncan** are only a few of the more recent ISFPs who have made a major impact on the NBA.

Outstanding Guards

ISFPs and ISTPs tend to dominate the guard positions in the NBA. As Sensing, right-brained players (SPs), they have superior court vision and the ability to make multiple, instantaneous decisions. As Introverts, they tend to play more under control than Extraverted guards.

ISFPs can be sterling ball-handlers. Their dominant Perceiving, right brain dictates that they keep their heads up, trying to see the "floor" at all times. (Judging Types [left-brain persons] will not have this natural tendency.) Seeing the floor is a must for being a first-rate ball handler of any Brain Type.

ISFPs innately possess the ability to spin and control the ball, thanks to the big muscles of the arm. Dribbling is more than utilizing the hands. The forearm, upperarm, and even the body muscles play a critical part. ISFPs coordinate all the necessary motor parts for effective ball-handling, controlling the ball like a yo-yo. ISFPs, like all SFs, will tend to use more of their upper arms in dribbling than other Types. When you combine this with ISFPs' natural ability to see the floor, it is no wonder they are such good ball handlers.

ISFPs are arguably the best jump shooters in the NBA. Their Introversion usually makes the tempo of their shot under control, and their right-brained, gross-motor-skill proficiency (SFP) makes them graceful jump shooters. When their shots begin to go awry, the main problem stems from their dominant Feeling function becoming too heavily engaged. This creates anxiety in ISFPs, resulting in their big muscles stiffening up.

Play Best without a Lot of Structure

ISFPs are one of four Feeling Perceiver Types (ISFP, ESFP, INFP, and ENFP). All these Brain Types are cerebrally designed to perform best in a more unstructured setting, reacting to matters by their adaptable Feelings. When forced to play in a regimented offense, ISFPs find it difficult to reach their potential. ETJ coaches (ESTJ and ENTJ) can especially inhibit their play. The freer style of some NBA teams has been career enhancing as well as career saving for many ISFPs.

One of the NBA's premier guards has been ISFP **Kevin Johnson**. Playing for coach and fellow FP (ENFP) Cotton Fitzsimmons, enabled Kevin to rise to the top of his game.

Defensive Players

The expression often used in basketball to describe a good defensive player, "quick hands," is somewhat of a misnomer. True, some hoopsters have quick hand responses, but the actual catalyst of such moves comes from the arm muscles. Try to swat or catch a fly sometime (the buzzing kind), and you will see that regardless of how quickly you can move your hands, your success is as dependent upon your arm muscles as your hand dexterity.

ISFPs can play exceptional defense when they want to (not always a top priority for them), thanks to their special ability to control their gross motor skills. They are able to steal the ball with hands that are attached to their lickety-split arms. They are also able to stay on the person they are guarding like glue, sliding their bodies with smooth, rapid leg movements. Uniquely gifted in controlling the large leg muscles, ISFPs learn quickly that defense is best played with legs, not arms or hands. **Joe Dumars, Scottie Pippen, Horace Grant and Derrick McKey** are some of the three ISFPs to make the NBA All-Defensive Team in recent years.

Shot-Blockers

Shot-blocking is not only fun but natural for ISFPs. Their control of the big muscles enables them to get high off the floor quickly. They often take great pride in this aspect of the game. Sometimes, however, in their zeal to send the ball back into the shooter's face or into the stands, they disregard their Thinking function. They leave their position in order to block another's shot when they should not or "leave their feet" on a fake shot. With time, ISFPs usually learn from their mistakes.

Energy Savers

Introverts do not possess the cerebral energy of Extraverts when it comes to action in the outer world. On the court, however, they can devote as much energy as an Extravert but not as consistently. Introverts have a built-in mechanism that regulates their expenditure of energy. They save energy until it is needed. ISFPs tend to save energy as much or more than any Type. This may take the form of not trying as hard as the coach wants in practice, or even in a game. The ISFP sees this tactic as a quick breather, whereas the coach may see it as lackadaisical behavior. Not all ISFPs come across this way, especially those raised with a strong work ethic.

The perceived nonchalance of ISFPs may be attributed typologically to their dominant Feeling function. The Feeling preference has a proclivity for harmony with self and others, not often for the "killer instinct" of Thinkers. ISFPs will not be as likely to make every move in basketball as would the "take no hostages" ISTPs (dominant Thinkers). Do not misunderstand, ISFPs may become angry and play with the intensity of an ISTP, but not for as long. Let us remember that ISFPs, as well as other Feeling Types, have a unique basketball giftedness that only they can bring to the game. ISFPs are definitely an asset to any team. They are great athletes and generally likable people.

Shy and Friendly Players

It would be wrong to say that all ISFPs are shy and amiable, but the majority are. As we have seen, Brain Types—including ISFPs, are constant, but their personalities are not. *Environmental differences make it possible to find an outgoing ISFP who is even comfortable among strangers.*

Introverts, by and large, are reticent near strangers and far more outgoing around friends. Anthony Cook, **Sean Elliott's** teammate in college at the University of Arizona, spoke of ISFP Elliott in 1989:

> People look at him and think he is shy, but when he's around the fellows, he's a different person.

Cook went on to say:

> We call him Silly because Sean is silly most of the time.[21]

Elliott was known as the team comedian when he played for the Wildcats. Jud Buechler, another Arizona teammate of Elliott, said:

> Sean has never been egotistical. He has one of the best personalities of anyone I've ever met. He could easily be pompous because it's so obvious that he's in another league. But Sean treats you like another guy.[22]

In 1988, when ISFP **Danny Manning** was playing his first season in the NBA, some media persons questioned his leadership skills and demeanor. Manning responded:

> I'm not shy. I've never been shy. The thing is when you get around the media and you're quiet, they assume you're shy. But I'm not shy at all.[23]

The *L.A. Times* said of Manning at this time:

> He has always been pleasant, unassuming, down to earth, most at home around his friends.[24]

As many Introverts, Danny Manning does not want to be labeled "shy." He may see it as boring and unfriendly. However, the best people to ask for an evaluation of a shy or constrained person are Extraverts. They know what it means to be outgoing and full of energy. Conversely, the best people to ask for an evaluation of someone who is outgoing are Introverts. They understand being more reserved and energy-saving. Generally speaking, ISFPs are very friendly folk who become more reserved in group gatherings—especially when it includes persons other than their friends. Their loudest expressions may be athletic artistry.

HELPING ISFPs

ISFPs can easily lose confidence. They are known to struggle as much as any Brain Type in the area of proper self image. When ISFPs become basketball stars, they will not have the confidence struggles of ISFPs who have yet to make their mark. Nevertheless, they can easily lose their confidence even at the professional level. It is wise for them to get objective, constructive input from those they trust.

ISFP **Sean Elliott**, playing under ENTJ coach Larry Brown of the San Antonio Spurs, said in his rookie season:

> I thought I would be doing better. It's a big adjustment. It's been a roller coaster, emotionally and physically. I play a good game, I feel good, then I have a bad game, and I'm really in the dumps. This league is tough enough without getting down on yourself.[25]

ISFPs, like INFPs, can also use guidance in controlling their Feelings and emotions when playing. Off the floor, they generally wouldn't hurt a fly, but in the heat of battle, they can act atypically. Some ISFPs have been accused of taking cheap shots (physically) at opposing players. This can happen when they get deep into their Introverted Feelings, losing their objectivity.

ESFP

We now look at basketball's "Entertainer," the lively performer, the magician, the consummate showman. The basketball court is the stage on which ESFPs perform. Things begin to happen when they step onto the hardwood. They love, more than any Type, to have their fingers on the ball. When they do, it's show time.

Gross Motor Skills

Like the ISFP, the ESFP is a right-brained athlete with proficient gross motor skills. The ESFP will demonstrate these skills even more than the ISFP. After all, the Extravert has more energy to expend. Consider former NBA All-Star and ESFP **Charles Barkley**. He stood 6-foot-5 yet played "bigger" than a lot of 7-footers in the NBA. Barkley was virtually unstoppable around the basket. Command over his big muscles combined with his high-energy Extraversion produced explosive strength and quickness. He was off the floor before other Types could relay the message from their brains to their legs to jump! If the competition tried to block his shot, they were no match for the energy, power, and control of his largest muscles. Barkley was once asked to rank his body parts. He said:

> Well, Number 1 has to be my legs. I've got supreme confidence in my legs. I'll put my legs up against anybody's . . . .[26]

Though few ESFPs have learned to maximize their legs as much as Barkley, their "wheels" are part of their SF package of gifts.

Consider another ESFP, Mr. Showtime himself, **Magic Johnson**. Over his career, Johnson won the NBA's Most Valuable Player three times while leading the Los Angeles Lakers to five World Championships. Not only was Magic bigger than other NBA guards, he dominated them with the control of his gross motor skills. He often seemed in slow motion as he drove the lane, able to control his entire body. Other Types break down in their gross motor skills in this same situation, often creating a turnover or a jerky shot. Not Magic, or his good friend and fellow ESFP, **Isiah Thomas**. ESFPs are wizards with their entire body movements.

Remember how well Johnson made the hook shot? He didn't use the wrist and fingers primarily as most Types, but used his entire body, enhancing the moves with the big muscles of his arms. Johnson's hook was probably his best shot; few people realize how good it was.

Consider one other tidbit about ESFPs' gross motor skills. Many basketball enthusiasts remember the 1990 NCAA Tournament and the heroics of Loyola Marymount's **Bo Kimble**. Having lost his best friend and teammate, Hank Gathers, to a tragic death on the court, Kimble honored his fallen comrade by shooting a left-handed free throw at the beginning of every game. Not only did he shoot these with his non-dominant hand, he hit them all, under pressure. If you looked closely at Kimble, you could see that he wasn't jerky or wristy with his shot. Instead, his SF mindset allowed him to shoot the ball with his major muscles. His delivery was simple yet highly efficient.

Scorers

Like other Perceiving Types, ESFPs love to shoot the ball and can be excellent shooters. The mechanics of their shot, however, are unique to their SF Type.

Shot mechanics are relatively simple, yet implementing them for a well shot ball is far more complicated. Most coaches dwell too much on the elbow to the finger tips; they would be wise to instruct more on the elbow to the toes. This comes naturally for SFs.

ESFPs, like other SFs, rely primarily on their large body muscles when shooting. They may or may not be aware of this when playing. Not all ESFPs shoot alike—depending on how they learned. Some will be much better shooters than others. They all, however, rely more on their gross motor than fine motor skills.

Getting back to Bo Kimble, he was able to shoot far beyond the range of most guards, even in the NBA. His big muscles enable to him to launch as far as the concession stand. Remember **Isiah Thomas's** outside shot? It was picturesque, graceful and could be accurate from long range.

ESFPs' outside shot can suffer under competitive pressure. The tension created in their Feeling function impairs the shot. The more control they exercise over their mind, the better their shot will hold up under pressure.

Foul Line Lovers

ESFPs can be experts at drawing fouls. They love to go strong to the basket, relying upon their quick reactions, superior peripheral awareness, and domination over their entire body movements.

ESFPs also exaggerate. They've been known to cry out and fall to the floor when bumped slightly. They have a special flair for the dramatic. **Magic Johnson**, as good as he was, still relied upon his thespian ESFP abilities to draw fouls, often hoodwinking referees by flailing his arms and hollering. No one in the NBA has been better at it than Johnson.

Magic Johnson not only learned the art of getting to the line but of making the precision foul shot. He raised his free-throw percentage from 76% in 1980 to nearly 91% in 1991. Johnson used his gross motor skills, especially when shooting foul shots. He pushed the ball with one arm, not relying on the wrists as have STs Larry Bird and Michael Jordan.

ESFP **Oscar Robertson** was named to the All-NBA eleven times in the 1960s and early 1970s. Robertson holds the NBA record for most free throws attempted, 22, and most free throws made, 19 in one half. Oscar is the all-time NBA leader in free throws made by a guard.

Assist-makers

Who comes to mind when you think of the top four, all-time assist leaders? Except for ISTP John Stockton, all are ESFPs. **Magic Johnson** established the all-time career assist record in 1991, formerly held by "the Big O," **Oscar Robertson**. (Stockton broke Johnson's record in 1995.) Robertson led the NBA in assists six times. Fourth on the list is **Isiah Thomas**. Assists are not limited to ESFPs, yet nobody enjoys dishing out the basketball more. Their statistics are the proof. Provided he stays healthy, newcomer **LeBron James** will become the next ESFP assist phenom.

The vital ingredient in being a top-notch assist maker comes from a man who holds the record for the most assist titles, eight. ENTP Bob Cousy, the inventor of the creative assist, has said: "Court awareness is the key."[27] According to Mr. Cousy, in conjunction with the material in this book thus far, which Brain Types would then be best at assists? If you answered right hemisphere dominant Types, the Perceptive Ps, you are correct. The top ten career assist leaders of all-time are all right-brained, spatial Ps. (By the way, even ESTP Wilt Chamberlain, all 7' 1" of him, led the league in assists in the 1967-68 season. He did it to prove to critics that he was not a selfish player. After demonstrating his point, he never reached the top 10 in assists again.)

Defense; Rebounders

ESFPs, like other Ps, generally prefer the offensive end of the floor. For the ESFP, it's pretty hard to do "showtime" on defense. Or so it was until defensive specialist and ESFP, **Dennis Rodman**, came along. Failing to develop his offensive skills when growing up (a rarity for ESFPs), yet tremendously athletic, Rodman found his place on the basketball floor. His leaping ability allowed him to score on shots close to the basket and be an outstanding shot blocker—even at 6-foot-7. Realizing his offensive skills would never get him recognized in the NBA, Rodman decided to concentrate his effort on defense. Gaining recognition in this area with Michael Cooper, Michael Jordan and other defensive aces, would be a major undertaking. But leave it to the highly-energetic ESFP Rodman; he won the NBA's Defensive Player of the Year in 1990 and again in 1991. By 1996, he made the NBA All-Defensive team 8 consecutive years.

Dennis played defense primarily with his feet and legs, sliding like a shadow on the man he is guarding. His ESFP body skills were used to "cut off the lane," "take charges," "block shots," and perform every other conceivable defensive feat. Anyone wanting to improve his or her defensive skills would do well to watch Dennis Rodman. If you have access to footage while he played, notice his prance as he ran the floor. He was like a show horse in competition. His major muscle control was something to behold. In addition, notice his Feeling smile. Although Rodman and other ESFPs have been known to "lose it," particularly in big games, it is sometimes refreshing to see some levity and charm amid the seriousness of the NBA. (Magic and Isiah were smilers, too. **LeBron James** is the latest heralded and smiling ESFP.) After all, it is only a game.

In 1992, Dennis Rodman demonstrated his ESFP potential in yet another way. At only 6' 7", he relied upon his desire and quickly reacting gross motor skills to lead the NBA in rebounding, with 18.7 per game! NBA executive Bob Bass said in 1992:

> I really believe that when the ball is two feet out of the shooter's hand, Rodman has the judgment to know if it's going to be short, long left, short right, whatever. He gets the best jump on the ball in the NBA, just like Willie [Mays] did in baseball.[28] (Insert added.)

(Bass was astute in his comparison of Mays and Rodman, both ESFPs!) Rodman continued his rebounding heroics by winning his seventh consecutive title in 1998.

Big-game Performers

ESFPs love to play in the big games, galvanized by the drama, excitement, and crowd approval. There are too many occasions to recall of ESFPs' big game heroics, but a few come easily to mind. I'll never forget **Magic Johnson's** Herculean effort in the final game of the 1980 Championship Series. Playing all five positions, he almost single-handedly beat the Philadelphia 76ers, giving the Los Angeles Lakers the title. He was a kid in a candy store, virtually unstoppable.

Isiah Thomas won the MVP of the 1990 NBA finals. He led his Detroit Pistons over the Portland Trailblazers for their second consecutive championship title. Thomas's regular season statistics had been below par, but the magnitude of the post-season play enabled him to show his true potential. He was awe-inspiring.

HELPING ESFPs

Pressure can also have a major negative impact on ESFPs in the closing moments of highly important games. ESFPs perform best by being aggressive and reacting to whatever comes their way. When they are forced to slow play down and do a lot of Thinking, their performances suffer. They must stay loose, not deviating much from their normal free-flowing style of play.

If ESFPs choose to play guard, they may have greater potential in the NBA at the point than the shooting guard. To play their best away from the basket, they need to handle the ball regularly, which the point position affords. To play the shooting guard, they must be willing to practice long hours on their outside shots.

ISTJ

Competitors

ISTJs who possess good round-ball skills enjoy the manifold ways basketball allows them to utilize their mental and physical dexterity. Their left-brain dominance will yield a more mechanical approach than the right-brained ISTP. Nevertheless, the ISTJ can perform as superbly and tenaciously as the ISTP, though not as often with the "killer instinct."

ISTJs need to have a substantial challenge to achieve peak performance. As dominant Sensates in their Introverted world, they prefer observing matters in a reflective, low-keyed way. They enjoy soaking up Sensing information. Yet all Introverts must deal with the outer, Extraverted world. For ISTJs, this pulls them into their secondary, Extraverted Thinking function, which requires additional loads of energy from them. ISTJs can supply the energy, but not for as long as Extraverts.

When a big game is on the line, ISTJs give their absolute best. Peak motivation comes from the meaning they have attached to the event. ISTJs' pain threshold is higher during important games. This pattern of behavior fits all Types but especially ISTJs.

Former UNLV (University of Nevada at Las Vegas) player Larry Johnson (ISTP) spoke in 1990 of teammate and ISTJ, **Stacey Augmon**:

> I remember the finals of the World University Games (in West Germany). It was [against] the Russians. Stacey had lost to the Russians on the Olympic team, and a couple of them were smiling at him, like they were remembering what happened. Well, Stacey just went crazy when the game started. He went dunking for the first 10 baskets of the game, seemed like. We won—it was like Stacey said, 'You can laugh now, but not later.' That's just him. He accepts all challenges.[29] (Insert added.)

Defensive Specialists

ISTJs are defensive specialists, but not because they possess the greatest motor skills for the task. Their proficiency comes from their "protector," conservative, defensive mindset and their hand-eye coordination. (Actually, all the SP Brain Types are as good, or even better, with their "defensive" motor skills than ISTJs. SPs, however, normally do not have the ISTJ's defensive mentality.)

Michael Cooper, who in 1990 left the Los Angeles Lakers after 12 seasons, was a true testimony to the ISTJ's defensive skills and mentality. Michael was named eight times to the NBA's all-defensive team, five times on the first team. He accomplished this though rarely being found in the starting lineup! Playing guard at 6 feet 7 and 175 pounds, Cooper is second in steals and third in blocked shots in the Laker record book. Teammate and close friend, Magic Johnson, said of Michael's team departure:

> One thing I won't miss, though, is getting smacked by Coop in practice.[30]

Magic knew, as well as anyone, the defensive skill and intensity of Michael Cooper, an ISTJ. Steve Springer, *L.A. Times* staff writer, said of Cooper:

> Abdul Jabbar was bigger, Magic Johnson more talented, Jamaal Wilkes smoother, James Worthy quicker and Kurt Rambis stronger, but none seemed to embody the spirit of the NBA's dominant team of the 1980s as much as Cooper.[31]

Assistant general manager Mitch Kupchak said at Cooper's last Lakers press conference:

> There's going to be something that's missing that can't be replaced. That's a special guy over there. There's an awful lot of heart over there that doesn't show up in the box score.[32]

These words typify many ISTJs. Larry Bird said that Michael Cooper was the NBA's best defensive player of Bird's era.[33]

Stacey Augmon, an ISTJ defensive specialist in college, said:

> I take more pride in my defense than my offense . . . my role on this team (UNLV) is as the defensive stopper and to put a little points on the board and that's what I did. I enjoy playing defense.[34]

ISTJ **Bobby Jones**, former Philadelphia 76er star, was named to the NBA All-Defensive First Team for a record 8 years straight. And who can forget **Kurt Rambis's** days with the L.A. Lakers? The Clark Kent look-alike was known for his kamikaze approach to the game, particularly on defense. Teammate James Worthy said of him:

> He had a style of his own. Nobody dove the floor like Kurt. Nobody got people going like he did.[35]

No Type overall is more committed to defense than the ISTJ. (It is no small wonder typological studies done in the U.S. military reveal more ISTJs than any other Brain Type.)

Potential Scorers

ISTJs can be scorers, too. They need to be encouraged, however, from the very beginning of their basketball careers to shoot the ball, not only in practice but in games. ISTJs **Jeff Hornacek** and **Steve Kerr** have proven their NBA offensive abilities, especially from long range.

Jay Burson, graduate of Ohio State University in 1989, knew how to put the ball in the hole. Unfortunately, a severe neck injury put a major road block to his NBA career. Jay stood barely 6 feet and weighed 155 pounds (another slender ISTJ). He averaged 22 points a game his senior year with the Buckeyes before his injury at the end of the season. And in his entire high school career, Burson averaged 33 points per game, more than one per minute! He also was twice named Ohio's Class AA Player of the year and became the top scorer in Ohio high school history.

If other players on the team are good shooters and smart players, ISTJs will often allow them to do the majority of scoring. Unselfishly, the ISTJ shores up the defense most others are unwilling to properly play. When a game with significant meaning takes place, however, the ISTJ is on immediate call to lend major assistance to the scoring machine.

Good Shooters

ISTJs are more mechanical in their shooting style than most Perceiving Types, but they can be dead eye shooters. Many observers can quickly see ISTJs' shooting accuracy but cannot figure out why they don't shoot more. Remember, ISTJs generally feel comfortable playing defense or sharing the offensive load. They do not like making mistakes and they find they make fewer on defense. ISTJs are normally outstanding team players; they do not mind feeding the ball to the more assertive, "give-me-the-ball" shooting Types.

ISTJs also like to please the coaching staff. They generally are obedient, supportive ballplayers. They will not fire up a shot or improvise a pass as readily as many other Types. Their desire is to accommodate the game plan.

ISTJs' dexterity and hand-eye coordination enable them to develop an outstanding shot. They love the open jumper or set shot which they can drill. They cannot naturally shoot the running fall-away or off-balance shot as well as the acrobatic Ps. They prefer squaring up to the basket, not rushing the shot.

During his NBA days, **Jeff Hornacek** was one of the premier shooting guards in the NBA. In 1990, he averaged nearly 18 points per game, leading all NBA guards in field goal percentage, hitting .538 from the field. In a poll of NBA managers, head coaches and assistant coaches, Hornacek was named the league's most underrated player. In 1991, Hornacek shot 51.8% from the floor, finished third in three-point field goal percentage in the NBA, and hit nearly 90% of his foul shots. In 1992, he virtually duplicated his previous year stats—shooting 51.2% from the floor, finishing third in three point percentage again, and hitting 88.6% of his foul shots. By 1996, Hornacek was still shooting with excellence, hitting 50.2% from the floor and 89.3% from the line.

ISTJs are excellent long range shooters due to their superb fine motor skills and dexterity. In 1990, ISTJ **Steve Kerr** led the NBA in three-point field-goal percentage at nearly 51%. By 1995, Kerr was still canning threes and even set the NBA single-season record at 52.4%. Retiring after the 2002-2003 season, Steve Kerr held the career record for highest three-point field-goal percentage at 45.4%.

ISTJ guard **Kyle Macy** led the NBA in free throw percentage twice (1981-82 and 1984-85).

Team Players

ISTJs, as much as any Type, exemplify team spirit. Their mindset is to consider the team's good ahead of personal benefit (unless their upbringing has instilled self centered ambition). This unselfish attitude will manifest itself on both ends of the court, something unique in a sport that is dominated by offensive minded Brain Types. Former hoopsters **John Wooden and Mike Krzyzewski** are just two ISTJs who carried their innate "team concept" into coaching.

HELPING ISTJs

In their formative years, ISTJs need to be encouraged to be assertive, to exorcise their reluctant leadership skills. They need to realize it's okay to make mistakes and miss shots. Even the best players have their periods of failure.

ISTJ **Jeff Hornacek** was a role model for his Type. He was a walk-on at Iowa State. He made the team and rode the pine until he got a chance to start a game. Performing so well that he played the entire 40 minutes, Jeff was named player of the game. He started from that point forward and went on to set Big Eight assists records for a season and a career. In a similar manner, Hornacek fought his way to NBA stardom.

ISTJs' fine motor dexterity can sometimes be counterproductive. ISTJs have a tendency to shoot the ball partly with the non dominant hand, which is meant to guide the ball, not to propel it. This somewhat two handed shot can lessen accuracy. Shooting exercises that emphasize the proper technique will be helpful.

ESTJ

Guess what happens to the style of play in basketball when you drop the I and add the E to STJ? You get a very different player. ESTJs play the game of basketball as they do any other sport—with zeal and aggression. Their philosophy of "overpowering is the best way to win" does not work well in hoops. ESTJs must learn that to progress in basketball, they must keep their aggression in check.

Good Outside Shots

ESTJs can develop a good shooting touch at an early stage. Their dominant ST fine motor skills make it possible to develop the necessary hand and wrist movements to perfect the shot—both with the shooting and guide hands. ESTJs have exceptionally strong hands and wrists, enabling them to shoot from long distance. With their superior fine motor dexterity and left-brained mechanical style, ESTJs can learn quickly how to place and control the guide hand for optimal shooting. As fine motor specialists, ESTJs must minimize the strength and action of the guide hand, keeping it from projecting the ball—which is the responsibility of the shooting and dominant hand. A way to measure if the guide hand is working properly on the shot is that it should not turn toward the basket on the follow through; rather, the side of the hand and little finger should still be facing the hoop. When this technique is learned, ESTJs are on their way to becoming very good shooters.

Sometimes ESTJs carry the outside shot too far. Big ESTJs often realize they lack finesse around the basket. They may then rely upon making their trusty fall-away jump shot than on taking the ball directly to the basket.

Pressure can greatly affect the ESTJ's shot. Not possessing the softer "P" touch of right-brained players, ESTJs easily become rigid at "nervous time." They're wise to take the high percentage shot or pass the ball when succumbing to pressure.

Insecurity in Disguise

Because ESTJs have strong convictions, aggressiveness, and orderliness in their lives, they appear self confident. But they aren't always. ESTJs are so in tune with reality and have such a drive to organize and control it, they often feel insecure in their abilities to do it all. Even though ESTJs look like bedrock, on the inside they're often like clay. In this condition, they will be less open to constructive criticism and may become verbally defensive.

Team Players

ESTJs, like other SJs, are strong supporters of the institution, organization, or team. They're conservators, normally committed to protecting the team. Though the larger ESTJs may make clumsy mistakes and play like football players on the basketball court sometimes, ESTJs usually think team first, personal glory second.

Much in Demand

Even though ESTJs do not have the graceful and offensive skills of many Perceiving Types, they're valuable, even to the NBA. Many teams want what an ESTJ has to offer and are willing to pay handsomely to get it. ESTJs have been known to sign big contracts even when their statistics and overall play seem not to warrant them.

OBSTACLES

Many NBA stars have a problem admitting when they foul. Understanding their Brain Type sheds light on this tendency. Left-brained ESTJs foul more than the average Type and don't perceive their actions as accurately as many right-brained players. They also play with such mechanical aggressiveness that they don't realize they've banged people.

HELPING ESTJs

ESTJs need as much help the mental approach as with the physical in virtually every sport. They need to learn how to control their anxiety, making it a priority to stay loose physically. (The mental section in this book will be of assistance.) You can imagine how difficult it is to dribble and shoot if your body is filled with tension.

Developing greater spatial awareness is helpful for ESTJs. Their nature is to rely too heavily on the left brain. By "seeing the floor" and responding, they will perform more smoothly and skillfully.

Big ESTJs need to work on their moves around the basket, giving extra effort to low-post moves and shots. This will help them overcome their preference to shoot fall-aways—sacrificing the higher percentage shots.

It is rare to find ESTJs in the NBA other than at the center position. Their Type is not as good at the other spots, especially point guard. The physical, mental, and spatial demands are not as high on ESTJs at the high school or collegiate level.

ISFJ

Defensive Mentality

Basketball is a sport that especially demonstrates the defensive talents of ISFJs. They normally play defense properly, using their strong, SF legs to keep the player they're guarding from the basket. Yet they need to work hard at developing lateral quickness—due to their mechanical SF movements. ISFJs are unselfish players, looking for ways to complement their teammates. They feel they can do this best by playing good defense. If ISFJs begin basketball at an early age and with good coaching, they can develop a finely-tuned offensive game.

Andrew Lang, Alton Lister, Acie Earl, P.J. Brown, and **Dale Davis** are ISFJs who have had success in recent NBA history. The few ISFJs found in the NBA will be at either the center or forward positions; you will never find one at point guard.

ESFJ

Not many ESFJs are in the NBA, but they can make their presence known. They're normally high-energy performers with good SF body strength and balance. Normally known for their defense, ESFJs value the team concept. As left-brained players, their movements may appear mechanical. ESFJs can be found at every NBA position except point guard. ESFJs in recent NBA history have included **Rasheed Wallace, John (Hot Rod) Williams, Eddy Curry, Charles Shackleford, Duane Causwell, Bobby Phills, Donald Royal, Alan Henderson,** and **David Wingate**.

Helping ESFJs

With a lot of practice, ESFJs can be good shooters in basketball. They tend to shoot more from the palm than the finger tips as they should. It is important to understand how ESFJs' proficient gross motor skills can sometimes be counterproductive. ESFJs will find it helpful to learn shooting exercises emphasizing the proper fingertip release and making sure the palm of the left or guide hand (in a right-hander's case) does not turn toward the basket on the shot, but rather the heel of the left hand stays lined up facing the basket. The ball should be released off the index and middle fingers, not the last two fingers. This will give them the proper rotation on the ball—something they often lack.

ESFJs can be good three-point shooters. When their shots begin to go awry, the main problem stems from their Feeling function, where it becomes too heavily engaged. This creates anxiety in ESFJs, resulting in their big muscles stiffening and the shot fading quickly. ESFJs must learn to relax when shooting.

ESFJs are *not* naturally gifted at "seeing the floor," being left-brained dominant players. Their innate peripheral awareness and spatial abilities are not as natural as some other Types. *If they place a premium on court awareness and making good passes, they can become proficient in these areas.*

ESFJs can play top-notch defense when they want to, utilizing their dominant gross motor movements and left-brained awareness. If they work on their quickness, they will be able to stay on opponents, sliding their body with SF leg movements. Uniquely gifted in controlling the large leg muscles, ESFJs learn that defense is best played with the legs, not the arms or hands.

ESFJs are usually good jumpers, thanks to their adept gross motor skills. Their Feeling function will inhibit them from being consistently aggressive on the boards, however. They do not like to punish others or get the ball at all costs as much as some other Types. ESFJs may also have to work on developing fingertip control. As SFs, the hands are not their best body strength.

ESFJs as Feelers often play according to their moods. It is important to regularly make sure that things are going well for them on and off the floor. SFs value expressions of appreciation that are personal. They respond best to praise and to people who really believe in them. SFs are Feeling Types, and are more sensitive to criticism than Thinking Types. Negative criticism often discourages SFs. If they must be dealt with sternly, a personal touch within 24 hours will help them understand their rebuke, and greatly aid in getting them back on track again, physically and emotionally. A wise coach can inspire ESFJs to play at high levels of intensity. ESFJs are results-oriented whereas the right-brained Ps are more process-driven.

ENTJ

Abstract Intelligence

ENTJs' strongest contribution to the game of basketball, as with other sports, is their conceptually logical Thinking. ENTJs are able to develop first rate motor movements, but it is their minds they trust most. Their NT mental acumen will tell them at any given point throughout the game what is the best possible shot, pass, defensive strategy, and so forth. Being master strategists, ENTJs use their intelligence to advance in life regardless of vocation. It is no small wonder that former basketball great, ENTJ, **Bill Bradley**, earned a Rhodes Scholarship and later became a U.S. Senator.

Competitors with Coordination

ENTJs are highly competitive people. As long as they believe they are competent in competition, they will not give up. ENTJs will practice for hours on end, doing whatever it takes to attain competency, striving to be the best at what they do. They bring their tenacity for succeeding to the hardwood. If there is any possible way to overcome the opponent with their minds, they will find it.

ENTJs can develop coordination in their moves and shots as well as, if not better than, ESTJs. With their fine motor skill proficiency, it would appear ESTJs have the advantage in these areas. Unfortunately, ESTJs tend to tense up too much when they play basketball, not allowing their body movements to perform as smoothly as they could.

ENTJs, on the other hand, do not have the strong motor control of the ESTJs. Yet ENTJs often perform more fluidly because their bodies are more relaxed and in sync. They may not play as smoothly as many right-brained P Types, but they are able to perform with excellent coordination.

Offensive-minded

ENTJs love to shoot the ball. To their minds, shooting and scoring demonstrate superior play over the defender, ensure victory by high percentage shooting, control the tone for the game, bring recognition for competent play, and establish one's leadership on the floor with fellow teammates. The points tallied have great depth of meaning to them.

Many ENTJs have revealed their offensive talents over the years. One of the best has been the indomitable Rick Barry. **Richard Francis Dennis Barry, III**, was elected to the Naismith Memorial Basketball Hall of Fame in 1986. He played four years in the now defunct ABA, averaging nearly 30 points per game. In the NBA, he made the All-NBA Team six times and was NBA Rookie of the Year in 1966. Rick led the NBA in scoring in 1967, with a 35 points per game average. Barry was not afraid to shoot the ball. He once set an NBA records for most field-goal attempts in a championship series game, with 48!

ENTJ **Jerry Lucas** was the *Sporting News* College Player of the year in 1961 and 1962. He led the NCAA for two seasons in rebounding and three years in field goal percentage. In the pros, he made the All-NBA Team five times and was NBA Rookie-of-the-Year in 1964.

Kevin McHale and Tom Chambers are two modern era ENTJs who were able to shoot and score. Playing in his first NBA All-Star game in 1990, Kevin Johnson was asked if he sought any advice from fellow Phoenix Sun teammate and three-time All-Star, ENTJ **Tom Chambers**. Johnson said:

> Yes. Tom just told me to get him the ball as much as I can.[36]

As I have said, ENTJs love to shoot the ball. The 6-foot-10 Tom Chambers scored a career-high 56 points in 1990 against the Golden State Warriors (Manute Bol and all). Chambers said:

> In my nine years in the league I haven't felt better about my shot than I did today.[37]

Opponent, Mitch Richmond, commented:

> We were playing pretty well, but he was on fire.[38]

ENTJs love to score and when they're on a roll, it's lights out.

Excellent Foul Shooters

Many ENTJs have been superb foul shooters over their careers, regardless of their form. **Rick Barry** has proven to be the best. Leave it to an ENTJ to be different, unique in his ways. Barry was the master of the underhand shot. He led the NBA in free-throw percentage six times and the ABA three times. Barry is ranked second in career NBA free throw percentage, at 90 percent. (Only ISTP Mark Price has been better.)

No one before or since Rick Barry has perfected the underhand foul shot. Have you ever wondered why? I have two guesses, the second being the more significant. First, players like to stay with their regular shooting style (and they think underhand looks kinda goofy).

Two, I believe only a certain Brain Type or two could pull it off. Because ENTJs are *not* born with the dominant motor skills of most other Types, they are quite capable of coordinating their body movements from both sides of the body with superb control. I have observed this with ENTJs in many sports. To excel at underhand shooting, the hands and arms must work in unison. One side of the body cannot dominate. Remember Wilt Chamberlain's underhand foul shot? Though Wilt's efforts were quite dismal, I am sure he was better at the shot in practice than in games. The pressure of the crowd often caused the fine-motor skilled ESTP to lose his two handed unity and revert to his dominant right side. Things got so bad for Wilt that Philadelphia 76ers' owner Ike Richman sent him to a psychiatrist to iron out his problems. Chamberlain later said:

> After two months that sucker, the psychiatrist, was a great foul shooter, and I was doing my same thing.[39]

If ENTJs opt to shoot the underhand foul shot, I believe the earlier in life they begin, the more proficient they will become.

Three-Point Shooters

ENTJs are among basketball's top three point shooters. They are able to control their motor movements superbly without too much tension. ENTJs can develop phenomenal confidence—an essential ingredient for good shooting.

Even 6-foot-10 **Kevin McHale** finally discovered, after ten seasons in the league, he could shoot "threes." In 1990, he became one of the NBA's leading three-point shooters. Quoting ENTJ McHale:

> I should have been shooting threes my whole career. I started late. I didn't realize how much fun it is to shoot threes. It's kind of like a guy on his death bed discovering ice cream.[40]

Kevin's NT wit often matched his extraordinary abilities on the floor, making him one of the most quotable players in the game. McHale utilized his strategic intellect for years in the low post and paint—mastering the pump fake, the drop step, the baby hook and various other moves. He used his head to trick more people than Orson Wells did on that memorable Halloween radio broadcast, many years ago. If you missed that one, he simulated an alien invasion to the alarm of many solid citizens.

High-Percentage Shooters

ENTJs can be high percentage shooters, particularly in the low post. They rely upon their smarts to take the highest-percentage shots. **Kevin McHale** led the NBA in field-goal percentage two different years, shooting over 60 percent. He has shot over 56 percent for his career.

ENTJs' shooting percentage will noticeably drop when they become less team-oriented. Those ENTJs who keep the team's welfare foremost in mind will generally take high percentage shots or look for the open shooter.

Potentially Good Defenders

ENTJs, when they have the desire, can be capable defensive players. **Kevin McHale** made the NBA All-Defensive Team six times and **Dave Cowens** three times. ENTJs can access their high energy and intelligence to play defense as well as offense—though they don't often care to. With speed and quickness becoming more valued in the modern NBA game, ENTJs are not found as often as they once were, nor are their defensive skills as effective.

Captains of Their Own Ships

There is no Brain Type that tries to be more in control of their destiny than ENTJs. They live for their future ambitions, relying upon no one but themselves to get there. To say they can be independent of others is an understatement.

ENTJs abhor being controlled by anyone but themselves. When they sense others are trying to manipulate them, they will do all they can to break that bondage, even if it sometimes means doing something radical to defy tradition or directives toward them.

Consider what some ENTJ NBAers have done over the years in pursing their goals. In each case, they felt they were doing what was best, long term, for their careers. Duke University graduate, **Danny Ferry**, the No. 2 pick overall in the 1989 NBA draft, decided to snub the Los Angeles Clippers in favor of the Italian basketball league. Only Ferry knows the real reasons he defied the NBA tradition, but he left no doubt as to who was in charge of Danny Ferry's life.

Graduating from Princeton University in the mid-1960s, **Bill Bradley** was recognized as the best college player in the land. Bradley also established himself academically, fully utilizing his ENTJ aptitude. Despite his hardcourt stardom, he chose to accept a Rhodes Scholarship over a chance to play professional ball. Upon completing his studies in 2½ years, Bradley joined the New York Knicks. He was not afraid to do what he thought was best for his life, even though it could have cost him a bundle. To this day, Bradley continues his ENTJ focus and drive. He is a former U.S. Senator from New Jersey with a chance of someday being addressed as "Mr. President." After all, his ENTJ Brain Type is the most formidable of politicians. (ENTJs include **Franklin Roosevelt, John Kennedy, Ronald Reagan, Bill Clinton** and **George W. Bush**.)

ENTJ **Rick Barry** captained his own ship and sat out the 1967-68 season with the San Francisco Warriors in order to play in the ABA in 1968. Suffice it to say, ENTJs are independent persons.

HELPING ENTJs

ENTJs need to persevere in developing their motor skills, including dribbling proficiently with both hands. The better motor movements are mastered, the more able they will be to implement their superior mental dexterity.

ENTJs, like ESTJs, will benefit by developing greater spatial awareness on the basketball floor. By keeping their heads up and responding to situations, they will enhance their performances. Sticking with inappropriate pre-planned movements may be their downfall.

ENTJs would do well not to admonish other teammates or referees in competition. Even if they're right with their corrections, they often end up winning battles and losing wars.

ENTP

The more I've researched ENTPs in the NBA, the more I've discovered their plentiful presence; they are one of the most frequently found Brain Types. For those familiar with typology, this may come as a surprise. One might ask, "How can the cerebral ENTP be so successful in such an athletic sport?"

ENTPs are frequently found on college teams due to their superior intellect, not necessarily true athleticism. Many players found among the top athletic Brain Types never make it to college; they fail to meet entrance requirements or maintain academic standards. (In pro baseball, for example, there are many more of the top athletic Types. They're often drafted out of high school.)

When NBA pre-Draft camps take place each year, ENTPs are invited more than any other Type. At the 1997 Chicago camp, witnessed only by NBA personnel, I determined that 30 percent of the invitees were ENTPs, compared to only 5 percent ISTPs. Yet ISTPs are clearly the NBA's most dominant Type, and they account for roughly the same percentage as ENTPs in the U.S. populace. Unfortunately, ISTPs and a number of other Types often have difficulty entering and staying in college.

ENTPs are rarely NBA superstars, but they can be very good players. They are high-energy people and possess tremendous agility and flexibility (due to their iNtuitive right-brained motor skills). ENTPs can be very smart players, understanding the game like those who coach them. As right-brained Perceivers with adept visual awareness, ENTPs can be top-notch passers. ENTP greats of yesteryear include **Bill Russell** and **Bob Cousy**. Contemporary accomplished ENTPs include high-flyin' **Vince Carter, Glenn "Big Dog" Robinson,** and **Michael Finley**. Other ENTP notables have included big men **Arvydas Sabonis** and **Vin Baker**, and European import and sharpshooter **Predrag Stojakovic**.

Point Guards

In recent NBA years, ENTPs have made an impact at point guard. Their quickness, high-energy efforts, passing abilities, and scoring mindsets are valued by many teams. Some ENTPs include **Damon Stoudamire, Nick Van Exel, Avery Johnson,** and **Sam Cassell**. Under pressure, ENTPs may not be as reliable as ISTPs, for ENTPs have a tendency to try to do too much with the ball, getting out of control. When ENTPs maintain the team focus and play within themselves, they can be among the best point guards.

HELPING ENTPs

ENTPs need to persevere in developing their motor skills, including dribbling proficiently with both hands. The better motor movements are mastered, the more able they will be to implement their superior mental dexterity.

Since ENTPs have exceptionally flexible body movements, they often have difficulty developing solid shot mechanics. Building shot fundamentals according to their unique Brain Type will yield more consistent and triumphant shots. ENTPs cannot be as successful as some other Types with unusual shot mechanics.

ENTPs would do well to let the coaches run the team and save their ideas for infrequent and appropriate times of discussion. Though ENTPs often have excellent insight, they must be cautious how and when they share it.

INFP

Finesse Scorers

No Brain Type in the game of basketball displays more finesse and body harmony than the INFP. INFPs are as smooth as silk. Their court demeanor is generally mild-mannered and not to be mistaken for the passion of your aggressive enforcers. It is remarkable how many INFPs have made it to the ranks of the NBA considering they approximate only 2 percent of the American populace. INFP **Julius Erving (Dr. J)** and Michael Jordan, ISTP, are two of the greatest players to have laced up the hightops. Yet can you think of ways in which they differed in their playing style?

John (Red) Kerr has watched Jordan play hoops ever since Michael's days at North Carolina. As general manager of the former pro team, the Virginia Squires, Kerr signed Julius Erving out of the University of Massachusetts. In 1990, announcing for the Chicago Bulls, Kerr said:

> There's no comparison. Michael is a vicious offensive player. Doc was never a vicious player. He was a finesse player.[41]

Dr. J is one of only seven players to average more than 20 points and 20 rebounds per game during their NCAA career. He then played five years in the ABA where he led the league in scoring three times. In 1976, he joined the Philadelphia 76ers where he finished out his 11-year NBA career, averaging 22 points per game. "The Doctor" made the All-NBA Team 7 times.

Another smooth INFP, **Kareem Jabbar**, has probably had the greatest impact on NBA history. Jabbar, voted the NBA's Most Valuable Player six times, made the All-NBA Team 15 times and the NBA All-Defensive Team 11 times. "Captain Hook" set NBA records for most seasons played, most games played, most minutes played, most points, most field goals attempted, most field goals made, and most blocked shots. Not bad for a low-keyed INFP.

Great Shooters

INFPs are outstanding shooters; they can compete with any Type. In the paint, near the basket, or beyond three point range, INFPs can shoot the ball accurately and artistically.

INFPs often shoot, particularly around the basket, with arms stretched high, whereas other Types usually bend the elbow more. Three INFPs have especially demonstrated this in recent NBA history: **Kareem Jabbar, Alex English,** and **Jeff Malone.** These three have played in the center, forward and guard positions, yet all were known for their finesse, soft touch, and shots with outstretched arms. Jabbar had his amazing hook. Dead-eye's English and Malone reached for the sky in their follow throughs. Not all INFPs shoot with extended upper limbs, but many do. They're the best Type at it.

Instant Scorers

INFPs are often known for their ability to score points quickly. This speaks well not only for their ability to score but also for their willingness to shoot the ball. Some bystanders even wonder if INFPs remember they have teammates because they're often reluctant to share the ball. Whatever the case, they can rack up points as fast as any Type.

INFP **Terry Teagle** demonstrated his ability to "light it up" while playing with the Golden State Warriors and Los Angeles Lakers. When Teagle was playing for Golden State, he once scored 36 points—in one half! I'm entertained by the way Teagle explained how he can have a spurt like that:

I consider offense my defense. I can run the court quicker than my man. I keep running and wear down the bigger guys' legs.[42]

When the 6-foot-5 Teagle played forward, he was usually guarded by bigger players. Nevertheless, INFPs love to run the floor, shoot the ball, and play offense more than defense. In his college days at Baylor University, Teagle became the Southwest Conference's all time leading scorer, averaging nearly 20 points per game over a four-year period.

INFP **Cedric Ceballos** knew how to score. Few could put the ball in the basket as fast as he could. INFP **Dennis Scott** was the fourth overall player selected in the 1990 NBA draft. He capped his first year in the pros by making the NBA All-Rookie Team, a first team selection. Following a 34-point performance against the L.A. Lakers, rookie Dennis Scott was lauded by Magic Johnson who guarded him:

> It didn't matter. Draped on him, hanging on him, oh man . . . It was one of the great exhibitions of shooting I've seen because nothing we did made a difference.[43]

Magic Johnson's teammate, James Worthy, spoke of newcomer Dennis Scott:

> He's a scorer. He reminds me of Purvis Short or Alex English or even Bernard King in his young days.[44]

INFP **Alex English** led the NBA in scoring in 1983 with a 28.4 point average. Over his 15 year NBA career, Alex tallied some 22 points a game!

Unorthodox Shots

Typology suggests that INFPs prefer showing their iNtuition to the outer world while generally hiding their more Introverted Feelings. I would concur. INFPs are able to show their creative side in a number of ways. INFP actor **Richard Chamberlain** has done a masterful job of performing virtually every conceivable kind of personality. INFPs in basketball are no exception. They can create highly productive shots, passes, and moves. Being orthodox is not of concern to creative INFPs.

Can you remember the accurate, unorthodox shot of former NBA star, INFP **Jammal Wilkes**? You'll never find a coach teaching that style of shooting. INFP Wilkes was a deadly shooter.

How about Dr. **Julius Erving**? Would you say he possessed some inborn creativity when he took the ball to the hole? The Doc's INFP dunks were great, but how he pulled them off was even better.

INFPs also practice unorthodox shots. Don Nelson coached **Terry Teagle** at Golden State:

> When Terry is on a roll he can make shots others shouldn't even try. The other guys might wonder why they're not allowed to shoot off the wrong foot or from some crazy angles, but Terry has shown he can make them. So I gave him carte blanche.[45]

Simply stated, INFPs are imaginative and accurate on the hardwood. Star **Grant Hill** (INFP) has proven this.

Three-point Shooters

It's debatable which Type is the best 3 point shooter. Arguably, ISTPs are the best under pressure. But INFPs are good, too. **Craig Hodges**, INFP, led the NBA in three-point field goal percentages twice, in 1986 and 1988. He placed second in 1990, keeping his career three point percentage above 40 percent. At the 1992 NBA's annual three-point shootout, Hodges won his third consecutive title and joined Larry Bird as the only three time winners.

INFP **Trent Tucker** was consistently one of the NBA's top three-point shooters, averaging more than 40 percent for his career. In 1986, he placed second in NBA three-point percentages, shooting .45055 to winner **Craig Hodges'** .45062. Less than one one-hundredth of a percent separated the two INFPs. **Dennis Scott**, despite his 6' 8" frame, was a superb three-point shooter in college and continued to demonstrate his INFP abilities in the NBA.

INFP **Vlade Divac**, the NBA's Yugoslavian transplant, measures in at 7-foot-1 and 250 pounds. His assigned position is center. Few people realize he is an excellent long range shooter. Most observers cannot explain Vlade's deft shooting touch and rare agility and quickness for a man his size.

The NBA's **Dirk Nowitzki** was the best INFP 3-point shooter in 2001, amazing for a 7-footer. Understanding his Brain Type puts it all in perspective.

Pickpockets

INFPs have the ability to be defensive aces. This is usually not their Number 1 love, however. When it is, watch out! INFPs are blessed with swift motor movements. Their hands can pick your pocket while you blink your eyes. INFP **Alvin Robertson** was the NBA's foremost bandit for a number of years. Robertson led the league in steals 3 times (1986, 1987, 1991) and was named NBA NBA Defensive Player of the Year in 1986 when he set the record for most steals in a season at 301. Robertson made the NBA All-Defensive Team 6 times in his first 7 years in the league.

Until ISTP John Stockton stole his record in the mid-1990s, INFP Maurice Cheeks was the all-time leader in career steals with 2,310.

Eric Murdock graduated from Providence in 1991. Not surprisingly, all this INFP did in his college career was to become the all-time NCAA leader in steals, tallying 376.

Adept Foul Shooters

INFPs, like some other Types, can achieve great accuracy at the charity stripe. **Jeff Malone** was an 87 percent free-throw shooter over his NBA career, placing him in the top ten of all time. In 1991, after eight seasons in the NBA, he shot 91.7% from the line.

Not only can INFPs hit the high percentage at the line, they are marvelous at drawing fouls with their creative, contorted moves and shots. To the delight of their coaches, INFPs spend a lot of time at the foul line.

Conceptually Smart

Not all INFPs do well in school work, but they certainly have the ability to be top-notch students. For some INFPs, poor study habits and lack of discipline become their downfall. When they do apply themselves, they excel academically. Lakers assistant coach Bill Bertka said of newcomer, Yugoslavian **Vlade Divac**:

> He's a very, very quick learner.[46]

L.A. Times staff writer Mark Heisler said of Divac:

> Given all that Divac has had to learn—including English—he's the next thing to a basketball Einstein, which is why the Lakers have reason to hope.[47]

Have you ever heard **Julius Erving or Abdul Jabbar** in an interview? These are two of many INFP athletes who have demonstrated their NF skills in language.

Deceptive Intensity

INFPs are sometimes perceived as lackadaisical, like their close cerebral relatives, the ISFPs. Because INFPs usually play with grace and control, preferring to save their energy for when they really need it, they generally perform at a lighter tempo than other Types do. Rest assured, however; when the big games come, or when they want to turn it on, they can perform.

Assistant Lakers coach Bill Bertka said of **Vlade Divac**, in 1990:

> He's kind of limp in practices, but he likes to play in games.[48]

HELPING INFPs

INFPs are similar to ISFPs in their playing confidence. As Introverted right-brained Feelers, they lean toward viewing their mistakes more negatively and subjectively than many other Types. If they play for a tough "Thinking" coach, their problems can easily be compounded. Encouraging slumping INFPs and ISFPs with positive reinforcement will do wonders to bring out their best performances. They generally perform according to how they feel.

INFPs are not always aggressive, particularly under the boards. It is helpful to provide them inspirational reasons for giving their best each time they play. Daily sharing the same song and dance will not cut it; INFPs respond best with creative variety.

Developing their motor skills will be helpful to INFPs. Considering the team's welfare will also go a long way in winning ball games and the acceptance of team members.

ENFP

ENFP "Gymnasts" bring their unlimited energy to the hardwood in the same way they approach life, vigorously. In hoops, they love to move, jump, shoot, and block shots. Rarely will they be accused of standing around. Not possessing the innate motor skills of the Sensates, ENFPs compensate by utilizing their right-brained dominance, coordinating their gross and fine motor skills. They perform with active grace and are well represented in the NBA.

Explosive, Quick

ENFPs perform quite unlike any other Type in basketball. They have a number of unique attributes. Explosiveness is one. The 1989-90 NBA season brought a flare of quickness the league had never seen in a big man. **David Robinson**, ENFP, joined the San Antonio Spurs after finishing a two-year Navy commitment. He was unanimously named NBA Rookie-of-the-Year in 1990. His explosiveness was an asset to every aspect of his game. He averaged 24.3 points, 12 rebounds, and nearly 4 blocks per game. No small wonder 7-foot-1 Robinson was the first unanimous selection as top rookie since Ralph Sampson (ISFP) in 1984.

All-Star forward, Jerome Kersey, said of ENFP Robinson:

> The best thing he does, he's so quick, you look and he's gone. You just don't see that in a big man.[49]

All Star center Patrick Ewing said:

> He's just a great player who works hard and comes up with big plays. He's very quick and uses his quickness.[50]

All-Star Charles Barkley, not always one to lavish praise on others, said of Robinson:

> He's going to be a monster. He can do it all: Play defense, shoot, rebound and block shots. Plus, he's the fastest big man I've ever played against.[51]

Robinson achieved his greatest achievement in 1995, winning the League's MVP Award.

Leapers

ENFPs' explosiveness, coupled with their ability to blend overall body movements, often produces athletes with remarkable jumping abilities. ENFP **Mike Powell** broke the long jump record in 1991 (held for 23 years), soaring 29 feet 4½ inches. ENFPs can play basketball like an Olympic gymnast performing a floor exercise. Consider the playing styles of **David Thompson, David Robinson, Kevin Garnett, Antonio McDyess,** and **Chris Webber,** to name only a few. ENFPs seem to prefer playing above ground level. They can be superb rebounders, too, especially on the offensive glass where they can score.

Like to Shoot

ENFPs possess large amounts of energy and prefer expending it by shooting. The 1990 NBA season saw the addition of rookie **Cliff Robinson** to the Portland Trailblazers. *L.A. Times* reporter, Mark Heisler, dubbed him the "shot-happy forward" before the season was over.[52] Appraising the upcoming 1991-92 season, Heisler spoke of the Houston Rockets:

> Shot selection from hell. For a start, Don Chaney should tie Vern Maxwell's [ENFP] right arm down.[53] (Insert added.)

It doesn't take long for observers to notice the ENFP's desire to put the ball in the basket.

Former NBA All-Star **Bernard King** not only proved his willingness to shoot the ball, but his ability to score. ENFP King led the NBA in scoring in 1985 with a 33 point average. Despite missing the entire 1986 season with a career-threatening knee injury, Bernard made a valiant comeback and continued his scoring pace. The 1991 season saw him complete his 13th year in the NBA. All he did was come in third in scoring (behind Michael Jordan and Karl Malone), with a 28.4 game scoring average, raising his career average to some 23 points per game. Retiring in 1993, Bernard King was a tribute to his Brain Type. Not all ENFPs can shoot the ball as accurately as King, but they sure have fun trying. **Glen Rice** was the NBA's best 3-point shooter in 1997, connecting on 47% of his attempts. This is a remarkable feat for one standing 6'8".

Intuitive, Good Learning Potential

ENFPs are most proficient at Extraverting their iNtuition. When performing, they communicate creativity to the world, both verbally and physically. Their iNtuition enables them to comprehend the grand scheme of things, understanding the big picture. Not always good students yet with the potential to be, they can be quick learners. Coach Larry Brown reported in

1990 on his Naval Academy graduate **David Robinson**:

> This is no ordinary kid. Asked why he blocked a shot, or defended a player so well, he says, 'Well, I couldn't let them drive the lane with impunity.' When's the last time you heard that?[54]

NBA coach Don Nelson commented on David Robinson during his rookie season:

> I think David's the best player in the league. It's clear-cut to me. He should be MVP and rookie of the year. I can only compare David to a guy I used to play with, Bill Russell. But Robinson is quicker.[55]

It's typologically noteworthy to consider Don Nelson's comments. INTJ Nelson, the conceptually astute Type, had the iNtuitive insight to see the similarities between Robinson (ENFP) and Russell (ENTP). The two Types play alike—with high energy and right-brained fluidity—yet they have noticeable differences. ENTPs rely more upon spatial logic, but they're not as motor skill adept as ENFPs. ENTPs are usually not as coordinated and graceful, yet they're less apt to make mental mistakes in pressure situations.

ENFPs are smart players too, relying upon their iNtuition to understand the scheme of things. Yet in pressure packed game situations, they are more apt to rely upon their athleticism and Feelings, the latter getting them in trouble if they're not careful.

Pressure Sensitive

Like all Brain Types, ENFPs are susceptible to performing poorly under pressure in a way unique to their individual Types. ENFPs tend to become too hyper, playing out of control. Loving to jump, they'll bound into the air to make a move without first surveying the floor. This can lead to untimely turnovers. Relying upon Feelings as their prime decision making function, they may make unwise choices, acting too hastily. ENFPs need to stay under control and access their visual logic.

At the end of his first regular season in the NBA, **David Robinson** said:

> I learned to be patient, not to fight things and [to] keep my stress level down. It's helped me greatly this season. I'm mellow and I refuse to let things bother me.[56]

It's good that Robinson began learning to combat ENFP obstacles early in his career. Although his quote seems to indicate he has matters pretty much under control, many more pressure situations lie ahead of him, particularly in the playoffs.

HELPING ENFPs

ENFPs should concentrate on developing ball handling skills, especially with their non-dominant hand. For ENFPs, the intricacies of the fine motor movements will not come naturally.

Shooting the ball with excessive arch or rotation can hurt ENFPs' accuracy. Because of their physical tendencies, they are prone to shooting in this fashion.

ENFPs need to learn to play under control, restraining their superman instincts to jump over a building in a single bound. Their overall performance will improve significantly when they learn to properly regulate their acrobatic moves, energy, and shot selection.

ENFPs are prone to think offensively first. When they set their minds to it, they also can be stellar defenders. Their basketball careers have greater potential when they stress defense as well as offense. **David Robinson** is one ENFP who has done this and was named the NBA's defensive player of the year in 1992. By 1996, Robinson had made the NBA All-Defensive team 7 consecutive years.

ENFJ

ENFJs do not possess the dominant motor skills of the Sensates or the smoothness of the right-brained Ps. Nonetheless, ENFJs relish competition and can make a major impact on the basketball floor. I believe their greatest assets in basketball are determination and hustle. Their zealousness is infectious to fellow teammates. They are the "Spark Plugs."

ENFJs possess much the same energy on the court as do ENFPs, but are not as coordinated and smooth. ENFJs set finesse aside and try to beat you running, jumping, diving, and overall hustling. Some have become very good shooters and complete ball players. As Feelers, ENFJs are generally personable and well liked by fellow teammates.

Polarized Shooting Percentages

When it comes to shooting, ENFJs are something of an enigma. On the plus side, they are able to develop a first class shot, both inside and outside. They can develop the motor movements to look good on the shot as well as make it. Challenge an ENFJ to a friendly game of horse, and you could easily come out the loser.

On the down side, ENFJs are noticeably affected by pressure. Their dominant, regimented left-hemisphere tries to gain control in pressure packed, big game situations. When this happens, the motor movements tense up, and the ENFJs' offense can greatly suffer. The infamous "brick" shot can rear its ugly head, or the turn-over may result due to rigid body movements or from the failure to utilize the spatial right brain.

ENFJs have the ability to be among the highest percentage shooters, or the lowest. Over his lengthy pro career, there is one ENFJ in the NBA who has wisely developed his Brain Type and motor skills. I am speaking of **Buck Williams**. Buck learned to rely upon his most proficient skills, sacrificing other abilities at which he is good, but not best, under pressure. By shooting the high percentage shots near the basket, the 6-foot-8 "Spark Plug" led the NBA in field goal percentage in the 1990-91 season, at 60.2%. He led the NBA again in 1991-92, shooting 60.4%. As of 1996, Williams had completed 55% of his shots during his 15-year career. Nonetheless, Buck has not been known for taking outside shots at the end of games. He knows that is not his strength. If Williams does take the outside shot when relaxed, however, he like other ENFJs, can hit it.

This leads us to the other end of the continuum for ENFJ shooters. When they take the lower percentage shots, especially in pressure situations, their shooting percentage made can take a nose dive. Their body movements have a tendency to get out of sync, and the shots will not fall. In the tense time of games, ENFJs must be careful in their shot selection, looking for high percentage attempts.

ENFJ **Marques Johnson** was one of the smoothest ENFJs to ever play basketball. Johnson developed his NF motor skills to complement his jumping ability, playing splendidly at both the collegiate and professional levels. He was a 52 percent field-goal shooter, averaging 20 points a game over his 11-year NBA career. He made the All-NBA Team 3 times.

Excellent Defenders

Because ENFJs are rarely relied upon as a team's leading scorer, they realize the importance of playing good defense to attain and retain their playing time. Their tireless work ethic and iNtuitive abilities pay top dividends in a defensive role.

Aggressive Rebounders

Going hard to the boards is a delight for ENFJs, being one of their favorite aspects of the game. Their NF fervor and jumping abilities produce numerous rebounds, both offensive and defensive. **Swen Nater, Buck Williams, and Rony Seikaly** all learned the art of cleaning glass.

Owing to their frequent, unchecked aggressiveness and hasty reactions to opponents' moves, ENFJs can rack up fouls in a hurry. They need to give high priority to overcoming this pattern.

HELPING ENFJs

ENFJs should rely on shooting high-percentage shots when experiencing anxiety on the hardwood. They also need to learn how to control their energies and enthusiasm when playing, minimizing turnovers, ill advised shots, and fouls.

Developing motor skills at an early age will benefit ENFJs, preparing them for any sport later in life. Their motor movements will be particularly tested in athletic pressure situations.

THE NBA's RAREST BRAIN TYPES

The **ISFJ, ESFJ, ISTJ, INFJ, INTJ,** and **INTP** Brain Types are the least represented in the NBA. Of these six, the INTP "Einstein" is the rarest. The INTP has the mental and physical skills to make it in the NBA over some of the eleven Types previously reviewed. Considering INTPs are knowledge seekers and approximate only 2 percent of the American populace, it is understandable why they are rarely found on the NBA hardwood; they prefer brains over brawn.

Dikembe Mutombo is one INTP who has overcome the odds. Through hard work and maximizing his NT mind, he's developed into one of the NBA's best centers. Playing within himself, Mutombo won the NBA's defensive player of the year award in 1997 for the second time in three years. He also led the NBA in shots blocked for three consecutive seasons (1994-1996).

Any players with Brain Types not frequently found in professional basketball should not give up their aspirations, but realize working harder and smarter will be necessary to reach the highest levels of basketball. They should consider the true life stories of persons who overcame unfavorable odds to attain athletic stardom. Reading the accounts of the disciplines and rigors that enabled them to reach their goals would be helpful.

If persons who constitute any of these remaining five Types are unwilling to undergo the hard work necessary to reach the upper limits of basketball, yet still desire to reach them, perhaps they should choose a sport more accommodating to their respective Types.

Conclusion:

We have considered some major attributes of the ten most commonly found Brain Types in the NBA. Each Type excels at specific phases of the game, mentally and physically. The more time you devote to observing and understanding these differences in Types, the more exciting and beneficial this study will become for you.

It is wise to investigate the players of your specific Brain Type. This will enable you to see the various ways persons of the same Type play basketball. Look for articles where they share their methods of success, mental and physical. If you have typed yourself correctly, you should relate to what they are saying. Remember the adage, "Different strokes for different folks." You will generally do best by emulating those most like yourself.

Though far from complete, here is a list of well-known players and their probable Brain Types that will provide a perspective on the most successful Types in professional basketball.

ISTP
Shaquille O'Neal, Alonzo Mourning, Ben Wallace, Derrick Coleman, Shawn Kemp, Tom Gugliotta, Mark Bryant, Rodney Rogers,
Tracy McGrady, Reggie Miller, Jalen Rose, Anthony Peeler, Jud Buechler,
Jason Kidd, Allen Iverson, Stephon Marbury, Mike Bibby, Tim Hardaway, Kenny Anderson, Mark Jackson, Dana Baros, Robert Pack, Mahmoud Abdul-Rauf, Brent Price,
Cynthia Cooper, Chamique Holdsclaw
  Retired: Moses Malone, Bill Walton, Jerry West, James Worthy, Larry Smith, Reggie Lewis, Pete Maravich, Nate Archibald, Ricky Pierce, Byron Scott, Doc Rivers, Scott Skiles, Mark Price, Dominique Wilkins, Detlef Schrempf, Terry Cummings, Rex Chapman, Muggsy Bogues, Larry Johnson, Chris Mullin, **Larry Bird**, Derek Harper, Bobby Hurley, Ron Harper, Gary Grant, Bryant "Big Country" Reeves, Hakeem Olajuwon, Patrick Ewing, Mitch Richmond, Dan Majerle, Terry Porter, **John Stockton**, *Michael Jordan*

ESTP
Tyson Chandler, **Karl Malone**, Charles Oakley, Robert Horry, Michael Doleac, Bob Sura, Ricky Davis, Mike Dunleavy, Steve Nash, Jason Williams, Chris Childs, Charlie Ward, Vinny Del Negro, John Starks, Michele Timms, Jackie Stiles
  Retired: Wilt Chamberlain, **Elgin Baylor**, Gail Goodrich, Walt Frazier, Tom Heinsohn, Maurice Lucas, Jim Paxson, Kelly Tripuckah, Mychal Thompson, James Edwards, Reggie Theus, Rodney McCray, Brad Davis, Danny Ainge, Sarunas Marciulionis, Antoine Carr, Michael Cage, Pete Myers, A.C. Green, Greg Anthony

ISFP
Tim Duncan, Kevin Willis, Elden Campbell, Juwan Howard, Horace Grant, Lorenzen Wright, Scott Williams, Calvin Booth, Dan Gadzuric,
Shareef Rahim, Joe Smith, Derrick McKey, Chris Crawford, Eddie Griffin,
Scottie Pippen, **Paul Pierce**, Walt Williams, Jonathan Bender, Darius Miles, Ed O'Bannon,
Kobe Bryant, Anfernee Hardaway, Eddie Jones, Steve Smith, Richard Hamilton, Wesley Person, Tracy Murray, Larry Hughes,
Chauncey Billups, Rod Strickland, Earl Boykins, Tyronn Lue, Dee Brown, Brevin Knight, Cory Alexander, Tyus Edney, Darrick Martin,
  Retired: Bob McAdoo, Bill Sharman, K.C. Jones, Dennis Johnson, Mike Dunleavy, Don Chaney, Robert Parish, Joe Barry Carroll, Ralph Sampson, Bill Cartwright, Sam Bowie, Larry Nance, David Rivers, Tree Rollins, Kenny Walker, Mark West, Kevin Duckworth, Benoit Benjamin, Sleepy Floyd, **Clyde Drexler**, Joe Dumars, Spud Webb, Brian Shaw, Sedale Threatt, B.J. Armstrong, Greg Grant, Keith Jennings, Charles D. Smith, Eddie Johnson, Chris Morris, Willie Anderson, **Kevin Johnson**, Dale Ellis, Sean Elliott, Doug West, Otis Thorpe, Terry Mills, Billy Owens, Danny Manning, Sam Mitchell

ESFP
Brendan Haywood, Kwame Brown, Jason Collins, Othella Harrington, Al Harrington, Gary Trent, Danny Fortson, **Jermaine O'Neal**, Elton Brand, Calbert Cheaney, Ron Artest, Rashard Lewis, Shawn Marion, Isaiah Rider,
Ray Allen, Latrell Sprewell, Allan Houston, Tariq Abdul-Wahad, Richard Jefferson,
LeBron James, Baron Davis, Steve Francis, Andre Miller, Antonio Daniels, Will Avery
Nikki McCray, Natalie Williams
  Retired: **Oscar Robertson**, **Magic Johnson**, Isiah Thomas, Calvin Murphy, Bob Lanier, Meadowlark Lemon, Darryl Dawkins, John S. Williams, **Cheryl Miller**, Bo Kimble, Wayman Tisdale, Stanley Roberts, Victor Alexander, Stacey King, J.R. Reid, **Charles Barkley, Dennis Rodman**, Sam Perkins, Oliver Miller, Horacio Llamas

ISTJ
Stacey Augmon
  Retired: **Michael Cooper**, Bobby Jones, Kyle Macy, Rick Adelman, Brian Winters, Jay Burson, Kurt Rambis, **Jeff Hornacek** Steve Kerr

ESTJ
Greg Ostertag, Eric Montross, Cherokee Parks, Vitaly Potapenko, **Kurt Thomas**, Greg Foster, Stanislav Medvedenko, Joel Pryzbila, Walter McCarty, Mike Miller
Lisa Leslie
  Retired: Rudy Tomjanovich, Mitch Kupchak, Chris Ford, Greg Kite, Frank Brickowski, Rick Smits, Joe Wolf, Joe Kleine, George Zidek, Olden Polynice

ISFJ
P.J. Brown, Dale Davis, Ervin Johnson, Nazr Mohammed, Rasaul Butler, J.R. Henderson, John Coker,
  Retired: Alton Lister, Andrew Lang, Acie Earl

ESFJ
Rasheed Wallace, Dickey Simpkins, Eddy Curry, Alan Henderson, Samaki Walker
  Retired: John (Hot Rod) Williams, Bobby Phills, Donald Royal, Charles Shackleford, David Wingate, Duane Causwell

INFJ
Chris Dudley, Jim McIlvaine,
  Retired: Mark Eaton, Adam Keefe

ENFJ
Rasho Nesterovic, Mark Madsen,
Maurice Taylor, Matt Bullard, Rex Walters,
Fred Hoiberg, Eric Washington
  Retired: **Marques Johnson**, Keith Erikson, Pat Riley, Dick Van Arsdale, Swen Nater, Matt Guokas Jr., Stu Lantz, Rony Seikaly, Buck Williams, Dan Schayes

INFP
Vlade Divac, Shawn Bradley, **Dirk Nowitzki**, Keith Closs, Brian Grant, Tayshaun Prince
Grant Hill, Shandon Anderson, Dell Curry, Doug Christie, Kerry Kittles, Tony Parker, Eric Murdock, Howard Eisley, Lee Mayberry, Bryce Drew
> *Retired*: Artis Gilmore, **Kareem Jabbar**, **Dr. Julius Erving**, Jamaal Wilkes, Alex English, Larry Drew, Terry Teagle, Trent Tucker, Craig Hodges, Jeff Malone, Roy Hinson, Rolando Blackman, Reggie Williams, Dennis Scott, Cedric Ceballos

ENFP
Yao Ming, Marcus Camby, Evan Eschmeyer,
Kevin Garnett, Antonio McDyess, Cliff Robinson, Chris Webber, LaPhonso Ellis, Anthony Mason, Tyrone Hill, Charles Outlaw, Dean Garrett, George Lynch, Antawn Jamison, John Wallace, Popeye Jones, Jerome Williams, Malik Rose, Robert Traylor,
Glen Rice, Jamal Mashburn, George McCloud, Bryon Russell, Rick Fox,
Jerry Stackhouse, Hubert Davis, Michael Dickerson, Terrell Brandon, Lindsey Hunter, Alvin Williams, Jamaal Tinsley, Speedy Claxton, Jay Williams
> *Retired*: Tommy Hawkins, Happy Hairston, David Thompson, Quinn Buckner, Orlando Woolridge, Ed Pinckney, John Bagley, Cliff Levingston, John Salley, Negele Knight, Craig Ehlo, David Benoit, Nate McMillan, Armon Gilliam, **Hersey Hawkins**, Vernon Maxwell, Chuck Person, Sherman Douglas, Rumeal Robinson, Loy Vaught,
> **David Robinson**,

INTP
Dikembe Mutombo

ENTP
Arvydas Sabonis, Michael Olowokandi, Erick Dampier, Todd MacCulloch, Scot Pollard, Keon Clark, Isaac Austin,
Vin Baker, Chris Gatling, Donyell Marshall, Antoine Walker, Jamie Feick, **Glenn Robinson**, Lamond Murray, Clarence Weatherspoon, Corliss Williamson, Jason Caffey, Darvin Ham, Marcus Fizer,
Shane Battier, Predrag Stojakovic, **Vince Carter**, Michael Finley, Manu Ginobili, Ron Mercer, Voshon Lenard, Bryant Stith, Randy Brown, Tony Delk, Cuttino Mobley, David Wesley,
Sam Cassell, Damon Stoudamire, **Nick Van Exel**, Travis Best, Derek Fisher, Jacque Vaughn, Avery Johnson,
Rebecca Lobo, Diana Taurasi
> *Retired*: **Bob Cousy**, **Bill Russell**, Rod Hundley, Kevin Loughery, Jeff Ruland, John Lucas, Frank Johnson, Mike Brown, Felton Spencer, Jayson Williams, Malik Sealy, Luc Longley, Sharone Wright, Matt Geiger, Mario Elie

INTJ
Keith Van Horn, Vladimir Stepania, Cal Bowdler
> *Retired*: Don Nelson, Phil Jackson, Jack Marin, Tom McMillen, Alvan Adams, Rick Carlisle, Bill Hanzlik

ENTJ
Pau Gasol, Raef LaFrentz, Brad Miller, Christian Laettner, Tony Kukoc, Don MacLean, Danny Ferry, Travis Knight, Andrew DeClerq, Pat Garrity, Todd Fuller, Chris Anstey, Austin Croshere, Chris Mihm,
Eric Piatkowski, Brent Barry, Wally Szczerbiak, Jon Barry, Brian Evans, Matt Maloney, John Crotty,
> *Retired*: Bill Bradley, Jerry Lucas, Dave Cowens, **Rick Barry**, Dan Issel, **Kevin McHale**, John Paxson, Tom Chambers, Todd Lichti, Brooks Thompson

11
Bowling, Boxing, and Cycling

Bowling

Surprising to many, bowling is one of America's favorite sports. Bowling is a sport I plan to cover more fully in the future, evaluating present and past stars (Dick Carter, Dick Weber and others, including women on the LPBA Tour).

Approximating perhaps 20 percent of the American populace, NTs (iNtuitive Thinkers) appear to be overly represented among the most successful professional bowlers. Their hard work ethic and mental giftedness contribute much to their success.

ENTP

ENTPs do exceptionally well on the PBA Tour; I have observed a number of them. Yet many ENTPs take a while to acclimate themselves to the physical and mental rigors of their profession. When they adapt, their NT competitive nature, cerebral skills, and right-brained dominance combine for smooth, intelligent play. ENTPs can develop good body coordination and fine motor adeptness, controlling the ball with precision and rotation.

Tour veteran **David Ozio** was the 1991 PBA Player of the Year. Having won only six scattered titles in the 13 previous years, ENTP Ozio finished '91 with the most individual tournament triumphs on tour, four, the money title, $225,485, and was ranked among the highest in game average, 215 for 1053 games. Ozio was in the money in 24 of 32 tournaments. The Texan commented on his '91 accomplishments:

> It was the kind of year you always hoped for, but never seems to come. I made key delivery adjustments on angle and speed. Concentrated on having more faith in myself at the line. Well, whatever, it worked. The pins started falling my way.[1]

In 1995, David Ozio was elected into the Professional Bowlers Association Hall of Fame. This same year, ENTP **Dave D'Entremont** won the prestigious Tournament of Champions and was the second-leading money winner on tour. Since joining the tour in 1982, the 34-year-old D'Entremont had struggled to be among bowling's best.

In 2000, ENTP **Norm Duke** won his second PBA Player of the Year award, averaging 219 per game.

ISFJ

Though infrequently found in professional sports, ISFJs can be exceptional bowlers. ISFJ **Walter Ray Williams Jr.** has dominated off and on for nearly 20 years on the Pro Bowlers Tour. Walter has captured the Player of the Year award four times—1986, 1993, 1996, and 1997. In 1995, he was inducted into the PBA Hall of Fame. Except for only a few months during the years 1993 to 2001, Williams held the PBA's number-1 computer ranking, an amazing record.

To physically direct a heavy ball down a long wooden lane with pinpoint accuracy requires excellent body control. Walter's style is not right-brain graceful, but more mechanical, SFJ gross motor regulated. His mastery over the body's large muscles has made him durable and bowling proficient.

Interestingly, Walter is also regarded as the best horseshoe player in the world, having won the World Horseshoe Pitching Championships six times. Williams estimates that he throws a bowling ball about 40,000 times a year and a horseshoe some 15,000 times. No Brain Type Grouping can endure these physical demands better than the SFs. ISFJ Walter Ray Williams Jr. has used his inborn big-muscle control to perfection.

BRAIN TYPES AND BOWLERS

INTJ   Danny Wiseman, Harry Sullins, Eric Adophson, Bryan Goebel

ENTJ   Brian Voss

ENTP   Nelson Burton Jr., David Ozio, Roger Bowker, Del Ballard Jr., Steve Cook, Norm Duke, Dave D'Entremont, Wayne Webb, Marshall Holman, Bob Learn Jr., Ricky Ward, Bob Belmont, Doug Kent, Randy Pedersen, Rick Steelsmith, Steve Hoskins, Jason Couch

ENFP   Marc McDowell, George Branham III

ISTP   Mark Thayer

ISFJ   Walter Ray Williams Jr.

Boxing

The preponderance of skilled boxers are of the SP (Sensing, Perceiving, right brain) Brain Type group. It is unusual for a professional champion *not* to be an SP. Generally speaking, ISTPs are the meanest and most feared fighters. ESTPs and the ESFPs are the showiest, biggest talking power punchers, and ISFPs are the most agile, graceful and best liked of the pugilists.

ISTP

No sport more than boxing reveals the ISTP's intensity and killer instinct. Boxing encourages its participants to beat up one another, something most ISTPs do easily when angry. They are generally the last to give up in a match. Willing to take three blows to deliver one, ISTPs love to attack, accepting the pain and scars that come with victory. ISTPs have included **"Smokin'" Joe Frazier, Larry Holmes, Thomas "Hitman" Hearns, Pernell Whitaker, and Mike Tyson**.

Consider three heavyweight champions of the world. From 1968 to 1973, **Joe Frazier** reigned. **Larry Holmes** held the title from 1978 to 1985. **Mike Tyson** wore the championship belt during the years 1986 to 1990 and again in 1995 and '96 (following his three-year prison term for rape). These ISTPs held the heavyweight title 16 of the 22 years between 1968 and 1990.

In 1991, **Mike Tyson** spoke of his ISTP aggressiveness:

> I wish I didn't feel that way. It scares me. It makes me think like there's something wrong with me. It's a miserable feeling. I hate it. But I also love it.[2]

In 1997, Tyson's ISTP sadistic instincts became known to the TV-viewing world. Challenging defending heavyweight champ Evander Holyfield for the world title, Tyson snapped in the third round and twice bit his opponent's ears—ripping off an inch of tissue and cartilage. Tyson's shocking behavior was atypical for ISTPs, but it did reveal what can happen when they stray from the beaten path. Though ISTPs will always struggle with their tempers when angry, they can ensure composure by having strong moral, ethical, and spiritual foundations.

ISTP **Pernell Whitaker** first became recognized nationally by capturing a gold medal at the 1984 Olympic games. Since then he has gone on to become the lightweight and welterweight champion of the world.

Over his career, **Thomas Hearns** won titles in the welterweight, super welterweight, middleweight, super middleweight, and light heavyweight divisions.

Whether in the ring or on the street corner, take caution if you plan to pick a fight with an ISTP.

ESTP

As in other sports, ESTPs have confidence and often share it openly. More often than not, they can back up their claims. ESTPs pack a wallop in their lightning-quick, supercharged wrists and fists. ESTPs aren't as willing as ISTPs to sacrifice their faces; after all, they don't want to alter their good looks.

ESTP **Sugar Ray Leonard** was one the showiest and most graceful fighters of all time. He retired (the first time) with a pro career record of 36-2-1, with earnings of more than $100 million. Like many ESTPs before him, Sugar Ray found retirement tough on his ego. In 1991, he hung up his gloves for the fourth time, supposedly this time for good. Yet six years later (1997), Leonard came back for another fix of accolades and a paycheck of $4 million. Despite the incentives, the 40-year old was sent to the canvas (fifth round) by fellow ESTP Hector Camacho. In his prime, Leonard was a rapid-fire, superb boxer.

ESTP **Ken Norton** held the World Boxing Council's heavyweight title in 1978. Of his three matches against Muhammad Ali, Norton fought brilliantly, winning one. Many say if it hadn't been for biased judging, he would have won all three.

No Pussycats in the Ring

Roberto Duran was one tough fighter. His former trainer, Ray Arcel, spoke of the mellow side of this ESTP:

> Roberto is like a Jekyll and Hyde character. Inside the ring, he's a lion. Outside, he's like a pussycat—a warm, beautiful human being.[3]

A pussycat? Not always. Boxing commentator Alex Wallau told of the time he interviewed Duran in Panama City:

> By coincidence, a cat walked on the set. Duran grabbed it by its tail, swung it over his head and smashed it against a wall. 'Gatos [cats] are bad luck,' he told me. It was just unbelievable.[4]

Unfortunately, Duran's upbringing didn't stress kindness to animals. Yet I believe Duran is a mellow person most of the time; ESTPs generally are. As Extraverted SPs, they live life mostly in their easy-going Sensing function. When fighting, however, their Thinking function is quickly engaged, activating their Jekyll persona.

Flashy and in Charge

Hector (Macho) Camacho was the World Boxing Council's lightweight champion in 1985-86. Hector was known to attend press conferences wearing such items as a sequined silver jacket, sparkling silver ankle boots over a black body suit, and enough gold around his neck to make Mr. T envious. Macho Camacho once said:

> My life is like a movie. I drive my Corvette up on the sidewalk, I race at 100 m.p.h. What do you want. I'm the Macho man.[5]

On his hopes for a movie career, he said:

> Give me a three-picture deal, one with me killing Rambo and two with me killing other guys. I'll be the biggest thing in movies.[6]

Like other ESTPs, Hector doesn't like to be told what to do. He explained that he once bought a model airplane and was told by the salesman not to fly it by himself. So? He says:

I flew it. It crashed and cost me $360.[7]

When Camacho successfully defended his International Boxing Council middleweight title in 1997—against Sugar Ray Leonard—he had a lifetime record of 64-3-1 with 32 knockouts.

ESFP

Are you old enough to remember **Muhammad Ali** (Cassius Clay)? From a typological and neuroscientific perspective, he was a classic ESFP. Unequivocally, Ali was the most flamboyant of all fighters, the ultimate showman, and considered by many to be the best boxer ever. Some ESTPs have attempted to challenge his charisma but still pale in comparison to his showy bouts and press conferences. As he said, "I am the greatest!" Ali held the heavyweight title eight different years, primarily in the 1960s.

A childhood friend of Ali gave us a glimpse of the young ESFP:

> He was just a playful person. He had a lot of friends. We'd eat in the cafeteria, and he'd come in and crack his jokes and say little silly things and have all the table laughing.[8]

Quick Reactions, Superior Vision

Ali's first boxing coach, Joe Martin, saw him win AAU titles, Golden Glove Championships, and his Olympic gold medal:

> His secret was his unusual eye speed. It was blinding . . . When he started fighting, Cassius was so fast with his eyes that you could give a guy a screen door and he wouldn't hit Cassius 15 times with it in 15 rounds. He was different. Quick as lightning for a big man, the quickest I ever saw.[9]

ESFPs, of all the Brain Types, potentially have the quickest reacting gross motor skills. Top notch ESFPs have demonstrated this in every sport: **Dennis Rodman in basketball, Tony Gwynn in baseball, Carl Lewis in track, Walter Payton and Reggie White in football**, to name a few.

The "Ali Shuffle" and his uncanny vision were patented ESFP. He compared to basketball's **Magic Johnson** (ESFP) with his phenomenal vision and instantaneous reactions.

ESFP **George Foreman** held the heavyweight title in 1973 and 1974. He embarked on a comeback in 1987 after 10 years of retirement. Four years and 24 opponents later (he knocked out 23), at age 42, he lost a championship fight with 28-year old Evander Holyfield. Foreman's natural ESFP abilities enabled him to use his gross motor skills to put up a noble, hard-fought fight. In ESFP fashion, he entertained the media and public like no fighter since, who else, Muhammad Ali.

In 1994, at age 45, Foreman became the oldest fighter to win a heavyweight championship. A single historic and shattering punch knocked out ENTP Michael Moorer. The boxing world was shocked, but those who know Brain Types realize SFPs can last longer in sports than any other Types. George's heroics were understandable. In 1997, the amazing 48-year-old Foreman won a heavyweight fight, earning $4.5 million for the day.

ESFPs tend to be overweight. If their occasional compulsion is food, it can get the best of them. Such has been the case with George Foreman. In 1991, he compared his eating habits to those of opponent Evander Holyfield:

> He's got a nutritionist, and I've got room service.[10]

And:

> I've got a strength coach. My wife. She gets big chains, and at night she puts them around the refrigerator. They are so strong, I can't break them.[11]

When ESFPs land a punch, their whole body is behind it; opponents feel as if they've been hit by a truck. Even Mike Tyson experienced the crashing blow of an ESFP when **Buster Douglas** floored him in Japan.

ISFP

Floyd Patterson was heavyweight champion of the world during the years of 1956-59 and 1960-62. Reserved and amiable, Floyd also collected a gold medal at the 1952 Olympics. Standing only 5' 11", and 185 pounds, he relied on his ISFP quickness, agility, and gross motor power.

Over a six year span, ISFP **Donald Curry** beat 25 opponents in a row, 19 by knockout. He was the welterweight champion of the world in the years 1983-86. The ISFP utilized fast feet, hands, and superb coordination. He packed SF thunder in both hands and defensive skills that left opponents delivering punches to thin air. He was regarded as invincible and invisible.

ENFP

It is doubtful that three of the four NF Brain Types—ENFJ, INFJ, and INFP—would ever win a championship belt at the professional level. For one, either their motor skills or mental/spatial abilities would limit their successes. Belying the NF image, however, ENFPs have the necessary tools to be world-class boxers. Despite their affable natures, they can be intensely competitive, physical, and lightening quick. ENFPs have tremendous unrestricted energies—difficult to match by any other Brain Type.

ENFP **Evander Holyfield** surprised the boxing world in the early 1990s. By dethroning Buster Douglas, Holyfield captured the heavyweight title of the world. The 6' 2", 210-pound Holyfield appeared to be chiseled from granite. He explained his 1990 victory over Buster Douglas:

> I won my fight even though I was the smaller man. It's not the size; it's the size of the heart. I'm a little guy, but I have a big heart and big determination. I work hard. I pray hard.[12]

As Holyfield alluded, ENFPs are driven by oversized hearts toward their goals. Serious ENFP athletes become superbly conditioned, able to handle intense pain in competition.

In 1996, Evander Holyfield shocked the boxing world again by defeating heavyweight champion Mike Tyson. The 34-year-old Holyfield, whose very presence in the ring was questioned due to past health problems, became the heavyweight champ for the third time.

Most NFs and ENFPs would never consider boxing; it doesn't fit their NF outlook on life. Nevertheless, Evander Holyfield became the best at boxing. He didn't leave his NF Brain Type behind, as he demonstrated in his address to disadvantaged children:

> Do you love yourself? The most important thing is to love yourself. You don't want to do anything to hurt yourself. You have to realize you want to be somebody. I knew I wanted to be important. Everybody can be important.[13]

Holyfield brought a refreshing image to boxing, not participating in the obligatory prefight hype and possessing many values worthy of modeling for youngsters.

Oscar De La Hoya demonstrated his Brain Type tendencies as a youngster, not retaliating with opponents in early ring experiences—even crying as he walked home. By 1992, however, Oscar had gained the world's attention by winning the gold medal at the Barcelona Olympics. Utilizing his ENFP motor skills, high energy and pain threshold, De La Hoya gained superiority in his weight class. By 1996, De La Hoya KO'd Julio Cesar Chavez and captured the World Boxing Council super-lightweight title. Yet at only 23, Oscar talked of retirement, preferring a life of golf or possibly architecture to the brutality of boxing. He's never enjoyed violence—atypical for boxers, but not for ENFPs.

Though far from complete, here is a list of well known boxers and their probable Brain Types

ISTP Rocky Marciano, Joe Frazier, Larry Holmes, Mike Tyson, Thomas Hearns, Pernell Whitaker, Michael Dokes, James Toney

ESTP Sugar Ray Leonard, Roberto Duran, Donny Lalonde, Hector Camacho, Ken Norton, Carlos Palomino, Roberto Duran, Riddick Bowe, Julio Cesar Chavez, Peter McNeeley, Tommy Morrison

ESFP Joe Louis, Muhammad Ali, George Foreman, James Buster Douglas

ISFP *Retired*: Floyd Patterson, Donald Curry, Eric Griffin

ENFP Evander Holyfield, Oscar De La Hoya

ENTP Lennox Lewis, Michael Moorer, Roy Jones

Cycling

Who would have ever thought cycling would be a sport that athletes would pursue as a career? After all, how much money can one make riding a bicycle around a track or the countryside? One cyclist who knows is American **Greg LeMond**. Following his victory at the Tour de France in 1989, Greg signed a three-year contract estimated at $5.5 million with the French-based Z team. As we're now in the 21st century, who knows where pay scales will go?

ENFP

Without question, there are many Brain Types who can make superb cyclists. Greg LeMond possesses one of the top Types, if not the best. LeMond is one of the few cyclists I have researched due to his fame and riding success. His cycling achievements include winning the grueling Tour de France three times—becoming the first American to win it, in 1986. (He finished third in '84 and second in '85.) The Tour de France covers 2,112 miles! It requires super human effort for victory.

Despite Greg's phenomenal success, many misfortunes befell him during his career. In 1987, he was accidentally shot while hunting turkeys. About two months later he had an appendectomy and his 1987 season went kaput. In 1988, he crashed in a race in Belgium, required arthroscopic surgery, and lost another year of competition. Greg developed an iron deficiency in 1989, leaving him listless until he rebounded at the Tour de France. On the final day of competition, LeMond overcame an improbable 50-second deficit to win in one of the year's most exciting moments in sports.

Physical afflictions affected Greg again in 1990, where he suffered through a miserable spring during which he could barely train without becoming exhausted. He was diagnosed as having the Epstein Barr Syndrome, an illness which includes fatigue. Following treatments, Greg pulled off another Houdini act by capturing his third Tour de France (TdF). Think of it! LeMond finished first in the TdF every time he competed between 1986 and 1990, winning 3 times! Still suffering the side effects of the Epstein illness in 1991, Greg finished 7th in France.

Just who is this athlete who seemed to defy human limitations? What sort of Brain Type can handle the rigors of cycling with such proficiency? It is no surprise that Greg LeMond is an ENFP, for this Type and ENFJs put extraordinary body energy into their sporting endeavors. They normally exude the energy of "Beep-Beep" the road runner. Greg LeMond transferred his supersonic energy to the bike pedals.

ENFPs also excel at cycling because they are the last Brain Type to sense pain when performing (ENTPs are close). Typologically, they are opposite ISTJs, one of the first to experience pain's sensations. Whereas ISTJs are dominant Sensates in their Introverted world and keenly aware of physical sensations, ENFPs are oriented to their iNtuitive outer world of Extraversion.

Introverted Sensing is their least developed cerebral function. Typologically, ENFPs actually have the highest pain threshold of all Types, a distinct advantage for cyclists.

Greg LeMond spoke of the various demands of cycling:

> I think this is the toughest sport in the world. No other sport combines both endurance and intensity the way this one does. You have a triathlon, which is nine hours long—running, swimming and cycling—but that is endurance. Who can last? You have running events that demand intensity but not endurance. Here you have everything. You're tested on all of your levels of athletic ability.[14]

Numerous injuries and inclement weather occur during the Tour de France, yet many cyclists continue the race. One's pain threshold must be almost robotic.

Ambassadors, Personable

ENFPs are often great ambassadors for their sport. A personable, pied piper style makes them athletes the public wants to follow. Sometimes, however, their amiable personalities can hurt their concentration and performance. In 1990, Greg LeMond's attorney, Nathan Jenkins, said of his cycling client:

> He will try to accommodate everyone, and that makes it difficult to train at the same time. He'll never say no to the public. He'll sign every autograph. But that always wears you down in a sport that requires such high levels of conditioning.[15]

LeMond also used his NF speech and hearing skills to develop a command of the French language, endearing him to the natives.

As an inspiration to aspiring cyclists, LeMond honed his skills in Reno, Nevada, after taking up the sport to help rehabilitate a leg from a ski injury.

ENTPs

ENTPs, like ENFPs, are Extraverted and dominant iNtuitives of the right brain. Thus, both Brain Types have the potential for extremely-high pain thresholds, as well as vast amounts of energy to expend. Considering these cycling assets, it wasn't surprising to discover that cycling phenom **Lance Armstrong** of the U.S. is an ENTP. In the year 2004, Armstrong won his record-setting sixth consecutive Tour de France! He and Greg LeMond are the only Americans to have won the prestigious and grueling race. And as LeMond overcame adversity to achieve stardom, Armstrong defied all odds and overcame a near-fatal bout with cancer to win his second Tour de France; he obviously proved to the world that his first victory was no fluke.

Though far from complete, here is a list of well known cyclists and their probable Brain Types

ENFP: Greg LeMond

ENTP: Lance Armstrong

Ultra-endurance cycling:

ENTP: John Stamstad

12 Football

Determining the Brain Types of football players is more difficult than discovering Types in most other sports. Obscured by helmets, uniforms, pads and tape, players spend most of their time in piles of humanity. Evaluating linemen is especially tough for they're rarely separated from the pack and they demonstrate few fine motor movements. It is easiest to type the players interviewed on national TV, who are normally the stars. Since few players get this opportunity, in order to get a good representation of the successful Types in the NFL, I've also had to attend the Pro Bowl and work for pro teams in recent years. Let's consider the patterns I've observed thus far.

To begin with, at the professional level it is unusual to find a left hemisphere J at a runningback position. (Fullback is where you might find an occasional one.) Instead, you will find the fluid, right-brain P— particularly at halfback.

ISTP

The consummate athletic Type also excels in football. Nonetheless, ISTPs tend to play some positions better than others. In the NFL, not many are found along the interior line, defensively or offensively.

Many ISTP athletes struggle academically (from a lack of interest rather than mental aptitude) and often fail to enter, much less graduate from, college. This explains why few enter the NFL (or NBA) draft each year.

Quarterbacks

Since ISTPs are often the top pitchers in baseball and point guards in basketball, one might think they would be the best quarterbacks. Though very good, they are not as consistent as a few other Brain Types at QB. They can be tops for a season or two, but tend to develop erratic play. Their ESTP relative is the NFL's best QB, historically.

ISTPs have an arm strength second to none; they can throw the ball long and hard. Yet this is often *not* the optimal way to move a football team. Smaller ISTP quarterbacks tend to throw more easily and accurately, relying upon finesse.

ISTPs lack nothing physically as quarterbacks; they have all the tools. Where they tend to go awry is between the ears. ISTP quarterbacks think too much, particularly when they feel pressure. In situations where the ESTP quarterback might lightly entertain three thoughts under pressure, the ISTP would be apt to seriously consider six, or fixate on only one. ISTPs are often too smart for their own good. Locking in on their right-hemisphere Thinking causes them to tighten up physically, restricting otherwise smooth, fine motor and gross motor skills; it also impairs their spatial abilities.

Because football seasons bring tremendous change from year to year, ISTPs are affected more than the hang-loose ESTPs. ISTPs take matters more intensely. As a result, ESTP quarterbacks are more apt to be consistent throughout their careers. If ISTP quarterbacks can relax and maintain the right perspective, however, they make top-notch quarterbacks.

In his sixth year in the NFL, ISTP **Mark Rypien** became a star performer and led the Washington Redskins to the 1992 Super Bowl, where he won the MVP. Coach Joe Gibbs spoke of Rypien:

He has that great arm, he's tough, but the main

thing is that he's so bright.[1]

Super Tough Competitors

When we consider that ISTP boxers have included **Smokin' Joe Frazier and Mike Tyson**, it makes it easier to understand the toughness of this Brain Type. Football is a natural fit for the ISTP's competitive spirit and ferociousness. **Ronnie Lott,** ISTP, was one of the hardest hitting defensive backs in NFL history. In 1991, Lott led the NFL in pass interceptions.

Joe Gibbs spoke of **Mark Rypien**:

> The first thing I remember about Mark in the beginning, the very first scrimmage he was in, he really got racked about five times and got right back up. So the first thing I remember about him was he was tough.[2]

Running Backs

ISTPs **Barry Sanders**, 5'8", 200 pounds, and **LaDainian Tomlinson**, 5'9", have proven little men can excel in the NFL. In college, Sanders set 13 NCAA season records and won the coveted Heisman Trophy Award (1988). As a rookie, he dazzled the NFL with 1,470 yards. By 1997, Sanders had become the first back in NFL history to run for 1,000 yards nine straight years. Not only could All-Pro Sanders elude tacklers, he ran them over.

When ISTPs get a lot of playing time, they're not apt to fumble the ball. Their Introversion and fine motor skill proficiency provides them hands that act like vices.

Despite Barry Sanders' greatness, many football fans are still troubled by his sudden and inexplicable departure from the NFL. "What happened to Sanders!?" they ask. Searching the web for comments from pigskin fans discovered one of the following opinions:

> "We used to watch him when he played for Oklahoma State, and he was sensational. He was even better in the NFL. I can't find anyone who will explain why he quit so early, when he would have surely broken Walter Payton's record. Did someone threaten him? (Anybody out there know?)"

Well, it's doubtful anyone knows all reasons for Barry hangin' up the cleats, but those familiar with Brain Types should know one major reason for it: Sanders' innate ISTP wiring.

Of all the Brain Types, ISTPs can (and often do) bolt the fastest from the public limelight—especially the ones with the humble, low-keyed personalities. In 2003, the purest point guard of all time retired from the NBA, following an incredible 19-year career. With no farewell tour, John Stockton just slipped into the night.

On the other hand, the normally more energized and outgoing ESTP has a tendency to stay too long, desiring to hold on to all the public attention.

Defensive Aces

ISTPs can be excellent defenders. Their willingness to suffer pain as well as inflict it makes them favorite players for their coaches. ISTPs have tremendous visual awareness that is regulated by their logical Thinking function.

ESTP

ESTPs, like ISTPs, can excel at most positions. Their dominant right hemisphere makes them adaptable players, having finesse to complement their ESTP strength.

ESTPs love to be in the spotlight and play to the crowds. **Joe Namath** rightfully earned his nickname "Broadway Joe." **"Neon" Deion Sanders**, the "ambi-dresstrous" defensive back, has been one of the NFL's more flamboyant ESTPs in recent years.

Number-1 Quarterbacks

I regard ESTPs as the best Brain Type at quarterback. They tend to be the most consistent QBs throughout their careers. If football coaches were aware of only this one fact from Brain Typing, they would be greatly aided. (This is not to say that a few other Types can't be top-flight quarterbacks.) Consider some ESTP quarterbacks, past and present: **Johnny Unitas, Joe Namath, Ken Stabler, Terry Bradshaw, Joe Montana, Dan Marino, John Elway, Brett Favre,** and **Peyton Manning**.

ESTPs' potential for excellence comes from a number of factors. As Sensing, dominant right brain athletes (SPs), they have superb visual awareness and athletic nimbleness. Their ST body functions master fine motor skills. With experience, ESTPs can throw a football with exceptional velocity, accuracy, and quickness. As Extraverts, ESTP quarterbacks generally relax more under pressure than ISTPs and other Types. They don't introspect too much or take their mistakes too seriously; their confidence is the last to wane. If

ESTPs throw an interception, they're not afraid to come back and call the same play again. ESTP QBs love to excite the crowds. They are energized by the audience frenzy and the chance to show their daring.

When ESTP **Joe Montana** retired in 1995, many believed him to be the greatest NFL quarterback of all time. The Comeback Kid was a 4-time Super Bowl champion, 3-time Super Bowl MVP, and a regular season MVP. Former San Francisco coach Bill Walsh spoke of Montana's early days with the 49ers:

> When he was first breaking in with us, whenever the thrust of what he was doing was by instinct, he played very well. Even watching Joe warm up, there was something hypnotic about him. That look when he was dropping back; he was poetic in his movements, almost sensuous, everything so fluid, so much under control.[3]

Though they can lose their concentration during routine games, ESTPs rise to the occasion when the game is on the line. The miracle endings pulled off by ESTP QBs are largely responsible for football's popularity.

John Elway has been recognized as one of the most formidable quarterbacks in the closing minutes of a game, when his team was behind and the ball deep in their own territory. In 1999, Elway led his Denver Broncos to their second straight Super Bowl victory; he also won the game MVP.

ESTPs desire the freedom to call their own plays. When ESTP **Jim Kelly** was allowed to call his own plays and run the no-huddle offense, Buffalo Bills General Manager, Bill Polian, said of him in 1991:

> The no huddle suits his personality well. He's an aggressive guy, and that up-tempo approach suits his personality.[4]

When interviewed in 1994, retired quarterback great **Ken Stabler**, ESTP, spoke of the increasingly controlling style of NFL coaches:

> I wouldn't like playing like that. I'm glad I played when I played. I'm glad I got the opportunity to call the plays and the show the way I wanted to. Win or lose, it was my decision. I made an airplane out of my game plan. I flew by the seat of my pants. I didn't study game film. I didn't do any of that stuff. I just wanted to know if it was zone [defense] or man, and who there good players were. You can't put a bit in a racehorse's mouth. You've got to let him run if he's going to be the best horse he can be.

Stabler also commented on the coaching virtues of his former Raider boss, ESFP John Madden:

> He threw me the playbook and told me, 'Go win. Do whatever.' We were basically in the thing together, but I ran the game. John never said a word to me about play-calling. He never yelled at me. John let me do whatever the hell I wanted to do and he backed me up.[5]

If coaches hope to get the most out of their ESTP quarterbacks, they'll consider Madden's relationship with Stabler. This doesn't mean that regulations can't be placed on ESTPs, but the tighter the reins, the less likely they'll perform at peak performance.

Johnny Unitas, ESTP, is often regarded as the greatest quarterback of all time. He was most known for his aggression and daring. In 1993, **Boomer Esiason** surpassed **Ken Stabler** as the NFL's leader in passing yardage among left-handers. It's not surprising that ESTPs kept the record between themselves.

In 1997, ESTP **Brett Favre** won his third consecutive NFL Most-Valuable-Player award. The 1996-97 season saw Favre lead his Green Bay Packers to their first Super Bowl victory in 29 years. Despite ESTJ coach Mike Holmgren's attempt to keep Favre in a non-audible, conservative game plan at the game's beginning, Brett, in classic ESTP fashion, threw caution to the wind and audiblized on only the second play of the game—resulting in a 54-yard TD pass. This, along with his second quarter audible—resulting in an 81-yard TD pass—made the difference in the game.

In 1996, **Dan Marino's** career totals reached 4,000 completions and 50,000 yards. By 2003, young ESTP star **Peyton Manning** was the NFL's co-MVP, a 4-time Pro Bowl selection and the only QB in NFL history to produce five consecutive 4,000 yard passing seasons.

Any professional team that doesn't have an ESTP somewhere among their quarterbacks is truly playing at a disadvantage.

Superb Running Backs

ESTPs are generally the most prominent running backs in pro football, particularly at the tailback position. A few ESTP greats have included **Jim Brown, O.J. Simpson, Eric Dickerson, Tony Dorsett, Marcus Allen,** and **Eddie George.**

Though most gifted with their fine motor movements, ESTPs adeptly control their big muscles with right-brained artistry. ESTPs are cunning and powerful runners, loving to fake out tacklers or just run over them.

ESTP **Jim Brown** rushed for 12,312 yards and scored 126 touchdowns in nine seasons with the Cleveland Browns. **Eric Dickerson,** ESTP, gained at least 1,200 yards in each of his first full seven seasons. In 1996, **Marcus Allen** became the first player in NFL history to rush for at least 10,000 yards and to catch for 5,000 yards.

Unless ESTPs make it a high priority to hold on to the football, they will fumble. It is common to see them play an excellent game, only to become the goat by losing the ball in the fourth quarter. In their zeal to outrun the defense and dazzle the crowd, ESTPs can forget to give proper attention to their fine motor giftedness.

Defensive Aces

ESTPs can be defensive aces, especially as defensive ends, middle linebackers, and defensive backs. Like their ISTP counterparts, ESTPs enjoy hitting hard and often. ESTPs **Junior Seau** and **Ray Lewis** have carried on the tradition of ESTP and former All-Pro linebacker **Dick Butkus,** relishing their licks on Sunday afternoons.

Tough Customers

Not all ESTPs play as did Butkus, yet they are aggressive players. Speaking of Butkus, he once spoke of his pro football career:

> I never set out to hurt anyone deliberately . . . unless, it was, you know, important, like a league game, or something.[6]

In 1991, Ron Heller spoke of ESTP teammate and quarterback **Jim McMahon,** saying McMahon was in:

> . . . tremendous pain. His fingers were all swollen. He had lost control of his right wrist. They had to put his arm in a splint just to make the trip to Cleveland.[7]

The *L.A. Times* continues the story:

> But after the Eagles had fallen behind, 23-0, McMahon rallied his team to a 32-20 victory, throwing for 341 yards with an arm he couldn't lift before kickoff.[8]

If ESTPs can control their multiple interests and make football a high priority, they are assets to any team.

ISFP

Excellent Receivers

ISFPs are among the top two wide receiver Types in the NFL. They are naturals as receivers—running with the speed, agility, and the spring of an antelope across the plains. **Robert Brooks, Isaac Bruce, Carl Pickens, Kevin Williams, Gary Clark,** and **Marvin Harrison** are just some of the ISFPs who have excelled in recent history. ISFPs are among the fastest runners. Olympic gold medalist and sprinter **Michael Johnson,** ISFP, was ranked first in the world at both 200 and 400 meters through most of the 1990s.

As receivers, ISFPs are unsurpassed in body control, balance and rhythm. Their fine motor abilities (hands) are secondary to their gross motor's, yet ISFPs often find success by clutching passes to the chest rather than relying on the hands alone. When practicing, young ISFP receivers should give extra attention to catching balls with the fingers. This will come in handy later in their careers.

Offensive Linemen

ISFPs are arguably the top Brain Type for offensive tackle in the NFL; they also fare well at other line positions. Some All-Pro ISFPs who come to mind, past and present, are **Art Shell, Doug Smith, Lomas Brown, Larry Allen, Erik Williams, Randall McDaniel, William Roaf,** and **Jonathan Ogden.** ISFPs are blessed with extraordinary body strength and balance. Couple these with right-brained-fluidity and grace and it isn't difficult to understand their superior offensive line talents.

Art Shell, former Oakland Raider, was a bulwark on offense. *People* magazine wrote of Shell:

> His speed and bulk made him an overpowering blocker, and he missed only five games through 15 seasons in which the team won the super Bowl twice.[9]

Former teammate and Raider Lyle Alzado once said of Shell:

> I never knew a defensive lineman who got the better of him.[10]

Former L.A. Ram **Doug Smith** played in 6 consecutive Pro Bowls at center. In 1997, **Lomas Brown** made his 7th consecutive Pro Bowl appearance—having played in the NFL 12 years. **Randall McDaniel,** in 1997, played in his 8th consecutive Pro Bowl after only nine years in the league.

Good Defenders, too

Don't let ISFPs' calm exterior fool you. When they get popped in a football game, their dominant, Introverted Feelings react with intensity. Their amiable personas can vanish quickly. ISFP **"Too Tall" Jones** led the Dallas Cowboy pass rush during much of the Coach Tom Landry era. The Miami Hurricanes' **Russell Maryland** was the 1990 Outland Trophy winner (best interior lineman), and became the No. 1 pick in the 1991 NFL draft, selected by the Dallas Cowboys.

In the NFL, ISFPs are not found as often at linebacker as they are in the secondary. Nonetheless, **Levon Kirkland** and **Brian Urlacher** have made their mark in the 21st century. In the 1900s, **Mel Renfro** was selected to the Pro Bowl an impressive 10 times. **Carnell Lake** was a 1990's All-Pro, playing both strong safety and cornerback.

Running Backs

ISFPs are among the best running backs, relying upon smooth moves and superb body balance. They often run effortlessly—with speed, quickness and surprising leg power. ISFPs usually don't do as well at NFL running back as the other SPs (ESFP, ISTP, ESTP), but they're definitely one of the best.

ESFP

ESFPs are often easily recognizable, tending to be outspoken and high-profile. ESFPs have included **Muhammad Ali, George Foreman, Charles Barkley, Dizzy Dean, Carl Lewis, and Lee Trevino**. Pro football has had its share of prominent ESFPs, a Brain Type that can be one of the best in football.

The Ultimate Performers

ESTPs and ESFPs are similar in their quests as crowd pleasers, though ESFPs generally have the advantage. As Feelers, ESFPs relate more to matters on an animate basis than inanimate, as would Thinkers. ESFPs are keenly aware of the fans and usually desire their approval. All-Pro defensive end **Bruce Smith** (1990 NFL Defensive Player of the Year) was one ESFP who did. Smith's celebrations after sacks drew the ire of opposing players and the NFL office. Smith was quoted in 1991:

> To be out there now in front of 80,000 people and millions more on TV, and just take control of a situation. . . . It's like addictive. No, it is addictive.[11]

Gross Motor Superiority

No Type better demonstrates big muscle control in an artistic, rhythmical fashion than ESFPs. They are incredibly strong and agile. Consider **Walter Payton, Edgerrin James, Emmitt Smith, Lawrence Taylor, Warren Sapp**, and **Reggie White**.

Perennial All-Pro **Reggie White** was voted the 1990 NFL Defensive Lineman of the Year. The 6' 5", 285-pound licensed preacher was dubbed the "Minister of Defense." *Sports Illustrated* wrote:

> No one, it seems, has ever heard him curse. He won't fight on the field.

White responded:

> Maybe a little pushing or shoving sometimes, but that is it.[12]

It's been refreshing to have role models for our youth like Reggie White.

The highlight of White's career came in 1997. Of all the football miles he's traveled, none was as sweet as the victory lap he took around the New Orlean's Super Dome—following his Green Bay Packers' Super Bowl victory. The most productive sacker of quarterbacks in NFL history was finally able to be on a championship team.

Quickness and Agility

Columnist Mike Downey wrote of **Bruce Smith** in 1992:

> But Smith also had mobility, with a first step that sometimes beat the snap the way a sprinter out of the blocks jumped the gun, too close to call.[13]

Perennial All-Pro **Anthony Munoz** is a more subdued ESFP. Considered the premier offensive tackle of the 1980s, he preferred to let his stellar play do the talking. Munoz retired in 1993, having been voted to the Pro Bowl 11 times. His wife DeDe said:

> Ever watch him? It's an artistic way of playing the offensive line. He makes it look easy.[14]

Defensive end William Fuller, ESFP, said of Munoz:

> He has the best feet of any tackle I've gone against.[15]

Fellow ESFP Bruce Smith, on Munoz:

> There are no comparisons between him and other tackles. He's proven it year after year that he's the best.[16]

What was most impressive about Munoz was not his size or football skills. Rather, it was his Christian character. Sam Wyche said when he coached Munoz at Cincinnati:

> If pro sports could point to one guy who would be the ideal to look up to, Anthony would be it. All of us try to set examples until something goes wrong, and then we reveal our true selves. Anthony's real self is the one the rest of us try to be.[17]

Outstanding Defenders

ESFPs are the consummate Brain Type on the defensive line. This is not to say others can't make All Pro, but ESFPs are wired the best. Some ESFPs include **Bruce Smith, Reggie White, Neil Smith, William Fuller, Cortez Kennedy, Sean Gilbert, Michael Dean Perry,** and **Warren Sapp.** As high energy, gross motor, right-brained players, ESFPs can be very quick, agile, and strong with the large muscles, possessing optimal body balance. They're strong enough to throw offensive lineman aside and agile enough to slip by a blocker to sack the ball carrier. ESFPs usually prefer games over practice, being highly motivated by big crowds.

This inborn design has great vision and peripheral awareness, lower body strength, and fluidity. On slick, wet, or muddy surfaces, they can excel over other Types. ESFPs can get highly emotional and tackle hard.

ESFPs are also one of the top few linebacking Types in the NFL. **Lawrence Taylor, Ken Norton Jr.,** and **Bryan Cox** are ESFPs. Few ESFPs in the NFL play in the defensive secondary. Their strengths are not as conducive for these positions.

Grade-A Runners

ESFPs are undeniably one of the top few running back Types in the NFL; they've included **Walter Payton, Emmitt Smith, Thurmon Thomas, Ricky Watters, Jamal Anderson,** and **Edgerrin James.**

Walter Payton rushed for an amazing 16,726 yards over his career, gaining more yardage than anyone in the history of the National Football League. He played 13 seasons in a league where the average running back lasts less than five. Payton was once asked to analyze his running style. He responded in ESFP fashion:

> I'm not feeling a thing when I'm running and cutting on the field. I don't even know what I'm doing. My aggression fuels my burning desire. I block out everything. I'm an *artiste*! Everything I do is spontaneous and creative.[18]

Thurman Thomas was voted the NFL's MVP in 1991, where he led the league in combined rushing and receiving yardage for the third consecutive season.

Emmitt Smith was the NFL's most productive rookie ballcarrier in 1990 and became one of the league's premier rushers. Nate Newton said of his perennial All-Pro teammate:

> He can stop on a dime and give you $9^1/_2$ cents change.[19]

In 2000, young running star **Edgerrin James**, ESFP, was the NFL's leading rusher, racking up 1,709 yards.

Agile, Strong Quarterbacks

Quarterbacks **Randall Cunningham, Rodney Peete, Jeff Blake,** and **Donovan McNabb** have shown their ESFP motor skills. ESFPs generally find it difficult to stay in the pocket when passing. Their wandering nature and athleticism make them roam the field. ESFP **"Dandy Don" Meredith**, so dubbed for partying and free-living ways, was not as mobile as Cunningham and Peete, yet he had many successful years with the Dallas Cowboys. Quarterback **Jeff Blake** played in his first Pro Bowl in 1996.

Though ESFPs are only once removed from the ESTP Brain Type, this is a significant difference when it comes to playing quarterback. ESFPs have the upper hand in whole body control, balance, and running. When tackled, they are more apt to stay on their feet than ESTPs. ESFPs usually have stronger arms overall, throwing the deep ball more easily. One other important aspect to consider is that ESFPs and ESTPs have the best spatial awareness of all 16 Brain Types. It's no small wonder to see why they have both done so well over center.

On the other side of the coin, ESTPs excel over ESFPs in the most crucial areas for QB. The Thinking ESTPs are better at logical reasoning (especially spatial logic) than the Feeling ESFPs. When game pressure rises to its highest levels (particularly in the playoffs), ESTPs have a significant advantage. They will usually make wiser decisions. Also, ESTPs have better fine motor abilities. They can have more compact throwing deliveries while releasing the ball sooner. Many ESFPs have had long arm throwing motions—Randall Cunningham, a case in point.

Especially in "big" games, if ESFPs can be aware of their ill-advised tendency to both throw logic out the window and rely on gut-level instincts and feelings, they will play better.

OBSTACLES

Many ESFPs have to fight the battle of the bulge their entire lives. When they enact personal disciplines and are in harmony with their Feeling function, they find greater success at keeping their weight down. **Bruce Smith** recalled his childhood:

As a kid I'd eat at my mother's house, then go down the road to my girlfriend's and eat, and then sometimes go to my friend's house and eat again. I could gain five pounds in a day. In a week, there wouldn't be a scale to weigh me.[20]

ISTJ

ISTJs are not as prominent in professional football as they once were. Today they are infrequently found in the NFL, and when they are, it's normally at quarterback. ISTJ QBs generally do not throw the ball hard, nor are they as accurate as some other Types. As left-brained quarterbacks, they won't be as mobile or visually aware as the right-brained Ps.

Miami Hurricane graduate **Steve Walsh** was an ISTJ quarterback who attempted to establish himself in the NFL. Veteran quarterback **Jeff Hostetler** led the New York Giants to victory in the 1991 Super Bowl. This ISTJ typified his Type as a signal caller.

The odds of finding ISTJs at running back in the NFL are remote.

ESTJ

Like ISTJs, ESTJs are not frequently found in professional football. Of the two, there are more ESTJs. The odds are extremely remote for finding ESTJs as NFL running backs; they lack agility and mobility. They are normally linemen or quarterbacks. As quarterbacks, however, their chances for NFL prominence is not high. Success at the high school and college level is more probable. **Scott Mitchell** and **Ryan Leaf** are two contemporary ESTJs.

When ESTJs are relaxed, they can pass as well as any Brain Type. They usually have strong arms and are quite athletic (Consider ESTJ Nolan Ryan.) They can be tough competitors, hating to lose. The more they feel pressure, however, the more acute their tunnel vision becomes, and the more mechanical their throwing motion—with accuracy suffering. The higher the competition level, the more their performance wanes. In the NFL, ESTJ quarterbacks can have good games, but they will lack consistency. ESTJs throw best from the pocket and are less adept at throwing on the run. (ESTPs are best at throwing on the run.) ESTJs are normally responsible, compliant players—though there are exceptions. This often makes them more attractive to coaches than the more talented but lackadaisical, undisciplined Types. From my observations, left-handed

ESTJ quarterbacks appear to have higher potential than righty ESTJs. In body movements, lefty ESTJs use their right brain more.

Keith Millard was one of the NFL's best defensive tackles until he injured his knee in 1990. In 1989, his fifth NFL season, he was named the NFL Defensive Player of the Year by the Associated Press. His 18 sacks were third in the league. In 1991, *Sports Illustrated* wrote:

> Millard's uncanny knack for anticipating the snap, combined with an explosive first step, makes him very difficult to block one-on-one. . . . Millard says his style of play is as much studied as instinctive, and it's not always foolproof, as his 20 offside penalties in 1988 attest. Still Millard's most effective asset may be his intensity, even though it is highly combustible. Millard works himself into a violent rage before a kickoff . . . .[21]

Keith Millard himself said:

> I used to get so fired up that I wore myself out before the end of the game. I was slapping my own guys around. My energy was ready to burst. By the fourth quarter I had used up my tank. I'd lose my temper and play bad because I was out to beat up the other guy rather than do my job, and that hurt me.[22]

As dominant left-hemisphere Thinkers, ESTJs become highly intense in situations that are important to them. I witnessed this firsthand in my ESTJ brother. When I was a child, I saw him, as a high school defensive back, knocked out cold two times in one football game. Smelling salts were used to revive him, and he went right out to play again. His tackling style was to lower his head and crack helmets with the offensive back. He and his opponents resembled mountain goats ramming heads. My brother played with intensity.

Needless to say, ESTJs are much more emotional in life and their football-playing style than ISTJs.

ISFJ

ISFJs are rarely found in pro football and the chances of them becoming household names are not high. The most likely position for NFL success is offensive tackle. One rare ISFJ with NFL stardom has been offensive tackle and All-Pro **Richmond Webb**. In 1997, the 6'6", 300-pound Webb played in his seventh consecutive Pro Bowl. He was recognized as the prime protector on his Miami Dolphin team for superstar quarterback Dan Marino.

ISFJs are capable of greater football success at the college level than pro, but their positions for success are limited. The skilled positions are the hardest for them to excel at.

INFP

INFPs can be top notch NFL receivers, relying upon their speed, agility, graceful movements, and phenomenal leaping abilities. In track and field, INFPs excel in the hurdles and high jump; they often emulate these moves on the gridiron.

In 1989, **Flipper Anderson** caught 44 passes for 1,146 yards, leading the NFL with an average of 26 yards per catch. He also set a record by catching 15 passes for 336 yards in one game. *Sports Illustrated* wrote:

> Anderson was not considered to be much of a pro prospect. One service that rated college players for the draft had him sixteenth behind even Don McPherson, who was a quarterback at Syracuse.[23]

Not knowing the innate abilities of INFP receivers can prove costly for scouts and coaches. When he was coach of the L.A. Rams, and of Anderson, John Robinson said he was impressed with:

> . . . the enormous number of catches he [Anderson] made with the guy right on him. He has the speed to threaten the defensive back but more than that, he can time the ball and go up and get it.[24]

Receiver **Yancy Thigpen**, INFP, had an All-Pro year with the Pittsburgh Steelers in 1995. In the NFL, however, INFPs are not found as often as ENFPs at receiver; ENFPs generally play with greater effort.

ENFP

ENFPs are loaded with energy, ever ready to expend

it on the gridiron. Consider ENFPs in other sports: boxing's **Evander Holyfield**, cycling's **Greg LeMond**, basketball's **Kevin Garnett**, baseball's **Sammy Sosa**, and track and field's **Gail Devers**. ENFPs consistently expend more energy in athletics than any other Brain Type, and they're one of the most commonly found Types in the NFL.

Agile, Explosive Running Backs

Roger Craig was a punishing runner and famous for his high knee kick. He was one of the NFL's all-time best receiving backs, becoming the first player to go over 1,000 yards in both rushing and receiving (1985). Craig was best known for his devout work ethic (a common trait to ENFPs).

By 2000, **Kimble Anders** had played in three Pro Bowls. The ENFP fullback was recognized as a specialist at running, receiving, and blocking.

Terrell Davis lasted until the sixth round of the 1995 NFL Draft. Surprising the talent scouts who don't understand Brain Types, ENFP Davis won the 1996 AFC running crown with 1,538 yards! He not only exuded ENFP energy and running savvy, he demonstrated his ENFP receiving talents.

In his first 7 years in the NFL, **Marshall Faulk** won a Pro Bowl invitiation 5 times. In 2000, Faulk won the NFL's Most Valuable Player award.

Superb Receivers

Arguably the best receivers in pro football, ENFPs utilize their vitality and acrobatic skills to overcome defenders. Some ENFPs include **Jerry Rice, Tim Brown,** and **Shannon Sharpe**. ENFPs can make acrobatic catches, fight defenders for the ball, catch passes in traffic without worrying about getting hit, and break tackles with their illusive movements and speed.

Jerry Rice, ENFP, has set himself apart as the premier NFL receiver of all time. It was reported in 1989:

> Super Bowl XXIII proved that Rice is in the same class with basketball's Michael Jordan. They both make plays that astonish even the game's best players.[25]

In 1994, Rice set the NFL career record of 127 touchdowns. In 1995, he broke the NFL's single-season record for receiving yards and most catches in a career. In 1997, Jerry Rice was chosen to the Pro Bowl for the 11th consecutive season. Amazingly, despite the wear and tear of playing so many seasons, he continued to be the league's most feared receiver.

Energetic Defenders

ENFP defensive specialists have included **Charles Mann, Leonard Marshall, Jerry Robinson, Albert Lewis, Derrick Thomas, John Randle, Ken Harvey, Hardy Nickerson,** and **LeRoy Butler**. Veteran player **Jerry Robinson** was a three-time All-American at UCLA and was named NFL defensive rookie of the year in 1980. His career was virtually injury free, remarkable for his 10-plus years in the NFL. Prior to his tragic death, linebacker **Derrick Thomas** was a perennial selection to the Pro Bowl. Consistent with his ENFP Type, Derrick was a specialist at stripping the ball from quarterbacks. Having met him, I found he was exceptionally personable.

ENFPs are among the best defensive secondary players. Their high energy play, high pain threshold, right-brained motor movement fluidity, quick feet, mobility and flexibility (they're excellent at backpeddling) give them high NFL potential.

NFL Quarterbacks?

At quarterback, ENFPs are mobile runners and capable of throwing the ball as hard and far as nearly any Type. They have physical tools to excel but must work very hard at the mental, spatial aspects to be NFL quarterbacks. Being iNtuitive and conceptual, ENFPs have a tendency under game pressure to see what "could be" rather than "what is;" they also falter in logic (especially spatially) as Feeling Types. Few ENFPs have been successful quarterbacks in recent NFL history.

Outstanding Punt Returners

It's difficult to imagine a Brain Type better suited to returning kicks than ENFPs'. They have been among the top returners in NFL history. ENFPs can be excellent provided they learn how to catch and hold onto the ball. **David Meggett** and **Desmond Howard** were first class ENFP returners in the latter 1990s. In 1997, **David Meggett** played in his second Pro Bowl. Standing only 5'7", Meggett was one of only two AFC players for the season to be ranked in the top 10 in both punt and kickoff returns. **Desmond Howard** was the 1991 Heisman Trophy winner—an award rarely given to a receiver. In 1996, Howard was the NFL's premier return man, highlighted by his 1997 Super Bowl return of 99 yards. His run deflated the New England Patriots' attempt at a second-half rally and earned him the game's MVP.

Helping ENFPs

ENFPs are not born with the best hands of the 16 Brain Types—they are once removed from the fine motor dominant STs (ISTP, ESTP, ISTJ, and ESTJ). NFs excel at coordinating fine and gross motor skills, making ENFPs the supreme acrobats. Nonetheless, if ENFPs work hard at developing their hands and improving concentration and self confidence, they can be the best of receivers.

ENFJ

ENFJs have played virtually every position in NFL history but are not as apt to be found today in pro ball as in yesteryear. As Extraverted NFs, ENFJs' style of play normally brings enthusiasm and fervor to the game.

ENFJs have been successful quarterbacks in NFL history. Those large in stature usually have had strong arms, able to throw hard and deep. ENFJs are intelligent and team players. They have included **Bob Griese, Pat Haden, Danny White,** and **Vince Ferragamo.** Hall-of-Famer **Griese** guided the Miami Dolphins to two Super Bowl victories. He passed for 25,092 yards and 192 touchdowns over his 14 seasons. ENFJs' odds for QB success are perhaps not what they once were. Nevertheless, recent ENFJs have included **Vinny Testaverde, Drew Bledsoe,** and **Gus Frerotte.**

As left-brained iNtuitive quarterbacks, ENFJs tend to develop tunnel vision under pressure. Their peripheral awareness suffers and throwing motion becomes more mechanical. Thus, it's paramount for ENFJs to control their strong emotions. Relaxation techniques and visual drills can be of much benefit.

In the NFL, very few ENFJs are found in the running back position. Receiver is a better position for ENFJs, though not many are found here, either. One ENFJ and former NFL receiver established himself in the record books. During the 1992 season, **James Lofton** (ENFJ) broke Steve Largent's all-time receiving record of 13,089 yards. (ENFP Jerry Rice currently holds the record.) Lofton, a former long jump champion at Stanford University, ended his NFL career with 14,004 career receiving yards.

ENTJ

ENTJs have excelled in pro football from its inception. They're arguably the best of the left brain Js in football. ENTJs are one of the best quarterbacks, receivers, linemen, and sometimes linebackers.

Former All-Pro **Reggie Williams**, ENTJ, of the Cincinnati Bengals was once one of NFL's top linebackers, and ENTJ **Greg Lloyd** became one of the top linebackers of the 1990s. Former All-Pro offensive lineman, **Dan Dierdorf**, has since taken his ENTJ talents to the broadcasting booth. Middle linebacker and perennial All Pro, **Mike Singletary**, was the main fixture in the Chicago Bears' defense during the 1980s. From 1983 to 1991, Singletary was annually named to the Pro Bowl. *Sports Spectrum* wrote in 1992:

> Singletary has developed a reputation around the league for knowing an opponent about as well as his coaches on game day. He reviews hours of films. He doesn't hesitate to work on a certain aspect of his game over and over until he gets it right.[26]

All-Pro safety and roommate of Singletary for 8 seasons, Shaun Gayle, said:

> Mike has a good understanding of what it takes to be the best . . . he's a guy who's committed to winning, to understanding the game.[27]

Regardless of the sport, ENTJs rely especially upon their cerebral acuity.

Smart Quarterbacks

Playing quarterback is prized by ENTJs. Desiring to lead people and be in control of situations, no position on the gridiron can offer more opportunities. As NTs, ENTJs prefer to engage their brain prior to exercising their brawn. They innately know that their mind is one of their special gifts. Some ENTJs to have played the game include **Len Dawson, Jack Kemp, Roger Staubach, Steve Bartkowski, Steve Young, Jim Harbaugh, Trent Green** and **David Carr.**

When they possess physical mobility, ENTJs are good running quarterbacks. They realize that interceptions can be avoided by tucking the ball in and going for the necessary yardage. ENTJs desire and *tend to complete a high percentage of their passes*. Their left-hemisphere dominance lends itself to a more calculated approach to the game, minimizing risk.

In 1963, **Roger Staubach** won the Heisman trophy as a running QB for the Naval Academy. This Hall-of-Famer took his running and winning ways to the NFL, leading the Dallas Cowboys to two world titles and ten winning seasons in as many years. Hall-of-Famer **Len Dawson** played 19 years in pro ball. He quarterbacked 3 AFL championships and a Super Bowl victory. *Len led the AFL a record eight seasons in pass completion percentage.* His final season, 1975, saw him lead the NFL in passing accuracy.

Following his successful pro career, **Jack Kemp** decided to exercise his mental dexterity in politics. In 1995, **Steve Young** won a record fourth consecutive passing title and was named the Associated Press' most valuable player for the second time in three years. Having played 15 NFL seasons, Young retired in 2000. He played in seven Pro Bowls and in classic ENTJ fashion, he left the game with the *NFL's all-time leading pass rating*.

Receivers

ENTJs normally do not possess the speed and mobility of other top receiver Types. They compensate for this deficiency by outsmarting defenders, and with precise, well rehearsed moves. Former Seattle Seahawks' wide receiver, **Steve Largent**, posted a number of records during his 14-year NFL career, becoming the league's all time number-one receiver in total yards.

ENTP

ENTPs are the most frequently found Brain Type in the NFL. For those familiar with typology, this will probably come as a complete surprise. You may be thinking, "How could the cerebral ENTP be so successful in such a brawny sport?"

The prime reason for so many ENTPs in the NFL became apparent to me when attending the 1996 Combine in Indianapolis, Indiana. This annual NFL event features the top several hundred college football players—demonstrating their talents in anticipation of the upcoming NFL Draft. This tightly guarded event is restricted to observers from NFL teams only.

Over the week-long workouts, I was able to evaluate nearly 250 players. ENTPs were the most commonly found Brain Type. Considering they're believed to approximate only 5 percent of the U.S. populace, an astounding 49 percent of the players were ENTPs! How could this be? ENTPs are frequently found on college teams due to their superior intellect, not necessarily true athleticism. Many players found among the top athletic Brain Types never make it to college; they fail to meet entrance requirements or maintain academic standards. (In pro baseball, for example, there are many more of the top athletic Types. They're often drafted out of high school.)

As a whole, ENTPs did better in their Indianapolis workouts than any of the other 15 Types. They are high-energy people and possess tremendous agility and flexibility (due to their iNtuitive right-brained motor skills). Many of the Indy drills were ideal for the ENTPs. Though they can look great at the Combine (without pads), they normally don't perform as well in NFL games. ENTPs are much better, however, at some positions than others.

As an aside, a large number of potential pros who aren't ENTPs never make it to college, or for that matter, the Combine. I'm convinced this disparity will lessen in the years ahead. Brain Typing will make universities and pro organizations more aware of overlooked and talent-latent players—providing them strategies for developing individual potential.

Place Kickers and Punters

ENTPs are arguably the top place kicking Type in the NFL. There appear to be more ENTPs than any other Type in kicking, especially among the best. Some ENTP place kickers include **Morten Andersen, Jason Elam, Steve Christie, John Carney, Cary Blanchard, Jeff Jaegger, Adam Vinatieri,** and **Mike Vanderjagt**.

ENTPs do not have the best natural motor skills, but with the proper training, they can become excellent kickers. Mentally, no Type is better at kicking in poor weather conditions. ENTPs' right-brained dominant iNtuition is the least sensitive Perceiving function to external weather conditions. As Extraverts, ENTPs are anxious to come into a game after sitting around for long periods; they've plenty of energy to release. (Introverts have greater difficulty getting to the optimal energy and mental levels.) As right-brained Ps, ENTPs are fluid and loose kickers, not mechanical or rigid. (Interestingly, ETPs are usually the top relief pitchers in baseball. As a reliever, fine-motor dominant ESTP

Dennis Eckersly went 150 innings without a walk!)

ENTPs can develop tremendous whip in their legs and arms. (For instance, ENTP Pete Sampras once had one of the fastest serves in tennis.) ENTPs' loose and flexible motor skills can generate extra snap to the pitch, serve, or kick. Conversely, gross-motor dominant SFs are more apt to be slower and short on kicks due to the tightness in their legs—especially when they experience pressure.

Though ENTPs will not always be great kickers, they have high potential when developing their physical and mental place-kicking and punting skills. Some ENTP punters include **Darren Bennett, Chris Gardocki,** and **Matt Turk**.

Quarterbacks

Having studied NFL quarterbacks quite carefully for many years now, I must include ENTPs among the top few Brain Types. Their smarts, potential for toughness, and physical and spatial skills all contribute to a high QB aptitude.

If ENTPs begin athletic endeavors as youngsters, they can develop the motor skills to be top-notch QBs. **Dan Fouts** played 15 years in the NFL, leading the league in passing 4 successive seasons. He once attempted 608 passes in a season, and 300-yard games were often routine. ENTP Fouts once held the dubious record of most fumbles in an NFL career, 106, until ENTJ Dave Krieg passed him.

Steve DeBerg surprised the pro football world by making his 14th season his best. In the 1990 season, he was the league's third rated passer, throwing only 4 interceptions in 444 attempts. ENTP quarterback **John Brodie** played for 17 seasons in the NFL, becoming one the top passers of all time. He led the league in both completions and total yardage in 1965, 1968, and 1970.

Contemporary ENTP QBs include **Neil O'Donnell, Jeff George, Rich Gannon, Kerry Collins, Charlie Batch, Jay Fiedler, Brian Griese, Jeff Garcia, Kurt Warner** and **Chad Pennington**. Though these players have had quite different personalities, careers, and playing abilities, they all share the ENTP inborn hard wiring.

Since ENTPs are least developed in their gross motor skills, young and aspiring ENTP QBs will be wise to develop their big muscle movements and to perfect their mechanics. This will come in handy when they are confronted with big-game pressure. In these situations, ENTPs' body skills can break down, and their passes can become errant.

ENTP QBs should also give high priority to visual awareness. Having a Type tendency to *imagine* "what could be" more than *seeing* "what is," ENTPs must give attention to seeing the complete field of play. Under pressure, they'll tend to lose their spatial abilities. Mental/visual exercises can be of appreciable benefit in overcoming this dilemma.

Versatility

ENTPs demonstrate wide versatility in the NFL. Areas of least success appear to be offensive tackle, halfback, and outside linebacker. Nonetheless, with much hard work, they're capable of making All-Pro at these positions.

One of the ENTPs' greatest attributes in football (and sports) is that they're often willing to sacrifice their bodies to achieve success. For example, their high threshold for pain and drive to achieve personal goals impel them to put a hit on an opponent, even if means personal sacrifice.

Unorthodox

Sometimes known for their audacious and zany ways, ENTPs have impacted the NFL in many areas. Former players and ENTPs include **"The Mad Stork" Ted Hendricks, John Matuszak, Tim Rossovich,** and **Lyle Alzado**. Former All-Pro **Lyle Alzado** once said:

> If me and King Kong went into an alley, only one of us would come out and it wouldn't be the monkey.[28]

ENTPs' sometime atypical behavior has easily fit the Oakland Raider image. When **Lyle Alzado** was battling brain cancer in 1992, Raiders' executive assistant Al LoCasale said of him:

> Lyle had always been a loony guy, and he stood out in Denver and Cleveland because of it, but when he came here, he was just one of the guys.[29]

Conclusion

We have considered some major attributes of the most commonly found Brain Types found in professional football. Types not mentioned should not give up their aspirations, but realize working harder and smarter will be necessary to reach the highest levels of the game.

Each Brain Type excels at specific phases of the football, mentally and physically. The more time you devote to observing and understanding these differences in Types, the more exciting and beneficial this study will become for you.

It is wise to investigate the players of your specific Brain Type. This will enable you to see the various ways persons of the same Type play football. Look for articles where they share their methods of success, mentally and physically. If you have typed yourself correctly, you should relate to what they are saying.

Though far from complete, here is a list of well known players and their probable Brain Types—providing a perspective on the most successful designs in professional football.

BRAIN TYPES AND FOOTBALL

ISTP
Mark Brunell, Brad Johnson, John Kitna, Ty Detmer, Cade McNown, Billy Joe Tolliver, LaDainian Tomlinson, Terry Allen, Fred Taylor, Jevon Kearse, Earl Holmes, Dale Carter, Shaun Williams, Jeff Feagles
Retired: Mark Rypien, Jim Taylor, Mike Ditka, Dick Anderson, Jack Lambert, Ronnie Lott, Lin Elliott, Bill Bates, Stan Humphries, Wade Wilson, Bryce Paup, Charles Haley, **Barry Sanders**

ESTP
Brett Favre, Peyton Manning, Michael Vick, Jake "The Snake" Plummer, Chris Chandler, Trent Dilfer, Eddie George, **Ricky Williams**, Curtis Martin, Andre Rison, Quinn Earley, Mark Stepnoski, **Junior Seau**, **Ray Lewis**, Kevin Greene, Donnie Edwards, Blaine Bishop, James Hasty, Ty Law,
Retired: **Joe Montana**, Johnny Unitas, **Joe Namath**, Ken Stabler, Terry Bradshaw, Fran Tarkenton, Joe Theismann, Phil Simms, Billy Kilmer, **Jim Brown**, Tony Dorsett, O. J. Simpson, Deacon Jones, "Mean" Joe Greene, **Dick Butkus**, Jack Youngblood, Howie Long, Mark Gastineau, Brian Bosworth, Dennis Byrd, Eric Dickerson, Jim McMahon, Dan Marino, John Elway, Marcus Allen, Herschel Walker, Merton Hanks, Deion Sanders, Troy Aikman

ISFP
Warren Moon, Steve McNair, Daunte Culpepper, Tony Banks, Chris Redman, Tee Martin, Warrick Dunn, Isaac Bruce, Carl Pickens, Marvin Harrison, Kevin Williams, Terance Mathis, Raghib "Rocket" Ishmail, Wesley Walls, Erik Williams, William Roaf, Larry Allen, Randall McDaniel, Lomas Brown, **Jonathan Ogden**, Levon Kirkland, Brian Urlacher, Anthony Morgan, Leon Lett, Russell Maryland, Aaron Wallace, Fred Strickland, Harlon Barnett, Greg Biekert, Doug Evans, Steve Atwater, Scooter McGruder
Retired: **Lynn Swann**, Doug Williams, Jeff Rutledge, John Cappelletti, Art Shell, Doug Smith, Ed "Too Tall" Jones, Mel Renfro, Lake Dawson, Gary Clark, Robert Brooks, Carnell Lake, Earnest Byner, Harvey Williams

ESFP
Donovan McNabb, Randall Cunningham, Rodney Peete, Jeff Blake, Byron Leftwich, **Emmitt Smith**, Jamal Anderson, Thurman Thomas, Edgerrin James, Natrone Means, Ricky Watters, Larry Centers, Jamal Lewis, Eric Green, **Keyshawn Johnson**, Randy Moss, Terrell Owens, Frankie Sanders, Troy Brown, Jermaine Wiggins,
Orlando Pace, Tre' Johnson, Bruce Armstrong, Ruben Brown, Ron Stone,
Bruce Smith, Neil Smith, Willie McGinest, Michael Strahan, Hugh Douglas, Cortez Kennedy, Sean Gilbert, Michael Dean Perry, William Fuller, Gilbert Brown, Warren Sapp, Richard Seymour, Darrell Russell, LaVar Arrington, Bryan Cox, Jessie Armstead, Micheal Barrow, Kevin Hardy, Greg Townsend, Tedy Bruschi
Retired: **Walter Payton**, Don Meredith, Dexter Manley, Chris Collinsworth, Jerome Brown, Ottis Anderson, Anthony Munoz, William (The Refrigerator), Perry, Lawrence Phillips, Ken Norton Jr., **Reggie White**, Nate Newton,

ISTJ
Jeff Hostetler, Steve Walsh

ESTJ
Scott Mitchell, Danny Wuerffel, John Walsh, Pat Barnes
Retired: Keith Millard, John Alt, Sean Salisbury, Ryan Leaf

ISFJ
Richmond Webb, Trezelle Jenkins

ESFJ
Craig Whelihan
Retired: Mark Collins, Sean Jones

ENFJ
Vinny Testaverde, **Drew Bledsoe**, Elvis Grbac, Gus Frerotte, Gino Torretta, Danny Kanell, Steve Wisniewski, Dave Szott, Eric Swann, Matt Stover, John Kasay
Retired: Pat Summerall, Frank Gifford, **Bob Griese**, Vince Ferragamo, Danny White, Pat Haden, Jim Hill, James Lofton

INFP
Retired: Mike Garrett, Flipper Anderson, Mike Sherrard, Yancy Thigpen

ENFP
Kordell Stewart, Akili Smith, Damon Huard, Drew Brees,
Jerry Rice, Tim Brown, Shannon Sharpe, Desmond Howard, Anthony Miller, Scott Turner, Charlie Jones, Qadry Ismail, Terrell Davis, **Marshall Faulk**, Garrison Hearst, Mike Anderson, Robert Edwards, Tiki Barber, Ron Dayne, Sam Gash, Dave Meggett, Keith Sims, John Randle, Tony Bennett, Mike Jones, Ken Harvey, Hardy Nickerson, Steve Smith,
Albert Lewis, Darryll Lewis, LeRoy Butler, Tim McDonald, Darren Perry, Ray Buchanan, Ashley Ambrose, Ike Reese
Retired: Willie Gault, Tom Jackson, Roger Craig, Jerry Robinson, Charles Mann, Leonard Marshall, Greg Bell, Keena Turner, Andre Ware, Brett Perriman, Gaston Green, **Derrick Thomas**, Kimble Anders

ENTP
Kurt Warner, Rich Gannon, Brian Griese, Jeff Garcia, Neil O'Donnell, Jeff George, Kerry Collins, Charlie Batch, Bobby Hoying, Koy Detmer, Jay Fiedler, Chad Pennington, Chris Weinke,
Jerome Bettis, Errict Rhett, Dorsey Levens, Charlie Garner, Cris Carter, Antonio Freeman, Herman Moore, Amani Toomer, Rickey Dudley, Terry Glenn,
Dermontti Dawson, Tim Grunhard, Frank Winters, Andy McCollum, Will Shields,
Morten Andersen, Gary Anderson, John Carney, Steve Christie, Jason Elam, Cary Blanchard, Jeff Jaeger, Pete Stoyanovich, Adam Vinatieri, Sebastian Janikowski, Mike Vanderjagt
Darren Bennett, Chris Gardocki, Matt Turk, Lee Johnson,
Peter Boulware, Keith Hamilton, Chad Brown, Rod Woodson, Eric Allen, Rodney Harrison, Eric Davis, Ryan McNeil, Keenan McCardell, Michael Bates, Jason Sehorn
Retired: **Dan Fouts**, John Brodie, Ron Jaworski, Joe Gilliam, John Matuszak, Lyle Alzado, Randy Cross, Jack Ham, Tim Rossovich, Paul Maguire, Mike Curtis, Bob Golic, Tony Mandarich, Bart Oates, Mike Lansford, Steve DeBerg, Steve Bono, Keith Jackson, Leslie O'Neal, Dan Saleaumua, Alfred Williams, Lamar Lathon, Terry McDaniel, Louie Aguiar, Tony Siragusa

ENTJ
Trent Green, David Carr, Rob Johnson, Steve Stenstrom, Keith Poole, Bruce Matthews, Tony Boselli,
Retired: **Roger Staubach**, Jack Kemp, Len Dawson, Steve Bartkowski, Neil Lomax, Jeff Kemp, Mark Malone, Dan Dierdorf, Reggie Williams, Steve Largent, Ahmad Rashad, Todd Christensen, Bob Chandler, Gary Fencik, Pat Leahy, Pat McInally, Mike Ademle, Mike Singletary, Greg Lloyd, Dave Krieg, Mark Kelso, Sterling Sharpe, **Steve Young**, Jim Harbaugh

13 Golf

The popularity of golf has seen significant growth in recent years. Courses cannot be built fast enough to keep up with the demand. Television coverage plays a major role in golf's appeal. Beautiful, lush courses amid bodies of water make golf an alluring sport to our senses. The players are fashionably dressed, appearing to leisurely enjoy themselves as we would a stroll through the woods. Serious golfers are pursuing a professional career for more than the aesthetics, with the number of million dollar purses on the PGA Tour increasing from one in 1983 to nearly 50 in 1997—where some $70 million in prize money was available.

There is another side to the links besides the fun and beauty, which most of us never consider. Golf involves all the physical and mental challenges of other top sports, despite its apparent lack of physical exertion. Golf includes more physical and mental aspects than just about any sport. The swing and putting intricacies are endless, while the mental side is enough to bring any world class athlete to his or her knees. When one's living is dependent upon golf, it is indeed a sporting challenge.

Golf is often played by great athletes representing all sports. **Hockey's Wayne Gretzky, Tennis' Pete Sampras, basketball's Michael Jordan, and even former NFL star Lawrence Taylor love the game.** When Taylor arrived six hours late the opening day of training camp in 1991, he said:

Don't blame me. Blame the foursome ahead of me.[1]

Golfing great **Lee Trevino** said:

You can talk about baseball, apple pie and fried chicken, but man, don't leave out golf. This is America's sport in my opinion. Baseball players retire, football players retire, hockey players retire, basketball players retire, [then] they play golf, don't they?

I've never seen a golf pro retire to take up hockey, baseball or football. This is it. This is the game.[2]

What Brain Types do you think would fare best in the 18 hole outing? Could a Feeler handle the game's logical aspects? Could a left-brained (J) implement the short game's finesse?

Based on my knowledge of Brain Types and golfers, any of the 16 Types can achieve a low handicap. Yet effort beyond the normal rigors must be given for some of them to attain this. Playing on the professional Tour is another story.

Professional golf is another sport where only select Brain Types are consistently found in the winner's circle. Nevertheless, one or two do not dominate. The winner each Sunday could be one of a number of Types. Let's briefly look at pro golf's top Brain Types.

ISTP

ISTPs, as we have already seen, are consistently the best overall athletes. I'm aware of no sport in which they cannot excel. Their brain design and body dexterity are made for athletics. Golf is no exception—yet it is not a sport they dominate.

Fantastic Short Game

ISTPs are perhaps the purest strikers of the ball. Their hand-eye coordination is the best; they can make a ball do almost anything. ISTPs right-brained fine motor (STP) proficiency is also suited to playing on and around the green—though putting is often their nemesis. It's not uncommon for ISTPs to get too handsy, especially under pressure. Tour player Ben Crenshaw said of ISTP **Mark Calcavecchia**, in 1990:

> He has great hands and knows what to do with them. He hit some unbelievable shots off the greens last year and he's a terrific putter.[3]

Finesse

Calcavecchia has been one of the best-known ISTPs on Tour. Many can't understand his finesse game, considering his 6-foot, 200 pound stature. He's also known as an aggressive player and one of the longest hitters. Knowing Mark's ISTP Type provides insight into his game.

ISTPs' intense logical minds, generally tremendous assets, are sometimes their worst enemies. ISTPs have difficulty controlling their incisive and temperamental moods on the golf course, although some hide it well. Nevertheless, they are the ultimate competitors and take the game most seriously.

Ben Hogan is considered by many to have had the consummate swing of all time. He was also the ultimate ball-striker, as well as one of the game's greatest thinkers. It is no surprise that Hogan demonstrated his God given gifts in this way. His right-brained dominance (P) enabled him to master the athletic swing of other great ISTPs.

Hogan implemented his mental as well as his physical dexterity on the links. He often said, "Management is 80 percent of winning." ISTPs are dominant Thinkers in spatial matters, logically synthesizing what is observable. They literally are scientists in their respective sports, Einsteins, in athletic attire. (The ISTP Brain Type, by the way, also qualifies as a chief architect, surveyor, and meteorologist.) Hogan combined the constituent mechanical elements of the game into a unified artistic swing.

Other ISTP impact players on the PGA Tour, past and present, include: **Jim Colbert, Mike Hill, J.C. Snead, Corey Pavin, Mark O'Meara, Tom Lehman, Craig Stadler, Steve Pate, Lee Janzen,** and **Jim Furyk,** to name several. **Corey Pavin and Craig Stadler** were the No. 1 and No. 2 wage earners on the 1991 PGA Tour, collecting $979,430 and $827,628. In 1996, **Tom Lehman** was voted PGA Player of the Year and set an official earnings record of nearly $1.8 million.

ISTPs are well represented on the Women's Tour. **Pat Bradley**, ISTP, became the first LPGA player to reach $2 million, $3 million and $4 million in career earnings. She captured her 30th career win in 1991, becoming only the 12th woman to make the LPGA Hall of Fame. This same year, at age 40, Pat was named the Ladies Professional Golfers' Association player of the year. She led the Tour with earnings of $763,118.

Beth Daniel is another ISTP star who has at times dominated the LPGA Tour. She was a two-time U.S. Women's Amateur champion, LPGA Tour Rookie of the Year in 1979, Player of the Year in 1980, and leading money winner in 1980 and 1981. Between 1983 and 1989, Daniel won only one tournament. Physical problems were partially to blame, but the mental side of golf became a major factor in her life. She joined the ranks of other ISTPs who introspect too much, and her putting suffered. Things abruptly turned around for her at the end of 1989 when she won four of six tournaments. The assault continued into 1990, when she won seven Tour events, including her first major, and pocketed a record $863,000.

PGA Tour player, Davis Love III, said of Beth Daniel:

> I'll tell you why she wins so much. It's that swing. She's got the world's prettiest swing.[4]

Daniel, like Hogan, has perfected the golf swing. Not only is it sound mechanically, but it has that distinctly right-brained grace.

In 1996, Australian ISTP **Karrie Webb** became the first woman to win over $1 million on the LPGA Tour and Britain's **Laura Davies**, ISTP, was voted the female player of the year.

OBSTACLES

Introspection

ISTPs often lack year in and year out consistency. They tend to introspect too much. As perfectionists, they can negatively affect both their swing and potentially phenomenal putting touch. Following his second place finish at the 1990 U.S. Open, ISTP **Mike Donald's** game steadily eroded. A year later, he began to get it back and explained the time in between:

> For the first time in a long time, I actually feel like I'm trying to play golf instead of trying to figure out what the heck I'm doing wrong.
>
> I was hitting shots that I wouldn't have hit if I would have just walked up to the ball, stood over it and just hit it. But by trying to make the perfect swing, my shots became awful.[5]

ISTPs tend to improve their games as they age—having learned the debilitating effects of overthinking and unnecessary frustration. **Mike Hill** of the Senior Tour provides hope for introspecting ISTPs. In 19 years on the PGA Tour, Hill won three tournaments and $573,000, total. In his first 3 years as a Senior player, Hill captured 12 titles and earned more than $2 million. Hill attributed his remarkable success to a better attitude:

> I believe the pressure I put on myself when I was young was too great for my brain to handle. I don't worry about playing well anymore.[6]

Jim Colbert had 8 victories over 21 years on the PGA Tour. In 1996 alone, Colbert won 5 tournaments and pocketed a Senior Tour record for earnings of $1.6 million. In his first six years as a Senior player, Colbert pocketed nearly $7 million. **Tom Lehman** failed eight times to get his PGA Tour card. His ISTP determination and ability to improve with time were instrumental for success.

At age 41, **Mark O'Meara** made 1998 his best year on the PGA Tour. In addition to winning the Player of the Year award and nearly $1.8 million, he captured two major titles, the Masters and British Open.

Intensity

ISTPs have the tendency in sports to become too intense in competition. They must learn to keep their fervency in check, particularly in a methodical game like golf. **Beth Daniel** had a standing rule with her caddie in 1990 to remove the club from her hands as soon as she hit a bad shot. She explained:

> If I'm upset, the longer I hold that club the more I want to beat it into the grass.[7]

Her caddie Greg Sheridan concurred:

> We've battered a few trash cans. I can usually measure how mad she is by how deep the clubface is buried in the ground.[8]

Golf Legend Mickey Wright once said of Beth Daniel:

> She's a marvelous player if you can just control her head.[9]

ISTP golfer **Tim Simpson** came on the PGA Tour in 1977, only to incur many disappointing years. Yet, in 1989 and 1990, he turned things around, winning $761,597 and $809,772. In 1991, Tim spoke of his frustrating years:

> In the first eleven years out here, I worked so hard and I was so intense that basically I couldn't get out of my own way. I tried so hard and wanted to be good so bad, I was just too tough on myself.[10]

Things changed for Tim when he received sound advice from a sports psychologist. He was told to relax more in his putting, sound advice for all uptight ISTPs.

Helping ISTPs

It is reported that a significant factor in **Beth Daniel's** turn around was her new caddie. He is said to have been a calming influence, something she needed. The knowledge of Brain Types can help not only in improving one's game, but it can lend assistance in choosing caddies or coaches best-suited for the athlete (for example, see ENFJ, Jim Courier, in Tennis chapter). Parents or guardians of ISTPs must be careful not to push them too hard in golf or any sport.

Beginning when they're young, help ISTPs keep their

cool. If you don't emphasize relaxation and self control early, ISTPs will struggle with excessive intensity for a long time to come. ISTPs experiencing pressure (like all STs) will be most affected in their arms, hands, and wrists. They must learn to be aware of this pattern and relax these areas.

ESTP

ESTPs are often the crowd drawers and pleasers—no one could rope in the spectators like ESTP **Arnold Palmer**. ESTPs possess charisma and often sport the latest or classiest fashions. Consider the late and great **Payne Stewart** and how he fashioned his trademark knickers, or how **Greg Norman** over his illustrious career has sported a variety of hats, threads, neck chains, along with his ever-present tan.

Caring about their bodies as well as their clothes, ESTPs generally are in top shape when appearing before crowds. Their often Hollywood or Herculean looks and persona will draw a gallery. The crowd responds to ESTPs by providing them additional motivation. ESTPs rise another notch when they feel the energy of their audience. Crowds and ESTPs are made for one another.

ESTPs employ their right brains with proficiency. They have superior vision that synthesizes matters expertly, and are generally super smooth with their swings (like **Fred Couples**), long hitters, great up and down players, and outstanding-to-inconsistent putters. In 1998, **Se Ri Pak** stormed the Women's Tour by winning two of the first three LPGA majors of the year. She possessed solid swing mechanics (unlike many ESTPs) and rhythmical, fluid strokes, Pak's golfing future is bright.

The best courses for ESTPs are those that allow for mistakes, where there's still a shot even when it's hit off-line. When their errant shots get them in trouble, ESTPs can play like Houdinis, pulling off the impossible while acting as if it were no big deal. They will acknowledge the gallery's excitement, but do so with the coolness of an actor entering LA's Dorothy Chandler Pavilion on the night of the Academy Awards.

Aggressive Players

A 1985 article in the *L.A. Times* reported:

The seemingly sudden emergence of foreign golfers in events traditionally dominated by Americans doesn't surprise **Arnold Palmer**.

The reason, Palmer says, is that players such as Spain's **Severiano Ballesteros**, West Germany's **Bernhard Langer** and Australia's **Greg Norman** have adopted the same gambling style that Palmer made famous in the 1960s.[11]

Remember the childhood saying, "It takes one to know one?" It would be fair to apply this in Mr. Palmer's case. ESTP Arnold instinctively recognized the aggressive playing styles of three other ESTPs. They "adopted" this style not so much from nurture as they did from nature.

Since the U.S. Open normally requires great accuracy and a more conservative approach, ESTPs do not fair as well in this tournament. They can win, but it is the toughest challenge in golf for their Brain Type. It depends on the Open course, but ESTPs must generally adjust their style of play. (U.S. Open courses and conditions most often suit the more conservative-playing left-brained Js.)

ESTPs play their best with controlled aggression, usually incurring trouble when they play otherwise. ESTP **Ray Floyd**, at age forty-seven, played fabulously well for three and one half days at the 1990 Masters. Having fun and subduing the Augusta National until Sunday's back nine, Floyd became too introspective and altered his ESTP style. He played with atypical caution and care—"even though it's not my nature," he later commented.[12]

Though Floyd lost, he had nothing to be ashamed of; after all, he was about to become the oldest to win a major on the PGA Tour. Floyd was far from finished, however. At age 49 in 1992, the ageless ESTP nearly won the Masters again, finishing second to ESTP **Fred Couples**.

Greg Norman's ESTP style of play enabled him to be golf's first $11 million dollar man—making him the PGA's career money leader in 1997.

Big Hitters

The 1991 PGA Championship at Crooked Stick is a tournament that will not easily slip from memory. An unknown, long haired Arkansan captured the admiration of millions of golfing fans. He routinely knocked the ball from sight, well beyond 300 yards. "Long **John**" **Daly**, age 25, subdued the course that Pete Dye built.

Daly made his first PGA win a major tournament, in classic ESTP gambling style. He finished the 1991 season as the longest hitter on Tour, averaging some 290 yards.

According to his fiancée in 1991, Daly made the year a turnaround time for himself. Known as a "party animal" and "Wild Man," Daly was in the process of tempering some of his ESTP attributes.[13]

Daly's unorthodox swing is not one to emulate unless you are an ESTP, and even then I would advise caution. He taught himself to play and was not as interested in mechanics as he was in competing. His unique ESTP swing takes extraordinary flexibility, timing, fine motor skills, and balance. Unless you possess these attributes, save your back and body a lot of trouble.

Davis Love III and **Fred Couples** have been two American ESTPs consistently near the top in the PGA Tour Driving Distance category. When **Love** first joined the Tour, his play was similar to Daly's current style. Love learned to temper his swing and length off the tee, however, in order to develop greater consistency.

Fast Players

More often than not, ESTPs play quickly. They have so many opportunities to pursue, and with few exceptions, they are in high gear, even on the golf course. (**Bernhard Langer** is one ESTP exception.)

As it will be repeatedly discussed in this book, one's environment plays a significant role in shaping behavior and personality. In fast-moving **Lanny Wadkins**' case, he reflected on his childhood:

> We'd play 27 to 36 holes in the morning, then go swimming, have lunch, and play 18 more holes.[14]

No one traverses the links like Lanny. Combine his Type and early style of play and you have a plausible explanation for his course persona. (I doubt that ESTPs Langer and Wadkins learned golf under similar circumstances.)

Superb Short Game Players

ESTPs and ISTPs are similar in their game near and on the green. They both possess right brain controlled fine motor skills, enabling them to be masters with the short sticks. ESTP **Ben Crenshaw** was long regarded as one of the top putters on Tour. When he and other ESTPs access their golfing zone, they'll chip in from off the green and routinely snake long putts.

ESTPs are more likely than ISTPs to develop the putting yips as they advance with age. They will be forced to adjust their stroke and mental outlook when this occurs.

HELPING ESTPs

ESTPs would do well to take the advice of fellow ESTP **Fred Couples**, who said in 1991:

> I would rather have a shorter swing, which I'm working on, and not hit the ball as far. I'm trying to be more accurate, and if I'm accurate, I'm a much better player . . . I think I could win 20 times a year if I hit every fairway.[15]

Fred followed his own advice in 1992. He blitzed the PGA Tour and achieved a Number 1 ranking in the world. The Masters was his first major title.

Learning patience, how to concentrate, and how to control one's anger are also helpful for ESTPs.

Last, ESTPs (like all STs) must learn to control their arms, wrists, and hands when experiencing competitive pressure.

ISFP

ISFPs could be more prominent on the pro Tour if they learned to better master their thought processes and emotions. ISFPs have all the physical skills; they are marvelous, graceful athletes. Swinging the golf club with sound mechanics and a smooth tempo need not be a problem. Conquering their minds is the challenge.

Successful ISFP golfers in the 1990's have included **Ernie Els, Steve Jones,** and **Duffy Waldorf**.

Self-effacing Golfers

ISFP **Kathy Whitworth** is the most honored player in LPGA history. Her 88 official Tour wins exceed the victories of PGA players Sam Snead (81) and Jack Nicklaus, who won 70. Despite her string of successes, the gentle and private Kathy has always been hard on herself. Sonja Steptoe, of *Sports Illustrated*, wrote of Whitmorth:

> "Dang it, Kathy, they should take your card!" she would say to herself after an errant shot. And thus would begin the masochistic mind game that Whitworth played during a round, the object

of which was to browbeat herself into hitting shots that would prove she belonged on the LPGA Tour. There was no letting up. Even as the ball rolled into the hole, she would shake her lacquered bouffant [hair] in disgust and mutter in her Southwest twang that she didn't deserve a good score. Carol Mann, who used to play the Tour with Whitworth, called it her "dark side."[16]

Many talented ISFP golfers never make it through the pro qualifying schools. They often lack confidence telling themselves that they don't belong on Tour and thus play that way, especially under pressure. If they find successes, however, their confidence will grow appreciably. They all have the potential of Kathy Whitworth. Like Kathy, however, they will forever tend to have these self deprecating tendencies.

Gross Motor Skills

Thanks to their adept large muscles, right-brained ISFPs can hit a long ball with fluid motion. Their wrists hinge naturally, as if they've been lubricated with WD-40. ISFPs do not struggle with the domineering wrists and hands of the STs. My oldest son and I once observed the pros on the practice range at the L.A. Open. He was particularly impressed with the graceful swing of ISFP **Wayne Grady**. Most of us would be wise to observe and emulate such swings.

Wonderful Short Game

ISFPs are able to chip and putt superbly. Their gentle touch and innate feel resemble an artisan developing a masterpiece. As long as they can maintain their composure, they're hard to beat in the proximity of the green.

Excel at Match Play

Evidence suggests ISFPs are especially gifted for match play. Their Type, which has a dominant Feeling function, tends to be less confidant playing against a large field of players than only one other player—which happens in match play. Competing against one person a round tends to raise an ISFP's game to a higher level of performance.

South African **Ernie Els** joined the PGA Tour in 1994. He surprised many by winning the U.S. Open Championship his first year on Tour and continued his excellence by becoming the first player to win 3 consecutive World Match Play Championships (1994-1996). This astounding feat was largely lost among the media reports describing Els's "final-round flops" in regular tournaments. They couldn't understand how the 6-foot-3 golfer with the smoothest swing on Tour hadn't performed better at the end of medal-play tournaments. Until 1997, when Ernie silenced most of his critics by winning his second U.S Open. As he has improved at the mental aspects of his ISFP game, the more consistent he's become. (By the way, match play has been good to Els for some time. As a youngster he beat Phil Mickelson for the Junior World Golf title in San Diego.) In 1997, Els rose again to the top by winning his second U.S. Open title, a remarkable feat for a 27-year-old. In 2002, Els won the British Open. In 2003, Els won a record-tying fifth World Match Play title.

ISFP golfer **Jim Thorpe** won back to back match play championships at Tucson in 1985 and 1986—before the tournament was cancelled.

HELPING ISFPs

ISFPs often need to develop a better self image. They must remember they have infinite value, independent of any sporting success, because they are hand-crafted uniquely by God. They have innumerable personal talents but assume lower profiles than the talented high-powered Extraverts. Having stability in their personal lives is important for optimal golf.

ISFP youngsters should seek to have fun when they play. They shouldn't focus negatively on their golfing weaknesses, but look for fun ways to improve them.

When ISFPs experience pressure, it is important to guard against letting their heads move too far forward in the swing before they hit the ball. Their big muscles will have more of a tendency to move their body farther forward than other non SF Types.

ISFPs also need to work hard on developing their fine motor movements. Being gross motor dominant, their hands will not be as quick as many of the other Brain Types. Interestingly, after **Steve Jones** won the 1996 U.S. Open (much to the surprise of golf pundits), he told how his dirt-bike accident in 1991 was responsible for his new-found golfing success. He no longer could grip the club normally with his left hand. His new and lighter left-hand grip made his right hand more dominant—eliminating a left-to-right fade and introducing a right-to-left draw. Steve's serendipitous discovery was ideal for ISFPs and their tendencies for slow hands, particularly the dominant hand sitting farthest down the shaft. Remember, however, many

ISFPs prefer to play their natural tendencies and fade the ball. Individual preferences must be taken into account.

And last, some SFP golfers have had much success at throwing the right arm—thus moving the club into the ball at impact mainly with the right side of the body (for right-handers). These kinds of golfers are sometimes described as "throwers." LPGA sensation **Annika Sorenstam** (ESFP) has been described as a playing this way. ST or fine motor dominant golfers need to be cautious when employing this technique. They already have a tendency to use too much of the dominant arm and hand in the swing.

ESFP

Their numbers are fairly small on Tour, both PGA and LPGA, but ESFPs are highly successful golfers. Perhaps their Extraversion prefers more team-oriented sports. Regardless of why there aren't more ESFPs on Tour, they are capable of playing superior, consistent golf. **Lee Trevino, Chi Chi Rodriguez, Jerry Pate, Notah Begay III, JoAnne Carner, Nancy Lopez, Annika Sorenstam, Michelle McGann, and Meg Mallon** have enabled us to view the ESFP in golf.

Lee Trevino won 27 tournaments on the regular Tour, including four majors (two U.S. Opens and two PGAs). Lee, as expected, dominated the Senior Tour after he joined in late 1989. He received the inaugural Senior PGA Tour Player and Rookie of the Year awards in 1990. For that year, Trevino pocketed nearly $1.2 million dollars in earnings and won 7 tournaments. By 1994, he became the first Senior to have three million-dollar seasons (1990, 1992, 1994). In 1997, Trevino became the first Senior player to pass $7 million.

Trevino, like other ESFPs, is good natured about life. Once struck by lightning, he explained in 1992 why he holds his one iron over his head when there's a storm on the golf course:

> Because even the good Lord has trouble hitting a one-iron.[17]

The only man who can compete with Lee Trevino's fun loving personality on the course has been another ESFP, the affable **Chi Chi Rodriguez**. Chi Chi was the ninth PGA player to reach the $3 million level in earnings. He, too, became a dominant player on the Senior Tour.

In 2003, ESFP **Annika Sorenstam** won her fifth player of the year award, winning 11 titles and $2.8 million. In 1991, Sorenstam was the college player of the year.

Feelers

ESFPs often wear their hearts on their sleeves. You can easily sense their mood. Their Feeling function drives their actions in life and on the course. **Chi Chi Rodriguez** said:

> There are people with classic swings, but they don't have a heart. It's what's inside you that matters.[18]

Meg Mallon won a lot of friends but no tournaments in her first five years on the LPGA Tour. Not surprisingly for an ESFP, however, she was voted the Tour's "friendliest player" in a poll of fellow players in 1990. When she won the Women's U.S. Open in 1991, she collected her third victory of the year (two were majors!).

Nancy Lopez is irrefutably one of the best LPGA players in history, a four time player of the year. She was one of the first athletes I attempted to type from viewing TV in the early 1980s. Her ES_P ways were obvious to me, yet with a determined and competitive drive, I wrongly assumed she was an ESTP. Evaluating her more closely many years later, I was surprised to discover she was an ESFP. Not only has Nancy demonstrated superior motor skills throughout her career, but emotional and people skills, too.

Long Hitters as Seniors

ESFPs generate more power with the gross motor skills than any other Brain Type. This especially begins to show itself in the senior years. Other Types begin to lose their gross motor abilities long before the SFs. Consider **Chi Chi Rodriguez**. Have you noticed his swing on the Senior Tour? Talk about using the big muscles! Only an SF could replicate his swing and walk the next day.

Yet Chi Chi's swing is highly productive. Standing only 5-feet-7, and around 135 pounds, he drove the ball much farther than other players, especially those of his size. He was comparatively much longer off the tee now than when he played the regular Tour—thanks to his enduring gross motor adeptness.

And **Lee Trevino**, at age fifty-four, was hitting tee shots as long as anyone in professional golf in 1994. Injuries have since hampered his game.

Visualizers

Although ESFPs' typological iNtuition is less developed than their Sensing function, they are quite capable of picturing matters in their minds.
Chi Chi Rodriguez said:

> People see me playing so fast and wonder why I don't slow down. I already played those shots the night before, so when I get up to them I'm ready.[19]

Like to Play Quickly

ESFPs, like ESTPs, don't care to spend extra time on the course. When **Chi Chi Rodriguez** was asked why he plays so quickly, he said:

> Successful people do things fast. There are some people in this world who take two hours to watch "60 Minutes."[20]

OBSTACLES

ESFPs golfers must guard against analyzing too carefully, something ISTJs and INTJs are more likely to get away with. ESFPs are primarily "feel" players. Once their swing is grooved, they must especially rely on touch. **Chi Chi Rodriguez** was once one of the best putters on the regular Tour. He said he lost his touch when asked to write a $50 magazine article on putting. He explained:

> I always just walked up to the putt and knocked it in the hole. But when I stopped to analyze it, I started to think about it. Sure enough, I got the jitters and it really hurt my career on the regular Tour. That $50 cost me a lot of money.[21]

Lee Trevino has similarly spoken of his hesitancy for getting too introspective. When asked if he had a regular golf teacher or guru, he replied:

> I've never had a coach in my life. When I find one who can beat me, then I'll listen.[22]

HELPING ESFPs

Meg Mallon said, after capturing three victories in 1991:

> I know it sounds funny for someone who has played golf a long time, but before you've won—or been in a position to win—it can make you extremely nervous to be under par.[23]

Most of us would experience shock, not nervousness. Nevertheless, Mallon's advice is particularly sound for ESFPs who find themselves playing better than they expected. Rather than panicking, they should enjoy the fruit of their labor while realizing they can be as good as any golfer.

ISTJ

The ISTJ Brain Type is ideally suited for golf—possessing the ability to regulate golf's physical and mental processes. ISTJs, as we saw in the Body Skills chapter, have superb dexterity. Their Type coordinates the fine motor skills with precision, providing them a distinct advantage over many other golfers. ISTJs approach golf as they do life—deliberately, thoughtfully, and persistently.

Concentration

Jack Nicklaus is considered by most to be the greatest golfer of all time. As a left-brained ISTJ, Nicklaus has taken a more deliberate, *mechanical* approach to the game. (How many players could crouch and concentrate over a putt as long as Nicklaus?) His Introverted preference has been instrumental to his success. Golf normally requires deep concentration in times of tremendous pressure, and ISTJs excel with the mind, loving to consider all the nuances of the game and course, analyzing matters thoroughly with great patience.

Motivation

ISTJs are competitive performers but lack the daily "killer instinct" of ISTPs. It usually takes the big matches, games or tournaments to fire up the ISTJ. When the Ryder Cup, majors, or an important tournament rolls around, watch out. ISTJs' calm, easygoing manner becomes highly motivated and focused. Jack Nicklaus, as well as a number of other ISTJs, has shown us this pattern over the years. Three of the four major tournaments of 1987 were won by ISTJs: the U.S. Open (**Scott Simpson**); the Masters (**Larry Mize**); and the PGA (**Larry Nelson**). The fourth major tournament, the British Open, was won by Nick Faldo, ESTJ. **Jack Nicklaus's** performances in the four pro major tournaments is unmatched—winning 18!

Accuracy

Nicklaus's stature is a major factor that has enabled him to play at a level above other ISTJs. ISTJs are conservative players, trying foremost to keep the ball in play. Nicklaus's size allowed him to hit a long ball with accuracy (he was the longest straight driver in the game). Many of the current ISTJs on Tour have the accuracy but lack the distance of the big hitters, which are often SPs. When ISTJs attempt to go for greater distance, their precision suffers.

ISTJ **Mike Reid**, nicknamed "Radar" on Tour because of his accuracy off the tee, won the Driving Accuracy category on the PGA Tour in 1980. He's been splitting fairways ever since. Suffice it to say, ISTJs are generally down the middle.

Lawrences of Arabia

Extricating themselves from sand difficulties is an ISTJ specialty. Their deft, ST fine motor skills and controlled swing are ideal for bunker play. ISTJ **Paul Azinger** led the PGA in Sand Saves three times between 1986 and 1990. Even as youngsters just taking up the game, ISTJs possess sand-playing skills.

Hand Dexterity

ISTJs are innately gifted to perform well in sports that require hand wrist proficiency. No Brain Type can develop faster in golf proficiency than the ISTJ.

Consider **Larry Nelson**, who didn't take up golf until he was age 21. Within six months he turned pro, and $3^1/_2$ years later he made the PGA Tour! Nelson had to spend many hours practicing to improve so quickly. Nevertheless, he had an optimal Type. Among his 10 PGA tournament victories, his major accomplishments include a U.S. Open and two PGA Championships. In 2000, Larry was the leading money winner on the Senior Tour, pocketing a cool $2.7 million. Larry Nelson has proven that it's never too late for ISTJs to begin and excel at golf.

OBSTACLES

Arms, Wrists, and Hands

Throughout this book, we will see evidence that one's greatest physical asset may also become one's nemesis. Because ISTJs are proficient with their fine motor skills, they have a tendency to use them too much in the golf swing, particularly when under pressure. **Jack Nicklaus** addressed this problem following his 1986 Master's victory (a record breaking sixth green jacket):

> I was playing more with my hands. When I played well, I was very quiet at the top and very quiet at the finish. I had been too violent with my hands going through the hitting area.[24]

It was written: "Once Nicklaus `took his hands out of the swing,' he started hitting the ball with full body force."[25]

Speed of Play

The PGA has a rule against slow play which can be a hindrance to ISTJs. Especially when under pressure, ISTJs tend to require additional time to consider matters. Their basis for evaluation is so precise that it often makes speedy decision making difficult.

For right-brained Extraverts (Arnold Palmer, Lee Trevino, Lanny Wadkins and Fuzzy Zoeller), playing with an ISTJ can be disconcerting. It is important to realize, however, each person plays according to his or her unique Type. Generally speaking, the more experienced ISTJs become, the less time they will require to play their rounds.

Paradoxical to ISTJs' slow play, they have been known to play too quickly. Their customary concentration and patience wanes when they lose interest, resulting in hitting the ball without adequate thought. ISTJs play faster in rounds where they lose concentration. When their minds are focused on golf, however, they will be deliberate.

Experiment too Much

ISTJs are the Thomas Edisons of the links. If something goes wrong with the swing, they often alter or experiment with it. This can be a bad habit. ISTJs can easily place too much emphasis on the mechanics and not enough on the swing tempo. **Larry Nelson** commented on his ever changing putting methods, following his 1983 U.S. Open victory:

> I must have tried 499 different things to correct it.[26]

When ISTJs finish an outstanding round of golf, they rarely remember the mental state they were in; their left-brained Thinking kicks in again when they surface from their Introverted Sensing function. Naturally, then, ISTJs believe their success came in perfecting some technique, and subsequently try to replicate it.

Overemphasis on Mechanics

Proper mechanics are crucial, yet can be emphasized to an excess. The relaxed, focused mind and smooth swing will bring the greatest success to the pro golfer, not messing with his good enough swing. The fluid swing maintains sound mechanics, whereas focusing on too many techniques or thoughts destroys the swing and the parts being worked on. One cannot break down the intricate pieces of the swing consciously when playing without becoming too mechanical. Following his 1991 victory at Pebble Beach, **Paul Azinger** commented:

> I was making it [golf swing] too complicated. It's really not that hard.[27]

Underemphasis on Imaging

As left-brained Sensates, ISTJs are among the least likely to instinctively use visualization. It requires utilizing their least developed brain preference, right-brained iNtuition. **Jack Nicklaus** has long been known for using imagery to perfect his golf game. This would seem unusual, considering his ISTJ makeup, had he not been taught this skill in his early years of golf. Nicklaus readily espouses his acquired skill of visualization.

Not all ISTJs are open to considering how to utilize harder-to-access portions of the brain. **Betsy King** has been hesitant. King, the LPGA's all-time money winner of the 20th century, has been regarded by many as the Jack Nicklaus of women's golf. She won 23 tournaments between 1984 and 1990, including six in 1989, winning the Women's U.S. Open and earning a record $650,000 in prize money. Betsy successfully defended her U.S. Open title in 1990. In 1995, she won her 30th career victory to gain entrance into the LPGA Hall of Fame.

Winless in her first seven years on Tour, King believes her golfing turnaround stemmed from improved mechanics. She said:

> I think the mental part of golf is overplayed. The mechanical part is more important than the mental part. Visualizing success is fine, but I can beat any 18-handicapper in the world. I don't care what the person's attitude is. He can picture hitting it 250 yards all he wants, but if he doesn't have the swing to do it, he can't do it.[28]

I could write a chapter on Betsy's comments, but let's only consider some brief points. *First*, Betsy's comments were in typical ISTJ fashion. I've already mentioned that ISTJs have the tendency to shun imaging. (Interestingly, some ENTP and ENFP pro golfers I've spoken with say that golf is over 90% mental! This belief is not surprising considering pros have already developed top-notch body mechanics, and that both Types are right-brained, dominant iNtuitives—the optimal visualizers.)

Second, proper mechanics are crucial for excelling in any sport, including golf. I know of no one who believes he or she can play expertly without mastering the mechanics, or beat a professional by simply visualizing.

Third, the mental part of the game *can* be overplayed, as Betsy says. Though few persons overstress the importance of the mind, many use inappropriate methods. (More on that in the Visualization chapter.) Conversely, the mechanics can be and are overplayed, far more often than the mental. Just go to the driving range and watch and listen, or pick up a golf magazine and read the articles. In contrast, how often do you discover or hear of others working hard on the mental side of golf?

Seeing that not every Brain Type excels on the pro golf Tours should convince us all how important the mind is in golf. *If the mind weren't so important, all the Types would be represented in the winner's circle.*

Every Type can perfect the mechanics to the degree of being able to win. I know; I've witnessed them. Only the mind inhibits many Brain Types from victory. Neuroscience and typology will continue to shed light on this issue in the years ahead.

Fourth, both mental and mechanics aspects are critical for excelled play. They go hand in glove.

Fifth, it appears Betsy King does not realize she has a Brain Type that naturally excels in golf. She may be unaware her mind is inherently able to focus in a golfing appropriate way, according to her Type. She reminds me of the INTP genius who could not understand why the other students in the physics class didn't excel or grasp concepts easily.

Sixth, Betsy's improved mechanics helped turn her game around! When one strikes the ball better through proper technique, one's confidence improves, bolstering the mind. Mechanics and the mind critically interrelate.

Last, Betsy's proclaimed spiritual conversion has had both a spiritual and mental impact. Prayer and meditating on Scripture will work wonders for a person's attitude on and off the golf course.

Ironically, soon after I wrote this piece on King, I noticed she was severely challenged in the mental part of her game. It happened at the 1990 Nabisco Dinah Shore in California, considered a major on the LPGA Tour. Betsy's previous comment about "the mental part is overplayed" may have taken on new meaning after the final round. Having bogeyed four holes during a five hole stretch on the back nine, King said:

> I haven't had a collapse like that in a long time. I kept looking at that leaderboard and noticed a five stroke lead with five to play. Then it was four and four, then three and three. I was just relieved when we ran out of holes.[29]

King went on to say: "Those last two hours seemed like an eternity."[30] She acknowledged to the media that she was nervous down the stretch. (Who wouldn't be?) I am glad for her sake and other golfers' that she addressed this often overlooked, critical dimension within sports. Her expertly-designed Brain Type for golf (and solid mechanics) got her to where she could be leading a major by five holes with five to go. Yet Betsy became caught up in her Introverted analysis and SJ cautious, defensive play. She allowed her natural strengths to become counterproductive.

For many years I have been a believer in Betsy King's golfing game (even if she's stated the mind is overplayed). I have similar confidence in other ISTJs who devote their time to golf, particularly to the mental side of the game.

A final chapter to the Betsy King story came when I read the April 7, 1997 issue of *Sports Illustrated*. It communicated the comeback of the 41-year-old King—with her first tournament victory in 20 months, the Nabisco Dinah Shore. Commenting further, *SI* reported that King revealed she had consulted a sports psychologist in 1994 (for competitive help among other things.) It's good to see that Betsy has placed additional emphasis on golf and the mind.

HELPING ISTJs

ISTJs are helped by learning golf imaging techniques. This can also assist them in attaining and maintaining a smooth swing tempo.

ISTJs should attempt to take the rigid arms, wrists, and hands out of the swing as much as possible.

ISTJs need to keep positive thoughts when playing, eliminating their inclinations for finding fault with their games.

ESTJ

I devote space to ESTJs not for their numbers on Tour but for their accomplishments. I have typed hundreds of the top PGA players, and ESTJs are infrequently found at the highest level. Nonetheless, they're capable of being the world's best. They play the Senior and LPGA Tours as well.

I believe ESTJs are uncommon on Tour because of their inability to control tension at the Qualifying School. Their swing mechanics are generally not the problem; ESTJs have extraordinary energy, regulated in a Thinking, left-brained fashion. They often have difficulty balancing their mental and physical energies in big events, exhibiting nervous, mechanical motor movements.

A prominent ESTJ on the PGA Tour in the 1980s was a fella whose two of three career wins were majors; he captured the U.S. Open, twice! I'm speaking of ESTJ **Andy North**, whose Brain Type was instrumental in those Open victories.

Those who follow the game of golf know the U.S. Open is played under the most stringent course conditions. There are speedy greens, slender fairways, and roughs often reminiscent of the pampas-covered plains of South America. The spray hitters do not fare well at the U.S. Open. Winners are sometimes better known as survivors. Winning scores often rest in the over par column.

ESTJs are survivors in golf. They hang in there, often without the sub par rounds. For most tournaments this approach isn't successful; the birdie shooters can leave ESTJs in the dust. At the U.S. Open, however, sub par scores are not the norm, fitting the ESTJ's game perfectly. Left-brained, Judging (J) golfers in general are better designed to play conservatively, while their aggressive, right-brained, Perceptive (P) counterparts tend to go for birdies and eagles.

Faldo vs. Foldo

Nick Faldo is another ESTJ who played in the 1980s. As a Brit, he wasn't often seen on my tube, and he began to excel only late in the decade. Golf followers used to know him as "Foldo" in the 1980s until his game reversed. Unfortunately, "Foldo" is often the ESTJs' golfing style until they overcome some major mental hurdles. Let's look a little closer.

Anxiety

Jack Nicklaus, Faldo's playing partner at the 1990 Masters, said:

> I couldn't believe how nervous he was, especially on the front nine. He couldn't pull the trigger, couldn't even play sometimes. He'd just walk around, lining up his shots, trying to calm down.[31]

> It was at the 15th hole [where Faldo got a birdie] that he began to relax.[32]

Remember, this was the year Faldo won his second consecutive Masters title. Considering his anxiety level, you might have thought it was his first professional tournament. He has learned to control tension enough to win many top tournaments—6 majors as of 1996—gaining him the reputation as one of the world's best golfers in the 1990s Faldo has become a consummate golf technician.

Former President **Gerald Ford** has been another well known golfing ESTJ. His play on Tour was limited to Pro-Am events, where he quickly gained a hacker's reputation. Can you imagine in those early years, how he felt as a high-handicap ESTJ on the first tee with a huge gallery lining the fairway? I'm sure he did a lot of hoping or praying. Tom Watson, who was often paired with Mr. Ford, was asked how he helped the President with his golf game:

> First, hitting the ball. Second, finding out where it went.[33]

In fairness to Mr. Ford, I'm sure he was a better player when not under the pressure of TV and crowds. Nonetheless, tending to take life too seriously at times, ESTJs will always battle the nerves on the course.

More Experienced, the Better

Baseball's **Nolan Ryan** is another well known ESTJ who experienced difficulty in balancing his mental and physical energies. Just ask the batters who faced him his first twenty years in the big leagues. Some are still afraid of a baseball because of his wild pitching. Ryan, however, was a much better pitcher at 40-plus than he was as a 20-year-old. The longer ESTJs participate in sports, the better they control their mental energies. (For more information on Nolan Ryan, see Baseball chapter.)

Experience similarly paid off for **Nick Faldo**. Faldo dropped his "Foldo" reputation when he learned to handle pressure and his putting improved. Faldo became one of the best putters (inside 10 feet) in the world.

Conservatives

ESTJs have a proclivity for conservative play. They want others to make the mistakes. At the 1987 British Open, **Faldo** defeated ISTJ Paul Azinger with 18 pars on the final day. Faldo said:

> I try to play a golf course down the middle, on the green and into the hole.[34]

> Golf tournaments aren't won by making great shots, they're won by making the fewest mistakes.[35]

I know a lot of Ps and even some Js who would argue Faldo on that one. Yet, for the ESTJ, conservatism works well. In 1996, Faldo was second in driving accuracy on the PGA Tour.

Hard Workers

When ESTJs make golf their focus, extraordinary time commitments and discipline are given. Faldo again commented:

Sometimes it's amazing. I'll work for three hours hitting bunker shots and get this overpowering urge to stay in there for three more. So I will.[36]

Personality vs. Brain Type

It is my intention to repeatedly give examples contrasting an athlete's personality with Brain Type. Consider **Nick Faldo**. If asked, most folks who follow Faldo's game would probably label him an Introvert. After all, he is regularly reported by the press as a reclusive, unsociable individual. Granted, he does convey that aura frequently, but we must look behind the image.

I will mention a few of the signs that Nick is classified Extraverted. (To understand the ESTJ's many faces better, read the ESTJ chapter.) The best way to discover an Extravert is to measure their innate, highly sustained energy level. Nick rates an "A" here.

Second, ESTJs are persnickety when choosing friends and acquaintances. ESTJs go through life judging most everything they confront with their discriminating Thinking function. They can find it hard to appreciate flawed things and people. Typology tells us that ESTJs will be least critical in their Introverted state (which can also occur when they're with people they like), when they cerebrally engage their non judging Sensing function. ESTJs often see themselves as Introverted.

Faldo vs. Hogan

Many golf pundits have compared Faldo to Ben Hogan. Hogan was a right-brained Introvert. Faldo is a veritable left-brained Extravert. This observation is obvious when one becomes proficient at Brain Typing. Hogan had the smooth, artistic swing, especially manifested in his short game. In Faldo, we also see a solid swing, though it is much more mechanical, especially in his short game.

Hogan and Faldo share two similar Brain functions, Sensing and Thinking. Both STs, they are most adept with fine motor functions and hand-eye coordination. They differ, however, in the E/I and J/P preferences. Hogan, as an STP, would master the artistic positioning of his hands where Faldo, STJ, would master hand dexterity.

Both Hogan's and Faldo's Types are dominant Thinkers, with Sensing auxiliary, according to Jungian typology. They therefore look quite similar. Neuroscience, however, reveals their vast differences in brain hemisphere dominance.

Too Much of a Good Thing

The inability to perform a body skill can be innate, substandard performance of that skill or it can be overuse of another. For the ESTJ (and ISTJ), innate dexterity of the hands and wrists can go too far. When the STJ feels pressure, the forearms, wrists, and hands tighten up like rigormortis. The whole golf game suffers, particularly the short game. Every Brain Type can, and will, carry its natural strengths to excess when succumbing to pressure.

HELPING ESTJs

ESTJs need to learn how to relax before and during a round. Rather than trying to blast the first drives on holes one and two, they would be wise to swing a little easier and hit the fairway.

ESTJs need to consciously relax their arms, wrists, and hands in pressured competition. Otherwise, their clubs are going to feel as if they spent the day with the Boston Strangler. Their greatest focus should be on a smooth, rhythmical swing.

Putting can be an ESTJ's nemesis, though it needn't be. When ESTJs are relaxed, they can putt superbly. Their fine motor dexterity and left-brained attentiveness to detail pay off well on the greens. Unfortunate for ESTJs, when they allow their keenly conscious left brain to become too fixated on the moment, considering all the potential consequences of a possible bad stroke or shot, they tighten up in mind and body—particularly in the wrists and hands. ESTJs will do well to emphasize a rhythmical, pendulum stroke at these moments, not a mindset considering every little angle and that they MUST make the putt.

ESTJs can derive long term benefit from learning to appreciate as well as critique. Applying tolerance to others' shortcomings and appreciating their strengths will not only enhance personal relationships but add joy to life.

ENTJ

What golf attributes come to mind when you think of **Tom Watson** in his prime? Tom has personified the ENTJ golfer: tremendous competitor, intellectually precocious, aggressive yet keeping game under control, playing superbly—even in foul weather, and competent with the long as well as short game.

ENTJs can be excellent performers in virtually any sport. They are more likely to be found on the pro Tour than ESTJs, primarily because of their mental approach. Taking up and sticking with golf is not always easy for ENTJs. One reason would have to be their Extraversion. Becoming professionally proficient in golf requires much Introverted activity. There are many lonely days on the driving range. Golf doesn't offer the team camaraderie of other sports, and ENTJs naturally tend to be drawn to team sports. ENTJs are uncommon on the women's Tour. This is not a result, however, of their inability to perform there.

ENTJs are great competitors. Not liking to lose in anything they care about, they will scrap to the very end. They want control more than any other Type, feeling best when they see themselves in charge. Tom Watson once said, "The biggest person I have to overcome is myself."[37] Watson, like other NTs, sets his own high standards, not needing others for motivation. Jack Nicklaus commented:

> The best part of Tom Watson's game is his mental toughness. Above all, he doesn't like to lose.[38]

Watson's accomplishments include winning eight major tournaments (five British Opens and two Masters), earning PGA Player of the year six times, and being leading money winner on Tour five years.

ENTJ **Johnny Miller** won a whopping 14 Tour events between 1974 and 1976 (ISTJ Nicklaus tallied nine). Miller said, in his prime:

> I turn mean with a 6-stroke lead. I'm not happy with a two shot win. I want more. I want to demoralize them. People used to say I didn't have the killer instinct. Well, most people don't know me very well.[39]

Well, John, I don't know you well either, but I believe you have a killer instinct. First, my research of ENTJs, and second, my experience of competing against ENTJs reveals there's no doubt you're a relentless competitor.

Curtis Strange dominated the PGA Tour as much as anyone in the latter 1980s, including back-to-back U.S. Open titles in 1988 and 1989. And let's not forget **Gary Player**, now on the Senior Tour. Gary has won, at last count, around 160 tournaments world-wide.

Value Consistency

ENTJs are always attempting to catch and maintain the illusive "consistency" in golf. Tom Watson has said:

> One thing is of primary importance to me—my swing, my improvement as a golfer, my consistency.[40]

ENTJs' success and consistency stems from their tenacious, erudite minds. Former great **Byron Nelson**, a mentor for **Tom Watson**, spoke of the Watson he's known:

> Tom's got such a brilliant mind that his intelligence always saves him.[41]

The ENT part of the ENTJ Type is aggressive, desiring to get in the lead as soon as possible. The J part seeks to maintain that lead but is more conservative, not wanting to blow the advantage. The ENTJ normally has a good balance for how the game of golf must be played.

Easily Motivated

ENTJs tend to finish high in the major tournaments. Their iNtuitive function looks forward with great anticipation to such special events. Visualizing the game is often as helpful for the iNtuitive as playing it. ENTJs come ready to play the big events, with minds primed as well as bodies—all the makings of a high finish. This helps explain why ENTJs often begin the season with a bang. They cannot wait to get back and demonstrate their superiority.

Tireless Workers

ENTJs have a work ethic second to none. When others are sipping lemonade at the pool side, ENTJs are advancing their profession. They'll work into the wee hours of the night as typical night owls. Lanny Wadkins, a go-with-the-flow ESTP, said Tom Watson:

> [Tom] would never tolerate a weakness. He'd go to the practice tee and beat at it till the darn thing went away.[42]

Watson commented:

> The range is my place. I practice after every round. Even if I'm leading by five shots.[43]

Leave it to the right-brained, spatially logical Lanny

Wadkins to make this astute observation:

> By and large your golf game mirrors your personality. Tom's [Watson] certainly does. We all approach things differently. Tom's methodical, organized, mechanical.[44]

Left-brained ENTJs are into mechanics and analyzing the game like other TJs. Right-brained golfers, especially EPs, are more rhythm, touch, feel and visual learners. Lanny Wadkins contrasted his approach with Watson's:

> When my swing is in trouble, I go back and look at old films when I was hot.[45]

It is also reported the Extraverted Watson rarely practices alone on the range. Someone is there to answer his questions regarding his swing. That's being analytical!

Creative Analysis

The 1990s brought the next ENTJ into stardom. An ENTJ who quickly became recognized as a star did not wait to turn pro before making his presence known. While still in college, **Phil Mickelson** won the Tucson Open, a PGA Tour event. He added this accomplishment to his three NCAA golf titles, a U.S. Amateur championship, and the Haskins Trophy (the Heisman trophy of college golf).

Mickelson gained a reputation as an inventive shot maker. This should come as no surprise considering he is typologically iNtuitive. Phil experimented endlessly with his golf game as a kid, reflecting:

> What that type of practice instilled in me, though, was imagination, a kind of resourcefulness and creativity that has become the strongest part of my game.[46]

Mickelson's devoted practice, linked with his innate iNtuition and Brain Type, produced an ENTJ PGA superstar by 1995. He was the Tour's second-leading money winner in 1996. Much could be written about Mickelson, but one aspect of his game deserves special mention.

Phil began playing golf at age 2! The natural right hander decided to swing a golf club as a lefty, despite his father's insistence to the contrary. (Mickelson's ENTJ bent couldn't have had anything to do with this power struggle, could it?) As we come to the present, Phil is right handed except for playing golf. This is significant.

If you happened to watch Mickelson play before his swing change in 1994, you probably noticed how much his right arm bent on the backswing, and how far beyond parallel he dipped the club, even on short irons. This was a result of his naturally dominant right hand holding the top of the club shaft. (Try this yourself and see if you aren't like one of the majority for whom this occurs.) Golfers ordinarily place their dominant hand below the non-dominant hand on the club. For amateurs, the dominant hand is one of the, if not the, major hindrance to their game. The dominant hand continually plays too big a role in the golf swing, including putting. This is truer for some Types more than others.

Phil Mickelson will not experience this problem like other golfers, even among professionals. He is a rarity in this regard on Tour. A major reason for Phil's past and future success is that he's an ENTJ playing with a subdued dominant hand. His non dominant left hand will help guide the club with right-brained contralateral control.

ENTJ **Tom Watson** has discovered the evils of the dominant hand as he has aged. Playing from his natural right side throughout his career, he said, in the late 1980s:

> Sometimes I wish I could cut this right arm off. I grip it [club] too tight.[47]

Phil Mickelson shouldn't have to struggle with this particular part of his game as he ages. Last, in case you are wondering what personas ENTJs employ as kids, Phil Mickelson's mother gives us a glimpse into a fairly common one:

> You know, Phillip was what you would call a strong willed child. He always knew what he wanted. He learned to get it by talking . . . I'd go to the parent-teacher conferences at school and his teacher would tell me that Phillip would come up to her, put an arm around her and say, "You are my favorite teacher." I'd go to the next class and the teacher would say, "Now I suppose you know I'm Phil's very favorite teacher."[48]

This illustration also gives you an idea why ENTJs are so prolific in politics.

Picturesque, Efficient Swings

Seeking perfection in the golf swing, ENTJs attempt to make it as efficient as possible. Because their motor movements do not dominate like those of Sensates, ENTJs are able to develop a swing that is compact and unified. In a 1991 survey of his peers, ENTJ **Tom Purtzer** was voted as having the best swing on the PGA Tour. **Steve Elkington**, ENTJ, was voted second.

HELPING ENTJs

The sooner in life ENTJs take up golf, the better their motor skills are in the long run. ENTJs need extra practice to develop the motor skills of Sensates. ENTJs should be encouraged not to quit, to keep at golf until they experience improvement. Once they gain greater skills, they feel more competent, and gain the desire to stick with the game.

Learning to relax before and during competition is important for ENTJs. Because their greatest body skill is using their minds, it is imperative they remove tension from analysis. Relaxing mentally will also relax their swings, producing fluid motions.

INTJ

Though there are few INTJs in professional golf (and a low percentage in the U.S. populace), they have made a profound impact. INTJs do not possess the Sensing Types' inherent motor skills, yet they can eventually master the swing and body skills in golf. INTJs must begin developing motor coordination at an early age to effectively play sports later. When this occurs in golf, they can be outstanding players.

Great Swing

Many golfers make the swing too complicated, with counterproductive, superfluous movements. We have discussed the prowess of the SF's gross motor skills and the ST's fine motor abilities. Nevertheless, these innate strengths can create problems (such as ISTJ Jack Nicklaus excessively using his hands). Many obstacles athletes experience in sports are natural strengths gone amok, carried to an excess. This is not the case with INTJs and their motor skills. They won't have the struggles of the Sensing athletes with overemphasizing motor skills.

My oldest son played on the golf team in high school. At one of his matches, he and I witnessed the ideal swing follow through. A fellow competitor, an INTJ, swung like Tom Weiskopf in his prime. This young man did not struggle with the ST fine motor dominance of my son; instead, his wrists cocked and uncocked easily, allowing his arms to extend into a smooth follow-through.

The INTJ's formative years in golf will be a time of developing and coordinating motor movements. As he or she becomes proficient, neither gross nor fine motor movements will dominate, even when under pressure. This is a marked benefit to INTJs in golf. Their finely tuned swing can achieve fluidity as it operates as a whole, with no exaggerated motor movements. INTJ **Tom Weiskopf** had one of the finest and most fluid swings in golfing history.

Conceptually Analytic

INTJs are in the "owl" family, relying on their mental acumen as an edge over the competition. **Tom Kite**, the cerebral Texan, has mastered his motor skills over the years, complementing his greatest asset—his indelible mental skills. This amalgamation of strengths propelled Kite's recognition as the most *consistent* golfer on Tour through much of the 1980s and 1990s. In addition to numerous victories, Kite once held the record for making the most consecutive tournament cuts. He's also been a Tour leader in career earnings and became golf's first $8-million man.

Consistency

Hale Irwin, another INTJ, was known as Mr. Consistency on the PGA Tour. From 1975 to 1978, Irwin went 86 tournaments without missing a cut! His streak is the third best ever on Tour. In 1986, Irwin dropped out of the money list's top 50 for the first time since 1969. But in 1990, glory again returned to Irwin's career. Counted out by most as a serious contender, Irwin came alive at the U.S. Open. Granted a special exemption as a former Open winner (his 10-year exemption for winning at Inverness in 1979 had expired), Irwin was allowed to play when failing to officially qualify. He again played like "Mr. Consistency."

As Medinah (the course) disposed of inaccurate golfing Types and players, Irwin was tied for the lead after regulation 72 holes with ISTP Mike Donald. Nineteen extra holes later, Irwin won with a sudden-death birdie. At age 45, he became the oldest player to win the U.S. Open. Irwin's mental and physical states were at such an optimal level that he played and won the Buick Classic the following week. He became the first player to win consecutive Tour events since (who else?) **Tom Kite**, in 1989. Irwin's exceptional play broke a five year victory drought, and followed his 1989 season as 93rd on the money list.

What happened to Hale Irwin? Did he discover a new golfing trick or swing mechanic? Not to my understanding. Irwin just once again accessed portions of his brain that hadn't been relied upon for years. At least three mental phenomena took place that U.S. Open week for Irwin. *First*, after he found himself in contention following an opening round 69, he envisioned a chance to win. His confidence was restored and boosted by specific neurons being reenergized.

Second, Irwin had great affection for the U.S. Open. INTJs attach deep iNtuitive meaning to valued matters in life, and I'm sure the Open was significant to Irwin, especially having won it twice before.

Third, on Monday, the playoff day at Medinah, something changed in Irwin's mind at hole 14. He later explained to the press that he was two strokes down and:

> Up to that time I wasn't concentrating. I was concerned with other things, like what Mike [Donald] was going to hit. But then I had to focus on what I was going to do.[49]

Irwin's dominant iNtuitive function had been considering *wrong* possibilities, such as what "Mike was going to hit," versus what "I had to do." It was only after focusing his iNtuition constructively that his game improved. Regardless of one's dominant brain function (S,N,T, or F), one must focus on the positive aspects of it, not the negative.

In 1994, at age 49, Irwin ended up 10th on the PGA Tour money list, pocketing over $800,000. He carried his golf excellence to the Seniors Tour in 1995 and quickly became its hottest player—winning rookie of the year honors. In 1997, Irwin's domination on the Seniors Tour included his second consecutive PGA Championship and ten victories—making him golf's first $2 million winner for a year's effort.

Excellent Putters

INTJs are generally regarded as top notch putters. **Bob Charles, Hale Irwin,** and **Tom Kite** have demonstrated the mastery of the blade. A major explanation for their putting success can again be attributed to INTJs' passive, relaxed motor skills. They are not "wristy" or "handsy" putters.

OBSTACLES

As we have read, INTJs' grandest gift is mental, not physical. As NT "owls," intellectual abstraction is their niche. In golf, they will utilize their minds to the utmost advantage. Conversely, this asset can become a liability under the rigors of tournament pressure.

For example, **Tom Kite's** INTJ iNtuition enabled him on the PGA Tour to focus on the big picture, playing week-to-week with a near perfect perspective on the game. Unfortunately, Kite's iNtuition was also his greatest nemesis. When intense pressure hit, as in the majors, Kite's weakest cerebral function, Sensing, was necessary to help handle the severity of high-pressure reality. (Sensing has been Nicklaus' strongest function.) Acute pressure dictates that iNtuitive athletes keep a realistic perspective. This can desert them when they are exposed to traumatic times. INTJs tend to use their minds excessively under pressure, as ISTJs would their hands.

Can you now understand why Nicklaus handled the majors and pressure differently than Kite? Kite was accused of not handling the pressure of the major tournaments, never having won any of the big four in his long career on Tour, until the 1992 U.S. Open. Nevertheless, Kite could have won more majors with the proper mental approach, as INTJ **Hale Irwin** has proved. (Kite's mechanics have not been the chief problem.)

Research suggests that our less-developed brain functions become more developed as we age. INTJs would therefore improve in Sensing, helping them to better handle intense pressure. I believe Hale Irwin experienced this in his victories in 1990.

Irwin overcame his INTJ susceptibility to pressure and won three U.S. Opens in his career. Conversely, INTJ **Tom Weiskopf** was an enigma to golfing fans over his 20 year PGA Tour career, having won only one major, the British Open. Yet that same year, 1973, Weiskopf won five Tour events over an eight week period! Tom also finished second at the Masters four times. Week in, week out, no Brain Type is more *consistent* than the INTJ. The majors are just not as easy for them. (It was great to see Weiskopf win his second major championship—22 years after his first—at the 1995 U.S. Senior Open. This time the runner-up was none other than Jack Nicklaus.)

HELPING INTJs

Encourage INTJs to get involved in athletic activities as children. Expose them to golf; see if they like it. Tell them they can be as competent and consistent as anyone. In their youth, help them to control their frustration and anger in golf. If you don't, they can act unbecoming on the links.

Expose them to the relaxation and mental techniques in this book. They must learn how to control their superior mental dexterity.

ENTP

ENTPs generally have a wonderful sense of humor, illustrated by the number of ENTP comedians in Hollywood (see ENTP section). ENTP golfers, without a doubt, add a personality injection into the pro Tour. Their golfing skills can also be first rate, evidenced by **Dave Stockton, Bruce Lietzke, Mike Weir, Brad Faxon, Colin Montgomerie, Justin Leonard, Jesper Parnevik, Fuzzy Zoeller, Rocco Mediate, Wayne Levi, Darren Clarke,** and **Rosie Jones**.

Arnold Palmer said of **Rocco Mediate**:

> I think he has a great personality for the game.[50]

For some 25 years, **Fuzzy Zoeller** was the good-natured comedian amid the many serious PGA players. Who can forget his mock-surrender, towel-waving incident at the 1984 U.S. Open when he beat Greg Norman? Fuzzy has continually entertained the golfing galleries as his ENTP counterparts play the Strip in Las Vegas.

Streaky Players

When iNtuitives access their mental zone, they seem to get on an extraordinary roll. ENTP **Wayne Levi** won four tournaments in 1990, three in only 36 days. No one on Tour had accomplished this since ENTJ Tom Watson won six tournaments in 1980. **Fuzzy Zoeller** won three titles in 1986. Texan **Bruce Lietzke** roped three tournaments in 1981. **Rosie Jones** captured four tournaments in her first 8 years on the LPGA Tour; three were in 1988.

Scotland's **Colin Montgomerie** has proven ENTPs can be consistent golfers, provided they play within their capabilities. Montgomerie led the European tour's money list five consecutive years (1993-1997).

Hard Workers

Rocco Mediate's mother spoke of her son, when he decided to play golf seriously:

> He was so determined. And when he decides to do something, he does it. He was like that with everything.[51]

Rocco was known to practice from 9 a.m. to 9 p.m. every day in the summer, hitting balls even in the dark. Mediate's college coach, Charlie Matlock, spoke of Rocco:

> He's a pure product of work. He had a tremendous ability to concentrate . . . But the main thing? He never let anybody or anything interfere with what he was going to do.[52]

Hard work is not uncommon for ENTPs in their vocational pursuits. If they enjoy their job, their all is given. (You can read of former ENTP tennis great **Guillermo Vilas'** work habits in the Tennis chapter.)

OBSTACLES

Putting can become a problem for ENTPs. This is not necessarily a result of motor skill ineptitude. Instead, when they allow their minds to monopolize in the wrong fashion, their putting suffers. When relaxed and focused, they can be superb putters.

In only his second year on the Senior PGA Tour, **Dave Stockton** won five tournaments and nearly $1.2 million, was leading money-winner and was named Player of the Year. He attributed his success primarily to recent mental exercises, not physical. Perfecting his mind strengthened his game in all phases. Stockton said in 1994:

> My strengths are my mental ability and my putting.[53]

Dave Stockton became the first senior player to post consecutive million-dollar seasons and won the U.S. Senior Open in 1996.

Many ENTPs have benefited from the unorthodox long putter. (The vast majority of Tour players who use the stretch putter are ENTPs.) With it, their hands aren't as dominant, they get a better view of the green, and anxiety seems to affect them less. On the pro Tours, **Bruce Lietzke, Rocco Mediate, Rocky Thompson,** and **John Brodie** are some ENTPs that have had success with the elongated putter.

Mental Gridlock

Because iNtuitives tend to live life in their minds, whereas Sensates tend to live life with their bodies, NTs are most apt to overload their *mental* circuit breakers. ENTPs, whose dominant function is right-brained iNtuition, consider myriad thoughts and possibilities under pressure. **Rocco Mediate** explained his poor showings in major championships:

> I let too many little things bother me before I play in those tournaments.[54]

HELPING ENTPs

ENTPs, like all NTs, will be well served by participating in sports at an early age. The sooner they can develop their motor movements, the better for them athletically.

ENTPs will want to have fun in learning the game. Therefore, allow them latitude. Don't bore them with excessive instruction, the perfecting of technique. Those will come in time.

Developing smooth tempo in their shots will help ENTPs appreciably. They tend to swing too fast.

ENFJ

ENFJs are sports enthusiasts, both as spectators and participants. As golfers, they innately possess the more methodical, left-hemisphere dominant motor skills, specializing in the mechanics of the swing. **Nick Price, Stuart Appleby, Chip Beck, Ian Baker Finch,** and **Julie Inkster** are ENFJs. This Type can be excellent golfers, though it usually takes more development time than normal to play near their potential.

ENFJs, like ESTJs, have extra difficulty making it through the pro Qualifying (Q) Schools. Under this kind of intense pressure, they often become too mechanical and play poorly. ENFJs most likely to do well on the PGA Tour have been foreigners. Foreign tour standards are easier than America's, thus allowing foreign ENFJs more opportunities to play and gain valuable experience. As they find success, they come to play the prestigious U.S. Tour and, before long, find success here as well.

Ian Baker-Finch and **Nick Price** are examples.

Australian **Baker-Finch** turned professional in 1979, yet did not join the PGA Tour until 1988. His improvement on Tour was significant. Baker-Finch won over $600,00 in 1990 and his first major at the 1991 British Open.

In 1983, South African **Nick Price** won the World Series of Golf in Akron, Ohio. This gave him a 10-year exemption for PGA Tour events. He used eight of those years to get his next U.S. victory. By the 1990s, Price was twice PGA Player of the Year (1993, 1994). In '94, Price won an amazing 6 titles—including the British Open and PGA Championship.

If it were easier to qualify for the American Tour, more American ENFJs would be in the winner's circle. Until the standards relax, they will continue to find it difficult to qualify for the Tour. Nonetheless, as American mini-tours develop, more hope is in store for ENFJs.

All Around Players

All phases of the game can be mastered by ENFJs. **Ian Baker-Finch** was once regarded as one of the premier putters on Tour, and most accurate off the tee. **Nick Price** had a long reputation for superb tee and iron play, but his game didn't soar until he corralled his putting. Both Baker-Finch and **Chip Beck** were listed among the top 20 players in the PGA Sand Save category in 1990. Hall of Fame member **Julie Inkster** won her 2nd consecutive LPGA Championship in the year 2000. The remarkable 40 year-old mother continued as one of the game's top shotmakers.

Affable

Getting along with others is high on the priority list of ENFJs. Their dominant Feeling function values people. They make good conversationalists and good interviewees. **Nick Price** has been accused of being so nice—trying to please people, especially off the course—that it's reportedly hurt his golf game. **Chip Beck** has been another amiable ENFJ who joined the PGA Tour in 1979, though it took him a while to reveal his potential. In 1987, Beck won in excess of a half-million dollars. Over the next five years, he equaled or bettered that figure, establishing himself as one of the most consistent players on Tour. Beck put himself into golfing history in 1991, becoming only the second player to shoot a 59 in PGA competition.

Hard Workers

What they may lack in physical skills, ENFJs make up for in extra hours on the course or driving range. Devoting themselves to a cause is not out of the ordinary for ENFJs. When golf becomes their focus, they are diligent workers.

HELPING ENFJs

ENFJ youngsters are less critical of their golfing game than ENTJs. ENFJs are more patient in their learning process and are excellent students, attentive, responsive and hard working. They can easily get hooked on golf.

ENFJs, like other iNtuitives, are well-served by developing their motor movements at an early age. If they do, they're capable of being splendid athletes.

The greatest hindrance to golfing stardom for ENFJs is mental. They will find assistance through the mental section in this book. Learning to relax and playing within themselves is paramount.

INFP

In the early 1990s, I wrote a portion of the following section for the first edition of *Your Best Sport*. Entering the 21st century, it's again intriguing to consider the INFP golfer previously highlighted, and the next stage of his career. Let's return to 1992:

Venture a guess who will be the most talked about player on the PGA Tour in the year 2000. Will it be one of the young bucks gaining fame such as ESTPs John Daly or Robert Gamez, or ENTJ Phil Mickelson? Or, maybe it's someone who's still in high school at this time.

Only time will tell, but there is a high school youngster that could well be this future player of renown. I seldom highlight youngsters as models of Brain Types, but one young INFP comes to mind. He began swinging a golf club at 11 months old. By 2, he had putted against Bob Hope on the "Mike Douglas Show." At age 5, his golfing wizardry was shown on the TV program, "That's Incredible", where he said he would someday beat Jack Nicklaus. That same year he won his first Junior World Championship.

At age 11 he quit counting his golfing trophies, 110 at the time. In 1991, at age 15, he won the Optimist Junior World Golf Championships for the sixth time. No one else has claimed more age group titles. He was the first 15-year-old to win the 15- to 17-year-old division of the twenty-four-year old event. In 1991, he became the youngest winner in the history of the USGA Junior Amateur Championship. He won the 1991 California High School CIF Southern Section Golf Association Championship (36 holes) by 10 shots—as a freshman! In 1992, he became one of the two youngest players ever to compete in a PGA Tour event, the L.A. Open. This young man is regarded by golf's cognoscenti as the finest junior golfer ever.

Who is this young prodigy? His name is **Eldrick (Tiger) Woods***. Not only is Tiger's INFP Type seldomly found in the U.S., it's rarely found on the pro Tour. INFPs can be excellent athletes, yet their numbers in pro golf are considerably lower than those in other major professional sports.*

Mimes

INFPs can be master mimics. As dominant Feelers, animate objects, such as people, preoccupy their thoughts. Their secondary function is visually oriented, right-brained iNtuition. INFPs look at people with creativity and appreciation, keenly noticing their mannerisms and moods. INFPs will demonstrate these spatial abilities early in life.

As a toddler, **Tiger Woods** *used to sit in the garage and watch his father hit shots at the practice net. At 11 months old, Tiger took his first swing with a shortened club. His dad recalled:*

> *He set up and he looked at the target, and he waggled and he looked back at the target and then he waggled again and then he pulled the trigger and swung.*
>
> *I almost fell out of the chair and I ran and got my wife and by the time we returned he had picked up another ball and he was repeating the drill just like I had.*
>
> *He had assimilated my swing through visualization.*[55]

Mr. Woods was rightfully astonished. Had he known Types, he would have understood Tiger's INFP penchant.

Incredible Torque

Tiger Woods, *at age 14, was 5-foot-9 and 120 pounds. In a driving contest in Texas, he drove the ball 310 yards! I followed him in the 1991 California State High School Championships where he continually outdrove one of the state's top golfers, a muscular ISTP standing 6-foot-3. Tiger, only a freshman, confounded everyone.*

INFPs can contort their bodies as few others can. Their big shoulder turns and lithesomeness in the golf swing can generate awesome power. The number one asset for hitting a golf ball a maximum distance is the ability to coordinate large and small muscle groups with the greatest velocity. Achieving high speed with the gross or fine motors independently will never achieve optimal distance. For example, though "P" gross motor golfers can hit the ball a long way, they'll never maximize distance until they can relax the big muscles and coordinate them with their fine motors. NFP golfers have the greatest potential for coordinating the two muscles groups. Yet unless they begin developing this harmony of body movements early in life, chances are they'll never reach their potential for power golf. Tiger Woods is a model case for the NFP potential.

Tiger's Future?

Receiving a college scholarship poses no problem for Tiger. His parents will be glad for the assistance. Golfing doesn't come cheap for Wood's family. His father estimated travel expenses for the 1991 summer alone would run $20,000.[56]

Tiger is unique. To my awareness, there's never been a great INFP golfer before. I believe that mental and emotional, not physical, obstacles have thwarted previous INFP golfers from achieving stardom. With Tiger's extensive experience and tutoring, I believe he could be the most talked about player on the PGA Tour in the year 2000. For his sake, I hope he is. I have a special affinity for INFPs.

Tiger's Pro Career?

Since the preceding story on Tiger Woods, written in 1992, much has since transpired. In 1996, at the age of only 20, Tiger made history by turning professional. Leaving college early, he was rewarded with an estimated $60 million in product endorsements. Though amateur Woods never came close to winning one of the many pro tournaments he'd been allowed to play in, corporate sponsors believed he was a sure bet.

Before turning pro, Woods captured a record third consecutive U.S. Amateur title. He was clearly the world's top amateur player. After playing his first PGA tournament as a professional, his fellow pros were awed at his talents. He drove the ball farther than anyone, his iron game included a hole-in-one, and his short game with remarkable finesse, was equally impressive. It only took Tiger 9 PGA Tour events to win $1 million and 3 titles. His fourth title came at the 1997 Masters, where he became the tournament's youngest champion and won by an amazing 12 shots. Woods fifth title came after 16 Tour events, where he pushed his career PGA earnings over $2 million—a mark achieved faster than any player in history.

The entrance of the new millennium was historic for humanity but meteoric for Tiger. In 2000, he won in excess of $9 million, with an amazing nine victories on the PGA Tour, six of them in a row! In only 3-plus seasons of play, his career PGA wins totaled 24 and earnings over $20 million. Included in these accomplishments were titles from the four major championships.

According to Woods, his success in 2000 came primarily from a revamped swing. Devoting over a year to redo and improve his body mechanics, while continuing to develop a more compact swing, Tiger honed his game to near perfection. (For many years I had suggested to others such an overhaul based on his _NFP Brain Type.) He did what was essential for his inborn motor skills to optimize his potential.

In 1997, I penned the following advice on how Woods could also improve his mind and emotions:

With so much talent, Tiger's future is seen by many as dominating the PGA Tour. This appears the case, but it's important to remember that he's an INFP. His pliable body will require continued mechanical soundness, and his mindset will need help in the ST categories—where Hogan and Nicklaus have innately excelled. Though Tiger's Type can be extremely competitive (hating to lose), it can also be very emotional and lose perspective.

A Thinking (T) caddie will be of much help to Woods. Interestingly, Tiger began his professional career employing "Fluff," an ENTP Brain Type who had caddied on Tour for 21 years—equal to Tiger's age! Fluff's experience and ENTP strategic mindset have been highly complementary to Woods. Tiger appropriately recognized his competent assistant after their Masters victory:

> *Here's to you, Fluff. You were strong for me, and you were calm for me. I couldn't have done it without you. And I want to thank you.*

The appreciative and "Feeling" Woods went on to say:

> *I think Fluff's the best caddie in the world.*[57]

Jumping back to the first few years of the 21st century, Tiger's physical abilities placed him in a class alone; he drove the ball so far that most courses were 2-4 shots easier for him than for his competition. Multiply this advantage by four rounds per tournament, and his superiority was easily understood. Yet as golf equipment improved and players worked harder at physical conditioning, Tiger's advantage lessened; he became vulnerable.

Woods is also extraordinarily competitive, a result of both his INFP wiring and childhood upbringing—particularly the drive instilled in him by his career-military father. Tiger's I_FP Type is arguably among the two best at match play. Though nearly every tournament is medal play, he relishes the opportunity to challenge one or two of the top competitors each day of the event. Despite these bonuses, Woods has some innate INFP golfing deficiencies which he must overcome to achieve his best.

Though Tiger has demonstrated many aspects of mental toughness, his INFP Brain Type is not as emotionally stable and logical as the eight Thinking Types. (Over Tiger's short career, he's already demonstrated some less-than-mature outbursts—a tendency for INFPs who allow pressure to get the best of them.) As already stated, his length and improving accuracy have enabled him to dominate most foes, yet his mind hadn't been as tested as has his competitors'—until 2003 and 2004. For instance, it's discouraging to play with someone who consistently hits 9-iron to the green when you have to hit 4. It is not only much harder physically, but mentally, to accurately hit a 4- than 9-iron. The short hitter is always taxed more than the long knocker. If Tiger were limited to others' distances, his mind would be much harder pressed; that is, the ability to remain calm and logical. Here, the Thinking mind one-ups the Feeler, particularly under intense pressure.

Progressing into the 21st century, Tiger's greatest challenge should come at the revered U.S. Open, where Thinkers "Ts" and the more conservative left-brained Js have an advantage over gamblin' right-brained Ps. (Js won an amazing 16 Open titles between 1972 and 1992. More startling, Thinkers won every Open but one spanning these 2 decades!) A victory at America's most-prized tournament normally requires driving accuracy, putting adeptness, and emotional stability. (The U.S. Open at Pebble Beach in 2000 and New York's Bethpage in 2002 were atypical for past Opens. These courses favored Tiger's length. Thus, it was not surprising that he won.)

The years 2003 and 2004 were frustrating for Tiger in his quest for additional major championships; he failed to capture even one as he had every year since 1999. His mind and body got out of sync, causing his swing coordination and mental outlook to suffer.[58]

Another rarely found INFP on Tour is **Vijay Singh.** At age 35, he established himself as one of the world's top players in 1998. In addition to winning the PGA Championship, his Tour earnings were $2.2 million. Vijay didn't miss a cut for 53 tournaments—a record which lasted until fellow INFP Woods later surpassed it. Singh continued his excellence by winning the Masters in 2000.

In 2004, however, the 41-year-old elder Vijay stunned the golfing world. He ended INFP Tiger Woods' *five years-plus run record run as the No. 1-ranked golfer in the world* and racked up 8 PGA Tour wins and nearly $9.5 million in earnings—all by October! Singh also broke Woods' single-season money record and had the lowest scoring average on Tour.

Golfing fans wouldn't have been so shocked at Vijay's 2004 success had they known Brain Types. Understanding Singh's size, excessive work habits, experience and so on, *along with his INFP inborn genetic design*, one can easily identify an optimal formula for golfing stardom. And by the way, Vijay was listed as an INFP in this book as early as the mid-1990s. *At that time, the unheralded and over 30-year-old had won only two of his now 20-plus PGA tournament victories.*

Yet many ask, what separates the two INFP greats from one another? Beyond golf swings, the two have different upbringings. The reserved and easygoing INFP from Fiji is a more stereotypical INFP. On the other hand, Tiger was raised in the action-packed life of Southern California, and by a high-energy and former green beret father. Tiger was consumed by golf and displayed his special abilities before audiences since he was almost a toddler. Though possessing the same

Brain Type (nature), the nurturing parts of their lives have been seemingly opposite. Vijay's mellowness has actually been a golfing blessing as he has tempered the deeply emotional makeup of the INFP.

Body Flexibility is Double-edged Sword

Though INFPs benefit from marvelous body coordination and flexibility, they must realize they can take a good thing too far. For example, INFPs must be careful avoiding the injuries to which their Brain Type is prone. In 1996, Cary Middlecoff, former U.S. Open and Masters champion, spoke of Tiger Woods in *Golf Digest*:

> He is going to hurt himself physically. He can play, but the way he swings, he is going to tear his back up. A bad back put me out of business. He jerks his hip and e`verything so quick right at contact.[59]

Though Middlecoff was not considering Woods' Brain Type, he noticed the INFP's tendencies and potential for golf injury. To Tiger's credit, his swing has become compact and efficient, minimizing the chances for injury. His hip turn is very restricted, yet his massive shoulder turn is estimated at 120 degrees. Like all INFPs, Tiger Woods needs to be mindful of the body's limits and exercise caution when going beyond its boundaries. After all, INFPs can be the top contortionists.

HELPING INFPs

INFPs can develop coordinated motor movements as early as any iNtuitive Types, yet they still need to devote extra time to them. In the long run, however, the mental/emotional side of golf will be their greatest obstacle to peak performance. Learning to keep their emotions in check will also be of major benefit to them. The mental section of this book can be of assistance.

ENFP

Arguably the world's top acrobats, figure skaters, and divers, ENFPs can also play golf. Their numbers on the pro Tour are few, however. They, as NFs, essentially struggle with the mental and emotional aspects of the game. ENFPs are not ones to give deep concentration to slow moving activities. ISTJs, their opposite Brain Type (such as Jack Nicklaus), are much better suited for golf. ENFPs are one of the, if not the, last Types you would expect to find in a more solitary sport like golf. Nonetheless, if they stick with the game, they can be among the top players on Tour.

Able to coordinate large and small muscles as NFs, ENFPs can develop flexible and graceful swings. Power and finesse are attainable for these high energy, righted-brained players.

Personable **Billy Andrade**, the Bob Hope of the PGA Tour, was regarded in 1981 as the No. 1 junior player in the nation as a 17-year old. He played college golf at Wake Forest, winning All-American honors 3 times. After going through Qualifying School twice and a shaky first year on Tour, he made $200,000 in 1989. His 1990 season replicated '89, but Andrade hit it big in 1991. Billy got into an iNtuitive "zone" and won back-to-back PGA Tour victories at the Kemper Open and Buick Classic. The golfing public quickly noticed a dynamic personality as well as a shining golfer. *Golf Magazine* wrote in 1991:

> Andrade is a bit of fresh air. CBS likes his bubbly personality so much that they had him up in the broadcast booth several times last year, long before he won. Andrade reminds you of a college kid who has stumbled upon the ultimate summer internship. And now, although suddenly rich and famous, he's still a big kid.[60]

Andrade majored in sociology, a natural course of study for ENFPs. After all, they are keenly aware of people, desiring to inspire and help them.

David Duval is another rare ENFP on the PGA Tour. Having a father and uncle as golf professionals was both motivational and instructional for young David. He became the American Junior Golf Association Player of the Year in 1989 and the collegiate Player of the Year in 1993. Duval turned professional in 1993, and by 1995, he ranked 11th in Tour earnings for the year. Nonetheless, he was considered an underachiever on the PGA Tour (having seven second-place finishes) until he won his first event in 1997. And in ENFP style, just like his Brain Type sidekick Billy Andrade had accomplished six years prior, Duval won back-to-back tournaments. But going one step beyond Andrade, Duval captured his third consecutive PGA event at the year's end Tour Championship! (This rare occurrence in pro golf is most probable when Extraverted players lock into the right brain—accessing the "zone" for weeks on end.) As one of the Tour's longest hitters, Duval took his game even further in 1998, winning the

PGA money title with earnings of nearly $2.5 million. The more David controls his ENFP mindset in the years ahead, the greater success he'll have.

(Updating this in 2004, Duval as much as anyone on Tour has fallen from past success. His NF mental-emotional makeup has been significantly challenged. ENFJs as much as Brain Type have taken this unexpected plunge in pro golf, yet both ENF_s are susceptible to it. Nonetheless, with the right approach, David Duval has the potential to make a major comeback.) And last, only a knowledge of Brain Types—versus personality/psychological types—explains how the low-keyed David Duval can be an ENFP.

HELPING ENFPs

ENFPs are often supercharged individuals, continually looking for something or somebody to whom to devote their interests. Golf is not a gregarious sport, particularly for beginners on the driving range. ENFPs may find it difficult to channel their enthusiasm to the links unless someone encourages them along the way.

ENFPs, as right-brained iNtuitive Feelers, commonly video their practices or performances in sports, ever critiquing and learning visually.

Once ENFPs become low handicappers, they need to restrain their boundless energy on the course. One way this can be done is by swinging in a smooth, rhythmical motion. ENFPs tend to swing too quickly, especially under pressure. Proper swing tempo is crucial for this high-energy Brain Type. As right-brained Ps, ENFPs should give extra attention to proper swing mechanics—not something that comes naturally. Practicing the mental side of the game is will also be of appreciable benefit.

Conclusion

Any golfers possessing the Types found infrequently on Tour should *not* give up their aspirations, but realize working harder and smarter will be necessary to reach the highest levels of golf. They should consider the true life stories of persons who overcame unfavorable odds to attain athletic stardom. Reading the accounts of the disciplines and rigors that enable them to reach their goals will be helpful.

If persons constituting any of the Types found seldom on Tour are unwilling to undergo the hard work necessary to reach the upper limits of golf, yet desire to reach them, perhaps they should choose a sport or recreation more accommodating to their respective Types.

Each Type excels at specific phases of the game, mentally and physically. The more time you devote to observing and understanding these differences in Types, the more exciting and beneficial this study will become for you.

It is wise to investigate the golfers of your specific Brain Type. This will enable you to see the various ways that persons of the same Type play golf. Look for articles where they share their methods of success, physically and mentally. If you have typed yourself correctly, you should relate easily to what they are saying. Remember the adage, "Different strokes for different folks." You will generally do best by emulating those most like yourself.

Though far from complete, here is a list of well known golfers and their probable Brain Types.

ISTP
Tom Lehman, Mark O'Meara, Jim Furyk, Lee Janzen, Craig Stadler, Corey Pavin, Steve Pate, Mark Calcavecchia, Scott Hoch, John Huston,
Karrie Webb, Pat Bradley, Beth Daniel, Patty Sheehan, Laura Davies
   Seniors: Babe Zaharias, Ben Hogan, Mike Hill,
      Jim Colbert, Walt Zembriski, J.C. Snead,
      Tom Wargo, Moe Norman,
      Kemp Richardson

ESTP
Seve Ballesteros, Jay Don Blake, John Cook, Fred Couples, Ben Crenshaw, John Daly, Robert Gamez, Bill Glasson, Nolan Henke, Bernhard Langer, Davis Love III, Greg Norman, Jose Maria Olazabal, Jumbo Ozaki, Paul Stankowski, Payne Stewart, Steve Stricker, Hal Sutton, Bob Tway, Willie Wood,
Se Ri Pak, Dottie Mochrie, Jan Stephenson
   Seniors: Arnold Palmer, Ray Floyd, Lanny Wadkins

ISFP
Ernie Els, Retief Goosen, Duffy Waldorf, Steve Jones, Billy Ray Brown, Paul Lawrie, Craig Perks, Wayne Grady, Gene Sauers,
   Seniors: Kathy Whitworth, Dr. Gil Morgan,
      Jim Dent, Charlie Sifford, Jim Thorpe

13....Golf

ESFP
Notah Begay III, Shigeki Maruyama, Omar Uresti, Jerry Pate,
Annika Sorenstam, Nancy Lopez, JoAnne Carner, Michelle McGann, Meg Mallon, Caroline Keggi, Leta Lindley, Christie Kerr
Seniors: Lee Trevino, Chi Chi Rodriguez, Jesse Patino

ISTJ
Paul Azinger, Scott Simpson, Larry Mize, Mike Reid, Jodie Mudd,
Betsy King, Chris Johnson
Seniors: Jack Nicklaus, Larry Nelson, Al Geiberger

ESTJ
Nick Faldo, Dave Barr,
Seniors: David Graham, Andy North, Don Pooley

INFP
Tiger Woods, Vijay Singh

ENFP
David Duval, Billy Andrade, Sergio Garcia, Heather Farr

ENFJ
Nick Price, Stuart Appleby, Chip Beck, Ian Baker Finch, Julie Inkster, Cindy Rarick

INTJ
Bob Estes, Casey Martin, Matt Kuchar
Seniors: Hale Irwin, Tom Kite, Bob Charles, Tom Weiskopf, Kermit Zarley, Mike McCullough, John Mahaffey, David Ledbetter

ENTJ
Phil Mickelson, Steve Elkington, Peter Jacobson, Jeff Maggert, Curtis Strange, Keith Clearwater, Jeff Sluman,
Seniors: Johnny Miller, Tom Watson, Gary Player, Bruce Crampton, Ken Venturi, Bobby Nichols, Deane Beman, Wally Armstrong

ENTP
Fulton Allem, Bobby Clampett, Darren Clarke, Chris DiMarco, Brad Faxon, Todd Hamilton, Tim Herron, Mike Hulbert, Justin Leonard, Wayne Levi, Bruce Lietzke, Billy Mayfair, Rocco Mediate, Colin Montgomerie, David Ogrin, Jesper Parnevik, Loren Roberts, Clarence Rose, Greg Twiggs, Jean Van de Velde, Mike Weir, Fuzzy Zoeller
Rosie Jones
Seniors: Dave Stockton, Rocky Thompson, John Brodie, Larry Laoretti, Gary McCord, Roger Maltbie

14
Gymnastics, Hockey, and Ice Skating

Gymnastics

The names of **Nadia Comaneci** and **Olga Korbut** bring fond memories for members of the Baby Boom generation. Who can forget their Olympic flights of perfection in the 1970s? Gymnastics has changed radically since. Many more youngsters are now involved in the sport. Before the days of Nadia and Olga, men gymnasts greatly outnumbered the women. In the 1990s, women outnumber men seven to one, with little girls beginning gymnastics as early as two or three years old, reaching their peak in their middle to late teens. Men start their careers later, not hitting their prime until their 20s.

ENFP

The most naturally acrobatic of the Brain Types are ENFPs. Coordinating motor skills in poetic grace, they charm their audiences by their physical and personable skills.

ENFP **Olga Korbut**, the petite Soviet in pigtails, was a multi winner at the 1972 Olympics in Munich. Not only did she win the hearts of the world with daring routines and radiant charm, she won gold medals for the balance beam and floor exercise and a silver for the uneven bars. Olga's innovative and revolutionary back flips on the beam and uneven parallel bars astonished everyone, including the judges. No one had ever performed such a risky maneuver. Today the move is commonplace, and necessary to find success in Olympic competition.

Californian **Cathy Rigby** played a major role in gymnastics awareness stateside; the ENFP was a medalist on the balance beam at the 1970 World Championships. In the 1979 World Championships, **Kurt Thomas** won the gold medal on the horizontal bar, while **Bart Conner** won for the parallel bars. Both are ENFPs.

Ukranian **Grigory Misiutin** (ENFP) was the "all-around" silver medalist at the '92 Barcelona Olympics.

ISTP

It is difficult to find a sport at which the ISTP does not excel; gymnastics is no exception. ISTPs, along with ENFPs, can make a strong claim for being the top gymnastic Type.

In the 1976 Montreal Summer Olympic Games, fourteen-year-old **Nadia Comaneci** captivated the world with her airborne gymnastics. Her exercises were known for their level of difficulty and risk. Nadia finished with seven perfect 10-point scores and three gold medals. She went on to capture 21 gold medals in Olympic and world championship competitions between 1976 and 1984. Demonstrating strength, flexibility, and artistry, Comaneci is one of the greatest gymnasts, and athletes, of all time. Comaneci's ISTP manner was contrasted with Olga Korbut's in *Everybody's Gymnastics Book*:

> Comaneci, a highly trained thoroughbred of an athlete, looked upon gymnastics more as an opportunity to excel than an opportunity to perform. Very interested in winning, she displayed the quiet and thorough intensity usually attributed to adult professionals of other sports. The public had some difficulty coming to grips with her intensity. After all, Korbut had cried when she failed on her bar routines in the 1972 Olympics and appeared to wear her emotions on her shirt sleeve. Comaneci was machine like in her performance.[1]

ISTP **Kim Zmeskal** has been one of America's answers to Nadia Comaneci. In 1991, Zmeskal won her second U.S. Championship and the women's all around at the World Gymnastics Championships. At 4' 7", she became the first U.S. woman ever to win the gold medal in that event at a world championships. For an encore, in 1992, Kim became a double winner at the World's, winning the floor exercise and balance beam. World-famous coach Bela Karolyi spoke of his prodigy:

> Kim is a little shy, but her mind is like a computer and she has nerves of steel. She is the best in this area I have ever coached in my life. She has excellent coordination, self discipline and concentration when everyone else is shaky.[2]

America's second answer to Nadia Comaneci, typologically, has been 4' 6", 70 pound **Shannon Miller**. At the '91 World Gymnastics Championships, the diminutive Oklahoman qualified for all four individual apparatus finals, the only U.S. gymnast to do so. Shannon shared the silver medal in the uneven parallel bars, the youngest American medalist ever. In 1992, Miller won five Olympics medals, including a silver medal in the all-around. At the 1996 Atlanta Summer Olympics, Shannon Miller captured the gold medal in the difficult balance beam.

Ukranian **Tatiana Gutsu** (ISTP) won the all-around women's title at the '92 Barcelona Olympics. ISTP Romanian **Simona Amanar** won the gold in the women's vault at the '96 Atlanta Games. On the men's side in Atlanta, **Li Donghua** (ISTP) of Switzerland earned the gold medal on the pommel horse.

Gutsy

ISTPs are universally known for their willpower and intensity, regardless the sport. This never came more apparent than at the '96 Atlanta Olympics, where the diminutive 4'9", 87 pound ISTP **Kerri Strug** captured global attention. When her more acclaimed teammates had succumbed to the intense Olympic pressure—relinquishing a strong lead in team competition—Kerri, the final participant, ran on a severely sprained ankle and soared over the vaulting horse to a perfect landing on one leg. Told by Bela Karolyi moments before that she needed a 9.6 to beat the Russians, Strug believed the excruciating pain was well worth the team victory.

Two important lessons can be learned from this historic event. First, don't ever count out ISTPs in gymnastics. Strug's coach Bela Karolyi said of his new starlet:

> She is just a little girl who was never the roughest, toughest girl, always a little shy, always standing behind someone else. I could never predict this scenario. She is so little. She is not a fighter like the others.[3]

If Bela knew Brain Types and had read my first edition of this book, published in 1992, he could easily have forecasted Kerri's potential and gutsy determination. I listed Strug in my ISTP section on gymnastics, having only watched her on TV in the '92 Olympics. Though her performance was far from spectacular at the time, I knew her upside was as high as any one in the world. She arguably had the optimal Brain Type for gymnastics. I even had people say to me prior to the Atlanta games, "What is Kerri Strug doing in the ISTP section. No way!" I'd just smile and say she had a wonderful upside.

The second lesson from this example is for coaches who, regardless of their greatness, need to rely on other Types to complement their deficiencies. As a Feeling coach (ENFP), Karolyi would want to be extra careful trusting his mathematical genius under the pressure he found himself in, with only seconds to minutes to calculate the score Strug needed to win. A Thinker (T) would have been good to consult at that time—a Type best in calculating inanimate matters. It turned out that it wasn't necessary for Strug to complete her final vault. On the other hand, who would know of Kerri Strug without Bela Karolyi?

ESTP

Though not found as often in advanced gymnastics as ENFPs and ISTPs, ESTPs can excel. At the 1984 Summer Olympics in Los Angeles, **Mary Lou Retton**, the 4-foot-9 West Virginia dynamo, captured the all around women's gymnastics title, giving the U.S. its first Olympic gold medal in the event. Retton utilized her ESTP athleticism, aggressiveness, and love for crowds to turn in her gold-medal performance. The vault was her strongest phase of the competition, requiring a sprinter's speed, a diver's lift, a gymnast's grace, and a stuntperson's daring. Retton scored a perfect 10 on her final vault, the first American woman ever to score one in gymnastics.

As an 8-year-old, gymnast Kim Zmeskal recalled training with Retton:

> She was always smiling, even when she got hurt. She was always happy and motivated.[4]

In ESTP style, Mary Lou was not one to hide her emotions when performing. After scoring a perfect 10 on her final '84 Olympic vault, Retton, in her own words, "went nuts." She said:

> Since then, they passed a rule that gymnasts cannot show emotion on the podium [floor]. They call it the Mary Lou rule. It's similar to pro football, where you can't spike the ball and you can't dance in the end zone after a touchdown.[5]

ESTPs excel in gymnastics by utilizing their right-brain-powered, fine motor skills. They can be the "lords of the rings." ESTP **Vitaly Scherbo** won five individual gold medals at the 1992 Summer Olympics, including the coveted men's all-around! He became the most decorated Olympic gymnast in history. At the '96 Atlanta Olympics, Scherbo again demonstrated his gymnastic' prowess. He won four medals (all bronze) in the: all-arounds, vault, parallel bars, and horizontal bar. Though he was disappointed with his results (and the judges' scoring), he retired from gymnastics showing the world his amazing ESTP talent. Vitaly had given up the sport for 7 months, following his wife's car wreck which left her critically injured. Coming out of a month-long coma, she begged him to return to gymnastics. (By then, it was reported he'd gained weight and couldn't even do a handstand.) Vitaly consented and that same year (1996) won 4 Olympic medals.

Russia's **Alexei Nemov** was another big-time ESTP performer at the '96 Atlanta Games. He won the gold medal in the men's vault, took a silver medal in the all-around, and earned bronzes in the floor exercise, pommel horse, and horizontal bar.

Like Mary Lou Retton, another American ESTP female captured the gymnastic world's attention in 1995. **Dominique Moceanu** won the coveted senior women's all-around title at the U.S. National Gymnastics Championships. Only 13-years old, Moceanu became the youngest woman to win the title—remarkable considering it was her first senior event. Some two months later, Moceanu earned the only individual medal for the U.S. in the World Championships. Her nearly flawless routine on the balance beam won her a silver medal.

One more ESTP female gave notice to the world of her expertise, in 2000, at the Sydney Summer Olympics. Long and lanky **Svetlana Khorkina** of Russia won the gold medal in the uneven bars.

ENTJ

Svetlana Boguinskaia won four Olympic gold medals (two gold) in 1988. In 1989, she was the all-around world champion and continued her excellence through the '92 Olympics. Svetlana modeled her ENTJ indomitable will, choreographic elegance, and acrobatic precision.

ENTP

Entering the 21st century, ENTPs have become among the top gymnasts. At the 2004 Athens Olympic Games, American ENTPs **Carly Patterson** and **Paul Hamm** won individual gold in the women's and men's all-arounds. ENTPs can be athletic, coordinated, hard working, smart, and endure much pain.

Conclusion

Gymnasts who are dominant right hemisphere "Ps" have a distinct advantage over dominant left hemisphere "Js." The Ps are more graceful, less rigid, tending to be more concerned about the process than the results of the performance, particularly under pressure. Js can win gold medals, but not as easily.

14....Gymnastics, Hockey, and Ice Skating

Though far from complete, here is a list of well known gymnasts and their probable Brain Types

ENFP Olga Korbut, Cathy Rigby, Bart Conner, Kurt Thomas, Grigory Misiutin
ISTP Nadia Comaneci, Shannon Miller, Kerri Strug, Simona Amanar, Tatiana Gutsu, Roza Galieva, Gina Gogean, Kim Zmeskal, Jaycie Phelps, Li Donghua, Scott Keswick
ESTP Mary Lou Retton, Svetlana Khorkina, Lavina Milosovici, Dominique Moceanu, Wendy Bruce, Vitaly Scherbo, Alexei Nemov, Blaine Wilson
ESFP Lilia Podkopayeva
ENTJ Svettlana Boguinskaia, Kathy Johnson, Jarrod Hanks
ENTP Carly Patterson, Paul Hamm, Trent Dimas, Tim Dagget

record with 215 points in 1985-86 and most goals in a season, 92 (1981-82). Atypical for an ISTP's athletic behavior, Gretzky won the Lady Byng Trophy five times as the league's most gentlemanly participant. The lefty is considered the greatest hockey player of all time.

Perfectionistic, Hard Working

Walter Gretzky once shed light on his son and behavior normal for other ISTPs:

> I've seen him spend hours and hours and hours that no other boy would do, just practicing one little move. Sometimes he spends a year or two before he'll even try something in a game.[6]

Walter Gretzky continued:

> He wasn't the kind of kid you would have to send out to practice. With Wayne, you'd have to make him come in. I'd be out there yelling, 'Don't be shooting at the side of the house. Look what you've done to the foundation!'[7]

Hockey

Though player salaries lag behind those in major league baseball, the NBA and the NFL, the National Hockey League (NHL) has a strong public following. Lack of national television coverage keeps many Americans from enjoying this exciting and rough game on ice. Let's take a look at the sport that advertises with the bumper sticker "Give blood, play hockey!"

Of the few hockey players I have studied carefully, certain Brain Type patterns stand out. Let's begin with the ISTP, the most dominant Type in the NHL.

ISTP

Upon **Wayne Gretzky**'s retirement in 1999, after 20 years in the NHL, he had amassed 61 individual records. The athletically-gifted ISTP won four Stanley Cups, three Canada Cups, nine Hart Trophies as NHL Most Valuable Player, ten NHL scoring titles (Art Ross Trophies), and achieved the all time points and assists records. Gretzky holds the highest single season scoring

Prior to retirement in 1997 (and his surprise return in 2001), ISTP **Mario Lemieux** won six NHL scoring titles, two Stanley Cups, three most-valuable player awards, and displayed great courage in athletic competition. Lemieux led his Pittsburgh Penguins to Stanley Cup Championships in 1991 and '92. Standing 6' 4", Mario was awarded the Conn Smythe Trophy as the MVP of the '91 playoffs. His 44 points were the second best in league history, behind the 47 points of ISTP Gretzky in 1985. Despite the back and cancer troubles that plagued Lemieux at the end of his career, he was still one of the game's all-time best. In 1995, Mario scored 161 points in 70 games—after taking a year off to recover from radiation treatments. In his final season (1996-97), Lemieux led the NHL in scoring with 50 goals and 122 points. The ISTP's determination is hard to overcome.

Intense Competitors

Though it doesn't always show, ISTPs are intense

competitors. *Sports Illustrated* once wrote of Mario Lemieux:

> Was Mario a well behaved child? 'It was as if he had one of these, says Pierrette [his mother], indicating a halo over her head. When young Mario's halo slipped, it uncovered a stubborn streak more suited to a pack mule than a cherub. He was, and is, a rotten loser, whether at Monopoly, cards or basement hockey. Tantrums followed losses. 'If Mario lost, it would be as if a hurricane went through the basement,' says Jean Guy [his father].[8] (Inserts added.)

ESTP

Any hockey buff recognizes the name Hull, dating back to the 1960s, when **Bobby Hull** first made his impact in the NHL and later became known as the best left-winger in history. Along came another hockey-playing Hull in the 1980s, but **Brett Hull** began his career unimpressively. Folks around the game said he would never compare with his dad; he just didn't have it.

It wasn't until the late 1980s that the younger Hull demonstrated he was very much like his dad. He, too, could score. And they were both ESTPs.

In three seasons, 1989 1991, Brett tallied nearly 200 goals. He quickly joined the ranks of superstars Wayne Gretzky and Mario Lemieux. (In 16 NHL seasons, Bobby Hull scored 610 goals.) In 1991, Brett racked up 86 regular season goals, capping the third best individual goal scoring season in league history. Hull was given the Lester Pearson Award (NHL's best player) by the NHL Players Association, and the Hart Trophy as the NHL's MVP. (Bobby Hull won the Hart Trophy twice.) In the 1991-92 season, Brett Hull scored 70 goals, becoming the second player in NHL history to score 70 or more goals in three consecutive seasons. (Wayne Gretzky was the first.) After 15 seasons in the NHL, Brett finally surpassed his father's goal total (610) in October of 2000. There is no doubt that Brett, as was his dad, is a scorer. *Sports Illustrated* wrote of Brett Hull:

> He is a pure goal scorer, a home run hitter in a league starved for such glamour boys. Hull is a major reason why the Blues [St. Louis] franchise . . . has increased its average attendance by almost 2,000 per game and is now profitable.[9]

In 1992, St. Louis Blues assistant coach Bob Berry said of Hull:

> Brett has the quickest delivery of any shooter I've ever seen. And he doesn't waste anything. A lot of big scorers kill goalies in practice. He saves his stuff for the games.[10]

Berry touched on some important aspects of ESTP athletes. They have strong, lightning quick fine motor movements, and they generally expend a lot more energy in games than they do in practice.

Though Brett and Bobby Hull have the same genetically predisposed Brain Type, I am not saying they have the same personalities or the same values in life. Many have said their styles of hockey play and living are polar opposite. As a compliment to Brett, he won the NHL's most gentlemanly player award in 1990. As we have repeatedly seen in this book, Brain Types show similarities in people that other methods do not. Both Hulls have achieved hockey stardom, largely as a result of their ESTP Brain Type.

Czechoslovakian import **Jaromir Jagr** has proven that Europeans can become among the NHL's best. His ESTP Type and flair quickly surfaced. Not possessing the deep-thinking game of the Introverted STP (like Mario Lemieux), Extraverted Jaromir has played with aggression and instinctive ESTP reactions, unpredictable. He's played the game at breakneck speed and dares the opposition to do the same. The prowess of his fine motor skills has enabled him as an NHL big guy (6'2", 230) to use his reach to great advantage. In the 1995-1996 strike-shortened season, Jagr won the Art Ross trophy, awarded annually to the player who leads the NHL in scoring. This was some accomplishment, considering ISTPs had won the Ross trophy the 14 previous seasons. Jagr won his third scoring title in 1998-99 when he tallied 44 goals along with 83 assists for 127 points, earning the Hart Trophy as League MVP. By 2000, he had appeared in six NHL All-Star Games.

ISFP

ISFPs continue their outstanding sports performances in hockey, too. As SPs, they possess exceptional body and spatial skills. ISFPs are the Methuselahs of sports, playing long beyond the norm. Their big muscle adeptness and right-brained fluidity enable them to compete longer than any other Brain Type.

Bobby Orr and **Gordie Howe** are two of hockey's all-time great ISFPs. Howe was regarded as hockey's best until the advent of Wayne Gretzky. Howe spent 25 seasons with the Detroit Redwings and retired. At age 45, Howe rejoined the NHL to play with his two sons in Houston. Playing seven more seasons, Howe retired again at age 52! His final season with the Hartford Whalers was no fluke; he was a productive performer among players half his age. In 1997, at age 69, Howe made a brief game appearance (with 20,000 cheering and admiring fans) to become the only pro in his sport to compete in six decades!

ESFP

I do not believe ESFPs are plentiful in the NHL, yet there is one I want to mention, retired **Marcel Dionne**. Dionne's career spanned 17 seasons. He is third in NHL history in points (1,771), goals (731), behind only Wayne Gretzky and Gordie Howe. Marcel Dionne was also one of the top assist-makers in NHL history. ESFPs, like basketball's Magic Johnson, have superior visual abilities and can be excellent at assists.

ENTJ

It appears a fair number of ENTJs have had NHL success. One such player has been **Eric Lindros,** who took the professional hockey world by storm with his play and behavior. Before turning pro, Lindros demonstrated his ENTJ independence by refusing to play for the Quebec Nordiques, the professional team holding his draft rights. The French speaking corner of Canada did not find favor with this, to put it mildly.

Precocious Lindros has penned his autobiography, *Fire on Ice*. In it, the indomitable one compares himself to a bird on a wire:

> People want you to do this. People want you to do that. . . . I'll be on that wire for life, and it doesn't matter how hard they pull because I'm the strongest bird and I'm not budging.[11]

As a player, the 6' 4", 230 pound Lindros has been an intimidator on skates. Rather than relying on the spatial and fine motor skills of the ISTPs and ESTPs, he has excelled with his NT intelligence, brute strength, fierce determination, and aggressiveness. His style has been unlike the many great SPs.

In 1995, Lindros ensured his place among hockey's elite when he was voted the Hart Trophy as the NHL's MVP. As of 2000, he was a six-time NHL All-Star. Lindros had scored 40 or more goals in four different seasons.

ENTP

The more I research hockey, the more I witness the prevalence of ENTPs. The game fits them in numerous ways. For starters, ENTPs relish speed, action, creativity, strategy, and physically demanding activities. ENTPs play all positions in hockey, and they especially excel at goalie.

Though far from complete, here is a list of well known players and their probable Brain Types

ISTP Wayne Gretzky, Mario Lemieux, Paul Kariya, Steve Yzerman, Guy Carbonneau,
Retired: Clark Donatelli

ESTP Brett Hull, Jaromir Jagr, Theoren Fleury, Rob Blake
Retired: Bobby Hull

ISFP Steve Duchesne
Retired: Bobby Orr, Gordie Howe, Bernie Nicholls

ESFP *Retired*: Marcel Dionne

ESTJ *Retired:* Dave Taylor

INFP Luc Robitaille

ENTP Dominik Hasek, Jeremy Roenick, Dave Karpa, Ray Ferraro
Retired: Larry Robinson, Al Iafrate, Kelly Hrudey, Jay Miller, Pierre Larouche

ENTJ Eric Lindros, Tony Granato, Owen Nolan,
Retired: Jim Craig, Mike Gartner, Danny Quinn

Ice Skating

Though competitive ice skating exists in various forms, Americans have a special affection for the graceful, balletic figure skaters. From the days of **Sonya Henie** (1920s and '30s) to the present, adults and children have been mesmerized by the skills and personalities of figure skaters.

Many Types are capable of superior skating, yet two Brain Types in particular dominated competitive figure skating in the latter 1900s, ENFPs and ENTJs. This pattern is being altered, however, by a rules change that eliminated compulsory figures from international competition. It took full effect before the 1991 season.

Compulsories have been the left-brained dimension of skating. The detailed movements of compulsories have been mastered by ENTJs and disliked by Ps. As you might imagine, the contextual, hang-loose ENFP would not be as interested or proficient in the exacting figures as the more controlled ENTJ. With compulsories now removed, ENTJs will be hard pressed to compete with the right-brain Ps who are exceptionally gifted at freestyle skating. Figure skating is becoming more like gymnastics, with an emphasis on jumps and athleticism. In this realm, ENFPs usually reign.

ENFP

ENFPs are particularly superb at sports with prearranged routines requiring energetic, flowing whole body movements. Figure skating is such a sport. ENFPs are able to unleash their spirited energy into demanding performances, utilizing their jumping and gymnastic abilities. Knowing every necessary movement beforehand works well with the ENFP's preference for synthetic Feelings. Many other sports demand instantaneous, logical, Thinking decisions, but these do not confront the performer on skates.

Of the contemporary renowned skaters I have studied, most are ENFPs. Some of them include **Brian Boitano, Kurt Browning, Scott Hamilton, Viktor Petrenko, Paul Wylie, Todd Eldredge, Kristi Yamaguchi, Michelle Kwan,** and **Midori Ito**.

In 1991, Canadian **Kurt Browning** became the first man to win three consecutive World Figure Skating Championships since **Scott Hamilton** of the United States (1981-84). Both are ENFPs! Hamilton won the men's gold in the 1984 Olympics at Sarajevo, Yugoslavia.

Brian Boitano won the gold medal in men's figure skating at the 1988 Winter Olympics in Calgary, Canada. His performance ranks among the best in sports history.

Midori Ito of Japan won the women's 1989 World Championships and dominated until ENTJ Jill Trenary took the women's gold at the 1990 World Championship. Although Trenary took first and Ito second overall, Trenary won neither of the free skating phases of the competition. (More on this when we look at the ENTJ skaters.) Ito's hang-time on jumps compared with pro basketball's slam dunk champions. Midori won the women's figure skating silver medal at the '92 Winter Olympics.

In 1992, Ukrainian **Viktor Petrenko** won Olympic (Albertville, France) and World Championships gold medals in men's figure skating.

American ENFP **Kristi Yamaguchi** won the women's 1991 World Figure Skating Championships and the '92 U.S. Figure Skating Championships. She achieved her greatest success, however, by capturing the gold medal at Albertville, becoming the United States' first women's skating champion at the Winter Olympics since Dorthy Hamill in 1976. Shortly thereafter, Kristi won the '92 World Championships, becoming the first U.S. woman to defend her world championship since Peggy Fleming in 1968. In 1997, Yamaguchi won her fourth World Professional Figure Skating Championship. Kristi was recognized as the epitome of grace, beauty, athleticism, and style.

Ukrainian **Oksana Baiul**, clothed in a furry pink bunny suit, won the gold medal in women's figure skating at the 1994 Winter Olympics in Hamar, Norway. Her ENFP artistic impression swayed the judges to choose her over American Nancy Kerrigan.

In 1996, two young women skated near perfection

at the world championships in Canada. American **Michelle Kwan** edged out competitor **Chen Lu** of China, both ENFPs. Kwan became the third-youngest world champion behind two other ENFPs, Sonia Henie and Oksana Baiul. At the '98 Winter Olympics in Nagano, Japan, Kwan was awarded the silver medal, despite skating superbly. In 2001, the 20-year-old Kwan won her fifth U.S. title, only to follow that up with her fourth world figure skating championship. In 2003 and at the ripe age of 22, **Michelle Kwan** won her fifth world championship in near-flawlless fashion.

Minimize Thinking

American **Paul Wylie**, ENFP, surprised the skating world at the 1992 Albertville Olympics. He was considered the least likely U.S. hope to earn a medal. Following Wylie's silver medal performance, coach Mary Scotvold spoke of her pupil:

> For seven years, I've thought he was one of the most magnificent skaters I've ever seen. . . . I was just praying that everyone in the world would see what we've seen for seven years, and they did.[12]

Until his silver medal performance, Wylie had never finished higher than ninth in international competition. Nonetheless, he had always been an ENFP, capable of winning a gold medal.

A Harvard graduate with a degree in political science, Paul carried a reputation of not skating well under pressure. He was said to think too much before competition. Paul's other coach, Evy Scotvold, once said that Wylie needed "a lobotomy" to be a better competitor. Scotvold added, "I mean that in a nice way."

I imagine the academic rigors of Harvard taught Paul to use his Thinking function and introspect more than many ENFPs are accustomed. Whatever the reasons, Paul hindered his ENFP Brain Type from performing optimally in competition until the '92 Olympics.

After placing a successful third in the original program at Albertville, Paul Wylie said:

> It was a matter of reducing my brain.[13]

Paul's comment is helpful to all athletes in competition. To understand why it has neuroscientific merit, refer to the section on Zoning.

ENTJ

In recent history, ENTJ women have had much greater success in singles' figures than ENTJ men. Elegance and precision have been the trademarks of female ENTJs. Some of them have included **Peggy Fleming, Dorothy Hamill, Katarina Witt,** and **Jill Trenary**.

Peggy Fleming was America's skating sweetheart for years as she demonstrated her precise, artistic talents. Fleming won the first of five straight national titles in 1964 at age 15. By 1968, she was the only U.S. gold medalist at the Winter Olympics in Grenoble, France. Taking an insurmountable lead in the Olympic compulsories, Fleming cried two days later when she felt she failed to do her best in the free skating performance. Nonetheless, she still won the gold, while capturing the world with her polished charm, elegance, and beauty.

Dorothy Hamill won a gold medal in women's figure skating at the 1976 Winter Olympics. Her success and beauty created a myriad of Dorothy wannabes as women all over America cut their hair in the short, Hamill style.

Glamorous **Katarina Witt** of East Germany became the first women's singles figure skater since Sonja Henie in 1936 to win back-to-back Olympic medals (1984 and '88). Olympic gold medalist Brian Boitano spoke of Witt, providing us greater insight into her persona and Brain Type:

> . . . Katarina was a great actress on the ice. That's why the judges really loved her. Nobody acted like she did. Katarina knew how to flirt even when she was nervous. Not to mention, she's beautiful. She's gorgeous. And she knew she could get away with anything. . . . She's very tough. She's a fighter.[14]

ENTJs, as has often been stated, can be exceptional athletes. NT intelligence is their greatest asset, dominated by the ENTJ's left hemisphere, which regulates their body movements with creative structure. One might wonder how a left-brained skater could fare so well in such an artistic, fluid sport. Let's consider only one reason.

Before retiring from amateur figure skating at the ripe old age of 23, **Jill Trenary** won three U.S. national titles and the world championship in 1990. Trenary announced her retirement less than 2 months before the 1992 Winter Olympics. The *L.A. Times* reported:

> But perhaps the most significant factor in her decision was the change in the sport's rules this year that eliminated compulsory figures.
>
> Despite failing to finish first in either freestyle skating phase of the competition, she won the world championship in 1990 because of her edge in the figures.[15]

Trenary, like all ENTJs preceding her, found an advantage in the compulsory figures. Contemplating retirement in 1990, she said:

> The sport is changing, not to my advantage. I'm not saying that I can't do well, but all know that the figures helped me out.[16]

To repeat, the International Skating Union's decision to legislate away the most mechanical aspect of the sport, compulsory figures, lessens the once-dominant ENTJs' chances for future skating success. Figures were meant to be mathematically precise, favoring the exacting skater. On the plus side for ENTJs, many judges are Js, having innate preferences for exactness.

Ex Olympian and double gold medalist, **Katarina Witt**, spoke prior to the '92 Olympics of another factor that lessens the ENTJ's chances while increasing the ENFP's:

> It is going more in the athletic direction. They jump more. I did four triples. They do six or seven.[17]

No Type is more naturally acrobatic than the ENFP.

Cool, Calm and Susceptible to Anxiety

Though they appear calm on the outside, ENTJs are not always serene on the inside, particularly prior to big events. **Peggy Fleming** spoke of her 1968 gold medal performance at Grenoble:

> I look at the tapes. I look as calm as anything. Inside, I was just going, 'Aughhhhhhhh! Get me out of here! Yikes! Yikes! But I knew I couldn't leave the building until I'd been through my routine.[18]

Dorothy Hamill was known as an intense and nervous perfectionist. This tension did not prevent her from winning a gold medal, wowing the world in 1976 at Innsbruck.

ENTJs have been, and will continue to be, among the world's finest skaters. No longer will it be as easy for them in single's figures. Their winning ways in ice dancing, however, remain steadfast.

ENTP

ENTPs have not had the favorable recognition in figure skating as have the ENFPs and ENTJs. Nonetheless, they are among the world's top skaters. In recent years, **Rudy Galindo**, **Tara Lipinski, Sarah Hughes, Christopher Bowman**, and **Tonya Harding** have shown their special ENTP abilities.

ENTPs and the top-notch ENFPs share many similarities. As skaters they possess: reservoirs of energy, highly flexible and graceful motor movements, personas that enjoy entertaining, and creative minds that excel at visualizing performance and success. ENTPs are not as innately gifted at body coordination, balance, or acrobatics as ENFPs. Therefore, ENTPs need to give special attention in shoring up these specific areas.

In 1996, ENTP **Rudy Galindo** became the oldest man since the year 1926 to win the U.S. figure skating championships. At the ripe old age of 26, he was considered two years beyond his peak. Galindo won national pairs titles in 1989 and '90 with Kristi Yamaguchi, but he struggled for years in singles before winning the nationals. Galindo had not experienced such a notable single's triumph since capturing the world junior championship in 1987.

In 1997, young phenom **Tara Lipinski** took the women's skating world by storm. First, the 14-year-old upset the reigning world titlist Michelle Kwan and won the U.S. national championships—becoming the youngest female to win the title. Within two months, Lipinski upstaged Kwan again and captured the prestigious World Figure Skating Championships—again being the youngest female to win this title. In 1998, Lipinski attained her greatest accomplishment yet, winning the gold at the Winter Olympics in Nagano, Japan.

Lipinski began her quest for skating superiority at age 6, working seriously throughout the years. Her agent Mike Burg said in '97:

> She's all business. I think Tara is a fierce competitor, and people can take that a variety of ways. She's not here to party or to make friends with the world. She has a job to do.[19]

Tara's coach Richard Callaghan said he frequently has had to drag Tara off the ice to end practice sessions. Most ENTP skaters lack the focus Lipinski has demonstrated over the years, but she's a prime example of what her Type is capable of doing when focusing on a single task.

Tonya Harding won the '91 U.S. Figures title (her first) with an unprecedented triple axel, and placed fourth at the '92 Olympic games at Albertville.

Another top-notch ENTP skater became well known as much off the ice as on. At the 1990 Figure Skating World Championships in Halifax, Canada, **Christopher Bowman** of the U.S. took third place. It was highly amusing to watch him in action. Highlights of his final week in training for this event were shown. Bowman and his coach, both ENTPs, related like Felix Unger and Oscar Madison of "The Odd Couple" days on TV. Bowman seemingly didn't care for what he perceived as an overemphasis on detail by his coach, and his coach was at wit's end trying to get his capricious student to toe the line. The dialogue between the two was classic ENTP. (ENTPs are not nearly as enthusiastic in receiving instruction, especially on details, as they are at giving it.)

Bowman's week at the '90 World's had not gone well and it appeared to be over for this comedian-showman on blades. Leave it to the ENTP to save his best for last. His final routine began tenuously with apparent jitters. As he focused more on the crowd than on his anxiety, Bowman surged with inspiration, aggressively attacking the remainder of his performance. In characteristic ENTP fashion, he threw in unplanned jumps and one upped everyone—the crowd, his coach, even himself. He won the bronze medal.

Christopher Bowman also won a second U.S. national championship in 1991, and placed fourth at the '92 Winter Olympics. Prior to retirement, he earned a reputation as having undisciplined training habits, a hedonistic lifestyle, and a self-proclaimed title of "Hans Brinker from Hell." Olympic medalist Paul Wylie recalled his roommate days with Bowman at the '88 Calgary Olympics:

> It was like living with somebody who works the graveyard shift and then comes home at 7 a.m. after spending a couple of hours at the bar. I was awakened at 5 in the morning eight straight days. On the morning after the short program, he came into my room, threw on the light, danced on the bed and yelled, 'Good Morning, Vietnam!'[20]

John Nicks, **Christopher Bowman's** coach prior to the '92 Olympics, spoke of his pupil's performance in a pre Olympic event:

> I think having Christopher Bowman follow coaching instructions for two minutes and 40 seconds is the most remarkable achievement of my 31 years of coaching. I really thank him for that.[21]

These Christopher Bowman anecdotes illustrate there are few dull moments with most ENTPs in sports, in or out of competition. Nonetheless, many personalities accompany ENTPs, some subdued, many animated. Tara Lipinski and Christopher Bowman are contrasting ENTPs in many respects. They, like all ENTPs, however, share similar inborn mental and motor skill proficiencies. ENTPs can be superb skaters, yet the road may be bumpy for them and their associates along the way.

ESFJ

Figure skating's **Nancy Kerrigan**, ESFJ, demonstrated her SF gross motor control, balance, and smoothness in the 1990s, culminating her amateur career with a silver medal at the '94 Winter Olympics in Lillehammer. Few ESFJs have been top-notch skaters, but Nancy demonstrated what her Type can do through hard work, perseverance, and learning to control her anxiety level.

Conclusion

I have written only of singles figure skaters, devoting my efforts to understanding them first. My future goals include studying ice dancers and speed skaters. Other Brain Types beyond those already mentioned can excel in singles figure skating, though they probably will be found less often.

Here is a list of some well known skaters and their probable Brain Types.

Figure Skating:

ENFP   Kristi Yamaguchi, Michelle Kwan, Oksana Baiul, Chen Lu, Yuka Sato, Midori Ito, Irina Stutskaya, Jayne Torvill, Tracy Wilson, Janet Lynn, Scott Hamilton, Kurt Browning, Brian Boitano, Elvis Stojko, Todd Eldredge, Viktor Petrenko, Aleksandr Fadeyev, Paul Wylie, Randy Gardner, Mark Mitchell, Scott Davis

ENTJ   Peggy Fleming, Dorothy Hamill, Katarina Witt, Jill Trenary

ENTP   Rudy Galindo, Christopher Dean, Philippe Candeloro, Peter Carruthers, Christopher Bowman, Jozef Sabovcik, David Pelletier, Timothy Goebel, Tara Lipinski, Sarah Hughes, Tonya Harding

ESFJ   Nancy Kerrigan, Jamie Sale

ESFP   Nicole Bobek, Surya Bonaly Elizabeth Manley, Rosalynn Sumners

Speed Skating:

ISTP   Bonnie Blair

ENFJ   Dan Jansen

ENTP   Apolo Anton Ohno, Christine Witty

Skateboarding:

ENTP   Tony Hawk

ISFP   Ben Pappas

15
Racing (auto), Snow Skiing, Soccer, Swimming and Diving

Racing (auto)

Between 1990 and 1994, NASCAR's attendance increased more than any other major sport. While Major League Baseball's attendance was dropping 9 percent, the NFL was holding its own, and the NBA attendance was rising 10 percent, NASCAR was up an amazing 47 percent. What was once a regional sport is now an international multi-billion dollar business. Auto racing is not the "good ol' boy" sport that many believe it to be. 1996 statistics revealed that women accounted for 38 percent of NASCAR's attendance.

Though many Brain Types have been successful, two in particular have made a lasting impact on auto racing. Let's consider the first.

ISTP

Prior to his tragic death in 2001, at the age of 49, **Dale Earnhardt** qualified as one of auto racing's all time greats. In 1994, 43-year old Earnhardt won his record-tying seventh NASCAR Winston Cup driver's award, earning again the $1 million season championship bonus. Performing fiercely like superstars of his Brain Type in other sports, ISTP Earnhardt, not surprisingly, was known over the years as "the Intimidator."

A.J. Foyt has been regarded as the greatest American race car driver in history. Over a career that spanned some 35 years, ISTP Foyt won four Indy 500s along with numerous other races, requiring many different kinds of cars. Junior Johnson, one of NASCAR's legends said:

> A.J. Foyt is the greatest driver that I ever knew. The best all around. He could drive anything, anywhere, any time. Won in about everything he ever sat down in.[1]

Chris Economaki, editor and publisher emeritus of *National Speed Sport News*, said of Foyt:

> He almost never made mistakes. Never put a wheel wrong. He never overdrove into a corner, or when conditions were bad. Never spun out, to speak of. Never overshot his pit. He judged his equipment. He won so many races with the canvas showing through a right rear tire that would have blown in another lap. He really understood the business he was in. Just never made mistakes.[2]

Though A.J. was known for his intensity and tempestuousness, his racing style belied that image. He was a cool operator behind the wheel, patient yet willing to be aggressive when necessary.

ESTP

As you might well imagine, ESTPs have used their aggressive daringness to be among auto racing's best. "The King" **Richard Petty**, ESTP, won a record seven Winston Cup championships.

ENFP

ENFPs are infrequently found on the NASCAR circuit. Nonetheless, one in particular has excelled: **Jeff Gordon**. In 1998, Jeff won his third NASCAR championship in four years! The energetic, affable, and go-for-it Gordon has shown that nice guys can master auto racing—a sport often dominated by impersonal or caustic characters.

Conclusion

Auto racing is represented by many Brain Types. Nonetheless, it appears that specific Types tend to excel, particularly demonstrated on the NASCAR circuit.

Though far from complete, here is a list of well known racers and their probable Brain Types

ISTP   A.J. Foyt, Dale Earnhardt

ESTP   Richard Petty

ISFP   Dale Earnhardt Jr.

ESTJ   Al Unser

ENTP   Emerson Fittipaldi, Arie Luyendyk, Dale Jarrett, Ernie Irvan, Joe Nemechek, Kyle Petty

ENFP   Jeff Gordon, Bill Elliott

MOTOCROSS:
ESTP   Greg Albertyn

Snow Skiing

American **Billy Kidd** was a silver medalist in the slalom at the 1964 Winter Olympics and a gold medalist at the 1970 World Championships. Kidd commented:

> To be a great ski racer, natural athletic ability is not enough. You also have to be mentally strong. You have to have courage, confidence, concentration, discipline, perseverance, and, most important, desire.[3]

Kidd spoke of world-class skiers:

> Some of them are good at it naturally; others have acquired that ability after years of hard practice. What separates the great ones from the also rans are the mental factors.[4]

Expert Billy Kidd pinpoints critical elements of great skiers, accentuating the importance of the strong mind. Two Brain Types in particular have competed well internationally in recent skiing history, both possessing physical and mental fortitude. Though not limited to them, ESTPs and ENTPs have made their mark. Sharing three typological similarities (ETP), they rely upon aggressive energies (E) and logical, synthetic, spatial, fluid abilities (TP). The vast majority of world-class skiers are either SPs or ENTPs.

ESTP

Aggressive

The most recognized skier in the world in the late '80s and 1990s was Italy's **Alberto Tomba,** a three-time Olympic gold medalist. At the '88 Calgary Olympics, Tomba won gold medals in the slalom and giant slalom. At the 1992 Winter games in Albertville, France, Tomba won the Olympic gold in the men's giant slalom for an unprecedented second consecutive time. He captured the silver medal in the slalom. At the '94

Lillehammer Olympics, Tomba won the slalom silver medal, missing the gold by 0.75 seconds. In 1995, Tomba won his first overall World Cup title. (This title had eluded him mainly because he skipped the speed races.) Never in his eight-year career had Tomba skied so wisely, or so well.

Earlier in his career, Tomba won races through pure aggression, strength, agility, and reflexes—all ESTP traits. As he approached retirement, he learned how to minimize risks and apply better strategies. Many believe Tomba to be the top skier of all time. Five-time overall World Cup champion, Marc Girardelli, not one to be easily impressed by skiers' feats, said of Tomba following his amazing seventh World Cup slalom victory of the '95 season:

> Right now, he seems to be from another world.[5]

Generally speaking, ESTPs approach skiing as they do life, with reckless abandon. They thrive on action and risk taking, valuing fun and freedom in their choices. Snow skiing and jumping are custom-made for ESTPs. Alberto Tomba's comments sum up the ESTPs sporting mindset and behavior:

> I don't know myself how I do it. Seven slaloms and two giant slaloms in one season; that's enormous.[6]

As high energy, right-brained athletes, ESTPs usually give marginal thought to mechanics and technique or conscious awareness during competition. They're immersed in the process, not results. By making the process their focus, results are best achieved—as a by-product, not the goal.

Braggadocios

It has been written of Tomba:

> He doesn't merely win races, he wins hearts and minds, not only of his countrymen—and women—but of everyone who likes to watch a great athlete capable of delivering on his boast.[7]

Prior to the '92 Winter Games, Alberto appeared as cool and cocky as ever. He later said:

> I was pretending to be confident, saying that these were the Alberto-ville Olympics. But inside I wasn't at all sure, believe me.[8]

ESTPs are often boastful, using this tack to express their self confidence, to intimidate their opponents, and to hide their own insecurities.

Bill Johnson was the first American man to win a gold medal in an Olympic downhill race. At Sarajevo, Yugoslavia (1984), ESTP Johnson brashly predicted his win before the race:

> I am going to win the downhill medal, no question.[9]

In youth sporting activities, ESTPs are not as apt as many other Types to practice strong self-disciplines. They prefer to have fun and not go through laborious practice sessions. Thus, ESTPs often develop their skills with unorthodox techniques—not knowing what they're actually doing. Unless ESTPs grow up on the slopes, they're not as likely to be world-class skiers as some other Types who have stronger work habits.

ISTP

Intense

Four days after striking gold in the '94 Winter Olympic downhill, American skier Tommy Moe mined silver in the men's supergiant slalom. The 23-year-old redeemed his career after years of unfulfilled promise. A skiing prodigy with superb STP motor skills, Moe's career was sidetracked by substance abuse in his teen years and an inability to overcome his intense ISTP Type.

To access the "zone" region of the brain in most sports (where athletes perform their best), one must minimize reasoning centers and access the primary visual/spatial regions of the right hemisphere. Extraverted Perceivers (EPs) are innately best at this, particularly engaging the anterior right brain. When Tommy Moe went before the eyes of the world at Lillehammer, he became energized and more like the ESTP. (I witness this phenomenon regularly in sports, especially with ISTPs.) Moe became more like ESTP Alberto Tomba, letting it all hang out with his STP mental and motor skills. As Moe became more concerned with the process than results, he finally achieved his long-held dream. All ISTPs can benefit from this strategy.

Considering ISTPs are often exceptionally principled people, it was not surprising to read that Tommy Moe declined all endorsement offers after winning the Olympic gold. Passing on dollars that few could resist, he didn't want his gold medal effort to be considered a fluke.

ESFP

ESFPs are rarely found among the top skiers in the world—not as a result of skiing inabilities; rather, few endure the self-disciplines and rigors necessary to excel. The gregarious **Picabo Street** is one ESFP who overcame the odds. She won the silver medal in the 1994 women's downhill at Lillehammer. In 1995, she was finally validated as a top skier—winning six of nine downhills to become the first American to win the World Cup season downhill title. Street repeated her brilliance in 1996, again winning the season downhill World Cup title. Her '97 season was ruined by knee surgery, but 1998 became Picabo's year of crowning glory. She won the Olympic gold in the women's supergiant slalom at Nogano, Japan.

Street found the Nagano conditions perfect in the super-G race. The snow was soft, ideal for her liking. Known as a "glider," she used her big muscle strength and daring style to barrel down the mountain to victory. The race favorite, Katja Seizinger of Germany, was a hard snow specialist and finished sixth.

When Picabo first became well-known in 1994, I was asked by many to guess her Brain Type. Having only a 10-second TV interview to go by, I perceived some ENTP qualities (a Type which can often initially resemble the ESFP). It wasn't until the 1998 Winter Olympics that I saw her SF traits and could clearly evaluate her. I was excited that an ESFP had excelled at skiing. To all ESFPs, let Picabo be your inspiration on the slopes.

ENTP

ENTPs can present a case for being the most dominant skiers in the world. For one, NTs usually have stronger work habits than SPs, and they're willing to endure greater hardships to achieve personal goals. Desire and tougher work habits often provide a competitive edge.

In achieving elite status, it is of great advantage to be a risk-taking, right-brained fluid skier. ENTPs have these inborn attributes. Their least-developed body skills are the gross motors. Thus, their legs are soft rather than stiff shock-absorbers. With this kind of flexibility, moguls are less of a challenge, whereas gross motor dominant SFs tend to lift off over bumps, flying too far due to their more tightly wound big muscle groups. ENTPs are also one of the top two visualizing Types. Though seeing the course in competition is important, visualizing the run can be even more crucial. If ENTPs work hard at developing and coordinating their motor skills at an early age, they have the potential to be among the world's consummate skiers. ENTPs are also considered the optimal Type for sports performance in poor weather. As dominant right-brained iNtuitives, they are the least likely to be negatively affected.

ENTPs captured two of the three American women's medals at the 1994 Lillehammer Winter Olympics. At only age 17, **Diann Roffe-Steinrotter** won a giant slalom gold medal in the 1985 World Championships in Bormio, Italy, becoming the second youngest skier (by four days) ever to win a world or Olympic title. Nonetheless, her career didn't meet expectations, and she never placed better than fourth in the super-G in World Cup competition. But in 1994, nine years after her Bormio gold, Roffe-Steinrotter captured the Lillehammer Olympic gold in the women's super-G—this in an event where she was ranked 36th in the world.

Liz McIntyre won the Lillehammer Olympic silver in the women's freestyle moguls.

In the '98 Nagano Winter Games, Austrian **Hermann Maier** overcame the mental and physical trauma from a spectacular alpine crash only days before, and won the men's giant and supergiant slaloms. Nicknamed the Hermannator, ENTP Maier dominated the 1997-98 World Cup circuit in the giant slalom and super-G.

Aggressive

ENTP **Jean-Claude Killy**, the debonair Frenchman, won three Alpine gold medals at the 1968 Winter Olympics in Grenoble, France. His technical mastery, raw speed, and French mystique brought him legendary status, still evident a generation later. Former ski coach Bob Beattie spoke of Killy's daredevil style:

Killy had that dash to him, always attacking,

looking like he was going to hell. People at home watching, most of whom would never think about skiing, could associate with that.[10]

Intelligent

ENTP **Billy Kidd** was regarded as a thinking man's skier. He spoke of his skiing travels prior to attending college:

> As I traveled through Europe, I tried to absorb some history, geography, geology, political science, economics, and languages.[11]

Determined, Pain Enduring

Following his Olympic silver medal, Billy Kidd persisted with unmitigated determination for six more years on the world circuit, seeking to be the best. Despite painful injuries, Kidd finally won the World Championships in Val Gardena, Italy.

Conclusion

I have only scratched the surface in my study of snow skiers. The observations I have made are worth noting, though much more research is necessary. It is good to remember that skiing takes many forms: slalom, giant slalom, downhill, cross country, ski jumping, and so on. Therefore, I expect a variety of Types to participate and excel in snow skiing.

Here is a list of a some well known snow skiers and their probable Brain Types.

ENTP   Jean-Claude Killy, Hermann Maier,
　　　Billy Kidd, Andy Mill, Bill Koch, Bode Miller,
　　　Simon Ammann,
　　　Liz McIntyre, Diann Roffe-Steinrotter

ESTP   Alberto Tomba, Bill Johnson

ISTP   Paul Accola, Katrin Gutensohn, A.J. Kitt,
　　　Tommy Moe

ESFP   Picabo Street

ENFP   Jim Shea Jr. (skeleton)

Soccer

Soccer is one of the truly "world sports." At the adult level, professional leagues exist in many countries. The grand event of soccer occurs every four years, when teams from around the globe—made up of the world's greatest players—come together to compete for the World Cup. In 1986, more than two-and-a-quarter million people attended World Cup matches in Mexico.

Soccer is also a sport loved by youngsters. In 1997, the *L.A. Times* reported that the U.S. Youth Soccer Association had 2.8 million members—approximately 41 percent were females. From 1985 to 1995, student participation in high school soccer jumped 81 percent—the single largest increase of any sport.

Having never played organized soccer, my principal exposure to the game came from watching and reading about it, then finally coaching youth soccer for six years. For this book, I only want to consider a few prominent players and Brain Types found within the sport. Since professional soccer has elevated slowly in America, I have had few opportunities to view the world's best players.

ENFP

Born Edison Arantes do Nascimento, Brazil's world-renowned **Pelé,** is considered the greatest soccer player of all time. Pelé began his pro career at age fifteen. At seventeen, he led the Brazilian National team to the World Cup championship. He later led them to two more. Pelé's career spanned 22 years, in which he scored an incredible 1,281 goals. Standing only 5 feet, 8 inches, Pelé was soccer's ambassador, visiting popes, emperors, kings, and other heads of state. After a brief retirement, Pelé was lured to America to play for the New York Cosmos.

Don Kowet wrote in his book, *PELÉ*:

> Even then, at seventeen, Pelé could dribble the

ball through a crowd of players, easily sidestepping their futile tackles. The path of his passes was as perfect as any computer could program. His shots were so powerful, opposing goalies guarded their nets even when Pelé was sixty or seventy yards away, defending his own. He was accurate when he headed the ball, too, but—as his Cosmos teammates were now learning—his greatest asset lay within that head.

> 'A good player will be thinking maybe two moves ahead,' said Gordon Bradley, who was promoted from head coach to vice-president after the season ended. 'Pelé can think six or seven moves ahead.'[12]

Studying Pelé's life many years ago, virtually everything I read led me to believe he was an ISTP. (I never recall seeing him play.) But as time has elapsed and looking deeper into his life, I must admit, I was wrong; Pelé is an ENFP—one who developed his ENFP skills to the utmost. As the above article states, Pelé was expert at looking ahead. His dominant iNtuitive function enabled him to visualize future player movements. Don Kowet writes further:

> What the Cosmos were learning, in fact, was that Pelé's qualities as a master tactician transcended even his uncanny skills at scoring. Cool, unruffled, even when being rushed, he had the ability to plot offensive strategies on the spur of the moment. At any instant, his intuitive radar told him the position of every other player on the field. Pelé's greatest talent wasn't scoring goals; it was turning eleven individuals into a team.[13]

On and off the field, Pelé's affable personality galvanized teammates to set self interests aside for the betterment of the team. Kowet provided two more insights into Pelé by which we should remember him:

> Perhaps no man in modern history was ever confronted by so many temptations to arrogance. No man ever rejected them so completely.[14]

And Pelé assessed himself:

> My talent is a gift of God; I am only what he made me.[15]

ESTP

Argentinian **Diego Maradona**, like sound alike rock star Madonna, is an ESTP. Their reputations have become similar, too. *Sports Illustrated* said that Maradona has been described by sports writers worldwide as:

> ... 'indiscreet,' 'flawed,' 'explosive,' 'vulgar,' 'spoiled,' 'surly,' 'mercurial,' 'petulant,' and plain 'rubbish.'[16]

Maradona has said:

> If at times I get angry or I complain, it's because I don't know how to keep my feelings quiet ... and I don't want to learn.[17]

Like some other ESTPs in the sporting world have done, Diego Maradona has made a name for himself, on and off the field. His problems heightened in 1991 when he was suspended from professional soccer for drug possession, to which he replied:

> I won't play professional soccer again. It's an irrevocable decision.[18]

Yet in ESTP fashion, Maradona had difficulty leaving the limelight and came out of retirement. Despite his controversial reputation, Maradona's teammates found him to be a good-natured and likable comrade.

Assuming the "world's greatest soccer player" recognition when Pelé retired, Diego Maradona thrilled fans with his uncanny skills. It was written:

> When he is at his best—dribbling impossibly between two, three, half a dozen opponents, starting and stopping like a jackrabbit, the ball magically attached to his foot, shin or knee—Maradona pleases all who see him.[19]

In the 1980s Maradona was the dominant soccer player in the world, leading Argentina to the 1986 World Cup championship in Mexico City. He became the world's highest paid soccer player, earning roughly $10 million annually from his many sports and business deals. Have hope all short soccer players; Maradona is only 5' 5".

Superb Soccer Players

ESTPs and ISTPs are two of the best Brain Types for soccer. They are able to play any position on the field. ESTPs generally do not enjoy playing on the defensive end of the field, unless it is as the goalie.

How Can the ESTP be So Good?

We have witnessed throughout this book the physical and mental strengths of each Type. In soccer, ESTPs' fine motor precision is not of much help (except at goalie), whereas their right-brain controlled motor and visual skills are. Spain's respected soccer coach, Helenio Herrera, spoke of **Diego Maradona**:

> He has an instant, spontaneous vision of the entire game, which permits him to put the ball exactly where he wants it. He's capable of inventing shots that have never been seen before.[20]

Diego's vision was supported by his synthetic, logical Thinking function, enabling him to make intelligent split second decisions.

ENTJ

ENTJs can be expert soccer players. Though they do not possess the speed and finesse skills of the right-brained players, ENTJs excel by hard work, aggressiveness, precision moves and intellect.

ENTJ **Kyle Rote, Jr.** was an outstanding soccer player. He won the NASL's Rookie-of-the-Year award, and is the only American born player to ever win a major professional soccer league scoring championship. In 1999, ENTJ **Mia Hamm** gained national stardom by leading the U.S. Women's national soccer team to a World Cup title.

Conclusion

All Brain Types have the potential to play superbly in youth soccer. In order for this to happen, some Types must begin developing their body coordination and motor skills at an early age. SFJs, particularly ISFJs, need to overcome their timidity. The older youngsters get, however, the more difficult for some Types to excel. As we see in the preponderance of other sports, only select Types dominate at the highest levels.

I view soccer and hockey as somewhat alike. The sixteen Brain Types tend to play the two sports similarly. Generally speaking, at the pro level: all SPs are represented, with ISTPs and ESTPs the top scorers; the successful SJs play defensive positions; the iNtuitives are well represented by ENTJs, ENTPs, and ENFPs.

Here is a list of some well known soccer players and their probable Brain Types.

ESTP	Diego Maradona
ESFP	Michelle Akers
ENTJ	Mia Hamm, Kyle Rote, Jr.
ENTP	Alexi Lalas, David Beckham
ENFP	Pelé, Freddy Adu

Swimming and Diving

The Summer Olympic Games elevate the sports of swimming and diving to high profile status, with many water athletes achieving celebrity recognition and rewards. Four Brain Types in particular, which are closely related, have especially excelled in swimming. They are the Extraverted iNtuitives (EN).

Extraverted iNtuitives have super charged energies to endure the rigors of swimming, high pain-thresholds, flexible and elastic motor movements, and goal-oriented minds that continually drive them.

ENFJ

NFs (iNtuitive Feelers) are masters at coordinating large and small muscle groups—a major benefit in excelled swimming. Yet a lot of finesse is not required in swimming. Therefore, ENFJs as left-brained athletes can "let it all hang out," without the fear of making mistakes like they might in other sports. Their powerful strokes and leg actions are hard to compete against. ENFJs have included **Donna DeVarona** and **John Naber**.

Donna DeVarona won two Olympic gold medals and broke eighteen world records during her celebrated career.

John Naber was a four-time Olympic gold medalist and the first man to break the two minute mark in the 200-meter backstroke.

ENFP

Californian **Janet Evans** captured the hearts of Americans at the 1988 Seoul Olympics, collecting three gold medals (the 400 and 800 frees and 400 individual medley). That same year, at age 18, she won the Sullivan Trophy, awarded to the outstanding amateur athlete. In 1990, for the third time in her career, ENFP Evans was named *Swimming World's* female World Swimmer of the Year. At the '92 Olympics, she won gold once again in the 800 freestyle. The '96 Atlanta Olympics was Evans' third and final. The vibrant, easy-going charm of Janet Evans was a major asset to swimming.

Matt Biondi, "the California Condor," captured seven medals (five gold) in the 1988 Seoul Olympics, breaking four world records. He continued his swimming excellence through the 1992 Barcelona Olympics. ENFP Biondi collected 11 Olympic medals over his career, tying with Mark Spitz for the most in Olympic history.

Rowdy Gaines, ENFP, won the gold medal in the men's 100-meter freestyle at the 1984 Olympics in Los Angeles.

ENTP

Leave it to the comedic and audacious ENTP to one up the swimming world, too. Virtually every sport has its precocious ENTPs among its stars, and swimming had **Melvin Stewart** in the early 1990s. Among other achievements, the clown prince of American swimming was a world record holder in the 200 meter butterfly.

Known for an occasional intentional false start at the beginning of a race, Stewart was asked about his practice of psyching out the opponents. He lightheartedly told a reporter:

> If I told you everything [about my strategy], I would have to kill you.[21]

Stewart was also unorthodox by swimming the butterfly with his head turned to the side. Butterflyers typically lift their heads straight up to breathe.

The self-described "swimmer geek" once discussed a typical ENTP athlete's work and play ethic:

> I'm not a fool, but if you knew my lifestyle, you'd say, 'Is he really an athlete?' I think you work hard and you play hard.[22]

Preparing for the 1992 Barcelona Olympics, Stewart put in nearly three times the swimming effort of most butterflyers, sometimes swimming 8,000 meters in a lone workout. ENTPs are known for their tireless efforts in both work and play, often burning the midnight oil to get them in.

An ENTP with a calmer demeanor than that of Melvin Stewart was exceptional at the '96 Atlanta Olympics. America's **Amy Van Dyken** won individual gold medals in the women's 50-meter freestyle and 100-meter butterfly.

At the 2000 Sydney Summer Olympics, Australian and ENTP **Ian Thorpe** won gold in the 400-meter freestyle and silver in the 200-meter free, while ENTP **Lenny Krayzelburg** (USA) won 2 individual golds in the 100- and 200-meter backstroke.

The 2004 Athens Olympics introduced ENTP phenom **Michael Phelps**. Pursuing the legacy of Mark Spitz, Phelps tied an Olympic record by winning eight medals—six gold and two bronze.

ENTJ

At the '92 Barcelona Olympics, **Mike Barrowman** won the gold medal in the 200-meter breaststroke, breaking his own world record. Barrowman capitalized on his ENTJ work ethic and intellect, swimming a race of perfection.

Conclusion

Select Brain Types appear to excel in swimming as they do in other sports. Nonetheless, a number of Types have turned in gold medal performances.

DIVING

Diving is appreciated by nearly all sports enthusiasts. The grace, guts, and gymnastics required are extraordinary; diving is not a sport that is easily mastered.

I loved diving as a child. I would ride my bicycle 4-5 miles a day in the hot, steamy summers of Southern Indiana just to swim and dive. The Surf Club, the closest I ever got to the surf as a Midwesterner, had a diving pool—including a 3 meter board. Here I had a chance to test my skills. I soon found myself doing better than most kids, yet lacking the grace and gymnastic abilities of the best divers. Guts I had, demonstrated by my doing a $3^1/_4$ forward somersault, not quite completing the $3^1/_2$. I had to be helped from the pool, temporarily blinded and stunned by the force of the water. My body stung for over 20 minutes. Something told me this was not my sport.

As a Brain Typist and sports researcher, I now understand why I didn't have it as a diver. Had I been one of several other Brain Types, I probably would have pursued the sport. One of those optimal Types is the gymnast par excellence, the ENFP.

ENFP

American **Greg Louganis** won back to back Olympic gold medals in the springboard and platform diving events (1984-88). ENFP Louganis was unparalleled in recent diving history. He began his ascent to the top with a gold medal effort at the 1978 World Diving Championships.

In 1996, ENFP **Fu Mingxia** won her second consecutive Olympic gold medal on the platform. Regarded as the female equivalent to Greg Louganis, China's Mingxia also captured the gold in the 3-meter springboard to sweep the women's diving competition. At the 2000 Summer Olympics, Mingxia took her third consecutive gold on platform! Unexpectedly winning gold on springboard was ENFP **Laura Wilkinson** of the USA.

ENFP **Wendy Williams** is a former women's U.S. National Champion on the 10-meter platform.

American **Kent Ferguson**, ENFP, won the men's springboard competition at the 1991 World Championships.

ENTJ

At the '92 Barcelona Olympics, **Mark Lenzi** brought home (to Fredricksburg, Va.) the gold from the men's springboard diving competition. His ENTJ determination, zeal for winning, exacting form, and high-level confidence brought him through any before-the-world nerves, and made him number one.

Conclusion

Diving is mastered by select Types. Further research will provide additional clues. For now, ENFPs can know they are among, if not, the best. ENTJs appear to be among the best J (dominant left-hemisphere) divers.

Here is a list of some well known swimmers and divers and their probable Brain Types.

ENFJ   Donna DeVarona, John Naber

ENFP   Janet Evans, Matt Biondi, Rowdy Gaines, Greg Louganis, Kent Ferguson, Fu Mingxia, Laura Wilkinson, Becky Ruehl, Wendy Williams

ENTP   Lenny Krayzelburg, Ian Thorpe, Melvin Stewart, Martin Zubero, Amy Van Dyken, Anita Nall, Scott Donie, Troy Dumais

ENTJ   Mike Barrowman, Mark Lenzi

ESFP   Summer Sanders

16 Tennis

The sport which began with a racket strung with catgut (not derived from kitty innards but different quadrupeds, particularly sheep) and a spheric fuzzy ball, has grown significantly in popularity over the years. The ambition of acquiring sizable paychecks plays a role in this growth.

In 1996, the ATP Tour's global outreach extended to 83 tournaments in 39 counties; the Tour is the No. 1 worldwide professional sports circuit. American **Pete Sampras** was the APT's leading money winner in 1996, pocketing $3.7 million in prize money (excluding endorsements). German **Steffi Graf** earned a whopping $2.66 million on the women's tour.

The total purse at the 2003 U.S. Open totaled $17 million. The singles men's and women's winners won a cool $1 million each.

Tennis is a sport I have played off and on throughout my life (like many of you), in which I hold my own only with other novices. My tosses often end up out of reach, my serves in the net, and my ground strokes in my doubles partner's backside.

Nevertheless, I can utilize my Brain Type awareness with tennis and reveal insight to those who want to know more this challenging sport. I won't tell you much on how to improve your mechanics, but I can give you some mental and physical approaches that will indirectly affect your whole game.

Brain Type Versus Personality

I have repeatedly attempted to convey the difference between these two issues throughout this book; I obviously want to stress the point. Two seemingly dissimilar persons can share similar cerebral inner workings which, in effect, will yield similar perception and decision making patterns, as well as motor movements. Some of these factors are genetic and not affected by one's environment at all. Conversely, we must remember that upbringing and environment will have a pronounced impact on many aspects of one's personality. *Thus Brain Types and personality can be quite different.*

Let's take, for example, two persons who share the same Brain Type (ISTP), but have distinctly different personalities. They are **Martina Navratilova and Steffi Graf**. Unless you have been off the planet in recent years, you already know these are two of the most dominant female tennis players in recent history. First, Martina is 12 years older than Steffi and has activated parts of her brain that only come as a result of age and experience. (Typological Function theory has a partial explanation for this.) Second, these two European born women have had different upbringings and environments throughout their lives. These factors clearly influence personality styles.

Before her retirement in 1994, Martina was regarded as one of the most personable "star" athletes in the world. Reportedly, she consistently found time for her friends, fans, and the media. Steffi has been regarded as more aloof and shy.

This book will tell you how the different Brain Types function, but understanding these two women's personalities adequately requires more information than I possess on them. What little I know sheds light on their personas. Steffi's father was reported to be highly restrictive and domineering, one who wanted her to remain completely focused on being the best tennis player in the world. Scott Ostler of the *L.A. Times* repeated in 1987:

> When Stephanie Maria Graf was only hours old, her father proclaimed that one day she would be a champion, and that he gave her that [a] sawed off racket before she turned four. He tied a string between two living room settees and that was their net. They played.

If Steffi would keep a rally going for ten hits, she would earn a bread stick. For 25, her reward would be ice cream and strawberries.[1]

Osler concludes his article by posing the question, "Is Steffi's dad a monster?" Peter Graf, Steffi's father told a London paper:

I don't think monster is the right word. I just want what is best for Steffi, and sometimes I have to fight for it.[2]

Whether being subservient to her father's wishes or her own, Steffi spent her time engulfed in tennis instead of social activities—prior to her father's imprisonment for tax evasion in the mid-1990s. According to Osler in 1987:

Steffi probably practices longer and harder than anyone else on the tour. On the court, she is extremely business like, with none of the outward exuberance of fellow countryman Boris Becker. Steffi has no boyfriends. She doesn't hang out much with the girls on the tour. She doesn't spend much money.[3]

In fairness to Steffi, one decisive reason she was not as outwardly exuberant as Becker is that he's an Extravert (ESTP) as opposed to her Introversion. Graf's unusual upbringing and environment have also shaped her personality, making it different from Martina's. Many Introverts are often misread and misunderstood.

John Feinstein was complimentary to Graf in his 1991 book, *Hard Courts*. Feinstein said his biggest surprise in doing research on and meeting pro tennis players was how much he admired Steffi Graf. He found her different than he expected, and said:

She is not only bright and interesting, but a warm and sensitive person. The remarkable thing is that she turned out the way she has with the father she has.[4]

As we look at the best Brain Types for professional tennis, keep in mind the differences in their physical and mental traits, even with those of the same Brain Type. All persons of one specific Type will share similar and dissimilar characteristics with others of their same Type. For example, all ISTP tennis players who have worked at their game will have special hand-eye coordination, spatial logic and awareness, and right-brained motor movements.

ISTP

Once again we find the ISTP at the top of the ladder in another area of athletics. ISTPs have normally been the predominant Brain Type found on the professional tennis circuit, particularly the women's tour. (With the advent of new rackets, the power game has especially changed both the men's and women's circuit in recent years. Certain tennis skills are not as necessary as they once were.) We will see there are some other Types that can give ISTPs a run for their money, but essentially none is better designed to play top notch, consistent tennis.

Consider ISTPs **Rod Laver, Ivan Lendl, Stefan Edberg, John McEnroe, Jimmy Connors, Michael Chang, Lleyton Hewitt, Martina Navratilova, Steffi Graf,** and **Monica Seles.** You will also see a potpourri of personas all within one ISTP Brain Type.

From 1978 to 1996, the Women's Tennis Association Player of the Year Award has gone to ISTPs 16 out of the 18 years! All four of the 1991, 1993, and 1995 women's Grand Slam events were won by ISTPs.

Many more ISTPs are being given the chance to play tennis than in former years. Tennis, like golf, has long been regarded as a rich person's sport. Many ISTPs have not been raised in this environment and thus have not played the game. Of all places, communist or socialist nations, in the last 20 years, have given all 16 Brain Types the most opportunities to play. Consider the ISTP tennis greats who did *not* come from affluent households. They usually are from the former Iron Curtain countries.

Upon retirement in 1994, **Martina Navratilova** had accumulated some $20.3 million in career tournament winnings. In 1992, she broke Chris Evert's record of 157 tournament titles. Martina finished with 167 singles titles, more than any other man or woman player. She also holds a 165 doubles titles.

Navratilova won 90 of 93 matches in 1982, followed by 86 of 87 in 1983! By 1986, she had captured her one-thousandth match victory, becoming the second player in modern history to do so. Navratilova almost consistently held the No. 1 women's ranking in the world for nearly 10 straight years (1978-1987). She won six consecutive Wimbledon singles titles between 1982-1987. Navratilova set a record by winning 74 consecutive matches, breaking Chris Evert's record of 55. Tennis legend, Tony Trabert, said of Navratilova:

> Martina is stronger, is faster, and has a more complete game than any other female player in history. She's a terrific volleyer, especially with her backhand, a shot I've yet to see any other woman make as consistently. She also smashes and simply moves better than anyone else before or currently.[5]

Navratilova has been a phenomenal athlete, even an expert skier. As an ISTP, she could have excelled in a number of sports.

At the ripe old age of thirty-nine, **Jimmy Connors** captured the heart of America and New York City with his tennis at the 1991 U.S. Open. Connors made it to the semifinals, spectacularly winning two come from behind, five set matches along the way. Following his defeat to Jim Courier, Connors walked off the court at the U.S. Open for the 113th time, and to the thunderous applause of 20,000 spectators.

Connors found consistent athletic success at an early age. He held the No. 1 ranking on the Association of Tennis Professionals computer several times, including one stretch of 159 consecutive weeks, from July 29, 1974 to August 16, 1977—longer than any other man. Connors retired with a 109 singles titles, including five U.S. Opens, two Wimbledons, and one Australian championship.

Although Connors often appeared outgoing over the years, especially on the court, his Brain Type is Introverted. I was amused by an article from the *L.A. Times* in 1990:

> Pat Calabria of Newsday wrote this week that during the French Open, NBC was having trouble getting commentator Jimmy Connors to interview male tennis players.
>
> 'I can't interview that guy,' Connors would say. Or: 'He's stupid.' Or: 'I don't even know that guy.' Or: 'That guy hasn't talked to me in years.'
>
> Finally, the network people asked Connors if there were any players whom he got along with and could interview. Connors thought about it, then said: 'Yeah. Eddie Dibbs.'[6]

Remember, personality and Brain Type do not always appear the same. Jimmy Connors acted Extraverted at times, but cerebrally his design is Introverted. His concentration and motor skills strongly supported this conclusion.

Monica Seles, the ISTP Yugoslavian import, has proven to be one of the greats of all times in women's tennis. In May of 1990 and at only 16 years of age, Seles became the youngest player ever to win a Grand Slam, the French Open. She defeated Steffi Graf in the finals. Only weeks before, Seles upset No. 1 ranked Graf in straight sets to win the German Open and end Graf's 66 match winning streak. (Graf had not lost a match for a year!) Seles' German victory put her into the No. 3 spot in the rankings (being No. 88 only one year before) and extended her own match winning streak to 24. She finally lost at Wimbledon, ending her streak of winning six straight tournaments and 39 matches.

Seles took the 1991 tennis scene by storm, capturing the WTA Singles Player of the Year award. Monica completed a sweep of all three of the 1991 Grand Slam events in which she played: the Australian Open, French Open and U.S. Open. She won seven other titles, including the Virginia Slims championship. Her single season earnings from tournaments totaled $2.45 million. All this at the ripe old age of 17!

Seles has been well known for her grunts when striking the ball. At the 1990 Wimbledon, a newspaper ran a sound check on Monica, supposedly using a "gruntometer." The tabloid *Sun* wrote:

> At a range of 15 feet, the machine recorded her service at 71 decibels—about the same as heavy road traffic.
>
> Grumph! She drops to a more ladylike 54 decibels, like a loud TV set, as she settles into easy rally.
>
> Graagh! She roars back at 82 decibels to deliver a powerful double backhand.[7]

According to the newspaper, the grunt that registered highest was somewhere between a pneumatic drill and a diesel locomotive. Monica responded to those who dislike her audible sounds:

> I'm working on it. I still don't know what the big deal is. Jimmy Connors grunted just as loud as I did, and a lot longer. But if it's going to bother everybody so much, OK, I'll work on it.[8]

(I haven't attempted to figure the Types of the grunters on tour, but it initially looks like the ISTPs could win here, too.)

Whether or not Seles's grunting has bothered you, she has become one of the greatest female tennis players in history. Tragically, a spectator stabbed her at courtside in 1993. Monica had won seven of the last eight Grand Slam events before the bizarre attack! Following over two years of physical and emotional rehabilitation, she returned to the courts at the Canadian Open in 1995. Amazingly, Seles won the tournament; she demonstrated her ISTP resolve more than ever, and showed that she was still one to be reckoned with.

Seles has revealed another aspect of her Brain Type. She's said:

> I never wanted to be a tennis player anyway, I wanted to be a basketball player. I'm a lot better at basketball than I am at tennis.[9]

I don't know much about Monica, but I know her Type, and it is the best in basketball. (Michael Jordan and Larry Bird are ISTPs. Refer to the Basketball chapter for more ISTPs). If Seles says she's good at hoops, I believe her. Better than at tennis, that I doubt.

Prior to his retirement in 1996, ISTP **Stefan Edberg** of Sweden was perceived by the press as being quite withdrawn. Some writers said his personality was so low keyed that it was almost off the scale. He has been called "Edberg the Iceberg," "Stoic Swede," "Emotionless," even "monotonous as a dial tone." If reporters learned more about his cerebral makeup, they would have been more understanding.

Stefan's personality was shaped in part by his father, a policeman. One might speculate that unsportsmanlike conduct was not tolerated as much in the Edberg household as it has been in some of America's well known tennis families. How refreshing it was to see Edberg not complain over line calls, and to be given the "Sportsmanship" award three straight years by his tennis peers. It is a tribute to Stefan for him to have behaved in such a manner, knowing his intensely determined and competitive Brain Type.

It was good to read the newspaper comments following Edberg's winning the '90 Newsweek Champions Cup:

> There is something to be said for the quiet, if not the meek, among us. There is a serene beauty in the subtle and—as of Sunday—a reward for the modest. There is Stefan Edberg.[10]

Upon his retirement, Edberg had six Grand Slam victories. His winning performance at the 1991 U.S. Open was magnificent (he also won in 1992!), culminating with a near perfect match against Jim Courier. Edberg never lost his serve, winning 68 points in 94 approaches to the net, disposing of Courier in three straight sets. In addition to perfecting his innate, fine motor skills and logical, spatial right brain, Edberg was able to attain the level of concentration at which ISTPs can excel. Edberg said after the match:

> It was like a dream out there. I feel like I could do anything. It's fantastic you can play such a good match in a Grand Slam final without losing your concentration.[11]

Though Edberg once had the same coach as Bjorn Borg, he developed his own style of play (custom fitting his own Brain Type, might I say). Rather than staying back and hitting from the baseline with top spin a la Borg, Edberg developed an aggressive game of serve and volley, incorporating an attack on the net and a one handed backhand. His game is now the combination of power and grace.

Consider how ISTP **Steffi Graf** impacted the tennis world since her debut. She was awarded twice the WTA Singles Player of the Year for four consecutive years (1987-1990 and 1993-1996). In 1988, Steffi became the sixth player to win the Grand Slam. She won three Grand Slam titles in 1989, '93, '95 and '96. As of the 1990 U.S. Open, Steffi had won nine of the 15 Grand Slam events since her first major title, the 1987 French Open. She also made the '90 U.S. Open her 16th consecutive appearance in a Grand Slam semifinal.

At that time Steffi also began a record 160th consecutive week ranked No. 1, breaking ISTP Jimmy Connors' mark of 159. (Steffi's streak finally ended in 1991 at 186 weeks!) ISTP's Ivan Lendl and Martina Navratilova held No. 1 for 156 consecutive weeks. It could be some time before another woman dominates the tour as has Steffi. She was clearly the dominant player of the '90s.

ISTP **Ivan Lendl** was one of the top three-ranked players in the world for ten straight years. From 1985-88, he had an uninterrupted stretch of 156 straight weeks at No. 1. His career earnings totaled over $21 million.

Rod Laver hung up his tennis shoes in the late 1970s. Before retiring, the ISTP racked up 47 career pro titles (after 1968) and was the first male to reach $1 million in official earnings. The Aussie with the shy persona was the only player in the history of tennis to win the Grand Slam twice, in the years 1962 and 1969.

Laver was known for a Popeye sized left forearm, his racket hand. All tennis players will enlarge their dominant arm, but STPs often develop theirs the most due to their fine motor emphasis.

Michael Chang, ISTP, is presently known for his oversized forearm. In 1997, Chang achieved a No. 2 world ranking, his highest ever.

Concentration, Intensity, Consistency

Regardless of the sport, ISTPs are able to muster phenomenal intensity and concentration. In these areas, no Type can outperform them overall. This pays big dividends in lengthy matches. In professional tennis, the Grand Slam events require the men to capture three sets in order to win a match. Many times these matches go five sets, lasting up to five hours long! This places tremendous stress on the athletes, both mentally and physically. When other Types break down in their minds, ISTPs are usually as strong mentally as they were at the beginning of the match, provided they have kept their emotions in check. ISTPs are ready to go on until their opponents drop. They're able to play or perform at a remarkably consistent pace.

At the 1990 U.S. Open, **Ivan Lendl** lost a five-set match, after dropping the first two sets. Perhaps his thirty years caught up to him as he lost to the nineteen-year old and eventual winner, Pete Sampras. But what a remarkable nine years of ISTP intensity and pace of play.

The *L.A. Times*' Jim Murray wrote of **Martina Navratilova** in 1990:

> Martina never seems to come to a game in emotional disarray. She is as tough and focused as Mike Tyson with his man on the ropes . . . .[12]

Murray accurately correlated Tyson and Navratilova's intensity and, unknowingly, their Brain Type (both ISTPs).

Tony Trabert recalled the days of **Rod Laver**:

> Laver was technically sound and played consistently at the same high level, match after match.[13]

Mary Joe Fernandez said, after losing to **Monica Seles** in the women's finals of the 1992 Australian Open:

> The best part of her game is her tenacity. Under no circumstances does she play tentatively. I think that's what wins her most of her matches.[14]

ISTPs' motor and mental skills (particularly concentration and intensity) enable them to play at a remarkably consistent rate.

Competitive, Perfectionistic

At the age of 33, **Martina Navratilova** was asked about her motivation to play pro tennis. She said:

> It used to be that I just wanted to be No. 1. I didn't care how. Now it's a combination of the competition, and the ability to do with a ball what I want with it. I mean exactly. To put it on a dime, with the right speed and the right spin. I love that. And giving it everything, my heart, my soul and my body too.[15]

Fine Motor Skills

Not only do ISTPs possess exceptional, innate, fine motor skills, they continue to maintain this adeptness throughout the match. When the mental and physical strains take their toll on most other Brain Types, they break down in their motor skills (particularly the NTs). The STPs are last to weaken in their fine motor movements.

Another benefit of the ST skills is highlighted by Trabert's description of **Rod Laver**:

> Although he was fairly slight, he packed a wallop in his game because he used a lot of wrists in his shots. This gave him additional pace and deceptively masked his shots until the last second.[16]

The two best Types for using their wrists in tennis (as in all sports) are the ESTP and ISTP. Although the left-brained STJs are naturally gifted in their wrists, they tend to be more mechanical, unable to produce as much spin, velocity, or control over the shots.

In his book, *Trabert on Tennis*, Tony Trabert advises against the part time tennis players overusing their wrists:

> "But Rod Laver always uses a lot of wrist when he hits," you might say. Yes, but Laver also hit eight jillion tennis balls in his career, practicing as much as five hours a day. A player who puts in only two hours on a weekend can never expect to duplicate the shots of a top pro like Laver.[17]

Although I agree with Tony's assessment, even the pro tennis players who have one of the other 14 Brain Types (not including ESTPs and ISTPs), will never develop Laver's wrist proficiency. Rod maximized his God given fine motor skills through extensive practice. No Type is better able to do this than STPs.

Volleyers

ISTPs have all the physical and mental tools to be the best volleyers, especially at the net. Their quick fine motor movements, deft touch, and logically spatial, right brain provide them this advantage. **Martina Navratilova and Stefan Edberg** are just two of the ISTPs who have demonstrated their superb volleying. In the early 1990s, many tour pros believed Edberg was the best volleyer in the world. After losing to Edberg in the Volvo/Los Angeles tournament, Aaron Krickstein commented:

> I think he's the best when he is on. His backhand volley is by far the best. He has such good net coverage up there and his reach and anticipation are amazing.[18]

Able to Develop Complete Game

It is hard to find an area of tennis in which ISTPs cannot excel. As we have seen, they have all the mental and physical tools. Not all professional ISTP tennis players, however, have mastered the various parts of the game. Like every other Type, they too must devote endless hours to perfecting each phase of the game. Good coaching will be important in this process.

OBSTACLES

As with all Types, ISTPs have their potential obstacles. It is just that they do not have as many or have them as often as the others in tennis. With the ISTP, and the other Brain Types discussed in this section, I will touch on only a couple of weaknesses.

Too Introspective

When ISTPs' dominant Thinking function (rather than their secondary Sensing function) takes over in a match, they synthesize matters too much, creating a more mechanical left-brained look and touch. If they are playing a left-brained (J) opponent who is relaxed, the opponent can appear to be the smoother, fluid player. ISTPs become paralyzed by thinking too much.

Overly Emotional

Although some ISTPs act as cool as cucumbers, they all have the cerebral potential to vent their anger. Basketball's **Bobby Knight** and football's **Mike Ditka** have shown the emotional side of the ISTP outside of tennis. **John McEnroe** has been perhaps the ultimate displayer of emotions in tennis. Tony Kornheiser, a *Washington Post* columnist, wrote of McEnroe in 1990:

> Watching him play, you see a balloon that's been blown up to the bursting point and suddenly let go, and the air escapes, making it do those loony circles until it falls to earth limp and exhausted.[19]

Tennis' Ion Tiriac said of McEnroe:

> Half come to see him win. Half come to see him lose. Half come to see what happens.[20]

And half of you are wondering if Tiriac ever passed mathematics. Despite his quote, I imagine the ENTP Tiriac did.

Curry Kirkpatrick of *Sports Illustrated* once wrote of **Jimmy Connors**:

> Connors has earned the reputation for nastiness while wearing his heart, not to mention his middle finger, on his sleeve.[21]

Returning to the emotional side of ISTPs, if they have spiritual or cultural values that restrict their sometimes emotional Thinking function, they can coach, perform, or play tennis as calmly as any. (This does not mean, however, they still do not become emotionally involved in their thoughts, whether or not this is shown outwardly.) Did you know **Martina Navratilova** was once known for her inner emotional stress and blowing big matches?

HELPING THE ISTP

ISTPs must keep their intensity and dominant Thinking in check. Carrying these to extreme can result in anger and frustration, eventually causing their fine motor skills to go awry. ISTPs' greatest assets can easily become their greatest liabilities. When ISTPs tense up, they must try to utilize more of the large body muscles, remaining loose and fluid with their dominant arm, wrist, and fingers.

ISTPs, like all Types, need to utilize their adept right brain and concentrate on being as spatial as possible. This will allow their Thinking function to operate at ease and lessen the left hemisphere's control, enhancing right brain performance.

Parents would be wise to have their ISTP children model **Stefan Edberg's** court demeanor. Not only will this benefit their tennis games but their personal lives as well. ISTPs battle their intensity throughout life, on and off the court. They will eventually be grateful for any assistance you can offer them.

ESTP

ESTPs love the limelight. Drawing attention to themselves is something they find natural. Appearance alone will often distinguish the ESTP among the 16 Brain Types. **Andre Agassi** has been the ultimate trendsetter in the modern tennis world. His long hair and beard today—gone tomorrow, earring, and bright and unorthodox clothes tell you a little about Agassi's persona and Brain Type. Not all ESTPs will be this flashy or have this personality, but all ESTPs have an inner drive to be recognized for how they look or perform. Agassi once said:

> People come to have fun. They come . . . since they don't know what's going to come out of me, whether I'm going to lose my mind or whether I'm going to laugh.[22]

Some of the ESTPs, past and present, include: **Ilie Nastase, Boris Becker, Andre Agassi, Michael Stich, Goran Ivanisevic, Patrick Rafter, Martina Hingis,** and **Jana Novotna.**

Ilie Nastase won 57 career pro titles, earning over $2 million. The tempestuous Romanian won a French and U.S. Open singles title before retiring in 1986.

German **Boris Becker** jumped into the top 10 rankings in 1985. The ESTP teenage prodigy stunned the tennis world this same year by becoming the youngest ever to win Wimbledon. By 2000, Boris had won 49 singles titles, 6 majors, and $25 million.

Andre Agassi stormed the professional tennis scene in 1987, achieving a No. 3 ranking by 1988. Andre won nearly $2 million in 1990. In 1992, he won his first Grand Slam singles title at Wimbledon. Agassi finally attained his goal of the No. 1 ranking in the world, in 1995.

Arantxa Sanchez Vicario of Spain, the youngest sister in a family whose four children are professional tennis players, started playing tennis at age 4. By 13, she was a pro. By 15, she was playing in Wimbledon and at only 17 years of age, Arantxa won the 1989 French Open. In 1994, she captured her third Grand Slam title, the U.S. Open.

Sanchez Vicario went on to become one of the best female tennis players in the world. By 1996, ESTP Arantxa had been ranked in the top ten for eight years—achieving a No. 1 ranking in both singles and doubles in 1995.

A very young **Martina Hingis** became the next ESTP female tennis star. Ironically, the 15-year-old beat

Sanchez Vicario in the fourth round of the 1996 U.S. Open. Hingis began 1996 ranked No. 20 and by early 1997, she had risen to the No. 1 position in the world—surpassing Frauline Graf. Hingis became the youngest player in history to earn that distinction. Also in '97, the 16-year-old and Czech-born sensation won three Grand Slam singles titles and $3.4 million.

Automatic Pilots

No Type consistently begins competition in a better state of mind and body than ESTPs (provided they haven't been up late doing the town). Their right brain controlled muscles are usually relaxed, and their energy level and confidence are high as they look forward to competing and winning. **Andre Agassi** has said:

> There's nothing mental about tennis. Once I get out there my body takes over.[23]

Agassi's statement is essentially accurate and classic for ESTPs. It is true that ESTPs normally perform best when they rely upon their spatial abilities, reacting with their inborn and learned instincts. In this mode they are much more process than result oriented. Their right-brained Sensing function is in charge. It is assisted by their secondary Thinking that provides the logical, split second answers they need on the tennis court. These inherent brain functions are essentially subconscious for ESTPs. They do not give attention to what is going on in their brains. Even if Agassi and other ESTPs believe there is little or nothing mental about their games, there most certainly is. We know from the study of Brain Types that not all Types perform and reason alike. Can you imagine INTJs identifying with Agassi's statements about the mind and body in tennis?

Hand-Eye Coordination Skills

Like ISTPs, ESTPs demonstrate remarkable, innate fine motor and visual skills. Positioning the hands in the proper place at the proper time is the primary skill of Sensing, Thinking, right-brained persons (STPs). Ken Flach, tour player and Davis Cup teammate of Agassi, said Agassi's natural ability:

> . . . disgusts me. His hand eye must be extraordinary. It's just the power of visualization. He just visualizes himself {whipping the competition} and taking names.[24]

ESTPs are wristy in their play, creating exceptional spin on the ball.

Powerful Serves

In recent years, a man regarded as having one of the most intimidating serves in tennis was ESTP **Boris Becker**. Becker's Brain Type and physical stature explain this special ability. The ESTPs' supersonic energy level, fine motor proficiency, and go for it attitude all contribute to their powerful serves.

When ESTP **Michael Stich** won the 1991 Wimbledon men's singles title, his serves consistently hit the 120 m.p.h. range on the radar gun. His maximum was 126. (This was before the new and improved "power" rackets.) He cranked up 15 aces in his finals win on Centre Court against fellow ESTP Boris Becker.

ESTP **Goran Ivanisevic** lost to Ivan Lendl in the 1991 U.S. Open. Ivanisevic blamed the loss in part to his sore back. Lendl commented later when he heard of the excuse:

> Yeah, he looked [hurt] serving at 125 miles an hour. I would like to have that back pain every day.[25]

Competitors

Arantxa Sanchez won the 1989 French Open in dramatic style, upending highly favored Steffi Graf. When about to face ESTP Sanchez again in the 1990 U.S. Open semifinals, Graf stated:

> She will fight for every point. She won't give me anything like some other players do.[26]

After losing to **Boris Becker** at the '91 French Open, Michael Chang said:

> Guys like Boris tend to play better and better the longer big tournaments go on. Once he's this far in the tournament, it's difficult to beat them.[27]

Good Net Coverage

ESTPs have the potential for fabulous net coverage. Provided they are healthy and svelte, their quickness and right-brained, fine motor skills are deadly. They can make a ball do just about anything.

Powerful Forehand

Bar none, no Brain Type can equal the consistent power of the ESTP's forehand and still have control over the racket and ball. Not every ESTP chooses to play this way. **Andre Agassi**, however, has been one who does. Agassi was said to have cannon forehand at age seven! Tour pro Jimmy Arias, once regarded as having the hardest forehand in tennis, has said:

> Andre hits the ball harder than anyone else by far. It's not even close. It's like a slap shot, the kind of shot I hit if I'm mad about something and I smash the ball over the fence. That's his regular stroke.[28]

Agassi's forehand has been clocked in excess of 100 mph.

It is said that Agassi's unorthodox forehand defies most of the laws of teaching. Considering that iNtuitive, Thinking Judgers (NTJs) write most teaching laws, it is understandable why Agassi doesn't fit their mold. Nevertheless, he has learned to hit the forehand the way his ESTP body and mind feel most comfortable.

We have learned how and why the ESTP is able to hit the ball so hard, whether serving or in the groundstroke. ESTPs' ability to generate power with a sporting object in their hands is not limited to tennis. In golf, the most consistent big hitters on tour are normally ESTPs. Some have included **John Daly, Fred Couples, Davis Love III,** and **Greg Norman**. In baseball, several ESTPs past and present are **Jose Canseco, Dave Winfield, Mickey Mantle, Mike Piazza, Juan Gonzalez,** and **Mike Schmidt**. Wherever you see ESTPs in athletics, you will almost always find power in their performances.

OBSTACLES

Though ESTPs are smooth, right-brained Thinkers, they are susceptible to pressure like every other Brain Type. When tension strikes in tennis, ESTPs access parts of the brain that debilitate their games. They can become mechanical and rigid like left-brained Js are apt to do. This happens when ESTPs leave their Sensing function and fixate on their less preferred synthetic Thinking function.

Three ESTPs demonstrated this liability at the 1990 U.S. Open, beginning when **Aaron Krickstein** lost to **Boris Becker**. Then defending champ Becker lost to Agassi in the semifinals. Agassi's game rattled Becker. The *L.A. Times* reported, following the match:

> Becker is regarded as wielding one of the best serves in the game, but during one period spanning the last two games of the second set and all of the third set, he lost his serve six consecutive times.[29]

Becker made only 56% of his first serves while committing 53 unforced errors. Unfortunately, rather than relax, he tensed more as his game waned. At one point the normally cool Becker even did a John McEnroe impersonation when line calls went against him.

Agassi had a great tournament until he met his Waterloo in the finals. The winner, Pete Sampras, spoke of Agassi:

> I thought he would go for more shots and winners, and he just seemed tentative. He wasn't being the aggressor. He was letting me dictate play and I think that was the difference.[30]

What Sampras forgot to mention was his 120 m.p.h. serves that shook every opponent he faced in this U.S. Open. Few thought Agassi could be defeated in this tournament, but when he became intimidated by Sampras' play, Agassi's game virtually broke down. He no longer had control over his customary and comfortable anterior right hemisphere.

Lack of Concentration

Andre Agassi said in 1989:

> One thing I lack is concentration, but that's my life story and I'm getting used to it. If I could answer that [why he loses concentration], I would already have corrected it. Maybe I'm an immature player some people might consider it that way.[31]

Agassi was quite honest in his personal assessment. The ESTP brain was designed to be action oriented, capable of dealing with and handling many practical matters in a short period of time. Therefore, it is easy for ESTPs to get sidetracked from the task at hand, considering there are always many other exciting opportunities and thoughts to be had.

Can Lose Their Cool

ESTPs have been known to lose their tempers. This is not always the case, for some have learned to keep their irritations in check. By and large, however, they will be one of the most vocal players on the court.

Too Much Attention?

ESTPs' desire to be recognized can sometimes go too far. Their awareness of this tendency will help them maximize their abilities. The ESTP baseball player may try to hit the home run when he should hit for a single, the ESTP quarterback may force a pass when he shouldn't, and the ESTP tennis player can easily attempt a difficult shot or even put on a temper show when he shouldn't. Although ESTPs can sometimes use this to their advantage, it still hurts their overall games.

ESTPs, like all SPs, tend to live for the moment. After all, they figure, tomorrow may never come, or it may not bring as many opportunities as today. Particularly for ESTP celebrities or athletes, it is most difficult to leave the limelight. They do not want to be forgotten. Sometimes this translates into them continuing to play even when it means taking a cut in pay or playing or performing beyond the time for retirement. For some ESTPs, this may become an obstacle. At the end of ESTP **Ilie Nastase's** career, he said:

> Now I am there just to be in the game. It is like a fashion for me. But I have to be there or else the people, they forget you.

He continued:

> I suffer when I lose, but I want to be where the show is . . . because tennis is my life. I know people say I should retire, but what do I do then? I don't care about opinion; it's my own life. To tell me to retire tomorrow is like saying I must die tomorrow. And I don't want to die.[32]

Peter Bodo wrote in *Tennis World*, 1981:

> One of Nastase's lawyers, Peter Lawler of Donald Dell's firm, told me that his client was booked to play 47 weeks this year. The figure is preposterous, the itinerary of a homeless man. But that's how Nastase wants it. He admits he's a 'yo yo' and claims that if he stops for two weeks, he gets sick.[33]

The ESTP's desire for recognition can sometimes go too far, regardless of the sport.

HELPING ESTPs

As previously stated, ESTPs are the, or among the, smoothest and most ready when beginning an athletic event. (Of course, they must have proficiency with their sport for this to be true.) Generally, the best thing you can do for ESTPs in tennis is to help them maintain their cool and collected ways throughout a match. Unless the match is close, they will tend to get impatient and lose their concentration. When this happens they will go for winners when they shouldn't. *Mental drills practiced over time can significantly aid their concentration skills.*

When ESTPs succumb to big time pressure, they will begin to think too much rather than rely upon their smooth, logical instincts. Their fine motor skills will tighten up, jeopardizing their success. When this happens ESTPs will be best served by trying to involve more of the gross motor skills. Also, a concerted effort will be necessary to make fluid and loose the dominant arm, wrists, and fingers.

The ESTP is often difficult to coach. Ion Tiriac, **Boris Becker's** manager in 1986, said of his young ace:

> But he is difficult. He is the most stubborn character I have ever met. You cannot tell him anything. Everything he has to find out for himself. Sometimes you have to remind him he isn't as good as he thinks he is.[34]

You may need the wisdom of Solomon to effectively coach an ESTP. If you lack this insight, have your ESTP read the book of Proverbs (written primarily by Solomon) in the Bible. It could do wonders for his or her life and game.

ISFP

ISFPs are top notch athletes and can perform superbly in almost any sport. In tennis, however, their numbers are not as prominent as in many other sports, particularly among the top performers.

The most successful ISFP tennis player in recent history has been Swede **Bjorn Borg**. Before retiring in 1984, Borg won the French Open six times, Wimbledon five consecutive times, but never the U.S. Open. He holds the dubious U.S. Open record of the most singles finals without a victory (four). Many tennis enthusiasts always wondered why he came up short at the U.S. Open.

Russian **Yevgeny Kafelnikov** was a rare ISFP among the world's best (in singles and doubles) in the late 1990s. His game has paralleled Bjorn Borg's, especially as an outstanding rallyer and baseline player. In classic ISFP style, Kefelnikov has been known for body endurance, playing the most matches in a season on the APT Tour.

Best on Slower Surfaces

Tony Trabert once said of Bjorn Borg:

> He was in the habit of producing a good shot from the baseline, letting his opponent come to the net, and then assuming the burden of trying to come up with a passing shot of pinpoint accuracy. This was a tough assignment for Borg, mentally and physically fatiguing, and one that became even tougher when he left the normally slow clay surface that he liked so much and tried the same tactics on grass or any other fast surface.[35]

Trabert's comments tell us much about the ISFP Borg. For one thing, he was able to achieve pinpoint accuracy with his shots. Borg's innate right-brained, SF gross motor skills enabled him to use his body and upper arms primarily, supple wrists secondarily, all with fluidity.

The fact that he played better on slow surfaces would be indicative of the ISFP who doesn't like to play the game as aggressively and fast paced as many other Types. Because ISFPs' demeanors are more low keyed, and they rely mostly upon the big muscles, slower surfaces are ideally suited for them. They like clay courts. From what I understand, retired pro and ISFP **Jose Higueras** was once a good clay court player himself.

Due to their specialized "P" gross motor skills, ISFPs are masters at creating rotation or spin on the ball. In tennis, ISFPs often revolve their game around spinning shots, like **Bjorn Borg**. Borg was superb at playing from the baseline, imparting tremendous rotation on the ball.

Determination

Do not let the generally mellow, laid back personas of ISFPs fool you. When they want something badly, a tennis win for instance, their Introverted Feelings generate tenaciousness, much like ISTPs. Whereas ISFPs are less apt to want to inflict punishment on their opponents than ISTPs, they can be no less determined to win. In a tribute to ISFPs, Bjorn Borg was known as a battler.

OBSTACLES

Self-punishers

Arthur Ashe spoke of Borg at the 1974 Wimbledon:

> He finished beating Snake Case today and was mumbling 'I'm so lucky' afterward—which I've heard often enough not to pay any more attention to—but now he really does appear whipped and drawn.[36]

I am confident that Borg was speaking more honestly regarding his self deprecation than Ashe gave him credit for. ISFPs often lack confidence in their abilities. Typology matriarch, Isabel Myers, wrote of them:

> They consistently tend to underestimate and understate themselves. Probably ISFP is the most modest type.[37]

ISFPs must remember that *modesty and confidence are not necessarily mutually exclusive*. ISFPs need to combine confidence with their special humility.

HELPING ISFPs

ISFPs respond and learn best when they are *treated with sensitivity, commended for their efforts, and encouraged to keep succeeding*. They often fail to see their potential. ISFPs love to have fun in whatever they do.

SFPs (ISFP and ESFP) are capable of developing expert and powerful, two handed backhand shots. Adeptness with their big muscles makes this possible. Yet, unlike many other Types, SFPs are often strong enough to play the one-handed backhand—such as once highly-ranked Conchita Martinez (ESFP).

ESFP

Tennis's Tony Trabert has said:

> It would be exhilarating to discover and help develop a future Magic Johnson and see his raw athletic talents adapted to the skills of tennis.[38]

Just how would a person with Magic Johnson's mental and physical skills do in tennis? Are the games of tennis and basketball similar?

First, Trabert and the rest of us need look no further than someone with Magic's ESFP Brain Type. Until the late 1980s, I knew of no ESFPs near the top of the current tennis world. That was until the advent of the Florida fireball, **Jennifer Capriati**.

Capriati was superb in her Junior tournaments. At 12, she won the U.S. Tennis Association's 18 and under national championship, the youngest to take that age group's title. At only 13, she won the junior championships at the French Open and the U.S. Open. At 14, she burst onto the pro circuit with as much fanfare as any female player in history. Some already compared her with Chris Evert. Ironically, her first coach was Evert's father, Jimmy. Capriati began her tutelage under him at age 5. Chris's brother, John, recalls this era:

> Dad came home one night and said to Chrissie, "I think I've finally found someone as talented as you." My dad said this when Chrissie was No. 1 in the world.[39]

Jimmy Evert's next assignment was to be Capriati's business manager. (Before winning a professional tournament, Capriati received two endorsement contracts worth an estimated $5 million.)

Accomplishments came quickly for Capriati after entering the pro circuit. She made *Newsweek's* cover, only the third female tennis player to do so (Chris Evert and Navratilova were the others). She became the youngest seeded player and youngest to win a match at Wimbledon—in 1991 she reached the semifinals.

Capriati was the youngest Grand Slam semifinalist with her French Open showing in 1990. In August of 1991, she won the Mazda Tennis Classic, defeating in the finals the Number 1 player in the world, Monica Seles. A month later, Capriati lost a heartbreaker to Seles (the eventual champ) in the semifinals of the 1991 U.S. Open. In 1992, Capriati won the Olympic gold medal. She rose to a Number 6 ranking in the world. Jennifer Capriati had served notice to the world that she was for real.

Unfortunately, Jennifer's fame turned to infamy within a few months. Failing to keep her ESFP impulsivities in check, she was arrested for shoplifting. Later she was arrested for drug possession and underwent court-mandated drug treatment. She adorned herself with nose ring and hair dyed purple and orange.

Had those close to Jennifer known of her Type's unorthodox behaviors when unregulated, they could have been better prepared for this adversity and better equipped to work through it. Perhaps other "Jennifer Capriati's" will be spared as a result of this information. I hope so.

In 1996, Jennifer began her comeback after a 2½ year layoff. With hard work she has the potential to be successful again.

Well, it's been years since I wrote the previous paragraph and sure enough, Jennifer's revamped mindset and diligence on the practice court paid off majorly. Though it took five years, in 2001, her first comeback victory was the Australian Open—the first Grand Slam event of her entire career!

Energy and Power

Let's consider Jennifer Capriati further, particularly during her first attempt on the pro circuit, and how this may help us to better understand the ESFP in tennis. Billie Jean King said of 14-year-old Capriati:

> She is the most powerful person of her age I have ever seen, without any question.[40]

Following her defeat to Capriati in the '90 French Open quarterfinals, Mary Joe Fernandez said:

> Her strategy is just to hit the ball as hard as she can.[41]

Martina Navratilova spoke of Capriati:

> Jennifer hits the ball harder than anybody I've

played from both sides, which is amazing at that age. She's nailing the return and I'm going back saying, "I can't hit it that hard." I could, but it may hit the cheap seats. The fact that she can hit it that hard and make the shot is amazing. She's just a phenom.[42]

Having read this far in the book, you have been continually reminded that SFs are most adept in their gross motor skills, utilizing and maximizing the big muscles throughout the body. Whether SFs are swinging a baseball bat, golf club, or tennis racket, they will use the large muscles more than any of the other three Brain Type or temperament groupings (ST, NF, and NT). Using the major muscles creates tremendous velocity and power. Couple this with Capriati's Extraversion and it's not difficult to understand how and why she often served a tennis ball over 100 miles per hour.

ESFPs have the lightning quick physical responses to external stimuli. This affects the game of tennis in many ways, including increased racket speed which in turn gives additional speed to the ball.

Right-brain, Fluid SF

Capriati's coach in 1990, Tom Gullikson, spoke of his teen prodigy:

> She's very receptive to coaching, and she is a very advanced player for her age. Certainly her backhand is her real strength, but she's also got a very good first serve. She's got a great service motion—a nice, smooth, continuing swing. She is definitely a power dictating type of player. She is extremely good.[43]

Let's consider some aspects of Gullikson's comments, applying the knowledge of Types. Her coachablilty spoke well for 3 major issues: her upbringing, to those to whom she was subordinate; her Feeling function, which desires to please and maintain harmony; and her SF Type, which learns best by experience and receiving practical, hands-on instruction. SFs do not have the natural NT capabilities that grasp matters quickly through conceptual logic. These are only three of perhaps many factors that played a role in her being "receptive to coaching."

Consider Capriati's serve. We just discussed the impact of the gross motor skills on the power of her game. Add her right-brained dominance and you get a powerful and graceful serve. Gullikson accurately pointed Capriati's Brain Type without knowing it when he said, "She's got a great service motion—a nice, smooth, continuous swing."

Her continuous swing was a result of *not* breaking down her body muscles and joints as the other Types would be much more prone to do. (For instance, the STs may get too wristy or armsy.)

ESFP's power on the serve and ground strokes come more from the big muscles, whereas the plethora of STs on the pro tennis circuit derive their primary strength and power from the arms and wrists. An ST with big legs and trunk, however, will often utilize the gross motor skills more easily than the slender ST.

Other Successful ESFPs

Four other ESFPs who made an impact in the 1990s were **Conchita Martinez, Lindsay Davenport, Serena Williams,** and **Anna Kournikova.**

Martinez from Spain achieved a career-high world ranking of Number 2 in 1995. She won 6 tournaments that year—four of them in a row.

When **Lindsay Davenport** graduated from high school in 1994, she was ranked in the world's top 10. By summer's end she was ranked 6th. But somewhat like Jennifer Capriati, she became affected by critical comments and SFP self doubts. In 1995, she fell out of the top 10 and experienced discouragement. She explained:

> I freaked out when I read some of the things about me. Like that I was too fat. And too slow. That I didn't belong in the top 10. Some people made it sound like all I did was sit around eating cheeseburgers. I hated it so much that I wanted to quit playing tennis.[44]

At the end of 1995, Lindsay realized she needed help and convinced a friend and former touring pro to be her new coach. Robert Van't Hof became a hands-on coach, implementing many new rigors. Fortunately for Davenport, she found ways to work through her difficulties and made a strong comeback. She was *Tennis* Magazine's Most Improved Female Pro in 1996 and surprised many by winning the women's gold medal (singles) at the '96 Atlanta Summer Olympics. By 1998, Lindsay had gained the women's number 1 ranking in the world!

ESFP's Pro Potential

ESFPs have the motor skills to accomplish greatness on the modern pro circuit. A major question will be whether their mental skills, specifically their decision making Feeling function, can handle the demands of tennis at the top of the professional world.

ESFPs need to develop more logical awareness on the court. They will be required to draw upon their Thinking function in difficult situations. Their power games alone will be insufficient to consistently beat the best players.

ESFPs also need to slow down their games somewhat. This will be hard considering their ESFP bent, but should come with time. One thing is for certain: ESFPs will continue to improve with experience. The more comfortable they feel with their games and minds, the better they will perform. This would be true for any players but especially for ESFPs.

We began by considering how a person possessing Magic Johnson's talents would fare in tennis. The motor skills required in tennis are not exactly the same as they are in basketball or many other sports. Nonetheless, Lindsay Davenport and other ESFPs have shown us that they can handle the physical aspects of tennis. I hope we see more ESFPs on the circuit in the years ahead—especially more men, where they're rarely found. ESFPs have the magnetic personalities that make sports popular. As for the their potential, if they place greater emphasis on the aforementioned issues, the upside is unlimited.

HELPING ESFPs

Another area requiring attention is ESFPs' need to practice patience. No Type is more prone to following impulses and delighting in the moment. ESFPs can get *bored easily* when they aren't enjoying themselves. Parents and coaches need to help ESFPs focus on their goals, with many of them being short termed. Long term goals often seem like an eternity to ESFPs. They also like perks or rewards for goals accomplished, so try to make it fun for them along the way.

ISTJ

Two names stand out when considering great ISTJs of the past: **Chris Evert and Stan Smith**. Evert turned pro in 1972 and retired in 1989, having never been ranked lower than the top four. Her career of 17 years includes 157 singles titles (surpassed only by Martina Navratilova's 167 titles) and 18 Grand Slam singles victories. She was named the Greatest Woman Athlete of the last 25 years by the Women's Sports Foundation in 1985. (Evert reminds me of another great ISTJ in another individual sport, golf. His name is Nicklaus.)

Chris Evert holds numerous U.S. Open records: most consecutive years seeded—18, most championships won—6, most singles finals—9, and highest percentage of matches won, career—.894. She won seven French Open titles out of nine finals. Evert was taught to play by her father who coached her from the time she was five.

ISTJ **Stan Smith** won 39 career pro titles, capturing a U.S. Open and Wimbledon singles title. Smith attained a No. 3 world ranking (his highest) in 1973 and retired ten years later.

Determined

No Brain Type is more capable of single mindedness than ISTJs. They manifest this trait in all sports and aspects of life. Martina Navratilova said just prior to Evert's retirement:

> Images come into my head about Chris. I think for me, the main thing is her determination, her single mindedness. I guess because of the kind of game that she has, she has had to [be that way], otherwise she would have been just another player.[45]

Superb Groundstroke

Navratilova spoke of Evert's stroke:

> People say that it's all in the mind, that everybody's stroke is the same and the rest is mental. And that's bull. Her strokes are better than just about anybody.[46]

Martina has touched upon a very good point. We have been learning from this book the importance of the brain in sports, physically and mentally. As we have seen, each Brain Type differs in motor skills and mental skills.

This has nothing to do with coaching or practice. It is a God given proclivity. Evert had the fine motor skills of the ISTJ. *Dexterity* is the key word we learned for STJs from the Body Skills section of this book. No one demonstrated that better than the queen of the two handed backhanders, Chris Evert.

Tony Trabert assessed Evert:

> I have tremendous respect for Chris Evert, the consummate groundstroke specialist. Looking closely at her game, however, she doesn't play as well as Navratilova on all surfaces. Her serve isn't a weapon, and she doesn't like to volley. It's been Evert's strong groundstrokes, along with her tough will, marvelous concentration, and determination, that have carried her to the top.[47]

Trabert encapsulated the basic tennis mentality and game of the ISTJ.

We will see throughout this book the defensive prowess of ISTJs. Regardless of the sport, this can be their greatest area of expertise. It often translates into conservative play, making the opponents beat themselves.

OBSTACLES

Little known ISTJ, **Andrei Cherkasov** of the former Soviet Union, was an unexpected participant in the 1990 U.S. Open men's quarterfinals match against Andre Agassi. He advanced to this round by surprising and upending Michael Chang in an earlier match.

Two Type factors struck me as I watched a portion of this tournament on TV. One, Cherkasov advanced throughout the tournament due to his ISTJ dexterity, tenacity, and defensive play. Second, he was no match for the free wheeling, confident, loose as a goose, right-brained Andre Agassi. Andre's ESTP style of play made Cherkasov even more mechanical than usual; he was intimidated. On a different day and set of circumstances, Cherkasov could possibly have prevailed. But this day, he was first physically overpowered, then mentally.

Knowing Agassi's and Cherkasov's Types clearly revealed their styles. If the TV broadcasters and audience were privy to this information, it would have added greater clarity to understanding the match.

The 1991 U.S. Open brought another little known ISTJ to the limelight, Dutchman and ex Florida State Seminole, **Paul Haarhuis**. Like ISTJ Cherkasov had done the year before, Haarhuis unexpectedly made it to the quarterfinals. He got there by disposing of No. 1 seeded Boris Becker. (In the 1989 U.S. Open, Haarhuis upset John McEnroe. ISTJs tend to play their best in important events.) Haarhuis's reputation mushroomed over night with his victory over Becker, even though he lost his quarterfinal match to the persevering and ageless wonder, Jimmy Connors.

In 1993, Haarhuis established himself as one of the world's top doubles players with 7 titles. By 1995, he and fellow Dutch countryman Jacco Eltingh ranked as the No. 1 doubles team most of the season. Haarhuis also achieved a No. 19 world ranking in singles.

HELPING ISTJs

ISTJs, like all dominant left hemisphere Js, need to learn to relax on the tennis court. They should develop smooth, fluid movements and swings. Working on good tempo is important. As much as anything, ISTJs must work on developing their spatial awareness. Rather than predetermining their next move too early, they will do best by focusing on the ball, thereby allowing the logic of the visual right brain to determine where to play the next shot.

ESTJ

ESTJs are aggressive players, generally specializing in defense more than offense. They prefer to perfect the offensive side of their game but often find it cannot be trusted as much as their defensive side, especially when they experience pressure. Though they have superior fine motor dexterity skills, their movements tend to be more mechanical than fluid and loose. A few ESTJs in tennis have included **Pam Shriver, David Wheaton, and Manuela Maleeva Fragniere**.

Defensive Specialists

A classic example of the ESTJ's tennis game was the 1990 U.S. Open Tennis Championships in New York. **Manuela Maleeva Fragniere** demonstrated her ESTJ Type in both victory and defeat. First, seeded No. 9 overall, she played superbly to defeat someone she had never beaten before, second ranked Martina Navratilova. Maleeva-Fragniere caught her by surprise, upsetting the highly favored Czech born superstar. Navratilova made only 55 percent of her first serves and committed 37 unforced errors. Even though Navratilova self destructed, her opponent's aggression paid off. Her defensive prowess (recognized as one of the world's best at the time) kept her in the hunt until Navratilova folded. Maleeva-Fragniere expressed her determination and drive following the match:

> It is probably what I have lived for in my tennis career.[48]

Overcoming Mental Barriers

Less than 48 hours later, Maleeva-Fragniere found herself playing Mary Joe Fernandez. One might have thought this match would be easy so soon after a major upset. This was not the case. For one, Maleeva-Fragniere had to overcome the mental barrier that she had never been beyond the quarterfinals of a Grand Slam event, having been stopped short 9 previous times. Second, she had to overcome the pressure of everyone's expectations.

Third, she had to overcome the ESTJ jitters, as strong as any around, especially at the beginning of a match or event, whatever the sport.

Maleeva Fragniere demonstrated significant pressure and tension through the first set. (A TV commentator even mentioned how nervous she looked before the match.) She racked up unforced errors and lost 2-6. The second set she calmed down, renewed her confidence and allowed Fernandez to beat herself. The third and final set Maleeva-Fragniere tensed up again when the lithesome INTP, Fernandez, regained her confidence, stamina, and right-brained flow. Maleeva-Fragniere became mechanical, allowing her dominant Thinking function to get the best of her. She dropped the final set 1-6, losing the match and still not reaching the semi finals.

Though ESTJs can be excellent tennis players, they're highly unlikely to achieve a consistent No. 1 singles ranking in the world. Their brain design, which choreographs their game, is better made for doubles.

David Wheaton, Stanford University and Nick Bollettieri Tennis Academy alum, turned pro in 1988. Having won the 1987 U.S. Open Juniors and the U.S. Boys' 18s National Claycourts, high hopes were in store for Wheaton's pro career. Though he has since won a few singles Tour titles (as of 2000), his game has never reached expectations. This tall ESTJ Minnesotan has needed to devote many hours to the mental side of the game if he is to reach his potential, particularly in major tournaments.

Doubles Players

Doubles seem to allow the ESTJ to play more loosely and aggressively. Here you'll see them at the net (which normally wouldn't be their style in singles) where their energetic dexterity reaps dividends. The higher paced doubles gives ESTJs less time to use their left-brained analytic Thinking and more time to draw upon their right hemisphere vision and synthetic Thinking.

Pam Shriver arrived on the tennis scene as the youngest U.S. Open finalist in history, establishing the record as a high school sophomore in 1978. Shriver has been ranked as high as No. 3 in singles and had one of her best years in 1987, winning four singles titles and reaching the finals of four others. Despite her successes, she never went as far as many they thought she would.

She established herself instead as one of the premier doubles players in the world, teaming up with ISTP Martina Navratilova to win 20 Grand Slam doubles titles by 1989. The Navratilova Shriver doubles team was probably the best ever in women's tennis.

Shriver has shown that Navratilova was not the only reason for her success. At the 1988 Olympic Games at Seoul, Shriver took the gold medal in women's doubles with Zina Garrison. The 1991 U.S. Open saw her team with Natalia Zvereva of the Soviet Union. Once again, she added a Grand Slam victory.

ESTJs, whether professional or amateur, can be top notch players, particularly in doubles.

Traditional Values

1991 saw a couple of ESTJs manifest traits of their Brain Type. **David Wheaton** became known for his red, white and blue headband during matches (precipitated by the gulf war crisis). **Pam Shriver** represented the U.S. in the Pan American games in Cuba, quite atypical for a wealthy tennis pro in a no pay amateur event. ESTJs exhibit strong convictions as well as athletic tennis games.

HELPING ESTJs

ESTJs need as much help with the mental approach as with the physical in virtually every sport. They need to learn how to control anxiety and minimize physical tension.

At the 1990 Virginia Slims tournament in Florida, **Pam Shriver** got so angry following a loss that she kicked a chair. So what, you say? The chair was said to be okay, but Shriver broke her toe. Had she been a graceful, dominant right brain person, she probably wouldn't have injured herself. By caring more about the process than the result of her game, she could have kept her anger in check. The moral is that ESTJs, and all left brain persons, need to be more synthetic and process oriented, trusting the right brain. It will lessen their tensions and chances for injury.

When ESTJs are under the control of tension (of which they are often unaware), their fine motor skills tighten up and their game suffers. A simple anti tension check for ESTJs is to see if their grip is light, their wrists loose and fluid, and their tempo smooth.

As they age and gain experience, ESTJs become more relaxed and learn to control their competitive anxieties. When many other maturing Types begin to lose their composure, ESTJs often do the opposite.

ENTJ

Again we witness the extreme competitiveness of the ENTJ, this time in tennis. ENTJs believe they must be in control of every situation they care about, including their tennis game. They can be overmatched in talent on the court, yet prevail due to their distaste for being second to anyone. We again see how ENTJs rely upon their greatest skill, their indomitable mind and will. **Billie Jean King, Jack Kramer, Tony Trabert, and Gabriela Sabatini** are a few ENTJs who have played the game.

The 1960s and 70s saw the emergence and stardom of Californian, **Billie Jean King**. The 5' 4", energetic and outgoing King won six times at Wimbledon, and had four U.S. Open Championships. She was ranked in the Top 10 a total of 17 years, and ranked No. 1 on the U.S. doubles list for a record 12 years. She was said to have a devastating backhand.

Hall-of-Famer **Tony Trabert** was a two time U.S. Open, Wimbledon, and French Open champ. He has coached two winning Davis Cup teams but is best known today for his tournament tennis analysis on TV.

High Energy

ENTJs expend tremendous amounts of energy in their play. After all, they possess as much energy as any Type, and are iNtuitive enough to not sense exactly how hard they are playing. They can develop a high threshold for pain. Sometimes in a long match, however, they can run out of gas, not realizing until too late they forgot to save some fuel. (ISTPs are more apt to preserve their energy supply.)

ENTJs play somewhat similarly to ESTJs but generally with greater success. They both play aggressive games of tennis, but ENTJs are usually more proficient in their offensive skills. There are a few obvious reasons for this.

Once they have become accomplished, ENTJs have greater confidence in their game than athletically comparable ESTJs. ENTJs' "N" function is generally more optimistic and positive than ESTJs' "S" function.

Second, ENTJs are not as naturally skilled as ESTJs in fine motor movements, yet in tennis this helps them. ESTJs, under pressure, tend to stiffen up their forearms, wrists, and hands which can be devastating. Conversely, ENTJs are generally more relaxed and supple in these areas of the arm, to their advantage.

Third, the only typological distinction between ENTJs and ESTJs are their preferences for perceiving matters (S and N). This difference, however, makes these Types dissimilar in many ways.

Creative, Focus on Goal

ENTJs play with more creativity than ESTJs, both mentally and physically. They are not as easily bothered by pressure, tending to live life in their minds first, anyway. ENTJs focus more on the long term goal, the end result, more than the mechanics or pressure of each stroke, game or even set. They can usually mask their nervousness much better than the ESTJ. (ENTJs are excellent actors.) ESTJs tend to focus more on the short term results, which can obviously create more pressure if things are going poorly.

Indomitable Wills

Billie Jean King once said of herself:

> And if you want to know about my ego, which is obviously big, it operates this way: every time you tell me I can't do something, that ego tells me I not only can, but must.[49]

ENTJs believe they must be in control of every situation they deem important. When given a challenge to accomplish something they value, watch out. Few things or people can stand in their way.

OBSTACLES

Although ENTJs are able to perform less mechanically than most left-brained Types, they still are susceptible to rigidity and deficiency in their motor skills, particularly in pressure situations. With the influx of more ISTP and ESTP women in tennis in recent years, ENTJ women will find more pressure matches and more difficulty than ever in gaining and maintaining a No. 1 ranking in the world. Let's consider ENTJ, **Gabriela Sabatini**.

It was only weeks after her 15th birthday that Sabatini reached the semifinals of the 1985 French Open. Although she lost to Chris Evert that day, Gabriela became the new darling of women's tennis. Tennis buffs felt Grand Slam titles would soon and easily arrive for her.

Unfortunately, the striking Argentinian (in tennis and looks) found the big events most difficult to win. Up until the 1990 U.S. Open, Sabatini was without a title after 20 Grand Slam tournaments. Only once had she reached a Grand Slam final, where Steffi Graf beat her in the 1988 U.S. Open.

It was interesting to read of Sabatini's comments following her disappointing fourth round loss in the 1990 French Open. She mentioned two specific reasons for her poor showing, hitting the ball too late, and not moving her legs. Both of these can, in part, be related to her innate NT deficiencies in motor skills and her J, left hemisphere tensing up under mental and physical stress.

But at the 1990 U.S. Open, Sabatini broke her jinx by upsetting her long time nemesis, Frauline Graf. (Prior to this, she had only beaten Graf 3 times in 21 tries!) At fifth seed, Gabriela was the lowest seeded female player to win at Flushing Meadow in 22 years. A few notable things helped her to bring this about. One was her attitude, enabling her to play more loosely. Sabatini said afterwards:

> Nobody was expecting me to win the tournament. The way I was playing, I was so confident. But I think that really helped a little bit. I didn't feel any pressure. I was just playing my game.[50]

I believe it helped Gabriela more than just a little bit to be relaxed. This attitude enabled her to access and maintain a high level of activity in her brain's right hemisphere, particularly the anterior region. One must do this to play optimal tennis.

Other factors instrumental to Sabatini's U.S. Open success included (but were not limited to her): a recent change of coaches, changing tennis tactics, and receiving mental help on the tennis game.

Her new coach stressed that she play more aggressive offensively, attacking the net. Sabatini did this to perfection while surprising her last two foes in the Open, Mary Joe Fernandez and Steffi Graf. Throughout her career, Gabriela got close to the net only on changeovers, but this changed appreciably, beginning with her match with Fernandez. Sabatini approached 92 times, winning 56 points.

Sabatini was able to finally add a Grand Slam title to her previous tournament wins since being ranked in October of 1984, when she was the top junior in the world. (Following her Open victory, Sabatini beat Graf 4 of the next 6 times they played, contributing to dropping Graf from her No. 1 ranking.) Nonetheless, from 1991 until her retirement, Sabatini was unsuccessful in winning another Grand Slam title.

In 1996, at the youthful age of 26, Gabriela Sabatini hung up her tennies. Her outside business interests and innate CEO abilities enabled her to leave the game that had served her so well (court earnings of $8,785,850.). Knowing her ENTJ Brain Type makes it much easier to understand why she pursued another career.

HELPING ENTJs

In her match against Lori McNeil at the 1991 Virginia Slims Tournament, Gabriela Sabatini again showed what can happen to an ENTJ experiencing pressure. Although she won the match, Sabatini fell apart in the third set when she completely lost her serve. Several of her first serves were clocked in the 40 m.p.h. range!

She was similarly affected a month later at the 1991 U.S. Open, losing in the quarterfinals to Jennifer Capriati. Against Capriati, Sabatini had 43 unforced errors, six double faults (she had 12 double faults in a previous match), and no aces. At the 1994 U.S. Open, Sabatini once again hit some serves in the 45- to 50-m.p.h. range.

ENTJs feeling pressure must focus on right-brained functions, that is, playing smoothly and gracefully while being as spatial as possible. They must avoid being self critical and focusing on their mistakes.

ENTJs will be wise to work on developing motor movements, especially hand eye coordination skills and spatial visual aspects of the game.

ENTP

ENTPs are goal oriented, energetic, imaginative people. They love life and engage it with their adaptable right hemisphere tendencies. Prior to 1990, **Suzanne Lenglen, Pancho Gonzales, Vitas Gerulaitis, and Guillermo Vilas** were four of the best known ENTP tennis professionals.

Creative Genius

Guillermo Vilas, the Argentinian, was a multi-talented, top seeded tennis player. Curry Kirkpatrick of *Sport's Illustrated* wrote of Vilas in 1978:

> Besides being one of the three best tennis players in the world, Vilas is a published author of prose and poetry. He has written a screenplay and collaborated on songs to be recorded in Argentina. He is a philosopher, a musician, a reader, a thinker . . . .[51]

Not all ENTPs are published poets, philosophers or musicians, yet these endeavors often characterize the persona of the ENTP Brain Type. ENTPs speak of matters poetically and philosophically. If they lack formal education, their syntax and vocabulary may be lacking, but they still possess these traits, if one looks closely enough. Vilas happened to be an educated, out and about ENTP.

It is interesting to note how Vilas viewed the game of tennis:

> I remember when I started tennis, it was considered a sissy game. We used to walk down the street and hide the rackets in our bags. Everybody whistled at us . . . . But I liked the creativity of the game. A tennis player could create more than a painter. Create combinations of things. Nothing was secure. There were the variables of the racket, the surface, the weather, the opponent, the spin and the speed of the ball. Where you were. Who you were. For me this was an unbelievable attraction. When someone said, "Come, go to court," it was like saying, "Come, paint." Only better.[52]

Vilas won 61 titles during his pro career, winning nearly $5 million. He won 4 Grand Slam singles titles and retired in 1989.

New Yorker **Vitas Gerulaitis** won 27 titles in his pro career, including the Australian Open singles in 1977. He retired in 1985 and died at the young age of 40. Gerulaitis was widely known for his carefree, fun-loving, and precocious nature.

Suzanne Lenglen was said to have changed the face of women's tennis more than any other person. This ENTP instigated change, emancipating women from their corsets, petticoats, and long sleeved blouses. Her personality captured the tennis world with her personal magnetism; she was its biggest draw. Lenglen was theatrical and dramatic in everything, including her clothes and playing style. Playing tennis like Baryshnikov dances, she used her NT acumen to outfox her opponents. Her many moods ranged from tantrums to merriment. Lenglen captured six Wimbledon titles despite her many maladies and died at just thirty nine years of age.

ENTP **Pancho Gonzales** held the U.S. singles grass, clay, and indoor championships in his day, putting a lock on all major titles. From 1953 to 1962, Gonzales dominated the professional tour. He is regarded as one of the premier players of all time.

There is a contemporary ENTP who came on tour with a bang; he was essentially unheard of until the 1990 U.S. Open. **Pete Sampras**, who at 19 became the youngest men's U.S. Open winner in history, beat a record that had stood for 100 years!

Sampras turned pro at 16 and dropped out of high school following his junior year. He wanted to devote his career to tennis. Yet this is the same youngster who had never gone beyond the sixteenth round in his eight previous Grand Slam appearances. He began the 1990 tennis season ranked No. 81, rose to No. 12 by the

U.S. Open, and achieved a No. 6 ranking following his first Grand Slam victory. In 1993, Sampras attained the number-one ranking in the world. He not only won his second U.S. Open title, but was the leading money winner on Tour. By 2001, Sampras had captured 13 Grand Slam titles, including 4 U.S. Opens.

Cool, Calm, and Collected

Sampras said, after his first U.S. Open victory:

> I had absolutely no nerves or anything about being in my first Grand Slam final. It was great, I had a great time out there.[53]

Pete was fortunate to have been taken so lightly by others in the Open. He was never was forced to spend much time in his least developed function, Introverted Sensing, a brain function that could create high anxiety. Rather, he cruised through the tournament in his basic ENTP mode, something not easily done by ENTPs who take an event with great seriousness.

Powerful Servers

Entering the 1990s, Boris Becker's serve was the most intimidating shot on tour. Pete Sampras changed that. The biggest weapon in his 1990 U. S. Open arsenal was a bazooka serve; he tallied 100 aces during the tournament. Sampras won 92% of his first serves against Andre Agassi in the finals, winning 35 of 38 points! Agassi said:

> If you look at the [videotape], you'd see all the aces are on the line. That's just tough. The chances of returning serves that are hit 100 m.p.h. when it hits the line are slim, not to mention when he can blast one 120 m.p.h.[54]

In 1997, **Pete Sampras** won his fourth Wimbledon, the tenth Grand Slam title of his career. Not only were his high-powered serves ever present, he had uncanny accuracy—placing the ball almost at will. Sampras told the press he had never served better. From the first Wimbledon round to the semifinals, Sampras went 97 consecutive service games without being broken. He held an amazing 116 of 118 service games during the two-week event.

Not many ENTPs have served as hard as Pete Sampras, but they have the potential to be big hitters—provided they possess sufficient physical stature. In 1997, ENTP **Greg Rusedski** had a record service speed at the U.S. Open, clocked at 143 mph. By 2003, up-and-coming 21-year old **Andy Roddick** smoked a 149 mph service and also won his first Grand Slam singles title at the U.S. Open. In the 2004 Davis Cup quarterfinals, Roddick powered a record serve at 152 mph!

Pancho Gonzales had the biggest serve in his era. (Extraverted Perceivers [EPs] would be the top servers for speed due to their high energy, smooth physical abilities, and go for it mentality.)

Typing Sampras

Sampras' court demeanor wasn't typical ENTP at the '90 U.S. Open. He was rather expressionless and quiet. He certainly wasn't "one upping" anyone with his behavior. It became obvious during the latter stages of the tournament, and the week after, that Pete was in a mental zone. He had to keep pinching himself to see if what was going on was real. The dominant iNtuitive had a solid dose of Sensing reality that he had never faced before. This was witnessed repeatedly that week. Following his quarterfinals victory over Lendl, Sampras said:

> I don't believe what's happening now. I can't really believe what's going on.[55]

After his Sunday win over Agassi in the finals, he stated:

> It doesn't seem real. It's going to take a while for it to sink in.[56]

On Monday, the day following his stunning championship, Sampras told reporters:

> I couldn't get any sleep because it's still unreal. I don't believe it still.[57]

Naturally, any 19-year old would be stunned to pull off the U.S. Open. But for the young and inexperienced ENTP, it would be twice as hard to believe.

It was the week following the Open that Sampras finally began to show some ENTP colors. He honored a commitment to play in the All American Tennis Championships in Florida (something for which to commend him, considering the previous week). Only American men played, with eight entered. Sampras played Jay Berger in a first round match, losing the opening set 6-0. It was obvious he was still stiff and "buzzed" from the Open. He rallied back to win the second set 6-1, but lost the final set 7-6, and the match. Once Pete warmed up in the middle of the match, however, he demonstrated some one up moves. He resembled Fred Astaire (and Suzanne Lenglen) on some volleys, and played some most unusual shots. The *coup de grace* was when he tried to hit an easy shot at the net by turning his racket upside down, attempting to use the handle to hit the ball. He completely missed the ball. That shot alone may have cost him the match. But as far as he was probably concerned, he had a good time anyway. Though Pete Sampras demonstrated a persona through the 1990s unlike Lenglen, Vilas, or Gerulaitis, he possessed the innate mental and motor skills of the ENTP.

By 2004, Switzerland's **Roger Federer** (another composed ENTP) was dominating the men's pro tour. The world's No. 1-ranked player won 3 of the 4 Grand Slam single's titles!

Hard Working, Strong

Romanian Ion Tiriac, known for his tough persona and coaching style, coached both Ilie Nastase and **Guillermo Vilas**. He and other tennis aficionados regarded the ST Nastase as having the superior talent. But Tiriac knew more than talent was necessary to have a champion. He said:

> For Nastase, tennis was all a game, all play. For Vilas, it is all work. Vilas worked hard, four, five, six hours a day of running and exercises and hitting balls. . . . Vilas strong? I play ice hockey. I think I am strong. If we arm wrestle, this guy snap my arm off quick. Laver strong? This guy snap Laver in two pieces.[58]

Arthur Ashe once said of Vilas:

> Guillermo trains like nobody I've ever seen.[59]

Again, I say that iNtuitives, as a rule, must work harder to develop their motor skills than Sensates. Vilas found this to be true. Not all ENTPs will be strong like Vilas, but they have loads of energy to expend, and motor skills not as likely to tighten up as Sensates and Judgers.

OBSTACLES

One Upping too Much

ENTPs are the Masters-of-One-Upmanship, always looking for an opportunity to conquer. This does not always work to their advantage.

On a positive note, some years ago musician Luis Alberto Spinetta of Argentina shed light on his fellow countryman, ENTP **Guillermo Vilas**:

> Willie is, you know, counterclockwise. You tell him what's white, he'll tell you what's black. You act hard on him, he'll be sweet. It's all reversed. He's contradictory. But he is young, a champion, sensible. He has fun. His future is now. He has found the world already.[60]

Sporadic

ENTPs are often up and down players. They can show greatness one match or tournament and mediocrity the next. ENTPs play according to their mental state as much as any Type. Therefore, it is imperative they approach each tennis event with as much positive mental preparation as possible.

Conclusion

Who, in your own mind, stands out as the greatest one upper in tennis history? Being a post World War II baby denied me the opportunity to witness many great tennis moments of the past. But in my lifetime, one ENTP stands alone, the irrepressible **Bobby Riggs**. It was Riggs, in 1973, at the ripe age of 55, who instigated the "Challenge of the Sexes" exhibition match against Billie Jean King. An estimated 40 million viewers watched on TV, with another 30,000 in person. Bobby got his comeuppance by losing three straight sets to Billie Jean. But it was Riggs who got the last laugh. Even though he lost the match, he one upped America by gaining an inordinate amount of attention and a sizable paycheck.

HELPING ENTPs

ENTPs are generally precocious children, much like 15-year old brains in 7-year old bodies. They may prefer conversations with adults than kids their own age. They are able to grasp concepts and information far beyond their years. Though their motor skills may be lacking, their mental skills are advanced, enabling them to learn the mental phases of tennis at an early age. If they continue to work hard as they get older, their physical skills will gain greater parity with their mental game, resulting in high performance tennis.

ENTPs, like all iNtuitives, should work hard on developing their motor skills, particularly hand-eye coordination. Numerous drills can be implemented.

INTP

Finding the cerebral INTPs in professional sports is rare. Normally, their mental acumen takes them into vocations such as science, medicine, or research. They are capable of developing motor skills but usually rely upon developing their more innately proficient cerebral skills, but every now and then, an INTP will choose to doggedly pursue a sport.

As NTs, they will be at a disadvantage with the Sensates. NTs need to give extra time and effort to developing their motor movements. The younger they can do this, the better. Right-brained NTPs, however, will have a greater advantage in smoothness and suppleness than their left-brained, NTJ counterparts.

INTP **Arthur Ashe** achieved a Number 2 world-ranking in 1976, only three years before his retirement. He tallied 33 career pro titles, including singles titles at the U.S. and Australian Opens, and Wimbledon. Ashe was once president of the Association of Tennis Professionals (ATP) and regarded as one of the most respected players in all tennis.

Ashe's cosmopolitan mind endowed him to write, philosophize, reason, and appreciate—to become deeply involved with his passions and concerns for this world. He was far more than a tennis player. Arthur succumbed to the AIDS virus in 1993, contracted through a blood transfusion.

Ashe once recalled Wimbledon, 1974, and the opinion that Australian, John Newcombe was favored:

> It's amazing how people can talk themselves into something and then reinforce a false opinion. Everyone is saying the rain delays will help Newcombe because it will condense the last rounds into a few days' play, and that Newc is such a big, strong guy, this will profit him. Virtually every newspaper has played this same angle—and everybody you talk to is repeating the theme. The facts are completely opposite. Newc is big and strong, sure, but there's no correlation between strength and the kind of sustained energy that everybody's talking about. He might yet win, but if he does, it will be in spite of the rain schedule, not because of it.[61]

Ashe, in INTP fashion, was disturbed by the illogic of favoring Newcombe. This same NT reasoning played a major role in his high level tennis achievement. INTPs are able to logically consider matters, without equal. This does not mean INTPs are always right, or that they always consider the proper facts, but when they objectively consider accurate, inanimate data, they are the "Einsteins."

Mary Joe Fernandez is a rare INTP on the circuit. She turned pro at only 14; but unlike other teenage prodigies (who have a traveling tutor), Fernandez remained in school and worked her tennis schedule around her education. Can you imagine the grades a typical student would get with Fernandez's tennis and school schedules? From what I have read, she was a straight A student.

It was comical to hear Billie Jean King and Tracy Austin comment on the USA's TV network broadcast of the 1990 U.S. Open. They remarked how good and encouraging it was for young players to stay in school while developing their tennis careers. They felt it was important to develop high school relationships and keep that balance of life. What amused me was when they used Mary Joe Fernandez as an example of staying in school and getting excellent grades to boot. Certainly other Brain Types can get straight A's (virtually every Type can if they study hard enough), but no Type is better suited cerebrally than the INTP for excelling academically.

Fernandez turned age 29 in 2000. She has rarely played with animation. Essentially, she's expressionless. This outward persona is generally how the INTP athlete will perform. (Frankly, I find it refreshing in a sports world often dominated by outgoing antics and animation.) INTPs partly perform this way due to their concentration and desire to save energy. After all, they are not as supercharged as the Extraverted athletes.

HELPING INTPs

I do not know any professional sport in which INTPs can achieve greater success than tennis. Yet, the odds are not high for INTPs being among the best the pro circuit. Thus, they should give special attention to schoolwork as well as tennis, in the event they decide to give up their vocational tennis pursuits.

INTPs take to academics naturally. They have an

aptitude for learning and find great satisfaction excelling in school. They can find the formative years of lower education quite a bore, however. The subject matter is often too rudimentary and the pace of learning too slow. Helping an INTP to develop an interest in school and in learning solid study habits is the first step to helping an INTP vocationally. No Brain Type has greater cerebral potential.

INTPs, like all iNtuitives, should work hard on developing their motor skills. Lots of running and learning body balance will improve the gross motor skills, while performing hand eye coordination drills will enhance the fine motor movements.

ENFP

Can you picture the game of Chris Evert for a moment (in her prime). What do you see? Try to see more than cute Chrissie methodically beating her opponent and remember her playing style. Now picture a gal playing tennis who is the exact opposite of Evert's Brain Type. This does not mean her tennis style will be exactly opposite Evert's but definitely contrasting. Make this gal a professional, too. We don't want to see balls flying over the fence. Which of the top women's players in the 1990s would you consider to have Evert's opposite Type?

If it's the player who ended Evert's career in the quarterfinals of the 1989 U.S. Open, you are correct. She had never beaten Chris in a Grand Slam match. Her name is Zina Garrison. (Other ENFPs have included **Tracy Austin, MaliVai Washington, Evonne Goolagong, Chanda Rubin,** and **Venus Williams.**)

Zina Garrison began playing tennis at age 10, later than most pros. She earned the ITF Junior of the Year Award in 1981, as she won both Wimbledon and U.S. Open junior titles. Zina turned pro in 1982 and has been ranked in the Top 5 in women's tennis. She became the first black female to reach the final of a Grand Slam event since Althea Gibson won Wimbledon in 1957 and 1958. During her career, Garrison was been known for giving motivational speeches to youngsters at schools. It is wonderful to see how she exercised her ENFP talents in life as well as sports.

Another ENFP with a contrasting playing style to Chris Evert's came from down under. This Aussie once said:

> I've never seen anyone so self assured as Chrissie [Evert], so businesslike and intense in her concentration. If she smiles while she's playing, it's rare. If I don't, check my pulse and send flowers.[62]

This player wrote in her autobiography of the time she won her first Wimbledon. Recalling when she was playing favored Margaret Court and was ahead two games in the first set:

> I was starting to feel looser, freer, and stronger with every point. I was enjoying myself. It was glorious running on grass. Like dancing, fast dancing. Everything seems faster on a grass court .... Your reflexes have to be sharper and quicker to cope. There's less time to make the stroke; you're lunging, leaping, sprinting instead of loping. It's like being part of a speeded up movie, and that's my style: fast.[63]

ENFP **Evonne Goolagong** made a lasting impact on women's tennis. The radiant bundle of energy won 92 major titles over her ten-year career. Evonne was inducted into the International Tennis Hall of Fame in 1988.

Until ENFP **Venus Williams** came on the scene, **Tracy Austin** was the most famous American ENFP, man or woman, in recent tennis history. Tracy came from a tennis family that produced four professional players. She was a young prodigy, with a record 25 national junior titles. She defeated Chris Evert to become the youngest player to ever win a U.S. Open (1979), at the age of 16. Tracy won two U.S. Open titles by the time she was 18. She had a No. 1 ranking in the world for five months in 1980. From 1983 to 1988, Austin played a limited schedule due to nagging neck and back injuries. Misfortune struck again in 1989 when she broke her leg in an automobile accident. Tracy Austin won 28 singles titles in her limited career. She, like ENFP Zina Garrison, has also used her ENFP communication skills in motivating others. Besides TV commentary, Austin gives numerous speeches and clinics.

MaliVai Washington, ENFP, left the University of Michigan after his sophomore season, turning pro in 1989. In 1991, he pushed Ivan Lendl to the limit at Wimbledon and Michael Stich at the U.S. Open, before losing both hard fought matches. Washington ended 1993 with a Number 13 world ranking.

Entering the 21st century, ENFP tennis prodigy **Venus Williams** was the world's top female performer. She capped off a great 2000 by winning the revered women's U.S. Open singles title, having won

Wimbledon earlier in the year. Williams brought a new look to women's tennis, the power game. In 2001, she became the first woman since Steffi Graf in 1995-96 to win back-to-back Wimbledon championships.

Extraverted (High energy Level)

Extraversion does not always mean talkative. Extraverts can even be reserved. The primary characteristic of healthy Extraverts is a high-energy level. They are action oriented, particularly with their bodies.

From what I've read, many have described **Zina Garrison** as shy or Introverted. Some of this insight is probably well-founded, but Brain Types add another dimension to a person's behavior. In light of this, it was interesting to read of Garrison's experience at the 1988 Seoul Olympics. She performed superbly, taking the bronze medal in singles competition and the gold in doubles. *Sports Illustrated* said of her actions at the games:

> ... she was appropriately bubbly, chatting blue streaks with athletes and strangers alike.[64]

Even though Garrison and other Extraverts may not be recognized for what they are, if you look closely, you will witness their Extraverted side. ENFPs are exceptionally energetic performers in athletics. Their sociability level is not a major consideration when I attempt to identify them.

Sports Illustrated (*SI*) also spoke of Zina's early days in tennis:

> Her style of play was the opposite of the dependent inner child. She was agile and bold.[65]

I'm confident, as *SI* has alluded, that Garrison demonstrated her high energy Extraversion on the court as a child. ENFPs Goolagong and Austin never hid their Extraversion from the public, nor has Venus Williams. As adults, ENFPs are generally enthusiastic, friendly and outgoing.

Acrobatic

ENFPs are at the top of the gymnastic, figure skating and diving world. They dominate in these as ISTPs do in many other sports. Unfortunately for ENFPs, tennis cannot be planned and choreographed as thoroughly as a number of other sports. Tennis requires much unplanned, split second decision making. Nevertheless, ENFPs can attain great success in tennis by just following their natural, highly energetic acrobatic style. It's been written of Zina Garrison:

> Wilkerson gave Garrison a wooden racket and turned her loose. The kid was fast, and she hit the ball with might and pleasure. Tennis was running, dancing and batting all rolled into one.[66]

Tennis aficionado, Bud Collins (ENTP), wrote of **Evonne Goolagong**:

> I think of her as a South Seas princess dancing, a gazelle gliding—she is all grace and lyrical motion. The theme of her performances is "Let the Sunshine In."[67]

Visionaries, Highly Intuitive

ENFPs are masters at utilizing the anterior region of the right hemisphere. Neuroscience confirms one function of this area involves facilitating iNtuition, inflection/intonation, and Extraverted creativity. Visualizing, particularly people and animate matters, is natural for ENFPs. **Zina Garrison's** brother, Rodney, recalled their childhood:

> When we were growing up, she used to trip us out. She always saw visions, and when she was away she always seemed to know when something was happening at home. We called her the Vision Girl.[68]

OBSTACLES

Capricious

Sports Illustrated commented on Chris Evert's previous long standing dominance over Zina Garrison in a simulated dialogue with Evert:

> She [Chrissie] has never had anything like your speed, yet almost always has kept you at bay with deft placement and unwavering consistency.[69] (Insert added.)

SI accurately described Evert's ISTJ tennis game, and the normal energy and speed of the ENFP. They also alluded to the inconsistent play of ENFP Garrison. The crowd, as well as the ENFP, is not always sure what and where the next shot will be. *SI* continued:

Over the years Garrison has lost so many late round matches to elite opponents that she has allowed the doubtful and demanding collective minds of tennis to conclude that she is a hopeless choker. She has been ranked among the top dozen women for six years, but has never made the finals of a Grand Slam event.[70]

The dominant iNtuition of ENFPs seems to propel them early in their careers, where they play matches with minimal introspection, and tend to dominate the opposition with their athletic zeal. As ENFPs age, however, and develop their Feeling and Thinking functions, they become more susceptible to the throes of pressure in some sports. Tennis appears to be one of them.

ENFPs can develop mental blocks toward certain players or events. For instance, playing style alone didn't give ISTP Martina Navratilova such an advantage over Zina Garrison. At the 1990 Virginia Slims in Los Angeles, Zina lost to Navratilova for the 29th time in 30 matches. Following the match, Garrison was quoted as saying, "It's devastating."[71]

Anxiety, Fears

As long as ENFPs stay in their Extraverted world, they are generally highly optimistic persons. Their iNtuition focuses on the myriad of positive possibilities. ENFPs are most susceptible to anxieties and fear when they are alone, in their Introverted Feeling mode. This is where they make subjective judgments on their lives. These Feeling judgments often supersede their less developed objective, logical judgments. The results range from anxiety to despondency if things are not going well.

Zina Garrison's childhood had some traumatic times. Her father and a brother died when she was very young. Zina clung to her mother, sharing a bed until she was 16. She reflected:

> My mother was so strong. She had come through all this death.[72]

When stressful reality hits, the ENFP's dominant iNtuition does not always handle it well. Rather than wanting to deal with the situation as a Sensate would be more apt to do, the ENFP wants to vamoose, to flee. That can be debilitating in life and on the tennis court.

Zina Garrison's traumas remind me of ENFP I met in the 1980s. Before the Iron Curtain came down, I had the privilege of traveling in one of these countries secretively with an itinerant missionary. His ministry, at great risk to himself and the persecuted Christians, brought them great encouragement.

On one rendezvous, we met an ENFP pastor I will never forget. The ENFP told us of his incredible fears growing up. So great was his fear of persecution that he did not leave his house until 12 years of age! When we met him, he told of how God had given him victory over his fears, and that he was now speaking openly of his Christian faith, even though it often meant prison for doing so.

ENFPs, like other Types, can overcome their fears and bouts of depression. I have found that mental exercises can provide transitory help in time of stress, but that having a strong spiritual foundation is the optimal way to deal with life's biggest issues.

Improvisational

No Brain Type is more gifted at responding immediately and creatively to an Extraverted situation involving people and relational matters than ENFPs (versus inanimate matters where the ENTP excels). Their brains are specifically wired to facilitate this. Reflect on how ENFPs **Oprah Winfrey, Goldie Hawn,** and **Bob Hope** have acted on stage.

ENFPs learn soon in life that they have the innate ability to improvise. This asset becomes a liability when carried too far. The propensity for ENFPs is to put things off until the last moment (like all Ps) and then handle it with their iNtuitive, creative flair. This will work in many situations, but life and the tennis game often pose situations that necessitate advanced planning and analysis. ENFPs need to have a thought out game plan before each tennis match if they hope to reach their potential.

Zina's Garrison's former and long time coach, John Wilkerson, spoke of his former pupil:

> Zina relied on her intuition instead of analyzing. She always wanted to go out there without a game plan, wanted to just let it happen.[73]

Wilkerson accurately spoke of Garrison's iNtuition, which is her dominant function, typologically. According to Type function theory, Thinking (or analyzing, as he put it) is the third preferred function, following Feeling, of the ENFP. Thus, it is understandable why Zina didn't prefer this mental function as Wilkerson wished she had.

Second, Wilkerson accurately described the ENFP tendency to avoid certain kinds of planning. I hope you can see the importance of knowing the Type of the person you are trying to encourage in athletics. Even, and especially, if the person happens to be you!

Garrison revealed her ENFP proclivities from an early age. *Sports Illustrated* said:

> Not until her third tournament did he [Wilkerson] realize that she wasn't even keeping score. She watched her opponent between points to see where she should serve or receive serve.[74]

Garrison did not find it a priority to use logic in her initial tournaments as a youngster. Rather, she relied upon her spatial right hemisphere to see her opponent's next move, then adapted accordingly.

HELPING ENFPs

ENFPs will never master the cerebral functions and motor movements of their opposite Brain Type, the ISTJ (Chris Evert's Type). ENFPs will need special instruction and hands on help developing these areas. At the same time, they should be allowed to freely exercise the skills of their own bent. (They, like all Types, need to strive for a healthy balance of mental and physical skills between their and their opposite Type's.)

Channel the ENFP's enthusiasm and coordinated movements into more specific learning phases of the game. Develop hand eye skills. Help the ENFP to understand the importance of having a master plan for each tennis match. See that the ENFP regularly practices proper mental techniques necessary for later match pressure situations. If ENFPs can get a good handle on their mental game, with lots of practice, their physical game will not let them down.

If ENFPs begin tennis at an early age, with proper coaching, their potential is among the best, particularly in adolescence. With the proper mental supervision and focus, they can be among the world's best for a long time.

ENFJ

Were it not for one particular ENFJ, I wouldn't be devoting the following length of information regarding this Brain Type. By my estimation, the likelihood of an ENFJ being ranked among the world's best in tennis is not high. Despite the odds, an ENFJ has achieved world class status: **Jim Courier**.

The ENFJ is the opposite Brain Type of the preeminent ISTP (for example, Edberg, Lendl, McEnroe, Connors, Navratilova, Graf, and Seles). The mental processes of the two Types are appreciably different. This will be visible on the tennis court, particularly when the two Types experience pressure. Nevertheless, the contrasting physical skills of the ISTP and ENFJ are not as diverse as the mental skills. NFs are capable of developing unity with the body's motor movements, large and small. ENFJs can achieve superior racket skills, powered by their Extraversion and fine motor adeptness. They may not always appear outgoing socially, but ENFJs generally demonstrate high-energy Extraversion in their athleticism. The ENFJ I have in mind certainly does; he's been known for his "nuclear powered" groundstrokes.

Jim Courier took the 1991 tennis world by storm. Ranked 25th at the end of 1990, Courier surprised many in '91 by capturing the French Open and making it to the finals of the U.S. Open. By February of 1992, Courier captured his second Grand Slam title (Australian Open), earning him a No. 1 ranking in the world! Having attended the Nick Bollettieri Tennis Academy with Andre Agassi, Courier took longer to make an impact on tour than the same aged ESTP Agassi. Their difference in Brain Types is one major reason.

High Strung

Jim Courier excelled in a tennis academy by the age of 11. By 14, he was off to Bollettieri's Academy, where he continued to learn until he was 20. Nevertheless, it is said that Courier's mental game was not on par with his physical. *People* magazine stated:

> Courier often seemed as tight during matches as an overstrung racket.[75]

ENFJs are often high strung, regardless of the sport. They frequently take their Extraverted, NF drive to the tennis court incorrectly.

Things began to change for Courier at the end of 1990. He got a new coach, Jose Higueras. Before long, Courier was playing much differently. It appears that Higueras' main contribution was mental assistance, not physical. Courier was learning to relax, and rightfully gave Higueras the credit. Jim's mother, Linda, said of her son following his French Open Grand Slam win:

> He's so relaxed, he's almost a different human being than he was a year ago.[76]

Courier said of Higueras:

> I'm a very competitive person, but Jose made me understand that you can't think if you're too excited . . . .[77]

Courier's assessment is correct. Competent reasoning is diminished under mental duress. In Courier's case, accessing his typologically less developed ENFJ Thinking function would be extra difficult under pressure. Therefore, especially for ENFJs, achieving and maintaining mental composure is essential for optimal athletic performance. Courier admitted he didn't begin to really use his head until he played Andre Agassi in 1991:

> That was the first match I ever won with my head. I'm calmer, more cool headed. Of course, I'm still a hitter, but now I can hit and think at the same time.[78]

An additional insight is worth mentioning, Jose Higueras' Brain Type. Coaches in tennis (like caddies in golf) can have a major mental and emotional impact on their players. If you're a player, it is wise to consider the Brain Types of coaches who assist you. Depending on each situation, it is sometimes wise to have a coach or caddie of the opposite Brain Type. This was nearly the case with Courier and Higueras. Jose is an ISFP, the mellowest Type. Couple his Type with his persona and experience, and you got a coach who was best for Courier at that stage of his career.

Hard Working, Tenacious

Jim Courier has been known for his ambition and hard work habits. Exerting tremendous effort is typical for ENFJs who want to fulfill ambitions. Veteran tour player Brad Gilbert said of Courier:

> Jim does one thing that a lot of athletes don't do when they get to the top. He works even harder.[79]

What Courier lacked in talent and finesse, he made up for in determination. He assessed himself:

> To me, tennis is trench warfare. I'm constantly digging, grinding and gutsing matches out.[80]

Australian pro Mark Woodforde said of Courier:

> He won't quit even if he's down five love in the final set. No one on the tour has more tenacity or a stronger will to win.[81]

Language Specialists

As members of the NF temperament group, ENFJs are gifted in speech and hearing skills. Jim Courier demonstrated his penchant for language in 1992, entertaining the Parisians at the French Open. Courier spoke phrases of fractured French to the delight of fans. It was reported that in preparation for his Normandy invasion, he:

> . . . bought some language books and tapes and has been studying seriously.

One of Courier's coaches said:

> He goes to his room for hours, and when he comes out he's just fried.[82]

Admirable for a high paid athlete, Jim Courier has placed an appreciable value on people and the languages they speak.

Another Jimmy Connors?

Sports Illustrated wrote about Jim Courier after the 1991 U.S. Open:

> Courier fights. He hustles. He works hard. He wants it. Could he be the next great American champion? Does he remind you of anybody? Say, of Jimmy Connors?[83]

The two Jimmys have had similarities: competitiveness and high energy. Yet they are quite dissimilar in motor and mental functions. *I wrote in 1992 that Jim Courier would be hard pressed to accomplish the feats of a great ISTP. Time has proven this to be true. By 1994, Courier's game was in decline. At age 24, he finished out of the Top 10 and did not win a title for the first time since 1990.* Nonetheless, there's always hope for ENFJs. They must, however, continually improve their mental and motor efforts in order to perform their best.

HELPING ENFJs

ENFJs especially need to learn how to control their energy, enthusiasm, and anxiety when playing. With this control, their motor movements will become more fluid and their awareness on the court increased.

ENFJs should try to develop their motor movements as early as possible. If ENFJs begin athletics for the first time at age 10 or beyond, their motor skills can be quite slow and clumsy. By encouraging them to begin exercise athletically at an early age, they can become first rate athletes, bringing coordination to their body movements.

OTHER BRAIN TYPES
(ISFJ, ESFJ, INFJ, INFP, and INTJ)

We have considered some major attributes of the most commonly found Brain Types in professional tennis. Of the five remaining Types, the INFP, INTJ, and ESFJ would most likely be found on the pro tennis circuit. INFPs would probably be most successful of these three. **Guy Forget** of France, INFP, cracked the ATP top 10 rankings for the first time in his 10-year career in 1991. Forget's power serve and newly found self confidence propelled him to win 6 tournaments and more than $1 million in earnings, while leading the French over the U.S. in Davis Cup competition. In 1993, INFP **Cedric Pioline** of France had over $900,000 in tournament earnings, while breaking into the Top ten for the first time in his career and reaching the U.S. Open finals.

Any tennis players possessing these remaining five Brain Types (or Types mentioned already but infrequently found excelling in professional tennis) should not give up their aspirations, but realize working harder and smarter will be necessary to reach the highest levels of tennis. They should consider the true life stories of persons who overcame unfavorable odds to attain athletic stardom. Reading the accounts of the disciplines and rigors that enabled them to reach their goals would be helpful.

Conclusion

It is wise to investigate the players of your specific Brain Type. This will enable you to see the various ways persons of the same Type play tennis. Look for articles where they share their methods of success, mentally and physically. If you have typed yourself correctly, you should relate to what they are saying. Remember the adage, "Different strokes for different folks." You will generally do best by emulating those most like yourself.

Though far from complete, here is a list of well known players and their probable Brain Types that will provide a perspective on the most successful in professional tennis.

ISTP
Lleyton Hewitt, Thomas Muster, Richard Krajicek, Miloslav Mecir, Petr Korda,
Monica Seles, Mary Pierce, Leili Meskhi
   Retired: Rod Laver, John McEnroe, Jimmy
          Connors, Ivan Lendl, Stefan Edberg,
          Martina Navratilova, Michael Chang,
          Steffi Graf

ESTP
Andre Agassi, Patrick Rafter, Boris Becker, Marcelo Rios, Michael Stich, Goran Ivanisevic, Vince Spadea, Carlos Moya, Arnaud Clement
Martina Hingis, Jana Novotna
   Retired: Ilie Nastase, Vic Seixas, Aaron Krickstein

ISFP
Yevgeny Kafelnikov, Magnus Norman
   Retired: Bjorn Borg, Jose Higueras,
          Gardner Mulloy

ESFP
Serena Williams, Jennifer Capriati, Lindsay Davenport, Anna Kournikova, Conchita Martinez,
  Retired: Pancho Segura

ISTJ
Paul Haarhuis, Andrei Cherkasov
   Retired: Chris Evert, Stan Smith

ESTJ
David Wheaton,
   Retired: Ted Schroeder, Pam Shriver,
               Manuela Maleeva Fragniere

ESFJ
 Gigi Fernandez

INFP
Guy Forget, Cedric Pioline

ENFP
Jonas Bjorkman, MaliVai Washington
Venus Williams, Chanda Rubin,
   Retired: Tracy Austin, Evonne Goolagong
             Zina Garrison

ENFJ
Jim Courier, Alexander Volkov

INTJ
   Retired: Tim Mayotte, Jeff Tarango

ENTJ
Todd Martin, Alex Corretja, Karel Novacek, Todd Witsken, Amos Mansdorf, Javier Sanchez, Rick Leach, Jay Berger,
Amelie Mauresmo
   Retired: Billie Jean King, Gabriela Sabatini, Mary
             Carillo, Tony Trabert, Jack Kramer,
             Harold Solomon, Cliff Drysdale,
             Brad Gilbert

INTP
 Mary Joe Fernandez   *Retired*: Arthur Ashe

ENTP
Roger Federer, Andy Roddick, Gustavo Kuerten, Marat Safin, Greg Rusedski, Emilio Sanchez, Jimmy Arias, Henri Leconte, Justin Gimelstob, Scott Draper, Scott Davis, Robert Seguso,
Irina Spirlea
   Retired: Suzanne Lenglen, Pancho Gonzales,
             Guillermo Vilas, Vitas Gerulaitas, Yannick
             Noah, Ion Tiriac, Leif Shiras, Bobby Riggs,
             Derrick Rostagno, Luke Jensen,
             Patrick McEnroe, **Pete Sampras**

17
Track and Field, Volleyball, Water Polo, Wrestling

Track and Field

Track and field is no longer limited to amateur athletics. Professional track athletes now compete internationally, in some cases making substantial amounts of money. A diversity of Brain Types excel in track, though certain Types are best designed for specific events. Let's consider some popular track athletes.

ENFP

In the thin air of Mexico City at the 1968 Olympics, **Bob Beamon** shocked the world with a long jump record of 29' 2½". In 1991, **Mike Powell** broke the longest-standing (23 years) and most respected record in track, which belonged to Beamon. In order to win this event in Japan, Powell had to beat Carl Lewis who had not lost a long jump competition in 10 years.

Powell was known by fellow long jumpers as "Mike Foul," resulting from his many fouls at the take off point of his jumps. In fairness to Powell, this pattern would not be uncommon for the iNtuitive, emotional, energetic ENFP. Following Powell's record setting jump in Japan, his coach Randy Huntington commented:

> Mike is an emotional jumper. His technique often depends on the height of his emotions.[1]

Powell consulted a psychologist to help him contain his emotions in competition.

Mike Powell's long jumping success was directly related to his Brain Type, along with determination and hard work. Powell's former college coach, Steve Lang, said of him:

> The thing that makes Mike so talented in the long jump is that he has the ability to jump so high. He can get up higher than anyone I've ever seen.[2]

Powell's 1991 efforts earned him the AAU Sullivan Award as the nation's outstanding amateur athlete.

Whether it be in basketball, football, baseball, or even ice skating, ENFPs are often tremendous leapers. It is understandable why Mike Powell became so successful.

Right-brained Visualizers

ENFPs are spatial persons. Regardless of the sport, they often rely on reviewing video tapes of their performances or practicing visualization techniques. Mike Powell spoke of his world record performance:

> I've imagined that moment in my living room a hundred times.[3]

Sprinters

ENFPs could make a strong case for being the fastest of all Brain Types. (This isn't to say that every ENFP is fast; other individual genetic and environmental factors must be considered.) As super high-energy, fine and gross motor coordinated, right-brained people, they possess optimal body qualities for sprinters. In every sport where speed has great importance, ENFPs are usually found among the best.

Sprinter **Leroy Burrell**, ENFP, was recognized as one of the world's fastest men. In 1991, Burrell broke Carl Lewis' world record in the 100 meters, lowering it to 9.90 seconds (only to have Lewis break it again some 3 months later at 9.86). In 1994, Burrell again set the world mark at 9.85.

ENFPs proved to be the fastest Olympians at the '92 Barcelona games. Californian **Gail Devers** won the women's 100 meters, and Great Britain's **Linford Christie** captured the gold in the men's 100. Devers continued her excellence at the '96 Atlanta Olympics, again winning the 100 meters.

Hurdlers

Combining their speed and graceful leaping abilities, ENFPs often attain world-class status in the hurdles. ENFP **Greg Foster** was a three-time winner in the 110-meter high hurdles at the World Championships (1983, 1987, and 1991).

INFP

Long-distance Runners

INFPs are arguably the top runners in the world at 1,500 to 5,000 meters. Superior NFP body coordination and flexibility enable them to stay loose and fluid, Introversion provides concentration and patience, and iNtuition can keep their mind on the goal or allow them to escape body pain by envisioning themselves elsewhere.

A former world-record holder in the 1,500, 2,000, 3,000, and 5,000 meters, INFP **Said Aouita** of Morocco was the elite long distance runner in the 1980s. INFP Algerian **Noureddine Morceli** followed in Aouita's footsteps, ranking first in the world through much of the 1990s—setting world records in the mile, 1,000, 1,500, 2,000, and 3,000 meters. Entering the 21st century, Moroccan and INFP **Hicham El Guerrouj** was the new world record-holder in the mile, 2,000, and 1500 meters. He has been recognized as the world's fastest miler and 1500-meter runner in history. In 8 years, he only lost 5 races—two of them Olympic finals. In 1996, he was tripped and fell on the final lap. At Sydney in 2000, El Guerrouj was so overwhelmed by the pressure that he cried—before the race began! Coming down the stretch on the final lap, he had little energy left, finishing a disappointing second. The emotional drain before the race coupled with his reported overtraining prior to the Olympics, caused El Guerrouj to seemingly defeat himself.

With universal pressure to prove he could win before the world's largest stage at the 2004 Athens Olympics, El Guerrouj courageously met the challenge. What was most impressive and revealing, however, was not his physical heroics, but his INFP emotions. Though dominant Feelers, INFPs rarely show their deeply personal emotions in public. (El Guerrouj's demonstration in Sydney was one of those exceptions.) The 2004 moment was again too big for El Guerrouj to again hide his innately sensitive makeup. After crossing the finish line, the sensitive victor fell to his knees in tears, overwhelmed. Still on the ground, he then hugged a fellow competitor (another Feeler) as his deeply-touching emotions continued like Yellowstone's "Old Faithful." It was humble sensitivity at its best. When El Guerrouj later stood on the victory platform as his country's anthem was played, he again revealed the warm and tender side of the INFP—this time with more composure.

ESFP

The SFP Types (ESFP and ISFP) can be among the world's best in shorter races. Longer distances are not conducive for their gross motor skill dominance. SFP muscles become tight and restrictive in the long hauls. The hurdles can also pose problems for ESFPs at the highest levels of competition.

ESFP **Carl Lewis** won four gold medals at the 1984 Olympic Games in Los Angeles. His success matched Jesse Owen's historic performance in 1936. Over his career, Lewis held numerous world records in the sprints and long jump.

Leroy Burrell said of competitor Lewis and his ESFP persona:

Carl is very glamorous. He enjoys the spotlight.[4]

The 1996 Atlanta Summer Olympics began Lewis's departure from track and field. There he captured his 9th Olympic gold medal and his 4th in the long jump. His outstanding career included many controversies—many involving his self-promotional ways which are not unusual for ESFPs. For over a decade, Lewis was at the top of international sprinting, twice the length of a normal career. (SFP Types [ESFP and ISFP] can last longer in sports than any other Types—thanks to their gross motor superiority.)

With stunning looks to match her performances, ESFP **Florence Griffith-Joyner** or "Flo Jo" collected three golds and a silver medal at the 1988 Seoul Olympics.

In 1998, at the age of only 38, Flo Jo died unexpectedly. From the poor conditions of childhood, she rose to become the world's fastest woman, living a life marked with extraordinary accomplishment and grace. And she did it in ESFP style.

The Next Track. Star?

In 1992, when I first published the forerunner to this book, *Your Best Sport*, I wrote the following:

*"In 1991, as a 15 year-old high school sophomore, Californian **Marion Jones (ESFP)** recorded the fastest female outdoor prep marks in the nation at 100, 200, and 400 meters! I've seen her run, and she was phenomenal. Barring unforeseen difficulties, she'll replicate the accomplishments of fellow ESFP, Flo Jo."*

The Marion Jones story picks up again five years later—where she was finally beginning to fulfill her star potential. Sidetracked in the college years by pursuing basketball ambitions at the University of North Carolina (where she was a star point guard, leading her team to the NCAA championship), Jones at last devoted undivided interest to track and field in 1997. Within months, she was running world-class times in the sprints and excelling at long jump. Jones surprised her competitors and won the 100 meters at the 1997 World Championships in Athens. It was interesting and humorous to read a newspaper quote by her new track coach, Trevor Graham, in 1997:

She'll probably end up being the biggest star in track and field. She's just like Carl Lewis.[5]

Brain Typing allows Marion Jones to be compared with Carl Lewis more deeply than how coach Graham and many others view her. As an ESFP, Jones possesses the same inborn mental and motor skill design as Lewis and Flo Jo. Besides their generally outgoing personas, ESFPs excel in gross motor rhythm and fluidity and bring more energy and explosiveness to their sports than their close counterparts, the ISFPs. Yes, "She's just like Carl Lewis," in many more ways than people would ever imagine. As I stated in 1992 (it's now 1997), "Barring unforeseen difficulties, she'll replicate the accomplishments of fellow ESFP, Flo Jo." *Well, it's now the 21st century and Marion Jones was finally given the chance to challenge Flo Jo's records in Olympic competition (the 2000 Summer Games in Australia). Marion met the challenge in ESFP fashion by winning 3 gold medals and two bronze, and yes, eclipsing Flo Jo's medal tallies!* In the men's sprints, ESFP **Maurice Greene** won the 100-meter dash.

ISFP

The 1990s saw **Jackie Joyner Kersee** as the world's best female athlete. As an Olympic gold medalist (1988 and 1992) and world record holder in the seven event heptathlon, ISFP Joyner-Kersee was accustomed to grueling, two day competitions. At the 1988 Olympics in Seoul, she also won a gold medal in the women's long jump. Joyner-Kersee had to withdraw from the 1996 Summer Olympic heptathlon due to a strained hamstring yet, despite her injury, the gutsy ISFP managed a bronze medal in the long jump.

Another American who achieved the world's fastest man recognition is ISFP **Michael Johnson**. Michael was chosen male Athlete of the Year for 1990 by *Track and Field News*. *Sports Illustrated* wrote of his 1991 season:

. . . Johnson accomplished in one season what

no one had ever done in a career: He ended the year ranked first in the world at both 200 and 400 meters.[6]

SI also shed light on Michael's ISFP ways, writing:

> Johnson is modest to a fault.[7]

Johnson's coach at Baylor University, Clyde Hart, said:

> Michael's not comfortable being pampered or treated like a star. It's very important to feel like an athlete and not like a business entity.[8]

Johnson continued his star performance into the 1996 Summer Olympics. Capturing two individual gold medals, he also set a world record in the 200 meters. The 2000 Summer Games in Sydney saw Michael win 2 more golds (the 400 meters and the 4x400 relay).

Though not all ISFPs' running styles are identical, Michael's unusual and confounding style has not been surprising for his Type. His former high school coach said:

> They say he runs like a statue, straight up. They say his feet never leave the ground.[9]

Michael has demonstrated his reliance on his SF gross motor skills in an Introverted fashion, not expending unnecessary energy. His big muscle dominance has also been revealed in his upright and stiffer running technique. Not surprisingly, legendary ISFP **Jesse Owens** was also known for his upright running style.

ESTP

Though ESTPs are exceptionally athletic and probably the most natural decathletes, they find it difficult to endure the hardships associated with this event. **Dan O'Brien** has been an exception. Having failed unexpectedly to make the 1992 Olympic team, decathlete O'Brien set out on a four-year mission. At the Atlanta Summer Olympics in 1996, he finally realized his dreams—winning the gold medal. May his determination and discipline be an encouragement to other ESTPs who face arduous tasks.

In 1990 ESTP **Randy Barnes** set a world record in the shot put at 75' 10¼". The 1988 Olympic silver medalist predicted it would happen and made good on his boast. At the 1996 Atlanta Summer Olympics, the 30-year-old Barnes finally won his long sought-after gold medal.

ISTP

ISTPs do not dominate track and field as they do so many other sports. Nonetheless, they are capable of excelling in most track events. **Mary Decker Slaney**, ISTP, was America's female premier long distance runner for over 20 years! In 1973, at age fifteen, she ranked fourth in the world at 800 meters and within a year broke the world record.

As of 1997, Decker Slaney held five women's American records in the 800 and 1,500 meters, mile, 2,000 and 3,000 meters! Despite her numerous injuries and lower leg operations, Decker Slaney proved that her ISTP mind was as strong as, if not stronger than, her body. (In 1994, she had 25 percent of her left Achilles tendon removed.)

Amazingly at age 38, Slaney ran a 4:26.67 indoor mile, even though she had not stepped on an indoor track in eight years. It was the best time for a woman in two years.

Decker Slaney is legendary as a feisty competitor, which is not surprising for an ISTP. Consider the time as a teenager when she threw a baton at a Soviet runner. At another event, she and a competitor were racing side by-side to the finish line. The opponent lunged for the tape and fell face first, receiving cuts and bruises; Decker Slaney won. At the ceremonial banquet that night, Decker Slaney was asked if she felt bad for her opponent. She commented:

> Hell no. You can bet she wouldn't have felt bad for me if I fell across the finish line.[10]

In 1991, battling Patti Sue Plumer on the final stretch of a 1,500 meter race, Decker Slaney threw an elbow as Plumer tried to pass, knocking her off stride.

ISTPs rarely "take prisoners" in competition; their primary focus is to win. Mary Decker Slaney was one tough competitor who demonstrated extraordinary physical and mental toughness.

NTs

ENTP

Of the four NT Types, ENTPs are the fastest overall and have the greatest physical flexibility in track and field. They're capable of being among the world's top sprinters. The high energy ENTPs have remarkable body mobility and potentially quick feet. Though ENTPs are among the few top sprinter Brain Types, they normally don't hold world records. The 1996 Atlanta Olympics highlighted their potential, however. Canadian **Donovan Bailey**, ENTP, set a world record in the 100 meters. ENTP **Michael Marsh** won the men's 200-meter dash at the 1992 Summer Olympics, and **Konstantinos Kenteris** won the event at the Sydney Olympics in 2000. ENTP **Kevin Young** won the gold medal and broke the world record in the 400-meter hurdles at Barcelona. **Mike Conley** (ENTP) captured the gold in the triple jump at the '92 Barcelona Games.

In 1995, Britain's **Jonathan Edwards** broke the 18-meter barrier in the triple jump, leaping 60 feet 0¼ inches. The humble and Bible-toting Edwards broke his own world record by more than one foot! He even gained the admiration of competing triple-jumpers through his graciousness and overcoming the debilitating Epstein-Barr virus. At the '96 Atlanta Olympics, Edwards won a silver medal in the triple jump, finishing behind ENTP Kenny Harrison.

ENTPs have also excelled at high jump, utilizing their explosive, limber and fluid body movements. ENTP **Charles Austin** won the high jump gold medal at the 1996 Atlanta Olympics—the first U.S. Olympian to win the event since 1968.

ENTJ

ENTJs have reigned in the decathlon in modern track (**Bill Toomey, Bruce Jenner, Dave Johnson,** and the 2000 Summer Olympic gold medalist, **Erki Nool**). Their intellectual and physical athleticism, empowered by a supreme work ethic, make them decathlete champions.

INTJ and INTP

INTJs and INTPs tend to do best in long-distance running, yet rarely do INTPs excel in the Olympics. At the 2000 Sydney Games, Australia's Aborigine **Cathy Freeman**, INTP, defied the odds by capturing the gold medal in the women's 400 meter run.

Though far from complete, here is a list of well known track and field athletes and their probable Brain Types.

ENFP: Gail Devers, Madeline Mims, Mike Powell, Leroy Burrell, Linford Christie, Lawrence Johnson, Greg Foster, Jack Pierce, Steve Lewis, Danny Everett, Charles Simpkins

INFP: Edwin Moses, Renaldo Nehemiah, Said Aouita, Hicham El Guerrouj, Noureddine Morceli, Dalton Grant, Frankie Fredericks

ENTJ: Bruce Jenner, Dave Johnson, Bill Toomey, Erki Nool, Frank Shorter, Francie Larrieu

ENTP: Jeremy Wariner, Tom Pappas, Joanna Hayes, Donovan Bailey, Konstantinos Kenteris, Charles Austin, Jonathan Edwards, Kenny Harrison, Mike Conley, Michael Marsh, Kevin Young, Chris Huffins

INTP: Cathy Freeman, Kathy Ormsby

ESFP: Carl Lewis, Maurice Greene, Florence Griffith Joyner, Marion Jones, Sandra Farmer-Patrick, Lauryn Williams, Perdita Felicien

ISFP: Jackie Joyner Kersee, Jesse Owens, Michael Johnson, Butch Reynolds, Hollis Conway, Henry Carr

ESTP: Randy Barnes, Dan O'Brien, Dennis Mitchell, Quincy Watts, Werner Gunthor, Stacy Dragila (pole vault)

ISTP: Mary Decker Slaney, Doug Kennedy (wheelchair Olympian)

ESTJ Sergei Bubka, Tom Petranoff (javelin)

Volleyball

Volleyball has expanded its venues to include the indoor courts as well as the sandy beaches. Pro indoor leagues exist internationally, along with doubles tournaments stateside. College and even high school competition is serious business at the amateur level.

Though many Brain Types can become proficient at volleyball, I only want to mention a few of America's best players.

ENTJ

Karch Kiraly has been regarded as the world's best volleyball player. He grew up playing volleyball on the beaches of Southern California. Karch was a four time All American at UCLA and a two time Olympic gold medalist. The 6' 3" ENTJ has been a dominant player on the Association of Volleyball Professionals (AVP) tour. In 1990, Karch played in 23 tournaments, winning seven and finishing second nine times! His fellow players voted him the tour's MVP and best offensive player. In 1992, Kiraly earned $1 million playing pro indoor volleyball in Italy.

ENTJs are ultra competitors in every sport they play, utilizing their superb intellectual skills. Newcomer Brian Lewis said, in his second season on tour:

> Everyone out there is physically blessed, but the guys who are winning are so mentally tough. Knowing what to do and when to do it is 90% of the game.[11]

Lewis pinpointed an area in which ENTJs excel. They also seek to master all the elements of the game through hard practice. In addition to their individual talents, ENTJs make excellent doubles partners in volleyball. In 1992, ENTJs Karch Kiraly and **Kent Steffes** set a Pro Beach Volleyball record for most consecutive titles. In 1993, the dynamic duo won an AVP-record 18 events.

Steffes made history on the beach tour by becoming the youngest player to have won more than $1 million in prize money. Prior to his retirement at age 30, he was known among his peers as the hardest and smartest worker on tour. His dedication and preparedness were vintage ENTJ.

ISTP

ISTP **Steve Timmons** is a two time Olympic gold medal winner in volleyball (1984 88). At 6' 5", he was named the most valuable player of the 1984 Olympic Games in Los Angeles. In college, Steve led the University of Southern California (USC) to the NCAA championship in 1980.

Back in 1981, Steve Timmons became good friends and volleyball partners with ENTJ Karch Kiraly. Timmons spoke of those days and a typical scenario when these two Types associate:

> Karch was a very serious guy and I was always the jokester. I loosened him up and he educated me.[12]

ESTP

ESTP **Randy Stoklos** became the first pro beach volleyball player to reach $1 million in career earnings. He spoke of his accomplishment in ESTP fashion:

> People are going to look back at this milestone, and it will be talked about forever.[13]

VOLLEYBALL PLAYERS AND PROBABLE BRAIN TYPES

ENTJ   Karch Kiraly, Kent Steffes, Tim Walmer, Mike Whitmarsh

ENFJ   Sinjin Smith, Adam Johnson, Al Janc

INFP   Mike Dodd

ISTP   Steve Timmons, Misty May

ESTP   Randy Stoklos

Water Polo

Prior to 1995, my knowledge of water polo was quite limited. Thanks to the winningest water polo coach in NCAA history, Ted Newland (U.C. Irvine), my interest in this water world activity was elevated. Newland asked that my son and I help him to better understand Brain Types and its relevance to his sport. (Even at the age of 67, grand master Newland continued to show the signs of a great coach; he was highly successful yet continually searching for the best coaching methods. For an entertaining profile of ISTP Newland, refer to the Dec. 9, 1996 issue of *Sports Illustrated*.)

Historically, water polo in America has been a sport for high school and above athletes. Yet in the mid-1990s, it became popular enough with youngsters (ages 8 to 14) to form youth leagues. California has been the sport's biggest participant. Women's water polo has shown unparalleled advancement in recent years; it has become the fastest growing women's sport in America. Among many enticements, polo affords team camaraderie and freedom from major injuries suffered in many other sports.

Water polo is taxing, a sport that requires tremendous stamina and exertion. Not surprisingly, the majority of water polo athletes are former competitive swimmers. (Some believe as many as 90% began as swimmers.) Most of them found swimming too boring, spending so much time with heads under water and finding little time to interact with others. According to Coach Newland:

> In swimming, you're in a closed environment that resembles a concrete prison—where you can't look around—and there's little change in sound, smell, or vision. So when swimmers find a new sport that takes their head out of the water and is more enjoyable both physically and mentally, they jump into water polo with enthusiasm. Most polo players swim because they know they have to, so they can get up and down the pool, but water polo becomes their real love.[14]

Researching the water polo athletes at U.C. Irvine over a 2-year period was quite revealing, not only regarding the team itself but for all upper level teams. The preponderance of Brain Types at Irvine (whose polo teams normally rank in the top 10 every season) were iNtuitives. From these, ENTPs were predominant—constituting over half the team members (a percentage much higher than in the general populace). In addition, nearly 90% of the players were Extraverts.

ENTPs are not only the most frequently found Type but certainly one of the top Types in water polo. Many of America's top players have been ENTPs. In his prime, Spain's **Manuel Estiarte** (ENTP) was considered the world's top player.

Let's consider some reasons for the ENTP's excellence in water polo. First, significant and continuous amounts of energy are necessary. Not only do the players' feet rarely touch the pool bottom (it must be at least 7'6" deep), but constant energy is necessary to keep moving up and down the pool—all the while banging into and out-muscling one another. Practice sessions often last 2-3 hours (twice a day!), with the players seldom resting or leaving the pool. The high energy (Extravert) performer is ideal for water polo since it necessitates the constant use of both arms and legs.

A high-pain threshold is also required. As dominant iNtuitives, ENTPs have extraordinary abilities to play through pain. (Sensates are more pain sensitive.) ENTPs' iNtuition enables them to keep the goal of winning in mind and not be too present minded. As P's, they're not fixated on instant results. The process of the sport is more their interest. As Thinkers, ENTPs are superb strategists and aggressive athletes.

There are generally more ENTPs on college polo teams than any other Types. They can be athletic but more importantly, ENTPs can be good students. As a Type, they can study less and generally do better academically than the other athletic Brain Types.

SJs (Sensing Judgers)

SJs tend to have difficulty dealing with the varied hardships experienced in water polo. The rigors of swimming become painful and monotonous. Though ESTJs are infrequently found in polo, they're capable of being "Nolan Ryans" in the water. Ryan, the former big league fireballer, could throw a baseball nearly 100 mph. ESTJs can really zing the ball in the pool, too, as well as play extra physical.

Summary

Water polo competitors come in all Brain Types, yet some Types are found much more frequently than others. The sport is great for body and mind conditioning, and is especially productive for developing gross motor skills. Properly utilizing the legs and torso is essential for competent polo play. Fine motor movements are also placed at a premium—for swimming, treading, positioning, catching, and throwing.

WATER POLO ATHLETES & PROBABLE BRAIN TYPES

ENTP   Manuel Estiarte, John Vargas, Gary Figueroa
ENTJ   Jody Campbell, Mike Evans
ENFP   Omar Amr
ESTJ   Ryan Bailey

Coaches:
ENTJ   Steve Heaston
ENTP   John Vargas
ISTP   Ted Newland

Weightlifting

ESTP

In 1996, the man they call "Pocket Hercules" (Turkey's Naim Suleymanoglu) won a record third Olympic gold medal (1988, 1992, and 1996) in the clean and jerk, setting a new world mark at 413 pounds—nearly 3 times his body weight! The 4'11", 141-pound ESTP has consistently demonstrated his Brain Type's superior upper body strength.

Wrestling

Amateur and professional wrestling are essentially two different sports. There is little "show" in amateur wrestling; these participants mean business.

ISTP

One serious wrestler has been **Aleksandr Kareline** of the former USSR. Weighing in at 286 pounds, Kareline was the 1988, 1992, and 1996 Olympic heavyweight gold medalist in Greco Roman wrestling! He astounds his audiences with his phenomenal upper body strength, as he routinely lifts huge men off the floor before taking them down. Aleksandr's arms resemble a derrick lifting its load, not surprising for an ISTP who possesses graceful, powerful fine motor skills.

ESTP

Professional wrestling owes its success primarily to ESTPs; they are the icons of the sport. ESTPs, more than any other Type, care about their physiques, have the most muscular bodies, boast of their prowesses, and love to play to the crowds. **Hulk Hogan, Jake "The Snake" Roberts, and Brutus "The Barber" Beefcake** are only three of the many ESTPs in professional wrestling.

Though pro wrestling is entertaining, it isn't without its risks. Hulk Hogan, 6 feet 7, 290 pounds, has had his nose broken 11 times at last count.

Wrestlers and probable Brain Types

ISTP   Aleksandr Kareline
ISFP   Dennis Koslowski
ESTP   Hulk Hogan, Jake "The Snake" Roberts, "Macho Man" Randy Savage, Ric Flair, Brutus "The Barber" Beefcake, Sid Justice, Mr. Perfect
ESFP   Rulon Gardner

ENTP   The Undertaker, Jesse "The Body" Ventura, Cael Sanderson

PART FOUR

COACHES AND THE SPORTS MEDIA

18
Coaches
(and Officials)

The purpose of this chapter is to identify the Brain Types of many of America's famous coaches, professional and amateur. This information enables you to associate coaches with specific Types, and to witness and appreciate the various yet successful approaches to coaching.

ISTP

ISTPs approach coaching as they do any other sporting interest—with unparalleled zeal and intensity. They are master tacticians and attack the opposition as ISTP **Norman Schwarzkopf** did in Operation Desert Storm. They love the element of surprise and are risk takers, normally unorthodox in their game plans.

Andre Dawson spoke of his former ISTP baseball manager, **Don Zimmer**:

> Suicide squeeze, safety bunt, hit and run, just about anything anytime. I've seen him hit and run with the bases loaded, and I've only seen that twice in my entire career.[1]

ISTPs managers can have short fuses when it comes to team errors in competition. Picture football's **Mike Ditka** or basketball's **Bobby Knight**—each railing on one of his players. Their wrath has not been limited to players; umps or referees have incurred it as well.

Not all ISTP coaches are as demonstrative as these two, nor have these two always been erupting volcanoes. ISTPs have difficulty keeping their dominant, intense, Introverted Thinking in check. Non ISTP Types might find this hard to understand, yet in fairness to ISTPs, it takes great effort. Generally, strong convictions or spiritual stability is required to control their intensity in the heat of battle.

As a super tough NBA competitor, and a mercurial coach in his early NBA coaching career, ISTP **Jerry Sloan** has mellowed. He now restrains his critical thoughts and remains noticeably cool (as well as being an excellent coach).

Off the field, ISTP coaches display a milder side. They spend more time in their non judgmental Sensing function. John Feinstein, author of a book on **Bobby Knight** and another on modern tennis players, compared the two:

> Bobby Knight was the sweetest, kindest, gentlest person in the world compared to dealing with tennis players.[2]

Visual Coaches

Able to make logical split second decisions with their right hemisphere Thinking, ISTPs also rely upon their spatial giftedness to assess the field of play. **Bobby Knight** was once asked, "Is there a part of the way you played the game that translated into the way you coach it?" He responded:

> Not really. I saw the game really well as a player. I could see where guys were open. I knew how to play. I could see how the game was developing and knew where guys were and had a feel for who could play and who could do what and who couldn't. I've always had that.[3]

In 1997, 46 of major league baseball's top executives were asked to pick the best manager in the game. ISTP Jim Leyland easily outdistanced his competition. He achieved this special distinction despite having coached many teams with marginal players and records.

ESTP

As they do in every area of life, ESTPs bring a flair and excitement to coaching. Generally verbose, ESTPs like to motivate their players with uplifting speeches, inspiring action.

ESTP coaches are known for their upbeat style of play; conservatism is minimized, particularly on offense. In football, ESTP coaches are ideal for ESTP quarterbacks. Here, the footloose QB isn't afraid when he makes a mistake that he'll be reprimanded. Instead, ESTP coaches usually sense their ESTP quarterbacks are much like themselves, providing their charges latitude and encouragement even when mistakes are made. Instilling confidence in their players yields success to ESTP coaches.

Tommy Lasorda, ESTP, purveyed this coaching attitude. He used his ESTP penchant for risk-taking by using the suicide squeeze as much as anyone in professional baseball. Like all SPs, ESTPs like to capture the moment; they're the consummate tacticians. Former Dodger Don Sutton spoke of his ex skipper Lasorda in 1988:

> He goes for the jugular. Each game is a season in itself. [Pitcher] Valenzuela will pinch hit. Orel Hershiser will relieve. The game is right now, at this moment, to win or lose.[4]

Tommy Lasorda managed the L.A. Dodgers for 20 years and was enshrined in the Hall of Fame in 1997.

Playing with the Cowboys, running back Herschel Walker compared ESTP newcomer **Jimmy Johnson** with ISTJ Tom Landry:

> With Coach Landry, we used to play book football. We would stick our heads in the playbook, draw the play in our mind and then try to go through it.
>
> Coach Johnson has set us free. Now, we're playing the kind of football that we were taught as little kids and everybody just loves it.[5]

Right hemisphere Ps would especially enjoy this aspect of Johnson's coaching style. Remember, however, ESTPs' approach to coaching is no better than ISTJs'. Each does best by implementing what fits their Type, even if not all the players are happy.

Highly successful ESTP football coaches include **Bill Parcells**, who coached the New York Giants to two Super Bowl championships. (As an aside, the risk-taking ESTP Parcells usually leads the league in fourth down attempts for first downs. Punting is not always his favorite tactical maneuver.)

Prior to coaching his first Super Bowl win with the Dallas Cowboys in 1996, **Barry Switzer**, ESTP, coached the Oklahoma Sooners for 16 seasons, capturing three national championships and 12 Big Eight titles.

Survivors in Coaching

ESTPs love coaching and are winners, truths that provide them tenure in a vocation which lacks longevity. Football's **Don Shula**, ESTP, racked up his 325th NFL win in 1993, overcoming George Halas's record. Once a player under coach Shula, Bubba Smith said:

> If a nuclear bomb were to be dropped, the only two things I bet would survive would be AstroTurf and Don Shula.[6]

ISFP

Personable

Low keyed, ISFP coaches use a different tact than STPs. ISFPs get the most mileage out of their players by granting them respect and extending friendship. Though generally taciturn, ISFPs are able to convey devotion to their players, inspiring them to give their all in return. Brow beaten players often find a new start when getting a chance to play for an ISFP. In modern sports, however, players often take advantage of these coaches, forcing ISFPs to withdraw from fraternizing as they once did.

ISFP coaches have included **Lenny Wilkins, Mike Dunleavy, Paul Silas, K.C. Jones, Ray Meyers, Jerry Tarkanian, Art Shell, Gene Stallings, Jack Pardee, Cito Gaston and Don Baylor**. Though personable, ISFPs can be highly competitive in sports.

When ISFP **Mike Dunleavy** took over the coaching reins for the NBA's Los Angeles Lakers in 1990, veteran Byron Scott said of his new coach:

> I like his personality more than anything. He gets along with people. He listens. I think one of the big things everybody likes, [is that] he listens to

suggestions.[7]

In 1989, former All Pro **Art Shell** was named head coach of the L.A. Raiders. *People* magazine wrote of Shell's approach to coaching:

> Even in the bad games, his communion with the players is obvious. Unlike more mercurial coaches, Shell doesn't scream or throw tantrums. When things go wrong, he gently pulls the offender aside, wraps a beefy arm around his shoulder and speaks his mind quietly.[8]

ISFPs have been known to vent their wrath in coaching, though it is generally mild compared to some other coaching Types. Laker Byron Scott compared a Mike Dunleavy exhortation to his former coach Pat Riley (ENFJ):

> This wasn't even close.[9]

K.C. Jones coached the Boston Celtics for five seasons (1983-88) and guided them to NBA Championships in 1984 and 1986. Sensation Larry Bird spoke of his former coach:

> He's the type of guy that allows you to be relaxed, lets you play the game you can play. I admire the guy. He's one of those dreamlike coaches. He treats you like a person. He rarely raises his voice.[10]

Among **Lennie Wilkins's** accomplishments are the NBA's all-time winningest coach, head coach of the 1996 Olympic Dream Team, and a nine-time NBA All-Star as a player. His ISFP coaching style has been well chronicled. Tim Talevich wrote in 1996:

> As a coach, Wilkins is considered more of a great motivator than a great strategist. He emphasizes encouraging individual contributions to a common goal.[11]

Three-time Olympian and NBA All-Star David Robinson spoke of Wilkins's coaching approach:

> He has such a laid-back personality, it's almost deceiving, because he's a fighter. He has a great understanding of the game, and you have to listen closely to what he says.[12]

Sometimes Conservative

Surprisingly, for an SP, ISFPs are sometimes conservative and defensive minded in their approach to coaching. Generally less aggressive than the other three SPs, ISFPs' coaching can demonstrate a cautious side (particularly in football). On the other hand, if their players have great talent, ISFPs will usually let them play at their own pace.

ESFP

Though there many ESFPs in professional sports (and the general populace), few are pro head coaches. Many reasons account for this, but some are that ESFPs are not into detailed analysis or the structuring of self or groups. They're outwardly emotional and try to avoid conflict as much as possible. Playing the game was not a problem for them—it all came so naturally; organizing teaching, strategizing, and disciplining others is a much bigger ordeal—particularly at the pro level. When they are coaching, ESFPs are entertaining to watch in action. ESFP broadcaster **John Madden** carried his lively persona to the booth following a successful coaching career, much to the amusement of millions of football fans.

Former basketball great and **ESFP Magic Johnson** tried coaching in the NBA, lasting only 16 games. Player Tony Smith commented on his former L.A. Lakers coach:

> It was kind of weird. He wasn't cut out to be a coach. He was way too intense. His emotions were up and down. He probably would have had a heart attack sooner or later.[13]

Not all ESFP coaches act and react alike, but they do parallel Magic Johnson's style. They cannot sit as passively as former college coach, ISTJ John Wooden. My hope is that more ESFPs will get pro head coaching jobs; they're not only players' coaches, they're media and fan attractive.

ISTJ

ISTJs can be the best of coaches. They have established great reputations and winning records in most major sports. Some sports suit their coaching makeup better than others. Consider the likes of **John Wooden, Mike Krzyzewski, Tom Landry, and Walter Alston**. No Brain Type knows the intricacies of the games they coach like ISTJs. They are disciplined, methodical, realistic and logical strategists, easy going until game time—where their emotions run high but are kept hidden.

While highly successful, ISTJs regularly plan for impending doom. Tending to be pessimistic, they believe Murphy and his laws are always nearby. They never want to take the opponent too lightly.

No-Frills Coaches

John Wooden is regarded as the greatest college basketball coach who ever lived. The ultimate perfectionist, he won 10 NCAA titles and had a career record of 664-162 for a winning percentage of .804. His autobiography, *They Call Me Coach*, was appropriately titled.

ISTJs are not high profile persons; they avoid the limelight. It even reflects in their coaching. John Wooden believes that players and coaches often favor style over substance. He once said:

> To me, there's entirely too much showmanship. I don't think there's any question about it: There are coaches who play to the cameras, just as there are players who are wrapped up in [showing off].[14]

Winning Coaches

Hall of Fame coach **Tom Landry** played and coached in the NFL for 40 years. With the Dallas Cowboys, he had 20 straight winning seasons, 18 playoffs, 5 Super Bowl appearances, and 2 Super Bowl championships.

Hall of Famer **Walter Alston** coached seven pennant winners and four world championships in his 23-year career as manager of the Brooklyn and Los Angeles Dodgers.

Basketball coach **Mike Krzyzewski** (shuh-shef-skee), recognized for his success with the Duke Blue Devils, has carried on the ISTJ winning tradition of the venerable John Wooden. Coach "K" has quietly led Duke to seven Final Four berths in nine years, from 1986 through 1994!

Coach K is second among active coaches in NCAA Tournament winning percentage, just behind his former coach, huggable Bobby Knight (ISTP). Unlike his former mentor, ISTJ Mike only throws chairs and chastises players in his mind or in private, not in public. His left-brained J approach will generally be much more under control than Bobby's spontaneous right-brained P.

Coach K finally got his due reward by winning the 1991 NCAA Tournament. He had acquired the players who could show the coaching genius of their coach. Duke won in style, beating the team many were calling the best college team of all time, UNLV. In 1992, Coach K and his Blue Devils won the NCAA Championship again, the first set of back to back college basketball titles since UCLA in 1972 73.

Following the '92 championship game, Duke player Brian Davis spoke of Coach K:

> It begins with Coach. At the start of the year, he laid out the game plan we needed to win the national championship and stuck to it . . . I don't think we were ever mentally fatigued because Coach puts us on the mindset that we never feel tired. And, at the same time, he doesn't whip us.[15]

Another ISTJ coach in the 1991 NCAA tournament demonstrated his coaching excellence. Kansas coach **Roy Williams** took a team of unknowns to the final game, losing to Coach K and his Blue Devils. In the process, the Jayhawks upended many favorites.

Coach Williams got his first head coaching position in 1989, taking over a decimated Kansas program on probation. By the next season, 1990, Williams was named national coach of the year, after leading Kansas to a 30-5 record. In 1991, he led his Jayhawks to the NCAA Finals! Only one coach in NCAA history has won more games in his first three seasons. For an encore in 1992, Coach Roy won coach of the year again. Roy Williams knows, like any good coach, you've got to have the horses to consistently win. His future success will certainly depend on recruiting, too.

To say that ISTJs can be good high school and college basketball coaches is an understatement. With experience and proper tutelage, they develop their innate expertise.

Perfecters

Roy Williams sat under his mentor, North Carolina's Dean Smith, for ten years. Here he gained valuable knowledge and insight. Out on his own, he has had a chance to do what ISTJs do best, perfect something already in existence.

Long time Temple coach, John Chaney, said of Williams' style of coaching:

> I think [Kansas] runs Dean's system better than he does.[16]

One of Williams' players at Kansas said of his coach:

> Coach Williams is a perfectionist. We have all our drills scheduled out in practice, but we usually go over the time set aside for each drill because coach Williams wants to get it perfect.[17]

Dandy Don Meredith, ESFP, once described his former coach, **Tom Landry**:

> He's a perfectionist. If he was married to Raquel Welch, he'd expect her to cook.[18]

Comprehensive Playbook

Despite their conservatism, ISTJ coaches break the game down so minutely they can end up with vast offensive schemes. Though leery of change in their personal lives, they're known to throw in new looks when coaching. Though not strong in typological iNtuition, ISTJs are often considered creative coaches.

Humble Mentors

The *L.A. Times* wrotes of coach **Roy Williams**:

> Williams is humble to a fault, always crediting players and downplaying his role. He doesn't display his awards in his office, which is decorated instead with portraits of six previous Kansas coaches and the Jayhawks' two national championship teams.[19]

Disciplinarians

ISTJs coaches give a high regard to discipline. NBA star Sam Perkins said Roy Williams was instrumental in getting him to go to North Carolina:

> He's a disciplinarian type coach . . . You have to do it his way. Once you did that, he was not only a coach but a friend.[20]

Perkins' remark hits the ISTJ nail on the head. Unfortunately, this coaching Type will incur more problems in modern times than in former years. As many young players become more independent and disrespectful to their coaches, the ISTJ's job becomes more difficult. Some sports institutions and organizations will not support coaches who have a balanced view of discipline, yielding instead to the independent young stars that could make a name or buck for their team or school.

ISTJ coaches will not stay in an environment that does not allow them to exercise discipline. They just do not have the mental energy to continually combat those who disagree. (Their Brain Type cousins, ESTJs, are much better at sticking in there to break the wild stallions. ESTJs are more likely to let everyone else quit before they give up trying to establish disciplines and order.)

ESTJ

"Logically pragmatic" describes the ESTJ coach. With a minimum of bells and whistles, they win games working harder than the opponent. ESTJ coaches stress fundamentals while valuing knowledge of their sport. They are logistical specialists.

Many ESTJ coaches are known for their "My way or the highway" personalities. They can be tough, candid, tactless, and matter-of-fact. On the other hand, there are some, due to their nurtured upbringings and being influenced by "Feeling" people, who are much more personable and diplomatic.

In the year 2000, veteran NBA coach, **George Karl** (ESTJ) demonstrated his Type tendencies. Columnist Michael Bauman wrote:

> In his first two years as coach of the Milwaukee Bucks, Karl took a fairly conventional approach in public discussions about his players. He was generally protective, paternal, upbeat. But this

season, as the Bucks fail to meet Karl's standards for not only performance but commitment, the coach has removed the rhetorical gloves. No more feelings will be spared. No more unpleasant truths will be shaded.[21]

Coach Karl said to the media:

> [Team owner] Sen. (Herb) Kohl's paying these (expletives) $50 million. Don't they have to have some degree of accountability?
>
> Our fundamental habits got to change. We've done it by film, we've done it by putting our arm around them, we've done it by compromising. Now it's got to change, or we're just going to be in this pool of mediocrity.[22]

ESTJs' relationships become most strained with right-brained Perceiving Types, considering that the ESTJ is the most structured of the here-and-now Brain Types—focusing on inanimate matters. EPs sometimes butt heads with ESTJs. EPs are the least apt to want someone else's structure imposed upon them.

ESTJs also get their share of gray hair from Feelers (F). They often view them as too soft, sensitive, or emotional. **George Karl** spoke of his ESFP starting 2 guard:

> I see Ray Allen smile when he makes a mistake. He missed a layup in the Atlanta game, one-point lead, missed a layup and laughed about it. I don't see great players laughing. And it drives me crazy. Am I wrong?[23]

Virtually every Brain Type has smiled after a mistake in hoops, but it is true that some Types will appear more nonchalant and carefree than others. ESFPs, in particular, are happy-go-lucky people, and prone to behaving in basketball as did Ray Allen. It isn't that they don't care, they're just not critical folks and prefer to treat matters more lightheartedly. As a matter of fact, ESFP Magic Johnson was known to smile after making mistakes—but when you coach a perennial All-Star, it's easier to accept his happy go lucky demeanor after a snafu.

Legendary football coach **George Allen**, ESTJ, demonstrated toughness, yet doled out affection for those who gave it their all. Allen's daughter, Jennifer, recalled her father:

> Dad hated being nice. He hated interviews. He hated questions. . . . Dad's training camp was brutal. . . . He said it was his favorite time of year: everything was organized, structured, disciplined. He made his team practice three times a day in full pads at full speed under the full California summer sun. . . . He forbade drinking water on the field. . . Players called dad's training camp "concentration camp," and they nicknamed Dad "Hitler."[24]

ESTJ coaches also have reputations for not winning the big games. This is a fair appraisal in many cases. What many critics fail to recognize, however, is that ESTJs are often the coaches who make it to the final dance. They get there through imposed structure and an emphasis on fundamentals throughout the season. They play to win and don't settle for anything less. The teams practice self discipline: they win many close games. Making fewer mistakes than the opponent pays off. Yet playoff time is not quite the same. Even the most undisciplined players on other teams become more focused, and the ESTJ coach does not have the same advantage.

ESTJs tend not to adjust to the opponent come playoff time. ESTJs can get stuck in their ways of doing things. Their philosophy often is, "We'll play our game and they'll have to adjust to us." That's good, but it's only half the formula. Coaches must also improvise to overcome their opponents.

Longtime college football coach, ESTJ **Bo Schembechler** of Michigan, tended to be set in his ways. He retired with a Rose Bowl record of 2 wins and 8 losses. Many a football pundit wondered why Bo didn't adjust better to the West Coast style of play, particularly the passing game. Prior to understanding the inborn designs of people, I was always frustrated, wondering why certain coaches didn't try to adapt during games when opponents strongly had the upper hand. Understanding Brain Types has helped me deal with this former trauma.

Hope for the Inflexible

Now that I've dealt with my past in this brief catharsis, I want to say that ESTJs can be great coaches. They are best, however, when they make a concerted effort to adapt to others. Lightening their standards a little, while getting some help with their sometimes neglected iNtuition, pays off, especially at playoff time. They must not be afraid in football to have a free wheeling ESTP at quarterback. ESTP John Elway served ESTJ **Dan Reeves** well at Denver. Despite their strained relationship, they participated in 3 Super Bowls over a 4 year period. Reeves showed more latitude in the early 1990s by letting Elway call some of his own plays. Nonetheless, the two struggled with compatibility. Had coach Reeves understood Elway's ESTP Brain Type, their rapport and games would have been better.

A candidate for most flexible ESTJ coach of the 1990s is former Washington Huskies' coach **Don James**. Capturing their second straight Rose Bowl in 1992, the Huskies also tied for the national championship. *Sports Illustrated* offered a profile of James's Type:

> James is serious, stern, authoritarian. Adhere exactly to the schedule, write everything down, evaluate, calculate, make no exceptions, do it my way or the highway. He is depressingly well organized and has said a few thousand times, 'A tidy ship is a happy ship.'[25]

S.I. continued:

> And the reason James is so successful is that no other coach has demonstrated the willingness to change every one of his theories, plans and schemes as James has. And that flies in the face of everything James seems to be. When unmasked, one of football's most intransigent coaches is actually the ultimate flexible man.[26]

It seems that James began revamping his coaching philosophy around age 56, adapting it to his players and the changing times. He is living proof that ESTJs are capable of altering their coaching philosophy.

A coach James once fired discussed his boss's character:

> Coach James is an outstanding football coach and great human being. He's consistent, fair, honest. He's as good as there is.[27]

"The Future is Now"

ESTJ football coach **George Allen** was known for stressing the ESTJ motto, "The future is now!" Needless to say, ESTJs want instant results. When Allen took the Rams over, they hadn't won in 10 years. Allen turned things around, won every season, and was voted NFL Coach of the Year twice. He then took over the Redskins who hadn't won in 30 years and again won every season and earned Coach of the Year two more times.

George Allen went back to college coaching shortly before his death. The *L.A. Times* reported of his fitness and determination at 72:

> Despite his age, Allen put in 18 hour days seven days a week at Long Beach. He jogged daily and would always stretch and run sprints with his players during practice.[28]

George Allen was loved and respected by most of those who played for him. Though tough and disciplined, he didn't ask any more from others than he required of himself.

ESTJs are particularly gifted at getting the most out of ordinary players. Emphasizing hard work, self discipline, team unity, fundamentals, and never-say-die goes a long way with teachable players. Last, ESTJ coaches should give extra effort to communicating with and relating to players.

Durable

ESTJs are the most persevering of all coaches. They're born to supervise people and retirement doesn't come easily. As the old saying goes, they prefer to die with their boots on. In 1997, ESTJs **Dick Motta** and **Bill Fitch** were the only NBA coaches in the unwelcomed category of having lost over 1,000 NBA games. Yet these two men were regarded as top-notch coaches. Their logistical intelligence and experience enabled them to still be successful in the ever-changing world of the NBA. In 1997, Fitch also held the career coaching record for NBA wins.

1997 also saw **Dean Smith** (ESTJ) establish the NCAA career record for wins, surpassing basketball's legendary Adolph Rupp. After 35 years at North Carolina University, Smith retired with 879 collegiate wins.

INTJ

Though INTJs are not commonly found in the U.S. populace or professional coaching ranks, they have made their mark as one of the top coaching Types. Like all NTs, INTJs are most gifted with their abstract, logical intellect. Coaching is an ideal place for INTJs to exercise their smarts. As Introverted Js, they are capable of writing the most comprehensive, detailed books on their sport. Their brains rarely shut off, frequently keeping them up late to consider another coaching possibility. INTJ coaches have included **Don Nelson, Phil Jackson, Tony La Russa, and George Seifert**.

Heady, Independent

Basketball coach **Phil Jackson** won his first NBA title in 1991 with the Chicago Bulls by employing his erudite coaching ways and by relying on the game's all-time talented player—Michael Jordan. By 1997, Jackson had captured his fifth NBA title (all with Michael Jordan). Consider some of Jackson's background.

In college, he had a composite major consisting of psychology, religion, and philosophy. In 1975, in his more rebellious days, Jackson published a book (*Maverick*) about his basketball career. It was aptly named for the most independent of Types, the INTJ. An avid reader, Jackson has regularly given his players non basketball books to read, not a favorite pastime for many NBAers.

Jackson's former coaches shed light on INTJ Phil. Bill Fitch commented:

> Tell you the truth, I'm surprised he got into coaching.[29]

Red Holzman said:

> Not that he couldn't handle it, but because I thought he would be a Bill Bradley type, maybe a senator from North Dakota.[30]

Both Fitch and Holzman recognized Jackson's cerebral giftedness. (As an aside, INTJs are not as apt to get into politics as ENTJs, like Bradley. Constant interacting with people and expending lots of Extraverted energy is harder for INTJs.)

Basketball coach **Paul Westhead**, INTJ, instituted the creative run and gun offense at Loyola Marymount College. His intellect was quickly recognized. Former Alabama coach Wimp Anderson spoke of Westhead:

> Paul's a smart guy. Paul knows English, Shakespeare, drama, all that crap. He's too smart. He knows Longfellow, Shortfellow....[31]

Paradoxical to Westhead's mental giftedness and thoroughness, he and other INTJs like to do things as efficiently as possible, even if it means doing things simply. For instance, consider Westhead's playbook at Loyola. He once showed that it was three pages, double spaced, "with a lot of big pictures."[32] Paul has proved that he's a creative and scholarly teacher. Nevertheless he simplified the game to its essence.

Some folks wonder why Westhead and Magic Johnson had a rift when Paul was coaching the L.A. Lakers. Time has shown Johnson to be a superb player and Westhead to be a very good coach. Many wonder what could have possibly been the problem. I can see one obvious problem: They are opposite Brain Types (Westhead an INTJ and Johnson an ESFP). That in itself not only creates a communication problem but an understanding problem as well. Opposite Types have greater difficulty seeing eye to-eye under pressure than any other combination. As long as things are mellow, no problem, but when tension comes, you'd better find a conciliator.

In 1991, Oakland A's skipper **Tony La Russa** was known for being:

> ... a lawyer, vegetarian, balletomane, American Indian patron and animal shelter executive.[33]

Brainy and eclectic are words commonly used to describe INTJs like La Russa, often called the best manager in baseball. His wife said:

> On opening day, Tony checks out. The rest of the [season], his body may come home, but his head is always in baseball. He is consumed by it.[34]

INTJs and ISTJs are similar in many ways; both can be consumed by their interests to which they devote endless hours in study. La Russa spent 12 of his 16 off seasons as a baseball player in school, continuing his education.

Night Owls

INTJs tend to burn the midnight oil, especially when motivated to complete a task. Once getting into the habit of staying up late, they find it difficult to go to bed early. Television's Chris Sager commented after interviewing NBA coaches for a TV special:

> **Don Nelson** walked in, sat down, put his feet up on the desk, basketball shoes and all, and suddenly he was a member of the crew. He hung

out until 5 a.m., claiming it was 2 a.m. Golden State [Warriors] time.[35]

Value Knowledge

In 1992, Don Nelson was named NBA coach of the year for an unprecedented third time. When Nelson played for the Boston Celtics, he would visit coach Red Auerbach's office before games:

> I'd walk in during his nap [to talk basketball].[36]

This is definitely not a common practice among players in the NBA.

Unorthodox, Creative

Mike Dunleavy, friend and former coaching disciple of Don Nelson, spoke of his former boss, in 1991:

> Do I know his mind? Nobody knows his mind. He doesn't even know his mind. I don't think ultimately he knows what he's going to do until he does it. Then he'll try something different, just to be different.[37]

Dunleavy also commented, laughing:

> I don't think anything he does is original. I think he steals everything.[38]

Dunleavy's second comment could lead us to believe that Nelson is not original or creative. Nothing could be farther from the truth. INTJs are the supreme inventors. Because there is "little new under the sun," even highly creative people improvise primarily from that which is already known. Nelson, like all INTJs, is exceptionally creative with logical matters. Don has already left his inventive impact in pro hoops; he is regarded as the father of the modern NBA defense.

Nelson has shown his unorthodoxy in numerous ways. Coach Rick Majerus, former assistant to Nelson said:

> A lot of guys do what I call the NBA thing. They do the NBA thing in the draft, the NBA thing in the trades. Nelly's [Nelson] not afraid to push the parameters of what others would perceive as acceptable . . . .[39] (Insert added.)

Let's not forget that coach Nelson was independent enough in the 1980s to wear a suit and taped up tennis shoes on the sideline during NBA games. Somehow, I can't imagine the dapper ENFJ Pat Riley doing that, or most other Brain Types, for that matter.

Self-Critical

Don Nelson has had a reputation for taking losses hard. INTJs, like all NTs, and particularly Introverted NTs, do their utmost to avoid failure and incompetency. Because they are intellectually astute, they view a loss as something that could have been prevented if they had just been more competent. Coach Rick Majerus again spoke of Nelson:

> I think Nelly takes it home with him. He points the finger at himself. It's like, 'We won, but I lost.'[40]

ENTJ

ENTJ coaches typify their "Fieldmarshal," "C.E.O." descriptions. They can be superb strategists, teachers, motivators, and leaders. Combining their competitive aggressiveness with their NT smarts, ENTJs are normally victors in games and battles. Past and present ENTJ coaches include **Vince Lombardi, Paul Brown, Dennis Green, Larry Brown, Rick Pitino, Joe Torre, Lou Piniella,** and **Bobby Valentine.** In 1997, Rick Pitino set a new standard for coaches' compensation, racking up a 10-year contract worth a reported $50 million.

Legendary coach **Vince Lombardi** was obsessed with excellence and success, common goals for ENTJs. Taking over a Green Bay Packer team that had won only one game the previous year, Lombardi won seven in his first season. He captured a Western Division title in his second, and five NFL championships in seven years, including two Super Bowls. In his early years, Lombardi prepared for his future greatness by holding a full time job while attending law school, followed by coaching three sports and teaching high school Latin, chemistry, physics and algebra. Vince Lombardi fully developed his ENTJ abilities, culminating in coaching eminence.

In 1998, **Joe Torre** was voted baseball's manager of the year, guiding the New York Yankees to a record 125 victories and a World Series championship—his second in a three year period.

Always Improving

The *L.A. Times* reported on Bobby Valentine's efforts to prepare for the 1992 season:

> At least one major league baseball manager views the off season as an opportunity for self improvement. Bobby Valentine of the Texas Rangers, hoping to better communicate with Latin Players on his team, is studying Spanish at a Berlitz school. And he isn't learning just a few words and phrases. He's taking the intensive course—100 hours in 10 days.[41]

Innovative

In 1946, ENTJ **Paul Brown** formed a professional football team in Cleveland that bore his name. He coached the Browns to seven championships. Brown utilized his strong left hemisphere iNtuition by instituting training camps, college scouting, game films, inventing the playbook, and being the first coach to signal plays from the sidelines.

Not all ENTJ coaches are regarded as innovative. Nevertheless, they are adept with iNtuition, capable of being highly creative.

Critiquers

ENTJs, like ESTJs, routinely critique their players. (The Extraverted, Thinking, left hemisphere Judgers (ETJs) are most apt to do this.) Many athletes believe it is excessive. Assuming the L.A. Clippers' coaching position in 1992, **Larry Brown** shared his ENTJ sentiments:

> You've got to adjust to dealing with players now. A lot of guys, you can say things to, and the first thing on their mind is, 'Coach wants to make me better.' Then there's some who think you're getting on them all the time. I think there's a fine balance. My job now is to give these guys the confidence to get them to become better players.[42]

Though they mean well in demanding the best, ETJs (ENTJ and ESTJ) should regularly critique their communications with players. ENTJs (and all coaching Types) will do well to recognize athletes' successes as well as mistakes. They should at least be communicated with on a one to one ratio. Above all, what they do right should be stressed.

ENTP

Bright and Witty

We have already identified iNtuitive Thinkers (NTs) as the most logically abstract. ENTPs are most adept at Extraverting their creativity and wit, which explains why the plethora of well known comedians are this Type. ENTP coaches are known for their levity, though competition can inhibit it. Some ENTP coaches past and present include **Red Auerbauch, Frank Layden, Chuck Daly, Al McGuire, Jim Valvano, Leo Durocher, Earl Weaver, Doug Rader, Lou Holtz, and Digger Phelps**.

Former player Elrod Hendricks once spoke of his manager **Earl Weaver**:

> I saw him get thrown out of so many ball games because of the rules. Earl probably knew the rules too good for the umps. They don't like to hear others telling them the rules; they feel they know the rule book better than anybody else. He was an encyclopedia of baseball . . . .[43]

Pitcher Kirk McCaskill, ENTJ, spoke of his former ENTP coach **Doug Rader**:

> What I've discovered and what's important is his intelligence and how well read he is. He really helped me out a lot. He's helped me to learn how to relax and, at the same time, challenge me.[44]

Pitcher Mike Smithson said of Rader:

> He's very smart, scholarly smart. He's book smart and street smart . . . .[45]

Slugger Dave Winfield described Rader as:

> . . . a more verbal manager than any I've heard.[46]

And retired Winfield heard many.

Responding to Rader's past zany reputation (like urging Little Leaguers to eat baseball cards because "they have lots of information on them," or doing crazy things to get house guests to leave, Mike Smithson said:

It's not fair to say he's a flake or off the wall because he likes to have fun.[47]

All Ps like to have fun and the ENTP is no exception; they just apply more creativity to their fun than most.

Dr. Jekyll, Mr. Hyde

A common persona of ENTPs is one of "adjust to anything." Yet in matters of importance to them, they expect competency, giving little latitude for error. Football coach **Lou Holtz** was once asked if he were a hands on coach:

> I'm definitely a hands on coach. My hands are usually around a throat, I might add.[48]

Earl Weaver was thrown out of more games than any other manager in pro baseball history. Weaver's Baltimore Orioles finished first or second 13 times in his 15 years of managing.

Leo Durocher was one of baseball's most successful yet controversial characters. Nicknamed Leo the Lip, he was known for saying, "Nice guys finish last." Durocher was inspirational to his players and infuriating to opposing teams. Broadcaster Lindsey Nelson, who worked with Durocher for 3 years on TV, once said:

> There were two different Leos . . . he was a brilliant man, and a quick study. He would remember everything you'd tell him.[49]

Nelson said Durocher was pleasant and humble in their private breakfast conversations, explaining further, however:

> Then after breakfast, we'd get up and go to the hotel elevator. All it would take would be for one other person to be on that elevator, and Leo would switch into character—a loud braggart. But that wasn't the real Leo at all.[50]

ENTPs love a stage and an audience, and one person on an elevator will do.

Outwardly Candid

ENTP coaches can use their creative, logical skills to edify or demean. They often say things for shock value—intending to galvanize others into greater productivity. Often what they say is not what they mean. Nevertheless, if it'll get someone to move, they'll risk offending them. Like all Brain Types, sometimes strengths become weaknesses.

Innovative

In the late 1980s, football coach **John Jenkins** boldly made his presence known with the Houston Cougars. Employing the most wide open offense in college football, ENTP Jenkins uniquely expanded the run and shoot. Innovation comes easily for ENTPs like John; controlling it is another matter. Many coaches were unable to understand or tolerate Jenkins' idiosyncrasies. Understanding his Brain Type would help.

A long and entertaining book could be written on ENTP coaches. For now, let's remember they can be excellent coaches, though not always predictable on or off the field. When they leave coaching, they can always try their hand at comedy or commentating.

ENFJ

As coaches, ENFJs are usually fashionably dressed and personable to the public and press. Of all the iNtuitive Types, male and female, I have found ENFJs to be the most concerned about their appearance. They love to coach, utilizing their dominant, analytic left hemisphere. Preparing thoroughly for games, ENFJs love to motivate their players. Past and present ENFJ coaches include **Pat Riley, Matt Guokas, Lute Olson, Bill Walsh, John Robinson, Dick Vermeil,** and **Terry Donahue**.

Highly successful NBA coach **Pat Riley** articulated the role of professional coach:

> Being the leader is a very difficult thing. It's a fine line. While you have to be one of the fellas—you keep punching what I call that membership card—you have to motivate players. . . . Being a leader is a tough job 'cause you're out there alone.[51]

Riley coached the L.A. Lakers to four National Basketball Association titles in seven seasons. In 1997, he became only the second three-time NBA coach of the year. (INTJ Don Nelson was the first.) Riley is the first to win with three teams: the Lakers (1990), the Knicks (1993), and the Heat (1997).

Like to Impact People

Having coached his San Francisco 49ers to two Super Bowl titles and taking a shot at broadcasting, **Bill Walsh** returned to college coaching in 1992. While announcing for TV, Walsh interviewed many college players. He commented:

> We met some magnificent young people. That in itself reminded me that I might be of more value somewhere other than just remarking on 10 different ways on how to fumble a football on television.[52]

Columnist Larry Stewart wrote of Walsh's broadcasting:

> What's appealing about Walsh, besides his strong, candid opinions, is a relaxed, uncontrived style. He comes across as genuine, without an ounce of phoniness, and that counts for a lot. Walsh, a pleasant man both on and off the air, is someone you would like to invite into your living room to watch a game.[53]

Basketball coach **Lute Olson** has added his ENFJ touch to coaching at the University of Arizona. In addition to his NF interest in people, he has a master's degree in education psychology and guidance. Olson is known to pick up recruits at the airport personally, and allow his players the power of veto if they think a recruiting prospect will not fit into their program. Olson stresses strength of character and team camaraderie. In 1997, his efforts paid off with a NCAA Championship title.

Though usually highly optimistic, ENFJs can paradoxically be genuine worriers. This double edged sword can wear heavily on them in time.

ENFP

ENFPs are energetic, charming, persistent and innovative, coaching notwithstanding. Following a detailed game plan, like some other Types, is hardly their style. ENFP coaches love to improvise on the spot during the game, whether or not it makes sense. Feeling, not Thinking, is their favorite decision making brain function. Thus, they often follow their gut level iNtuition.

Basketball coach John MacLeod spoke of retired NBA coach and ENFP, **Cotton Fitzsimmons**:

> The amazing thing about him is, he not only changes his lineup game to game, but half to half.[54]

Cotton accurately sized himself up:

> Let's face it, I'm an unorthodox coach. I just change 'em around.[55]

Longtime Georgia Tech basketball coach, **Bobby Cremins**, personified his ENFP Type. Cremins was considered a good recruiter of players but rapped as a weak X and O man. He responded to a reporter in 1990, "I've heard that and it's crap." Pointing to his Yellow Jacket star players Scott, Oliver and Anderson, he said, "Ask them if I can coach." As the three were all on the verge of laughing, he said: "No, don't ask them."[56]

Let's consider Cremins as a recruiter. ENFPs are fabulous recruiters of people; a reason for dubbing them "Pied Pipers." **Bob Hope, Sammy Davis Jr., Rev. Robert Schuller, Oprah Winfrey, Goldie Hawn,** and **Richard Simmons** are just a few celebrities that have demonstrated their ENFP people magnetism. ENFPs exude optimistic warmth to their audiences. No one needs to convince me Bobby Cremins can recruit.

What about Cremins as a coach? Not being privy to his coaching methods, I do know something about how the ENFP Brain Type functions. Typology and neuroscience identify the ENFP as a right-brained, dominant iNtuitive. Creativity, seeing the "big picture," and adapting to the moment (especially with people) are among Cremins' major strengths. All of these traits are beneficial in coaching. Unfortunately, few basketball coaches are ENFPs—failing to fit the usual coaching mold of structure and deep analysis.

ENFPs are able to analyze (break down) matters, yet their preference is for synthesizing (putting together). They prefer to teach the whole, the concept, as a higher priority than the parts, the details. Both concepts and parts are important in coaching (and ENFPs would agree), but ENFPs stress the former because that is where they're most adept. Bobby Cremins took his Georgia Tech team to the 1990 NCAA Final Four, largely on his coaching skills. Give Cremins at least adequate talent and he knows how to win; he has proven this over the years.

Exuberant, Personable

When **Cremins** tried to recruit high school phenom Bruce Dalrymple, his former assistant George Felton said:

> Bobby sat down with him, started drawing plays on a piece of notebook paper, and got so excited he started punching holes in the paper. That paper looked like ashes before he got through. Bruce signed.[57]

Felton also related:

> They all sign with Bobby because he cares.[58]

ENFPs are similar to ENTPs in that they like to perform for an audience. If they get one, they can be quiet at home. If not, they'll make their family their audience. Cotton Fitzsimmon's wife spoke of her husband and his TV show, in 1990:

> He loves doing that show. It's fun for him. When that camera goes on, he's on. But at home, I have trouble getting him to open his mouth sometimes.[59]

Before retiring in 1992, ENFP **Lou Carnesecca** coached basketball at St. Johns for 24 seasons. The *L.A. Times* wrote:

> His teams, led by Chris Mullin and Walter Berry, might not have earned him as much notice as did his penchant for sweaters, some rather gaudy, instead of the traditional jacket and tie, and his ability to run and jump on the sidelines like a man 20 years his junior.[60]

Always on the Go

ENFPs are persons on the move, finding it difficult to sit still. Easily bored, they love to be involved in fun and inspirational activity. Former Yellow Jacket star Tom Hammonds once asked Bobby Cremins if he would like to go fishing sometime. His coach responded:

> Sure, how long does it take?[61]

Strong Values

ENFPs develop strong values in life. NBA star John Salley tells of going to play for Cremins in college:

> Everybody else had been telling me about the girls and the good times. Coach told me I would have to give up six hours of my social life each day. When you're a kid, you don't want to give up six hours of ANYTHING. But I went down there and spent almost my whole visit with the academic adviser.[62]

ENFPs bring a unique dimension to coaching that is often misunderstood yet tremendously refreshing.

Though far from complete, here is a list of coaches and team owners and their probable Brain Types.

ISFP
Baseball: Cito Gaston, Don Baylor, Tony Perez, Grady Little
Basketball: Lenny Wilkens, Mike Dunleavy, K.C. Jones, Paul Silas, Don Chaney, Jerry Tarkanian
Football: Art Shell, Jack Pardee, Gene Stallings, Eddie Robinson

ESFP
Football: John Madden, Wayne Fontes, Isiah Thomas

ISTP
Baseball: Don Zimmer, Jim Leyland Whitey Herzog
Basketball: Jerry Sloan, Larry Bird, Jerry West, Bobby Knight, Jim Keady, Scott Skiles, Pat Summitt
Football: Mike Ditka, Bobby Ross, Bill Cowher, Jim Haslett
Water Polo: Ted Newland

ESTP
Baseball: Tommy Lasorda, Dusty Baker, Rene Lachemann, Frank Robinson, Jim Lefebvre
Basketball: Doug Collins, Denny Crum
Football: Don Shula, Bill Parcells, Jimmy Johnson, Steve Spurrier, Barry Switzer
Hockey: Barry Melrose

ISTJ
Baseball: Walter Alston, Marcel Lachemann,
Basketball: John Wooden, Mike Krzyzewski, Roy Williams, Steve Fisher, Rick Adelman
Football: Tom Landry, Tom Osborne

ESTJ
Baseball: Bruce Bochy, Bob Boone
Basketball: Dick Motta, Bill Fitch, Rudy Tomjanovich, George Karl, Chris Ford, Dean Smith, John Thompson, Jim Boeheim, Dale Brown, Jim Harrick, Billy Tubbs
Football: Dan Reeves, Mike Holmgren, George Allen, Chuck Knox, Rich Brooks, Buddy Ryan, Andy Reid, Bo Schembechler, Don James
Golf: Jack Grout
Owners: Marge Schott

INFP
Basketball: Maurice Cheeks
Football: Tony Dungy

ENFP
Basketball: Cotton Fitzsimmons, M.L. Carr, Quinn Buckner, Johnny Davis, Bobby Cremins, Lou Carnesecca,
Gymnastics: Bela Karolyi
Tennis: Vic Braden

ENFJ
Basketball: Pat Riley, Del Harris, Matt Guokas Jr., Stu Jackson, Lute Olson, John MacLeod, Steve Lavin
Football: Bill Walsh, Marty Schottenheimer, Dick Vermeil, Ara Parseghian, Terry Donahue, John Robinson

INTP
Football: Tyrone Willingham

ENTP
Baseball: Leo Durocher, Earl Weaver,
              Doug Rader, Sparky Anderson,
              Stump Merrill, Butch Hobson
Basketball: "Red" Auerbach, Chuck Daly, Frank
              Layden, Kevin Loughery, Hubie Brown,
              Bernie Bickerstaff, Jimmy Lynam, Mike
              Fratello, Jim Cleamons, Jimmy Rodgers,
              Darrell Walker, Jerry Reynolds, Bill
              Russell, Al McGuire, Digger Phelps, Rollie
              Massimino, Jim Valvano, Pete Carril, Bob
              Huggins, George Raveling
Football: Lou Holtz, Jeff Fisher, Bobby Bowden,
              Gary Barnett, Rick Neuheisel,
              Jerry Glanville
Hockey: Larry Robinson
Tennis: Ion Tiriac
Owners: Ted Turner, Eddie DeBartolo Jr.,
              Bud Adams, Art Modell, Jack Kent Cooke,
              Dr. Jerry Buss, Jerry Reinsdorf, Pat Croce,
              Mark Cuban

INTJ
Baseball: Tony LaRussa
Basketball: Don Nelson, Phil Jackson, Bill Hanzlik,
              Rick Carlisle, Paul Westhead,
              Gary Williams, Dave Odom
Football: George Seifert, Jim Fassel
Owner: Al Davis, Bud Selig

ENTJ
Baseball: Joe Torre, Lou Piniella, Bobby Valentine,
              Jeff Torborg, Jim Riggleman,
              Mike Hargrove, Buck Showalter
Basketball: Larry Brown, Rick Pitino, John Calipari,
              Dave Cowens, Brian Hill, P.J. Carlesimo,
              Jeff Van Gundy, Dan Issel,
              Nolan Richardson, Mike Montgomery,
              Pete Gillen
Football: Vince Lombardi, Paul Brown,
              Bill Belichick, Brian Billick, John Gruden,
              Dennis Green, Dom Capers,
              Steve Mariucci, Mike White, Jim Mora

Referees and Umpires

It doesn't take long for serious sports fans to realize that game officials have their own styles. As Types relate to all other things people do in life, Types relate to officiating.

The referee or umpire can be as instrumental in the outcome of a close game as the star player or coach. I find it amusing when watching a game on TV (and irksome when I'm coaching!) to see officials lose their objectivity and go overboard with their Brain Types. Conversely, I enjoy seeing officials use their Types in a fair an objective manner.

Knowing the Brain Types of officials can be more than a cognitive benefit. When coaching, I have discovered that by trying to relate specifically to the officials' Brain Types (talking to them in their Type lingo and about their Type interests, before and during the game), I can get them to be more objective and fair to my team. This approach may not be as influential at the pro level (where officials are more closely evaluated for objectivity and accuracy).

For instance, I might address **NT** officials from an intellectual standpoint, while assuring them they are in control of the game. I try not to voice displeasure with NTs. (They disdain being told they're incompetent before others.) I appeal to **SJ** officials by asking them about specific rules, which they know and prize so dearly, allowing them to explain. (All Thinkers are big on rules.) I also try to grant SJs extra respect. I try to relate to **NFs** on a more personal basis. And for the **SPs**, I crack some jokes, try to find out what they've been up to in their sports lives, and try to make it a fast paced, fun time all around. They probably have lots of activities to get to afterwards.

Treating officials according to their Type uniqueness can make them your friends, which is desirable. This enables me to be more objective regarding them, understanding better why they may make a bad call. If I feel compelled to say something corrective, I try to communicate it a way they find acceptable.

Here are some prominent professional officials and their probable Brain Types.

SJs	SPORT	TYPE
Doug Harvey	MLB	ESTJ

SPs

Pam Postema	MLB	ESTP
Dee Kantner	NBA	ESTP
Mills Lane	Boxing	ISTP

NTs

Gene Tunney	NFL	ENTJ
Jeff Bergman	NFL	ENTJ
Earl Strom	NBA	ENTJ
Ted Bernhardt	NBA	ENTJ
Bill Spooner	NBA	ENTJ
Richie Powers	NBA	ENTP
Mike Mathis	NBA	ENTP
Ed T. Rush	NBA	ENTP
David Jones	NBA	ENTP
Paul Mihalak	NBA	ENTP
Woody Mayfield	NBA	ENTP
Al Clark	NBA	ENTP
Dick Bavetta	NBA	INTJ

19
Sports Media

This chapter offers sports fans an opportunity to better understand the people who report sports as well as the comments they make. Persons in the sports media includes radio, television, newspaper, and magazine personalities. They convey a multitude of styles while reporting sports. Most of us have our favorite and least favorite sports reporters. Interestingly, however, we will see that some of our best and least liked media persons are of the same Brain Types.

ENTJ

Competent

No Brain Type dominates TV sports broadcasting more than the ENTJ. After all, who is more competent to handle the requirements of the booth? ENTJs project sound logic and an expansive vocabulary imbued with creative commentary. Approaching sports media work as they would the presidency of a corporation, they master their work with knowledge, time commitment, and the ability to convince others. Even if it takes a great deal of Introversion to learn the athletes' or teams' statistics, ENTJs will take the solitary time to accomplish this task. A few media ENTJs include **Al Michaels, Chris Berman, and Bob Costas.**

Tell it Like it Is

Some ENTJs convey a warmer persona than others of their same Brain Type. This conscious Feeling emphasis, developed by a good relational environment or value system, will generally serve ENTJs better as they communicate with the public. The ENTJ, a dominant Thinker, will always need to be cautious of being abrasive or saying something that might offend others, especially Feelers. (Rarely will the sports audience find the Feeling ENFJ caustic.)

Television golf analyst and former golfing great, **Johnny Miller**, ENTJ, found himself in a few commentating controversies his first full year behind the microphone. At the 1990 PGA Seniors Championship, Miller responded to ENTJ broadcast partner Bryant Gumbel's remark that the caddies of Gary Player, Jack Nicklaus, and Lee Trevino were famous in their own right. Miller said, in 1990:

> Probably more famous than the guys leading at Heritage.[1]

He was referring to the Heritage (a regular Tour event) being televised on rival CBS. It ended in a three way playoff with Payne Stewart, Larry Mize, and Steve Jones. Do you think any of those three were laughing?

Now that Miller has completed a number of years in the TV booth, he does a first rate job of commentating. He has good NT insights, and appears to go out of his way, most of the time, to be gracious and fair to the players. ENTJ announcers soon learn that everything spoken will be closely scrutinized.

Creative

Are you familiar with these baseball names: Roberto (Remember the) Alomar, Todd (Mercedes) Benzinger, Mike (Nova) Scioscia, Greg (Appo) Maddux and John (I Am Not a) Kruk? If you are, then you know of whom I am about to speak, Mr. Wordsmith himself, ENTJ sportscaster **Chris Berman**.

If I had a buck for every athlete Berman creatively labeled, I could take an extended vacation. Not all ENTJs will use their left-hemisphere iNtuitive Thinking as has Chris, but they all have remarkable memories with word and numerical associations.

ENTJs In Sports Media

Various sports: Al Michaels, Jim Nance, Bob Costas, Chris Berman, Chris Myers, Jim Lampley, Jim Rome
Baseball: Tony Kubek, Jim Palmer, Tim McCarver, Don Drysdale, Steve Stone, Steve Garvey
Basketball: Billy Packer, Chick Hearn
Football: Dan Dierdorf, Ahmad Rashad, Len Dawson, Todd Christensen
Golf: Ken Venturi, Johnny Miller
Tennis: Tony Trabert, Mary Carillo, Roger Twibell, Cliff Drysdale, Barry MacKay, Bill Macatee, Barry Thompkins
Track: Bruce Jenner, Dave Johnson

ENTP

"Audacious" describes ENTPs and their sports reporting styles. Unafraid to take chances or tackle tough issues, they love to verbally problem solve. Their personas vary widely, yet they all employ their spontaneous, creative insight and wit. ENTP announcers have included **Howard Cosell, Dick Vitale, Al McGuire, Harry Caray,** and **Bud Collins.**

Outwardly Confident

ENTPs, like all NTs, are highly competent and diligent at learning in areas of their interest. A continual temptation for media ENTPs is to speak as if they are knowledgeable in all areas.

Forecasters

ENTPs occasionally get themselves in trouble by predicting future happenings. Their right brain iNtuitive dominance projects future events in a highly creative fashion. (ENTPs have a tendency to believe that if they've thought a matter through, they've actually lived it in reality.) Often they are correct in their forecasts, but when they error, it can be embarrassing.

In April of 1990, as the basketball went to Detroit's Isiah Thomas in the final seconds against the Atlanta Hawks, TV analyst **Kevin Loughery** (ENTP) commented: "I guarantee Isiah will shoot the ball." Results:

> Isiah passed the ball instead and Dominique Wilkins picked it off for the Atlanta win.[2]

Promoters of Hype, Excitement

Frank Layden, ENTP basketball aficionado, spoke of ENTP **Hubie Brown's** style of commentating:

> Sometimes he makes an inbounds pass seem like the invasion of France.[3]

Seattle Times columnist Steve Kelly, on basketball announcer **Dick Vitale**:

> Vitale might be the first commentator whose TV monitor comes equipped with an airbag.[4]

Industrious

ENTP Golfer **Gary McCord** never made it big on the PGA Tour. In 1985 he was flying to a tournament when he spotted CBS TV director Frank Chirkinian in first class. McCord told *USA Today*:

> I wasn't even playing in the tournament. I was broke. I had nothing to do, so I pleaded with Frank to let me help out that weekend, be a gofer.[5]

Chirkinian went beyond McCord's dreams. He assigned McCord to the 16th hole as an analyst, a capacity he's fulfilled ever since. Chirkinian probably didn't know Gary's ENTP Brain Type, but he did sense Gary was an excellent and humorous communicator.

Unpredictable

The only thing you can predict about ENTPs is that they are unpredictable. Gary McCord has proven this at CBS:

> McCord has done so many crazy things since joining CBS in 1985 that he keeps a running tab of the number of times that he has almost been fired by longtime golf producer Frank Chirkinian.[6]

In classic ENTP fashion, McCord responds to his near firings:

> It's been over 20 now. I've always begged my way back on the air.[7]

ENTP reporters generally provide us with the comedic side of sports, easily holding our interest during the slower parts of the game.

Probable ENTPs In Sports Media

Various sports: Roy Firestone, Jack Whitaker, Brent Musburger, Pete Axthelm, Charley Steiner, Keith Olbermann, Dick Stockton, Howard Cosell, Kevin Harlan, Fred Roggin
Baseball: Harry Caray
Basketball: Dick Vitale, Marv Albert, Jim Valvano, Hubie Brown, Kevin Loughery, Al McGuire, Mike Fratello
Boxing: Dr. Ferdie Pacheco, Bert Sugar
Football: Paul Maguire, Dan Fouts
Tennis: Bud Collins, Vitas Gerulaitis, Leif Shiras, Fred Stolle
Volleyball: Chris Marlowe

ENFJ

Wordsmiths

ENFJs, in life and sports reporting, seek to provide their audiences with personable, creative insight. They are poetic wordsmiths, hoping to find the best terms to fit the moment. Broadcaster **Vin Scully** has been the "Voice of the Dodgers" for over 40 years, having been tutored by broadcasting legend, Red Barber. ENFJ Scully has broadcast many sports, thoroughly preparing himself along the way. It was reported of him in 1987:

> Assigned to man the microphone at a Jimmy Connors Rod Laver tennis match a few years ago, Mr. Scully first read a variety of tennis books, milking them for pages of notes. He questioned tennis veterans Billy Talbert and Tony Trabert for hours, accumulating more notes. Finally, he played set after weary set with a pro who was familiar with both Mr. Connors's and Mr. Laver's games and tactics.[8]

From the Arena to the Booth

Former ENFJ athletes and coaches often try their hand at broadcasting. If given ample opportunity, they can be among the best. Some of these ENFJs have included **Pat Summerall, Frank Gifford, Bob Griese, Bill Walsh, Dick Vermeil, Pat Haden, Pat Riley,** and **Terry Donahue**.

Following his successful pro football coaching career, **Bill Walsh** commented, after his first year in broadcasting:

> Last year I may have worked too hard. I'd end up with notes everywhere, too many notes. Now I'm learning to edit out what isn't important.[9]

ENFJs rely more heavily on notes than the Extraverted NTs, particularly when recapping new information. NTs have exceptional mental abilities to think on their feet as well as memorize reams of information and numbers. I have listened to and watched NF and NT ministers for years. The Extraverted NTs prefer not using notes when preaching sermons. In fact, many will not use a note, memorizing their sermon word for word, often with numerous Bible verses and anecdotes. They are exceptional with their mental dexterity.

Extraverted NFs, particularly ENFJs, are far more likely to rely upon notes for sharing information. Relying upon notes too much, whether in the pulpit or broadcast booth, can lessen the effectiveness of the message.

Personable

ENFJs are usually well liked due to the warmth they convey to their audience. They are more likely to come across as caring people than the Thinking ENTs in the broadcast booth. When they feel comfortable and relaxed, they are more apt to share stories of players and people than statistics. Thinkers lean toward statistics.

Columnist **Larry Stewart** wrote of Bill Walsh during his broadcasting days:

> Walsh is courteous and easy to like. During a two hour interview over breakfast at an Anaheim hotel, a fan would occasionally come by to say hello or ask for an autograph. Walsh would go out of his way to make the person feel at ease, always saying, 'Have a nice day.'[10]

This isn't to say that ENFJs are always nice. Some can be troublesome at times, like all Types. Generally, however, when they are out of pressure situations, they are affable and charming.

In conclusion, ENFJs tend to say more than is needed, attempting to express the right words while putting the story in the proper context. Otherwise, they are easy to listen to.

Probable ENFJs In Sports Media

Various sports: Vin Scully, Pat Summerall, Pat Riley, Jim Hill, Leslie Visser, Gayle Gardner, Diana Nyad
Football: Bob Griese, Dick Vermeil, Pat Haden, Terry Donahue, Bill Walsh

ENFP

Often thought of as the "Pied Piper" in typology circles, ENFPs have a special ability to draw people to themselves. Ever optimistic, rarely critical, full of verve, ENFP commentators can make the dullest sporting event exciting. Their warm, light hearted approach makes you feel good, that it's worth the time to watch the game. **Dick Enberg** and **Bob Uecker** are ENFPs.

Personable, Promote Camaraderie

Broadcaster Bob Costas, ENTJ, spoke of **Dick Enberg**:

> I've never met anyone as prominent in broadcasting as Dick who is more of a team player.[11]

Columnist Larry Stewart wrote of Enberg:

> A lot of people in broadcasting, whether they are on air celebrities or behind the scene producers, executives or gofers, call Enberg a close friend. Some call him their best friend.[12]

It's too bad there aren't more ENFPs in sports reporting. They energize the event.

Probable ENFPs In Sports Media

Various Sports: Dick Enberg, Hannah Storm, Fred Hickman
Baseball: Bob Uecker, Joe Morgan
Basketball: Quinn Buckner
Gymnastics: Bart Conner, Janet Lynn
Tennis: Vic Braden, Tracy Austin

SPs

INtuitives dominate the principal roles in TV and radio broadcasting, being most capable of poetically improvising and speaking with decorous diction and syntax. They are master orators. Extraverted Sensing Perceivers (ESPs) are also found in the booth (though less often), but only as former jocks or coaches who can provide real experiences plus talk in the common vernacular. ESPs communicate well with simple to understand language and are often talkative. Introverted SPs are rarely found in broadcasting. When they are, it is in a secondary role, perhaps as an analyst. ISFPs will be much more laconic than ISTPs. In fact, once ISTPs get going, they can be talkative.

Probable SPs In Sports Media

ESTP

Baseball: Reggie Jackson, Don Sutton
Basketball: Tom Heinsohn, Reggie Theus
Football: Terry Bradshaw, Howie Long, Joe Namath, Joe Theismann, Bill Parcells, Jimmy Johnson, Dan Marino, Deion Sanders

ESFP

Though rarely found in the broadcast booth, ESFPs are generally regarded as the funniest, down home style broadcasters. Their speaking is simple and understood by the masses. ESFP **John Madden**, commentator for NFL football, has been a consistent winner as the outstanding sports personality analyst at the annual Sports Emmy Awards ceremonies.

ESFP

Baseball: Joe Garagiola, Dizzy Dean
Football: John Madden, Chris Collinsworth,
　　　　　Don Meredith
Golf: Lee Trevino, Jerry Pate

ISTP

Basketball: Bill Walton
Football: Ronnie Lott
Tennis: John McEnroe, Jimmy Connors

SJs

SJs (ESTJ, ISTJ, ESFJ, ISFJ) are rarely found in broadcasting, and if they are, it is in a subordinate role. They lack the humor and "shooting from the hip" style of speaking of the ESPs. If SJs get in the booth, they will be of a more serious nature, factual and accurate. They will not emulate the hype of the ENTPs, that's for sure. *L.A. Times* columnist, Allan Malamud, spoke of ISTJ **Chris Evert's** tennis commentary in 1990:

> Chris Evert is a rarity—a TV commentator who doesn't talk enough . . . .[13]

The more time ISTJs spend in front of a microphone, however, the more long winded they will become. They often resemble ISTPs, after the time it takes to overcome public speaking fears.

Probable SJs In Sports Media

ISTJ

Golf: Jack Nicklaus
Tennis: Chris Evert Lloyd

ESTJ

Football: Bo Schembechler
Tennis: Pam Shriver

PART FIVE

PORTRAITS OF THE 16 BRAIN TYPES

20
SPs

ISTP, ESTP
ISFP, ESFP

ISTP
(Introversion, Sensing, Thinking, Perceiving)
BEIR
(Back, Empirical, Inanimate, Right-brained)

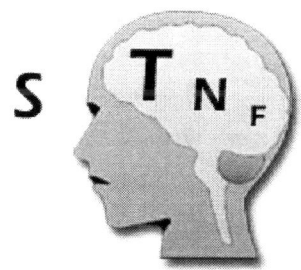

"Athlete"

Most athletes, if they knew the brain's functioning and then could choose a Brain Type, would choose ISTP. This Type is found in action oriented, coordinated, artistic people. They are masters with tools, no matter what kind—scalpel, chisel, brush, or baseball bat—no matter what size, tiny instrument or vast machine. When using instruments that require the use of the hands, the ISTP is a true artisan.

Putting the development of verbal skills on hold, ISTP children prefer activities requiring skill and strategy. They are risk takers, seemingly fearless as youngsters. On top of a jungle gym, out on a diving board, or in front of a pitcher, the courageous ISTP amazes peers and parents with his or her bravado.

Thriving on excitement and fast moving adventure, ISTPs usually appear quiet and reserved. It may take some years before anyone other than their parents can understand their mumbling. Not often conversationalists or communicators, they nevertheless win friends, limiting themselves to a few close ones. They tend to be generous, fraternal, and optimistic yet sometimes strongly resistant to authority; they love their freedom. At school, they generally apply themselves no more than necessary or as much as Mom and Dad insist, preferring to save their energy for another time.

Planning for the future does not appeal to ISTPs. They tend to plunge into matters, wanting to waste no time.

ISTPs are inquisitive and exploratory. They want to know "why," preferring a logical explanation. They will take things apart to investigate the inner workings. Fact gathering helps them learn many details about their interests.

If ISTPs learn submission and self control, they can fit into society well. If not, ISTPs can find themselves behind bars, losing the freedom they value so highly. ISTPs are capable of excelling in numerous vocations. No Sensing (S) Type has greater academic potential. The female ISTP may be seen as a tomboy if she follows her natural inclinations.

ISTPs are realistic, independent and spontaneous. They often need to improve communication with co-workers and loved ones, and stay on track with a course of action. Self expression will prevent them from "stuffing" frustrations to the boiling point.

ISTPs provide us some of the most thrilling ball games, the most daredevil exploits, some of the best art. ISTPs express life with color and adaptability.

ISTP Sports Profile

Consummate Athlete

We are talking the athlete par excellence, numero uno in the majority of sports! No Type is better designed, cerebrally and in the use of hand eye coordination, than the ISTP. Reflect on some of these performers, past and present: baseball's **Ty Cobb, Ted Williams, Henry Aaron, Pete Rose, Don Mattingly, Wade Boggs, and Roger Clemens**; basketball's **Jerry West, Larry Bird, Michael Jordan, Jason Kidd, and John Stockton**; football's **Barry Sanders and Ronnie Lott**; hockey's **Wayne Gretzky and Mario Lemieux**; golf's **Ben Hogan, Pat Bradley, and Karrie Webb**; tennis' **Rod Laver, John McEnroe, Jimmy Connors, Stefan Edberg, Martina Navratilova, Monica Seles, and Steffi Graf**; gymnastics' **Nadia Comaneci and Shannon Miller**; and boxing's **Mike Tyson and Larry Holmes**. As you have just witnessed, ISTPs can excel in virtually every sport. They are amazing, unparalleled athletes!

Young ISTPs

Coaching youth teams for the past decade, I have been able to view closely the fledgling traits of all 16 Brain Types. ISTPs are often *not* the top sport Type or athlete when young. Unless they are coached properly from an early age, awkwardness, uncertainty, and recklessness can characterize their performance in the formative years.

As Introverted, right-brained Thinkers, ISTPs often become fixed on thinking issues. This translates into freezing in the middle of an important play. A Little League shortstop catching a grounder with runners on base and then not knowing where to throw the ball is a good example. This normally happens because the inexperienced ISTP thinks before Sensing or seeing the play develop. Yet in the next inning, he or she is liable to get an extra base hit and make a spectacular catch, gaining restitution for previous error.

When you coach young ISTPs, your words often go unheard. ISTPs spend their thoughts picturing something in their minds rather than translating instructions into meaning. They learn best by doing, loving to get dirty and performing some daredevilry in the process. Do not expect them to answer your questions in a lengthy, articulate fashion as would an ENTJ or ENTP. ISTPs are laconic and generally answer in an inaudible mumble. They do their talking by performing boldly on the field.

Once the ISTP gets the "hang of it," he or she has the beginnings of a great athlete. Practice no longer becomes practice; it becomes necessary and fun. In fact, ISTPs often practice longer and harder than any other Type. Former basketball great **Bill Walton** (ISTP) recalled his playing days:

> As a player, I would spend all my time working at it, not knowing it was work because it was so much fun.[1]

My files are full of ISTP athletes and their tireless practice habits. Hours can seem like minutes when they get involved in the practice of their sport. All Types have phenomenal abilities to concentrate; their areas of interest differ, however. The ISTP is best at sports concentration.

A well known athlete personifies this intensely competitive Type when they become focused on a sport they love, and when they've had a challenging upbringing. His story is not atypical for an ISTP. His name is **Don Mattingly**, the former American League MVP, batting champion, and All Star first baseman. Just because Don and I grew up in the same burg along the sleepy Ohio River, Evansville, Indiana, does not mean I'm partial to a fellow Hoosier. I am, however.

Focused, Driven

Sports Illustrated ran a lengthy story on Don which described many of his ISTP characteristics. When looking back to his teen years and the newly constructed batting cage at his high school gym, Don said:

> I couldn't believe it—I could hit all day, all winter, and never have to chase balls. I was up there in lunch hours, recess, free periods, after school . . . .[2]

His then wife to be, Kim, said, "He was a ballaholic."[3] After graduation, Don and Kim, now married, moved in with her parents. Kim said:

> He wore the same woolen shirt every day and hardly ever showered or shaved. He just hit and worked out, hit and worked out. He was a maniac. No. Not was—is.[4]

Mike Pagliarulo, Don's ex teammate on the Yankees, spoke of Don's off season tenacity in his home batting cage:

> He gets locked in there the way he gets locked in during the season. I've never seen any other baseball player like him.[5]

Intense, Tough, Competitive

Mattingly also personified the intensely competitive ISTP when the cleats are laced up. Former Yankee pitcher Bob Tewksbury said:

> Check Donnie's eyes during a game. They're right out of a horror movie. He yells at opposing players. He paces in the dugout. I've never seen anyone compete with that kind of passion.[6]

Mattingly himself said:

> I don't actually dislike any opposing players, but I hate them when I play against them. Especially pitchers. You have to hate the guy. You have to get your mind into a sort of rage.[7]

ISTPs often play the Dr. Jekyll, Mr. Hyde routine like few other Types. When they get serious physically, watch out. Just ask a few of the guys who have tried to fight **Mike Tyson** in the ring.

Don Mattingly's ISTP competitiveness was told by his brother Michael:

> It doesn't matter if it's Wiffle Ball or chess, Don hates losing. I taught him to play chess when he was five. I wasn't bad for a ten year old, but he kept playing and playing and playing until he could beat me. He simply refuses to lose.[8]

The ISTP is not the only Brain Type who can have these traits. They will, however, possess them more strongly than any other Type in athletics. An ISTP's upbringing and present environment will play a major role in how pronounced these traits become.

ISTPs are intense competitors at whatever they value in life. Some control their outward emotions while some do not. An under control ISTP has been All Pro NBA guard, **Mark Price**. In April of 1990, however, Price was ejected supposedly for the first time in his life. Mark who lists the Rev. Billy Graham as his idol, insisted he didn't swear at the referee. Even Chicago's Michael Jordan, playing for the opposition, said the worst the language ever got was "Bull."[9] Aside from puns, ISTPs have the ability to remain cool, calm and collected.

(Coaching, however, can be a real test of control for the ISTP. See Coaching chapter for further insight.)

Contrast Price's court demeanor to that of former NBA hoopster **Scott Skiles** in college. After ISTP Skiles led his Michigan State team to an upset over the Georgetown Hoyas, Skip Bayless of the *Dallas Times Herald* wrote of Skiles:

> He did something I thought I'd never witness. He intimidated the pressing, breaking, taunting Hoyas. He simply took over . . . and even backed down 6-8, 240-pound Jonathan Edwards, who made the mistake of saying something to Skiles. Skiles answered by pointing at and cursing Edwards and ripping a jumper from maybe 30 feet.

Bayless continued:

> Like Bird [Larry], Skiles can be a jerk. A punk. A bully. A beer drinkin' blue collar redneck who won't take nothin' off nobody. He doesn't care if you're black or blue, he'll beat your butt in basketball.[10]

ISTPs, by and large, are the most dependable athletes under pressure, owing to their superior physical and mental skills.

Manager Sparky Anderson once told what it was like to take ISTP pitcher **Jack Morris** out of a game:

> Jack used to break blood vessels in my hand when I'd go out to get the ball.[11]

Fun-Seeking, Risk-Taking

Golfer **Chris Patton** was a hit at the 1990 Masters. The 6 foot-1, 300-pound Clemson student qualified for Augusta National by winning the 1989 US Amateur Championship. Patton played four days of superior golf and amazed the gallery with his ability to maneuver his corpulent ISTP frame. He told the press a story that would appear a tad risky to most Brain Types. It seems that he and his buddies would hold "range wars," in which they face off and exchange 4-iron shots from 100 feet ($33 1/3$ yards)! Patton said:

> Aw, it's easy to get out of the way unless they start hooking.[12]

I don't know what Patton's friends are like (although I'll bet a few are other SP risk takers), but I sure wouldn't want a 300 lb. ISTP hitting 4-irons at me!

Not all ISTPs are this venturesome, but be careful if you ever put a challenge to one; the ISTP just might take you up on it.

Scorers, Offensive-Minded

ISTPs are prolific at whatever they really enjoy doing and practicing. **Pistol Pete Maravich**, the ISTP hoopster phenom of the 60s-70s, is still the NCAA all time scoring champ with 3667 points in only three years, and without the 3-point shot! His 45 points a game average in college is almost unbelievable. Pete is now leading the fast break in heaven following his fatal, tragic heart attack. Maravich was a role model on how to play and enjoy basketball. He also modeled how to live, but only during the last years of his life—by his own admission. I recommend his autobiography, *Heir to a Dream*.

Varied Personalities

We have just looked at a number of factors that are directly attributed to the unique functioning of the ISTP brain. Their brains are especially adept at controlling fine motor movements. ISTPs share similar cerebral activities in that they: are gifted at delving deeply into matters, perceiving them in a factual and practical way, evaluating them logically and synthetically; and preferring to remain flexible in their outer world while more structured in their inner world.

Let's not forget, however, that ISTPs, as well as all other Types, can have many different personality styles within their respective Brain Type. Culture and environment play a major role in developing one's personality.

Many good ISTP athletes are seen as aloof, confident, as private persons who are not very sociable, withholding smiles unless with close friends. Conversely, other ISTPs demonstrate more outgoing personas.

Masters of Deception

Deception often connotes a negative or bad image. Deception, however, is not always wrong—particularly in sports. Picture in your mind the running back juking by the linebacker, the batter faking a bunt, but at the last second, squaring around to swing away. Or the point guard looking to pass one way but dishing off the other.

ISTPs are masters of logical deception. They often feign one move, only to set up their opponents for a different tack. Often the difference between winning and losing comes from deception. One thing you can count on if you are ever competing against ISTPs in sports, they'll try to outfox you with split second timing.

The whole world viewed the moves of a wily ISTP in the beginning months of 1991. Technically speaking, it had nothing to do with sports, but in retrospect, it was a game of sorts. The ISTP in charge was **Gen. H. Norman Schwarzkopf**, battlefield commander of the Allied forces against Iraq. In his successful military plan to free Kuwait, Schwarzkopf demonstrated his ISTP genius.

The *L.A. Times* said following the war:

> The battle plan for vanquishing the Iraqi army mapped out by Gen. H. Norman Schwarzkopf was one of the most complex military campaigns ever devised, yet it rested upon a fundamental principle as old as human conflict—deception.
>
> From the opening minutes of the air war in the pre dawn hours of Jan. 17 to the climactic battle with the Republican Guard, the plan was to render Iraq's army deaf and blind, deceive it on the allies' true intentions, and then suddenly—and—violently—encircle and annihilate it.[13]

Of course all the allied military personnel engaged in that massive conflict share in the victory, but Gen. Schwarzkopf was the mastermind behind it all. He clearly demonstrated his ISTP genius.

Whether you engage an ISTP in war, boxing, basketball, badminton, or tiddlywinks, you had better be on your guard. They come with the mind and body to beat you.

Superstitious

ISTP athletes are often known for their superstitions, which can be debilitating to their play and perspective on life. They must realize their superior physical and mental skills do not need the burden of groundless notions.

Principled

As Introverted dominant Thinkers, ISTPs place a high value on logic, right and wrong, and principles. Though they can have difficulty in areas of self-discipline, ISTPs are known for taking self-sacrificing positions. If they believe in something strongly, they are one of the first to lay down their lives for a cause.

When former baseball and Boston Red Sox great **Ted Williams** was closing out his career in the 1960s, he had his worst season at the plate, hitting under .300 for the first time. His $125,000 salary was baseball's highest at the time. The Red Sox sent him a contract for the next season, matching the previous year's. When ISTP Williams got it, he sent it back with a note stating that he wouldn't sign it until they gave him the full pay cut allowed! He felt undeserving of the $125,000. Williams ended up cutting his own salary by 25 percent and in the following and final season of his outstanding career, he raised his batting average 62 points to .316. When ISTPs believe strongly in a principle, they are unwavering.

Vocationally

ISTPs are capable of pursuing many careers. Direction and success depend upon their self discipline and studying habits early in life. If they apply themselves academically, they can make straight A's through school. (ISTP Gen. Schwarzkopf finished in the top 10 percent of his graduating class at West Point, measuring an IQ of 170.) ISTPs are often surgeons when they choose the medical profession.

ISTPs are highly adept at financial trading and investing (stock brokers, investment analysts, and so forth). Their risk taking, adaptable, logical minds serve them well in this capacity. I know a retired ISTP physician who has probably made more money in his stock investments than in his entire medical practice.

Ty Cobb, the renowned baseball player, was also regarded as a financial whiz. At his death in 1961, Cobb's estimated net worth was around $12 million, a ton of money considering his baseball pay in the olden days. (He began his career with Detroit in 1907 receiving $2,500, and got his biggest pay check in 1927, a whopping $85,000.) His portfolio was full of stocks, bonds, real estate, and mineral holdings. Ty didn't turn his finances over to a money manager; he strictly used his own financial savvy. Columnist Al Stump wrote of Cobb:

Comparing Cobb, the first man into the Hall of Fame, with the top paid stars of the period between World War II and free agency leaves little doubt that he was the richest individual in the game's history, club owners excepted. No one, active or retired, he believed could match his holdings—what he called "my annuities."[14]

If ISTPs choose *not* to apply themselves academically, their career choices become much more limited. They can appear ignorant and illiterate, and lack the self discipline necessary to stay consistently with a job. And, if they are not careful, their drive for expediency can land them in trouble with the law.

Type Tips

Despite their inherent superstar potential, ISTPs must devote many hours of practice to developing their athletic skills.

ISTPs will perform at their best when they keep their aggression and intensity under control. They must remember these assets can become counter productive if not kept in balance. ISTPs must make sure not to overuse their Thinking function. Excessive logical introspection will cause ISTPs to lose their fluidity and adaptability in sports.

The greatest assistance parents and coaches can provide ISTPs is mental and emotional. A calming influence in their lives will yield tremendous dividends. Teach sportsmanship to your ISTPs, not winning at all costs.

Read the various sports' chapters for additional insights into ISTPs.

PROBABLE ISTPs IN SPORTS

Baseball:
1st: Jeff Bagwell, Jim Thome, Wally Joyner;
   R: Lou Gehrig, Don Mattingly, Will Clark
2nd: Pokey Reese, Ray Durham, Jeff Treadway, Chad Fonville;
   R: Pete Rose, Steve Sax, Rob Thompson
ss: **R:** Robin Yount, Walt Weiss, Cal Ripken Jr., Greg Gagne, Shawon Dunston
3rd: Chipper Jones, Matt Williams;
   R: George Brett, Wade Boggs
C: **R:** Terry Steinbach
OF: Rusty Greer, Steve Finley, Jeromy Burnitz, Todd Hollandsworth;
   R: Ty Cobb, Ted Williams, Henry Aaron, Carl Yastrzemski, Roger Maris, Darryl Strawberry, Jim Eisenreich, Willie McGee, Mike Greenwell, Chili Davis, Eric Davis Brady Anderson, Jay Buhner,
P: Roger Clemens, Tom Glavine, Kerry Wood, Rick Helling;
   RP: Trevor Hoffman, Billy Wagner, Troy Percival;
   R: Dennis "Oil Can" Boyd, John Tudor, Dave Stewart, Steve Howe, Mitch Williams, Danny Jackson, Jim Abbott, Bret Saberhagen, Charles Nagy, Steve Avery, Randy Myers,

Basketball: Shaquille O'Neal, Alonzo Mourning, Derrick Coleman, Shawn Kemp, Larry Johnson, Tom Gugliotta, Mark Bryant, Rodney Rogers, Reggie Miller, **Tracy McGrady**, Anthony Peeler, Jalen Rose, **Jason Kidd**, Allen Iverson, Stephon Marbury, Tim Hardaway, Kenny Anderson, Mookie Blaylock, Mark Jackson, Mike Bibby, Dana Baros, Robert Pack, Mahmoud Abdul-Rauf, Brent Price,
Cynthia Cooper, Chamique Holdsclaw
   Retired: Moses Malone, Bill Walton, Jerry West, James Worthy, Larry Smith, Reggie Lewis, Pete Maravich, Nate Archibald, Ricky Pierce, Byron Scott, Kiki Vandeweghe, Scott Skiles, Doc Rivers, Mark Price, **Larry Bird**, **Michael Jordan**, Dominique Wilkins, Detlef Schrempf, Dino Radja, Terry Cummings, Rex Chapman, Muggsy Bogues, Hakeem Olajuwon, Patrick Ewing, Bryant "Big Country" Reeves, Chris Mullin, Mitch Richmond, Dan Majerle, Ron Harper, Derek Harper, Terry Porter, Bobby Hurley, Gary Grant, John Stockton,

Boxing: Rocky Marciano, Joe Frazier, Larry Holmes, Mike Tyson, Thomas Hearns, Pernell Whitaker, Michael Dokes, James Toney

Football: Brad Johnson, Mark Brunell, Ty Detmer, Cade McNown,
LaDainian Tomlinson, Mike Anderson, Terry Allen, Fred Taylor, Jevon Kearse, Earl Holmes, Dale Carter, Shaun Williams, Jeff Feagles
   Retired: Mark Rypien, Jim Taylor, Mike Ditka, Bo Jackson, Dick Anderson, Jack Lambert, Ronnie Lott, Lin Elliott, Bill Bates, Stan Humphries, Wade Wilson, Charles Haley, **Barry Sanders,** Billy Joe Tolliver, Bryce Paup

Golf: Tom Lehman, Mark O'Meara, Jim Furyk, Lee Janzen, Craig Stadler, Corey Pavin, Steve Pate, Mark Calcavecchia, Scott Hoch, John Huston,
Karrie Webb, Pat Bradley, Beth Daniel, Patty Sheehan, Laura Davies
   Seniors: Babe Zaharias, Ben Hogan, Mike Hill, Jim Colbert, Walt Zembriski, J.C. Snead, Moe Norman

Gymnastics: Nadia Comaneci, Shannon Miller, Kerri Strug, Simona Amanar, Tatiana Gutsu, Roza Galieva, Gina Gogean, Kim Zmeskal, Jaycie Phelps, Li Donghua, Scott Keswick

Hockey: Wayne Gretzky, Mario Lemieux, Paul Kariya, Steve Yzerman, Guy Carbonneau, Clark Donatelli

Racing (auto): A.J. Foyt, Dale Earnhardt

Rowing: Thomas Lange, Anne Marden

Snow Skiing: Paul Accola, Katrin Gutensohn, A.J. Kitt, Tommy Moe

Tennis: Lleyton Hewitt, Thomas Muster, Richard Krajicek, Miloslav Mecir, Petr Korda,
Monica Seles, Mary Pierce, Leili Meskhi
  Retired: Rod Laver, John McEnroe, Jimmy Connors, Ivan Lendl, Martina Navratilova, Steffi Graf, Stefan Edberg, Michael Chang,

Track and Field: Mary Decker Slaney

Volleyball: Steve Timmons

Wrestling: Aleksandr Kareline

Coaches:
baseball: Don Zimmer, Jim Leyland, Whitey Herzog,
basketball: Jerry Sloan, Larry Bird, Scott Skiles, Doc Rivers, Byron Scott, Bobby Knight, Jim Keady, Pat Summitt,
football: Mike Ditka, Bobby Ross, Bill Cowher, Ray Perkins, Jim Haslett,
water polo: Ted Newland

Sports Media: Bill Walton, Jimmy Connors, John McEnroe

PROBABLE WELL-KNOWN ISTPs:

Gen. Norman Schwarzkopf, Marlin Fitzwater, Carl Karcher

Popular Career Choices:
Construction, mechanics, machine operation, racing, aviation, surgery, sculpting, securities trading, finance, law enforcement, criminal investigation. ISTPs are the masters of tools and machines.

ESTP

(Extraversion, Sensing, Thinking, Perceiving)
FEIR
(Front, Empirical, Inanimate, Right-brained)

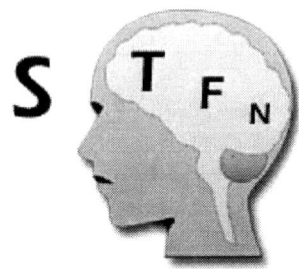

"Opportunist"

ESTPs, always in motion, may make you tired just by watching them. They are noted for their zealousness and for enjoying life to its fullest, having the gift for finding excitement in everything they do. Tackling life's opportunities head-first, they would not be considered gun shy or timid.

Young ESTPs may be called hyperactive. Always ready to move on to the next thing, they have a short attention span if the activity is not immediately rewarding. They want to be on the go, experiencing as much as possible. There never seems to be enough time to accomplish everything. They seem fearless, trying anything at least once. Living for the moment, they cash in now, content to pay later.

ESTPs like center stage and are entertaining to be with. They attract many friends, which can often play havoc with their family time, especially if there is any tension at home. They love life and exploration, but are less enchanted with school related challenges. They want learning to be relevant and immediately useful. As learners, ESTPs do better with guidance than control. They prefer to rely on common sense rather than follow directions. They are not anti-authority, but can easily find themselves in trouble.

As smooth operators, ESTPs are flirtatious and sophisticated, and suave at social functions. They are witty, fun, and unpredictable, and radiate charm and generosity. They are popular, but may find lasting commitments confining and boring. Being risk takers, they have keen senses of competition.

The female ESTP is athletic by nature. ESTPs are attracted to athletics whether they play or just watch. They derive great satisfaction from physical experiences and material possessions. ESTP Pop Rock star **Madonna** is appropriately called the "material girl." ESTPs may be inclined to be impulsive, taking advantage of whatever is expedient for them at the moment. ESTPs make decisions, however, with their Thinking, not Feeling function. If ESTPs use their skills and risk taking for good, they will not enter into antisocial behavior such as safe cracking, smuggling, drug selling, and swindling. ESTPs are men and women of action, getting things done in the here and now.

Action-Oriented

Former pro football quarterback **Ken Stabler** once said:

> People think all I do is drink, raise hell and stay out all night—and they're pretty close to the truth.[15]

ESTPs like to be on the move, enjoying their Sensing function to the fullest. Ken Stabler directed his to the wild life.

Duchess of York, **Sarah Ferguson**, defied the English role of royalty as an ESTP. The tabloids loved to report all the dutch the duchess got in. Unlike her traditional, ESFJ sister in law, Princess Diana, Fergie was the Cher of Buckingham Palace. She is known for her independence, high spirits, extravagant ways, provocative vocabulary, and part time parenting. Her Royal Badness once said:

> I relate to Americans because I'm a little wild.[16]

She's also stated:

> I'm too spontaneous, and I don't think before I act.[17]

Prince Andrew once lightheartedly teased her critics at a speaking engagement:

> Thank you for inviting me to take over from my wife, who is resting up at the moment and about to disappear again on another trip, leaving me behind to do all the work.[18]

ESTP women rarely fit the stereotypical role of a housewife. Consider ESTP **Cher's** comments:

> I don't know what I am to base myself on. When

do I have to cut my hair and quit wearing jeans and my leather jacket and going on motorcycle rides? When do I have to start wearing a bun and stay home?[19]

Not all ESTP women have exercised their freedoms as much as Cher and Fergie. Nonetheless, they tend toward action and independence.

ESTPs are not by nature drawn to the reflective inner world of the spiritual. They live independent lives of personal preferences, and less often stop to contemplate the hereafter. They are bold, verbally confident, and spontaneous persons, and not unlike the **Apostle Peter** of the Bible, need the miraculous call of God (or atypical self-discipline) to slow them down on any given day. Peter's impulsive faith eventually became rock-solid.

Actors

Sensates rarely play big time roles in Hollywood; acting is an iNtuitive profession. Yet when a Sensate does make it in the movies, he or she is invariably an ESTP. Though normally not regarded for their "acting" skills, ESTPs bring excitement, action, and down to earth reality to the big screen. They include **John Wayne, Sylvester Stallone, Arnold Schwarzenegger, Clint Eastwood, Burt Reynolds, Cher, Madonna,** and **Kim Basinger**.

Steve Kelly, a *Seattle Times* columnist, wrote of the acting ability of ESTP **Brian Bosworth**, former pro football player turned actor:

> Boz makes Arnold Schwarzenegger look like Laurence Olivier, and Sylvester Stallone is Rex Harrison by comparison.[20]

Kelly's tongue in cheek comment unwittingly contrasted three ESTPs.

Though ESTPs' right-brained dominant Sensing (or Empirical) function is not suited for an orator or Shakespearean actor, they nonetheless can learn to be capable communicators. When **Arnold Schwarzenegger** shockingly captured the California governorship in 2003, he also surprised many who previously didn't believe he could string words together so well.

Contemporary Musicians

ESTPs are infrequently connected with classical music, preferring modern melodies and lyrics. Some ESTPs who've made their recent marks in song include **Cher, Gloria Estefan, Madonna, Lorrie Morgan, Tanya Tucker, Tina Turner, Johnny Cash, Billy Ray Cyrus,** and **Tom Jones.**

Commentators

Retired ESTP athletes often become broadcasters. They like staying around sports, sharing their keen awareness of the game in witty and sometimes verbose style. ESTP **Reggie Jackson** once hosted TV's "Greatest Sports Legends." His executive producer said:

> Reggie is an excellent host. He comes prepared for each show, and his interviewing style is natural.[21]

Hate to Leave the Limelight

Retiring from the public eye can be difficult for well known ESTPs. This can be problematic in athletics. Continuing to play when the mind and body are no longer able to compete can do a disservice to the team and lead to injury. ESTPs' emphases on the physique and living life to its fullest often make growing old tough to handle. Not having other goals beyond one's athletic career frequently leads to depression.

Varying Personalities

General descriptions have been presented in this section highlighting each of the 16 Brain Types. Unfortunately, they are not always exacting. Though persons possessing the same inborn Type share specific cerebral functions and circuits, neuronal networkings, body skills, and so forth, personalities vary widely within each Type—especially due to "nurture." (This book emphasizes this fact.) Personas vary widely with ESTPs, too.

ESTPs are sometimes reserved and uncommunicative. As dominant right hemisphere persons, they don't always place a high value on talking—especially when feeling forced to. They prefer to rely more on the action they take or on their physical senses.

I once coached a nine-year-old boy in basketball. I could tell from our first practice he was an ESTP. As we went through the season, he demonstrated this repeatedly. Had I not been aware of the various idiosyncrasies within each Type, I would have guessed him to be an ISTP, not ESTP. He hardly spoke the whole season! Some adult ESTPs, including professional athletes, also convey laconic styles. They just don't fit the normal ESTP mold. Nonetheless, when they perform athletically, their Type is much easier to distinguish.

ESTP Sports Profile

Extraverted, right-brained STs are prominent and prolific in sports. Not every ESTP is brash or macho yet this is often the pattern. ESTPs are well conditioned and built, more so than any other Type. Whether male or female, they'll pump iron and, or exercise. Their lives are centered around their bodies, which often resemble Greek gods'. This fixation often leads them into sports, where they can excel in many fields. **ESTP athletes include wrestling's Hulk Hogan, baseball's Mike Piazza and Rickey Henderson, basketball's Karl Malone, football's Joe Namath and Brett Favre, snow skiing's Alberto Tomba, golf's Arnold Palmer and Greg Norman, tennis' Andre Agassi, boxing's Sugar Ray Leonard, gymnastics' Mary Lou Retton, hockey's Brett Hull, and soccer's Diego Maradona.**

ESTPs are often super-aggressive in the way they play sports. They learn they can't always be this way, but when aggression is required, they proceed energetically.

ESTPs, proficient with their fine motor skills, are masters of hand eye coordination. As dominant right-brained STs, they are able to spontaneously position their hands in the proper location at a given moment. Their quick understanding and agility helps explain why they are such gifted athletes.

Power Athletes

The Extraverted ESTPs, equipped with high powered fine motor skills, are the most powerful athletes, regardless of the sport. When they are tall and/or well-built, they usually have the longest hit in golf and baseball and the strongest serves and groundstrokes in tennis.

Spatial

As dominant right-brained STs, ESTPs have excellent visual acuity and peripheral awareness. They can see the complete playing field, though they may not always want to give up the ball or puck.

No. 1 Quarterbacks

I regard ESTPs as the premier quarterback (QB), tending to be the most consistent throughout their careers—especially in pressure-packed games. (This is not to say that some other Types cannot be top flight QBs.) Consider some ESTP QBs, past and present: **Johnny Unitas, Joe Namath, Ken Stabler, Terry Bradshaw, Joe Montana, Dan Marino, John Elway, Jim Kelly, Brett Favre** and **Peyton Manning**.

Type Tips

ESTPs are the, or among the, smoothest and most ready when beginning an athletic event. (Of course, they must have the proficiency with their sport for this to be true.) Generally, the best thing someone assisting ESTPs can do is to help them maintain their cool and collective ways throughout the competition.

In finesse sports, ESTPs have a tendency after a while to get impatient and lose their concentration. Mental drills practiced over time, such as suggested in this book, can significantly aid their concentration skills.

When ESTPs feel big time pressure, they often rely upon their Thinking function rather than their spatial and smooth abilities. This will cause their fine motor skills to tighten up, jeopardizing success.

As kids and adults, ESTPs are free spirits. They desire to steer their own ship, eschewing close supervision. They will best be served by listening to others' *constructive* suggestions and guidelines.

Coaches and guardians of ESTPs would do well to teach them aspects of humility and regard for others. This need not lessen ESTPs' competitive drive, only complement it. ESTPs have the potential to win awards and trophies as well as friends and admirers.

Read the various sports' chapters for additional insights into ESTPs.

PROBABLE ESTPs IN SPORTS

Baseball:
1st: **R**: Dick Allen, Jack Clark, Cory Snyder, Glen Davis, Eddie Murray
2nd: Craig Biggio;
  R: Bobby Grich, Juan Samuel, Mickey Morandini,
ss: Alex Rodriguez, Edgar Renteria
  R: Mike Gallego, Mariano Duncan, Jose Offerman, Rafael Belliard
3rd: Phil Nevin;
  R: Mike Schmidt, Pedro Guerrero, Steve Buechele, Gary Gaetti, Ken Caminiti
C: Mike Piazza, Benito Santiago;
  R: Gary Carter, Lance Parrish, Steve Yeager, Darren Daulton,
OF: Juan Gonzalez, Gary Sheffield, Rickey Henderson;
  R: Mickey Mantle, Reggie Jackson, Dusty Baker, Andre Dawson, Jesse Barfield, Dave Winfield, Kirk Gibson, Brian Downing, Dan Gladden, George Bell, Luis Polonia, Deion Sanders, Jose Canseco
P: Pedro Martinez, Todd Stottlemyre, Darren Dreifort, Ricky Bones;
  R: Don Sutton, Dennis Martinez, Gene Nelson, Greg Minton, Lee Smith, Dave Stieb, Doug Drabek, Dennis Ekersley, Juan Berenguer, Gregg Harris, Juan Guzman

Basketball: Karl Malone, Charles Oakley, Robert Horry, Michael Doleac, Pete Chilcutt, John Starks, Bob Sura, Ricky Davis, Jason Williams, **Steve Nash**, Chris Childs, Charlie Ward,
Michele Timms, Jackie Stiles
  Retired: Wilt Chamberlain, Elgin Baylor, Gail Goodrich, Walt Frazier, Tom Heinsohn, Maurice Lucas, Jim Paxson, Kelly Tripuckah, Mychal Thompson, James Edwards, Reggie Theus, Rodney McCray, Brad Davis, Danny Ainge, Sarunas Marciulionis, Antoine Carr, Michael Cage, Pete Myers, A.C. Green, Vinny Del Negro, Greg Anthony,

Boxing: Sugar Ray Leonard, Roberto Duran, Donny Lalonde, Hector Camacho, Ken Norton, Carlos Palomino, Roberto Duran, Riddick Bowe, Julio Cesar Chavez, Peter McNeeley, Tommy Morrison

Football: Brett Favre, Peyton Manning, Chris Chandler, Jake "The Snake" Plummer, Tim Couch Curtis Martin, Eddie George, Andre Rison, Quinn Earley, Willie Davis, Mark Stepnoski,
Junior Seau, Ray Lewis, Kevin Greene, Donnie Edwards, Blaine Bishop, James Hasty, Ty Law,
  Retired: Joe Montana, Johnny Unitas, Joe Namath, Ken Stabler, Terry Bradshaw, Fran Tarkenton, Joe Theismann, Phil Simms, Bert Jones, Billy Kilmer, Bernie Kosar, Jim Brown, Tony Dorsett, Paul Hornung, O. J. Simpson, Deacon Jones, "Mean" Joe Greene, Dick Butkus, Jack Youngblood, Howie Long, Mark Gastineau, Brian Bosworth, Dennis Byrd, Eric Dickerson, Marcus Allen, Jim McMahon, John Elway, Troy Aikman, Dan Marino, Herschel Walker, Merton Hanks Deion Sanders

Golf: Davis Love III, Greg Norman, Fred Couples, John Daly, Seve Ballesteros, Bernhard Langer, Jose Maria Olazabal, Jumbo Ozaki, Payne Stewart, John Cook, Paul Stankowski, Bob Tway, Hal Sutton, Robert Gamez, Jay Don Blake, Willie Wood, Nolan Henke, Steve Stricker Se Ri Pak, Dottie Mochrie, Jan Stephenson
  Seniors: Arnold Palmer, Ray Floyd, Ben Crenshaw, Lanny Wadkins,

Gymnastics: Mary Lou Retton, Lavina Milosovici, Wendy Bruce, Dominique Moceanu, Vitaly Scherbo, Alexei Nemov

Hockey: Brett Hull, Jaromir Jagr, Theoren Fleury, Rob Blake
  Retired: Bobby Hull

Racing (auto): Richard Petty
  (motocross) Greg Albertyn

Snow Skiing: Alberto Tomba, Bill Johnson

Soccer: Diego Maradona

Tennis: Andre Agassi, Patrick Rafter, Michael Stich, Goran Ivanisevic, Marcelo Rios, Ken Flach, Vince Spadea, Carlos Moya
Martina Hingis, Jana Novotna
 Retired: Ilie Nastase, Vic Seixas, Aaron Krickstein, Boris Becker

Track and Field: Randy Barnes, Dan O'Brien, Dennis Mitchell, Quincy Watts, Werner Gunthor, Stacy Dragila (pole vault)

Volleyball: Randy Stoklos

Weightlifting: Naim Suleymanoglu (Pocket Hercules)

Wrestling: Hulk Hogan, Jake "The Snake" Roberts, "Macho Man" Randy Savage, Ric Flair, Brutus "The Barber" Beefcake, Sid Justice, Mr. Perfect

Coaches:
baseball: Tommy Lasorda, Dusty Baker, Rene Lachemann, Frank Robinson, Jim Lefebvre
basketball: Doug Collins, Danny Ainge, Denny Crum,
football: Don Shula, Bill Parcells, Jimmy Johnson, Barry Switzer, Steve Spurrier
hockey: Barry Melrose

Sports Media: Terry Bradshaw, Joe Theismann, Howie Long, Joe Namath, Don Sutton, Tom Heinsohn, Dan Marino, Deion Sanders, Jimmy Johnson

Lyndon Johnson   Lee Iococca

POPULAR CAREER CHOICES:
Sales, real estate, investments, entrepreneur, automobile dealer, mechanic, athletics, dentistry, construction, multi-level marketing

PROBABLE WELL KNOWN ESTPs:

Lyndon B. Johnson, Lee Iococca, Sarah Ferguson (Duchess of York)

Clint Eastwood, Erik Estrada, Burt Reynolds, Arnold Schwarzenegger, Sylvester Stallone, John Wayne

Johnny Cash, Billy Ray Cyrus, Tom Jones, Merle Haggard, Buck Owens

Maria Conchita Alonso, Kim Basinger, Cher, Gloria Estefan, Madonna, Louise Mandrell, Lorrie Morgan, Tanya Tucker, Tina Turner, Yuri

ISFP
(Introversion, Sensing, Feeling, Perceiving)
BEAR
(Back, Empirical, Animate, Right-brained)

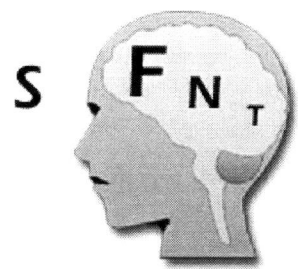

"Artisan"

The ISFP is an artist with athletic grace and an artist with interpersonal relationships. The ISFP is humble, kind, harmonious, skilled, artsy, serene, curious, impulsive, fun loving, visual, and sensing. This free flowing Brain Type dislikes routine and schedule.

As children, ISFPs are often noncompetitive, nonverbal, warm, and reserved. They do well in an atmosphere of freedom where they are nurtured and appreciated. They are sensitive to color, texture, and touch, learning best by hands on experiences. Under stress, ISFP's are prone to mood swings, people of sensitive and somewhat fragile emotions. ISFPs are subject to depression and need gentle, loving encouragement along with some helpful guidelines.

The ISFP may develop interest in art, photography, dancing, music, sports, clothing, food—whatever is sensory and visual. Like all SPs, ISFPs are perfectionists in their work. They are closely in tune with their bodies and enjoy the feelings they get from graceful movement. *US* magazine spoke of pop superstar ISFP **Janet Jackson**:

> Jackson comes across as charming and shy and, at the same time, talented and driven. In other words, she has illustrated the dichotomies that fuel her career: She's the perfectionist who leads her band and dancers through the split second choreography of "Miss You Much" with a fierce determination; she's also the withdrawn young woman who giggles girlishly, and nervously shifts on her heels around outsiders.[22]

To express themselves, ISFPs turn to action, intricate gift making and crafts, and written expressions of appreciation. As lovers of nature, they relate well to animals as well as with small children.

Bill Shoemaker, ISFP Hall of Fame jockey, rode for more than 40 years and won more races—8,883—than any other jockey. "Shoe," the most beloved jockey of all time, suffered a severe spinal injury in 1991. Following the accident, a man who knew him well said:

> He [Bill] was like Charlie Whittingham, he had that instinctive knack of knowing what to do with horses. He had a sixth sense about horses.[23] (Insert added.)

Being a "now" person, the ISFP lives to enjoy the moment, wanting excitement. The ISFP plans for and plans on having a lot of leisure and free time to enjoy simple pleasures. We often find the ISFP beautifying the environment, focusing on the needs of others, and coming to the aid of the less fortunate.

The ISFP has a few close friends and a larger group of friends who are attracted to the kind, quiet, easy to live with personality. ISFPs are peacemakers, promoting harmony and avoiding disagreements. They readily sense the needs and feelings of others and work to help them reach their goals. This constant interaction builds relationships, bringing people together in cooperation.

ISFPs may overlook their own needs. They need to be less self critical, being perhaps the most humble and most misunderstood of all the Types. They constantly underestimate their own abilities and accomplishments, which can keep them from doing something that a far less capable person will end up doing. ISFPs will be happiest in work deeply meaningful to them, keeping contact with the outside world, keeping their goals clearly in sight.

If you find someone who enjoys life, is reflective, compassionate, pleasant and kind, you may have found a good friend, an ISFP who will rarely judge you but help you in your personal pursuits.

ISFP Sports profile

ISFPs are Introverted, right-brained SFs. They are gifted in the use of their gross motor skills, specializing in body rhythm that produces an artistic, graceful flow. ISFPs are prolific athletes and prevalent in most American sports. In 1998, baseball's **Mark McGwire**, ISFP, broke the long-held single-season record for home runs.

ISFPs' Introversion enables them to concentrate deeply, to ponder their favorite sport thoroughly. Being Feelers, they do not possess the logical, hair splitting abilities of the Thinkers. Yet they can perform superbly in most sports. They tend to make their decisions from experience or synthetic reasoning. The less analysis involved in competition, the better they will perform under pressure.

Gentle Natures

In my sports consulting endeavors, I'm often asked why ISFP athletes aren't more aggressive. Coaches are normally looking for the energetic and aggressive mentality. By their innate natures, ISFPs don't consistently operate this way. This needn't be a liability, however. With regular, encouraging oversight and help in tapping into their individual motivations. ISFPs' energies can be extended. They are not the Type that regularly seeks to destroy the enemy/competitor with physical punishment. As dominant Feelers, they seek harmony with others. Yet if competitors make them mad, watch out; ISFPs can unleash inordinate amounts of energy, aggression, and emotion.

Track and field's world record-holder **Michael Johnson**, ISFP, has illustrated his Brain Type's natural style. When asked about his desire to play pro football in 1996, the speedster Johnson recalled his high school days in football-loving Texas:

> I didn't like contact, and I didn't like the whole football mentality. On a football team, you've got to be yelled at. Or, you've got to yell at someone. It's not football without some yelling or some hitting and all that kind of stuff. And that's just not me.[24]

Competitive

Do not let the gentle and caring ISFP fool you when it comes to competition. If they care about the activity, they can surprise you. In 1992, the *L.A. Times* wrote of ISFP **Jackie Joyner-Kersee** (heptathlon world record-holder and Olympic gold medalist):

> Remarkably, even with her titles and records, Joyner-Kersee says her competitors sometimes reveal a lack of respect. Perhaps they misread her friendliness as a lack of competitiveness.[25]

Once again, speaking of jockey **Bill Shoemaker**, horse owner Doug Atkins said:

> He was always very competitive. Whether it was riding horses, training them or just playing cards, he always wanted to beat you.[26]

When ISFPs get focused in their Introverted Feeling function, they can become intense and competitive. Generally, this doesn't happen around others, unless there is competition. I know a former NFL receiver and ISFP who is as gentle as a lamb, except when you do such things as invite him over for a friendly tag football game. He was a bloody mess the last time I saw him play for fun.

Cool, Calm, and Collected

ISFP athletes often have reputations of being calm operators in their sport (such as track and field's **Michael Johnson**, tennis' **Bjorn Borg,** and golf's **Ernie Els**). Following **Els'** back-to-back PGA Tour victories in 1997 (the U.S. Open and Buick Classic), fellow pro Brad Faxon said of the easygoing Els:

> What is his resting heart rate, like 35? I mean, he'll never die. He won't.[27]

ISFPs' laid back style and right-brained dominance (P) contribute to this perception. Yet little do fans realize the great emotion and inner concerns often dealt with by this Brain Type.

Energizer Bunnies

Television commercials portraying the long-lasting Energizer batteries parallel ISFPs as the most durable athletes in career longevity. They are the Methuselahs of sports. Since SFs are gross motor dominant, they rely on their large body muscles more than the other 12 Types (SJs, NFs, and NTs). Since SFPs are generally more athletic than SFJs, they're found much more often in pro sports. And between ISFP and ESFP, ISFPs appear to hang around pro sports the longest. Consider **Robert Parish**. In 1997, after playing his 21st NBA season as a 43-year-old, Parish retired as No. 1 on the all-time NBA list in number of games played. In 1997, at age 69, ISFP **Gordie Howe** (Mr. Hockey) made a brief game appearance (with 20,000 cheering and admiring fans) to become the only pro in his sport to compete in six decades!

At the age of 70, **Dr. Tom Amberry** became the world free throw record holder by hitting 2,750 free throws in 12 hours—without a miss! I was fortunate to get to meet and Brain Type Dr. Amberry, and to better understand how this remarkable feat could be performed—by a senior citizen no less. The answer can be summed up: ISFP.

In his 80s, former pro an ISFP **Gardner Mulloy** was the consummate player among the most senior tennis players. In 2000, 44-year-old NFL *quarterback* **Warren Moon**, ISFP, played his 24th year in professional football! Don't be surprised if you find an ISFP still going strong athletically when other Types of comparable age have faded.

Type Tips

Teach young ISFPs to "use their heads," to think of their sport and its strategies, rules, and so forth. This will help them when they enter competition and are more apt to rely upon their Feeling function.

ISFPs can be top notch football players. Though they can play every position, they especially excel at wide receiver.

ISFPs respond and learn best when they are treated with sensitivity and commended for their efforts. They often fail to see their potential. ISFPs love to have fun in whatever they do.

ISFPs easily lose confidence. They are known to struggle as much as any Type in the area of proper self image. When ISFPs become highly proficient at their sport, they will not have the struggles of other ISFPs who have yet to make their mark. Nevertheless, ISFPs can easily lose their confidence even at the professional level. It is wise for them to get objective, constructive input from those they trust.

Read the various sports' chapters for additional insights into ISFPs.

PROBABLE ISFPs IN SPORTS

Baseball:
1st: **R:** Mark McGwire, Fred McGriff, John Jaha, Jason Thompson, Sid Bream, Joe Carter
2nd Damion Easley; **R:** Harold Reynolds
ss: **R:** Ernie Banks, Maury Wills, Alfredo Griffin, Rafael Ramirez, Manuel Lee
3rd: Fernando Tatis, Dean Palmer
C: Charles Johnson, Jorge Posada; **R:** Yogi Berra, Roy Campanella, Pat Borders
OF: Moises Alou, Jermaine Dye, Richard Hildago, Henry Rodriguez, Devon White, Shane Spencer, **R:** Don Baylor, Lonnie Smith, John Shelby, Gary Pettis, Derrick May
P: Chuck Finley, Frank Castillo; **R:** J.R. Richard, Mike Scott, Mike Davis, Dave Smith, Bruce Hurst, Frank Viola, Storm Davis, Alejandro Pena, Ken Hill, Heathcliff Slocumb

Basketball: **Tim Duncan**, Kevin Willis, Elden Campbell, Juwan Howard, Horace Grant, Otis Thorpe, Lorenzen Wright, Terry Mills, Scott Williams, Shareef Rahim, Joe Smith, Derrick McKey, Chris Crawford, **Scottie Pippen**, Billy Owens, Paul Pierce, Walt Williams, Sam Mitchell, Anfernee Hardaway, Kobe Bryant, Eddie Jones, Steve Smith, Tracy Murray, Wesley Person, Larry Hughes, Richard Hamilton, Jonathan Bender, Rod Strickland, Dee Brown, Brevin Knight, Chauncey Billups, Cory Alexander, Tyus Edney, Darrick Martin

Retired: Bob McAdoo, Bill Sharman, K.C. Jones, Dennis Johnson, Mike Dunleavy, Don Chaney, Robert Parish, Joe Barry Carroll, Ralph Sampson, Bill Cartwright, Sam Bowie, Larry Nance, David Rivers, Tree Rollins, Kenny Walker, Mark West, Kevin Duckworth, Clyde Drexler, Joe Dumars, Kenny Smith, Sleepy Floyd, Spud Webb, Brian Shaw, Sedale Threatt, B.J. Armstrong, Lester Conner, Greg Grant, Tony Smith, Kevin Pritchard, Charles D. Smith, Eddie Johnson, Chris Morris, Willie Anderson, Kevin Johnson, Dale Ellis, Sean Elliott, Danny Manning,

Boxing: *Retired*: Floyd Patterson, Donald Curry, Eric Griffin

Football: Steve McNair, Daunte Culpepper, Tony Banks, Chris Redman, Tee Martin, Earnest Byner, Isaac Bruce, Carl Pickens, Marvin Harrison, Kevin Williams, Terance Mathis, Raghib "Rocket" Ishmail, Wesley Walls, Ernest Byner, Harvey Williams, Erik Williams, William Roaf, Larry Allen, Randall McDaniel, Lomas Brown, **Jonathan Ogden**, Anthony Morgan, Leon Lett, Russell Maryland, Aaron Wallace, Fred Strickland, Harlon Barnett, Greg Biekert, Doug Evans, Steve Atwater, Scooter McGruder
Retired: Lynn Swann, Doug Williams, Jeff Rutledge, John Cappelletti, Art Shell, Doug Smith, Ed "Too Tall" Jones, Mel Renfro, Lake Dawson, Gary Clark, Robert Brooks, Carnell Lake, Warren Moon,

Golf: Ernie Els, Steve Jones, Duffy Waldorf, Kenny Perry, Paul Lawrie, Craig Perks, Wayne Grady, Gene Sauers, Kathy Whitworth
Seniors: Dr. Gil Morgan, Jim Dent, Charlie Sifford, Jim Thorpe

Hockey: Bernie Nicholls, Steve Duchesne,
Retired: Bobby Orr, Gordie Howe

Skateboarding: Ben Pappas

Tennis: Bjorn Borg, Yevgeny Kafelnikov
Retired: Gardner Malloy, Jose Higueras

Track and Field: Jackie Joyner Kersee, Jesse Owens, Michael Johnson, Butch Reynolds, Hollis Conway, Henry Carr

Wrestling: Dennis Koslowski

Coaches: Lenny Wilkens, Mike Dunleavy, Paul Silas, K.C. Jones, Don Chaney, Jerry Tarkanian, Art Shell, Jack Pardee, Gene Stallings, Eddie Robinson, Cito Gaston, Don Baylor, Tony Perez, Grady Little

PROBABLE WELL KNOWN ISFPs:

Janet Jackson, Alan Jackson, "Puff Diddy" Sean Combs, Bill "Willie" Shoemaker, Don Williams, Chuck Yeager

Janet Jackson   Alan Jackson

POPULAR CAREER CHOICES:

Artist, dancer, athlete, musician, photographer, fashion designer, child care worker, nurse, animal care specialist, ministry, transportation operative, construction worker, farmer

ESFP

(Extraversion, Sensing, Feeling, Perceiving)

FEAR

(Front, Empirical, Animate, Right-brained)

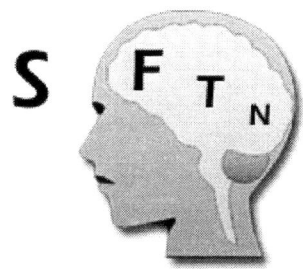

"Entertainer"

The ESFP is often the most outgoing and entertaining person in a crowd. He or she loves life and people, seeking attention and fun in every situation that arises. ESFPs are energetic, gregarious, sociable, charming and generous. Think of **Elvis Presley, Magic Johnson, Chi Chi Rodriguez, and Dolly Parton** and you will picture the ESFP's action packed, colorful persona.

ESFPs must have jobs relating to people. Being genuinely empathetic, they actively care about the welfare of others. ESFPs have a flair for style, dressing like "a million" whether they have it or not. They nonetheless often show a good deal of common sense, dealing well with the practical, immediate facts of life.

"Look at me" is the heart's cry of the ESFP. ESFPs thrive on being in front of others, displaying their showmanship. They are light hearted, romantic and optimistic. They need to feel the love and care of others more than most Types. Their generosity is hard to equal. They see gifts as symbols of love and affection.

ESFPs want their cake now and often forget to plan for later. They may need to plan for the future with strategy for saving and conserving. They can become anxious when tough times hit, fighting despondency when their careless living lands them in less than ideal circumstances. ESFPs must beware of compulsive behavior when experiencing anxiety. Controlling their weight is one area that can be a problem.

ESFPs are gross motor dominant; they rely mostly on their big muscle movements (versus fine motor). This translates to swaying their bodies to music (Elvis mastered this!), hugging friends, and exaggerating big muscle movements in sports.

ESFPs are fun to have as parents, providing a circus-like atmosphere and lifestyle. Their inconsistency, however, can be confusing to children. ESFP children live life with the same abandon as adults; this quality does not work well in school, where discipline is needed. ESFPs learn best by using their senses and by doing. The parent can help by being the "J" function for these lively performers. When their "F" function, or strong personal values, are engaged in school pursuits, ESFP children can achieve with honors.

ESFP children may be seen as hyperactive, messing up the house, being loud, always wanting to do one more thing. They love surprises and they love the limelight, the excitement of performing. Watch them, applaud them, and let them entertain you with their unique Brain Type.

ESFP Sports Profile

ESFPs are Extraverted, right-brained SFs and make some of the best athletes. Complementing their superior spatial skills, ESFPs master the big muscles of the body with speed, balance, rhythm, and timing. ESFPs generally do not have the patience or discipline to learn a sport the introspective way Introverted SPs do (ISTP and ISFP). It is helpful for them to take the time to learn the proper mechanics and techniques for their sport.

Outstanding, Entertaining Athletes

ESFPs are, and can be, among the best in the world at their chosen sport. **Muhammad Ali, Walter Payton, Magic Johnson, Tony Gwynn, Lee Trevino, Florence Griffith Joyner, Carl Lewis, and Marion Jones** have proven this.

ESFPs bring showmanship to the game as no one else can. If you want to sell tickets or draw large crowds, have an ESFP perform. The NBA's **Dennis Rodman** has probably stretched the ESFP's persona and behavior to its near limits. Few behave as has Rodman. (As mentioned repeatedly, the pronouncement of the Type traits will also be affected by upbringing and current environment.) ESFPs, genetically, have a penchant for performing with pizzazz. **Elvis Presley** and **Dolly Parton** have shown this on stage. ESFPs often play their sport as if they were on stage. They want to be noticed, and with flair.

Five years into his professional NBA career, **Magic Johnson** said:

> I just love the games. Just to be out there. Whenever I am, I'm in my own little world. It's the only place I can really relax, let it flow, be myself. Out there, I can let go of it all. That's me out there.[28]

ESFPs are born to play with spontaneity and style. They know of no other way. **Lee Trevino**, the incessant talking and clowning golfer known as the Merry Mex, was asked if he planned on changing his style when joining the Senior Tour:

> If I've got to change, give me a .45 and I'll blow my brains out.[29]

Suffice it to say, most ESFPs carry their personality into their performances.

Say What They Feel

ESFPs tend to share their feelings sometimes without a lot of thought first. This "FP" trait of ESFPs is especially perceptible to Thinking, left-brained persons. Boston Celtic coach, ESTJ Chris Ford, said of **Charles Barkley**, in 1991:

> I love Charles because he's so honest. You can see a thought form in his head and then come right out of his mouth without stopping in between.[30]

ESFPs are also playful and fun-loving. From the quotable **Charles Barkley** again:

> Life's got to be funny. If you're not enjoying it, you might as well be dead.[31]

Influence Others

Basketball player **Bo Kimble** has demonstrated the inherent, persuasive, ESFP communication style. Paul Westhead, Loyola Marymount coach of the 1990 NCAA tournament team, on why he left ESFP Kimble in the game after getting four fouls in the first half:

That's my style. Besides, Bo's a very good talker. If he'd gotten his fifth, he would have talked his way back into the game.[32]

Caring, Sensitive, Charitable

Not all ESFPs have the brashness of Charles Barkley. Some have much different values (or Feelings) and demonstrate a contrasting persona. **Tony Gywnn**, all-star outfielder, has been known for loving his family, honoring others, politeness, and being extraordinarily generous with his time.

Elvis Presley was known for his spontaneous generosity. His heart would often go out to the less fortunate, even to the point of buying them a new car on the spot.

When NBA super-star, **Magic Johnson**, announced his retirement in 1991, Los Angeles Mayor, Tom Bradley, commented:

> Magic Johnson has been the most charismatic, most caring, most kind sports figure I've known in my lifetime. He has never been too busy to help a good cause, and that's the legacy he has provided for us and will remain forever.[33]

Despite **Charles Barkley's** Extraverted, oft pert capricious behavior, he possesses the caring side of his Brain Type as well. Derek Smith, former teammate of Barkley's in Philadelphia, said:

> He is easily one of the most generous people I know. Guys come in for 10-day contracts, and Charles gives them his cars. He invites them into his home. He's a giver.[34]

Notice the ESFP athletes listed in this section and you will see a number of them who magnify the ESFP's normal behavior. Others are more reserved. Do not forget, upbringing and current environment affect external behavior and one's persona. What they do not influence is Brain Type and genetically predisposed cerebral activity.

Type Tips

ESFPs perform best by being aggressive and reacting to whatever comes their way. When they are forced to slow down and do a lot of thinking, their performances suffer. They must stay loose, not deviating too much from their normal free flowing style of play.

ESFPs need to practice. No Type is more prone to following impulses and delighting in the moment. Thus, ESFPs get bored easily. Parents and coaches need to help ESFPs focus on their short-term goals. Long term goals often seem like an eternity to ESFPs. They also like perks or rewards for goals accomplished, so try to help them have fun along the way.

When ESFPs lose interest in or don't feel good about their sport, for whatever reason, their attitudes go south in a hurry. Help them see the "big picture" and keep a good attitude. Things could easily turn around.

Read the various sports' chapters for additional insights into ESFPs.

PROBABLE ESFPs IN SPORTS

Baseball:
- 1st: Frank Thomas, Andres Galarraga, Carlos Delgado
- IF: **Nomar Garciaparra**, Barry Larkin, Roberto Alomar, Jose Vidro, Edgardo Alfonzo, Tony Batista, Junior Spivey, Miguel Tejada, Luis Castillo, Adrian Beltre, Luis Sojo;
  - **R:** Mike Sharperson, Lenny Harris, Jose Oquendo, Junior Felix
- OF: **Barry Bonds, Albert Pujols**, Ken Griffey Jr., Larry Walker, Manny Ramirez, Andruw Jones, Garret Anderson, Geronimo Berroa, Al Martin, Magglio Ordonez, Dimitri Young, Felix Jose;
  - **R: Willie Mays**, Willie Stargell, Dave Parker, Dave Henderson, Kal Daniels, Kirby Puckett, Willie Wilson, Bobby Bonilla, Brian McRae, Glenallen Hill, Albert Belle, **Tony Gywnn**
- C: Ivan Rodriguez; **R:** Joe Garagiola, Tony Pena
- P: Bartolo Colon, Livan Hernandez, Wilson Alvarez, Jose Rijo, Armando Benitez, Freddy Garcia;
- **R: Dizzy Dean**, Satchel Paige, Doc Ellis, John Candelaria, Ben Rivera, Alex Fernandez

Basketball: Brendan Haywood, Kwame Brown, Jason Collins, Othella Harrington, Al Harrington, Gary Trent, Danny Fortson, Jermaine O'Neal, Elton Brand, Calbert Cheaney, Ron Artest, Rashard Lewis, Shawn Marion, Latrell Sprewell, Allan Houston, Isaiah Rider, **Ray Allen**, Tariq Abdul-Wahad, Richard Jefferson, Baron Davis, Steve Francis, Andre Miller, Antonio Daniels, Will Avery,
Nikki McCray, Natalie Williams

Retired: **Oscar Robertson, Magic Johnson**, Isiah Thomas, Calvin Murphy, Bob Lanier, Meadowlark Lemon, Darryl Dawkins, John S. Williams, **Cheryl Miller**, Tony Campbell, Bo Kimble, Wayman Tisdale, Stanley Roberts, Victor Alexander, Stacey King, J.R. Reid, **Charles Barkley**, Dennis Rodman, Sam Perkins, Oliver Miller, Horacio Llamas

Boxing: Muhammad Ali, George Foreman, James Buster Douglas

Football: Donovan McNabb, Rodney Peete, Jeff Blake, Emmitt Smith, Jamal Anderson, Edgerrin James, Natrone Means, Ricky Watters, Larry Centers, Jamal Lewis, Lawrence Phillips, Eric Green, **Keyshawn Johnson, Randy Moss**, Frankie Sanders, Troy Brown, Jermaine Wiggins, Bruce Armstrong, Ruben Brown, Orlando Pace, Ron Stone, Bruce Smith, Neil Smith, Willie McGinest, Michael Strahan, Hugh Douglas, Cortez Kennedy, Sean Gilbert, Michael Dean Perry, William Fuller, Gilbert Brown, **Warren Sapp**, Darrell Russell, Bryan Cox, Jessie Armstead, Micheal Barrow, Kevin Hardy, Greg Townsend, Tedy Bruschi

Retired: **Walter Payton**, Don Meredith, Dexter Manley, Chris Collinsworth, Jerome Brown, Ottis Anderson, Anthony Munoz, William (The Refrigerator), Perry, Ken Norton Jr. Randall Cunningham, Thurman Thomas, Nate Newton, **Reggie White**

Golf: Notah Begay III, Shigeki Maruyama, Omar Uresti, Jerry Pate,
Annika Sorenstam, Nancy Lopez, JoAnne Carner, Michelle McGann, Meg Mallon, Caroline Keggi, Leta Lindley
  Seniors: Lee Trevino, Chi Chi Rodriguez, Jesse Patino

Hockey: *Retired*: Marcel Dionne

Skating (figure): Nicole Bobek, Surya Bonaly, Elizabeth Manley, Rosalynn Sumners

Snow skiing: Picabo Street

Swimming: Summer Sanders

Tennis: Serena Williams, Lindsay Davenport, Anna Kournikova, Conchita Martinez, Jennifer Capriati
  Retired: Pancho Segura

Track and Field: Carl Lewis, Florence Griffith Joyner, Marion Jones, Sandra Farmer-Patrick

Coaches: John Madden, Wayne Fontes, Isiah Thomas

Sports Media: John Madden, Chris Collinsworth, Joe Garagiola, Don Meredith, Jerry Pate

PROBABLE WELL KNOWN ESFPs:

Elvis Presley, Roy Clark, John Madden, Jennifer Lopez, Britney Spears, Dolly Parton, Sarah Brightman, Wynonna Judd, Aretha Franklin, Sandi Patti, Charo, Ivana Trump, Tammy Faye Bakker, Paris Hilton

Ivana Trump

POPULAR CAREER CHOICES:

Tour and travel, sales, public relations, catering, performing arts, athletics, nursing, child care, cosmetology, designing, transportation operatives, construction

21
SJs

ISTJ, ESTJ
ISFJ, ESFJ

ISTJ

(Introversion, Sensing, Thinking, Judging)
BEIL
(Back, Empirical, Inanimate, Left-brained)

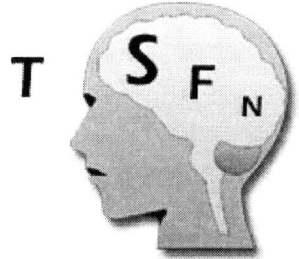

"Investigator"

The ISTJ is a serious individual, driven by duty, realistically encountering life as a project to be ordered and understood. The ISTJ is calm, self controlled, almost aloof to the needs of others until they become obvious. Then the ISTJ rushes to the rescue, determined to be of assistance even if the need is not completely identified with by the ISTJ.

As children, ISTJs are quiet, neat, obedient, and a source of pleasure to the adults in charge. They are often good at school, turning in neat work on time. They are cautious, particularly in new situations, not wanting to be center stage. ISTJs prefer structure, wanting well defined goals and procedures, a schedule. This preference then is imposed by them on others, especially on their parents. This means the ISTJ wants the parent to be responsible, dependable and on time. The ISTJ can appear bossy and controlling which he sees as being orderly and responsible. The room of the ISTJ gets increasingly neat as the child gets older.

The ISTJ can be described as hard working, dependable, persistent, analytical, traditional, pragmatic, conservative, honor bound, and more cautious than spontaneous. The rules must be followed and the work done before leisure can be enjoyed. Because he or she is organized and efficient, the ISTJ may be given a position of authority, though remaining a reluctant leader. At ease with logic and words, the ISTJ appears to have an outgoing nature, but is one of the most private of all sixteen Types. The ISTJ can mask vulnerability to criticism.

ISTJs show love by providing rock solid security and work with the certainty of the here and now over what may develop from stepping out into the unknown. They may marry irresponsible people and try to reform them. They are as demanding of those around them as they are of themselves. Though fiercely loyal, the ISTJ can seem cold and uncaring, needing to voice feelings of love and appreciation more often. Family affairs and holidays are usually important, as is being a provider or homemaker. ISTJs are happiest at home among family rather than meeting new people and approaching new situations.

The ISTJ does things right, is faithful and consistent in parenting, generous, painstaking, and decisive. ISTJs need to let loose a little, to take time for people so they don't become isolated, and to recognize and deal with their own personal feelings. Even free time must have a purpose for the ISTJ and be task oriented. As guardians of traditional values, ISTJs are useful with their careful planning and patient attention to detail. They need, however, to take time to have some fun and be willing to ask for help. ISTJs select friends carefully, being keen observers of things and people around them. Though seemingly aloof and distant, they need and blossom under encouragement and appreciation for who they are and for jobs responsibly completed. A little notice of their strengths goes a long way.

ISTJs are acutely aware of their Sensing environment. Temperature, odors, sounds, and sights preoccupy their conscious and subconscious minds. Physically, ISTJs are generally the thinnest or slightest of frame of the 16 Types. Their Introverted, dominant Sensing function regulates their appetites with the sensitivity of a spider with a bug on its web. Satiety is quickly experienced. Overweight ISTJs are exceptions to the rule.

In recent years, Jungian-based questionnaires have shown an increase in ISTJ respondents. Many who rely on the popular psychological types approach, and do not understand Brain Types, believe ISTJs are one of the most commonly found Types in America. They are greatly mislead. Men in particular score their quizzes as ISTJs—placing high value on the reserved, pragmatic, logical, and organized traits of the "Investigator." Utilizing Brain Types, especially its motor skill traits, quickly reveals the true ISTJ. In reality, the "Investigator" is one of the least found Types in the U.S.

ISTJs and Business/Vocations

The words "trustworthy" and "perfectionistic" typify the ISTJ. Organized and structured, ISTJs are an asset to almost any area of business. As dominant Sensates, they excel in hands on, practical occupations. Proficient with assignments placed before them, ISTJs enjoy problem-solving, especially when they must utilize their logical and analytical minds. They may go to great lengths ensuring that a project or assignment is completed down to the very last detail. They are collectors and articulators of facts to support views and projects. Overseeing and managing work that requires thoroughness comes readily to ISTJs. They appreciate guidelines and specifications and will stay within the boundaries of their position.

Although they aren't as controlling as Extraverted Js, ISTJs respect leadership and expect other coworkers to abide by the given rules. The ISTJ manager will keep things in order and delegate when necessity demands. Most are very dedicated and will not settle for mediocrity.

ISTJ Sports Profile

ISTJs are Introverted, left-brained STs. Found in many professional sports, they can be top-notch athletes. ISTJs tend to take a more defensive approach to their sport; this is where they excel most naturally. With hard work, they can master the offensive end as well.

Introspective, Protective

Relying heavily on their left brain, ISTJs prefer processing matters sequentially. They want to ensure things are done properly and with control. This generally gives them a more conservative, defensive approach to sports, and life. Don't be fooled, however, for when their skills, confidence, and motivation levels are high, they can be aggressive, with extraordinary concentration skills, as exhibited by ISTJs **Jack Nicklaus** and **Chris Evert** in their prime.

Golf normally requires deep concentration in times of tremendous pressure, and ISTJs excel with the mind, loving to consider all the nuances of the game and course, analyzing matters thoroughly with great patience.

ISTJ **Orel Hershiser** won the 1988 Gold Glove Award as the best fielding pitcher in the National League. He not only shut the opponents down at the plate with no runs for 59 consecutive scoreless innings this same year, but he captured this defensive award in classic ISTJ fashion.

Let's not forget Hershiser's unbelievable scoreless inning string. Few, if any, thought ENTJ Don Drysdale's record could ever be broken. With the pennant race on the line, Hershiser bore down and maximized his ISTJ concentration. (It's hard to believe, but ISTJs often find it hard to concentrate. Yet when something really gets their interest, no Brain Type can concentrate longer and harder on the present.)

ISTJs now retired from the NBA include defensive stars **Michael Cooper** and **Bobby Jones**. Michael Cooper's wife once said of her ISTJ mate, and ex NBA player:

> He doesn't spend, he doesn't want clothes. He got married in a T shirt and jeans and he has been that way ever since. He doesn't have a credit card, and he has only one gas card. That's a tough way to live.[1]

Tough Under Pressure

ISTJs generally handle sports pressure better than their other SJ counterparts. Their dominant Introverted Sensing function, supported by their auxiliary Thinking, enables them to maintain their composure and objectivity. ESTJs, generally second best of the SJs at handling pressure, show more effects of anxiety in the slower moving sports that require finesse.

Successful in Big Events

It often takes an important event for ISTJs to give full effort, particularly in an offensive mode. When the big event involves a team sport, ISTJs want to make sure they contribute their share. They give extra effort for the team's sake. In a major baseball game, ISTJs will normally bat for a higher average than in the normal season. If the event is basketball, they will score more points, especially if their teammates drop in their offensive production.

Major events in individual sports, such as tennis or golf, also bring out the reserved tenacity and competitive fire in ISTJs. **Jack Nicklaus's** performances in the four pro major tournaments is unmatched—winning 18! Winner of three majors on the PGA Tour, professional golfer **Larry Nelson** was particularly effective in pressure packed Ryder Cup play. In the year 2000, Nelson was the top money leader on the Senior PGA Tour. **Orel Hershiser** performed his best through the pressures of the Dodgers' pennant drive.

Lack Confidence

When ISTJs are exposed to new and challenging situations in sports, they often lack confidence, even when they have expert abilities. Unlike some Brain Types who relish such opportunities, ISTJs tend to be cautious and less than aggressive.

LPGA star **Betsy King**, ISTJ, did not win a golf tournament in her first seven years on tour. Nevertheless, from 1984-1989, she won 20 tournament titles—more than any other player on the men's or ladies' tour! She won back to back U.S. Opens in 1989 and 1990. In 1995, King won her 30th career victory to gain entrance into the LPGA Hall of Fame. As of 2000, King was the LPGA's all-time money winner—with earnings near $7 million dollars.

Paul Azinger, another ISTJ golfing great, was quoted after his 1988 victory in the Bay Hill Tournament at Orlando, Florida:

> I responded under pressure better than I ever thought I was capable of.[2]

These words came from the ISTJ who had been on Tour for 5 years, had won 3 tournaments in 1987—the same year he was named PGA Player of the Year.

Introverted

After winning the 1984 U.S. Open, golfer **Larry Nelson** was quoted regarding his personality:

> My wife's an extrovert, I'm an introvert. She wants to have people over to the house. I want to be alone.

So?

> So what she does is get me out of the house and have people over.[3]

Jack Nicklaus was voted player of the century in a poll by *Golf Magazine* in 1988. At a dinner honoring him, he said:

> All the finalists were asked to prepare a speech, but I thought that would be presumptuous. I said, 'I'll think of something when I get up there if I'm selected.' Well, I'm up here, and I don't know what to say.[4]

Thoroughness

Columnist Scott Osler wrote, in 1988:

> Every big league pitcher keeps a book on hitters. Some pitchers actually jot down the information in a book, some store it in their heads. Some, because of lack of storage space keep the information in their catchers' heads.
>
> Orel Hershiser may be the first pitcher ever to store his pitching secrets on a floppy disk. Orel is a child of the computer age. The Sultan of Software.[5]

Hershiser began using a computer in 1988 to keep track of all the baseball information that would be of interest to a pitcher.

Liked and Well-Mannered

ISTJ athletes are generally liked for their humble, low key demeanors. Fierce competitors when they want to be, they play within the rules. They don't pop at the mouth like some other Types; thus, they are liked and respected.

Great Coaches

No Brain Type has a better coaching mind than ISTJs. When considering all the facets of coaching, the deep thinking, analytic, logical, realistic and perfectionistic ISTJs are naturals. Regardless of the sport, they have an inherent ability to know how to teach and coach. ISTJs may not have been the best at performing the sport, but it is hard to find a Type that is better at coaching it.

Basketball's **John Wooden, football's Tom Landry,** and **baseball's Walter Alston** will long be remembered by true sports pundits as being among the greatest coaches of all time in their respective sports. To better understand the coaching techniques of ISTJs, and to learn of other ISTJ coaches, see the chapter on coaches.

Long-Suffering, Loyal, and Long-Lasting

SJs are inherently loyal and persevering. They feel obligated to stick through thick and thin until they see the job completed. Not ones to shun responsibility, SJs stand the tests of storms in their painstaking efforts to accomplish their tasks. They approach coaching with this same mindset.

Thinking SJs can handle criticism much better than their Feeling counterparts. Therefore, STJs would be more naturally suited to the rigors and pressures of coaching. As long as STJs believe they are doing the right thing with integrity, they are a bulwark. Couple these traits with Introversion (a preference not inclined to sudden changes) and we can see why ISTJs are among the most long lasting of the coaches, staying in the profession for as long as they are needed.

Type Tips

Development of spatial awareness will improve ISTJs' athletic skills, enabling them to minimize conscious thoughts and have for smoother motor movements in competition. Visualization techniques can help them to activate their less preferred right hemisphere.

ISTJs must learn to stay relaxed while performing, particularly in their forearms, wrists, and hands. They will have a tendency to tighten up in these areas when under pressure.

ISTJs must maintain positive thoughts to eliminate their tendency toward self-criticism. Further suggestions are highlighted in the various sports' chapters in this book.

PROBABLE ISTJs IN SPORTS

Baseball: Craig Counsell,
   Retired: Bill Russell, Mike Witt, Dick Schofield
         Orel Hershiser, Jeff Blauser

Basketball: Stacey Augmon,
   Retired: Michael Cooper, Bobby Jones, Kyle Macy, Rick Adelman, Jay Burson, Kurt Rambis, Jeff Hornacek, Steve Kerr

Football: *Retired:* Jeff Hostetler, Steve Walsh

Golf: Paul Azinger, Scott Simpson, Larry Mize, Mike Reid
      Betsy King, Chris Johnson
   Seniors: Jack Nicklaus, Al Geiberger, Larry Nelson

Tennis: Paul Haarhuis, Andrei Cherkasov
   Retired: Chris Evert, Stan Smith

Coaches: John Wooden, Mike Krzyzewski, Roy Williams, Steve Fisher, Rick Adelman, Tom Landry, Ted Marchibroda, Tom Osborne, Walter Alston, Marcel Lachemann

PROBABLE WELL KNOWN ISTJs:

Queen Elizabeth II, Pat Nixon, Sen. Alan Simpson, Tom Osborne

Queen Elizabeth II

Sen. Alan Simpson

Popular Career Choices:

Law, legal secretary, dentistry, banking, accounting, tax examining, financial planning, insurance, teaching, coaching, engineering, computer programming, physical sciences, supervising or managing, law enforcement, military, fire fighting, farming

ESTJ

(Extraversion, Sensing, Thinking, Judging)

FEIL

(Front, Empirical, Inanimate, Left-brained)

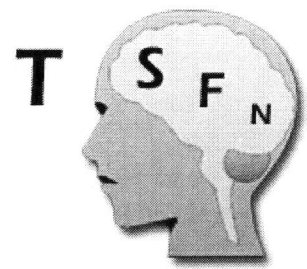

"Supervisor"

As children, ESTJs want their lives to be structured, predictable, and secure. They expect their parents to exercise authority over them, but they want them to be fair. ESTJ children play hard and may be "bossy," developing the aggressive, leadership style common to this Type. They are keen observers, organized and industrious, earning money at an early age and saving toward planned purchases. ESTJs are likely candidates for sports, scouting, holding school office, band, youth groups, anything that requires membership and organization. They want to keep moving toward a goal.

ESTJs are enthusiastic class members and are obedient to fair and sensible rules. They volunteer information, thinking quickly on their feet. At home, they can be both strong-willed and highly responsible. They can become high achievers if they invest time and effort—particularly in their pragmatic academics.

The ESTJ enjoys deciding what must be done and then putting into practice procedures that hasten the finished product. Managing an operation is a welcome stimulus for the ESTJ, yielding respect from peers and family for dependability and a job well done.

When describing the ESTJ, one may use terms such as logical, practical, industrious, capable, generally outgoing, dependable, efficient, traditional, critical, and conservative. They also do not want to change something unless there is a definite need. Taken to its end, this characteristic can lead to controlling, inflexible ESTJs. They need to remain open to new information and not become preoccupied with fear.

ESTJs often fear financial disaster and losing control of their lives and those of their families. Responsibilities are taken seriously with an assertive take charge attitude.

ESTJs have presidential tendencies, giving directives easily, yet they need to see and value the feelings of others. ESTJs frequently hold high positions, which they use to impose their judgments and opinions on others. To maintain balance, they need to plan for free time and relaxation, relinquishing their control over others for a time.

As long as ESTJs feel needed in their chosen work, retirement is postponed. They often live out the old saying of preferring to die with their boots on. In 1998, South Carolina's Strom Thurmond, ESTJ, set the longevity record of nearly 43 years for serving in the U.S. Senate. At 95, he also became the oldest senator in history.

ESTJs usually have a grasp on many facts and can communicate them well. They are ready with an opinion on most topics, making them easy to get to know.

Extraverted or Introverted?

ESTJs often do not see themselves as Extraverted. One reason for this is their standards for associates are high, and when these standards aren't met, ESTJs often choose to disassociate. They can enjoy their privacy. The telltale identification for ESTJs is their energy levels. Their personas may resemble ISTJs at times, but ESTJs have superior energies. When healthy, ESTJs are busy tackling one task after another.

Charming, Witty—Cold, Critical?

All of us know ESTJs, whether we recognize them as such or not. They occupy many leadership positions. Some are warm, fun, witty, and great conversationalists, while others of us know ESTJs (and perhaps these same ESTJs) as cold, judgmental and controlling. They can have wide swings in their personalities, demonstrating the mood they feel will best help them control a given situation. If they believe the tough side is necessary, you will most likely be treated sternly. Conversely, if they believe charm is best for the moment, you'll be charmed.

British golf star **Nick Faldo** is a case in point. In 1991, *Sports Illustrated (SI)* wrote of the ESTJ:

> What is it that makes him to be the world's most impeccable grouch?[9]

Yet, *SI* shared another side of Faldo:

> How come he's charming and witty and

emotional only when nobody is around to write about it?[10]

SI continued:

> In private, he could not be more polite, chatty and amiable.[11]

Not all ESTJs act like Faldo has, but they do have these tendencies. Faldo's poor relationship with the media and players, especially in the past, could have been due to a number of factors in his life. Regardless, he has not placed a high level of importance on winsomeness with the public.

There are other ESTJs who do care greatly about their public image. They can be charming and warm, possessing the best of social graces. Most ESTJs prefer this aura, but sometimes can find it difficult to maintain when trying to control matters.

An ESTJ with a wonderful reputation, particularly in Texas, is former baseball great **Nolan Ryan**. He intimidated major league hitters for 27 years with a fastball that exceeded 100 mph. Off the field, Ryan won numerous admirers as well. His down to earth, conservative, responsible, and personable character was a real plus for baseball.

One other characteristic of the ESTJ is worth noting. When ESTJs Extravert, they engage their Thinking function. Thus, it is understandable why their critical eye for right and wrong can be so active. ESTJs firmly planted in their Thinking will freely criticize, though they'll temper their opinions when they want or need to get along with others.

When ESTJs Introvert (which includes being with persons they enjoy), they actively engage their non judging, Sensing function. In this mode, they are caught up in perceiving matters rather than judging them and will tend to be more mellow.

ESTJs, like every other Brain Type, access different brain functions according to where their energies are directed. Therefore, large swings in behavior can occur.

ESTJ Sports Profile

Common to all ESTJ athletes is their meticulous bent. The ways they demonstrate it differs, but you can be sure: They all have it.

British golfer **Nick Faldo** shies away from hats for fear it will mess up his hair. He has trimmed his nails every Monday. He had his fireplace rebuilt, in his new house no less, because it was a little more than an inch off center.[12]

Hard Working, Hands on

ESTJs are arduous workers in matters they like. They will channel their Extraverted energies into controlling the present. **Nolan Ryan's** ranch manager in 1991 spoke of his famous baseball boss:

> He's a hands on owner, for sure. When he comes here, he gets right into it. He helps us castrate the steers, dehorn 'em, everything. Nothing fazes him. I'll see him reach into the shoot with that million dollar right arm and I'll say to myself, `Are you sure you want to do that?' But he'll never buckle. He'll go right in there.[13]

Routine Regimented

Naturally, all Brain Types develop routines that stay with them a lifetime, but the ESTJ is fixated on routines. Just hang around one sometime and you'll quickly get the point. Take Nolan Ryan, for instance. Following his 7th no hitter in May of 1991, at 44 years of age, Nolan was a creature of routines again. Only 4½ hours after getting to bed this memorable night, Nolan was up and at it again. He said:

> Once a game is over . . . Well, it's like this morning. I was down in the weight room preparing myself for my next start. That's what I have to concern myself with—my routine—so I'll be ready.[14]

Generous, Philanthropic

ESTJs like to maintain the time honored institutions of society. They will give freely of their time and money, if need be, to keep helpful organizations afloat and see legitimate needs met. *Sports Illustrated* wrote again of **Nolan Ryan:**

> He does not do the autograph shows, signing for money. He does not do speeches for money, but he does talk for certain charities he considers important.[15]

ESTJs are Extraverted, left-brained STs. Their physical dexterity makes them splendid athletes. ESTJs are intense competitors and are found at the professional level in many sports. They, like most Types, tend to excel in some sports more than others.

Great Dexterity

Sports Illustrated said of **Nick Faldo**:

> What he loved was sports. Nick was the kid you hated in school, the one who was good at everything. He was a county class swimmer, a wonderful canoeist and bicyclist, a terrific soccer goalie, runner, discus thrower, basketball player and cricket player. However no sport captivated him until he saw Nicklaus play in the 1971 Masters on the telly. Nick was 14.[16]

You may not find ESTJs at the top of every sport, but it's hard to find a sport at which they cannot be good, even at an early age.

The Fine Wine of Sports

ESTJs are analogous to fine wine; they improve with age. As ESTJs mature in athletics, they are better able to control their high energy levels. This translates into smoother motor movements and less tension in their wrist and hand area. Since STs are most gifted with fine motor skills, excessive energy and tension to this body area becomes counterproductive.

Baseball's **Nolan Ryan** became a much better pitcher in his forties than he was in his twenties. In the twilight of his career, he lost velocity in his fastball, but he could better control it, as well as his curveball and changeup, something not possible before.

Baseball's **Bob Boone** played his best ball and hit his highest the end of his 18-year professional catching career. **Nick Faldo** achieved his golfing best after many years on Tour.

Obstacles

To their disadvantage, ESTJs' dominant Thinking function can get out of control under competitive pressure. Since they do not possess the grace and flow of their Extraverted right brain P cousins (ESFP, ESTP), they can injure themselves and others. Many ESTJs in professional basketball have had reputations of letting their aggressions get out of control.

Former President **Gerald Ford,** ESTJ, developed a reputation for sending golfing galleries scurrying for cover (when his left-brained Thinking came under too much pressure).

ESTJ tennis pro **Pam Shriver** got so angry in her 1990 third round loss at the Virginia Slims tournament in Florida that she kicked a chair and broke her toe.

I coached a youth basketball team (13- and 14-year olds) that included an ESTJ. He was one of the bigger kids and was developing his skills. In typical ESTJ fashion, he enjoyed banging under the boards and giving full effort. Unfortunately, we had to stop nearly every practice to give first aid to a fellow teammate he had hurt. The ESTJ rarely realized how rough he was playing. His teammates wished he had. He, like other ESTJs, will develop greater body control as they practice and mature. Don't forget, Js (left brain persons) will generally have greater difficulty with graceful movements than their P counterparts.

Type Tips

ESTJs will find it helpful to seek out persons who can help them learn to relax and maintain their composure in competition. ESTJ pitcher **John Smoltz** was 2 11 with the Atlanta Braves in the first half of the 1991 season. At wit's end, he sought the counsel of a sports psychologist who could help him relax. The result? Smoltz went 12-2 the remainder of the year, helping his team make it to the World Series where they eventually lost in one of the hardest fought Series ever played. ESTJs, will battle anxiety as long as they play sports. Learning to remain cool in competition is of prime importance. (In 1996, Smoltz won 24 regular-season games and was voted the National League Cy Young Award.)

ESTJs need to consciously relax their arms, wrists, and hands in pressured competition. Otherwise, their superior fine motor skills will work counterproductively.

Like other dominant left-brained Js, they need to rely more on the their spatial right hemisphere. By developing greater visual awareness, they will perform more smoothly and skillfully.

Read the various sports' chapters for additional insights into ESTJs.

PROBABLE ESTJs IN SPORTS

Baseball:
IF: Ed Sprague
OF: Austin Kearns **R:** Tom Brunansky
C: Damian Miller, John Flaherty; **R:** Bob Boone, Brian Harper, Ernie Whitt, Ron Karkovice
P: John Smoltz, Jason Bere, Roberto Hernandez, Josh Beckett;
  R: Nolan Ryan, Jeff Russell, Bryan Harvey, Duane Ward, Kevin Gross, Jim Gott, Willie Frazier, Danny Cox, Mike Harkey Doug Henry

Basketball: Greg Ostertag, Eric Montross, Cherokee Parks, Vitaly Potapenko, Kurt Thomas, Greg Foster, Stanislav Medvedenko, Joel Pryzbila, Walter McCarty, Mike Miller
Lisa Leslie
  Retired: Rudy Tomjanovich, Mitch Kupchak, Chris Ford, Greg Kite, Frank Brickowski, Rick Smits, Joe Kleine, George Zidek, Olden Polynice

Football: Ryan Leaf, Scott Mitchell, Danny Wuerffel, John Walsh, Pat Barnes
  Retired: Keith Millard, John Alt, Sean Salisbury

Golf: Nick Faldo
  Seniors: David Graham, Andy North, Dave Barr, Don Pooley

Hockey: Dave Taylor

Racing (auto): Al Unser

Tennis: David Wheaton,
  Retired: Ted Schroeder, Pam Shriver, Manuela Maleeva Fragniere

Track and Field: Sergei Bubka, Tom Petranoff

Coaches:
Baseball: Bruce Bochy, Bob Boone
Basketball: Dick Motta, Bill Fitch, Rudy Tomjanovich, George Karl, Chris Ford, Dean Smith, John Thompson, Jim Boeheim, Dale Brown, Jim Harrick, Billy Tubbs
Football: Dan Reeves, Mike Holmgren, George Allen, Chuck Knox, Rich Brooks, Buddy Ryan, Andy Reid, Bo Schembechler, Don James
Golf: Jack Grout
Owners: Marge Schott

PROBABLE WELL KNOWN ESTJs:
Bob Dole, Geraldine Ferarro, Gerald Ford, Jesse Helms, Walter Mondale, Richard Nixon, Strom Thurmond, Harry Truman, Tom Bradley, Raisa Gorbachev, Rose Kennedy, George Shultz, Gen. Thomas Kelly, James B. Stockdale, Jim Lovell, Judge Joseph Wapner, Fawn Hall, Marla Maples

Harry Truman   Richard Nixon   Gerald Ford   Robert Dole

Popular Career Choices:
Employment that involves money, facts and objects: business, management, finance, banking, commerce, accounting, law, home economics, teaching, school administration, cosmetology, office administration, secretarial, law enforcement, military

ISFJ

(Introversion, Sensing, Feeling, Judging)

BEAL

(Back, Empirical, Animate, Left-brained)

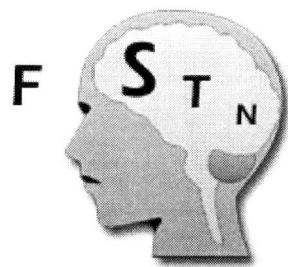

"Assistant"

Behind many successful, high powered men and organizations, one often finds the dependable, responsible, hard working ISFJ. ISFJs have a strong desire to be of service, to minister to individual needs, and to complete all work begun. To make things happen, they carefully follow handbooks and rules, trying to do everything themselves, tending to become overworked.

As a child, the ISFJ is quiet, obedient, loving, loyal, and hard-working, regularly trying to please the teacher. ISFJs do chores, are on time, and rarely behave improperly. They need routine, appreciation and gentle encouragement to venture out of their comfort zones, and recognition for consistency and diligence.

To ISFJs, work is good and must be finished before play can be enjoyed. They need to practice a skill alone before having the confidence to show it to others. They keep a few close friends, often for a lifetime, carrying a sense of history. They value tradition and loyalty.

The ISFJ is a devoted mate and family member, bringing up children to conform to society's expectations. A diligent homemaker, the ISFJ is neat, orderly, thrifty, and practical, with a high sense of duty. Because ISFJs are so conscientious, they are apt to be judgmental toward nonconformists and those whose behavior disagrees with the standards of the ISFJ. They may be filled with resentment toward these people, while being attracted to them in order to help change them.

ISFJs are known to marry irresponsible persons with the goal of reforming them. ISFJs are then often taken for granted or caught up in worry. Neglecting to take time off to have fun, they can develop anxiety and physical ailments. They may need encouragement to delegate some of the load they are carrying. In the face of trials, they need to reach out and confide in others. Wishing to please everyone can be a heavy burden.

Center stage and positions of authority over others are not enjoyed or sought by ISFJs. (It is rare to find an ISFJ who's been bold enough to become well known.) Rather, they are outstanding executing jobs involving repeated sequential procedures with tangible results. Though likely to take the first job offered them, they will do their best with it. They organize life around the people most important to them, usually family. Hopefully, they will not harbor intense feelings of being misunderstood or taken for granted, but will establish a positive lifestyle being a pillar of society, working loyally for the common welfare, and building a network of strong relationships.

ISFJ Sports Profile

ISFJs are Introverted left-brained SFs. They enjoy participating in sports, though they are not found frequently in professional circles. In athletics, they exercise great control over their gross motor movements. Their legs are their mainstay, their greatest source of strength. If ISFJs work at it, they can be leapers with excellent vertical jump. For example, the NBA's **Andrew Lang**, **Dale Davis**, and **P.J. Brown** have been top notch shot blockers.

Timid

ISFJs normally show timidity and caution in athletics, just as they do in life. As they progress athletically, these factors become less of a problem, though something always to be faced.

Three typological preferences contribute to ISFJs' lack of aggressiveness: their Introversion is generally conserving energy, not expending it; their Feelings are seeking harmony, not contention; and their left-brained dominance (J) will not let them "jump in and ask questions later."

Sports that cause high levels of fear are unwelcomed by ISFJs. Young ISFJs do not like to face the hard throwing pitcher on the mound. They may step into the batter's box, but they are not likely to crowd the plate. Yet, if they are unafraid of the pitcher, they are capable of hitting the ball hard, using their body to generate power. Defensively in baseball, they are reluctant to charge the ball or stick their nose down to snag a hard grounder.

On the other hand, some ISFJs are found playing football. A few have even made it to the NFL, but the chances of them becoming household names are not high. The most likely position for NFL success is offensive tackle. One rare ISFJ with NFL stardom has been offensive tackle and All-Pro **Richmond Webb**. In 1997, the 6'6", 300-pound Webb played in his seventh consecutive Pro Bowl. He was recognized as the prime protector on his Miami Dolphins team for superstar quarterback Dan Marino.

Basketball is a fun sport for ISFJs. They don't have to worry about a hard ball smacking them in the face but can enjoy playing with a ball that is much less intimidating.

Defensive Mentality

Basketball is a sport that especially demonstrates the defensive talents of ISFJs. They play defense properly, using their strong, SF legs to keep the person they're guarding from the basket. Yet they need to work hard at developing lateral quickness. ISFJs are unselfish players, looking for ways to complement their teammates. They feel they can do this best by playing good defense. If ISFJs begin basketball at an early age and with good coaching, they can develop a finely-tuned offensive game.

Bowling and Horseshoes

Though infrequently found in professional sports, two sports where an ISFJ has been the absolute best is in bowling and horseshoes. **Walter Ray Williams Jr.** has dominated off and on for over a decade on the Pro Bowlers Tour. Walter has captured the Player of the Year award four times—1986, 1993, 1996, and 1997. In 1995, he was inducted into the PBA Hall of Fame.

To physically direct a heavy ball down a long wooden lane with pinpoint accuracy requires excellent body control. Walter's style is not right-brained graceful, but more mechanical, SFJ gross motor regulated. His mastery over the body's large muscles has made him durable and bowling proficient.

Amazingly, Walter is also regarded as the best horseshoe player in the world, having won the World Horseshoe Pitching Championships six times. Williams estimates that he throws a bowling ball about 40,000 times a year and a horseshoe some 15,000 times. No Brain Type Grouping can endure these physical demands better than the SFs. ISFJ Walter Ray Williams Jr. has used his inborn big-muscle control to perfection.

Type Tips

ISFJs need to be encouraged to be more aggressive in sports, particularly on the offensive end. They need to realize it is okay to make mistakes; blunders are part of the process of sports maturation. Even the greatest athletes have their periods of failure.

ISFJs should become familiar with the mental section of this book. Learning to relax and alleviate fear is crucial to their athletic success.

Like all dominant left-brained persons, ISFJs need to develop their spatial awareness. Ways to do this are mentioned throughout this book.

If ISFJs can begin athletic activities at an early age, the more likely they are to succeed, not only by developing their motor skills but confidence and assertiveness as well.

Parents and coaches need to remember that ISFJs respond and learn best when they are treated with sensitivity, commended for their efforts, and encouraged to keep trying.

PROBABLE ISFJs IN SPORTS

Basketball: P.J. Brown, Dale Davis, Ervin Johnson, Nazr Mohammed, J.R. Henderson, John Coker, *Retired:* Alton Lister, Andrew Lang, Acie Earl

Bowling: Walter Ray Williams Jr.

Football: Richmond Webb, Trezelle Jenkins

PROBABLE WELL KNOWN ISFJs:

Since ISFJs rarely seek the limelight, few are household names in America. Conversely, ISFJs' opposite Type, the ENTP, normally seeks an audience—the reason so many are named in the ENTP profile.

Popular Career Choices:
Nursing, social service work, ministry, secretarial service, teaching (especially elementary level), counseling, child care, probation officer, veterinarian, physical therapy

ESFJ

(Extraversion, Sensing, Feeling, Judging)

FEAL

(Front, Empirical, Animate, Left-brained)

"Facilitator"

Is there someone you know who talks easily, conversing readily with each person he or she meets during the day? Is this person someone who is easy to call, sympathetic, helpful, warm, practical and down to earth? Is his or her concern for people evident to all? You are probably thinking of an ESFJ. An ESFJ is friendly and outgoing, deriving energy simply from mingling with people. Choices are generally made by considering how issues will affect others. Seven years before her tragic death (in 1997), *People* magazine wrote of England's ESFJ **Princess Diana**:

> People marvel at Diana's bearing, her warm and knowing smile, her aplomb, and they wonder, where does it come from? The answer is simple. It is there all the time, locked away like a kernel, wanting only the sunshine of public adulation for it to unfold.[17]

ESFJs express feelings easily. They radiate with confidence at social functions, enlivening the atmosphere wherever they go. They are natural hosts and hostesses, making everyone feel at home. ESFJs show their admiration readily, praising those they respect, defending their associates. They are devoted friends, using time and energy to keep up with their broad field of relationships.

As children, ESFJs are outgoing, rule following, and socially adept. They are high achievers, motivated early to please teachers and parents. They cooperate with structured programs, developing good study habits. At home, their strong wills may bring them in conflict with parental authority.

ESFJs are drawn to traditions and family. As nurturers, they need to be appreciated for their caring ways. They assume responsibility for the happiness and welfare of others, being harmonious and peacemaking. ESFJs are sought out for their willingness to listen, sympathetic hearts, and sensible advice. With practical knowledge of what to do, what to wear, and where to go, ESFJs actively assist others in need of direction.

Roger Singleton, representing a charity for orphans and handicapped children, spoke of **Princess Diana** in 1990:

> The Princess is a person of compassion rather than a working royal who has so many events to get through a week.[18]

John Mayo, director general of Help the Aged once said of Diana:

> She has a keen sense of humor and puts people at ease.[19]

ESFJs may avoid conflict to the point of permissive parenting or denial of the reality they know so well. There may be a situation that needs to be faced and dealt with. They may tend to want to be the "good guy" and let the spouse do the disciplining. Wanting things to run smoothly, the ESFJ will do much to pacify and compromise, and turn to self blame for problems that arise. As a spouse, however, the ESFJ can be quite domineering, wanting control over the family management. This is especially seen in wives who see the home and family as their area of responsibility and expertise.

People magazine reported on **Princess Di** during her marriage to Prince Charles:

> Most people think that of the two—Charles and Diana—Diana is the one with steel. She's her own woman, and she knows exactly what she wants to do, in the same way the Queen Mother did and does. She's a very tough lady. . . .[20]

To be described as tougher than an INTJ like Prince Charles is to be a person of strong resolve, which ESFJs are.

The ESFJ, when faced with illness symptoms or difficult situations, may fear the worst will happen, denial no longer being possible. As people of action, ESFJs will make every effort to personally solve the dilemma, sometimes even when the business is not theirs to solve. They just see a need and "go to it." Completion without delay is their goal.

ESFJs have a penchant for interior decorating and clothing style. Prince Charles once commented on Lady Di in a way that speaks of ESFJs:

> I like seeing a lady well-dressed. It was one of the things I always noticed about her before we got married. She had, I thought, a very good sense of style and design.[21]

So we see ESFJs as harmonious, outgoing, talkative, conscientious, responsible, orderly, practical, hard working, and encouraging. ESFJs earn the confidence of others, selling themselves before selling the product or idea. The careers of ESFJs follow those serving humanity, people oriented occupations. Without a lot of personal contact, ESFJs will wither away, being frustrated at their role in life. If, however, ESFJs are surrounded by family and friends, they flourish and help run the lives around them with structure and care.

ESFJ Sports Profile

ESFJs are Extraverted, left-brained SFs. Exercising great *control* over their gross motor movements is what they do best. Whether in golf, basketball, tennis, figure-skating, or bowling, they dominate with their big muscles. ESFJs can become very smooth in their motor movements, almost as if they were right-brained Ps. They can be very athletic. ESFJs, like ISFJs, tend not to pursue sports that instill fear. Therefore, basketball, tennis, golf, swimming, figure-skating, and so forth, are where they are often found.

Tennis' **Gigi Fernandez**, ESFJ, was ranked as one of the top female doubles players in the world for over five years. (At the highest levels of tennis, ESFJs do best at doubles' play.)

Figure skating's **Nancy Kerrigan**, ESFJ, demonstrated her SF gross motor control, balance, and smoothness in the 1990s, culminating her amateur career with a silver medal at the 1994 Winter Olympics in Lillehammer. Few ESFJs have been top-notch skaters, but Nancy demonstrated what her Type can do through hard work, perseverance, and learning to control her anxiety level.

Not many ESFJs are high profile athletes in professional baseball, basketball, or football. Nonetheless, some have made their marks through determination and long hours of practice.

In football, defensive secondary specialist **Mark Collins** played a role on two New York Giant Super Bowl teams. The NFL veteran of over 10 years received All-NFL recognition. Defensive end and veteran **Sean Jones** made his presence known in the NFL for over a decade.

In basketball, ESFJs **Rasheed Wallace, John "Hot Rod" Williams,** and **Bobby Phills** have impacted the NBA.

Type Tips

ESFJs, like all SJs, must be careful to keep tension at a minimum in athletic competition. Under pressure, as SFs, ESFJs will tend to tense the big muscles of the body, achieving too much control. The mental section in this book will be of assistance.

ESFJs, like all left hemisphere Js, should develop greater spatial awareness to improve their athletic skills.

Parents and coaches need to remember that all Feelers, including ESFJs, respond and learn best when they are treated with sensitivity, commended for their efforts, and encouraged to do their best.

PROBABLE ESFJs IN SPORTS

Basketball: Rasheed Wallace, Dickey Simpkins, Eddy Curry, Alan Henderson, Samaki Walker
 Retired: John (Hot Rod) Williams, Bobby Phills, Donald Royal, Charles Shackleford, David Wingate, Duane Causwell

Football: Craig Whelihan
 Retired: Mark Collins, Sean Jones

Skating (figure): Nancy Kerrigan

Tennis: Gigi Fernandez

PROBABLE WELL KNOWN ESFJs:
Princess Diana, Queen Mother (former Lady Elizabeth Bowes-Lyon), Barbara Bush, Loretta Lynn, Yoko Ono, Tipper Gore, Dr. James Dobson, Gary Smalley

Barbara Bush   Queen Mother   Princess Diana   Loretta Lynn

Popular Career Choices:
Sales, customer relations, business, residential real estate agent, personnel supervisor, secretary, teaching (especially elementary level), special education, ministry, nursing, psychology, social work; in general, jobs where contact with people is involved.

22
NFs

**INFP, ENFP
INFJ, ENFJ**

INFP

(Introversion, iNtuition, Feeling, Perceiving)
BCAR
(Back, Conceptual, Animate, Right-brained)

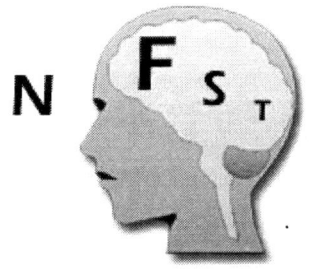

"Idealist"

INFPs are a caring, devoted, and often scholarly Type committed to special persons or causes. Apt to appear reticent and shy, they have strong values. They appreciate abstract feelings such as love, loyalty, and faith, responding to the beautiful and good in life. They like to live in harmony and tend to maintain an awareness of people and their feelings. INFPs are usually interested in books and new ideas, and they're adept at learning languages. They excel in vocations involving their personal values which they apply helping others live up to their possibilities.

The four Introverted iNtuitive Types (INFP, INFJ, INTP, INTJ) are considered the least commonly found Types in America, comprising an estimated 2 percent each.

The INFP is an idealist, always looking for perfection and rarely finding it. Rock star **Michael Jackson**, INFP, said of his mind set:

I don't think I'm ever totally happy. I am one of the hardest people to satisfy, but at the same time I'm aware of how much I have to be thankful for.[1]

As children, INFPs are daydreamers, creating a fantasy world to live in. This fantasy world is difficult for INFPs to leave behind, even as adults. With the world in an ever changing state of flux and turmoil, INFPs often wish they could return as did Peter Pan to Never Land, the place where children never grow up. (**Michael Jackson** named his multimillion dollar estate Neverland Ranch!)

INFP children desire to please teachers and parents, finding it difficult to express their own needs. They have thoughtful, delicate consciences and need a lot of approval and positive reinforcement. They make affirming and positive parents, remembering their own needs at the same age.

INFPs are congenial until their values are stepped on or threatened. At this point, they become emotional and demanding. This contradiction can be confusing to those close to them, who see it as strange and complex. INFPs, however, are their own worst critics, judging their skills and accomplishments as less than perfect, leaving them vulnerable to depression. They are happiest when doing meaningful tasks on their own, working behind the scenes for those people and causes they respect and value.

They seem hard to get to know, but INFPs are a joy to work with, and they're entertaining and humorous to those close to them. They want to communicate and to create and be appreciated for their uniqueness. They rely mainly on themselves, unwilling to ask others for assistance. They may have an independent stage in the teen years, though they are not aggressively rebellious, only intolerant of rules. They want to do things their own way.

Socially, INFPs can be very charming and personable, making an effort to reach out almost Extravertedly. They are reluctant leaders, using persuasion instead of dictation.

INFPs can be excellent musicians, vocalists, composers, and writers. Their poetic way with words and music is natural, and they should be encouraged as youngsters to develop these talents.

The foremost question INFPs take through life is "Who am I?" Life delivers far more questions for them than it does answers. INFPs can be philosophical and poetic, not particularly practical. They are committed family members, devoted friends in their small group, and loving and romantic spouses. You can expect them to start more projects than they finish as they idealistically search for life's purpose and meaning. They will use their inner prodding to make the world a better place.

INFP Sports Profile

By and large, INFPs are modest. Yet there are some INFPs who are downright aloof and cocky. The difference lies in how their values have been shaped. INFP's parents can greatly affect this attitude. Major league baseball's **John Olerud**, INFP, was labeled affectionately by *Sports Illustrated*:

> John's so modest, if he hit a home run, he'd apologize for hitting the ball.[2]

Mimics

INFPs, like other right-brained Ps, have extraordinary three dimensional spatial abilities. INFPs replicate others' movements and then spice them with their own creativity. They are adept at imaginatively illustrating what they view whether it be on canvas, stage, or on the athletic field.

I have personally witnessed this ability in my youngest son, Jordan. My two older children had swimming lessons as kids. Jordan decided to skip lessons. He just watched the other kids until he felt comfortable, then jumped in and swam. He did the same with diving. When Jordan was in the 2- to 3-year range, he would watch me teach my oldest son how to perform an athletic maneuver. Within a couple of minutes he was mimicking me, often with more grace than I demonstrated. Trust me, INFPs are extraordinary mimics.

See the Golf chapter of this book for how another INFP, golfer Tiger Woods, learned to mimic his father.

Remarkably Smooth

INFP children are gifted from the very beginning with natural coordination, blending the gross and fine motor skills. They are as smooth and silky as any Brain Type when they take up a sport for the first time. Their coordination gets even better with exercise, culminating in graceful athletes.

INFPs are generally quick (provided they're not overweight). Running down a pop fly, leading a fast break, or running a race, the INFP will be a contender whatever sport he or she chooses.

Competitors

Being dominant Feelers in their Introverted world, INFPs possess a strong passion for what they value. In athletic competition they usually give tremendous effort. Only when they feel they are not being treated properly, or when personal stress is too much for them, do they lack drive and initiative. Otherwise their dominant Feeling function, being a Judging preference, is ready to take action whenever it concentrates on the task at hand.

Type Tips

INFPs are similar to ISFPs in their athletic confidence. As Introverted right-brained Feelers, they lean toward viewing their mistakes more negatively and subjectively than many other Types. If they have a tough "Thinking" coach, their problems can easily be compounded. Encouraging slumping INFPs with positive reinforcement will do wonders to bring out their best performances. They generally perform according to how they feel. As iNtuitives, they need their motor skills developed as early as possible.

INFPs are not always aggressive. It helps to provide them inspirational reasons for giving their best each time they play. Sharing the same song and dance every day will not cut it; INFPs respond best to creative variety. Those of us who assist INFPs need to broaden our motivational techniques.

For further insights into how INFPs perform athletically, read the various sports' chapters.

PROBABLE INFPs IN SPORTS

Baseball:
1st: John Olerud; **R:** Rod Carew
ss: Derek Jeter; **R:** Chris Gomez, Tony Fernandez
OF: Raul Mondesi, Earnest Riles, Lance Johnson, Dave Martinez, Doug Glanville;
   R: Roberto Clemente, Fred Lynn, Dave Justice, Harold Baines,
P: Mariano Rivera, Steve Trachsel, Kevin Foster, Jose Melendez

Basketball: Vlade Divac, Shawn Bradley, Keith Closs, Brian Grant, **Dirk Nowitzki**, Grant Hill, Shandon Anderson, Doug Christie, Kerry Kittles, Eric Murdock, Howard Eisley, Lee Mayberry, Bryce Drew,
   Retired: Artis Gilmore, Kareem Abdul-Jabbar, Dr. Julius Erving, Jamaal Wilkes, Alex English, Larry Drew, Terry Teagle, Trent Tucker, Craig Hodges, Jeff Malone, Roy Hinson, Rolando Blackman, Reggie Williams, Maurice Cheeks, Cedric Ceballos, Keith Askins, Dennis Scott, Dell Curry

Football: Yancy Thigpen,
   Retired: Mike Garrett, Flipper Anderson, Mike Sherrard

Golf: Tiger Woods, Vijay Singh

Hockey: Luc Robitaille

Tennis: Guy Forget, Cedric Pioline

Track: Edwin Moses, Renaldo Nehemiah, Said Aouita, Hicham El Guerrouj, Noureddine Morceli, Dick Fosbury, Dalton Grant, Frankie Fredericks

Volleyball: Mike Dodd

Coaches: Tony Dungy, Maurice Cheeks

PROBABLE WELL KNOWN INFPs:
Richard Chamberlain, Michael Jackson, Jim Henson, Charles Schulz, Ron Shelton, Mother Teresa, Christian Riese Lassen

Mother Teresa   Charles Schulz

Popular Career Choices:
Psychology, psychiatry, medicine, science, teaching (prefer higher education), counseling, religious education, ministry and missionary work, literature, art, music, composing and writing, poetry

ENFP

(Extraversion, iNtuition, Feeling, Perceiving)
FCAR
(Front, Conceptual, Animate, Right-brained)

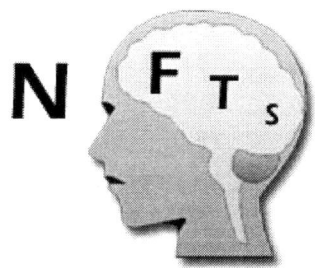

"Motivator"

The ENFP is an initiator of new ideas and projects. Every day new possibilities come into view and are acted upon. These new enterprises are not undertaken alone. The ENFP recruits others, with persuasive enthusiasm, to embark on the newest venture. A highly active imagination drives the ENFP to bounce from one activity to the next, creating even more energy and bringing passengers along. There is never a dull moment. Could the Pied Piper have been an ENFP?

With a high dose of Extraversion, the ENFP feels concern for others and the need to help and affirm them. In doing so, the ENFP needs affirmation on a constant basis. Going to great lengths to please and gain approval, the ENFP never slows down until exhaustion hits. This hyperactivity makes the ENFP fun to live with, yet unpredictable to the point of sometimes frustrating others.

ENFPs are dynamic, highly skilled, and usually can do anything they set their minds to. They can be marvelous musicians and vocalists. Some ENFPs include: **Whitney Houston, Diana Ross, Reba McEntire, Barbara Mandrell, Kenny Rogers, Amy Grant,** and **Ricky Skaggs**. If they have been in a successful occupation, they may have been in numerous others.

As children, ENFPs are delightful and entertaining, but very sensitive to criticism. They can charm their way out of most difficulties which they get into when being impulsive, wanting to do things their own way and not fitting neatly into structured schedules. Self expression is of the utmost concern their whole lives. One might be chosen for leadership due to recognition of the ENFP's persuasive powers and energetic ideas. They enjoy reading and exploring possibilities, deriving great satisfaction from living in the future.

ENFPs are value oriented, distracted at work or school by disharmony, and often late because of a vague awareness of time. They are social, charismatic, generously giving of themselves and their affection to all around them. They idealize relationships. Perceiving the world through possibilities, the ENFP explores and implements one idea after another, one experience after another, improvising and creating. Work is play and needs to be unstructured with constant interaction. They can spend hours researching subjects that interest them. The next day, however, the interest may have flown, replaced with new pursuits and new stimuli.

ENFPs can reach overload, getting too many projects going and being torn in too many directions. They need to establish priorities, to face reality and deal with it instead of running when things get routine or threatening. Balance is needed. If they have a good relationship, they should accept its imperfections and stay with it. The ENFP helps make the world go around for others, "decorating" home, work and schools with a warm, colorful touch.

As born cheerleaders, ENFPs use their unfettered enthusiasm to prompt others to success. As a reserve player on the great Boston Celtic teams of the 1980s, **M.L. Carr**, ENFP, was known for his towel-waving activities to inspire his teammates and crowd. And last, ENFPs' laughter is often distinctive and infectious.

ENFP Sports Profile

Energetic Acrobats

ENFPs participate in athletics with a high degree of energy. They are often like volcanoes ready to erupt, not emotionally as much as physically. They find it hard, however, to separate their emotions from sports, which generally provides them additional impetus.

ENFPs are among the best at figure skating, diving, and gymnastics. Their right-brained dominance provides them grace, flow, and spontaneity. INtuition lends tremendous creativity to their routines, and Extraversion fuels tremendous energy. Performing before a world wide audience, such as the Olympic Games, creates such an adrenaline rush that ENFPs usually forget the difficulty of their routines and attempt them with uncharacteristic boldness. They tend to go outside themselves, utilizing abilities they never knew they had.

All-Star **David Robinson** impacted the NBA with his speed and gymnastic abilities, not merely height and strength. In 1990, All Star Charles Barkley said of the ENFP newcomer:

> He's going to be a monster. He can do it all: Play defense, shoot, rebound and block shots. Plus, he's the fastest big man I've ever played against.[3]

ENFPs have been among the top track and field athletes. ENFP **Leroy Burrell** set the 100-meter dash world record in 1991. In 1994, Burrell again lowered the world mark, at 9.85 seconds. **Gail Devers**, ENFP, won the 100 meter dash in both the '92 and '96 Summer Olympic Games. **Mike Powell** broke Bob Beamon's 23-year old long jump record in 1991, soaring over 29 feet.

High Pain Threshold

There is no Brain Type with a higher threshold for pain than the ENFP. Typologically, the least developed function of ENFPs is their Introverted Sensing, the preference most in touch with physical pain. When ENFPs are in athletic competition, they kick their dominant iNtuitive function into high gear. They focus on the event with all their mental and physical energies. Discomfort in the process is given little regard. I have witnessed this in ENFPs many, many times. It is incredible to me how oblivious they can become to the physical travails in the heat of competition.

Greg LeMond demonstrated this repeatedly in the process of becoming the world's best known cyclist. After ENFP tennis pro **Zina Garrison** played a 1990 U.S. Open match with a badly sprained ankle, against the advice of a tournament physician, she said:

> I have a very high tolerance for pain. I just wanted to stay out there and finish. I wanted to at least make her work for the money she is getting in the next round.[4]

Though Garrison lost the match, Arantxa Sanchez Vicario and the fans witnessed the unrelenting physical drive of an ENFP.

Hard Workers

Extraverted NFs are known for their work ethic in athletics, particularly those who learned self discipline as youngsters. In 1990, San Francisco conditioning coach, Jerry Attaway, spoke on why the 49er stars sustained fewer injuries than most other NFL teams. *Sports Illustrated* reported:

> . . . he points to the training habits of [Jerry] Rice and [Roger] Craig, who work out like a couple of Evander Holyfields in the off season . . . .[5] (Inserts added.)

How fitting to have three ENFPs compared with one another.

Visualizers

EN_Ps (ENFP and ENTP) are highly adept at visualizing. Their dominant and spatial right-brained iNtuition preference is used to imagine events in their lives, including athletics. By visualizing, ENFPs build confidence, perfect technique, and activate regions of the brain that are important for athletic success. (Refer to the Visualization chapter for further clarity.)

It was reported that ENFP Olympic diver and gold medalist **Greg Louganis:**

> . . . 'mind scripted' each dive an estimated forty times, sometimes imagining it in real time, sometimes going through it in slow motion, to check out how different parts of his body behaved and felt at different moments.[6]

Other ENFPs are mentioned in this book who depend upon visualization techniques to achieve top performance.

Type Tips

Hobby and recreational pursuits for ENFPs include juggling. It's difficult to find a Type that surpass the juggling proficiencies of ENFPs.

ENFPs must remember to use their mental as well as athletic talents in certain kinds of competition. Though ENFPs perform best by not over analyzing in sports that have preset routines, it is sometimes necessary for them to Introvert and analyze in other key situations. As point guards in basketball, they must decipher if a pass is safe to make, or in baseball, whether to stretch a base hit when behind by one run.

ENFPs need to learn to perform under control, restraining their superman instincts to jump over buildings in a single bound. Their overall performances will improve when they learn to properly regulate their acrobatic moves and energy.

Like other iNtuitives, ENFPs will be well served by developing their motor skills at an early age. For additional insights on how ENFPs perform athletically, refer to the various sports' chapters. In summary, ENFPs can be superb athletes.

PROBABLE ENFPs IN SPORTS

Baseball:
IF: Omar Vizquel, Joey Cora,
  R: Lou Whitaker, Terry Pendleton, Cecil Fielder, Tony Phillips, Ozzie Guillen
OF: **Sammy Sosa**, Vladimir Guerrero, Darin Erstad, Bernie Williams, Kenny Lofton, Reggie Sanders,
  R: Jackie Robinson, Hubie Brooks, Shane Mack, Billy Hatcher, Milt Thompson, Mel Hall, Ron Gant, Roberto Kelly, Greg Vaughn
C: Sandy Alomar Jr.; **R:** Bob Uecker, Lenny Webster
P: Pedro Astacio, Chan Ho Park, Dontrelle Willis, Carlos Perez,
  R: Dwight Gooden, Alvin Morman, Chuck McElroy

Basketball: Marcus Camby, Evan Eschmeyer, **Kevin Garnett**, Antonio McDyess, Cliff Robinson, Chris Webber, LaPhonso Ellis, Anthony Mason, Tyrone Hill, Charles Outlaw, Dean Garrett, George Lynch, Antawn Jamison, John Wallace, Popeye Jones, Jerome Williams, Malik Rose, Robert Traylor, Glen Rice, Jamal Mashburn, George McCloud, Bryon Russell, Rick Fox, Jerry Stackhouse, Hubert Davis, Michael Dickerson, Terrell Brandon, Lindsey Hunter, Alvin Williams, Jamaal Tinsley, Speedy Claxton, Jay Williams
  Retired: Tommy Hawkins, Happy Hairston, David Thompson, Quinn Buckner, Orlando Woolridge, Ed Pinckney, Cliff Levingston, John Salley, Craig Ehlo, David Benoit, Nate McMillan, Armon Gilliam, Hersey Hawkins, Vernon Maxwell, Chuck Person, Sherman Douglas, Loy Vaught, **David Robinson**

Bowling: Marc McDowell, George Branham III

Boxing: Evander Holyfield, Oscar De La Hoya

Cycling: Greg LeMond

Diving: Greg Louganis, Kent Ferguson, Fu Mingxia, Laura Wilkinson, Wendy Williams

Football: Kordell Stewart, Akili Smith, Drew Brees, **Jerry Rice**, Tim Brown, Shannon Sharpe, Desmond Howard, Anthony Miller, Scott Turner, Charlie Jones, Terrell Davis, Marshall Faulk, Kimble Anders, Garrison Hearst, Robert Edwards, Sam Gash, Dave Meggett, Keith Sims,
John Randle, Tony Bennett, Mike Jones, Ken Harvey, Hardy Nickerson, Steve Smith,
Albert Lewis, Darryll Lewis, LeRoy Butler, Tim McDonald, Darren Perry, Ray Buchanan, Ashley Ambrose
  Retired: Willie Gault, Tom Jackson, Roger Craig, Jerry Robinson, Charles Mann, Leonard Marshall, Greg Bell, Keena Turner, Andre Ware, Brett Perriman, Gaston Green, Derrick Thomas

Golf: Billy Andrade, David Duval, Sergio Garcia, Heather Farr

Gymnastics: Bart Conner, Kurt Thomas, Grigory Misiutin, Olga Korbut, Cathy Rigby

Racing (auto): Jeff Gordon, Bill Elliott

Skating (figure): Kristi Yamaguchi, Michelle Kwan, Oksana Baiul, Chen Lu, Yuka Sato, Midori Ito, Irina Stutskaya, Jayne Torvill, Tracy Wilson, Janet Lynn, Scott Hamilton, Kurt Browning, Brian Boitano, Elvis Stojko, Todd Eldredge, Viktor Petrenko, Aleksandr Fadeyev, Paul Wylie, Randy Gardner, Mark Mitchell, Scott Davis

Soccer: Pelé, Freddy Adu

Swimming: Janet Evans, Matt Biondi, Rowdy Gaines

Tennis: Venus Williams, Chanda Rubin, Jonas Bjorkman, MaliVai Washington
Retired: Tracy Austin, Evonne Goolagong, Zina Garrison

Track and Field: Gail Devers, Madeline Mims, Mike Powell, Leroy Burrell, Linford Christie, Lawrence Johnson, Greg Foster, Jack Pierce, Steve Lewis, Danny Everett, Charles Simpkins

Coaches: Cotton Fitzsimmons, Bobby Cremins, Lou Carnesecca, M.L. Carr, Quinn Buckner, Bela Karolyi, Vic Braden

Sports Media: Dick Enberg, Bob Uecker, Hannah Storm, Fred Hickman, Joe Morgan, Bart Conner, Vic Braden, Tracy Austin, Quinn Buckner

Bob Hope   Sammy Davis Jr.   Barbara Mandrell

Popular Career Choices:

Sales, public relations, entrepreneur, human services, health related professions, music, acting and entertaining, play and screen writing, journalism, advertising, ministry, counseling, psychology (note the great latitude in career choices)

PROBABLE WELL KNOWN ENFPs:

Fred Astaire, Todd Bridges, Ted Danson, Sammy Davis Jr., Michael Gross, Arsenio Hall, Dorian Harewood, Bob Hope, Mark McEwen, Bronson Pinchot, Roy Rogers, Richard Simmons, Martin Short, Ben Vereen, Montel Williams

Glen Campbell, Hammer, Johnny Mathis, Kenny Rogers, Ricky Skaggs, Mel Tillis

Rep. J.C. Watts Jr., Robert H. Schuller, Oral Roberts

Julie Andrews, Susan Anton, Delta Burke, Carol Burnett, Jamie Lee Curtis, Julia Louis-Dreyfus, Sandy Duncan, Barbara Eden, Kathie Lee Gifford, Goldie Hawn, Michelle Lee, Marilyn Monroe, Ginger Rogers, Suzanne Somers, Connie Stevens, Oprah Winfrey

Reba McEntire, Lola Falana, Debbie Gibson, Amy Grant, Whitney Houston, Cyndi Lauper, Barbara Mandrell, Minnie Pearl, Diana Ross

INFJ
(Introversion, iNtuition, Feeling, Judging)
BCAL
(Back, Conceptual, Animate, Left-brained)

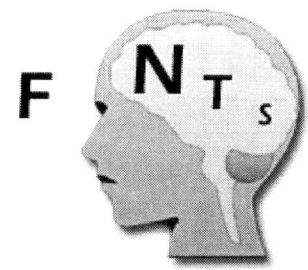

"Wordsmith"

Though Introverted, here are truly "people persons," ones so concerned with others that they may appear Extraverted. They have endless ideas, always considering possibilities, being happiest when these ideas are helping and bettering others.

As children, INFJs are often quiet and day dreamy, maybe even complacent. They want to understand and be understood—which helps them enjoy academic activities. They tend to be excellent students, high achievers, dependable and steady. Finding school rewarding, they quickly learn that their minds are a key to the world of learning and creativity.

INFJs are likely to be seen as mystical, so great are their vivid imaginations. They live to intuit, with visionary abilities with which few can completely relate. Their ideas are expertly expressed in writing and in verbal communication.

INFJs are usually organized and decisive, with a willingness to work long and hard. They tend to have clear goals, are skilled at working with people, and relate to others with empathetic and compassionate skill. They often feel compelled to render service to humanity. While carrying heavy inner burdens of their own, they can become overburdened with the world's troubles. Because they can be easily hurt by others, they may retreat into a private, safer world.

So much of what is inside INFJs is hidden, not fully tapped for our appreciation. Their caring affection may not be outwardly shown, but their quiet strength is felt by others. They may not prefer to lead, but spread their ideas in a deliberate and quiet way.

The extreme end of this tendency is that INFJs have ideals and causes to fight for and may become rigid and demanding, with streaks of stubbornness. Their visions deal with human welfare. However rigid their projects begin, harmony is usually reached as the goals near.

The INFJ tends to choose occupations in counseling, clinical psychology, psychiatry, teaching, clergy, medicine, social work, architecture, and media specialties. INFJs seek harmony in every part of life. They make loving spouses and fiercely devoted parents, becoming deeply bonded to their children.

The four Introverted iNtuitive Types (INFP, INFJ, INTP, INTJ) are considered the least commonly found Types in America, comprising an estimated 2 percent each.

INFJ Sports Profile

Intelligent, Hard working Athletes

Studious by nature, INFJs reflect deeply and creatively in sports. They use their heads with a grasp of the "big picture." Methodically and painstakingly, they work to improve their skills.

INFJs are Introverted, left brain dominant NFs. Though not commonly found in professional sports, they are capable of athletic success. Like other NFs, they are able to develop body harmony, but must begin athletics at an early age if they hope to do the best for their Type. If they do not start young, INFJs can be awkward in their motor skills.

Very few INFJs have been successful in professional sports. The ones that seem to make it are found in pro basketball, and they are tall. Not relying on smooth body coordination or a shooting touch, they primarily have made it through hustle and attitude. **Chris Dudley** and **Jim McIlvaine** are two recent NBA INFJs.

Smaller INFJs who have devoted their lives to athletic endeavors can become successful in their chosen sports. The higher in competition they go, however, the more difficult it will be to excel against the competition. Yet INFJs are fortunate to have great minds for numerous vocations in the event their pro sports dreams don't pan out.

Though INFJs and INFPs are exceptionally close in their typological letters, they are far removed in their athletic movements. The right-brained INFPs are born with more fluid athletic skills. Consider INF"P" **Shawn Bradley**, the 7' 6" NBA basketball player. His father said:

He was always coordinated despite being tall. When he was 4 years old, we gave him a bike and he was riding it around after about an hour.[7]

In junior high, Bradley played football—quarterback and receiver. In high school he played baseball—a .400 hitter, and golf. These were in addition to basketball! The *L.A Times* reported:

He was blessed with enough coordination for his favorite sports hobby to be water skiing.[8]

Not all INFPs are as gifted as Shawn Bradley. If, like Shawn, they began sports at an early age, however, they would perform similarly. Neither would all INFJs have as much difficulty in developing their skills as would tall INFJs. (Exceptionally tall persons reveal the Brain Type differences in motor skills most noticeably.) I have played sports against INFJs who had excellent motor coordination. They started sports at an early age.

No person of any Brain Type should ever give up on his or her athletic dreams. Yet it is good to know beforehand the potential difficulties that one's inborn design will experience along the way. This ensures a wise aproach to the decision of going forward or not, as you realistically face the obstacles. This illustration can also teach differences in Types, and how some must work harder and smarter to achieve success.

The NBA's **Chris Dudley** is another tall INFJ. Through hard work, good defense and INFJ intelligence (a Yale graduate), Dudley has also achieved basketball success. Unfortunately, he's been recognized as the NBA's worst free throw shooter. He once missed 17 in a row in an NBA game. Near the end of the 1992 NBA season, shooting a horrific 32% from the line, Dudley answered some of his critics. To insure victory at the end of the game, opposing coach Don Nelson had his Golden State Warriors foul Chris intentionally. Dudley responded by making all eight of his free throws!

Chris talked about his charity stripe tosses:

I can make them in practice, but when I get into a game I start thinking about making the perfect shot. I have too many things on my mind and can't relax.[9]

INFJs, like all 8 dominant left-hemisphere Brain Types, will tend to get more mechanical in their motor movements under pressure. Reading the mental section in this book should help them to learn to relax more. As a note of encouragement to all INFJs, Chris Dudley's shot has gotten progressively better over the years. Since he didn't develop his motor movements in youth the way most athletes do, body synchronization has not come easily—especially considering his nearly 7-foot frame.

I played a pickup basketball game recently and was completely outplayed by an INFJ my size (6'3"). His shot was sound and deadly and his defense was exceptional. If INFJs start young enough and work hard at their sport, they can be very good athletes.

Conclusion

I desire to research INFJs more in the future. Because they do not have the high sports profile of many other Types, I have more to learn regarding their abilities in the various sports.

Type Tips

INFJs should begin developing motor skills as early as possible. They should play the sports most fun for them to insure a continuation and commitment to exercise.

Learning to control their emotions and anxiety in competition is essential for success. The mental section of this book will be helpful.

As Introverts, INFJs often lack the sports energy of the Extraverted Types. In the more active sports, it is important that INFJs place an emphasis on energetic play.

PROBABLE INFJs IN SPORTS

Basketball: Chris Dudley, Jim McIlvaine

PROBABLE WELL KNOWN INFJs:
Lamar Hunt

Popular Career Choices
Psychology, counseling, therapy, ministry, religious educator, scientific research, medicine, journalism, writing and editing, teacher.

ENFJ

(Extraversion, iNtuition, Feeling, Judging)

BCAL

(Back, Conceptual, Animate, Left-brained)

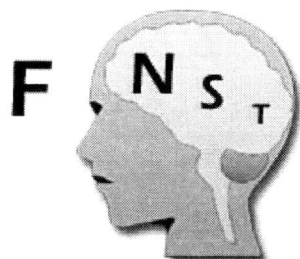

"Educator"

This well liked person is a leader who nurtures growth and maturity in others. The ENFJ is gifted in persuasive speech, setting out to improve the lives of those around him or her, and the world in general. Creatively visualizing the direction a group should go, ENFJs are able to motivate many to follow. Cooperation and harmony are valued by them, and they consider personal relationships to be of utmost importance. Prone to depression as they overload themselves with the concerns of others as well as self, ENFJs struggle to keep emotions under control. They are idealistic when it comes to love and friendship, and can become disillusioned with a less than perfect mate or friend.

Charismatic speakers, ENFJs use fluent language skills to communicate their visions. They frequently become ministers, politicians, and teachers and are often found in the favorite teacher category.

ENFJs like to plan and organize their areas of interest. They honor their commitments, do well in school, and have the ability to see what is needed for the welfare of the whole group. If individuals differ in opinion from the ENFJ, however, he or she takes it personally as failure and rejection.

As one of the more Introverted of the Extraverts, ENFJs may appear less outgoing on a one to one basis. Given leadership and an audience, however, the ENFJ will shine and mature into an expressive communicator.

ENFJ children are warm and friendly, obedient to rules and teachers. They know how to appeal to both children and adults. Being attracted to athletics, literature, history, drama, music, and art, they put a great deal of energy into their interests.

One way to detect ENFJs is to notice how much they care about their appearance. This makes them almost seem like Sensates. They want to be thin, contemporary, fashionable, well-coifed and beautiful (or handsome). Many ENFJs go into acting and become leading ladies and men. They act attractive, suave and alluring. **Farrah Fawcett, Julia Roberts, Tom Selleck, Tom Cruise, Linda Evans, Heather Locklear,** and **Robert Redford** fall aptly into this brain pattern.

Placing people high on their priority lists, ENFJs become nurturing and responsible leaders. They are sensitive and tolerant. Freely relating what is important to them, they share their hearts with the world. They initiate friendships, seeking the good in others and building upon it.

ENFJs are "value" driven persons, defenders of ideals and other matters that arouse an emotional response. In 1988, ENFJ **George H. Bush** used as the mainspring to his presidential campaign the issue of "values"—the '88 buzzword for a candidate's bedrock beliefs. For Mr. Bush, it came easily.

Being a dominant "value" person, the ENFJ can become fiery when personal beliefs are trod upon. When criticized, they may lose a logical perspective. Desiring harmony, they need to learn that the cost may sometimes be too high. ENFJs are diplomatic and energetic, leading the way to improved relations, peace, and joy. Burn out may occur if the ENFJ does not learn to say "no" in the service of others. Even Extraverts need time to relax and regroup. (ENFJs and ENFPs, I've observed, are prone to depression when hope is not on the horizon.)

Charmers, Conciliators, Chiefs

Tom Selleck once responded to his reputation:

> It bothers me when people equate niceness with being dull and wishy washy. It makes me sound like a wuss.[10]

In 1991, *People* magazine wrote of former Secretary of Transportation, and Labor, **Elizabeth Dole** (ENFJ):

> With her shrewd instincts and rich North Carolina drawl as her most formidable weapons, Dole excelled at the art of negotiating with congressional committees, so much that around Capital Hill she earned the nickname Sugar Lips.[11]

McCall's magazine wrote of Dole:

> But because of her immense charm and magnetism, press reports about her tend to have a soft focus. *Business Week* compared her to **Jacqueline Kennedy Onassis**, calling her 'a glamorous, feminine presence, draped on a frame of steel.'[12]

The comparison of Jacqueline and Elizabeth was accurate (both ENFJs). And, as described, Mrs. Dole and other ENFJs have tremendous resolve. By the time **Nancy Reagan** (ENFJ) left Washington in 1988, she thoroughly convinced Capital observers of her resolution.

After **President Bush** had spent nearly a year in office, it was written:

> Yet, for all of Bush's overt personal contacts with the outside world, beneath the surface he has concentrated more power in the White House and placed it in fewer hands than any President since Richard M. Nixon.[13]

Often Feel Shy

ENFJs have been known to act and feel Introverted. Part of this relates to their, at times, lack of self confidence. ENFJs' dominant Feelings operate primarily on gut level analysis; logic isn't essential for decision making. Their iNtuition allows for unlimited possibilities. Thus, ENFJs are prone to second guess themselves. Their NF bent is rock solid in certain deeply cherished values; otherwise, they are prone to vacillation on lesser matters.

ENFJs approach life somewhat cautiously, similar to all left brain, analytic Js. This attribute lends itself to a quasi Introverted persona. Conversely, their right-brained, synthetic, ENFP cousins release their ENF in a spontaneous mode, appearing more Extraverted.

Nevertheless, when ENFJs stand before people, particularly on stage or in a public setting, they come alive. They can range from splendid to verbose communicators.

All-American People

ENFJs rapidly ascend to leadership positions by their Extraverted, charming personas and orderly "J" ambitions. They represent stability and hold strong values. Valuing democracy in groups, they seek to get along with others.

ENFJ Pop star **Paula Abdul** followed in the footsteps of many ENFJ females who preceded her. In high school she was class president, Homecoming princess, and May Queen.

In 1997, actor **Jimmy Stewart** died at age 89, leaving an endearing impact on Hollywood and the movie-viewing world. He was quintessential ENFJ, with the innate ability to communicate warmth, values, and winsome language.

Having already established himself in motion pictures (with an Academy Award in 1940), Stewart pursued his patriotic ideals and joined the army during World War II, at age 32. (He took a five-year wartime hiatus from acting.) He and his draft board even bent the rules to allow his military entry (he was underweight). Stewart's army duty involved 25 combat flying missions, and he achieved full colonel status. Returning to Hollywood, he was greatly admired for the rest of his life.

Jimmy Stewart and George Bush have had many similarities: ENFJs, Ivy League grads, intelligent, personable, good communicators, hard working, military enlistees, World War II pilots with combat missions, and men who strongly pursued their goals and held deep values. Each achieved remarkable success and public recognition. They have been positive modern examples of ENFJs.

Emotional

In the 1988 presidential campaign, **George Bush** spoke of desiring a kinder, gentler nation. Despite any political overtones of his theme, he (and other NFs) truly hope for harmony in their lives. They are greatly influenced by how others feel about them.

In 1991, President Bush told an audience that he shed tears as he prayed just before ordering the start of the war against Iraq. The *L.A. Times* reported:

> For Bush, who said he tries to keep his emotions in check in public and who appears uncomfortable when questioned in interviews and other settings about personal values, it was an extraordinary display: His voice choked up, he stumbled over

his words and he paused to run his fingers across an apparently moist cheek as he recounted the deeply personal moment.[14]

In his speech, Mr. Bush said:

> So, if I show some emotion, that's just the way I am.[15]

In 2001, President Bush's son, George W. Bush (an ENTJ), was elected as the 43rd President of the United States. His wife, **Laura Bush**, is another dignified ENFJ First Lady, once again showing the contribution these energetic and structured NF women have on their husbands' political successes.

ENFJ Sports Profile

Passion, Determination

ENFJs often develop a passion for sports. They see more than perfecting their game or winning and losing; they relate to the people involved in sports in a special way. Collecting trading cards can almost be like collecting people. They personalize sports.

ENFJs do not possess the natural motor skills of the Sensates or the smoothness of the right brain Ps. Nonetheless, they can become excellent athletes, particularly if they begin sports early in life.

ENFJs' greatest assets in athletics are determination and hustle. Their zealousness is infectious to fellow teammates. ENFJs can be viewed as "spark plugs." They usually set finesse aside and beat their opponents by more running, jumping, diving, hustling—whatever it takes. ENFJs are extra hard workers, blue collar athletes. Defense is often their speciality. Some ENFJs have included tennis' **Jim Courier**, golf's **Julie Inkster**, baseball's **Jeff Kent**, volleyball's **Sinjin Smith**, football's **Drew Bledsoe**.

Throw and Hit Hard

Throwing hard in baseball and football or hitting the ball hard in tennis or baseball is common for ENFJs. Their Brain Type imparts great passion in their games; they love to expend energy.

Regard for Others

Having moved frequently in his formative years, former Olympic swimmer **John Naber** recalled his empathetic ENFJ ways:

> Since I was always the stranger in town, I would look at the guy who was the last one picked on a team because he reminded me of me. As an outsider, I knew I had value and I knew I had worth, so I sought out those who weren't very popular. I assumed that they, too, had worth and personal value and that there was something to discover about them.[16]

Type Tips

ENFJs, like other iNtuitives, are well served by developing their motor movements at an early age. If they do, they're capable of being splendid athletes.

If motor skills are developed, ENFJs' greatest hindrance to athletic stardom is usually mental. They will find assistance through the mental section of this book. Learning to relax and playing within themselves is paramount. They especially need to learn how to control their energy, enthusiasm, and anxiety when playing.

ENFJs are susceptible to losing confidence in their abilities when things are not going well. They view their circumstances more subjectively than Thinkers, having a tendency to get down on themselves. They welcome encouragement and a positive outlook from their associates.

Reading of ENFJs in the various sports of this book will provide further insight.

PROBABLE ENFJs IN SPORTS

Baseball:
1st: Mark Grace
2nd: Jeff Kent
ss: Gary DiSarcina
3rd: Robin Ventura, Kevin Seitzer
     R: Doug DeCinces
P: Andy Benes, Dan Plesac,
     Bob Scanlan, Shawn Boskie;
     R: Mark Langston

Basketball: Rasho Nesterovic, Mark Madsen, Maurice Taylor, Matt Bullard, Rex Walters, Fred Hoiberg, Eric Washington
  Retired: Marques Johnson, Keith Erikson,
    Pat Riley, Dick Van Arsdale, Swen Nater,
    Matt Guokas Jr., Stu Lantz, Rony Seikaly,
    Buck Williams, Dan Schayes

Football: Vinny Testaverde, Drew Bledsoe, Elvis Grbac, Gus Frerotte, Gino Torretta, Danny Kanell, Steve Wisniewski, Dave Szott, Eric Swann, Matt Stover, John Kasay
   Retired: Frank Gifford, Bob Griese, Vince Ferragamo, Danny White, Pat Haden, Jim Hill, James Lofton

Golf: Nick Price, Chip Beck, Stuart Appleby, Ian Baker Finch, Julie Inkster, Cindy Rarick

Skating (speed): Dan Jansen

Swimming: John Naber

Tennis: Jim Courier, Alexander Volkov

Volleyball: Sinjin Smith, Adam Johnson

Coaches:
basketball: Pat Riley, Del Harris, Matt Guokas Jr., Lute Olson, Randy Ayers, Stu Jackson, Stan Morrison, Steve Lavin
football: Bill Walsh, Marty Schottenheimer, Dick Vermeil, Ara Parseghian, John Robinson, Terry Donahue

Sports Media: Vin Scully, Pat Summerall, Bob Griese, Pat Haden, Terry Donahue, Dick Vermeil, Gayle Gardner, Diana Nyad

PROBABLE WELL KNOWN ENFJs:
George H. Bush, Tom Brokaw, Dick Clark, Gary Collins, Tom Cruise, Billy Graham, Merv Griffin, Michael Landon, Prince Andrew, Robert Redford, Christopher Reeve, Pat Robertson, Fred "Mr." Rogers, Tom Selleck, Rick Shroder, Jimmy Stewart, John Tesh, Robert Wagner

Elizabeth Dole, Jacqueline Kennedy Onassis, Nancy Reagan, Crystal Bernard, Christie Brinkley, Laura Bush, Lynda Carter, Cindy Crawford, Lorianne Crook, Bo Derek, Angie Dickinson, Linda Evans, Farrah Fawcett, Cristina Ferrare, Annette Funicello, Leeza Gibbons, Linda Gray, Mary Hart, Jenny Jones, Grace Kelly, Cheryl Ladd, Heather Locklear, Sophia Loren, Joan Lunden, Alexandra Nichita, Chelsea Noble, Deborah Norville, Stefanie Powers, Lee Remick, Donna Rice, Julia Roberts, Brooke Shields, Dinah Shore, Jaclyn Smith, Kate Smith, Kathy Smith, Elizabeth Taylor, Cheryl Tiegs, Raquel Welsh, Betty White, Vanna White, Paula Zahn

Paula Abdul, Debby Boone, Holly Dunn, Crystal Gayle, Eydie Gorme, Olivia Newton John, Naomi Judd, Kathy Mattea, Anne Murray

Pat Boone, Paul McCartney, Donny Osmond, Randy Travis

Jacqueline Kennedy Onassis   Elizabeth Taylor   Crystal Gayle

Tom Cruise   Mr. Rogers   Rev. Billy Graham

Popular Career Choices:

Teaching, counseling, psychology, ministry, news media, advertising, acting, writing, photography, health-related professions, sales, business, coaching

23
NTs

INTJ, ENTJ
INTP, ENTP

INTJ
(Introversion, iNtuition, Thinking, Judging)
BCIL
(Back, Conceptual, Inanimate, Left-brained)

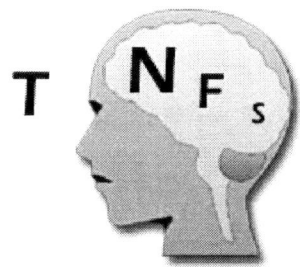

"Inventor"

INTJs are one of the rarest birds in the U.S. population, estimated at 2 percent. They make their presence known by inventing, researching, writing, practicing medicine, and doing a variety of highly skilled pursuits well. Though Introverted, they can develop a facility for teaching and speaking, working well with language. As for foreign languages, an INTJ has linguistic capabilities that few can duplicate. (Naturally, they are left-brained dominant iNtuitives.) One INTJ learned fifteen foreign dialects quickly and easily as he set out for the mission field.

INTJs are exceptionally independent. They appear cold and aloof unless they purposely develop a warmer method of relating. They may appear arrogant and "know it all," even argumentative. This characteristic may alienate others who are intimidated by the "superiority" of the INTJ.

With skill and confidence, INTJs enter areas of work and interest that require creating, constructing, and applying technology to complex problems. They like to be originals, coming up with new thoughts, ideas, inventions, and ways of doing things. The critical minds of INTJs question everything, logically pursuing every avenue of doubt. Tactfulness may not seem necessary to INTJs as long as they are persuaded in their own minds.

The independence of the INTJ can lead to isolation and eccentricity (Howard Hughes was an INTJ). The INTJ needs to take the time to develop friendships that will help keep a balanced perspective.

As a child, the INTJ's active imagination and aggressive independence can be challenging for even the best parenting. The child seems almost like a miniature adult, competent in decision making, or at least confident in it. Consider Calvin in the comic strip of "Calvin and Hobbes" if you want to see a juvenile INTJ in action. (Bill Watterson, Calvin's creator, illustrates the INTJ masterfully. No small wonder; he, too, is one.) INTJ children are driven in pursuit of exploration and experimentation.

Though scoring well at school on formal tests, INTJs may be less motivated to learn by way of the usual, factual, step by step methods. They may daydream a lot, but can be high achievers if they want to be. Their most difficult years, academically, come in grade school. If they persevere and study in college, they will often be near the top of the class. It may be quite a turnaround from their formative years of education.

INTJs want to improve and correct everything that comes along. They research and redesign continuously. Seeking challenges and disdaining routine, they may ignore the feelings of others, complicating their lives at school and work. They need to work at appreciating the views of others, or at least being harmonious. Their desire to control may be unwelcome.

To bring about change, INTJs follow their inspirations. Their insights are deep and technical. They specialize in the challenges of the impossible. They prize learning, and are willing to invest time, energy, and money in education for themselves and for their children. Otherwise, INTJs can be quite frugal and thrifty. (Some INTJs end up being life time students; they love to learn.)

INTJs have much to offer in innovation and theoretical reasoning. They love to present models for strategies of how things should work. They are sometimes missionaries of the greatest sacrifice, or international spies and con artists. Their special skills can be used for the good of all or for the promotion of their own selfish pursuits.

INTJ Sports Profile

Win with Head

INTJs are Introverted, left-brained NTs. They are methodical and strategic in their athletic pursuits, just as they are in life. INTJs feel a need to master their sport of interest in their heads as soon as possible, innately knowing their minds are their greatest athletic tools. Former major league pitcher **Eric Show** once spoke of his INTJ ways in college:

> I was playing ball, playing guitar and taking courses in calculus, biology, chemistry, philosophy and physics. I accepted the fact that there was a God, but which God—Allah, Buddha, Sri Chimnoy? I studied the Allen Watts movement, Zen, everything you can name. I studied the great works of St. Augustine, Freud, Russell, Marx.[1]

In 1988, completing his 7th year in the big leagues, Show stated:

> I have dedicated my life to learning.[2]

When asked, "learning what?" he stated:

> Learning *what*? What should I learn? I should learn *everything*! The question you should ask is, What should I leave out?[3] (Emphasis his.)

Not many INTJs are found in America's most popular sports. Why so few? First, one wouldn't expect to find many, considering INTJs small percentage of the U.S. populace.

Second, sports are very much in the here and now, strongly utilizing the Sensing function. Accessing the "S" function does not come naturally for the highly iNtuitive INTJ.

Third, INTJs do not possess the natural gross and fine motor skills of the Sensates. INTJs must work harder to develop these skills. If INTJs pursue sports tenaciously, they can become very proficient at a number of them, particularly if they start early in life. They will quickly learn to take advantage of their superior mental skills, often making up for less-developed body movements. As we all know, proficiency in athletics requires both mental and physical dexterity. INTJs will learn to use their heads masterfully.

Any sport or recreational hobby that challenges the mind will be of interest to the INTJ. Sailing, wind surfing, flying (full-size planes or models), and target shooting are just a few that they enjoy. Yet the more popular sports can be of interest too.

Type Tips

Encourage INTJs to get involved in athletic activities as children. They will require more time to develop their motor skills than Sensates.

Golf is probably the most popular sport suited to INTJs. (INTJ Tom Kite was the PGA's most consistent player of the 1980s.) Pitching is another area of expertise, allowing INTJs to excel in major league baseball.

Mental and emotional exercises should be given high priority. (See mental section in this book.) Considering INTJs live life in their minds as much as any Type, it is crucial they learn to keep their tensions and thoughts in check.

When INTJs succumb to pressure in sporting events, their visual awareness can suffer appreciably; as left-brained dominant iNtuitives—especially adept at analyzing language—spatial matters in sports are hindered by physiological processes. Thus, it's paramount that INTJs learn to relax and place high priority on the visual elements of their sport.

PROBABLE INTJs IN SPORTS

Baseball: Randy Johnson, Mike Mussina, Mark Wohlers, Gregg Olson
   Retired: Eric Show, Tim Burke, Ed Whitson, David Cone

Basketball: Keith Van Horn, Vladimir Stepania, Cal Bowdler,
   Retired: Don Nelson, Phil Jackson, Jack Marin, Tom McMillen, Alvan Adams, Rick Carlisle, Bill Hanzlik

Bowling: Danny Wiseman, Harry Sullins, Bryan Goebel, Eric Adophson

Equestrian: Michael Plumb

Golf: Bob Estes, Casey Martin, Matt Kuchar
   Seniors: Hale Irwin, Tom Kite, Bob Charles, Tom Weiskopf, Kermit Zarley, Mike McCullough, John Mahaffey, David Ledbetter

Tennis: Tim Mayotte, Jeff Tarango

Coaches:
Baseball: Tony LaRussa
Basketball: Don Nelson, Phil Jackson, Rick Carlisle, Greg Popovich, Bill Hanzlik, Paul Westhead, Gary Williams, Dave Odom
Football: George Seifert, Jim Fassel

Sports Media: Peter Gammons

Team Owners: Al Davis, Bud Selig

PROBABLE WELL-KNOWN INTJs:

Abraham Lincoln   Jimmy Carter   Nancy Kassebaum   Prince Charles

Warren Beatty, Jimmy Carter, Prince Charles, Warren Christopher, Justice Ruth Ginsburg, Howard Hughes, Bobby Ray Inman, Nancy Kassebaum, Charles H. Keating Jr., Dr. Jack Kevorkian, Abraham Lincoln, Bruce Lindsey, Tom McMillen, Ralph Nader, Justice Sandra Day O'Connor, William J. Perry, Harold C. Simmons, Justice David H. Souter, Thomas Sutherland, Paul Tsongas, Peter Ueberroth, Markus Wolf

POPULAR CAREER CHOICES:

Engineering, computer science, law, science (life and physical), research, medicine, inventing, entrepreneur, business analysis, consulting, management, languages, and careers involving the management of human resources.

ENTJ

(Extraversion, iNtuition, Thinking, Judging)

FCIL

(Front, Conceptual, Inanimate, Left-brained)

"Chief Executive Officer"

The ENTJ is a person with a strong desire to lead. This Brain Type has the ability and drive to harness people or groups toward a goal. ENTJs see the future with vision, relishing the leadership roles in that vision. They are natural leaders who work hard, delegate well, and accomplish much. With iNtuition and Thinking, ENTJs formulate brilliant strategies. They're born Chief Executive Officers (CEO's).

With firm persuasion, ENTJs maintain control even in the midst of crisis. Rarely wavering from their convictions and objectives, they epitomize the characteristics of the commander in chief. They invariably assume the command awarded them due to their intelligence and competence. It has been said they cannot *not* lead. This pattern begins early in life, almost from the moment ENTJs come into contact with others.

"CEOs" have the ability to comprehend complex issues and relate to the layperson with ease. They can be outstanding communicators, public speakers, pastors, and presidents. They usually memorize their speeches and have eye contact with their audiences.

ENTJs desire to get tasks completed without delay. They despise inefficiency. They are drawn to solving problems with short and long term objectives. Others may resist their style of leadership if it is overbearing, lacking in tact, or impersonal. ENTJs need to take time to get all the facts, listen to those involved, consider the feelings of others and show appreciation. They should steer away from arguments and confrontations, being more winsome in their directives.

ENTJs' sometime quick tempers, impatience, and critical spirits can be directed at themselves as well as toward others. They are not naturally adept at relating to people even though their strong egos may deceive them into thinking they are. In fact, their high confidence level assists them in thinking they can do almost anything. An ENTJ teenager, for example, may be out driving immediately after passing a driving test even though those with him can clearly see his need for more practice.

Interpersonal skills must be learned by ENTJs if they are to have success in friendships and marriage. They actually do become good at relating to others, partly because of the desire to do so, and also because they are good actors and imitators. They quickly pick up the appropriate behavior seen in others. ENTJs may choose to use these learned skills to manipulate to get what they want, or they may genuinely work toward the welfare of others.

As children, ENTJs win friends easily, though they can be controlling and argumentative. They win friends who admire their many talents and abilities and their outgoing ways. They may, for instance, call their friends almost every day. Competitive and driven to be the best, ENTJs often achieve high honors. Self-critical ENTJ children may cause emotional scenes.

As we have seen, ENTJs are competent individuals with self assured and aggressive ways, quite easily recognized in typology. Their goals for learning and self growth for themselves and others are objective. They lead the way in their chosen fields, trusting they will be followed.

ENTJs have been significant leaders throughout history. Some of our more recent ones include **Franklin D. Roosevelt, Dwight D. Eisenhower, John F. Kennedy, Ronald Reagan, Martin Luther King Jr., Margaret Thatcher, Mikhail Gorbachev, General Colin Powell, Bill Clinton,** and **George W. Bush**. As you see, the values, interests, morals, and styles of leadership vary appreciably with these ENTJs. What they do share in common, however, is their inborn Brain Type which specializes in Extraversion, iNtuition, Thinking, and Judging.

Ross Perot, ENTJ and true CEO, proved he could not resist his innate leadership drive, by seeking the U.S. Presidency in 1992 and 1996. His debating skills and boldness captured a nation's attention in 1992.

The knowledge of Brain Types can enable each of us to see beyond the personas or reputations of each person. This knowledge helps us to understand the constructive as well as destructive potential of each Brain Type. The Bible's **Apostle Paul** demonstrates, in one person alone, the manifold behaviors of the ENTJ. As an anti-Christian religious leader prior to his conversion, he persecuted and put Christians to death. Following his new found faith, Paul never desired to kill anyone again, Christian or non. Instead, he promoted God's love to the world. The once zealous persecutor of Christianity became its greatest propagator. Paul penned the famous Biblical words on love, often recited today at weddings and found in I Corinthians 13 of the New Testament. Paul was once a misguided ENTJ who changed his values and mission in life, all for the betterment of the world.

ENTJs have an inborn desire to lead people. It is up to parents and society to instill in them the proper values. When this is done, there are no stronger, competent, effective or better leaders than ENTJs.

ENTJ Sports Profile:

ENTJs are among the best athletes and excel in most sports, which cannot be said of many other Brain Types. ENTJs are consistently the best of the left-brained (J) Types in most sports. Many would not expect ENTJs to do so well, considering they are iNtuitives whose fine and gross motor skills are not as innately proficient as Sensates. Yet, as we have seen with virtually all Brain Types (including iNtuitives), motor movements can be developed to compete in most sports at the upper levels. In addition, ENTJs' inherent strength of conceptual logic enables them to outfox most of their opponents.

"CEOs" utilize their drive and tenacity in athletics to great advantage. Their indomitable will perseveres until the game or match is over. They are not about to concede defeat as long as they can stand and breathe.

For further insights into how ENTJs perform athletically, read the various sports chapters.

Type Tips

When ENTJs first take up a sport, they may need extra encouragement to stick with it. Because they place such a high emphasis on competency, they do not like to play a sport in which they are behind in skills. Until they can develop the necessary talents, they may need regular morale boosts. With their superior work ethic, however, it shouldn't be long before they achieve success.

ENTJs would be wise to develop their motor skills. Any activities or exercises that improve hand eye coordination and smooth motor movements are advisable. The earlier in life these can begin, the better.

ENTJs are gifted with typological iNtuition. Thus, they can achieve rapid success through positive visualization techniques. The younger they can begin mental training, the greater athletic success they will find.

ENTJs should not be critical (of themselves and others) when playing sports. This can be excessively debilitating early in their careers. Such emphasis creates undue tension, resulting in motor and mental rigidity.

ENTJs can easily focus too much on the *results* of their actions more than on the *process*. They are best served by being less critical of the results, while concentrating on and developing smooth motions, coordinated motor movements, and tempo. Rather than fixating on striking out the batter, hitting the shot, or completing the pass, ENTJs should develop awareness of body processes needed to complete their actions.

Read the various sports chapters for additional insights into ENTJs.

PROBABLE ENTJs IN SPORTS

Baseball:
1st: Eric Karros, J.T. Snow, Jeff Conine, Travis Lee; **R:** Steve Garvey
2nd: **R: Ryne Sandberg**, Marty Barrett, Jody Reed
ss: Jay Bell, **R:** Tony Kubec
3rd: Travis Fryman, Todd Zeile, Russell Branyan; **R: Paul Molitor**, Dave Hollins, Dave Magadan
C: Javy Lopez;
 R: Joe Torre, Tim McCarver, Carlton Fisk, Mike Scioscia, Damon Berryhill, Mike Stanley, Mike MacFarlane
OF: Tim Salmon;
 R: Bobby Valentine, Dale Murphy, Kevin McReynolds, Brett Butler, Paul O'Neill, Chad Curtis
P: **Greg Maddux,** Barry Zito, Mark Prior, Denny Neagle, Jeff Fassero, Scott Erickson, Shawn Estes, Bobby Witt, Kevin Tapani;
 RP: Robb Nen, Matt Mantei
 R: Don Drysdale, Jim Palmer, **Tom Seaver**, Dave Dravecky, Steve Stone, Tom House, Ken Brett, Joe Magrane, Kirk McCaskill, Scott Sanderson, Jimmy Key, Jay Howell, Ron

Darling, Mike Boddicker, Rick Aguilera, Roger McDowell, Tim Belcher, John Wetteland

Basketball: **Pau Gasol**, Raef LaFrentz, Brad Miller, Christian Laettner, Tony Kukoc, Don MacLean, Danny Ferry, Travis Knight, Andrew DeClerq, Pat Garrity, Todd Fuller, Chris Anstey, Austin Croshere, Chris Mihm, Eric Piatkowski, Brent Barry, Wally Szczerbiak, Jon Barry, Brian Evans, Matt Maloney, John Crotty,
Retired: Bill Bradley, Jerry Lucas, Dave Cowens, **Rick Barry**, Dan Issel, **Kevin McHale**, John Paxson, Tom Chambers, Todd Lichti, Brooks Thompson

Bowling: Brian Voss

Football: Trent Green, David Carr, Rob Johnson, Steve Stenstrom, Keith Poole, Bruce Matthews, Tony Boselli,
Retired: **Roger Staubach**, Jack Kemp, Len Dawson, Steve Bartkowski, Neil Lomax, Jeff Kemp, Mark Malone, Dan Dierdorf, Reggie Williams, Steve Largent, Ahmad Rashad, Todd Christensen, Bob Chandler, Gary Fencik, Pat Leahy, Pat McInally, Mike Ademle, Mike Singletary, Greg Lloyd, Dave Krieg, Mark Kelso, Sterling Sharpe, **Steve Young**, Jim Harbaugh

Golf: Phil Mickelson, Steve Elkington, Peter Jacobson, Jeff Maggert, Curtis Strange, Keith Clearwater, Jeff Sluman,
Seniors: Johnny Miller, Tom Watson, Gary Player, Bruce Crampton, Ken Venturi, Bobby Nichols, Deane Beman, Wally Armstrong

Gymnastics: Svetlana Boguinskaia, Kathy Johnson, Jarrod Hanks

Hockey: Eric Lindros, Tony Granato, Owen Nolan,
Retired: Jim Craig, Mike Gartner, Danny Quinn

Skating (figure): Katarina Witt, Peggy Fleming, Dorthy Hamill, Jill Trenary

Soccer: Mia Hamm
Retired: Kyle Rote Jr.

Swimming-Diving: Mike Barrowman, Mark Lenzi

Tennis: Todd Martin, Alex Corretja, Karel Novacek, Todd Witsken, Amos Mansdorf, Javier Sanchez, Rick Leach, Jay Berger
Retired: Billie Jean King, Gabriela Sabatini, Mary Carillo, Tony Trabert, Jack Kramer, Harold Solomon, Cliff Drysdale, Brad Gilbert

Track and Field: Bruce Jenner, Dave Johnson, Bill Toomey, Erki Nool, Frank Shorter, Francie Larrieu

Volleyball: Karch Kiraly, Kent Steffes, Mike Whitmarsh, Tim Walmer

Coaches:
Baseball: Joe Torre, Lou Piniella, Buck Showalter, Bobby Valentine, Jeff Torborg, Mike Hargrove,
Basketball: Larry Brown, Rick Pitino, John Calipari, Dave Cowens, Brian Hill, P.J. Carlesimo, Jeff Van Gundy, Dan Issel, Nolan Richardson, Mike Montgomery, Pete Gillen, Mark Gottfried
Football: Vince Lombardi, Paul Brown, Bill Belichick, John Gruden, Brian Billick, Dennis Green, Dom Capers, Steve Mariucci, Jim Mora

Sports Media:
Various sports: Al Michaels, Jim Nance, Bob Costas, Chris Berman, Chris Myers, Jim Lampley, Jim Rome
Baseball: Tony Kubek, Jim Palmer, Tim McCarver, Don Drysdale, Steve Stone, Steve Garvey
Basketball: Billy Packer, Chick Hearn
Football: Dan Dierdorf, Ahmad Rashad, Len Dawson, Todd Christensen
Golf: Ken Venturi, Johnny Miller, Curtis Strange
Tennis: Tony Trabert, Mary Carillo, Roger Twibell, Cliff Drysdale, Barry MacKay, Bill Macatee, Barry Thompkins
Track: Bruce Jenner, Dave Johnson

PROBABLE WELL-KNOWN ENTJs:

Bill Bradley, Patrick Buchanan, Bill Clinton, Hillary Clinton, George W. Bush, Dick Cheney, Mario Cuomo, Howard Dean, Dwight D. Eisenhower, Dick Gephardt, Newt Gingrich, Mikhail Gorbachev, Albert Gore, Jack Kemp, John F. Kennedy, John F. Kennedy, Jr., Alan Keyes, Benjamin Netanyahu, Ross Perot, Dan Quayle, Ronald Reagan, Franklin Delano Roosevelt, Margaret

Thatcher, Justice Clarence Thomas, Oliver North, Gen. Colin Powell, Ron Brown, Martin Luther King Jr., John Chancellor, Connie Chung, Katie Couric, Brit Hume, Peter Jennings, Jim Lehrer, Jane Pauley, Dan Rather, Diane Sawyer, Maria Shriver, Kathleen Sullivan, Bryant Gumbel, Barbara Walters, Judy Woodruff, Leona Helmsley, Anita Faye Hill, Marcia Clark, Johnnie Cochran Jr., David Duke, Daryl Gates, Dr. Laura Schlessinger, Donald Trump

Lucille Ball   Geraldo Rivera   Demi Moore   Rush Limbaugh

Martin Luther King Jr.   Margaret Thatcher   Colin Powell

Bill Clinton   Jack Kemp

POPULAR CAREER CHOICES:

ENTJs have the drive and intellectual aptitude to excel in virtually all vocations, yet they seem to derive their greatest satisfaction from jobs that allow them to exercise their abstract logic while leading and inspiring others. Some of these careers include:

Law, management in business or industry, educational administration, politics, sales, medicine, entrepreneurial endeavors, financial planning, banking, ministry, consulting, public speaking, writing, organization executive, coaching

Charlie Chase, Ralph Emery, Bob Eubanks, Rush Limbaugh, Sally Jessy Raphael, Geraldo Rivera, Alex Trebek, Chuck Woolery

Mark Harmon, Charlton Heston, Dolph Lundgren, George Strait, Jean-Claude Van Damme, Lawrence Welk

Barbara DeAngelis, Tom Peters, Zig Ziglar, Denis Waitley, Tom Vu

Lucille Ball, Meredith Baxter, Candice Bergen, Courteney Cox, Bette Davis, Patty Duke, Jane Fonda, Robin Givens, Valerie Harper, Mariette Hartley, Katharine Hepburn, Linda Lavin, Shelley Long, Susan Lucci, Demi Moore, Michelle Phillips, Brigitte Neilsen, Phylicia Rashad, Connie Sellecca, Jane Seymour, Marlo Thomas

La Toya Jackson, Chynna Phillips

INTP
(Introversion, iNtuition, Thinking, Perceiving)
BCIR
(Back, Conceptual, Inanimate, Right-brained)

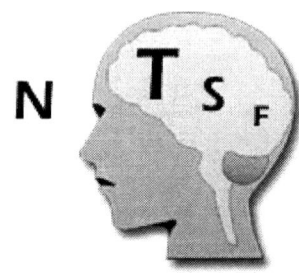

"Logician"

INTPs are usually precocious children, synthetically logical and reserved. They may be solemn and independent, with a passion for asking why or seeking to find out why? all by themselves. They are obedient in matters to which they are indifferent, provided they think the rules are fair. They think physical punishment is violating to their dignity.

Hands-off parenting that allows constructive experimental behavior can be productive with INTPs. Ridicule and sarcasm concerning their abilities will be devastating and will promote their ready tendency for self doubt. Others may ridicule them for their ability to be lost in thought. They may use personal isolation as a defense mechanism. INTPs often feel they are very different from others until they find more commonality in a college setting.

INTPs may appear to be somewhat socially slow, needing to work hard to develop interpersonal skills. They are original thinkers, enjoying logical reasoning for its own sake. Having a passion for questions that begin "What would happen if . . . ," they are highly effective in organizing themselves to research and plan. As premier problem-solvers, any project, big or small, presents itself as a stimulating challenge. INTPs are sought after for their creative ideas and theories.

INTPs, as we can see, live in the creative world of concepts and ideas, placing greater value on the principles behind the facts than on the facts themselves. Even existence can be an abstract to INTPs. They have been known to pursue the impossible theory, the grand idea, to the disregard of reality or those closest to them. They make excellent writers, artists, computer programmers, scientists, professors, philosophers, and mathematicians. Because of their extremely competent cerebral abilities, INTPs are most often attracted to academic pursuits (INTPs are generally valedictorians, especially at the college level), and less to athletic activities, unless motivated by parents, siblings, peers, and so forth.

INTPs are rare and complicated individuals indeed. Relating to them can be an intellectual challenge. If you can persuade INTPs to simplify their thought processes and slowly unweave their complicated conclusions so that you can follow their intricate logic, the trip will be worthwhile. They seek precision, you see, qualifying to the nth degree what they are expressing. INTPs with a handle on truth can be persuasive geniuses. As teachers, they need to take extra care to talk on the student's level. They make supportive parents, wanting children to develop their own abilities, preferring not to push or control. It's estimated that INTPs approximate 1-2 percent of the American population.

INTP **Albert Einstein** spoke little prior to the age of three. His family even believed him to be retarded at a stage in childhood. His mother once wrote to a friend:

> I don't know what we are going to do with Albert, he doesn't seem to learn very much.[4]

Yet Einstein was not unusual for a young INTP, who finds the rigorous discipline of Sensing reality in lower education to be boring and militaristic. His precocious mind was not interested in rote learning.

Einstein never respected those who automatically submitted to the establishment; he valued those who were independent thinkers. He considered it stupid to learn things by heart. Remembering matters was a process of understanding why and how things worked or were. Just to know was not enough; he had to understand. This thinking is common for INTPs.

Einstein, like other INTPs, was best designed for unscrambling the unknown complexities of this world and universe. INTPs normally do not get exposed to these complexities until college and beyond. When they do, they are unparalleled in problem solving, relying upon conceptual logic.

Honors and recognition had no meaning for Einstein,

though he received many. He said:

> The value of a man resides in what he gives and not in what he is capable of receiving.[5]

INTP Sports Profile

American **Lori Norwood**, the 1989 women's world pentathlon champion, depicts the INTP. (Pentathlon events include swimming, running, riding, fencing, and shooting.) Let's look at Norwood to better understand some aspects of the INTP Brain Type.

Generally Reserved

Coach Janusz Peciak told *Sports Illustrated*:

> Lori is very shy. She never acts like she's a big star. It doesn't matter whether she's the world champion or in last place, she has the same personality. I really like that about her. She's a very nice person.[6]

Norwood's Introversion not only gives her personality a "shy" aura, but allows her to reflect deeply. One interest of hers is sculpting. She said:

> I can't just sculpt for an hour or two. Once I get into the studio, I live there.[7]

Erudite, Driven, Disciplined

Sports Illustrated reported:

> She is a sweet-faced, soft-spoken, introspective woman who spends a great deal of time reading and thinking about things besides pentathlon—things like art, life, the environment. Her serene countenance belies the fact that Norwood is a driven, focused competitor who came back after a two-year layoff to win the world championship in Wiener Neustadt, Austria, in August 1989.[8]

Coach Peciak spoke again of Norwood:

> She's very disciplined. And she has a talent for work. Lori is a person who hates to lose. She's much tougher in the brain than the men.[9]

How would you respond to her coach's comment of Lori's mental toughness being superior to men, (I'm sure he means most rather than all), based on what you've learned thus far in the book? I would have to agree with him. We have repeatedly seen the ISTP's superiority in most sports, both physically and mentally. The INTP shares the same Introverted, Thinking, right-brained dominance, with only iNtuition differing from the ISTP's Sensing. INTPs will not possess the ISTP's superb motor skills but will share similar mental intensity and toughness. INTPs normally attack and dominate the books (using iNtuition) the way ISTPs dominate sports (using Sensing). In the case of Norwood, she has demonstrated her prowess in some sporting events as well. Norwood claimed:

> I'm not an amazingly talented or gifted athlete. I'm just more able to stay concentrated on something for a long time and be consistent.[10]

ITPs (ISTP and INTP) are able to concentrate longer and deeper, and reason more in the inanimate, logical realm than any other Brain Type. If the reported percentages of Types in America are roughly accurate, with ISTPs accounting for 5% and INTPs 2%, then approximately 93% of the population (including men) is not as mentally tough as ITPs. *SI* stated:

> . . . Norwood is [Peciak's] favorite student. She would be any coach's dream—she follows orders without question and never complains, no matter how much she may be hurting. Her idea of fun is a 10-mile run. Other U.S. team members may straggle into practice 20 minutes late, but she's always on time. Although practice starts at 8 a.m., Norwood is up at 6:30 so she can be fully awake and focused for her workout.[11]

Bob Nieman, the only other American besides Norwood to win a pentathlon world championship, said:

> This sport may require more mental discipline than any other . . . Lori's got a real good head for the sport.[12]

In 1991, after observing his rookie player for only five days, **Dikembe Mutombo** (INTP), Denver Nuggets coach Paul Westhead made an assessment:

> Right away I could see that the guy could do a lot more things than people thought he could. And he could learn. Tell him something once and he

would learn it.[13]

Artistic, Spatial, Right-brained

Lori Norwood is an accomplished artist as well. Her INTP right brain preference enables her see and visualize creatively and in detail. Norwood said:

> I love the feel of clay. I always had a three dimensional sense as a kid. I was always making dogs and other animal figures, or building sand castles out of mud—always creating.[14]

It's fascinating to hear her speak of "three dimensional sense" and "always creating." We saw in the Neuroscience chapter how the right hemisphere has superior three dimensional perspective. Though left-brained Types do not possess this innate adeptness, they can appreciate the finished artistry of the Perceptive Types.

Lori's and other INTPs' iNtuition will be the catalyst for "always creating." Regardless of how they use their N, it will be a highly proficient brain function.

For other INTP profiles, refer to the Body Skills section and the Tennis chapter.

Type Tips

INTPs normally take to academics like ducks take to water. They have an aptitude for learning and can find great satisfaction in excelling in school. They can find the formative years of lower education quite a bore, however. The subject matter is often too rudimentary and the pace of learning too slow. Encouraging INTPs to develop an interest in school and learn solid study habits is the first step to help INTPs vocationally. No Brain Type has greater cerebral potential than INTPs.

INTPs can be very good athletes. Tennis is a great sport for them to pursue. I don't know of a professional sport in which INTPs can achieve greater success. They can also excel at long distance running.

INTPs, like all iNtuitives, should work hard on developing their motor movements. Lots of running and learning body balance will improve the gross motor skills, while performing hand eye coordination drills will enhance the fine motor movements.

PROBABLE INTPs IN SPORTS

Basketball: Dikembe Mutombo

Tennis: Mary Joe Fernandez
Retired: Arthur Ashe

PROBABLE WELL KNOWN INTPs:

Jermarr Arnold, Mikhail Baryshnikov, Dietrich Bonhoeffer, William F. Buckley Jr., George Washington Carver, Leonardo da Vinci, Jonathan Edwards, Albert Einstein, Jane Goodall (naturalist), Jascha Heifetz (violinist), Dr. C. Everett Koop, Gary Larson, John Lennon, C.S. Lewis, Nelson Mandela, Linus Pauling, Andrei D. Sakharov, Rudolf Serkin (pianist), Alexander Solzhenitsyn, Roger Sperry, Steven Spielberg, Garry Trudeau, Peter Yarrow

Dr. C. Everett Koop   Nelson Mandela   Jane Goodall   Steven Spielberg

POPULAR CAREER CHOICES:

Mathematics, philosophy, psychiatry, medicine, advanced sciences, university teaching, physics, research, strategic planning, creative writing, literature, music, art.

ENTP

(Extraversion, iNtuition, Thinking, Perceiving)

FCIR

(Front, Conceptual, Inanimate, Right-brained)

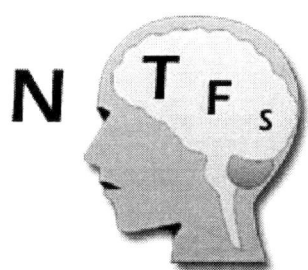

"Strategizer"

ENTPs are goal-oriented, energetic and imaginative. They love life and work well with people and are challenged by new ideas. They improvise quickly to avoid boredom, having the ability to think on their feet, entertaining the crowd with quick and witty responses. ENTPs are masters of one-upmanship. They do not like to do the same thing twice, never sing the song the same way, never follow directions precisely. They prefer to employ methods of their own, designing systems and carrying them on to completion. ENTPs who read this material may jot down notes in the margins as they scan the pages, looking for ideas to use in their many areas of interest.

ENTP children may be up and out of the crib at midnight for exploration. They use their toys in unique, inventive ways. Rushing through the day like whirlwinds of activity, they can ask a million questions. They want to be helpful. They want to relate to other children, children who may be resistant to the ENTP's unorthodox mannerisms.

ENTPs are dominant right-brained iNtuitives and highly adept in conceptual, visual matters. They learn computer technology easily and tend to dominate the industry as adults. (Microsoft's **Bill Gates** is an ENTP.) ENTPs also excel in technical mechanics. They may be found taking their toys apart to see how they work, or fixing the neighbor's car or VCR.

The ENTP child or adult likes to keep the options open. Changing one's direction, occupation, or mind is a regular practice. If the parent or spouse is not of similar Brain Type, the ENTP can be source of confusion and frustration. Understanding the ENTP mind and behavior may take patience and insight.

My years of research reveals that children diagnosed with Attention Deficit Disorder with Hyperactivity (ADHD) are commonly ENTPs. All four EP Types are susceptible to this categorization, but ENTPs usually have the severest forms. Though I reject most of the popular theories and drug remedies for treating this often misdiagnosed disorder, there is an irrefutable scientific explanation for it—in many cases. ENTP children in particular, have been shown through brain imaging and genetic testing to have inborn neurobiological factors that prompt ADHD-like behavior. Yet I also believe that when these children are given a consistently loving, creative, structured and disciplined environment—particularly by their parents—the vast majority of ENTPs can escape the diagnosis of ADHD. Applying Brain Typing can bring much benefit to this and other often misunderstood conditions.

ENTP children may not fit into the usual routine of our structured classrooms. The elementary teacher is likely to be of a very different Brain Type. ENTPs prize freedom and experimentation and challenge the teacher's methods and conclusions with logic and competence.

ENTPs love to travel and can be found away from home for extended periods of time. They are consulting, flying, doing business in the most exciting and varied ways possible. At home, they probably have begun a number of projects that are taking far too long to complete. The ENTP may be out pursuing even more interests, taking risks, relating to people.

Many people in the field of entertainment and show business are ENTPs. They account for most of the comedians and a good number of talk show hosts, singers, and musicians. Center stage is home for most ENTPs. *(Occasionally ENTPs can be found with low-key personas. Environment shapes the ENTP personality probably more than any other Brain Type—a major reason ENTPs can have so many varied looks.)*

Entertaining the world and getting the most out of every opportunity, ENTPs really do contribute to making the world revolve. They may need to learn to respect authority and practice self-control. Though they need to work on completing projects, ENTPs generally keep us laughing as we are shown the broad spectrum of possibilities by this creative Brain Type.

ENTPs are right hemisphere dominant—adaptable, spontaneous and open ended persons. They are inquisitive, energetic, and audacious in their endeavors. Resisting being "put in a box" or having to live the traditional way, they are free spirits who like to freely pursue their impulses. ENTPs do not have the cerebral desire to be as structured as the left-brained "Js" in society. That is perfectly okay; they must live the way they are cerebrally designed. They must acknowledge, however, that their "P" characteristics can go to excess.

A famous American family, the Kennedys, illustrates the subtle differences in Brain Types. Democrat **Edward Kennedy** has served in Congress for many years, supporting his party and convictions strenuously. Nevertheless, he has had his share of incidences that have caused many to question his stability. Ted is an ENTP who has had difficulty at times regulating his Type's tendencies. His older brothers, John and Robert, appear to have captured higher public esteem in their political careers. Even though President Kennedy was known for "extracurricular activities" while in Washington, he was regarded as structured in his political ways. This is understandable considering he was an ENTJ.

Each Brain Type has tendencies for improprieties. For instance, Introverted "Js" will be much more secretive in their improper activities than Extraverted "Ps", such as an ENTP. The public will become much more aware of the "EPs" indiscretions than the subtle "IJs".

Implicating one's Brain Type as an excuse for illegal or faulty behavior is never acceptable. Every normal person has the ability to live a moral, law-abiding, upstanding life.

Ted Kennedy has complied with protocol and tradition in the Senate, but his personal life has been more difficult for him to control. Mike Barnicle, a longtime Kennedy sympathizer and best-read columnist of the *Boston Globe*, predicted Kennedy could be beaten in the 1994 election because:

> People have grown tired of a man who is out of control.[19]

Paul Richter of the *L.A. Times* wrote that supporters of Kennedy:

> . . . paint a picture of a man whose party-going is part of an exuberant, spontaneous, sociable nature.[20]

Both columnists capture the tendencies of ENTPs. The degrees of self-discipline and structure vary with ENTPs, depending upon their upbringing, life values, spiritual convictions, and so forth. God specifically designed their precocious minds to keep society on the cutting edge.

ENTPs are conceptually brilliant people, including Ted Kennedy. When they use their charm, they are most persuasive. Columnist Paul Richter says that Kennedy's portrait in the Senate has been unlike that of his personal life:

> There, the talk is often of his hard work, subtle mastery of lawmaking, and the equable personality that enables him to cobble deals that unite wildly divergent interests.[21]

This insight into Ted Kennedy is intended to be used constructively in each of our lives. It is important that we try to understand what makes people tick humanly, spiritually, environmentally and neurologically. We then can lend assistance to others as well as ourselves.

Ted Kennedy, by his own admission, has said he is trying to improve his personal matters. For his sake, and our country's, I pray for his success.

I believe that **Solomon** in the Bible was an ENTP. Solomon provides an overview of his life in the Old Testament book of *Ecclesiastes*. He had an incredible life. To say that he sought wisdom, tried to live life to the fullest, and accumulated the material things of life is a grand understatement. Though a highly intelligent man, Solomon discarded the spiritual convictions of his formative years for the sake of political advantage and voluptuous living. He was the third and last king of united Israel.

Solomon was regarded as wiser than the wise men of the East and of Egypt. He wrote some 3000 Proverbs and 1000 songs. People came from distant lands to see and hear him. There was hardly an area of life in which he was not expert. Despite his unparalleled successes, he ended life a saddened man. He wished he had never neglected his relationship with God. Concluding his Ecclesiastes work, he said:

> Now all has been heard; here is the conclusion

of the matter; fear God and keep his commandments, for this is the whole duty of man. (NIV, Ecc. 12:13)

ENTP Sports profile

Found in virtually all professional sports, ENTPs can be top-flight athletes. As dominant right-brained persons, they have more naturally fluid motor movements than left-hemisphere NTJs. ENTPs have the potential for remarkable body flexibility and quick feet. Gross motor proficiency is their least least-developed inborn body skill (of the possible four).

ENTPs are generally high-energy performers, particularly gifted in logical abstraction skills—specializing in designing intellectual game plans. By master-planning attacks, their opponents are outfoxed. ENTPs are often known for their comedic and zany ways in athletics, a delight to the fans and sports media. (Their coaches are not always as thrilled.) Nonetheless, they can be serious athletes. As NTs, ENTPs have a strong drive to win and can generate enormous energy and will power.

To learn about their specific athletic habits, read the various sports chapters which tell in depth of ENTPs.

Type Tips

ENTPs are generally precocious children, much like 15-year-old brains in 7-year-old bodies. They may prefer conversations with adults than with kids their own age. They are able to grasp concepts and information far beyond their years. Though their motor skills may be lacking, their mental skills are advanced, enabling them to learn the mental phases of sports at an early age. If they continue to work hard as they get older, their physical skills will gain greater parity with their mental game.

ENTPs, like all iNtuitives, should work hard on developing their motor skills, particularly hand-eye coordination. Numerous drills can be implemented.

ENTPs will want to have fun in learning sports. Allow them latitude. Don't bore them with excessive instruction, the perfecting of technique. Those will come in time.

PROBABLE ENTPs IN SPORTS

Baseball:
1st: **Jason Giambi**, Mo Vaughn, Rafael Palmeiro, Tino Martinez, Todd Helton, Sean Casey, Lee Stevens, Richie Sexson, Doug Mientkiewicz;
  R: Frank Howard, Kent Hrbek, Bob Hamelin
2nd: Chuck Knoblauch, Delino DeShields, Todd Walker; R: Jose Lind
SS: R: Bill Ripkin, Pat Listach
3rd: Troy Glaus, Paul Konerko, Tyler Houston;
  R: Sal Bando, Doug Rader, Scott Brosius
C: Jason Kendall, Joe Girardi, Jason LaRue;
  R: Mike LaValiere, Jim Leyritz
OF: **Ichiro Suzuki**, Jim Edmonds, Luis Gonzalez, Shawn Green, Marquis Grissom, Brian Giles, Derek Bell, B.J. Surhoff, Ryan Klesko, Cliff Floyd, Johnny Damon, Turner Ward;
  R: Jay Johnstone, John Lowenstein, Steve Lyons, Otis Nixon, Chuck Carr,
P: **Curt Schilling,** Kevin Brown, David Wells, Andy Pettitte, Brad Radke, Hideo Nomo, Mike Hampton, Orlando Hernandez (El Duque), Dave Burba, Hideki Irabu, Eric Milton, Terry Mulholland, Joey Hamilton, Carlos Perez, Mike Remlinger, Ben Sheets, Rick Ankiel;
 RP: Eric Gagne, Mike Williams, Scott Sullivan, Norm Charlton;
  R: Gaylord Perry, **Phil Niekro**, Charlie Hough, John (The Count) Montefusco, Bill "Spaceman" Lee, Jeff Reardon, Tom Candiotti, Chad Ogea, Chris Bozio, Carl Willis, Jeff Montgomery, Sid Fernandez, Jesse Orosco, Doug Jones, Jeff Brantley, Rod Beck

Basketball: Arvydas Sabonis, Michael Olowokandi, Erick Dampier, Todd MacCulloch, Scot Pollard, Keon Clark, Isaac Austin, Vin Baker, Chris Gatling, Donyell Marshall, Antoine Walker, Jamie Feick, **Glenn Robinson**, Lamond Murray, Clarence Weatherspoon, Corliss Williamson, Jason Caffey, Darvin Ham, Marcus Fizer, Shane Battier, Predrag Stojakovic, **Vince Carter**, Michael Finley, Ron Mercer, Voshon Lenard, Bryant Stith, Randy Brown, Tony Delk, Cuttino Mobley, David Wesley, Sam Cassell, Damon Stoudamire, **Nick Van Exel**, Travis Best, Derek Fisher, Jacque Vaughn, Avery Johnson, Rebecca Lobo
  Retired: **Bob Cousy**, **Bill Russell**, Rod Hundley, Kevin Loughery, Jeff Ruland, John Lucas, Frank Johnson, Mike Brown, Felton Spencer, Jayson Williams, Malik Sealy, Luc Longley

Bowling: Nelson Burton Jr., David Ozio, Roger Bowker, Del Ballard Jr., Steve Cook, Dave D'Entremont, Wayne Webb, Marshall Holman, Bob Learn Jr., Ricky Ward, Bob Belmont, Doug Kent, Randy Pedersen, Rick Steelsmith, Steve Hoskins

Cycling: Lance Armstrong
John Stamstad (ultra-endurance)

Football: Kurt Warner, Rich Gannon, Brian Griese, Jeff Garcia, Neil O'Donnell, Jeff George, Kerry Collins, Charlie Batch, Bobby Hoying, Koy Detmer, Jay Fiedler, Chad Pennington, Chris Weinke,
Jerome Bettis, Errict Rhett, Dorsey Levens, Charlie Garner, Cris Carter, Antonio Freeman, Herman Moore, Amani Toomer, Rickey Dudley, Terry Glenn,
Dermontti Dawson, Tim Grunhard, Frank Winters, Andy McCollum, Will Shields,
Morten Andersen, Gary Anderson, John Carney, Steve Christie, Jason Elam, Cary Blanchard, Jeff Jaeger, Pete Stoyanovich, Adam Vinatieri, Sebastian Janikowski, Mike Vanderjagt
Darren Bennett, Chris Gardocki, Matt Turk, Lee Johnson,
Peter Boulware, Keith Hamilton, Chad Brown, Rod Woodson, Eric Allen, Eric Davis, Ryan McNeil, Keenan McCardell, Michael Bates, Jason Sehorn
  Retired: **Dan Fouts**, John Brodie, Ron Jaworski, Joe Gilliam, John Matuszak, Lyle Alzado, Randy Cross, Jack Ham, Tim Rossovich, Paul Maguire, Mike Curtis, Bob Golic, Tony Mandarich, Bart Oates, Mike Lansford, Steve DeBerg, Steve Bono, Keith Jackson, Leslie O'Neal, Dan Saleaumua, Alfred Williams, Lamar Lathon, Terry McDaniel, Louie Aguiar, Tony Siragusa

Golf: Fulton Allem, Bobby Clampett, Darren Clarke, Chris DiMarco, Brad Faxon, Tim Herron, Mike Hulbert, Justin Leonard, Wayne Levi, Bruce Lietzke, Billy Mayfair, Rocco Mediate, Colin Montgomerie, David Ogrin, Jesper Parnevik, Loren Roberts, Clarence Rose, Greg Twiggs, Jean Van de Velde, Mike Weir, Fuzzy Zoeller,
Rosie Jones
  Seniors: Dave Stockton, Rocky Thompson, John Brodie, Larry Laoretti, Gary McCord, Roger Maltbie

Gymnastics: Trent Dimas, Tim Dagget

Hockey: Dominik Hasek, Dave Karpa, Ray Ferraro
  Retired: Larry Robinson, Al Iafrate, Kelly Hrudey, Jay Miller, Pierre Larouche

Racing (auto): Emerson Fittipaldi, Arie Luyendyk, Dale Jarrett, Ernie Irvan, Joe Nemechek

Skating (figure): Rudy Galindo, Christopher Dean, Philippe Candeloro, Peter Carruthers, Christopher Bowman, Jozef Sabovcik, Tara Lipinski, Sarah Hughes, Tonya Harding

Skiing (snow): Jean Claude Killy, Hermann Maier, Billy Kidd, Andy Mill, Bill Koch, Liz McIntyre, Diann Roffe-Steinrotter

Soccer: Alexi Lalas, David Beckham

Swimming-Diving: Lenny Krayzelburg, Ian Thorpe, Melvin Stewart, Martin Zubero, Amy Van Dyken, Anita Nall, Scott Donie

Tennis: Roger Federer, Andy Roddick, Gustavo Kuerten, Marat Safin, Greg Rusedski, Emilio Sanchez, Jimmy Arias, Henri Leconte, Justin Gimelstob, Scott Draper, Scott Davis, Robert Seguso,
Irina Spirlea
  Retired: Suzanne Lenglen, Pancho Gonzales, Guillermo Vilas, Vitas Gerulaitas, Yannick Noah, Ion Tiriac, Leif Shiras, Bobby Riggs, Derrick Rostagno, Luke Jensen, Patrick McEnroe, Pete Sampras,

Track and Field: Donovan Bailey, Konstantinos Kenteris, Charles Austin, Jonathan Edwards, Kenny Harrison, Mike Conley, Michael Marsh, Kevin Young, Chris Huffins

Water Polo: Manuel Estiarte

Team Owners: Ted Turner, Eddie DeBartolo Jr., Bud Adams, Art Modell, Jack Kent Cooke, Dr. Jerry Buss, Jerry Reinsdorf, Pat Croce, Mark Cuban

Coaches: *Baseball*: Leo Durocher, Earl Weaver, Doug Rader, Sparky Anderson, Stump Merrill, Butch Hobson; *Basketball*: "Red" Auerbach, Chuck Daly, Frank Layden, Kevin Loughery, Hubie Brown, Bernie Bickerstaff, Jimmy Lynam, Mike Fratello, Jim Cleamons, Jimmy Rodgers, Darrell Walker, Jerry Reynolds, Al McGuire, Digger Phelps, Rollie Massimino, Jim Valvano, Pete Carril, Bob Huggins, George Raveling; *Football*: Lou Holtz, Jeff Fisher, Bobby Bowden, Gary Barnett, Rick Neuheisel, Jerry Glanville; *Hockey*: Larry Robinson; *Tennis*: Ion Tiriac

Sports Media:
Various sports: Roy Firestone, Jack Whitaker, Brent Musburger, Kevin Harlan, Charley Steiner, Keith Olbermann, Dick Stockton, Howard Cosell
Baseball: Harry Caray
Basketball: Dick Vitale, Marv Albert, Jim Valvano, Hubie Brown, Kevin Loughery, Al McGuire, Mike Fratello
Boxing: Dr. Ferdie Pacheco, Bert Sugar
Football: Paul Maguire, Dan Fouts
Tennis: Bud Collins, Vitas Gerulaitis, Leif Shiras, Fred Stolle
Volleyball: Chris Marlowe

PROBABLE WELL-KNOWN ENTPs:

Benjamin Franklin, Sir Winston Churchill, John Ashcroft, Joseph Biden, Tony Blair, Alan Greenspan, Howell Heflin, Jesse Jackson, Edward (Ted) Kennedy, Henry Kissinger, Ed Koch, Tip O'Neil, Paul Simon, Boris Yeltsin, Marion Barry, Dr. Joycelyn Elders, Michael Eisner, Webster Hubble, Joe Lieberman, Rupert Murdoch, David Stern, Ted Turner, Robert Bork, Betty Friedan, John Sununu, Peter Arnett, Carl Bernstein, David Brinkley, David Frost, Charles Jaco, Charles Kuralt, Robert Novak, Charles Osgood, Jack Perkins, Tom Pettit, Harry Reasoner, Andy Rooney, Willard Scott, Bob Woodward, Art Buchwald, James Carville, Mary Matalin, Allen Ginsberg, Ernest Hemingway, Irving Wallace, Andy Warhol, Armstrong Williams, William Gaines, Steven Jay Gould, Stephen King, Salman Rushdie, Alvin Toffler, Isaac Asimov, Chelsea Clinton, Alistair Cooke, Thomas Kinkade, Pablo Picasso, Oliver Stone, Al Hirschfeld, George Adamson (naturalist), Jacques Cousteau, Charles Darwin, Michael Dell, Bill Gates, Mel Gibson, Hugh Hefner, Don Ismus, Timothy Leary, Madalyn Murray O'Hair, Jake Steinfeld, Howard Stern, Gianni Versace, Dr. Ruth Westheimer, Larry Flynt, Don King, Frank Capra, Matt Groening, Norman Lear, Rex Reed, Gene Shalit, Gene Siskel, Roger Ebert, Melvin Belli, Deepak Chopra, Christopher Darden, Brian (Kato) Kaelin, Robert Shapiro, Gerry Spence, Tony Robbins, Roger Clinton, David Copperfield, Steve Irwin

Benjamin Franklin   Sir Winston Churchill

Tim Allen, Woody Allen, Jason Alexander, Dan Aykroyd, John Belushi, Victor Borge, David Brenner, George Burns, John Candy, George Carlin, Jim Carrey, Dana Carvey, Chevy Chase, Gary Coleman, Bill Cosby, Billy Crystal, Bill Daily, Rodney Dangerfield, Dom DeLuise, Bob Denver, Danny DeVito, Chris Farley, W.C. Fields, Redd Foxx, Jackie Gleason, Kelsey Grammer, Tom Hanks, Pee wee Herman, Benny Hill, Sam Kinison, Robert Klein, Jerry Lewis, Howie Mandel, Cheech Marin, Dean Martin, Steve Martin, Groucho Marx, Dudley Moore, Mike Myers, Eddie Murphy, Bill Murray, Bob Newhart, Joe Piscopo, Richard Pryor, Don Rickles, Paul Rodriguez, Mort Sahl, Soupy Sales, Jerry Seinfeld, Garry Shandling, Pauly Shore, Yakov Smirnoff, Tom Smothers, Jim Varney (Ernest P. Worrell), Gene Wilder, Robin Williams, Jonathan Winters

Groucho Marx   George Burns   Eddie Murphy   Bill Cosby

Alan Alda, Richard Dean Anderson, Desi Arnaz Sr., Edward Asner, Mark Linn Baker, Alec Baldwin, Marlon Brando, Michael Caine, James Cagney, James Coburn, Sean Connery, Kevin Costner, Russell Crowe, Robert Culp, Richard Dreyfuss, Charles Dutton, Peter Falk, Harrison Ford, Richard Gere, Mel Gibson, John Goodman, Elliott Gould, Hugh Grant, Charles Grodin, Gene Hackman, Larry Hagman, Alfred Hitchcock, Dustin Hoffman, Anthony Hopkins, Dennis Hopper, Michael Keaton, Robin Leach, Jack Lemmon, John Larroquette, Spike Lee, Christopher Lloyd, Lee Marvin, Walter Matthau, Robert Mitchum, Leonard Nimoy, Jack Nicholson, Carroll O'Connor, Ed O'Neill, Sean Penn, Luke Perry, Brad Pitt, Vincent Price, Rob Reiner, Wayne Rogers, Mickey Rooney, Telly Savalas, George C. Scott, Rod Serling, Donald Sutherland, Patrick

Swayze, Richard Thomas, Spencer Tracy, Jon Voight, Orson Welles, George Wendt, Bruce Willis

James Cagney

Harrison Ford

Kevin Costner

Wolfgang Mozart

Yanni

Mick Jagger

Willie Nelson

Roseanne Barr, Halle Berry, Celine Dion, Jodie Foster, Whoopi Goldberg, Shirley MacLaine, Penny Marshall, Bette Midler, Rhea Perlman, Gilda Radner, Bonnie Raitt, Joan Rivers, Barbra Streisand, Lily Tomlin, Judy Tenuta, Tracey Ullman, Mae West

POPULAR CAREER CHOICES:
Computers, strategic planning, law, politics, medicine, science, business management, entrepreneur, comedy, magic, sales, inventing, venture capitalism, art, music, school administration, teaching, languages, journalism, coaching.

Whoopi Goldberg

Barbra Streisand

Bette Midler

Johnny Carson, Dick Cavett, Morton Downey Jr., Jay Leno, David Letterman, Jack Paar, Pat Sajak, Wil Shriner, Larry King

David Letterman

Jay Leno

Bryan Adams, Michael Bolton, Sonny Bono, David Bowie, Eric Clapton, Kurt Cobain, Tom Cochrane, Nat King Cole, Alice Cooper, Phil Collins, Michael Crawford, Miles Davis, John Denver, Bob Dylan, Jerry Garcia, Gerardo, Jimi Hendrix, Don Henley, John Hiatt, Engelbert Humperdinck, Mick Jagger, Billy Joel, Elton John, Jon Bon Jovi, Ricky Martin, John Mellancamp, George Michael, Randy Newman, Prince, Bob Seger, Doc Severinsen, Tupac Shakur, Paul Simon, Rod Stewart, Curtis Stigers, Ice-T, Yanni

Garth Brooks, Charlie Daniels, Mickey Gilley, Kris Kristofferson, Jerry Lee Lewis, Eddie Money, Ronny Milsap, Willie Nelson, Marty Stuart, Conway Twitty, Clay Walker, Hank Williams Jr.,

Leonard Bernstein, Jose Carreras, Placido Domingo, Vladimir Horowitz (pianist), Wolfgang A. Mozart, Luciano Pavarotti, Itzhak Perlman, Andrew Lloyd Webber, Steve Lawrence

PART SIX

BIRDS, BEES, AND TEMPERAMENT GROUPS

Introducing the Four Flying Creatures

The four temperaments were first introduced in Chapter 5, "You Were Meant to Fly." There, a brief description was given of the SJ, the SP, the NF, and the NT. The next four chapters present a fuller treatment given to these temperaments and creatures.

It occurred to me that a vehicle from nature could be used to illustrate the abstract principles of Brain Typing. Nature so often supplies us with useful analogies. The bee, the hummingbird, the stork, and the owl emerged in my course of research as the best representatives of the SJ, SP, NF, and NT, respectively.

My purpose is not to offer a one to one correlation in all areas. Rather, I have tried to bring to life some of the more obvious similarities in each Type and its representative flying creature. I have discovered not only that children retain the information more easily as a result of these comparisons, but that they are a tremendous aid for adults as they learn to understand people and themselves through the study of Brain Types.

24
The SJ "Bee"

ISTJ
ESTJ
ISFJ
ESFJ

The SJ (Sensing, Judging) temperament is a stable one. The individual SJ is likely to be a pillar of strength and the backbone of society. SJs are dependable, industrious, independent and pragmatic. They feel obligated to perform some useful function daily in their social group.

The reliable SJ is a saver and conservator. Values, traditions, institutions, money, knowledge—just about anything, whether tangible or intangible—may be stored by the SJ. In preserving these valuables for society, SJs hope to transmit them to the next generation, fully intact and completely useful.

Because SJs must earn their play, the work ethic is valued. SJs find it difficult to refuse added responsibility. As a result, they may tend to take on more than they have time to accomplish. Looking at the mountain of tasks they have taken on and feeling the constraints of time, SJs may become depressed with the weight of their obligations.

In all, the pre eminent characteristic of SJs is *responsibility*. They seek to be useful in their families, their jobs, and in society. They have a strong sense of belonging and feel obligated to uphold time honored rules and traditions. Thus, in their supportive roles they prefer to be known as givers and not takers. As conservators, SJs assume the responsibility of preparing for the future, sometimes more out of pessimism than anything else.

The SJ and the Bee

The SJ family of Types parallels, in many ways, the flying creature known as the honeybee. A close look at the bee will uncover many behavioral characteristics it shares with the SJ. Just as there are four different Types of SJs, there happen to be four species of honeybees. Consider some similarities in SJs and bees in general.

Both are caretakers of their own societies. The little bee, like the SJ, gives far more he takes. The bee's cross fertilization efforts enable the plant kingdom to reproduce, thereby supplying food, oxygen, and other essentials to a dependent but grateful world. It is estimated that nearly thirty five percent of the world's food supplies is dependent on the bee. Some plants depend wholly upon the bee's cooperation for their existence. Bees also bless mankind with that sweet delicacy, honey.

SJs, by comparison, are the backbone of society. Hard working, dependable and persistent, the SJ serves as the caretaker of others, maintaining a low profile. In general, SJs find it difficult to receive. They prefer working for the benefit of others, feeling obligated to serve and feeling uncomfortable when they are being served.

The young bee learns responsibilities in the hive within

hours of hatching and carries out specific chores. It begins by clearing the cell from which it hatched. It then becomes involved in cleaning other cells and incubating unhatched eggs. The bee is a marvel from its first few hours on earth.

Similarly, SJ children learn obedience quickly. They follow routines well and assume responsibilities from the time they are adolescents or younger. SJ children want to please others, and work diligently to seek approval from their elders. SJ children want to know what they are supposed to do and go to work on their tasks quite willingly.

Because of its short lifespan, the bee cannot afford to waste time. It lives each day as if it were its last. The bee works continually, requiring little time for rest. There is never a time when the bee is without something to do. The phrase, "busy as a bee" is an understatement.

early in life with the proper guidance. SJs assume new responsibilities for managing and maintaining organizations as they grow into each new phase in life.

Bees maintain an unending vigilance, guarding their hives unceasingly. It is virtually impossible for an intruder to enter and disrupt a hive. Entry guards insure round the clock protection. They maintain a sophisticated system for guarding their hive, having an excess of a thousand scent organs on their antennae. An unfriendly visitor is removed immediately. Poised and prepared, the bee watches and waits for imminent danger.

SJs are the guardians of time honored institutions. They value, support, and perpetuate the home, social club, church, company, and country. They like to be prepared and may be considered the most protective of all the temperaments. Their somewhat pessimistic bent prods them to prepare for the worst, or to expect impending doom and plan for its arrival.

Hard Workers

The little bee lives to work, whereas other creatures must work to live. Worker bees live as long as five or six months in winter. Their increased lifespan during winter is due to the decrease in their workload with no young bees to raise or food to collect. When summer comes, their lifespan drops to a period of four to six weeks. Bees will work themselves to the point of exhaustion and beyond. Their search for nectar is relentless. They "buy up every opportunity," even making pollen while in flight. There is no time wasted as the bee uses all six of its legs to work in unison to make pollen. By the time it returns to the hive, it will have made two large lumps of pollen that appear too heavy for it to carry.

SJs may also work as if there were no tomorrow. The SJ's insistence upon getting things done is puzzling to members of the other three temperaments. Not tending to be "open ended," SJs look forward to completing tasks and finishing projects while others around them are thinking of how to spend their free time. When Introverting, however, the SJ is usually more flexible.

The bee moves from one kind of responsibility to another as it matures. Within the hive, young bees help feed bee larvae for up to two weeks, then take on other jobs such as storing nectar to benefit other bees.

For the SJ, household chores, obedience at home and at school, and "stick-to-it-iveness" can be developed

SJs, in the course of establishing, maintaining, conserving, and perpetuating their society, hardly know when to stop working. SJs are likely candidates for becoming workaholics. Those who do not take needed breaks and vacations may shorten their lifespans or impair their own physical health.

In their social organization and constructive abilities, bees demonstrate superior intelligence. The forager bee uses sophisticated movements and techniques when returning to the hive from a visit to potential sources of nectar. At the hive, the bee uses circular movements, figure eights, tailwagging, and body tilting, referring to the position of the sun to communicate to the other bees where it has found a source of nectar. Its knowledge of direction and its accuracy in finding food sources put the bee at the top of the list of insect creatures for intelligent use of its abilities.

SJs possess an inner sense of direction, especially in comparison to others who might have their "heads in the clouds." They see what needs to be done (S) and find ways to get it done in the most efficient, direct manner (J). Thus, SJs are the ones who make a "bee line" directly to the task or responsibility and follow through to see the job completed. This kind of reliability along with their desire for accuracy makes them extremely useful and valuable to their social units.

SJs do not possess the same kind of "intelligence" their NT or NF friends might have. Yet SJs can be highly intelligent. They may not master the complex, abstract, theoretical world inhabited by NTs and NFs, but they have their own unique kind of intelligence. Their design mandates that they deal with the real world, here and now. They do not allow themselves the freedom or opportunity to consider countless possibilities with no specific deadlines. Therefore, they possess an unmatched degree of intelligence for dealing with immediate issues.

The bee and the SJ are the foundation stones of their societies. Their continual hard work and dependability are easy to take for granted. In human society, the squeaky wheel gets the oil, but the SJ "wheel" never has time to rust. The wheel may break down, however, and when it does, it usually does so without warning.

Showing Appreciation to the SJ

Being appreciated and receiving thanks at the proper time are important to SJs. Careful attention to their feelings will prevent discouragement. SJs will perform magnificently as long as they are appreciated for their diligence. While SJs do not need confirmation as often as some Types, they still appreciate a kind word so long as it relates to their production. They tend to be very "volume" oriented. By verbally recognizing their outstanding efforts, you will be able to retain your SJs for a long, long time. While they may feel awkward in accepting you praise (remember they are givers, not takers), they will bubble with joy internally when recognized for their efforts.

25
The SP "Hummingbird"

ISTP
ESTP
ISFP
ESFP

SPs (Sensing, Perceptive) love *action*, preferring to spend their time absorbed in activity. If action or excitement are unavailable, they store their energy in anticipation of some future activity, hoping it may not be too far off. Their central focus is upon doing, performing, and enjoying.

Freedom is of vital importance to SPs. Duty, obligation, restriction, or any kind of confinement can be positively detestable. Their love of freedom is demonstrated in their impulsiveness and search for excitement. Once SPs sense that rules, practice, or discipline will interfere with their activity or interest, they will grow restless and want to move on.

SPs live for today. They are oriented to the moment. Tomorrow may never come, so today's desires must be fulfilled. Goals are rarely considered. Thus, while they have "today," SPs will often be optimistic and lighthearted. SPs add excitement to the world and may be noted for their daredevil antics. Since they tend to become bored with the status quo, SPs will search out the new, the adventurous, and the stimulating.

Explorers, dare devils, performers, hunters, gamblers, and athletes are often SPs. This is not to say all SPs are so adventure oriented. One might say that they prefer vocations involving action, movement, and a thrill. Sitting behind a desk all day doing routine work would not appeal to SPs. They may be capable of filling such a position, but their interest and output would be minimal. SPs perform extremely well when a crisis occurs on the job. They are masters of expediency.

Of all the temperaments, SPs are pre eminently fond of tools. Tools allow SPs to express themselves. They have found many such tools that express their personalities in building, performing, creating, racing, or playing. SP athletes have their sports equipment; SP construction workers use hammers and bulldozers; SP doctors and dentists are skillful in their use of scalpels and drills; SP artists employ chisels and paintbrushes; SP racers maneuver airplanes, cars, and boats; and SP performers display their skills with musical instruments, props, or costumes.

SPs, when they are in possession of material goods, will often share their earthly treasures unselfishly. They want their friends and associates to share with them as they take pleasure in the fruits of their good fortune. This attitude, when coupled with the SPs flair for living, points to the characteristic tendency of the SP to live for the here and now.

The SP and the Hummingbird

The smallest bird in the world, the tiny hummingbird, weighs less than two pennies but displays such boundless energy and endurance that it is capable of migrating thousands of miles. Many wonderful parallels can be found when the SP and the hummingbird are closely studied.

Ounce for ounce, the little hummingbird has the greatest energy output of all God's creatures. Its tiny frame loses heat faster than larger birds so that it must burn energy just to keep itself warm!

Similarly, SPs can "wear you out" with their energy. They possess incredible endurance, providing the activities they engage in are not boring.

Hummingbirds are the quickest of all birds to seek new feeding spots. They dart away swiftly from predators or any attempt to restrict their movement. So, too, SPs are quick to move if they see a threat coming to hamper or inhibit their free and easy lifestyle. Once they feel their circumstances becoming too restrictive, as if the walls were closing in, SPs will take off to find more open country.

Hummingbirds enjoy variation, moving among the countless flowers and selecting various insects. Their insatiable appetites are only briefly appeased before they engage again in their search for variety.

SPs will become disenchanted without variety. They thrive on variety, their spice of life, moving from opportunity to opportunity, from possibility to possibility.

The hummingbird is the performer par excellence. It can fly forward, backward, vertically—like a helicopter—and even upside down! It can also stay suspended in midair. Almost any maneuver possible is accomplished with grace and precision, effortlessly.

In comparison, the SPs tend to be among the world's greatest athletes and performing artists. Picture **Michael Jordan, Carl Lewis, Emmitt Smith, and Muhammad Ali** in their primes, and how they resembled the hummingbird, defying normal human limits. The great SP dancers, sculptors, painters, contemporary instrumentalists, and vocalists, entertainers, and adventurers use their performing skills with flawless precision. Their work is really play, and practice may be shunned for taking pleasure in the act of performing. To practice in a routine way is boring. The SP performer is far more interested in the new, the lively, and the exciting.

The hummingbird knows how to conserve up to half the energy expended by other flying creatures. Its wing structure and the angle of use of its wings in flight provide both propulsion and lift more efficiently than for any other bird. When it becomes necessary to "turn on the juice," the little "hummer" has reserves of energy stored in advance, ready to meet any challenge.

The hummingbird uses its long, needle like bill as a tool of great importance. It can thread a nest with great artistry, pick insects from flower petals or from the air in mid flight, and gather nectar. Using its bill as a weapon, the hummingbird repels intruders from its territory.

shrewdness, artistry, and dexterity. Recognizing these qualities will greatly encourage the SP.

The final product or result is not as important to SPs as the activity itself. They perform in wonderful ways while they have an audience or group showing its appreciation. They can learn to direct their activity to more profitable results if given direction. As risk takers, SPs will occasionally encounter defeat. Encouragement from others who have experienced similar defeats will be greatly appreciated by SPs needing to bounce back before tackling another challenge.

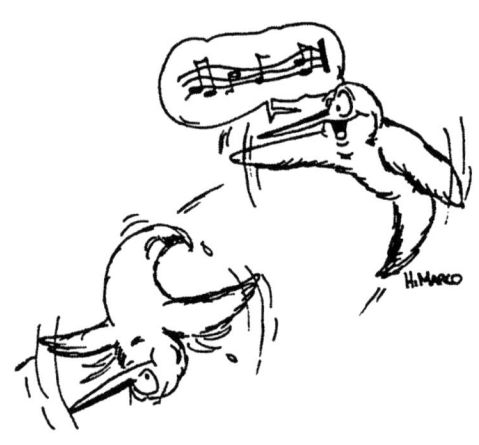

THE HUMMINGBIRD IS THE PERFORMER PAR EXCELLENCE!

SPs are capable of using various kinds of tools just as the hummingbird uses its "tool." They are masters of tools.

Hummingbirds tend to stay close to the ground in their everyday pursuits. Whether the little creature flitters from flower to flower or traverses the ocean to a new nesting place, it prefers to stay low to the earth. Hummingbirds fly just above the ocean swells.

SPs are not "high flyers" either. They do not frequent the upper atmospheres of the NTs and NFs. They prefer the immediate, real and practical matters of life rather than the future or abstract concepts. They are impulsive, active, free and graceful, enjoying today since tomorrow may never come. They remain close to reality and seem always to enjoy it.

The hummingbird is a phenomenal traveler. As often as twice a year, the little bird may travel from Canada to Central America. It can fly over wide bodies of water, sometimes as far as five hundred miles, non stop. In order to do so, the hummingbird must maximize its fuel and conserve its energy.

SPs are on the go. Many times SPs are seen as wanderers, traveling great distances in search of activities they find stimulating and interesting.

Showing Appreciation to the SP

Like all temperaments, SPs need to be shown appreciation in order to be motivated and to function to their fullest potential. They are not product oriented like the SJ, but *process* oriented. They especially appreciate recognition for the way or manner in which they do things. SPs are versatile performers, displaying excellent timing, adaptation, daring, bravery, finesse,

26
The NF "Stork"

INFJ
ENFJ
INFP
ENFP

NFs (iNtuitive, Feeling) prefer to live in a world of possibilities rather than facts. Their lives are always a search—a quest for purpose, meaning, and for finding themselves. Whether or not they display it outwardly, NFs tend to have high regard for the feelings and rights of others and feel a strong kinship with their fellow man. They value relationships and invest considerably in them as long as they feel there is some appreciation or response. They also require recognition, wanting the acknowledgment of another for a task or duty well performed. Without this, they will lose interest and find another worthwhile cause from which approval for their efforts can be obtained.

NFs tend to believe the best about others before entertaining suspicions of their motives. This comes both from being optimistic (N) and feeling (F) toward others. They will actively and directly work toward aiding in the improvement of others (serving as educators, counselors, ministers, and health related professionals), or somewhat indirectly, through various forms of communication. Having a flair for language, NF communicators excel in both the written and spoken word. Generally, ENFJs and ENFPs communicate orally, and INFJs and INFPs prefer the written word, although they often cross these boundaries. The expression of their ideas is found in television and drama, poetry, journalism, biography, fiction, and psychology. As creative writers, they usually forge innovative ideas and schemes, being the premier "wordsmiths" of culture, a trait that sets them apart from the other three temperaments.

NFs value harmony in relationships. They prefer tactfulness to truthfulness and will use their skills to preserve relationships rather than sever them. Inspiring and imaginative, NFs also enjoy creating, expressing their creations artistically and sensitively.

Type watchers will discover that NFs dominate the fields of creative writing, counseling, journalism, and health related professions. There are many NF theologians. Conversely, it is unusual to see NFs as accountants (though mine is), but you will find Extraverted NFs in sales or business related vocations.

The NF and the Stork

A majestic flying creature which best illustrates the iNtuitive Feeling Type is the incomparable stork. This bird, renown for ages, is even more appealing and fascinating than the common folktales make it to be: delivering babies, bringing good fortune, preserving marriages and families, and even guarding homes from lightning and evil spirits, to name just a few. Do these characteristics accurately describe the real stork of our times?

From folklore, the stork seems to possess a distinct popularity. Its reputation is backed by reliable, documented evidence from at least three thousand years of recorded history. Indeed, some of the volume of material about the stork antedates the birth of Christ by nearly a thousand years.

A number of civilizations took special notice of storks and sought to protect them from harmful influences. Laws were passed making it a crime to harm or kill the beloved bird. Many of its admirers were in awe of the supposed powers of this stately bird. Even Aristotle, as early as 300 B.C., wrote that the stork was revered in his day for its unique characteristics.

The Romans, too, became enamored with the stork's attributes. The Lex Ciconaria or "Stork's Law," was established, mandating that children provide for their parents when the latter became elderly and in need. The Romans, observing how the stork had cared for members of its family, both young and old, legislated their approval for the compassion, sensitivity, and lovingkindness demonstrated by the bird for its own.

The stork occupies a special place in the Bible, as well. In the sacred text of the Hebrews, the stork is described as the "pious one." The Hebrew word, *hasidhah*, is the word for stork. The root word is the noun *hesed* which means "lovingkindness, loyal love." *Hesed* is used some two hundred and fifty times in the Old Testament, particularly in the Psalms, to illustrate the many ways God demonstrates His infinite love for mankind and to depict man's kindness to his fellow man. The comparison of the stork's love for its family with God's love for mankind speaks supremely well for the stork. During biblical times, the stork was considered the most loving of all birds, a fact the Bible plainly recognizes.

Our word "stork" actually is taken from the ancient Greek *storge*, which literally means, "an innate, natural affection." This could be best understood by contemplating a mother's unconditional love for her child. The definition, however, is broader in meaning. It connotes an affection capable of being directed to anyone. C.S. Lewis in *The Four Loves*, states, "It is indeed the least discriminating of loves."[1] It isn't predicated upon looks, intelligence, blood relationship, or age. The illiterate, grotesque, and the homely can all be recipients of storge (affection) love. It is the humblest love.

Thus, whether we base our meaning of the word "stork" from the Hebrew or Greek, or accept the legendary accounts concerning its character, we find that the stork is truly a caring, loving creature.

The family of storks is made up of seventeen known species throughout the world. Their shapes, sizes and appearances vary from one region to another. To the surprise of many, America has its own stork. Ornithologists had been fooled until recent years about the true identity of the wood ibis, known now to actually be the wood stork. Nesting in Florida, the wood stork is the only such species in North America.

Let's compare the stork and the NF. NFs tend to center their focus on people rather than things. They see potential good in everyone. They are often willing to devote their entire lives to developing the potential they see in others. Missionaries, persons in the ministry, and other people related vocations are often made up of NFs.

The stork's focus is upon its family, devotedly caring for the needs of its own. Rather than flying off to meet personal needs, the stork dutifully serves. It will travel up to forty miles to locate food for the family. Despite the young stork's ability to fly at fifty days old, it will continue to return to the nest until it is around seventy five days old. Parent storks continue providing for their young even after the latter should be out of the nest. Similarly, NFs will devote themselves to others as long as there is a concerned response.

NFs and storks are able to manifest extra amounts of affection and concern. The stork will go to great lengths to show compassion. Parents will stand over their young and shelter them from the blowing wind and harsh sun. It is also believed the stork may be the only bird that will bathe its young during hot weather. The parents will act as a shower, spraying the young with water swallowed from cool ponds nearby. Parent storks have even been known to give up their lives in efforts to extricate their young from forests fires.

Storks have been observed caring for the elderly and weak of their species. When a stork can no longer fly with vigor or provide for itself, the younger storks will lend their assistance. This type of concern begins early in the stork's life since its species is *altricial*, that is, in need of care for some length of time because it is hatched in an immature and helpless condition. This might be contrasted with other species, such as the duck, who is *precocial*, capable of a high degree of independent activity from birth. Thus, from the time they are young to the time they die, storks are intensely devoted to the needs of their family and species.

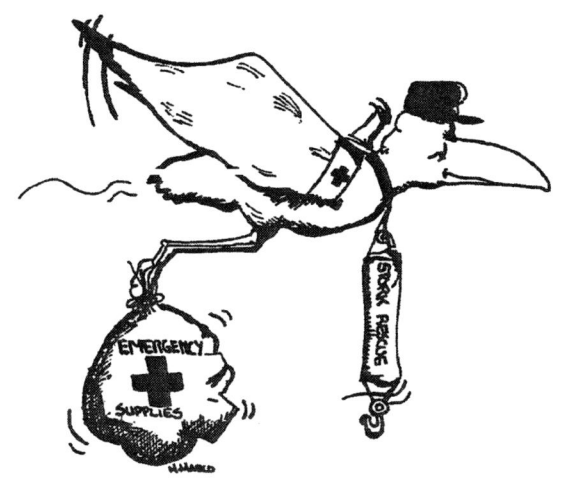

Unfortunately, it cannot be said that all NFs nor all storks are gentle, loving creatures. Their God given design, however, is such that if properly cultivated, their lives can manifest these qualities. There can be maladjusted NFs and storks who display seemingly contrary behavior patterns.

Immature, unmated storks have been known to fly through their own colonies, attacking unprotected nests. These marauders will kill younger storks and destroy eggs, displaying a kind of savagery that seems uncharacteristic for their species. This form of aberrant behavior has been documented. Similarly, maladjusted NFs are capable of wreaking havoc within their own society.

No matter what a person's temperament group or Brain Type might be, there remains the possibility that the individual will choose only to develop his or her strongest preferences and to ignore the development of a weaker yet important function. Such callous disregard usually leads to the formation of unbalanced persons who find they cannot cope with the world where there are so many unlike them. The remedy is to recognize our differences and seek to become more balanced in our own temperaments while displaying greater tolerance to those different from us.

The stork is the premier performer in the swamps. It can be a real "show stealer" as it struts majestically through the murky waters, looking for food. With its massive wingspan, in excess of five feet, the stork soars through the sky effortlessly and descends gracefully to make a landing, much like a "747" touching down on the runway. Standing erect in the tall cypress, dressed in its black and white robe, the stork appears judicial as it views the blue and green courtroom below. All the other creatures in the swamp seem to look up and take notice of the stork's appearance and performances.

Whether on solid ground or up in the clouds, the stork knows how to capture an audience. When descending to the earth, the stork is capable of displaying a wide array of maneuvers. It will dive at full speed, flip flopping from side to side, wings cupped. Or it will simply ride along with the thermal currents, moving like a glider in the heavens. Storks have been seen traveling up to a distance of fifteen miles without flapping a wing.

Like the stork, NFs can be performers and actors. They are capable of expressing themselves on paper or in front of others, whether on stage or at a podium, through their verbal and written communication skills. Tending to have a flair for language, NFs use their abilities to draw the attention of others, much like the stork in the swamp.

It may be said that both storks and NFs know how to use their heads. The stork is shrewd in its ability to procure food from the dark waters of its habitat. Its elongated bill is used with the coordinated efforts of its legs and feet. The stork can hunt for fish in muddy waters even after dark. It uses its feet to flush out the fish that feed in the shallow water. When a fish is detected, the stork swiftly flaps its wing into the water on the side where the fish is located. The noise and splash frighten the fish into the open and waiting mouth of the clever bird. Scientists have timed the wing reaction delay to be only one-fortieth of a second and the closing of the stork's bill at twenty-five milliseconds. This incredible reaction time is one of the fastest known among vertebrates.

The NF, like the stork, is also capable of intelligent behavior. Indeed, NFs tend to score high on tests and are found among National Merit Finalists, Valedictorians, and Rhodes Scholars. They enjoy the challenges of trying to comprehend complex global issues. In this they are akin to the NTs who are attracted to the abstract, theoretical world and help make it understandable to others. As the stork gathers a tangible substance (fish) from the dark murky waters of the swamp, so the NF searches the possibilities available within a world often dark, abstract and undefined.

The stork may appear clumsy, with its long, stilt like legs, large bulky bill, and unusual body. But appearances can be deceptive! Its gangly legs are actually powerful springs that catapult it into the sky where it masters the thermal currents. The stork can soar to incredible heights as it rides the warm air winds. High above the world, the stork gets a global perspective unlike many other creatures. European storks travel thousands of miles yearly, migrating to the south of Africa and returning via the upper atmosphere thermals. While they may not be as agile and coordinated on the ground as some of their feathered friends, the storks are masters of the warm air currents when they fly high.

NFs can be deceptive in appearance at times, too. Because they would rather be "flying high in the clouds," they may appear awkward or clumsy with more practical matters. Their preference is to obtain a global perspective on life. Thus, they resemble in their personalities the gangly stork who, although showing concern about practical matters, prefers to soar through the skies, drinking in the rich beauty of the landscape below.

Showing Appreciation to the NF

NFs are unique, just as members of the other three temperament groups are unique. NFs, too, must be treated carefully in order to help them reach their potential.

Appreciation can be best shown to NFs by acknowledging their individual uniqueness and contributions. NFs desire their creativity and feelings to be recognized by others. When someone fails to do this, it is often interpreted as a sign of rejection. Thus, NFs tend not to handle criticism and rejection as well as members of other temperaments. When recognition and appreciation are not demonstrated, NFs become disheartened. Their output and productivity will drop. It is essential for the NF's own well being and work output that we show our gratitude.

"An NF's preference is to obtain a global perspective on life."

27
The NT "Owl"

INTJ
ENTJ
INTP
ENTP

NTs (iNtuitive, Thinking) focus upon the possibilities the future may hold, but judge these with impersonal logic rather than feeling. Usually technically oriented, NTs are the scientists of society, probing, investigating, acquiring knowledge, and contemplating their findings. Lovers of intelligence and wisdom, NTs score high on IQ tests and may do well in school if they possess a fair degree of self discipline. Blessed with a certain giftedness for school, NTs often depend on their abilities to get by without study and preparation, relying upon their innate intelligence to pull them through.

NTs are tempted to carry logic to the extreme, assuming that others around them understand the logic involved in every situation. This may lead to high expectations of others or greater criticism of another's lack of understanding. NTs demand much of themselves and others, particularly in areas where NTs are strong. Thus, NTs tend not to express approval or seek approval whenever a task that seems ordinary is accomplished. They are comfortable with the phrase "Virtue is its own reward" and may take the work ethic to extremes. NTs become absorbed in their work, finding that work without play is not so dull after all. Indeed, some become so absorbed in their work or various projects that they may work late into the night with increasing energy and little sign of fatigue. These "night owls" are not necessarily the ones who haunt late night entertainment spots as they are the ones who burn the midnight oil.

NTs are adept at manipulating their environment, seeking solutions to a variety of problems. Methodical, ingenious and naturally inquisitive, NTs seek to develop and use skills of uncovering, deciphering, investigating, and probing. Curious, precocious, complex, inventive, self critical, remote, and impersonal are words that typically describe the NT. They are most commonly found in areas requiring the skillful adaptation of knowledge to problems. Thus, engineers, lawyers, computer experts, designers, analysts, architects, criminologists, physicians, technicians, and scientists of all sorts tend to be cast from the NT mold.

The NT and the Owl

Of all the flying creatures in the animal kingdom, the wise ol' owl best represents the iNtuitive Thinker. NTs are widely known for their accumulation of knowledge and wisdom. They are the most inquisitive of temperaments. What better creature, therefore, might there be to represent the unique NT Types than the bird who continually seems to ask, "Who?"? The majestic, poised bird seems to sit in reflective silence, pondering the mysteries of the deep woods late into the night. Similarly, the NT often sits in quiet repose, contemplating deep issues that begin with the questions who, what, where, when, why?

The owl has been popular for thousands of years, probably due to its unusual, almost human appearance. With its large head and deep-set eyes that stare forward, feathered tufts protruding like ears, and a beak that resembles a nose, the owl seems to possess a unique and ominous aura, setting it apart from other birds. But not all owls look alike. Over one hundred different species of owls are found the world over. Eighteen of these species live in North America. Their sizes vary greatly. The largest have wingspans measuring over five feet in length, while the smallest is tinier than a robin.

The owl can see things in the night like no other animal. An abundance of rod cells in the retina of its eye allows the creature to see clearly in the dark. As day draws near, the owl is able to contract its iris, adjusting to the available light. The size of its eyes are comparable to a human's, allowing it to take in a great deal of light, yet the bird weighs only one-fiftieth the weight of a human being.

The owl's uncanny vision is enhanced by a third eyelid that moistens and cleans each eye much like an automobile's automatic windshield wiper and pump. This feature allows the owl to use its eyesight with advantage over other night creatures upon which it preys, or those from which it must protect itself.

Similarly, the NT is able to see things with incredible perception. While not necessarily attracted to minute details, NTs enjoy the opportunity to make something clear and understandable from "foggy" or clouded issues. Like owls, the vision of NTs is sharp in all situations, enabling them to adjust their focus according to the need of the moment.

Owls will use the night hours to advantage, using the cover of darkness to pursue sources of nourishment. When other fowl are at rest, the owl is hard at work, not only feeding itself but its owlets as well. Here the owl's legendary night vision is continually exercised as it tirelessly searches for its family's food.

In like manner, NTs are known for gathering their "food" (knowledge) until late at night and into the wee hours of the morning. They are the typical "night owls" who become energized by intellectual challenges. In their quest for knowledge, NTs share much of what they find with their offspring, who often grow up to be unusually knowledgeable in many areas, particularly if these children are themselves NTs.

Young owls anxiously anticipate leaving the nest. It seems as though they cannot wait to develop their wings and practice hunting. They usually escape the nest before they can fly, unlike most other birds. They, like NTs, want to conquer their world as soon as possible.

Young NTs develop a passion for knowledge very early in life. It is typical to find that NT children are precocious. They are anxious to get out of the family "nest" and into the world where they can explore to their hearts' (and minds') content. Once a person becomes familiar with the differences found in the four temperament groups, it becomes rather easy to identify NT children whose exceptionally inquisitive minds set them apart from other children.

The owl's expressionless stare gives it an impassive, almost distant or aloof appearance. By it, one might think the owl is cold and remote. NTs, likewise, often give others the impression of being disinterested in the emotions of others. To many, the NT personality is an enigma. "What's going on in that complex mind?" wonders an observer. The answer to the question lies, and may remain, in the hidden recesses of the NT's often impenetrable mind. Stop and think for a moment. Do you know anyone who fits the NT description?

An owl's sense of hearing rivals its own legendary visual ability. Ironically, the feathered tufts that appear to the casual observer to be ears are not ears at all. The ears are below its eye level. They are not prominent, nor are they visible. Each ear possesses two flaps of skin which can be moved directionally to pick up sounds. This feature allows the owl to hear with pinpoint accuracy. When it is on the prowl and judges that the sound of its prey is the same in both ears, the owl calculates that its prey is in direct line to be attacked. The circle of stiff feathers around the owl's face, called a "facial disk," helps its hearing, too, funneling sound into its ears. The relative silence of the owl's own flight allows it to hear even the faintest of sounds.

Like the owl, the NT listens carefully and makes an effort to discern incoming data with great accuracy. The sense of hearing in NTs seems uniquely adjusted to picking up what they hear and storing the information with understanding. Being master logicians, NTs are capable of "splitting hairs" when required, and usually find no equal in intellectual debate. Considering the fact that so many NTs are engineers, scientists, mathematicians, philosophers and members of other occupations requiring high levels of abstract, intellectual aptitude, NTs seem to possess that same audio sensitivity and ability to interpret what is perceived that is found in the owl.

The owl possesses two sets of spear like claws on each foot. The movement of these claws resembles that of ice hooks, and their grip might be compared to the strength of a vise. So strong and powerful are the owl's claws that when it grasps its prey, the claws actually penetrate the flesh of the owl's victim. In a similar manner, NTs are endowed with a tenacious grip. Having a fondness for knowledge and the gathering of useful information, NTs do not easily forget the things they have heard and seen. Their grasp and retention of knowledge gained through listening and careful reasoning equip them for a variety of ideological tasks.

As a final observation, we see that two of the more prominent features of the owl are its eyes and the large size of its head. Without intending any reference to the physical appearance of NTs, the comparison might be drawn to the NTs' scope of vision and their characteristic "braininess."

Showing Appreciation to the NT

Appreciation may be shown to NT "owls" by recognizing their ideas and capabilities. It is necessary to listen to them. No matter what your own Type may be, listening attentively will help you grasp the essence of an NT's thoughts. It is often best to take these ideas and ponder them further. Showing NTs that you are willing to do this will be meaningful to them.

NTs are rarely moved by comments on their personal qualities, nor do they place much value on accomplishing routine tasks. They, like SJs, find it difficult to receive expressions of appreciation. Of course, they truly want them and, like all of us, genuinely need them; but in order to mean something special to them, appreciation must be given in an appropriate manner. It is best to remember that to the NT, conquering the complex is its own reward. Nevertheless, take care to recognize them when you see them succeed in a challenging venture.

PART SEVEN

HELPING THE MIND

Improving Performance

Bo Jackson was once said to know football, baseball, basketball, track, guitar—just about everything—at least according to Nike. The Auburn University star turned professional sports upside down in both football and baseball. Unfortunately, a hip injury curtailed careers. When quizzed in 1989 about the rigors of sports, Bo responded:

> I don't get tired. There is nothing physical about sports, it's all mental. If you can handle it upstairs, the rest is easy. There is nothing physical about what we do. You put it in your mind and go out and do it.[1]

I have mixed feelings about what Bo said. It is easy for Bo to say there is nothing physical about sports; it would be easy for the rest of us to say it if we also possessed a body builder's physique and the speed of a world class sprinter.

"If you can handle it upstairs, the rest is easy." Agreed—if an athlete has developed the necessary physical skills. Most athletes are capable of performing well at their current levels of competition.

Unfortunately, many physically capable are less prepared mentally. For those, competent help is needed.

Bo Jackson had a distinct advantage over most of us in sports. Thanks to his **E**mpirical, **R**ight-brained (SP) Brain Type, his marvelous body worked superbly both physically and mentally. (Baseball did not come as easily mentally for Jackson, however, as did football.) This does not mean that if we are not a top notch Type for athletics, we need throw up our hands in surrender. We are all capable of accessing and developing specific areas of our brains that in effect, create a simulated mental lobotomy. We may never experience the same degree of mental efficiency that some Brain Types do, but we can emulate their performances to a greater degree than we ever thought possible.

There are six topics we want to consider in this section on helping the mind: The Performing Mind, Zoning, Relaxation, Visualization, Philosophical or Spiritual Foundation, and Goal Setting. By getting a good handle on these, an athlete will improve his or her game appreciably.

28
The Performing Mind, Zoning, Relaxation, and Visualization

The Performing Mind

Perceiving, Not Judging

Athletes perform best in a Perceiving rather than a Judging mode. Neuroscientifically speaking, this is when they rely most on the right hemisphere. How can you help yourself be a Perceiver when you are playing your sport?

If you make a mistake, you should be aware of it (Perceive it) but not condemn or Judge it. Judgments such as "What an idiot I am" or "I can't throw a ball straight" debilitate and impair performance.

By Judging yourself in words, orally or tacitly, you utilize the Thinking or Feeling functions, which are generally in the left hemisphere. Regardless of which hemisphere is most used, heavily engaging the Judging function (T or F) ruins a top performance.

When you engage a Perceiving function (S or N) after a mistake, you will spatially see yourself repeating the error and noticing what must be done next time to avoid it. Verbal reprimands are not in order, only spatial replays.

Reasoning too Much

Excessive Thinking or Feeling when playing will hinder performance. Performing must essentially be done on automatic pilot, spontaneously, with a focus on visual Perception versus verbal Judgment. Negative thoughts, whether of the past or future, debilitate the present.

Contributors to Poor Performance

Some factors that hinder top performance are:

1. Placing too much emphasis on the results rather than on the process of performing. Overly utilizing the brain's Judging functions (T,F) causes body movements to become mechanical and rigid.

2. Analyzing past mistakes and fearing they will be repeated.

3. Getting too pumped for the game or competitive event.

4. Trying too hard, regarding out of control aggression more important than under control aggression and smooth tempo.

Learning/Teaching

All good coaching techniques can and should be used with any athlete, regardless of brain dominance or preference. The question is how much of each technique should be used on each Brain Type?

All athletes need to be instructed verbally and visually. Yet Judging, left-brained persons prefer the verbal, analytic aspects of the sport. Their best understanding comes from this approach. Conversely, Perceptive, right-brained persons prefer the visual, synthetic aspects of a sport. Ps learn fastest by watching others perform the skill they are to learn, or by visualizing the skill.

Nevertheless, both Js and Ps must be exposed to the teaching styles they don't prefer. Js should watch videos of athletes who have excelled in their sport and go to their games. Ps should have verbal instruction to complement their spatial dexterity.

Whatever your Type, watch stars in your chosen sport. Baseball's **Matt Nokes** hit 32 home runs as a Detroit Tiger rookie in 1987. He credited his success to teammate Darrell Evans:

> In '87, when I hit all those home runs, he hit in front of me. It's hard to explain, but it was like we were on the same wavelength. He would hit a home run and I could see how he did it, then more often than not I'd hit one.[1]

Activating the Right Hemisphere

Noncompetitive, rhythmic exercises are excellent ways to activate the right brain while suspending the left. Walking, running, swimming and dancing help the left hemisphere to become bored, thereby stimulating the right hemisphere.

Listening to music, especially when you do not concentrate on the words, is right brain effective. Athletes who listen to music before they compete have the right idea. Singing or humming are also effective.

The next time you go for a walk, notice the scenery. Stimulate your right brain by testing your peripheral awareness; try to see things out of the corners of your eyes.

Disengaging the Right Hemisphere

Disengaging the right brain is not something one would want to encourage in left-brained athletes. Obviously, it is much more difficult for dominant left-brained persons (Js) to rely upon the right hemisphere in times of mental pressure. If by chance they do achieve this difficult task, they shouldn't do anything to disrupt it.

Unfortunately, a verbal admonition or command will often cause the left brain to seize control again, especially in those who already have left-hemisphere dominance. Therefore, coaching from the sidelines should be short, simple, present-tense words that are encouraging and positive.

The secret to peak performance is learning how to efficiently use both sides of the brain, not just the right. Right-brained persons must work at efficiently utilizing their left brain.

Energy Cycles

Brain Types and hemispheric preferences are not the only mental matters to consider in sports. The brain operates in roughly 90-minute cycles which are called Circadian rhythms. Each hemisphere tends to be more active in one cycle than the next. Your verbal left hemisphere has its greatest energy flow in one cycle and your spatial right half dominates the next cycle. In addition to this rhythm, sleep habits, nutrition, attitude, and so on all play their parts in an athlete's performance and are reasons for his or her inconsistencies.

Zoning

The subconscious state of the zone is something that athletes often experience when they perform at their absolute best. In game 1 of the 1990 NBA Finals, ESFP **Isiah Thomas** sparked the Detroit Pistons with a come from behind victory. Thomas scored 14 points in a five minute span in the last quarter, demolishing the Portland Trailblazers. Thomas spoke of his exceptional performance:

> It just happens. It's like your total game comes together in those four or five minutes. I got an energy burst somewhere. A lot of energy. The crowd was into it. I was just trying to get over the hump. Right then, at that moment, you're not even thinking. Just feeling. Feeling good. It just happens. Boom, it's there. You just kind of smile.[2]

Because Thomas is a Sensing Feeler (SF), he is more in tune with his body feelings than the other Brain Type groups (ST, NT, and NF). Yet all Types, regardless of brain preferences, experience to some degree this same "feeling" when they enter their zone. When the spatial right hemisphere gains control over the verbal conscious left, the zone becomes accessible.

The most poignant words Thomas said were:

> It's almost like you're two steps ahead of every player. It's almost like slow motion. You get to see everything.[3]

Thomas touched on critical areas of the zone. Being "two steps ahead" indicates the spontaneous, synthetic, right brain is engaged. The mechanical, more slowly processing, analytic left hemisphere can not achieve this experience.

Consider Thomas's comments: "It's almost like slow motion. You get to see everything." We have spoken throughout this book of the spatial, visual aspects of the right hemisphere. As Thomas fixed on the Sensing function of the right brain, while highly engaging his visual cortex, he saw "everything." He was only aware of his spatial world, virtually unconscious of verbal thoughts.

Magic Johnson was as visually aware of the happenings on the basketball floor as any hoopster in history. Is it a coincidence that he, too, is a right-brained ESFP? Magic placed exceptional value on the properly timed and made pass. He fully utilized his right brain spatial abilities.

(As an aside, my guess for the ESFP's superiority in this particular aspect of athletic spatial matters is as follows: Perceivers are more spatially gifted than Judgers. Sensates are stronger at seeing what is, iNtuitives at what can be. Extraverted, right-brained Sensates have Sensing as their most active brain process, whereas Introverted right brain Sensates have the Judging functions T or F as their most active. Introverted Perceiving (IP) Thinking and Feeling will want to reason more than view when affected by pressure. Lastly, ESTPs (The other ESP Type) would tend to Think more about the game than just gut level respond to the moment as the ESFP would.)

One final aspect of Thomas's experience of "slow motion" implies the absence of the *time-oriented left brain*. The *right hemisphere is more event-oriented* and loses track of time without assistance from the left. When athletes are highly engaged in the anterior right brain, they focus on the event, not the clock.

Zoning as It Relates to Skill Level

The ability to enter the zone correlates to an athlete's skill level. The more skill-proficient one is, the more likely the zone can be accessed. Therefore, beginners in a sport have little or no chance to zone. They would be in complete disarray because they have not yet honed their physical and mental skills.

Efficient Brain Yields Top Performance

Dr. Monte Buchsbaum, former professor of psychiatry and director of the Brain Imaging Center at the University of California, utilizes brain-imaging technology to measure brain metabolism. Though he doesn't correlate his findings with athletic significance, Buchsbaum has researched components of the zone, such as heightened concentration, overall decrease in brain activity, and increase in visual awareness.

Reporting in the *New York Times Magazine*, Lawrence Shainberg wrote of Buchsbaum's 1988 published research on abstract reasoning:

> Working with subjects involved in problem

solving, he's found that during periods of intense concentration, there is a marked *decrease* in the overall metabolic rate of the brain. The research indicates that the more skill one brings to a task, the more efficient the brain becomes.[4]

Dr. Buchsbaum said:

> We have found that higher levels of [brain] metabolism correlate with worse performance.[5] (Insert added.)

Buchsbaum and his colleagues completed their research in 1991, and published their findings in 1992. Subjects practiced a video game during a one- to two-month period. As they *improved* their skills, PET Imaging Technology revealed cortical brain activity *lessened* significantly. This occurred despite a 7-fold increase in performance! The researchers reported:

> We believe that during the first attempts at playing the game, the subjects are trying out many different cognitive strategies for the task, thus using many different brain circuits involving varied brain areas. After much practice, it is likely that subjects have developed a set strategy for performance of the task and thus use fewer brain circuits and/or fewer neurons per circuit with the resulting less overall brain activity.[6]

They said their research:

> suggests then that those who honed their cognitive strategy to the fewest circuits improved the most.[7]

Active Visual Cortex Yields Top Performance

Studying subjects learning video games in 1989, Shainberg wrote of Buchsbaum and his colleagues' studies:

> Predictably, they have found that the metabolic rate decreases as the game is mastered, but there is one interesting exception. In the visual cortex, the part of the brain that processes visual imagery, the metabolic rate increases. Buchsbaum suggests that this is because the subject is able to process more visual information as his skill increases.[8]

Another possible explanation for increased visual activity is that the subjects found their skills increasing by relying more on subconscious spatial strategies than conscious, non spatial strategies.

These researchers have provided additional information to help access the zone. Though many helps are covered in other sections of this book, here are some basic steps that can be taken.

1. Start with developing your motor and mental skills, practicing properly and regularly. The better you get, the more efficiently your brain will operate, increasing your chances of entering the zone.
2. Try ridding yourself of verbal conscious thoughts, when you practice or play, which is best accomplished by becoming as visual as possible. Instead of trying to consciously eliminate thoughts, focus spatially on the event. "See" the golf course and its many nuances; "see" the basketball court and players, becoming as peripherally aware as possible. Proper visualization techniques are helpful, too. The time to perfect your conscious-thoughts technique is during practice, not during a game. During competition, many athletes introspect too much.
3. Seek an above-average energy level, maintaining an ultrarelaxed state, mentally and physically. Too much energy or adrenaline will cause the eyes to dilate (often experienced during anxiety) making it more difficult to see clearly. Relaxation can be assisted by tensing then relaxing each muscle group.
4. Work on concentration. Try reading a book with the TV on or practicing your sport at times when you know you'll be distracted. Practice positive concentration, with confident thoughts. Focus deeply on the event, believing you will do your best.
5. Utilize the methods suggested in The Performing Mind, Relaxation, and Visualization sections of this chapter.

Optimal athletic performances will resemble a peaceful, almost hypnotic trance. Remember, zoning is not a state that can be automatically turned on or off. When it is achieved, you want to ride it out for as long as possible. Do not disrupt the proceedings. Recalling and articulating the zone experience is difficult for athletes. The active right hemisphere does not allow for it. Remember:

The better you are at what you do, the more you can forget it; the more you forget it, the better you do it.[9]

Relaxation

Both cognitive and physical skills are greatly affected by tension. Regardless of an athlete's Brain Type, optimal performance cannot occur unless he or she is relaxed.

Any Type can achieve relaxation. Most athletes require considerable time and effort to develop the ability to handle pressure. Relaxation training can help them check the Judging functions (T,F) in both hemispheres when the pressure mounts.

One way to relax the mind is by relaxing the muscles. Inactivity is not relaxation, rather relaxation and tension exercises are more effective. They are accomplished by systematically tensing and relaxing various muscle groups of the body, one after another. Here you will experience sensory distinctions, enabling you to feel the tension state in different areas of your body.

This relaxation section is not comprehensive, but let's look at a few exercises.

Follow Your Body

This relaxation exercise enables you to follow your muscle and body sensations. Without describing these sensations verbally, attempt to feel them by going slowly, being sensitive to each and every sensory nuance.

1. Begin this process by sensing your breathing rate. Next, consider how your body feels. Now clench your fist and squeeze tightly. Slowly sense the feelings in your fist and progressively move on to your wrist, forearm, upper arm, shoulder, back, and chest.
2. Keep clenching. How has the clenched fist affected your breathing? What is its affect on your stomach muscles, legs, and the rest of your body?
3. At last, you may release your clenched fist and relax your hand, shaking it gently. Rest a minute before proceeding with the next step in this exercise.

Now that your body has returned to normal, get ready to "shake it up" again. You are going use the clenched fist exercise, but this time try to keep your thoughts in the arm area alone, particularly below the elbow. Before you start, think of some descriptive words for what you feel. Use one-word descriptions.

For instance, your *physical thoughts* might include words such as: burning, aching, tingling, weak, and so forth. *Emotional thoughts* might be: anger, worry, supercharged, or determined. Remember, use only one-word descriptions as you concentrate on your sensations. Try to keep a mental note of your chosen words.

4. Now clench your fist one more time and spend 30 to 60 seconds in concentration. Undo your fist when you are finished and relax it. What sensations are you feeling as you relax your arm and let it hang? Provide one-word descriptions for the next minute or two.
5. Can you recall the sensations and words experienced with the clenched fist? Try to identify some of them and see if you can experience any body feelings. These should remind you of tension. Conversely, the sensations and words felt when relaxing your fist should promote relaxation. This exercise, when practiced, will provide a beneficial mind and body memory bank.

Relaxation Response

The Relaxation Response, written by Harvard Medical School's Herbert Benson, has been instrumental in validating relaxation theory and its various techniques. Though many relaxation books and techniques exist, a general guideline is to find a quiet, peaceful setting. A passive attitude is necessary. Sit in a comfortable position and attempt to concentrate upon one thing for the period of relaxation.

Your area of focus should be anything that does not bring other stimulating thoughts to your mind (such as picturing yourself in God's care, resting by a stream, and so on). Speaking a word or phrase after exhaling is one of the best ways to keep extraneous thoughts from entering your mind. This is a time of relaxation—you do not want your mind to wander. Your goal is to achieve total relaxation, but you cannot force it. It is an exercise you should practice each day when possible.

1. Focus on a non stimulating subject.

2. Sit down in a quiet environment and get comfortable.
3. Read steps four through eight, then close your eyes and complete the exercise.
4. Relax your muscles as much as possible to relieve tension.
5. Breathe naturally but slowly, repeating your phrase or word when exhaling.
6. Seek a passive attitude; don't worry about anything. If your mind wanders, just bring it back in focus.
7. Continue for at least 10 minutes.
8. At the end of the exercise try to relax your body part by part.

This exercise can help you relax and gain greater control over your mind. By regularly practicing relaxation techniques, you can attain significant results. If possible practice your relaxation exercises at the same time every day.

Praying and meditating on Scripture or other material is another way you can achieve relaxation. Seek to find and implement ways that enable you to relax.

If relaxation techniques are practiced regularly, they can be beneficial before and during athletic competition. Being able to relax at these times will maximize athletic performance. Unless your skills far exceed your competition's, proper relaxation is difficult to achieve. Thus, practicing relaxation techniques is beneficial.

Next time you experience frustration as you practice your sport, stop and take a couple of minutes to relax. When you resume, try to be relaxed and loose in your motor movements. Be more concerned about the smooth process than the result of your exercise. Effective results are only achieved when you are relaxed and non judgmental.

Visualization

The 1980s accentuated the significance of weightlifting in athletics. Virtually every serious athlete was out to achieve muscle tone. We're now in an age that highlights a part of the body that has nothing to do with barbells or athletic equipment.

Athletes in all sports have begun to take seriously the mind's influence over physical skills. Relying on physical training alone no longer brings the success it once did. Many insightful athletes are now advancing their skills with mental techniques. Those who follow suit are finding themselves at a distinct advantage.

Various terms describe these avant guard mind methods include: visualization, mental imagery and focusing. It is believed that the former Soviet Union and eastern European countries originated mental practicing as standard training for their athletes. They discovered mental training is a vital adjunct to physical performance.

Does Visualization Have Scientific Merit?

Many people rightfully want to know if there is any solid evidence to support visualization techniques, other than the hoopla from visualization promoters. The answer is yes and no. Yes, there is evidence that supports visualization. No, not all suggested techniques are beneficial.

Visualization has direct physical and physiological influences on the body. Sophisticated imaging techniques monitoring cerebral activity enable us to understand the brain's functions during visualization. PET Scan research at Washington University School of Medicine in St. Louis has been one of many institutions to shed light on this subject.

Subjects were asked to imagine moving their hands. Since there was no actual movement, PET imaging revealed there was no activity in the brain's primary motor cortex. (The primary motor cortex activates body movements.) Neurology researcher Peter Fox states:

> But we did see activity in the motor programming region around Broca's area.[10]

Imagining movements, then, activates areas of the brain controlling actual movement. The motor programming center is at the base of the primary motor cortex. It acts as a primer to actual movements. Before the primary motor cortex can engage body movements, the motor-programming center must tell it what to do and how to do it.

Thus, an athlete can engage an area of the brain controlling actual body movements by imagining or visualizing movements first. Think of how this might be effective prior to a foul shot in basketball, a swing in golf, or a serve in tennis. Especially in sports with moments of downtime, when parts of the body have not been used for a while, it only makes sense to warm up the region of the brain that will be called upon to engage these body movements.

Pictures in Your Mind

The process of seeing pictures in your mind has been called *cinematics*. It enables you to easily engage the right hemisphere by visualizing matters and associating emotions with them.

Daydreaming is one aspect of cinematics. It can be experienced anywhere, anytime—as most of us have learned. Sometimes this practice gets us into trouble, for we lose track of what is going on around us. Calvin, of the "Calvin and Hobbes" cartoon strip, experiences this quite often, much to the chagrin of his school teacher and parents. In society or the classroom, daydreaming is often considered negative and counterproductive. Many fail to realize cinematics can increase productivity as well.

The left brain is often overloaded during a normal workday, needing periodic rest. A way to achieve this rest is to increase activity in the right brain. If this is not accomplished, one's concentration and productivity drops off. Therefore, defocusing on a specific subject can sometimes be as productive as highly focusing.

To effectively problem-solve in many situations, engaging the right hemisphere is necessary for additional insight. Daydreaming to the future or fast-forwarding to possible solutions to problems is often effective. Inspiration, inventing, performing optimally, and setting goals are only a few possible benefits from cinematics.

Mozart, known more for his music than motor movements, wrote his compositions directly from the musical images in his head. Without analyzing what he was doing, he sometimes distracted his left hemisphere by having his wife read to him as he used his right brain to write out the musical pieces in his mind.

Productive persons learn that daydreaming or distracting the left hemisphere is not slothful or irresponsible behavior. In fact, it is often necessary.

Here are some simple steps to help you.

1. Picture yourself in a particular sport, one perhaps in which you would like to do well.
2. Next, visualize yourself in someone's body who excels in that sport. Feel the body movements and sensations as you participate in his or her actions. See all the things that person sees performing.
3. Next, ask yourself if the person you just visualized yourself as has ever failed. Of course he or she has. Success never comes without the ability to handle failure. It does not mean you like failure, only that you can deal with it. Be realistic concerning your athletic mistakes. Even the pros make them every time they perform. So will you.

To be fully effective, mental training must be practiced regularly, preferably daily. It is not an exercise you perform once and then you've got it. It is similar to perfecting a sport. The more you practice the mental side, the better you get. There is no easy way to circumvent the process.

For many, success comes only after they see themselves that way. Focusing on their problems is debilitating. It is better for them to focus on where they could be and how that would feel, mentally and physically.

Visualizing and Brain Types

As you might imagine, some Brain Types have greater difficulty than others visualizing. The visual, spatial right-brained athletes definitely have an advantage over the verbal left hemisphere ones. Of the left-brained persons, the iNtuitives are able to image better than the Sensates. Therefore, left brain Sensates or SJs will have the greatest difficulty. This does not mean they cannot do it, only that they need more effort.

29
Philosophical or Spiritual Foundation

Take a moment and think of any well known athletes, past or present, who have tainted their reputations or ruined their lives for lack of character, morals, or ethics. Nearly every day, the sports section of my newspaper tells of another pitiful incident.

In 1997, pro golfer **John Daly** entered the Betty Ford Center for treatment of alcoholism. This followed a previous day of heavy drinking, doing damage to his hotel room, and complaining of chest pains. Daly has a history of drinking problems and unorthodox behavior, costing him millions of dollars in endorsement contracts.

At last count, former NFL All-Pro **Dexter Manley** has had 17 rehab treatments for substance abuse.

In 1996, All-Pro **Michael Irvin** was suspended 5 NFL games for breaking the league's drug policy.

1996 and 1997 saw the NBAs **Dennis Rodman** with one altercation after another, especially on the floor. His off the court antics also raised many eyebrows.

All-Star **Darryl Strawberry** was sentenced to 6 months of home confinement and three years probation following his conviction of federal tax evasion. He was

SORRY! EARTHLY TREASURES HAVE NO HEAVENLY VALUE.

also given mandatory drug abuse counseling.

Having had cocaine problems seven years prior, **Dwight Gooden** was suspended for the entire 1995 baseball season, after testing positive for drugs again.

In 1989, **Pete Rose**, baseball's all-time leader in hits was banned from baseball for life for betting activities—restricting him from entering the coveted Hall of Fame. In 1990, Rose served a 5-month jail term for income tax evasion.

What, if anything, could have averted these situations?

A while back I read of **Jose Canseco** agreeing to counseling to avoid aggravated assault charges. He was accused of intentionally ramming his car into one being driven by his wife. Unfortunately, this was not the first time Canseco had a brush with the law.

What drove college basketball star **Len Bias** to celebrate his 1986 professional signing with the Boston Celtics by taking a fatal dose of cocaine? What, if anything, could have averted this tragedy?

Do you think former track star **Ben Johnson** would like to turn back the clock an0d say "no" to his first use of steroids? Who can forget Johnson's humiliation when he was stripped of his gold medal at the 1988 Seoul Olympics? Johnson denied for nine months after his Seoul downfall that he ever knowingly took steroids. Faced with incriminating testimony from those who knew his drug habits, he finally told the truth. He told *Sport* magazine:

> I was terribly ashamed. It hurt because of my mom. It was hard to come back. I didn't know what to do, didn't know where to turn. I was standing on the edge of a cliff.[1]

It is estimated that Johnson's disqualification cost him $10 million in endorsements and appearances the next year alone. Did Ben have a strong philosophical or spiritual foundation?

The **Cincinnati Reds** were the Cinderella team of the 1990 World Series, knocking off the perennial world champ Oakland A's. The Reds' euphoria was short lived. Before the regular 1991 season began, noticeable discontent hit the Reds' squad, evidenced by reliever Rob Dibble's comments:

> Guys were at each other's throats in spring training about what guy got more money.[2]

Things degenerated further by the 1991 midseason. The Reds were on a dismal losing streak and were playing below .500 ball. Pitcher Tom Browning commented on his team:

> With struggling comes bitching. That takes away from team unity. Guys shouldn't be thinking about themselves. They should be thinking about what it takes to win games.[3]

What was the foundation for life on which these individuals built? Whose values did they borrow, or did they form their own?

Roy Tarpley, incurred a lifetime ban from the NBA in 1991. The potential superstar's five-year career was marred with bouts of alcohol and drugs. Following his banishment, he commented to the press:

> In the end, just say that I tried to be hip, slick and cool and get high on the sly. . . . I guess once I got hold of a lot of money, I thought, I could party, stop and do the job. It didn't work out that way. I just kept partying. As soon as I got hold of money, my decision making went all out of whack.[4]

Though Tarpley was reinstated to the NBA in 1994, I venture to say that he wishes he had spent more time on winning the game of life.

Sports and Life are Different Games

We have considered only some of the many unfortunate events that have transpired in big time sports. A series of books could be written on the personal life problems of well known athletes. Many of the greatest athletes of all time have had their personal lives run amok. Could the parents, guardians, coaches, friends, or sports organizations have done anything more to help ensure a strong moral fiber in the life of the athlete?

We usually figure that moral decay will not happen to our athlete; somehow he or she will be spared. On the contrary, unless we devote special effort to emphasizing upright character and the most important goals in life, our athlete will be more apt to experience personal downfalls.

For example, a 1990 study found that athletes committed date rape with more than four times the frequency of non athletes. The *L.A. Times* reported in 1992:

> What society has fostered is a segment of the population—elite athletes—that has learned from an early age that they are special. Often they form the idea that rules don't apply to them.[5]

In 1995, the *L.A. Times* published a study of criminal activity by U.S. professional and college athletes. They found these athletes had nearly 5 times the incidents of assault and rape as the general population. Scholars and social scientists concur that male athletes are much more likely to be abusive toward women than other males.

Let's try to put things in perspective. Sports are games. Life's focus should not be on whether we can bat over .300 in baseball, slam dunk a basketball, break par in golf, or bowl a 300 game. For many athletes and their overseers, sports goals become the primary focus. They fail to realize the futility of their focus until the athletes are out of sports. Whether their careers end in high school or after lengthy pro involvement, athletes will have their time of reckoning. If they have built their priorities on the proper foundation, retirement will be satisfying and joyful. If not, their latter years will be filled with insecurity, despondency, and a series of wrong choices. No Brain Types are spared.

There are a number of reasons to pursue sports. A few of the top reasons are to build character, to obtain exercise, to pay for education, and to build friendships. Seeking a pro career or stardom should be of lesser importance. Only an infinitely small number of athletes will ever get recognized or paid for their trouble and talents. For the great percentage of those who never make the pros, if their goals have been proper, they will be ready to tackle life head on, with stability. The same will occur for those who make pro and have their priorities in order.

Let's consider how solid rock instead of sand can undergird our personal foundation.

Beliefs and Convictions

Beliefs and convictions regulate at least two major areas in the context of this book: the level of intensity to continue in a sport or life pursuit and the behavior manifested in the pursuit, amid successes and failures.

Many athletes do not know how to handle *success*. They develop, among other things, attitudes of arrogance, boastfulness, and condescension toward teammates and fans. Conversely, many athletes do not know how to handle *failure*. They exude poor sportsmanship, derogatory remarks, blame, and criticism of teammates.

Having a strong belief system can prevent destructive behaviors that accompany both success and failure: drugs, violence, gambling, illicit relations, and so forth. Some of America's greatest athletes have fallen victim to such vices. On the other hand, there are positive stories to be told.

My son and I attended a California high school, all-star basketball game in 1990. We left the game saying that one player (unknown to us) had far greater potential than any of the other players, not because of his performance that night, but because of his Brain Type. Returning home, I put his name in my file of future NBAers. He was a 6' 4" guard by the name of **Earnest Killum**. Accepting a scholarship to Oregon State, Earnest was academically ineligible his freshman year. He was quoted as saying:

> School was never a big deal to me in high school.

I was going to class, but I wasn't paying attention to the teacher.[6]

Killum's attitude and beliefs gained greater footing in college where he responded to his academic challenge unlike the typical jock. He diligently pursued his studies and earned a 3.5 grade point average after his three semesters, making the honor roll. Earnest commented after his first year in college:

> Last year was rough. There were times when I wanted to give up, but my faith in God kept pushing me to be a better student athlete.[7]

Yet Earnest's trials had just begun. His convictions were to stand greater tests.

In the summer of 1991, Earnest suffered a mild stroke. He was restricted from playing ball again for six months. Though under the treatment of a blood thinning drug, he suffered a fatal stroke in January of 1992. Earnest's final game was in his native Southern California, against USC. Though doctors limited his playing time, he scored 13 points in only 16 minutes and played great defense against USC star Harold Miner. The following day he suffered his second stroke.

The story of Earnest Killum is applicable to all. He was beginning to show himself as the consummate basketball player, maximizing his God-given Brain Type. What's more, he had already won the game of life. Prior to his unexpected death, Earnest reflected on his academic and physical hurdles:

> It happened for a reason. I don't know why it happened, but God was probably telling me something. He was probably telling me that there's more [to life] than just playing basketball. There was nothing I could do about it except pray.[8]

He told his high school coach:

> If the Lord won't let me play basketball, then I'll get an education and carry on.[9]

Earnest Killum entered the presence of his God with deep convictions, after setting his earthly ambitions on spreading his faith to youngsters of the inner city. He, like **Pistol Pete Maravich**, will leave us marvelous legacies, not only of their basketball wizardry, but of their more important, eternal values.

29....Philosophical or Spiritual Foundation

What are Your Beliefs?

Every person is philosophical. Your life and mine are lived according to our personal philosophies, whether or not they are spiritual. We are driven by deep seated beliefs formed over a lifetime. When decisions are made, our true beliefs dictate the course of action.

Identifying our deepest convictions is necessary to achieve maximum potential in any area of our life, including sports. Each of us should identify our inner mission. What is it that really drives me? When pain, boredom, fatigue, sadness, or hopelessness raise their ugly heads, only a strong inner focus and motivation will overcome.

All persons must decide for themselves what their beliefs will be. Others may strongly try to influence us, but we are the only ones who can control and establish our beliefs.

I want to help you in this section identify your strongest inner convictions, regardless of what they are. This will enable you to achieve a greater focus and probability for success in your desired sports and life accomplishments.

- What are your deepest inner convictions or beliefs for life and sports?
- What are your goals for this year, the next ten years?
- Are your beliefs consistent with your goals and your behavior?
- Would those who know you best say your espoused philosophy is consistent with your behavior?
- Who do you give higher regard to, yourself or others?
    - -what about when you are under pressure?
    - -how do you show this?
- Who are your personal heroes, role models? What do they believe?
- On a scale of 1 to a 10, how would you rate your overall effort level, game in, game out?
- When you are exhausted or discouraged in athletics, what is your greatest motivation to keep going?
- Do you wish you had greater motivation at times in athletic competition?
- Do you wish you had greater motivation in life overall?
- Do you wish you had greater self discipline in life?
- Where are you in your spiritual pilgrimage?

Beyond this exercise of self-awareness, I want to illustrate how you can build upon your personal belief system or change it. You can use this approach in conjunction with your own personal convictions. I am not out to proselytize anyone. You must determine for yourself what your beliefs are and will be.

I believe, along with the vast majority of Americans, that man is not only a physical and mental being, but spiritual as well. The City University of New York Graduate School conducted an enormous survey in 1991, sampling 113,000 adults (Gallup normally polls 1200 adults). The figures collected through nationwide telephone interviews over a 13 month period revealed *92.5% of the American population believed in God. 86.5% considered themselves Christians,* 7.5% said they had no religion, 2.2% declined to name their religion, 1.8% were Jewish and "other faith groups, such as Muslims, Buddhists, and Hindus, each numbering only a fraction of a percent."[10]

Considering that over 90% of our populace acknowledges a deity, I take the liberty to emphasize the importance of a spiritual foundation in the life of an athlete. A 1991 Gallup survey disclosed that:

> ...82% of Americans say they believe that the Bible is either the 'literal' or 'inspired' word of God, and more than half of them read the Bible at least monthly.[11]

Thus, in siding with the majority, I will use Biblical passages in a sports and typological context, demonstrating their relevancy and usefulness in a personal belief system. They can form the core of a person's deepest motivations.

I have chosen to build my foundation on what I believe to be God's words, not man's. They are found in the Bible. Knowing Brain Types as I do and after years of appraising man's wisdom, I'm left with no confidence in deriving my eternal beliefs from other mortals' thoughts. Who or what has the greatest credibility to you?

To use the words of the **Apostle Paul** as he addressed the people of Athens in the New Testament book of Acts 17:22b-28:

> Men of Athens! I see that in every way

you are very religious. For as I walked around and looked carefully at your objects of worship, I even found an altar with this inscription: TO AN UNKNOWN GOD. Now what you worship as something unknown I am going to proclaim to you.

The God who made the world and everything in it is the Lord of heaven and earth and does not live in temples built by hands. And He is not served by human hands, as if He needed anything, because He Himself gives all men life and breath and everything else. From one man He made every nation of men, that they should inhabit the whole earth; and He determined the times set for them and the exact places where they should live.

God did this so that men would seek Him and perhaps reach out for Him and find Him, though He is not far from each one of us. For in Him we live and move and have our being. As some of your own poets have said, 'We are His offspring.'

The Apostle Paul was a person who submitted his life to God (becoming a Biblical Christian). He and all others who do this place their intellect, emotion, and will under God's control. They are then able to obtain the highest motivation, self-discipline, and love possible. Consider the following Bible verses written by Paul.

· Be devoted to one another in brotherly love. Honor one another above yourselves. Never be lacking in zeal, but keep your spiritual fervor, serving the Lord. . . . Do not be proud, but be willing to associate with people of low position. Do not be conceited (Rom. 12:10-11, 16b).

· Be very careful, then, how you live—not as unwise but as wise, making the most of every opportunity, because the days are evil. Therefore, do not be foolish, but understand what the Lord's will is (Eph. 5:15-17).

· Train yourself to be godly. For physical training is of some value, but godliness has value for all things, holding promise for both the present life and the life to come (I Tim. 4:7b-8).

· But you, man of God, flee from all this [love of money], and pursue righteousness, godliness, faith, love, endurance and gentleness. Fight the good fight of the faith . . . 1 Tim. 6:11-12a) [Insert added].

· Whatever you do, work at it with all your heart, as working for the Lord, not for men, since you know that you will receive an inheritance from the Lord as a reward. It is the Lord Christ you are serving (Col. 3:23-24).

· I consider my life worth nothing to me, if only I may finish the race and complete the task the Lord Jesus has given me—the task of testifying to the gospel of God's grace (Acts 20:24).

· Do you not know that in a race all the runners run, but only one gets the prize? Run in such a way to get the prize. Everyone who competes in the games goes into strict training. They do it to get a crown that will not last; but we do it to get a crown that will last forever. Therefore I do not run like a man running aimlessly; I do not fight like a man beating the air. No, I beat my body and make it my slave so that after I have preached to others, I myself will not be disqualified for the prize (I Cor. 9:24-27).

· Therefore, since we are surrounded by such a great cloud of witnesses, let us throw off everything that hinders and the sin that so easily entangles, and let us run with perseverance the race marked out for us. Let us fix our eyes on Jesus, the author and perfecter of our faith, who for the joy set before him endured the cross, scorning its shame, and sat down at the right hand of the throne of God. Consider him who endured such opposition from sinful men, so that you will not grow weary and lose heart (Heb. 12:1-3).

· Timothy, my son, I give you this instruction in keeping with the prophecies once made about you, so that by following them you might fight the good fight, holding on to faith and a good conscience. Some have rejected these and so have shipwrecked their faith (1 Tim. 1:18-19).

· You were running a good race. Who cut in

29....Philosophical or Spiritual Foundation

on you and kept you from obeying the truth? That kind of persuasion does not come from the one who calls you (Gal. 5:7-8).

· I have fought the good fight, I have finished the race, I have kept the faith. Now there is in store for me the crown of righteousness, which the Lord, the righteous Judge, will award me on that day—and not only me, but also to all who have longed for his appearing (II Tim. 4:7-8).

Other sayings may contain God's principles, too. Because we reap what we sow, following wise principles will have rewards in this lifetime on earth. We reap eternal blessings when we do what we do through the power of God. The main point I try to make with my clients is that to neglect the spiritual side of their lives is to leave them weakened. If you feel a need in your life to be enriched spiritually, I challenge you to seek truth and not rest until you have found it and built your life on it. Life is the only game you have to win. When we all stand before God someday, He won't ask to see our trophies, sports scrapbooks, or bank accounts. Find spiritual role models or heroes. Stand alone in your beliefs, if you have to. Build on solid rock that cannot be undermined.

Whatever the verses, sayings, or mottoes by which you live your life, write them out and keep them before you. Memorize them, know them forwards and backwards. If you find this difficult, more than likely you do not believe them strongly. You may think you do, but your true beliefs will be acted upon and known thoroughly. By keeping your beliefs ever before you, you soon discover whether you truly believe them.

You Have Purpose

Have you ever wondered why you are alive and on the earth? Do you believe that you are here by evolutionary process, the beneficial culmination of primordial ooze, or do you believe that a higher power planned and put you here? Is there any inborn *purpose* for your existence or is *purpose* optional in your thinking? Do you believe you are innately designed to perform in specific ways mentally, physically, and spiritually, or are you like putty, being molded by everything that happens to you, becoming a product of your background and environment, mentally and physically?

Whether we like it or not, science reveals that purpose, order, organization, and design exist throughout the universe and nature. Human beings (including their brains) are no exception.

This book will help you athletically whether or not you believe you are cerebrally designed with purpose, order, and uniqueness. Yet if you do see these aspects as real, this material will supply even greater meaning.

Who Should be Our Heroes?

Have you ever considered the bedroom walls of youngsters? Beyond the smudge marks and cave drawings, you will discover who and what are important to them. Children interested in sports often have a poster or some reminder of their favorite athletes. Wanting to emulate these athletes' physical skills is wise for athletic success, but what about success in life? Are there other posters or reminders that should be occupying the rooms of our children?

To achieve our best in life, it is good to model people of strong moral and spiritual character. There is no better life to emulate than that of Jesus Christ. Yet men and woman may be imitated, too, provided we realize they are only human. The Apostle Paul enjoined Christians to model his devotion to Christ:

> Whatever you have learned or received or heard from me, or seen in me—put it into practice. And the peace of God will be with you (Phil. 4:9).

There are persons in history and today who can serve as role models of upstanding character. As parents, we can help our children identify these persons.

Those of us who use the Bible as our source of guidance may look within its pages to find role models. Jesus Himself, being perfect, did not display the characteristics of any one Type but the quintessence of them all. God may well have given us a picture of the life of Christ from four different Brain Type group perspectives in the four Gospels. **Matthew**, the tax collector, provides us a record of Christ's genealogy and other SJ interests. *The NIV Study Bible* comments that **Mark** provides a:

> ...simple, succinct, unadorned, yet vivid account of Jesus' ministry, emphasizing more what Jesus did than what he said. Mark moves quickly from one episode in Jesus' life and ministry to another, often using the adverb 'immediately.'[12]

Mark strongly resembles the SP style, which also is the shortest of the Gospels. **Luke**, the physician, provides a rich NF flavor to the Gospels:

> The writing is characterized by literary excellence, historical detail and warm, sensitive understanding of Jesus and those around him.[13]

Lastly, **John** is the most theological of the gospels, holding special interest for NTs.

Regardless of the Gospel writers' Brain Types, and those of other Biblical authors, God has provided His word to us in many different styles.

The following list provides Biblical persons and their possible Brain Type groupings. Their lifestyles varied according to Type and their relationship to God. When they submitted their lives to the Creator, they became role models.

For wisdom is more precious than rubies,
and nothing you desire can compare with her.
(Proverbs 8:11)

Better is a patient man than a warrior,
a man who controls his temper than one who takes a city.   (Proverbs 16:32)

SJs   Matthew
           Timothy
           James
           Martha

When pride comes, then comes disgrace,
but with humility comes wisdom.   (Proverbs 11:2)

SPs   Peter
           John Mark

NFs   David
           Moses
           Luke
           Barnabas

NTs   Paul
           John
           Daniel
           Joseph (O.T.)

Consider choosing a Biblical person, or someone of high moral character as a hero to model. This will complement emulating an athlete's skills.

When choosing a Christian model, consider what Christian means. There is a difference between *American Christianity*, the kind to which you and I are commonly exposed, and unadulterated *Biblical Christianity*, straight from the original teachings. Its followers are morally and ethically upright, regard others more highly than themselves, and joyfully share all that God has given them, among other attributes. They let Scripture dictate their beliefs and actions.

30
Goal Setting

Are you a goal setter? Do you regularly plan your achievements, following through on specific goals you have set for yourself? If you do, you are in the minority. Many persons never set goals. Of those who do, most give up on them prematurely. Why is this?

I suppose it is like going on a diet, or sticking to any plan that includes prolonged difficulty. Only those who have high levels of motivation or self discipline follow through on their goals. If you are *not* one of these persons, do not despair, there is *hope* for you.

Goals are imperative if you desire to be a top notch athlete. You must establish what you want to achieve and how you will achieve it. This does not necessarily mean you have to write out your goals, although it is recommended.

Let's consider some important ingredients of proper goal setting. Goals should be:

A. *Realistic*—goals must be attainable for your abilities. Placing them out of reach guarantees failure and lessens motivation.

B. *Measurable*—you need to have ways of tangibly evaluating your progress. Set objective points and quantify matters along the way, measuring how you have done.

C. *Challenging*—though realistic, goals must require hard work. Setting them according to your Brain Type is helpful.

D. *Specific*—identify your exact goals. Generalizations won't work. State precisely what you want to accomplish.

E. *Timely*—specific and realistic deadlines are necessary, crucial in accomplishing your goals.

F. *Valuable*—linking goals to your value system (philosophical or spiritual beliefs) enables you to expend ultimate effort.

Goal-Setting Steps

Here are some steps to begin identifying and accomplishing goals.

1. Identify your goals and write them down in order of importance.

Physical:_____
_____
_____
_____
_____

Mental:_____
_____
_____
_____
_____

Mechanics-Technique:_____
_____
_____
_____
_____

Spiritual-Philosophical:_____
_____
_____
_____
_____

2. Why do you want to accomplish these goals?

3. What obstacles can prevent you from achieving your goals?

Physical: _____
_____
_____

Mental: _____
_____
_____

Mechanics-Technique: _____
_____
_____

Spiritual-Philosophical: _____
_____
_____

Financial: _____
_____
_____

Other: _____
_____
_____

4. Plan to remove obstacles by writing out in a sentence or two your approach to overcoming them.

Physical: _____
_____

Mental: _____
_____

Mechanics-Technique: _____
_____

Spiritual-Philosophical:_____
_____

Financial:_____
_____

Other:_____
_____

5. *Make a list of what you are willing to voluntarily give up to achieve your goals.*

    a.

    b.

    c.

    d.

    e.

6. *List the persons with whom you will share your goals.*

    a.

    b.

    c.

    d.

Reviewing your goals regularly is essential. Each morning you can remind yourself of what needs to be done; each evening can be used for evaluating your progress. Weekly, monthly and at other timely dates, you can make longer term appraisals. A monthly training schedule for your physical goals is provided as an example.

MONTHLY TRAINING SCHEDULE
(Physical)

	Sun.	Mon.	Tues.	Wed.	Thurs.	Fri.	Sat.
1							
2							
3							
4							
5							
6							
7							
8							
9							
10							
11							
12							
13							
14							
15							
16							
17							
18							
19							
20							
21							
22							
23							
24							
25							
26							
27							
28							
29							
30							
31							
Total							

Objectively evaluating yourself on a regular basis will help you achieve your goals. By comparing your plans with what you actually accomplished, you can grade yourself, seeing just how you are doing. Using a common school standard is one way of grading.

MONTH: _____

PLANNED:_____ ACTUAL:_____

MONTHLY GRADE_____

A= 90-100%

B= 80-90%

C= 70-80%

D= 60-70%

F= 59% and below

Though goals are only a means to an end, they are significant in enabling you to become all you can be in every area of your life. Without them, you may settle for mediocrity.

Conclusion

This section on Mental Helps was intended to demonstrate the importance of properly using your mind in athletics and life. There is appreciable value in devoting concerted effort to mental practice as well as physical.

PART EIGHT

FURTHER CONSIDERATIONS IN TYPE

31
Other Psychological Methods and Accurate Typing

A number of psychological or mental approaches are being used to determine an athlete's potential. A few of them have merit, but none compares to Brain Typing technology (an outgrowth of Jung-Myers typology). Other methods are far less accurate, scientific and dependable. Many reasons account for this.

We might correlate other methods to what the Wright brothers were able to accomplish at Kitty Hawk. They are like the first flight attempts from cliffs that ended after short duration. One would be better off walking (or not trying to analyze an athlete at all).

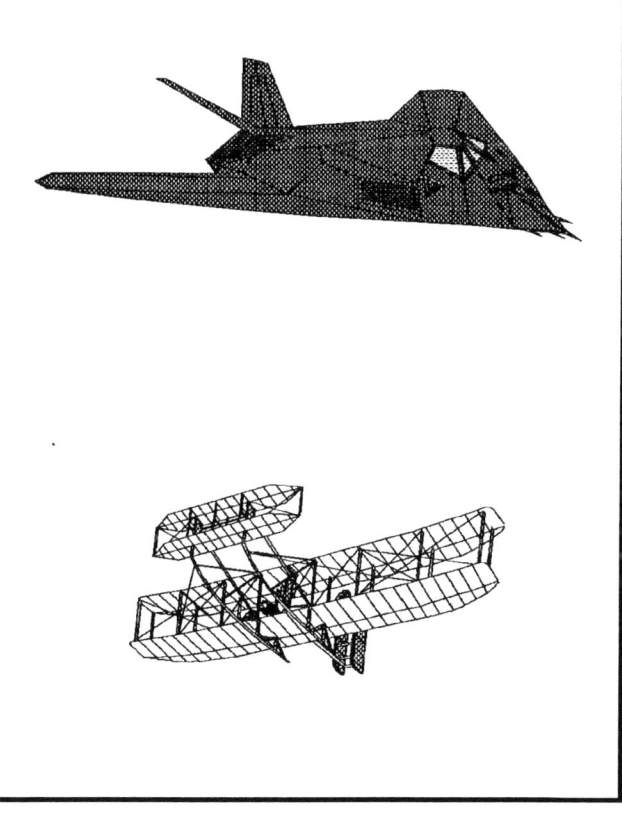

They shed light only on the truth that each athlete has a distinct psychological makeup. This is a positive step and a fact that all those associated with athletics need to recognize. Unfortunately, these approaches are still equivalent to early aviation forms.

Brain Typing brings us into the age of supersonic flight. Contrast the Kitty Hawk plane with the stealth technology of the F-117. During the 1991 Persian Gulf War, the F-117 fighter flew thousands of missions over Iraq's most heavily defended sites and was never scratched by enemy fire. Air Force officials say it was never even seen. The sophistication of typology, neuroscience, and genetics help us come out of the Dark Ages. Let's consider a few of the problems with other approaches. I will only generalize what the best of them offer.

I have some conflicts with even the best of these approaches. Often I see damage to organizations or athletes who have undergone these analyses. I once introduced Brain Types to a professional basketball organization but had to overcome their hostility toward psychological analyses. They once wanted to draft a player (but didn't) who later became a star in the NBA, being advised to pass on him because he was reported to *not have the proper mental makeup*. Had the reputable sports psychology service that gave this bad advice known the material in this book, they would have highly recommended the player. Instead, their superficial approach made it more difficult for the real truth to be known.

What are the basic drawbacks with other methods? First, except for Jungian typology, they do not reveal the eight preferences of the brain pertaining to energy flow (E,I), information gathering (S,N), decision making (T,F), and outward behavior (J,P). The assessment of these cerebral preferences are essential for determining which athletes will excel, and how to get the most out of any athlete.

Second, other methods (including Jungian typology) do not provide evidence as to which body skills each athlete is most proficient in (gross motor, fine motor, speech—hearing, and intellectual abstraction skills), which is especially essential to know when an athlete is under pressure. Neither do they provide the valuable information related to the distinct functioning of the brain's right and left hemispheres.

Third, approaches such as the popular *Athletic Motivation Inventory* (AMI) rely upon aspects such as drive, aggressiveness, determination, mental toughness, and emotional control. These are important to consider, but typology and neuroscience reveal that many Brain Types not designed for sports at the professional level can easily possess these positive mental characteristics. They can even be excellent college players, but do not possess the necessary superior mental and motor skills to play consistently at the pro level. Therefore, a player could easily be drafted or recruited who scored well on one of these other methods, but one who won't perform at his grading level.

Conversely, top Brain Types and future superstars can score poorly using these other methods, especially when the athlete's upbringing or environment has been substandard. In addition, some of your most natural athletes, including baseball pitchers with certain Brain Types, do not innately have mental toughness. These necessary mental skills, however, can be developed in some Types.

Fourth, the other methods of which I am aware utilize a questionnaire of sorts in order to determine the athlete's mental tendencies or patterns. (So does, in fact, the Jung-Myers method. With this I have concern.) Regardless of the accuracy of the particular mental analysis, subjective, self evaluating questionnaires such as these cannot be considered foolproof. Even when test takers answer as honestly as possible, they often do not see themselves as they truly are.

We must remember that persons answering a psychometric questionnaire often have an ulterior motive. When the boss, marriage counselor, prospective spouse, or other seekers-into-their-minds (including sports organizations) begin to probe, a natural protective mechanism activates. In order for one to expose personal, perceived weaknesses to others, one must normally feel unconditional acceptance. Therefore, questionnaire answers are often unreliable, even those related to Jung-Myers typology. (I am not saying Jungian typology is less than accurate, only the questionnaire methods for its evaluation.)

(*Take heart, however, there is a way for accurate analysis. We'll get there in the next section.*)

In addition, the law states that psychological inventories may be administered only on a voluntary basis. Many times, especially with your most highly recruited athletes, there is an unwillingness to undergo a mental profile. If they do not participate, they will still be highly valued by some team for their past accomplishments. If they do participate and their results prove negative, their stock may drop fast.

Benefits of Other Approaches

I would never rely upon other evaluations as my main source for measuring mental maturity or toughness, but only as extraneous helps. Their input would have to be evaluated in light of Brain Types.

Where I would possibly value some information from a few of these other inventories would be in the areas where they would measure an athlete's attitude, values, or ethics system. In part, this would be measuring the athlete's past and present environment. For instance, it would be better for a ballclub to have a talented ISTP, let's say, who would be coachable and a positive role model, than one who was a trouble maker, even if he or she were a top-notch player.

There are a number of environmental factors that can distort a potentially great athlete's performance. Many times, from just a change in a slumping athlete's environment, he or she will perform a remarkable turnaround.

Accurate Typing

In the early 1980s, I attended an International Biennial Conference of the Association for Psychological Type. There I heard from the most eminent typology spokespersons, adorned with their post graduate psychology degrees. Their presentations were polished and informative. I was impressed; these practitioners knew their subject. (Virtually every speaker was an iNtuitive Brain Type.)

I was also struck by their seeming inability to perceive the Types of well-known people of whom they spoke. It didn't make sense to me; how could these erudite "psychoanalyzers" be so ineffectual in typing others? But who was I to question their revelations? After all, I was a layman and had been a student of Type for less than five years. A panel of experts said that Adolf Hitler was an ENFJ (his values ran amok), John Kennedy, an ESTP (a deep-down party-er), and Abraham Lincoln, an ISFJ (ol' honest Abe). Other notables and notorious were typed in this interesting forum; some I knew were incorrect while for others I didn't have a clue. "Oh well," I thought. "Leave the evaluations to the experts. I had better learn to drive before I learn to take the engine apart." And so I did. (I later discovered Hitler was not an ENFJ, that Kennedy was an ENTJ, and Lincoln, clearly an INTJ.)

In 1984, I published my first book, on typology's relationship to salespersons. By this time, I had begun to feel comfortable in typing others. It seemed that there was something about my Brain Type that had a gift for this. Therefore, I included some well known persons as illustrations in my book. As I highlighted the temperaments, I even mentioned as an anecdote that Adolf Hitler was a maladjusted NF. I had never come to this conclusion for myself; my reliance was upon those who I thought knew more. It was only after a few times of trying to explain to those who asked why I thought Hitler was an NF that I opted to research him for myself, and changed my opinion. He was a definite Thinking Type who had gone severely awry. (Though I know his Brain Type, it's best left unsaid. Within every Type, rogues are possible when ethical standards are ignored.)

This instance taught me to be extremely careful in typing others. I must rely upon my own research as well as that of others. I have come to realize Type "experts" are often wrong with their appraisals of others, especially when they do not use the Myers Briggs Type Indicator *(MBTI®)*, such as in the speculations of John Kennedy and Abraham Lincoln. I say this not to demean typology's hierarchy, but to point out that their greatest service lies in understanding and articulating the dynamics of typology. Here they are unparalleled. (Some typologists do not attempt to evaluate anyone to whom they cannot administer a questionnaire.)

Unfortunately, when typing others, these mostly iNtuitive experts see too many possibilities and not enough of the Sensing, factual nuances. (We must remember, our brains excel in only one Perceiving function and one Judging function each. Thus, no Brain Type can master both Sensing and iNtuition, or Thinking and Feeling.) I have even come to realize that some of the most well known, highly educated leaders in psychological type circles have assessed *themselves* incorrectly. For many reasons, this exists and in the long-run will be unproductive for promoting the accuracy of typology.

Questionnaires

If we cannot always rely upon the typology experts, where else can we turn? Let me reiterate that when persons answer a psychometric questionnaire, they often try to portray how they want to be seen instead of how they really are. When the boss, marriage counselor, prospective spouse, or other seekers into their minds begin to probe, a natural protective mechanism activates. In order for one to expose personal, perceived weaknesses to others, one must normally feel unconditional acceptance. Most times, this is not the case. Therefore, questionnaire answers are often unreliable, even those related to Jung-Myers typology. (I am not saying Jung-Myers typological preferences are less than accurate, only the questionnaire methods for their evaluation.)

Many other possibilities exist for mistyping. Questionnaire takers need to make sure they understand the questions and the specific verbal terms. A multitude of connotations can be attributed to one word alone! Hasty answers may lead to incorrect conclusions. Persons lingering too long over questions may read too much into them, trying to outguess the questionnaire.

One's environment and frame of mind can also have a significant bearing on how one perceives self or answers a specific question. This can change daily, or even hourly, depending upon factors such as being tired, worried, cranky, or stressed.

I have witnessed first-hand that with hundreds of people who take Jungian typology questionnaires, of the four preference dyads, one if not more is often misevaluated. The first time I took the Myers Briggs questionnaire *(MBTI®)*, my Type was misdiagnosed as well. This is not to say you should avoid questionnaires, particularly the *MBTI*. Just remember the *MBTI*, the best of the lot, is an indicator, not absolute verifier. It can assist you, however, in the pilgrimage of better understanding your God-given mindset. The *MBTI* is intended for adult use and can, at times, provide accurate evaluations.

In 1991, four elite members of the Association for Psychological Type (APT) participated in a panel discussion, responding to a report issued by the National Research Council on the usefulness of the *MBTI®*. APT member and Senior Product Developer of Consulting Psychologists Press, Inc., Allen Hammer, stated:

We do need more validity research in developing the *MBTI*. I don't think any serious user would say that it is a complete and perfect instrument or ever will be.[1]

Myers and McCaulley (1985) reported that the accuracy of the *MBTI* in predicting "True Type" was 75 percent. In 1996, temperament guru David Kiersey, coauthor of *Please Understand Me*, reported in the *APT Western Region Newsletter*:

> My guess is that the various Jungian instruments—MBTI, [Keirsey Temperament] Sorter, Singer-Loomis, Gray-Wheelwright, MMTIC—are wrong about half the time, which is to say they misclassify about every other person.[2]

For many years I have believed the best of Jungian Type questionnaires are only 50-60 percent accurate. I strongly concur with Keirsey's estimate.

The Best Way

I do know of an approach that can provide 100 percent accuracy, if it is applied carefully. At the present time, *the best method for accurate evaluation is the same method Carl Jung used to discoverer six of the mental preferences (E,I,S,N,T,F), by empirically studying thousands of persons, observing and documenting their infinite genres.* Unfortunately, few are qualified to do this. It won't be long, however, before genetic testing and sophisticated brain mapping technology will be used to identify each Brain Type. With each passing day, this is becoming more of a reality.

Though Jung's empirical approach was best, he had trouble discerning psychological functions, except in "highly differentiated individuals." He only typed persons who demonstrated their functions in overt and "habitual" patterns. Jung said:

> When any of these four basic psychological functions [S,N,T,F] is *habitual*, thus setting a definite stamp on the character of the individual, I speak of a psychological type.[3] (Insert added, italics in the original.)

Speaking of those persons he did not type, he said:

> This group is the most numerous and includes the less differentiated normal man . . . .[4]

In other words, Jung chose not to "type" the majority. His INTP brain excelled at intellectual abstraction, not Sensing skills. Nevertheless, as he spent countless hours with his patients, he engaged his Sensing function sufficiently to discern the psychological preferences that make up the essence of this book. *Discovering* the mental preferences and *being able to assess* others easily and accurately are two different abilities.

A major problem exists. It is difficult to find those Brain Types in Type circles who are most gifted at typing others. Their interests are normally found elsewhere. I have been told repeatedly that I happen to be one of those Types. I have yet to locate many others with my cerebral makeup who are active in typology.

My empirical approach evidently combines a natural God-given gift with years of studying people, typology, body mechanics, neuroscience, and genetics. Certain Brain Types are better able to read or pick up on the nuances in people. I have an insatiable drive to type those I see or with whom I come in contact. Whether I'm watching TV, at the ball game, or casually meeting someone, I sense a natural, almost unconscious desire to know another's mental makeup.

Do you recall the Kevin Costner sequence in "Field of Dreams," where he and his daughter are spectators as "Shoeless Joe Jackson" and friends play ball? Costner's relatives arrive and question what he and his daughter are watching. They answer they're watching the players. The relatives think the two are crazed since they themselves cannot see anyone. I often find myself in the same kind of situation, recognizing the different Brain Types rather easily while others can't see much, if anything at all. (In contrast to Jung, I see most persons as appearing "highly differentiated.") And, as with Costner's reception, I find that others are not always thrilled when I do it. Therefore, I do *not* share my observations socially unless asked, and then with great caution.

I began my critical evaluations years ago with businesses. Before they would hire a new employee with a specific job description, they would seek my services. (One or two Brain Types are usually best for each job description.) To bypass often inaccurate questionnaires, and the cost in time and money of visiting distant companies, I developed another approach. The company would interview prospective employees and send me an audio tape recording of the session. I typed them accurately by their syntax, diction, inflection, and so on. I could not afford to make a mistake lest the employee fail to handle the job to the company's standards.

Absolute accuracy is necessary in typing athletes, particularly at the professional level. My typology/neuroscience analysis is highly specific; I rarely deal in generalities.

For example, if a pro basketball team is looking for a point guard, I can provide information on the specific Brain Type with the most adept motor and mental skills for the team's style of play. I have learned the specific Brain Types of over 95 percent of the players in the NBA (99 percent of the best ones), as well as many of the top college hoopsters. I also type players unknown to me, provided I'm able to see them perform in person or on video tape.

You, too, can become more and more proficient at evaluating people as you watch and learn and ask questions. Questionnaires may start you in the direction of accuracy, but you need to evaluate them with keen and experienced observation.

Insisting upon Accurate Typing

Those who require absolute accuracy in their typing include professional and college sports teams, and serious athletes who are out to perfect their abilities. Parents or coaches of young athletes who hope to reach professional status someday would want to be certain of the child's Brain Type. They would not want to place a square peg in a round hole. Similarly, those in all other areas of life have a strong need for complete Typing accuracy.

Many organizations are administering questionnaires to their personnel, hoping to learn more of their mental makeup. Though some of these instruments are useful in gaining further understanding, I repeat, none can match the insight of Jung-Myers typology and Brain Typing data. Unfortunately, those who want to use Jung-Myers typology cannot rely upon questionnaire answers. To ensure correct analysis, someone needs to be consulted who is expert in Brain Typing. (For more assistance, refer to the back of the book.)

Typing Someone Close to You

If you are only interested in typing a person or two, as a parent, let's say, your chances for accurate evaluation can be good—if you are willing to study your child thoroughly. It may not take long, but more than likely it will. In a relatively short period of time, you probably will determine one or two typological brain preferences. To accurately appraise all four is another story.

When asked many years ago by two parents familiar to me to assess their children, I consented. After this couple studied their children for some time, they reported I was in error regarding one of them. They held this belief for nearly five years, after which they finally came to believe my analysis. They had been close in their evaluation, only missing one preference, yet it was an appreciable difference pertaining to the child's potential, vocationally and athletically.

Do not assume you already know your child's cerebral makeup. Ask other adults who know him or her how they view your child in light of the eight brain preferences. Remember, your child can be an Introvert, for example, yet have an Extraverted persona with friends. And, it's not unusual to find Extraverts with Introverted personalities. If you are uncertain and have a high need to know, you need to consult an expert in Brain Typing.

If it is not imperative to immediately know someone's Type, then take your time and learn this Brain Typing information. Even if you can decipher only one preference, that should provide you many answers for your or another's behavior. Enjoy the process of learning others' traits, making sure you seek to value and appreciate them. Remember, you must seek to understand your own design for you to understand why you perceive others as you do. Understanding yourself and others, even seeking to do so, will make this world a better place.

32
Parents and Guardians

How important to you is good character development? Which do you spend more time considering, what your children will do for a living someday and where they will go to college, or what kind of persons they will be? Do you place a higher value on what your children *do* or what they *are*? True character is revealed in time, particularly during adversity.

Professional baseball's pitching ace Rob Dibble was involved in a number of unsportsmanlike incidents during his major league career. When the outbreaks heightened in 1991, Rob sought counseling, saying of himself:

> I'm a poor loser, a baby. I need to grow up. . . . I was taught to win at all costs.

He continued:

> It took 27 years for me to get like this, it's going to take a few years to unravel it all.[1]

Many factors were involved in Rob's behavior over the years. Nevertheless, had some persons taken an active role in tempering Rob's intensity, he would most likely have avoided his notoriety.

While coaching over 50 youth teams for more than a decade, I witnessed the gamut of parents. Their personalities, behaviors and, yes, Brain Types, are as varied as the kids'. Parents range from quiet and encouraging to loudmouthed and highly critical. Unfortunately, a number of young athletes have poor adult models in parents and coaches who instill or tolerate unacceptable behavior. Problems are assured later, down the road.

Depending upon their Brain Types, some children are more difficult to raise or coach than others. Parents have to exercise extra effort and wisdom. ISTP athletes are the most genetically predisposed to competitive intensity, even as youngsters. They often get angry or shed tears when failing to do things perfectly. In baseball, by striking out, grounding out, even hitting a ball up against the center field fence only to be caught, or producing anything but a solid base hit, they can become incensed. ISTPs are much different than young ISFPs who can walk back to the dugout smiling after a strikeout. After all, ISFPs reason, they had fun at the plate, and it's only a game!

In 1982, a sobering warning to parents was expressed in *Psychology Today*:

> The hero and the psychopath are twigs from the same branch. Both are relatively fearless. The more or less fearless child . . . will grow up to be either a hero or a psychopath, depending on how his parents rear him.[2]

Parents and coaches need to identify those children who are overly intense and channel that determination into positive experiences and sportsmanlike behavior.

How do You Rate?

In sports, how would you rate yourself as a motivator, encourager, coach, and parent of your child? Do you feel a need to improve in any of these areas? Most of us do. Either way, this chapter is still for you.

As parents or guardians, we need to seriously consider the ramifications of our influence on our aspiring athletes. Whether we are *active* or *passive* participants in their athletic endeavors, we are making a profound impression on their bodies, minds, and souls.

Participating Guardians

Tennis expert Tony Trabert wrote in his book, *Trabert on Tennis*, of inappropriate ways to oversee young athletes:

> When it comes to having youngsters play tennis, the biggest problem lies not with the kids, but with the hordes of parents who goad them to succeed, who tag along, often abusing their children and anyone else within earshot when things don't go their way on the court.[3]

We, as parents or guardians, tend to think it's the other folk who have these problems, not us. Sure, we aren't perfect, but our child is in good hands under our care.

How much do you want athletic success for your child? How much goading do you do? I must admit there is a fine line between encouraging one's child to participate in a sport versus insisting. What if the child wants to quit athletics for the wrong reasons? Pat answers are hard to find.

Most sports require starting at an early age if world class status is to be achieved. Yet five-year old youngsters are hardly in a position to know whether gymnastics is best for them. Thus, parents often determine what they believe is best. But is the parent or guardian qualified to make this decision? Will they be seeking the child's best interest or their own? As Trabert and other concerned sports experts are saying, many of us need to take inventory of our motives and methods for seeing our children succeed.

Trabert shares a specific incident where he sat next to a father who was watching his daughter play

competitive tennis. She corrected a bad call by the umpire so that the point would go to her opponent! (Yes, you read that right.) After the umpire thanked the girl for her honesty, the father said to Trabert:

> I'd never want Mary to admit something like that. She's not out there to win the damn sportsmanship award. She's out there to win. Period.[4]

Most of us would never condone the father's

comments, yet in reality we often are indifferent to the truth in sports for the sake of winning. How often do you or those near you at sporting events speak up for the truth when it is costly to your player or team? How often do you see coaches, parents, and fans, from youth athletics to the professional level, yelling to help out the opposition on a bad call? Not too often, or ever.

Two, if we fudge on the truth in sporting events, what are we modeling to our youngsters? Do you think they will go through life believing it's okay to compromise the truth in sports but not in other areas? In other words, it's okay to cheat in sports but not on my spouse, employer, and income taxes? When the truth is compromised in one area, it will be compromised in another. It is only a matter of time. Honesty is far more important in the overall game of life than winning.

Tony Trabert spoke again of this same father, after both his daughters lost at the tournament:

> Their father was castigating them for being losers and was pacing back and forth, ranting and raving at the two of them. He didn't stop this verbal assault until the girls, along with their distraught mother, walked away from him and his harangue, which started echoing off cold concrete walls.[5]

Tragically, this shoe fits many adults. Whether it takes place at the competition site or at home, it makes no difference. Berating a child is never appropriate; it only inflicts damage. If you ever wonder if you're one of these "beraters," just ask those people who know you best. Allow them to answer honestly.

Wrong Expectations

Some parents encourage their children to play fairly and be good sports but still criticize them. In coaching, I often see parents (generally dads) unmercifully chastise their youngsters for not performing better. As a self proclaimed expert, dad is quick to point out countless mistakes. If dad could only see videos of how he really played (they didn't have home videos that long ago!) instead of incorrectly recalling faint memories of how he wished he had performed. Dads (and moms) are often unrealistic in their expectations for their children.

Nothing points this out more quickly than for us fathers, as adults, to play the same sport as our child, with tough competition. We then blame our athletic ineptness on being out of shape or not having played the sport for a long time, when in reality we never could play the sport as well as we thought.

I have had this reminder a number of times. As my oldest son advanced into high school sports, I tried to help him both mentally and physically. I often expected him to perform better than he did, that is, until I went out and played with athletes of his caliber. Sure enough, I made more mistakes than I thought possible. Gee, it seemed so easy from the stands where my expectations were often too high. It's often wise to lower our expectations while increasing encouragement to our children.

Appropriate Correction

Correction or rebuke is sometimes appropriate for your child in athletics. We should remember a few basics, however.

First, correction should be done in private. Just as you do not want someone correcting you in front of others, neither does your child. ("Do unto others as you would have them do unto you.")

Second, stern correction should only be used for inappropriate behavior, attitude, or play. John McEnroe's past behavior would fall into this category.

Third, we must convey love for the child first, then offer our correction. If children do not sense our love in body language as well as words, our correction will not be nearly as effective. We must never punish the child verbally by berating them. Our correction should focus on what they should have done.

Lastly, reasonable disciplinary measures should be taken for the child's misdeeds, fitting and relevant to the crime. Writing the tennis linesman a letter of apology—for berating him—could be an example, and part of the discipline process. Youngsters learn their best lessons, not from verbal haranguings, but from implementing good deeds appropriate to the offense.

Being an active participant in your children's sporting life can be beneficial. *You can show how much you care for them, you can learn to be an encourager, you can teach them valuable lessons of life within the context of sports, and it can even be a way to get some exercise as you attempt to help your child.*

It is possible to be an active parent and not be vocal. A parent can attend a child's events without offering corrections afterwards, listening when the child wants to talk, and encouraging when the child gets down. This kind of parent is special; I know, my mother was one.

Pete Sampras, the 1990 U.S. Open Tennis Champion at age 19, said of his parents:

Growing up, they didn't put a whole lot of pressure on me. They let me develop as a player and not worry about winning every junior tennis match . . . and I will always be thankful.[6]

L.A. Times staff writer, Paul Dean, disclosed more on the Sampras' parenting style:

Sam and Georgia Sampras do not play tennis. But they know life and coached their son in some unusual values. Being a good winner is tougher than being a good loser. Playing well is even better than winning or losing.[7]

Sam Sampras commented:

There were some occasions when Pete would do like other kids, where he would get really upset and take his racket and just hit the ground. I told him: 'Do that one more time and I'll not support you in tennis.'[8]

That warning was never forgotten, "That's where I got my good attitude," says Pete.[9] Pete's inherited values can be seen in his statement, "I've always liked the attitude of [Rod] Laver, his fairness, his sportsmanship."[10]

Non-participating Guardians

Some parents are essentially not involved or interested in their child's sporting activities. Sports may conflict with their jobs. Maybe they don't like or understand sports, or maybe they just do not want to get involved. The child knows when the parent doesn't care. This can be discouraging to a youngster, making it harder to endure the rigors of his or her sport.

My belief is that parents should be involved, to some degree, in every genuine interest their child pursues. Moses said in the Bible that parents are to talk to their children when sitting at home, when walking along the road, when putting them to bed, and when getting them up (Deuteronomy 6). He instructed parents to teach their children about God, and to obey Him, within the context of living life. In other words, use all the events and interests in the child's life to introduce God. Regardless of your values or beliefs, going along side your child can be wonderful blessing for the both of you, even if it involves sports.

Typological Considerations

One obvious reason you want to be an active participant in your children's athletic endeavors is to help them understand their Brain Type. The benefits of this are numerous. Rather than getting down on themselves when they fail, they can find tremendous hope in discovering God's unique design for them—their innately superior motor and/or mental skills.

You will want to teach and encourage using your own Brain Type. If you as a parent are a Thinker and your child is a Feeler, you must be careful in your criticisms. Thinkers, by how and what they communicate, often dampen the motivation and hope of Feelers. I have been guilty of this and continue to see others be similarly insensitive at nearly every sporting event I attend. We as parents need to do some changing.

Self Image

As we head into the 21st century, the importance placed on sports is staggering. Athletics have become an obsession for millions of parents and fans. The star performers are revered as much as anyone in society; just consider their salaries. Notice the autograph seekers that now pervade sports circles. No level of athletics is unaffected.

The result is: children begin associating self worth by how they perform athletically. Many other areas of life deal in this same propaganda of performance determining worth, such as school and grades, vocation, and income. Parents and peers can be culprits in promoting this value system.

Do we as parents want to have our children's esteem based on something that can be taken away or fade into oblivion? Or do we want to have their esteem centered in something that is lasting and permanent? I believe as human beings created in the image of God, we receive our sense of worth in and from Him. In our short stay here on earth others may know us as athletes, maybe even great athletes at some point. But in God's eyes we are known and valued as persons who may happen to participate in sports.

Measuring self-worth by athletic achievements is inviting tremendous disappointment. As the saying goes, "You finally get to the top of the ladder only to see it is leaning against the wrong wall!" Few come to realize the futility of it all. One exception was basketball sensation, **Pete Maravich**. Prior to his unexpected death at age 42, Pete wrote in his autobiography, *Heir to a Dream*, of his futile attempt at finding esteem and fulfillment in sports and achievements. He finally found his self worth in spiritual matters.

Conclusion

As parents and guardians, we have been entrusted with children. It is imperative that we give due consideration to our involvement in their athletic lives. For us *active* parents, we must evaluate ourselves regularly, as often as we evaluate our children. Since we never arrive at being perfect overseers, just as our children will never be perfect athletes, we continually need to practice good parenting methods. *Passive* parents should begin taking an interest in their children's athletic pursuits, using these opportunities for nurturing, bonding, and teaching. When our children complete their organized athletic careers, which will rarely go beyond high school, we, as parents, will have been successful if we have built a close, supportive relationship with them.

Using Brain Type To Improve Communication

The various Brain Types communicate differently, much to the consternation of those attempting communication. For instance, ISFPs, who are primarily in tune with their Feelings and Sensing functions, might find it difficult to relate to ENTJs, who are most competent with their Thinking and iNtuitive functions. Two ISFPs in conversation would find their communication styles more compatible.

Now try to imagine how an ISTP (dominant Thinker) relates to the ISFP when trying to communicate strong logic or Thinking aspects. Conversely, an ISFP would have difficulty relating strong Feelings to an ISTP.

Much of the time, people are communicating with one another as if they spoke two different languages. It is like taking a person from America and sending him to Japan with no advanced warning. He is then expected to understand the language and customs of the people. The best that can be done for him is to get a translator; but even that will be insufficient in understanding the Japanese and their ways.

Most people operate in life like our American in Japan with a translator. They usually get by when communicating with other Types, yet fall far short of true understanding. Learning Brain Types is like learning Japanese. You still will not fully understand the Japanese and their many customs and vicissitudes, yet you will have a much better handle on understanding what they are trying to say and do.

Academically, I have amassed knowledge on why and how the 16 Brain Types operate. Yet with many years of studying, I am still unable to relate experientially (other than superficially). I just do not operate, mind and body, like the other Brain Types. Neither do they operate like my Type. Nonetheless, learning about the various Types has helped me immeasurably. I am now able to better understand others and seek to identify with their values and cerebral functions.

A good way to begin understanding other Brain Types and their communication styles is by reviewing the material in the typology section. After developing an understanding there, read the Brain Type and temperament sections. This should help you appreciably in understanding the other Types. Then, when you approach others unlike yourself, try to communicate from their perspective and preferences. The rewards will be well worth the effort. You will find out more about them than you ever knew before and your communication levels will markedly improve.

The wise in heart will be called discerning, and pleasant words promote persuasiveness.

(Proverbs 16:21)

33
Putting It in Perspective

The material in this book has far reaching implications. With each passing day, you will see additional ways in which it relates to life. It is impossible in one book to convey the full impact of Brain Types as they affect sports and life. In these many pages, we have only scratched the surface. (More information is available in additional books and tapes by the author.) For now, here are some minimum truths to take with you:

1. All persons are unique; no two are identical.
2. Though unique, all persons share similarities with others.
3. Some of these similarities have been identified as mental processes and others as body skills.
4. Understanding these processes and skills in yourself and others can yield many benefits.

A benefit I have not yet mentioned is the concept of brotherhood. It is enlightening to read of and view others of your same Brain Type. By doing so, you will gain a more objective perspective of some of your innate tendencies, and you will often find yourself rooting for those of your Type to succeed, while developing a greater kinship with them.

Constructive Uses

The 16 Brain Types complement one another, creating a synergistic effect—functioning better together than in isolation. Alone, each Type is only one-sixteenth of the puzzle; together, they have the potential to harmonize into a complete picture. If this world consisted of any fewer than all 16 Types, it would be incomplete. Each Type has an integral place in society.

God intended mankind to live together, work together, to interface at the deepest levels. The Bible's Apostle Paul enjoins people to function collectively as a physical body does (I Corinthians 12). His words were written for each one of us, regardless of which part of the body we are. Perhaps your Brain Type is not as glamorous as you would like. You need to see its worth, that society is in great need of your unique gifts, and how you can do certain endeavors better than any other Brain Type. We all need to be thankful for our special giftedness.

Conversely, you may be too high on yourself and condescending to others. The Scriptures tell us:

> Do not think of yourself more highly than you ought, but rather think of yourself with sober judgment . . . .(Rom 12:3)

The most honored body parts, or top Brain Types for a given sport or task, must objectively realize their limitations, while valuing the other Brain Types.

Tracy Patterson, the son of former heavyweight champion boxer, **Floyd Patterson**, was quoted in 1992:

> A lot of people don't understand my father. They think that because he goes quiet on them, he's staying a distance away from people, but it's the opposite. He's sensitive. I mean, real sensitive. He gets afraid before my fights. When things don't go good for people he knows, he gets upset . . . .[1]

Using Brain Types constructively enables one to know Floyd Patterson is an ISFP as well as understand him. His son's description of him is typically ISFP. The many people who "don't understand" Floyd Patterson, and the many of us who do not perceive others correctly, can be immeasurably assisted by Types.

Destructive Uses

Some persons are going to misuse Brain Typing; this is a given. Since the days of Adam and Eve, every aspect of life has been perverted to some degree. Our subject matter will not be an exception. I am hopeful that the readers of this book will do their part to share the proper uses of this material, encouraging others to value and appreciate one another.

In 1992, I read an article unrelated to our subject but with similar implications. The *L.A. Times* stated that doctors would:

> ... soon be able to predict a child's life span by taking a small blood sample and looking for telltale gene patterns that regulate heart disease.[2]

The article said geneticist, James Hixson, told an American Heart Association forum:

> We feel we can soon predict at a very young age the likelihood of an individual developing heart disease.[3]

The implications of this research are broad and potentially controversial. Geneticist Hixson said in an interview:

> The implications are profound for life insurance companies and employers. If we type individuals as being at high risk, it is conceivable that some companies, like airlines or trucking firms, might shy away from hiring them.[4]

Two sides to this issue surface. Airline passengers and motorists will be thankful for these findings; potential pilots and truckers might not. So we are forced to deal with this dilemma. Should this research and information not be used in order for people to avoid a form of discrimination? Or, because of its benefits to society, should we accept its use and consequences? Nearly every day another dilemma is brought on by the explosion of 21st century knowledge. Answers will not always be easy, but changes are inevitable and sometimes necessary.

There are other means of measuring, in our society, which discriminate or restrict people from achieving their desired goals. For certain kinds of jobs, there are stature limitations, mental requirements, racial or sociological quotas to meet, experience and educational requirements. Interviewers are using a variety of measurements, even psychological. This already takes place in sports circles from Little League and other youth programs to professional sports, with coaches relying on all sorts of criteria. This book provides a more scientific analysis to evaluate athletes. Though it is not yet possible to determine Brain Type by taking blood samples and DNA analysis, this amazing phenomenon should happen very soon. Until then, its best to rely on the helps in this book to determine Brain Type.

Like pilots and truckers, some athletes won't be chosen. Athletes with greater potential will be selected and groomed. Nonetheless, this does not have to be a negative experience for the dismissed athletes. They can approach athletics the way wannabe pilots and truckers will have to deal with their new obstacles.

Geneticist Hixson provides another side to the issue by saying that people at increased risk:

> ... would then adjust their diet or receive clinical treatments to limit development of arteriosclerosis over their entire life span.[5]

For truckers, pilots, or athletes, this may mean choosing an alternative vocation or sport. If a child knows at age ten he or she cannot qualify as a pilot or trucker, then another occupation can be sought. Similarly, by studying the information in this book, one might avoid rejection later by choosing one's best sport now. However, an athlete can also choose to pursue a sport he or she strongly prefers, realizing it will take more time, self discipline and diligence to master. In other words, a realistic choice can be made.

Like many new evaluative scientific approaches, Brain Typing is a 21st century form of athletic evaluation. It should be used constructively and wisely.

Freedom in Knowing Self

As Socrates repeated the Delphic maxim, "Know Thyself," and as the Biblical book of Proverbs suggests throughout, we need to get an accurate appraisal of ourselves if we hope to deal with life effectively.

More than once, I have desired to be a different Type and not possess the mental, emotional, and physical genetic traits I sometimes demonstrate. Yet, as I have attempted to honestly see myself as I am designed, God has given me great freedom and joy to be myself.

Great Potential for Each Type

Every Brain Type, regardless of their athletic giftedness, can improve and learn throughout their sports' careers—even the highly athletic ISTPs. It is often the hardest workers who become most successful in athletics, sometimes enabling less gifted Types to achieve the highest levels of success. This book provides numerous suggestions and ideas for improvement. In addition to these, other steps can be useful.

For instance, research strongly suggests right hemisphere dominant persons have superior spatial skills compared to left-brained persons. Nonetheless, both groups can significantly improve their vision. Optometrists have said that the average person utilizes only 30 to 40 percent of his or her visual potential. By practicing specific eye exercises, peripheral awareness and depth perception can improve, enhancing one's potential athletically. Left-hemisphere dominant athletes will especially find this helpful, regardless of their sport.

Trading-Card Collectors

A chapter was not devoted to card collecting since this book is one big chapter on the subject. By getting a handle on this material, card collecting will become much more exacting and profitable. I cannot offer insight into collecting cards of retired athletes, being unable to predict the future state of the U.S. economy or the subjective criteria that determine card prices.

When appraising rookie athletes, choose those who possess one of the top Brain Types for the sport(s) and position(s) in which you have interest. The same approach can be used for seasoned, unproven athletes, but you must also consider their environment and such things as their playing positions, coaches, teams, physical statures, athletic backgrounds and skills, and so forth. For further help in these areas, refer to the back of the book where additional information can be ordered.

You are not a "Lone Ranger"

Discovering and understanding your design should help you build confidence. Some who are not familiar with the study of Type might surmise that as individuals begin to identify the weaknesses within their own Type, they would become caught up with negative aspects. Consequently, they would think less of themselves. I have found this not to be the case. Rather, in identifying my own strengths, I have gained confidence I've never had in my entire life.

Over the years, I had frequently wondered, "Where do my true talents lie? Am I really exercising my best gifts in what I'm doing today? What am I capable of doing beyond what I'm doing now?" To a large degree, these questions have now been answered through my own investigation into Brain Types.

Many times in my past, I have felt rejected and even ostracized for the way I was or the way I behaved. I wondered, "Am I one of a kind? Aren't there others who are close to being like me?" I have come to learn that there are millions of other individuals, much like myself, who have the same Brain Type. We behave in similar ways. I have, since beginning my studies in Type, talked to many of these similarly designed individuals who have told me (much to my amazement) that they have felt the same feelings of "strangeness" and being out of step with others. What we've come to realize is that this is the way God designed us! We are all "Master planned" to function in specially designed ways to do our part in society. What a relief! I feel better about myself. I actually feel better about others, those who do not fit into my mold. I now know it's okay to be me, for you to be you, for differences to coexist. I only wish I had discovered these principles sooner in life. On the other hand, when I consider this information has never been available to any previous generation, I feel privileged.

Once an Owl, Always an Owl

At the University of Minnesota's Center for Twin and Adoption Research, painstaking analysis was devoted to the lifestyles and psychological profiles of 350 pairs of identical twins *reared apart*. It was found that most of an individual's leadership ability is inherited or genetic, and that shyness is one of the traits most strongly linked to heredity. These and other findings provide further evidence of inherited, indelible designs in people.

Direct your children toward their natural bents, that is, point them toward the areas in which they have God-given talents. We too often direct our children into our professions or towards doing what we'd like them to do. This book should have shown you that your children may not be cut out to do what you want them to do. I am not talking about discipline, religious training, learning a work ethic, or other values. The issue is to examine whether we might be trying to force our child or spouse or friend into our own mold or Type, or one of our choosing. This person may have been created an owl and you may be a bee. You can both fly, but *you will never change one into the other.* No genetic mutation or evolutionary process will ever make that happen! An owl will always be an owl, and a bee will always be a bee.

It's Okay to be Yourself

Many years ago I attended a luncheon to hear one of the most dynamic speakers in the country. From the moment he began speaking to the time he stopped, he delivered a stream of sensational jokes, stories, and humorous incidents. Witty, smooth, articulate and personable, he demonstrated everything a speaker would want to be. As he was speaking, I pondered how great it would be if I could speak in such a manner. I knew that if I practiced and gained enough experience, I could be a polished speaker, too. I also realized I could never be just like him. Not only were our backgrounds and philosophies different, but the speaker's Type was the opposite of my own. My mind would never naturally gravitate into the areas to which his went. We were different creatures entirely.

I left the luncheon excited about what he had said. As I drove home, I also felt a great sense of relief that I would never have to perform the way he did. I wished that I could, but it was more important to know that God made me to exercise my own special skills and gifts in my own way. That day was one of a few key turning points in my life. I learned that it was not only okay to be me, but that I was just as important in my role as he was in his.

A section from Pastor Charles Swindoll's book, *Standing Out*, beautifully illustrates this point. He quotes the following article, printed in the Springfield, Oregon Public Schools Newsletter:

> Once upon a time, the animals decided they should do something meaningful to meet the problems of the new world. So they organized a school.
>
> They adopted an activity curriculum of running, climbing, swimming and flying. To make it easier to administer the curriculum, all the animals took all the subjects.
>
> The duck was excellent in swimming; in fact, better than his instructor. But he made only passing grades in flying, and was very poor in running. Since he was slow in running, he had to drop swimming and stay after school to practice running. This caused his web feet to be badly worn, so that

he was only average in swimming. But average was quite acceptable, so nobody worried about that—except the duck.

The rabbit started at the top of his class in running, but developed a nervous twitch in his leg muscles because of so much make up work in swimming.

The squirrel was excellent in climbing, but he encountered constant frustration in flying class because his teacher made him start from the ground up instead of from the treetop down. He developed "charlie horses" from overexertion, and so only got a "C" in climbing and a "D" in running.

The eagle was a problem child and was severely disciplined for being a non conformist. In climbing classes, he beat all the others to the top of the tree, but insisted on using his own way to get there . . . .[6]

Dr. Swindoll's comments on this tale:

The obvious moral of that story is a simple one—each creature has its own set of capabilities in which it will naturally excel—unless it is expected or forced to fill a mold that doesn't fit. When that happens, frustration, discouragement, and even guilt bring overall mediocrity or complete defeat. A duck is a duck—and only a duck. It is built to swim, not to run or fly and certainly not to climb. A squirrel is a squirrel—and only that. To move it out of its forte, climbing, and then expect it to swim or fly will drive a squirrel nuts. Eagles are beautiful creatures in the air but not in a foot race. The rabbit will win every time unless, of course, the eagle gets hungry.[7]

Are we ever to make a conscious attempt to change parts of our personality? I think an important word to think of in this connection is "balance." Each of us is born with a particular Brain Type, one that I have chosen to compare with the owl, stork, bee, or hummingbird. No matter what happens throughout life, we will always remain the Brain Type with which we were born. Yet there is room for balance and growth in all of us, no matter what Type we are. In summary, you have been

blessed with a unique design from birth. Use your strengths; improve upon your weaknesses. Seek to be balanced. Look to adapt your preferences to others as the need arises. Be the best you can be. Take heart, God has wonderfully created you.

Listen to advice and accept instruction, and in the end you will be wise.
(Proverbs 19:20)

NOTES

Introduction

1. Dan Logan, "Mind Games." *Orange County Life*, 11 May, 1990, p. N3.

Chapter 1: A Manual for Athletes, Parents, Coaches, Recruiters, Scouts, Sports Organizations, Sports Media, and Trading Card Collectors

1. Bill Plaschke, "Now His Pride Is Hurt." *L.A. Times*, 30 April, 1991, p. C1.
2. Gene Mauch quoted in "Shortstop Choice Not Clear Cut." *L.A. Times*, 27 Mar. 1992, p. C4.
3. Rod Carew quoted in "Penner." *L.A. Times*, 6 Nov. 1991, p. C7.
4. Morning Briefing, *L.A. Times*, 23 May, 1990, p. C2.
5. Peter Pascarelli, "Baseball's Draft: The Future is Now." *The National*, 4 June, 1990, p. 28.
6. Tom Landry, letter to the author, 13 Jan. 1987. (used by permission)
7. Tom Landry, letter to the author, 6 Feb. 1989. (used by permission)

Chapter 3: Mental Preferences

1. Walter Lowen with Lawrence Miike. *Dichotomies Of The Mind*. New York: John Wiley & Sons, 1982, p. 1.
2. Calvin E. Hall and Vernon J. Nordby. *A Primer of Jungian Psychology*. New York: Mentor Books, 1973, p. 96.

Chapter 7: Neuroscience: How the Brain Works

1. Bagley, Wright, Church and Hager. *Newsweek*, "Mapping the Brain." 20 April, 1992, p. 70.
2. *Ibid.*
3. Sally P. Springer and Georg Deutsch. *Left Brain, Right Brain*. New York: W.H. Freeman and Company, 1985. pp. 151 152.
4. Thomas R. Blakeslee. *The Right Brain*. New York: Berkley Books, 1980, p. 45.
5. *Ibid.*
6. Springer and Deutsch. p. 173.
7. Richard Bergland. *The Fabric of Mind*. New York: Viking Press, 1985, p. 1.
8. Springer and Deutsch. p. 152.
9. *Ibid.*, p. 157.
10. *Ibid.*, p. 34.
11. *Ibid.*, p. 46.
12. *Ibid.*, p. 47.
13. *Ibid.*, p. 48.
14. Blakeslee. p. 12.
15. Springer ad Deutsch, p.52.
16. *Ibid.*
17. Donna Bruyere and Loretta Thirtyacre. "Sensitivity to Nonverbal Cues and Feelings in Groups by MBTI Type." *Journal of Psychological Type*, Vol. 19, 1990, p. 54.
18. *Ibid.*, pp. 56 57.

Chapter 8: Brain Types and Body Skills

1. *Sports Illustrated*, 1 June, 1992, p. 44.
2. Steve Jones, personal interview, 26 Aug. 1990.
3. *Random House Dictionary*, 1975.
4. Christine Brennan. "Friends Call Ormsby a Perfectionist." *L.A. Times*, 8 June, 1986, Part 3, p. 2.
5. *Ibid.*
6. *Ibid.*

Chapter 9: Baseball

1. *L.A. Times*, 10 Oct. 1989, Part 3, p. 1.
2. James G. Hay. *The Biomechanics of Sports Techniques*. Englewood Cliffs, N.J.: Prentice Hall, 1978.
3. *L.A. Times*, 15 June, 1991, p. C2.
4. *L.A. Times*, 10 July, 1991, p. C1.
5. Ross Newhan. "For Once, Rocketman Is Grounded." *L.A. Times*, 12 Oct. 1990, p. C1.
6. *Ibid.*
7. *L.A. Times*, 4 June, 1991, p. C1.
8. *L.A. Times*, 27 Aug. 1991, p. C2.
9. *L.A. Times*, 14 Aug., 1995, p. C12.
10. *L.A. Times*, 14 Aug., 1995, p. C12.
11. *L.A. Times*, 23 June, 1989, Part 3, p. 2.
12. *L.A. Times*, 2 May, 1991, p. C1.
13. *Ibid.*, p. C6.
14. *Ibid.*
15. *L.A. Times*, 19 June, 1991, p. C3.
16. *Ibid.*
17. *L.A. Times*, 3 May, 1988, p. C2.
18. *L.A. Times*, 28 May, 1991, p. C2.
19. *L.A. Times*, 6 Aug. 1991, p. C2.
20. *L.A. Times*, 1 July, 1990, p. C6.
21. Viewpoint/Letters. *L.A. Times*, July, 1989, p. 3.

22. Tim Kurkiian. "Inside Baseball." *Sports Illustrated*, 12 Aug. 1991, p. 56.
23. *Ibid.*
24. *Ibid.*
25. *Ibid.*
26. *L.A. Times*, 24 June, 1986, Sports Section, p. 3.
27. *L.A. Times*, 11 Aug. 1991, p. C10.
28. *USA Today*, 14 Oct. 1991, p. C4.
29. *L.A. Times*, 28 Oct. 1989, Part 3, p. 1.
30. *L.A. Times*, 24 May, 1990, p. C2.
31. *Ibid.*
32. *L.A. Times*, 17 May, 1991, p. C8.
33. *Ibid.*
34. *L.A. Times*, 17 June, 1991, p. C3.
35. *L.A. Times*, 18 Oct. 1991, p. C5.
36. *L.A. Times*, 27 Aug. 1990, p. C2.
37. *Ibid.*
38. *L.A. Times*, 20 July, 1989, Part 3, p. 4.
39. *L.A. Times*, 6 July, 1990, p. C5.
40. *L.A. Times*, 2 July, 1989, Part 3, p. 11.
41. *Ibid.*
42. *L.A. Times*, 3 May, 1991, p. C2.
43. *L.A. Times*, 2 July, 1989, Part 3, p. 11.
44. *Ibid.*
45. *L.A. Times*, 2 May, 1991, p. C1.
46. *L.A. Times*, 3 May, 1991, p. C1.
47. *L.A. Times*, 3 May, 1991, p. C1.
48. *Ibid.*
49. *Ibid.*
50. John Weyler. "Baseball." *L.A. Times*, 31 July, 1988, Part 3, p. 6.
51. *L.A. Times*, 25 Feb. 1987, Part 3, p. 1.
52. *Ibid.*
53. *Ibid.*
54. *L.A. Times*, 10 Oct. 1991, p. C1.
55. *L.A. Times*, 4 April, 1991, p. C8.
56. *L.A. Times*, 27 Feb. 1988, Part 3, p. 23.
57. *L.A. Times*, 28 July, 1991, p. C2.
58. *L.A. Times*, 4 April, 1991, p. C8.
59. *L.A. Times*, 3 Aug. 1991, p. C4.
60. *L.A. Times*, 6 May, 1984, Sports Section, p. 2.
61. *L.A. Times*, 28 Oct. 1991, p. C17.
62. *L.A. Times*, 21 Sept. 1990, p. C2.
63. *L.A. Times*, 10 July, 1990, p. C1.
64. *L.A. Times*, 16 May, 1991, p. C1.
65. *L.A. Times*, 10 July, 1990, p. C1.
66. *Ibid.*
67. *Ibid.*
68. *L.A. Times*, 5 March, 1991, p. C8.
69. *L.A. Times*, 10 Oct. 1990, p. C6.
70. Gene Wojciechowski. "Angel's McCaskill Balks at Removal but Wins Anyway." *L.A. Times*, 29 July, 1986, Part 3, p. 1.
71. *L.A. Times*, 11 Oct. 1991, p. C1.
72. *L.A. Times*, 15 May, 1996, p. C2.
73. E.M. Swift. "Moon Man." *Sports Illustrated*, 13 Aug. 1990, p. 59.
74. *L.A. Times*, 28 April, 1991, p. C2.
75. *Sports Illustrated*, 13 Aug. 1990, p. 63.
76. *Sports Illustrated Classic*, Fall 1991.
77. Hank Hersch. "A Gentleman and a Slugger." *Sports Illustrated*, 15 April, 1991, p. 86.
78. *L.A. Times*, 2 April, 1991, p. C1.
79. *L.A. Times*, 21 July, 1991, p. C3.
80. *Sports Illustrated*, 15 April, 1991, p. 86.
81. *Ibid.*
82. *Ibid.*
83. *L.A. Times*, 3 April, 1991, p. C1.
84. *L.A. Times*, 23 June, 1991, p. C6.
85. *L.A Times*, 23 Feb. 1997, p. C14.
86. *Sports Illustrated*, 15 April, 1991, p. 106.
87. *L.A. Times*, 7 Oct. 1991, p. C11.
88. Richard Hoffer. "Heeeere's Ozzie!" *Sports Illustrated*, 6 April, 1992, p. 94.
89. *Ibid.*
90. *Ibid.*
91. Ross Newhan. "Pendleton Gets Day Off, Still Wins Title." *L.A. Times*, 7 Oct. 1991, p. C11.
92. *L.A Times*, 27 June, 1997, p. C2.
93. *L.A. Times*, 7 May, 1991, p. C1.

Chapter 10: Basketball

1. *L.A. Times*, 7 Mar. 1988, Part 3, p. 2.
2. *Sports Illustrated*, 10 Feb. 1992, p. 43.
3. Larry Bird and Bob Ryan. *Drive*. New York: Doubleday, 1989, p. xi.
4. *L.A. Times*, 20 Dec. 1986, Part 3, p. 2.
5. Bird and Ryan, *Drive*. p. xi.
6. *Sports Illustrated*, 13 Mar. 1989, p. 35.
7. *L.A. Times*, 5 June, 1990, p. C7.
8. *L.A. Times*, 1 May, 1990, p. C7.
9. *L.A. Times*, 5 Mar. 1989, p. C3.
10. *L.A. Times*, 1 June, 1991, p. C1.
11. *L.A. Times*, 28 May, 1990, p. C2.
12. *L.A. Times*, 11 July, 1991, p. C5.
13. Mike Downey. "He Rules the Boards With a Mean Streak." *L.A. Times*, 4 Mar. 1991, p. C1.
14. Bird and Ryan. *Drive*. jacket cover.
15. Bird and Ryan. *Drive*. jacket cover.
16. *L.A. Times*, 17 Dec. 1990, p. C2.
17. Jack McCallum, *Sports Illustrated*, 10 June, 1991, p. 18.
18. *L.A. Times*, 14 Mar. 1988, Part 3, p. 2.
19. Bird and Ryan, *Drive*. p. 253.
20. *L.A. Times*, 16 April, 1987, Part 3, p. 2.
21. *L.A. Times*, 9 Mar. 1989, Part 3, p. 12.
22. *Ibid.*
23. *Ibid.*
24. *Ibid.*
25. *L.A. Times*, 25 Mar. 1990, p. C1.
26. *Sports Illustrated*, 9 Mar. 1992, Interview.
27. *L.A. Times*, 16 April, 1991, p. C1.

28. *Sports Illustrated*, 27 Jan. 1992, p. 39.
29. *Orange County Register*, 1 April, 1990, Sports Section, p. 1.
30. *L.A. Times*, 16 Aug. 1990, p. C1.
31. Steve Springer. "Lakers Send Off Cooper." *L.A. Times*, 16 Aug. 1990, p. C1.
32. *Ibid.*
33. Bird and Ryan, *Drive*. p. 243.
34. *L.A. Times*, 1 April, 1990, p. C5.
35. *L.A. Times*, 27 Jan. 1989, Part 3, p. 4.
36. *L.A. Times*, 6 Mar. 1990, p. C2.
37. *L.A. Times*, 19 Feb. 1990, p. C4.
38. *Ibid.*
39. *L.A. Times*, 28 Nov. 1991, p. C2.
40. *L.A. Times*, 4 April, 1990, p. C2.
41. *L.A. Times*, 30 May, 1990, p. C2.
42. *L.A. Sports Profiles*, Jan./Feb. 1991, p. 19.
43. *L.A. Times*, 11 Mar. 1991, p. C1.
44. *Ibid.*
45. *L.A. Sports Profiles*, Jan./Feb. 1991, p. 19.
46. *L.A. Times*, 18 Oct. 1990, p. C14.
47. Mark Heisler. "For Divac, the Payoff Bets Better." *L.A. Times*, 18 Oct. 1990, p. C14.
48. *Ibid.*
49. *L.A. Times*, 15 May, 1990, p. C4.
50. *L.A. Times*, 18 Jan. 1990, p. C3.
51. *L.A. Times*, 12 Mar. 1990, p. C2.
52. Mark Heisler. "Porter Slips Into Background." *L.A. Times*, 13 June, 1990, p. C5.
53. Mark Heisler. "The NBA." *L.A. Times*, 3 Nov. 1991, p. C10.
54. *L.A. Times*, 12 Mar. 1990, p. C2.
55. *L.A. Times*, 29 Mar. 1990, p. C2.
56. *L.A. Times*, 28 April, 1990, p. C4.

Chapter 11: Bowling, Boxing, Cycling

1. *L.A. Times*, 8 Jan. 1992, p. C2.
2. *L.A. Times*, 4 Nov. 1991, p. C2.
3. *L.A. Times*, 4 Dec. 1989, p. C2.
4. *Ibid.*
5. *L.A. Times*, 23 Mar. 1986, Part 3, p. 2.
6. *Ibid.*
7. *L.A. Times*, 4 Dec. 1986, Part 3, p. 2.
8. *Sports Illustrated*, 13 Jan. 1992, p. 74.
9. *Ibid.*, p. 76.
10. *L.A. Times*, 11 Mar. 1991, p. C2.
11. *Sports Illustrated*, 29 April, 1991, p. 25.
12. *Sports Illustrated*, 5 Nov. 1990, p. 85.
13. *USA Today*, 18 Oct. 1990, p. C1.
14. *Sports Illustrated*, 30 July, 1990, p. 18.
15. *L.A. Times*, 3 May, 1990, p. C3.

Chapter 12: Football

1. *L.A. Times*, 23 Jan. 1992, p. C1.
2. *L.A. Times*, 23 Jan. 1992, p. C2.
3. *Sports Illustrated*, 13 Aug. 1990, p. 77.
4. *L.A. Times*, 27 Jan. 1991, p. C3.
5. *L.A. Times*, 25 Nov. 1994, p. C1.
6. *L.A. Times*, 30 Nov. 1991, p. C2.
7. *L.A. Times*, 26 Nov. 1991, p. C2.
8. *Ibid.*
9. Jeannie Park and Lorenzo Benet, *People*, 4 Dec. 1989, p. 96.
10. *Ibid.*
11. *Sports Illustrated*, 2 Sep. 1991, p. 29.
12. Paul Zimmerman. "White Heat." *Sports Illustrated*, 27 Nov. 1989, p. 68.
13. Mike Downey. "Bills' Smith on Stairway to Greatness." *L.A Times*, 12 Jan. 1992, p. C3.
14. *Sports Illustrated*, 10 Sep. 1990, p. 79.
15. *Ibid.*
16. *Ibid.*
17. *Ibid.*
18. Mark Sufrin. *Payton*. New York: Charles Scribner's Sons, 1988, p. 33.
19. *L.A. Times*, 24 Sep. 1991, p. C2.
20. *Sports Illustrated*, 2 Sep. 1991, p. 29.
21. Jill Lieber. "Deep Scars." *Sports Illustrated*, 29 July, 1991, p. 39.
22. *Ibid.*
23. Richard Hoffer. "Look, Ma, Great Hands!" *Sports Illustrated*, 10 Sep. 1990, p. 98.
24. *Ibid.*
25. Walter Roessing. "Jerry Rice: Football's Miracle Receiver." *Boys Life*, Nov. 1989, p. 35.
26. Mike Sandrolini. "Bearing The Truth." *Sports Spectrum*, Jan./Feb. 1992, p. 13.
27. *Ibid.*, p. 14.
28. *L.A. Times*, 26 Jan. 1992, p. C2.
29. *Ibid.*

Chapter 13: Golf

1. *L.A. Times*, 16 Aug. 1991, p. C2.
2. *L.A. Times*, 13 June, 1991, p. C2.
3. *L.A. Times*, 22 Feb. 1990, p. C4.
4. *Golf Digest*, April, 1991, p. 125.
5. *L.A. Times*, 22 June, 1991, p. C16.
6. *USA Today*, 4 Oct. 1991, p. 3C.
7. *Golf Digest*, April, 1991, p. 126.
8. *Ibid.*
9. *Ibid.*, p. 128.
10. *L.A. Times*, 8 Feb. 1991, p. C1.
11. Morning Briefing. *L.A. Times*, 8 Aug. 1985, Part 3, p. 2.
12. *L.A. Times*, 9 April, 1990, p. C1.
14. *L.A. Times*, 12 August, 1991, p. C1.

15. *L.A Times*, 12 April, 1991, p. C16.
16. *L.A. Times*, 21 Feb. 1991, Section C.
17. Sonja Steptoe. "Playing Out of Deep Rough." *Sports Illustrated*, 23 Sep. 1991, p. 8.
18. *Golf*, Aug. 1991, p. 106.
19. *Ibid.*
20. *L.A. Times*, 8 July, 1991, p. C2.
21. *L.A. Times*, 9 Mar. 1991, p. C2.
22. *L.A. Times*, 1 Mar. 1991, p. C2.
23. *L.A. Times*, 26 Sep. 1991, p. C13.
24. Thomas Boswell. *Strokes Of Genius*. Garden City, NY: Doubleday & Co., 19S7, p. 31.
25. *Ibid.*
26. *Golf Digest*, Sep. 1983, p. 58.
27. *L.A. Times*, 4 Feb. 1991, p. C1.
28. *Sports Illustrated*, 12 Feb. 1990, p. 185.
29. *L.A. Times*, 2 April, 1990, p. C2.
30. *Ibid.*
31. *L.A Times*, 9 April, 1990, p. C10.
32. *L.A. Times*, 9 April, 1990, p. C1.
33. *L.A. Times*, 2 June, 1990, p. C2.
34. *L.A. Times*, 11 April, 1991, p. C3.
35. *L.A. Times*, 23 July, 1990, p. C13.
36. *Sports Illustrated*, 8 April, 1991, p. 86.
37. Boswell, *Strokes Of Genius*. p. 97.
38. *Ibid.*, p. 100.
39. *Sports Illustrated*, 3 Feb. 1975.
40. Boswell, *Strokes Of Genius*. p. 94.
41. *Ibid.*, p. 94.
42. *Ibid.*, p. 95.
43. *Ibid.*, p. 96.
44. *Ibid.*, p. 95.
45. *Ibid.*
46. *Golf Digest*, April 1991, p. 56.
47. Boswell, *Strokes Of Genius*. p. 105.
48. *L.A. Times*, 9 Feb. 1991, C15.
49. *L.A. Times*, 19 June, 1990, p. C6.
50. *Golf*, Aug. 1991, p. 74.
51. *Ibid.*, p. 75.
52. *Ibid.*, p. 124.
53. *L.A. Times*, 6 Sep. 1994, p. C2.
54. *L.A. Times*, 3 Jan. 1991, p. C4.
55. *L.A. Times*, 20 June, 1990. p. C8.
56. *L.A Times*, 19 Nov. 1996, p. C2.
57. Rick Reilly. "What a Trip." *Sports Illustrated*, 26 May, 1997, pp. 64-66.
58. *USA Today*, 18 August, 2003, p. 8C.
59. *L.A. Times*, 4 June, 1991, p. C7.
60. *Golf*, Oct. 1991, p. 49.

Chapter 14: Gymnastics, Hockey, and Ice Skating

1. Bill Sands and Mike Conklin. *Everybody's Gymnastics Book*. New York: Charles Scribner's Sons. 1984, p. 15.
2. *L.A. Times*, 15 Sep. 1991, p. C2.
3. *Sports Illustrated*, Atlanta 1996 (Special Commemorative Issue, p. 41.
4. *L.A. Times*, 15 Sep. 1991, p. C2.
5. *L.A. Times*, 28 Mar. 1992, p. C8.
6. *L.A. Times*, 16 Oct. 1989, Part 3.
7. *Ibid.*
8. Austin Murphy. "Make Room For Lemieux." *Sports Illustrated*, 6 Feb. 1989, p. 35.
9. Austin Murphy. "Shooting Star." *Sports Illustrated*, 18 Mar. 1991, p. 23.
10. *L.A. Times*, 30 Jan. 1992, p. C3.
11. *L.A. Times*, 17 Nov. 1991, p. C11.
12. *L.A. Times*, 16 Feb. 1992, p. C1.
13. *Ibid.*
14. *Sports Illustrated*, 10 Feb. 1992, p. 63.
15. Randy Harvey. "Trenary Retiring From Amateur Figure Skating." *L.A. Times*, 21 Dec. 1991, p. C1.
16. *L.A. Times*, 3 Aug. 1990, p. C4.
17. *L.A. Times*, 29 Jan. 1992, p. C2.
18. *L.A. Times*, 16 Feb. 1988, Part 3, p. 2.
19. *L.A. Times*, 20 Mar. 1997, p. C6.
20. *L.A. Times*, 10 Jan. 1992, p. C4.
21. *L.A. Times*, 11 Jan. 1992, p. C5.

Chapter 15: Racing (auto), Snow Skiing, Soccer, Swimming and Diving

1. *Sports Illustrated*, 30 Sep. 1991, p. 68.
2. *Ibid.*
3. Billy Kidd and Bill Grout. *Ski Racing*, Chicago, IL: Contemporary Books, 1984, p. 19.
4. *Ibid.*
5. *L.A. Times*, 9 Jan. 1995, p. C17.
6. *L.A. Times*, 23 Jan. 1995, p. C7.
7. Bob Lochner. "Italy's Tomba Has Toned Down Messiah Act, but Only a Little." *L.A. Times*, 9 Feb. 1992, p. C8.
8. *Sports Illustrated*, 2 Mar. 1992, p. 23.
9. *L.A. Times*, 9 Feb. 1992, p. C3.
10. *L.A. Times*, 1 Dec. 1991, p. C3.
11. Kidd and Grout. *Ski Racing*. p. 7.
12. Don Kowet. *Pele*. New York: Atheneum/ SMI, 1976, p. 47.
13. *Ibid.*, p. 45.
14. *Ibid.*, p. 61.
15. *Ibid.*, p. 89.
16. Rick Telander. "Prima Dona." *Sports Illustrated*, 14 May, 1990, p. 99.
17. *Ibid.*, p. 102.
18. *L.A. Times*, 2 August, 1991, p. C2.
19. Telander, p. 100.
20. *People*, 18 June, 1990, p. 110.
21. *L.A. Times*, 8 Mar. 1992, p. C3.
22. *Ibid.*

Chapter 16: Tennis

1. Scott Osler. "For Steffi Graf, Pappa Knows Best." *L.A. Times*, 29 June, 1987, Part 3, p. 24.
2. *Ibid.*
3. *Ibid.*
4. *L.A. Times*, 4 Sep. 1991, p. C19.
5. Tony Trabert and Gerald Secor Couzens. *Trabert On Tennis*. New York: Contemporary Books, 1988, p. 109.
6. *L.A. Times*, 25 July 1990, p. C2.
7. *L.A. Times*, 13 Aug. 1990, p. C6.
8. *L.A. Times*, 22 July, 1990, p. C2.
9. *Ibid.*
10. Julie Cart. "Edberg Silences Agassi With a Touch of Class." *L.A. Times*, 12 Mar. 1990, p. C1.
11. *L.A. Times*, 9 Sep. 1991, p. C1.
12. Jim Murray. *L.A. Times*, 16 Aug. 1990, p. C1.
13. Trabert and Couzens. *Trabert On Tennis*. p. 96.
14. *L.A. Times*, 25 Jan. 1992, p. C2.
15. *L.A. Times*, 25 Feb. 1990, p. C2.
16. Trabert and Couzens. *Trabert On Tennis*. p. 96.
17. Trabert and Couzens. *Trabert On Tennis*. p. 205.
18. *L.A. Times*, 3 Aug. 1991, p. C2.
19. *L.A. Times*, 19 July, 1990, p. C2.
20. *L.A. Times*, 10 Sep. 1990, p. C2.
21. Ronald Atkin. *For the Love of Tennis*. London: Stanley Paul & Co, 1985, p. 27.
22. *L.A. Times*, 31 Aug. 1990, p. C7.
23. *Sports Illustrated*, 13 Mar. 1989, p. 74.
24. *Ibid.*
25. *L.A. Times*, 2 Sep. 1991, p. C2.
26. *L.A. Times*, 7 Sep. 1990, p. C7.
27. *L.A. Times*, 5 June 1991, p. C1.
28. *Sports Illustrated*, 13 Mar. 1989, p. 74.
29. Thomas Bonk. "U.S. Handsome, Sabatini Stunning." *L.A. Times*, 9 Sep. 1990, p. C1.
30. *L.A. Times*, 10 Sep. 1990, p. C1.
31. *L.A. Times*, 3 Aug. 1989, Part 3, p. 4.
32. Atkin. *For the Love of Tennis*. p. 18.
33. *Ibid.*, p. 18.
34. *L.A. Times*, 25 June, 1986, Part 3, p. 2.
35. Trabert and Couzens. *Trabert On Tennis*. p. 96.
36. Atkin. *For the Love of Tennis*. p. 149.
37. Isabel Briggs Myers and Peter B. Meyers. *Gifts Differing*. Palo Alto, CA: Consulting Psychologists Press, 1980, p. 99.
38. Trabert and Couzens. *Trabert On Tennis*. p. 47.
39. *L.A. Times*, 27 May, 1990, p. C19.
40. *L.A. Times*, 27 May, 1990, p. C19.
41. *L.A. Times*, 6 June, 1990, p. C16.
42. *L.A. Times*, 27 May, 1990, p. C19.
43. *L.A. Times*, 29 Mar. 1990, p. C2.
44. *Tennis*, Jan. 1997, p. 31.
45. *L.A. Times*, 23 Feb. 1989, Part 3, p. 5.
46. *Ibid.*
47. Trabert and Couzens. *Trabert On Tennis*. p. 109.
48. *L.A. Times*, 3 Sep. 1990. p. C1.
49. Atkin. *For the Love of Tennis*. p. 61.
50. *L.A. Times*, 9 Sep. 1990, p. C1.
51. Atkin. *For the Love of Tennis*. p. 27.
52. *Ibid.*, p. 35.
53. *L.A. Times*, 10 Sep. 1990, p. C1.
54. *Ibid.*
55. *L.A. Times*, 6 Sep. 1990, p. C1.
56. *L.A. Times*, 10 Sep. 1990, p. C1.
57. *L.A. Times*, 11 Sep. 1990, p. C1.
58. *L.A. Times*, 6 Sep. 1990, p. C1.
59. *Sports Illustrated*, 16 Sep. 1991, p. 23.
60. Atkin. *For the Love of Tennis*. p. 28.
61. *Ibid.*, p. 151.
62. Evonne Goolagong and Bud Collins. *Evonne! On the Move*. New York: E.P. Dutton & Co, 1975, p. 159.
63. *Ibid.*, p. 72.
64. Kenny Moore and J.E. Vader. "Living a Dream." *Sports Illustrated*, 27 Nov. 1989, p. 76.
65. *Ibid.*, p. 74.
66. *Ibid.*, p. 72.
67. Goolagong and Collins. *Evonne! On the Move.*, p. 25.
68. Moore and Vader., p. 72.
69. *Ibid.*, p. 68.
70. *Ibid.*, p. 72.
71. *L.A. Times*, 19 Aug. 1990, p. C1.
72. Moore and Vader. p. 72.
73. *Ibid.*, p. 76.
74. *Ibid.*, p. 74.
75. William Plummer and Don Sider. "Pardon His Dust." *People.* 1 July, 1991, p. 76.
76. *Ibid.*
77. *Ibid.*
78. *Sports Illustrated*, 24 Feb. 1992, p. 54.
79. *Ibid.*, p. 51.
80. *Ibid.*
81. *Ibid.*
82. Elliott Almond. "Courier Has a Few Tricks Under His Hat in Opening Day Victory." *L.A. Times*, 26 May, 1992, p. C2.
83. Curry Kirkpatrick. "Open and Shut." *Sports Illustrated.* 16 Sep. 1991, p. 23.

Chapter 17: Track and Field, Volleyball, Water Polo, and Wrestling

1. *Sports Illustrated*, 16 Sep. 1991, p. 37.
2. *L.A. Times*, 31 Aug. 1991, p. C4.
3. *Sports Illustrated*, 16 Sep. 1991, p. 37.
4. *Sports Illustrated*, 1 July, 1991, p. 45.
5. *USA Today*, 31 July, 1997, p. 3C.
6. *Sports Illustrated*, 20 May, 1991. p. 48.
7. *Ibid.*, p. 48.
8. *Ibid.*
9. *Ibid.*, p. 49.
10. *L.A. Times*, 8 June, 1991, p. C2.

11. *L.A. Times*, 6 July, 1991, p. C12.
12. *L.A. Times*, 12 July, 1990, p. C16.
13. *Sports Illustrated*, 24 Feb. 1992, p. 8.
14. Ted Newland, fax to the author, 3 Oct. 1996. (used by permission)

Chapter 18: Coaches (and officials)

1. *L.A. Times*, 14 Oct. 1989, p. C2.
2. *L.A. Times*, 26 June, 1991, p. C2.
3. *L.A. Times*, 14 Jan. 1992, p. C2.
4. *L.A. Times*, 22 April, 1988, Part 3, p. 2.
5. *L.A. Times*, 7 Aug. 1989, Part 3, p. 2.
6. *L.A. Times*, 5 Oct. 1991, p. C2.
7. *L.A. Times*, 24 April, 1991, p. C2.
8. *People*, 4 Dec. 1989, p. 95.
9. *L.A. Times*, 7 Dec. 1991, p. C1.
10. *L.A. Times*, 19 Dec. 1989, p. C13.
11. *The PriceCostco Connection*, Nov. 1996, p. 19.
12. *USA Today*, 1 Aug. 1996, p. 13E.
13. *L.A. Times*, 1 April, 1997, p. C2.
14. *L.A. Times*, 14 Oct. 1990, p. C1.
15. *L.A. Times*, 7 April, 1992, p. C5.
16. *L.A. Times*, 27 Mar. 1991, p. C1.
17. *Ibid.*
18. *L.A. Times*, 14 Aug. 1991, p. C2.
19. Chris Baker. "Kansas Gets Next Best Thing." *L.A. Times*, 27 Mar. 1991, p. C1.
20. *Ibid.*
21. Michael Bauman. "Karl Continues Parade of Tirades." *Milwaukee Journal Sentinel*, 8 Dec. 2000.
22. *Ibid.*
23. *Ibid.*
24. Jennifer Allen, "Coach Dad." NFL Insider, 2000.
25. Douglas S. Looney. "Mr. Flexibility." *Sports Illustrated*, 30 Dec. 1991, p. 35.
26. *Ibid.*
27. *Ibid.*
28. Dick Wagner. "Fatherly Winner Is lost by Football." *L.A. Times*, 1 Jan. 1991, p. C1.
29. *Sports Illustrated*, 11 Nov. 1991, p. 118.
30. *Ibid.*
31. *L.A. Times*, 23 Mar. 1990, p. C1.
32. *Ibid.*
33. Bob Oates. "La Russa Has Many Tastes and Talents." *L.A. Times*, 5 Mar. 1991, p. C1.
34. *Ibid.*
35. *L.A. Times*, 6 June, 1990, p. C2.
36. *L.A. Times*, 5 May, 1991, p. C1.
37. *L.A. Times*, 5 May, 1991, p. C1.
38. *L.A. Times*, 8 May, 1991, p. C1.
39. *Ibid.*
40. *Ibid.*
41. Morning Briefing. *L.A. Times*, 7 Feb. 1992, p. C2.
42. *L.A. Times*, 7 Feb. 1992, p. C2.
43. Frommer. *Baseball's Greatest Managers*. p. 238.
44. *L.A. Times*, 9 April, 1990, p. C20.
45. *Ibid.*
46. *L.A. Times*, 11 Aug. 1991, p. C10.
47. *Ibid.*
48. *L.A. Times*, 1 Jan. 1991, p. C2.
49. *L.A. Times*, 8 Oct. 1991, p. C1.
50. *Ibid.*
51. *L.A. Times*, 31 Oct. 1991, p. C1.
52. *L.A. Times*, 17 Jan. 1992, p. C2.
53. *L.A. Times*, 10 Jan. 1992, p. C3.
54. *L.A. Times*, 17 Mar. 1991, p. C10.
55. *Ibid.*
56. *USA Today*, 20 Mar. 1990, Sports Section.
57. *Orange County Register*, 30 Mar. 1990, p. D1.
58. *Ibid.*
59. *L.A. Times*, 15 May, 1990, p. C1.
60. *L.A. Times*, 14 April, 1992, p. C2.
61. *Ibid.*
62. *Ibid.*

Chapter 19: Sports Media

1. *L.A. Times*, 17 April, 1990, p. C2.
2. *L.A. Times*, 13 April, 1990, p. C2.
3. *L.A. Times*, 27 Aug. 1990, p. C2.
4. *L.A. Times*, 18 Jan. 1991, p. C2.
5. *L.A. Times*, 2 June, 1990, p. C2.
6. *L.A. Times*, 12 April 1991, p. C3.
7. *Ibid.*
8. Jerry D. Lewis. "The Voice Of The Dodgers." *American Way*, 1 June, 1987, p. 50.
9. *L.A. Times*, 5 Sep. 1990, p. C7.
10. *Ibid.*
11. *L.A. Times*, 2 Nov. 1990, p. C3.
12. *Ibid.*
13. Allan Malamud. "Notes on a Scorecard." *L.A. Times*, 3 July, 1990, p. C3.

Chapter 20: SPs

ISTP

1. *L.A. Times*, 15 Mar. 1992, p. 8.
2. Peter Gammons. "The Hit Man Hits Back." *Sports Illustrated*, 6 Feb. 1989, p. 63.
3. *Ibid.*
4. *Ibid.*, p. 66.
5. *Ibid.*
6. *Ibid.*
7. *Ibid.*
8. *Ibid.*
9. *L.A. Times*, 17 April, 1990, p. 4.
10. *L.A. Times*, 17 Mar. 1986, Part 3, p. 2.
11. *L.A. Times*, 15 April, 1992, p. C2.
12. *Orange County Register*, 5 April, 1990, p. C3.
13. John M. Broder. "Schwarzkopf's War Plan Based on Deception." *L.A. Times*, 28 Feb. 1991, p. A1.
14. Al Stump. "Ty Cobb Was a Money Player." *L.A. Times*, 12 July, 1991, p. C1.

ESTP

15. *L.A. Times*, 15 Jan. 1989, Part 3, p. 3.
16. *People*, 20 Nov. 1989, p. 119.
17. *People*, Collector's Edition, Fall 1990, p. 88.
18. *People*, 20 Nov. 1989, p. 128.
19. *US*, Jan. 1992, p. 96.
20. *L.A. Times*, 29 May, 1991, p. C2.
21. *L.A. Times*, 31 Aug. 1990, p. C3.

ISFP

22. Steve Pond. "Jackson's Heights." *US*, 5 Mar. 1990, p. 22.
23. *L.A. Times*, 10 April, 1991, p. C5.
24. *L.A. Times*, 10 Aug. 1996, p. C2.
25. Julie Cart. "Easy Doesn't Do It." *L.A. Times*, 21 July, 1992, p. C1.
26. *L.A. Times*, 10 April, 1991, p. C5.
27. *L.A Times*, 27 June, 1997, p. C2.

ESFP

28. *L.A. Times*, 8 Nov. 1991, p. C2.
29. *L.A. Times*, 25 Jan. 1990, p. C4.
30. *L.A. Times*, 19 June, 1991, p. C2.
31. *L.A. Times*, 4 April, 1990, p. C2.
32. *L.A. Times*, 21 Mar. 1990, p. C2.
33. *L.A. Times*, 8 Nov. 1991, p. C5.
34. *L.A. Times*, 2 June, 1991, p. C2.

Chapter 21: SJs

ISTJ

1. *L.A. Times*, 18 Mar. 1987, Part 3, p. 2.
2. *L.A. Times*, 19 Mar. 1988, Part 3, p. 3.
3. *L.A. Times*, 27 June, 1984, Part 3, p. 2.
4. *L.A. Times*, 22 June, 1988, Part 3, p. 2.
5. Scott Osler. "Pitcher's Book Not Enough; Hershiser Prefers Interfacing." *L.A. Times*, 2 August, 1988, Part 3.

ESTJ

9. Rick Reilly."Not Bloody Likely." *Sports Illustrated*, 8 April, 1991, p. 80.
10. *Ibid.*
11. *Ibid.*, p. 82.
12. *Ibid.*, pp. 80 90.
13. *Sports Illustrated*, 15 April, 1991, p. 120.
14. *L.A. Times*, 3 May, 1991, p. C1.
15. Leigh Montville. "Citizen Ryan." *Sports Illustrated*, 15 April, 1991, p. 120.
16. Reilly. p. 86.

ESFJ

17. *People*, Collector's Edition, Fall 1990, p. 63.
18. *Ibid.*, p. 67.
19. *Ibid.*

20. *Ibid.*, p. 63.
21. *Star*, Summer 1991, p. 18.

Chapter 22: NFs

INFP

1. *Orange County Preview*, 8 August, 1991, p. 2.
2. Hank Hersch. "A Gentleman And A Slugger." *Sports Illustrated*, 15 April, 1991, p. 84.

ENFP

3. *L.A. Times*, 12 Mar. 1990, p. C2.
4. *L.A. Times*, 6 Sep. 1990, p. C8.
5. Peter King. "Inside the NFL." *Sports Illustrated*, 5 Nov. 1990.
6. Jack Maguire. *Care and Feeding of the Brain*. New York: Doubleday, 1990, p. 163.

INFJ

7. Gordon Monson. "Man on a Mission." *L.A. Times*, 28 Feb. 1991, p. C6.
8. *Ibid.*
9. *Sports Illustrated*, 20 Mar. 1989, p. 100.

ENFJ

10. *US*, 11 Dec. 1989, p. 8.
11. Bill Hewitt and Linda Kramer. "Dole On A Role." *People*, 24 June, 1991, p. 88.
12. Lorraine Dusky. *McCall's*, June 1990, p. 67.
13. Jack Nelson. "Bush Talks With Many, Shares Power With Few." *L.A. Times*, 6 Nov. 1989, p. A1.
14. James Gerstenzang. "Bush Tells of Crying Before Declaring War." *L.A. Times*, 7 June, 1991, p. A3.
15. *Ibid.*
16. *Creative Living*, Winter 1992, p. 12.

Chapter 23: NTs

INTJ

1. *L.A. Times*, 27 Feb. 1988, Part 3, p. 23.
2. *Ibid.*
3. *Ibid.*

INTP

4. Hilaire Cuny. *Albert Einstein*. Greenwich, Conn.: Fawcett Publications, 1962, p. 11.
5. *Ibid.*, p. 8.
6. Demmie Stathoplos. "Lori Norwood, Pentathlete And Renaissance Woman." *Sports Illustrated*, 16 April, 1990, Spotlight section.
7. *Ibid.*
8. *Ibid.*
9. *Ibid.*
10. *Ibid.*
11. *Ibid.*
12. *Ibid.*

13. *Sports Illustrated*, 9 Dec. 1991, p. 88.
14. Stathoplos. Spotlight section.

ENTP

19. Paul Richter. "Kennedy: A Public Private Life." *L.A. Times*, 7 June, 1991, p. A1.
20. *Ibid.*
21. *Ibid.*

Chapter 26: The NF "Stork"

1. C.S. Lewis. *The Four Loves*. New York: Harcourt Brace Jovanovich, Inc., 1960, p. 54.

Improving Performance

1. *L.A. Times*, 29 Sep. 1989, Part 3, p. 8.

Chapter 28: The Performing Mind, Zoning, Relaxation, and Visualization

1. *L.A. Times*, 1 July, 1990, p. C6.
2. *L.A. Times*, 6 June, 1990, p. C4.
3. *Ibid.*
4. Lawrence Shainberg. "Finding `The Zone'." *New York Times Magazine*, 4 April, 1989, p. 37.
5. *Ibid.*
6. *Brain Research*, 20 Jan. 1992, p. 142.
7. *Ibid.*
8. Shainberg. p. 37.
9. Shainberg. p. 38.
10. *Discover*, Mar. 1989, p. 65.

Chapter 29: Philosophical or Spiritual Foundation

1. *Sports Illustrated*, 22 July, 1991. p. 26.
2. *Sports Illustrated*, 22 July, 1991, p. 14.
3. *Ibid.*
4. *L.A. Times*, 6 Jan. 1992, p. C2.
5. Julie Cart. "Sports Heroes, Social Villains." *L.A. Times*, 2 Feb. 1992, p. C3.
6. *L.A. Times*, 18 Jan. 1992, p. C1.
7. *Ibid.*
8. *Ibid.*
9. *L.A. Times*, 26 Jan. 1992, p. A5.
10. George W. Cornell. "Surveys Reveal Religious Peculiarities." *L.A. Times*, 15 June, 1991, p. F21.
11. *Ibid.*
12. *NIV Study Bible*. Grand Rapids, MI: Zondervan Bible Publishers, 1985, p. 1491.
13. *Ibid.*, p. 1533.

Chapter 31: Other Psychological Methods and Accurate Typing

1. *Bulletin of Psychological Type*, Vol. 14, No. 4, Fall 1991.
2. "An Interview with David Keirsey," *APT Western Region Newsletter*, Vol. 6, No. 1, Sept. 1996, p. 1.
3. *Journal of Psychological Type*, Vol. 22, 1991, p. 8.
4. *Ibid.*

Chapter 32: Parents and Guardians

1. *L.A. Times*, 16 Aug. 1991, p. C3.
2. *Special Report*, Nov. 1990, p. 61.
3. Tony Trabert with Gerald Secor Couzens. *Trabert on Tennis*. New York: Contemporary Books, 1988, p. 8.
4. *Ibid.*, p. 9.
5. *Ibid.*, pp. 9,10.
6. Paul Dean. "Sampras' Parents Exult Behind the Scenes." *L.A. Times*, 20 Sep. 1990, p. 20.
7. *Ibid.*
8. *Ibid.*
9. *Ibid.*
10. *Ibid.*

Chapter 33: Putting It in Perspective

1. Michael Leahy. "Floyd Patterson: His Own Man." *Sports Illustrated*, 1 June, 1992, Boxing.
2. Joel Greenberg. "In Brief." *L.A. Times*, 20 Jan. 1992, p. B9.
3. *Ibid.*
4. *Ibid.*
5. *Ibid.*
6. Charles R. Swindoll. *Standing Out*. Portland, OR: Multnomah Press, 1979.
7. *Ibid.*

For Further Information...

Are you interested in the fascinating field of Brain Types as it relates to sports and life? Would you like to be included in upcoming announcements of tapes, seminars, workshops, literature, and new publications?

The Brain Type Institute offers you the opportunity to take part in the rapid-growing interest in Brain Types. If you would like to find out about new developments, please check the opportunities listed below.

I am interested in the following:

> SEND TO: B.T.I.
>   HC-71 Box 121-1
>   Thornfield, MO 65762
>   (417) 679-4748
>
> **ONLY FOR ORDERING MATERIALS**
> **WITH VISA AND M.C..........1-800-748-5549**
>
> http://www.braintypes.com

__ Other Brain Type products (books—*Get the Most Out of Life: with Your Inborn Brain Type*; videos and CD—*Who Am I? Who Are You?*; audio tapes—*Get the Most Out of Life; An Introduction to the 16 Brain Types*

__ Additional copies of *YOUR KEY TO SPORTS SUCCESS*.

__ Include me on your mailing or e-mail list.

__ I would like to arrange a seminar in my area.

__ I am interested in personal consultation.

__ I am interested in having a Brain Type assessment.

__ Other_____.

SEND INFORMATION TO:

Name_____

Address_____

City_____

State_____Zip_____ (optional) Phone _____
                                                                          Email _____